Good managers find ways to make their organizations successful. The ways to do this are to build competitive advantage in the forms of cost competitiveness, quality, speed, and innovation. Because of the importance of the four sources of competitive advantage—which really are goals that every manager should constantly try to achieve and improve upon—we refer to them frequently throughout the text. The idea is to keep you focused on a type of "bottom line" to make sure you think continually about "delivering the goods" that make both the manager (you) and the organization a competitive success.

The **four "bottom line" practices** are:

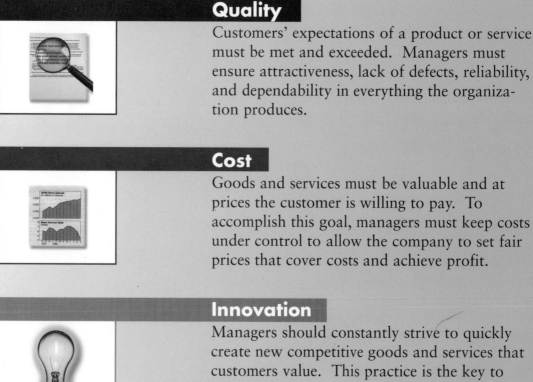

Quality

Customers' expectations of a product or service must be met and exceeded. Managers must ensure attractiveness, lack of defects, reliability, and dependability in everything the organization produces.

Cost

Goods and services must be valuable and at prices the customer is willing to pay. To accomplish this goal, managers must keep costs under control to allow the company to set fair prices that cover costs and achieve profit.

Innovation

Managers should constantly strive to quickly create new competitive goods and services that customers value. This practice is the key to staying ahead of competitors.

Speed

Organizations must respond to market needs quickly by introducing new products first; quickly delivering customer orders; and responding quickly to customer requests.

You will see evidence of these four practices called out occasionally in your text by the icons above. These icons will be in the margin, highlighting a paragraph where the particular practice is discussed.

Management
Competing in the New Era

Management

Competing in the New Era

Fifth Edition

Thomas S. Bateman
McIntire School of Commerce,
University of Virginia

Scott A. Snell
Cornell University

McGraw-Hill Irwin

Boston   Burr Ridge, IL   Dubuque, IA   Madison, WI   New York   San Francisco   St. Louis
Bangkok   Bogotá   Caracas   Kuala Lumpur   Lisbon   London   Madrid   Mexico City
Milan   Montreal   New Delhi   Santiago   Seoul   Singapore   Sydney   Taipei   Toronto

McGraw-Hill Higher Education

A Division of The McGraw-Hill Companies

MANAGEMENT: COMPETING IN THE NEW ERA
Published by McGraw-Hill, an imprint of The McGraw-Hill Companies, Inc. 1221
Avenue of the Americas, New York, NY, 10020. Copyright © 2002, 1999, 1996, 1993, 1990 by The McGraw-Hill Companies, Inc. All
rights reserved. No part of this publication may be reproduced or distributed in any form or by any means, or stored in a data base or re-
trieval system, without the prior written consent of The McGraw-Hill Companies, Inc., including, but not limited to, in any network or
other electronic storage or transmission, or broadcast for distance learning.
Some ancillaries, including electronic and print components, may not be available to customers outside the United States.

This book is printed on acid-free paper.

domestic   1 2 3 4 5 6 7 8 9 0 VNH/VNH 9 8 7 6 5 4 3 2 1
international   1 2 3 4 5 6 7 8 9 0 VNH/VNH 9 8 7 6 5 4 3 2 1

ISBN   0-07-240859-6

Publisher: *John E. Biernat*
Senior editor: *John Weimeister*
Developmental editor II: *Christine Scheid*
Marketing manager: *Lisa Nicks*
Project manager: *Laura Ward Majersky*
Senior production supervisor: *Lori Koetters*
Media technology producer: *Jenny R. Williams*
Cover and interior design: *Artemio Ortiz Jr.*
Supplement coordinator: *Betty Hadala*
Photo research coordinator: *Judy Kausal*
Typeface: *10/12 Times Roman*
Compositor and project management: *The GTS Companies, Inc.*
Printer: *Von Hoffmann Press, Inc.*

Library of Congress Cataloging-in-Publication Data

Bateman, Thomas S.
    Management: competing in the new era / Thomas S. Bateman, Scott A. Snell.—5th ed.
        p. cm.
    Includes bibliographical references and index.
    ISBN 0-07-240859-6
    1. Management. I. Snell, Scott, 1958- II. Title.

HD31 .B369485 2002
658.4—dc21

                                                    2001024859

INTERNATIONAL EDITION ISBN 0-07-112298-2
Copyright © 2002. Exclusive rights by The McGraw-Hill Companies, Inc. for manufacture and export.
This book cannot be re-exported from the country to which it is sold by McGraw-Hill.
The International Edition is not available in North America.

www.mhhe.com

For my parents, Tom and Jeanine Bateman
and Mary Jo, Lauren, T.J., and James
and
My parents, John and Clara Snell,
and Marybeth, Sara, Jack and Emily

About the Authors
Thomas S. Bateman

Thomas S. Bateman is Bank of America Professor and management area coordinator in the McIntire School of Commerce at the University of Virginia. Prior to joining the University of Virginia, he taught organizational behavior at the Kenan-Flager Business School of the University of North Carolina to undergraduates, M.B.A. students, Ph.D. students, and practicing managers. He also recently returned from two years in Europe as a visiting professor at the Institute for Management Development (IMD), one of the world's leaders in the design and delivery of executive education. Dr. Bateman completed his doctoral program in business administration in 1980 at Indiana University. Prior to receiving his doctorate, Dr. Bateman received his B.A. from Miami University. In addition to Virginia, UNC-Chapel Hill, and IMD, Dr. Bateman has taught at Texas A&M, Tulane, and Indiana Universities.

Dr. Bateman is an active management researcher, writer, and consultant. He has served 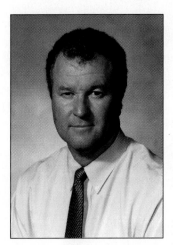 on the editorial boards of major academic journals, and has presented numerous papers at professional meetings on topics including managerial decision making, job stress, negotiation, employee commitment and motivation, group decision making, and job satisfaction. His articles appear in professional journals such as the *Academy of Management Journal, Academy of Management Review, Journal of Applied Psychology, Organizational Behavior and Human Decision Processes, Journal of Management, Business Horizons, Journal of Organizational Behavior, Decision Sciences,* and *Financial Times Mastering Management Journal.*

Dr. Bateman's current consulting and research centers around entrepreneurship in the United States, Central Europe, and Southeast Asia, and the pursuit of long-term, intrinsically-motivated work goals.

He is currently working closely with companies including Nokia, Singapore Airlines, Quintiles, and USPS.

Scott A. Snell

Scott A. Snell is Professor of Human Resource Studies in the School of Industrial and Labor Relations at Cornell University. He received a B.A. in Psychology from Miami University, as well as M.B.A. and Ph.D. degrees in Business Administration from Michigan State University. During his career, Dr. Snell has taught courses in human resource management and strategic management to undergraduates, graduates and executives. He is actively involved in executive education and has conducted international programs in Europe and Asia as well as Australia and New Zealand.

Professor Snell has worked with companies such as AT&T, GE, IBM, Merck and Shell to address the alignment of human resource systems with strategic initiatives such as globalization, technological change, and knowledge management. His research and teaching interests center on how leading companies manage their people for competitive advantage. This work focuses on the development and deployment of intellectual capital as a foundation of an organization's core competencies.

Dr. Snell's research has been published in a number of professional journals including the *Academy of Management Journal, Academy of Management Review, Human Resource Management, Human Resource Management Review, Industrial Relations, Journal of Business Research, Journal of Management, Journal of Managerial Issues, Journal of Management Studies, Organizational Dynamics, Organization Studies, Personnel Psychology,* and *Strategic Management Journal.* He is also co-author of two books, *Management: The Competitive Edge,* and *Managing Human Resources.* In addition, Dr. Snell has served on the editorial boards of *Journal of Managerial Issues, Digest of Management Research, Human Resource Management, Human Resource Management Review, Human Resource Planning,* and *Academy of Management Journal.*

Preface

The merger, approved by the Justice Department in January 2001, is a business block-buster: Internet powerhouse America Online merged with—or rather, most would say took over—old-line media giant Time Warner. It's a watershed event in the turn-of-the-millennium market mania. Some say it's a monopoly; alternatively, maybe it's just a merger between two famous companies that may or may not work out.

Actually, it's more than just a merger. It's a $97 billion dollar merger between two very different corporations that personify the old and the new economies.

But maybe there is no distinction between old economy and new. Perhaps we're just living and managing in a new era that has new types of challenges, and is very interesting indeed.

Will the merger work? All eyes are on Bob Pittman, the co-chief operating officer, to see if he can make it happen. The challenge for AOL, and for Pittman, is to take full advantage of the Internet. According to Pittman, the Net will transform business and social life every bit as profoundly as electricity did a century ago. Says Pittman, "With all its copyrights, Time Warner is in a marvelous position to take advantage of the Net and not be frightened by it. AOL's mindset, assets, and expertise help them in that path."

The merger could be phenomenally successful, but there are signs of trouble. Growth in 2000 was slower than expected, revenues were lower, and losses due to merger write-offs were steep. Moreover, by 2001 the macroeconomic environment was threatening. The new company faces continual governmental antitrust oversight, and the two companies could not have corporate cultures that are more unalike. *Business Week* describes the cultural difference between Time Warner's graybeards and AOL's twentysomethings this way: When it comes to making deals or launching new ventures, it's "Let's do lunch" versus "Let's skip lunch."

Short-term, investors are skeptical. AOL's stock dropped 48 percent in the year after the merger announcement. Time Warner's Gerald M. Levin was criticized for the timing and details of the sale to AOL. Analyst Henry Blodget says that Pittman won't convince Wall Street that the deal is working unless he boosts the stock price from $37.50 to $90 by mid-2002. Pittman says he's on the hot seat: "The company must hit the numbers expected of it." If it doesn't, "I'll be responsible." The company's CFO, Michael Kelly, says they can pull it off. "There are lots of dials and levers in achieving our results."

Strategically, Pittman must create valuable synergies between AOL and Time Warner and powerful new consumer services. Organizationally, he must blend two cultures, build bridges between units, create a new structure comprised of a series of interlocking teams, and get people to work together. The technological, strategic, and organizational challenges are daunting, to say the least.

Can Pittman succeed? Communication is a bedrock of his leadership style. He persuaded Time Warner executives to trade in their e-mail system for AOL's. He put all employee-benefit processing online, saving the company tens of millions of dollars. Time Warner folks resisted, but came to see the advantages to the company. Pittman has held regular meetings every two or three weeks with division chiefs. They have hammered out budgets and Web strategies. They agreed on technologies. Open discussions help reduce corporate intrigue in which people speculate about one another's motives, and help establish trust and mutual expectations for how the company will move forward.

Another bedrock in Pittman's approach is constructive conflict. Time Warner is known for its warring divisions, and managing the company is said to be like herding cats. Pittman encourages vigorous debate; several years ago at AOL his executives threw food at each other. But he bans personal attacks; the conflicts are to be over business issues, not personalities. Pittman's methods are cascading through AOL Time Warner.

Says Chairman Steve Case: "Bob has operational zeal." AOL-Time Warner CEO Levin says, "Bob Pittman blends the realism of a top-flight executive with the creative vision of an entrepreneur."*

Bob Pittman's task is to meld the yin and yang of old and new media, in this long-awaited convergence of the analog present and the digital future. But what does a lofty statement like that mean for the real people who worked in the former companies; the new, merged company; and for everyone else who works, manages, and must survive and thrive in today's world?

In many ways, the AOL story is a metaphor for today's management opportunities and challenges. Think of the topics reflected in the story—globalization, corporate strategy, the "human element" of business, leadership, decision making, mergers, culture, costs, speed, managing change, creating futures, and so many others—and learn more about them in the following pages.

Our goals

Our mission with this text hasn't changed from that of our previous editions: to inform, instruct, and inspire. We hope to *inform* by providing descriptions of the important concepts and practices of modern management. We hope to *instruct* by describing how you can take action on the ideas discussed. In other words, you will learn practical applications that will make you more effective in ways that benefit both you and your organization. We hope to *inspire* not only by writing in a positive, interesting, and optimistic way, but also by providing a real sense of the unlimited opportunities ahead of you. Whether your goal is starting your own company, leading a team to greatness, building a strong organization, delighting your customers, or generally forging a positive future, we want to inspire you to take positive actions.

We hope to inspire you to be both a thinker and a doer. We want you to think about the issues, think about how to become a better manager, think about the impact of your actions, think before you act. But being a good thinker is not enough; you also must be a doer. Management is a world of action. It is a world that requires timely and appropriate action. It is a world not for the passive, but for those who commit to positive accomplishments.

We also hope to inspire you to keep learning. Keep applying the ideas you learn in this course, read about management in sources outside of this course, and certainly keep learning about management after you leave school and continue your career. Make no mistake about it, learning about management is a personal voyage that will last years, an entire career, your entire lifetime.

Competitive advantage

Today's world is competitive. Never before has the world of work been so challenging. Never before has it been so imperative to your career that you learn the skills of management. Never before have people had so many vast opportunities with so many potential rewards.

You will compete with other people for jobs, resources, and promotions. Your organization will compete with other firms for contracts, clients, and customers. To survive the competition, and to thrive, you must perform in ways that give you an edge over your competitors, that make the other party want to hire you, buy from you, and do repeat business with you. You will want them to choose you, not your competitor.

To survive and thrive, today's managers have to think and act strategically. Today's customers are well educated, aware of their options, and demanding of excellence. For this reason, managers today must think constantly about how to build a capable workforce and manage in a way that delivers the goods and services that provide the best possible value to the customer.

---

* C. Yang with R. Grover and A.T. Palmer, "Show Time for AOL Time Warner," *Business Week,* January 15, 2001.

By this standard, managers and organizations must perform. Four essential types of performance, on which the organization beats, equals, or loses to the competition, are *cost, quality, speed,* and *innovation.* These four performance dimensions, when done well, deliver value to the customer and competitive advantage to you and your organization. We will elaborate on all of these topics throughout the book.

Good managers find ways to make their organizations successful. The ways to do this are to build competitive advantage in the forms of cost competitiveness, quality, speed, and innovation. Because of the importance of the four sources of competitive advantage—which really are goals that every manager should constantly try to achieve and improve upon—we refer to them frequently throughout the book. The idea is to keep you focused on a type of "bottom line," to make sure you think continually about "delivering the goods" that make both the manager (you) and the organization a competitive success.

Results orientation

An important theme of this book, then, is how to manage in ways that deliver *results*— results that customers want. When you deliver high-quality, innovative products, quickly, and at a competitive price, you are achieving the results that can give you the competitive edge. And keep in mind, these are the same results that your competitors strive for as they try to gain an edge over you.

This approach makes this book unique among management texts. Rather than offering only concepts and processes, which nonetheless are integral parts of this text, we have a clear results orientation that is essential to success. The concepts and processes are means to an end, or the ways by which you can achieve the results you need.

Competing in the new era

The subtitle of the book refers to the fact that managers must develop and sustain competitive advantage, and real results, in a time when the business world has been rocked by new developments. The Internet, globalization, knowledge management, the need to collaborate across organizational boundaries, and other changes in the business environment and business practice dramatically cast doubt on the relevance of the "old ways" of managing. In 2000, people were saying that the old economy was gone, giving way to a new economy in which a new game is played under very different rules.

But by 2001, the dot.com shakeout and economic slowdown had people saying that the old rules—including the need for profits!—are as vital as ever. Perhaps there is no distinction between the old economy and the new. Nonetheless, the context has changed, drastically. The AOL-Time Warner merger combines a company playing by the old rules with one that has forged some of the new rules, in an effort to combine the strengths (and avoid the dangers) of both. This effort describes our goal of teaching managers and aspiring managers how to compete successfully in the new era.

Topical currency

It goes without saying that this textbook, in its fifth edition, remains on the cutting edge of topical coverage, as updated via both current business examples and recent management research. Chapters are thoroughly updated and students are exposed to a wide array of important current topics.

We have done our very best to draw from a wide variety of subject matter, sources, and personal experiences.

Forging the future

By highlighting the sources of competitive advantage and using a clear results orientation, we continue our efforts to create a new generation of management texts. Our previous editions were more integrative than other texts and were the first to devote major coverage to the vital management topics of managing in our natural environment and managing workforce diversity. And, we have broken the traditional mold by encouraging students to "forge the future," including more coverage of career management in the first and last chapters.

Still, in this edition we retain the traditional functional organization. Even though the world has changed, it is not chaos. A functional approach still is useful in that it provides students and instructors with a framework within which to tackle dynamic issues. Moreover, we of course give full coverage to all of the topics all management texts emphasize: globalization, quality, change, ethics, teams, and so on.

As this textbook forges the future for management texts, we want to influence students to forge *their* futures. Throughout the text, a proactive rather than a passive approach to management is encouraged. For example, Chapter 7, New Ventures, doesn't merely describe small business management; it inspires readers to create new ideas and new businesses. Chapter 18, Managing and Creating Change, speaks to the importance of creating a great future, not just being ready for the future and adapting to it. We highlight the "genius of the *and*" and being both a leader and a learner.

With your help, we want to influence business in the future. Through our mission of informing, instructing, and inspiring, we hope you will apply these ideas to create your own organizations and/or make the organizations in which you work more successful and outstanding.

A team effort

This book is the product of a fantastic McGraw-Hill/Irwin team. Moreover, we wrote this book believing that we would form a team with the course instructor and with students. The entire team is responsible for the learning process.

Our goal, and that of your instructor, is to create a positive learning environment in which you can excel. But in the end, the raw material of this course is just words. It is up to you to use them as a basis for further thinking, deep learning, and constructive action.

What you do with the things you learn from this course, and with the opportunities the future holds, *counts*. As a manager, you can make a dramatic difference for yourself, and for other people. What managers do matters, *tremendously*.

Outstanding Pedagogy

Management: Competing in the New Era is pedagogically stimulating and is intended to maximize student learning. With this in mind, we used a wide array of pedagogical features—some tried and true, others new and novel:

• Learning Objectives, which open each chapter, identify what students will learn by reading and studying the chapter.

• Opening quotes provide a thought-provoking preview of chapter material. The quotes are from people like Peter Drucker (on management), Jack Welch (on strategy), Harry David Thoreau (on ethics), Julius Caesar (on leadership), and Charles Kettering (on change and the future).

• Setting the Stage describes an actual organizational situation and provides a rich introductory example of the chapter topic. Setting the Stage is placed before the text material as a practical application.

• Boxed inserts describing current examples and controversial issues are found throughout the text.

• "From the Pages of *Business Week*" highlights recent *Business Week* articles in each chapter.

• Icons representing the four running themes of the book—cost, quality, speed, and innovation—are placed at appropriate points in the text to indicate an extended example, best practice, or issue for discussion. The icons continually reinforce and enhance the learning of these important themes.

End-of-chapter elements

• Key terms are page-referenced to the text and are part of the vocabulary-building emphasis. These terms are defined in the glossary at the end of the book.

• A Summary of Learning Objectives provides clear, concise responses to the learning objectives, giving students a quick reference for reviewing the important concepts in the chapter.

• Discussion Questions, which follow the Summary of Learning Objectives, are thought-provoking questions that test the student's mastery of concepts covered in the chapter and ask for opinions on controversial issues.

• Concluding Cases provide focus for class discussion.

• Two Experiential Exercises are included in each chapter. Most of them are group-based, and some involve outside research.

End-of-part elements

• An Integrating Case appears at the end of each of the five parts of the book.

• Two short Case Incidents also focus on managerial problems that include issues from multiple chapters and are a stimulating arena for discussion.

• Part One has an in-basket exercise, which we believe is an excellent exercise for early in the course.

Comprehensive supplements

For the student

• **Student CD-ROM**—*Free* with the purchase of a new textbook. The Student CD-ROM contains interactivities, self-assessment exercises, chapter quizzes, and links for students to go above and beyond the boundaries of the printed textbook. One of the interactivities that will be included on the CD utilizes Flash technology with voiceovers and feedback to bring the concept to life in 3-D.

• **Online Learning Center**—www.mhhe.com/bateman

For the instructor

• Instructor's Manual, prepared by Thomas Lloyd, Westmoreland County Community College, contains chapter outlines, suggested discussion questions and answers for Setting the Stage, two lecturettes for each chapter, suggested answers to end-of-chapter Discussion Questions, suggested answers to the Concluding Case discussion questions, objectives and teaching tips for the Experiential Exercises, discussion questions and suggested answers for Case Incidents and Integrating Cases, and a Video Guide.

• Test Bank, prepared by Amit Shah, Frostburg State University, contains approximately 100 questions for each chapter and consists of true/false, multiple choice, fill-in, matching, and essay questions.

• PowerPoint Presentation software, developed by Michael Gordon of Rutgers University, contains tables and figures from the text plus additional graphic material. A self-contained viewer is packaged with each disk so that those who do not have the PowerPoint software can easily view the presentation.

• Color acetates from the PowerPoint slides are also available.

• Videos are available for each chapter. Corresponding video cases and a guide that ties the videos closely to the chapter can be found in the Instructor's Manual.

• Computerized Testing enables you to pick and choose questions and develop tests and quizzes quickly and easily on the computer. Available for Windows or Mac users.

Acknowledgments

This book could not have been written and published without the valuable contributions of many individuals. Our reviewers over the last four editions contributed time, expertise, and terrific ideas that significantly enhanced the quality of the text. The reviewers of the fifth edition are:

Janice Felbauer
Austin Community College

Randy Nichols
Oakland City University

David Foote
Middle Tennessee State University

Fred Slack
Indiana University of Pennsylvania

Carolyn Hatton
Cincinnati State Tech Community College

Carl Sonntag
Pikes Peak Community College

Jim McElroy
Iowa State University

Christina Stamper
University of North Carolina—Wilmington

Dot Moore
The Citadel

Jim Wachspress
New Jersey Institute of Technology

Our thanks to these members of our focus group:

Ray Aldag
University of Wisconsin—Madison

MarySue Love
Maryville University

Shawn Carraher
Indiana University—NW Campus

Granger Macy
Texas A & M—Corpus Christi

Al Crispo
Purdue University

Michael Vijuk
William Rainey Harper College

Marya Leatherwood
University of Illinois—Springfield

Ben Weeks
St. Xavier University

We would also like to thank those who reviewed for us in previous editions:

Debra A. Arvanites
Villanova University

Charles A. Beasley
State University of New York—Buffalo

Barbara Boyington
Brookdale Community College

Hrach Bedrosian
New York University

Diane Caggiano
Fitchburg State College

Charles Blalack
Kilgore College

Ron Dibattista
Bryant College

Mary A. Bouchard
Bristol Community College

Dale Dickson
Mesa State College

Eugene L. Britt
Grossmont College

William Jedlicka
William Rainey Harper College

Lyvonne Burleson
Rollins College—Brevard

Augustine Lado
Cleveland State University

Elizabeth A. Cooper
University of Rhode Island

Bert Nyman
Rockford College

Anne C. Cowden
California State University—Sacramento

Marc Siegall
California State University—Chico

Michael W. Drafke
College of DuPage

Robert J. Ash
Rancho Santiago College

J. F. Fairbank
Pennsylvania State University

Alan J. Fredian
Loyola University—Chicago

Elias Kalman
Baruch College

Steve Garlick
DeVry Institute—Kansas City

Gus. L. Kotoulas
Morton College

John Hall
University of Florida

Catherine C. McElroy
Bucks County Community College

Donald E. Harris
Oakton Community College

David L. McLain
Virginia State University

Frederic J. Hebert
East Carolina University

Joseph B. Mosca
Monmouth college

Durward Hofler
Northeastern Illinois University

James J. Ravelle
Moravian College

Thomas O. James
Benedictine College

Joseph C. Santora
Essex County College

Many individuals contributed directly to our development as textbook authors. Dennis Organ provided one of the authors with an initial opportunity and guidance in textbook writing. John Weimeister has been a friend and adviser from the very beginning. Welcome back, John! John Biernat was a great champion for the project, and is a talented publisher and good friend. Kurt Strand is, too. Christine Scheid is the consummate developmental editor, doing it all with great skill and professionalism. What a team!

Finally, we thank our families. Our parents, Jeanine and Thomas Bateman and Clara and John Snell, provided us with the foundation on which we have built our careers. They continue to be a source of great support. Our wives, Mary Jo and Marybeth, demonstrated great encouragement, insight, and understanding throughout the entire process. Our children, Lauren, T. J., and James Bateman, and Sara, Jack, and Emily Snell, are an inspiration for everything we do.

Thomas S. Bateman
Charlottesville, VA

Scott A. Snell
Ithaca, NY

Contents in Brief

Contents

Part One

Foundations of Management 2

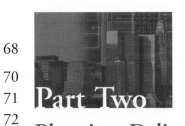

Part Three

Organizing: Building a Dynamic Organization 252

Chapter   Eleven
Managing the Diverse Workforce

Part Four

Leading: Mobilizing People   376

Chapter   Twelve
Leadership

Management

Competing in the New Era

Part One
Foundations of Management

Foundations of Management

Managing
The External Environment
Managerial Decision Making

Planning:
Delivering Strategic Value

Planning and Strategic Management
Ethics and Corporate Responsibility
International Management
New Ventures

Strategy Implementation

Organizing: Building
a Dynamic Organization

Organization Structure
The Responsive Organization
Human Resources Management
Managing the Diverse Workforce

Leading:
Mobilizing People

Leadership
Motivating for Performance
Managing Teams
Communicating

Controlling:
Learning and Changing

Managerial Control
Managing Technology and Innovation
Creating and Managing Change

The three chapters in Part 1 describe the foundations of management. Chapter 1 describes the imperatives of managing in the new era and introduces key functions, skills, and competitive goals of effective managers. Chapter 2 describes the external environment in which managers and their organizations operate. Chapter 3 discusses the most pervasive managerial activity—decision making. Sound decision-making skills are essential for effective managerial performance.

Chapter One
Managing

Management means, in the last analysis, the substitution of thought for brawn and muscle, of knowledge for folklore and tradition, and of cooperation for force.

—Peter Drucker

Chapter Outline

Learning Objectives

After studying Chapter 1, you will know:

1. The major challenges of managing in the new era.

2. The drivers of competitive advantage for your company.

3. The functions of management and how they are evolving in today's business environment.

4. The nature of management at different organizational levels.

5. The skills you need to be an effective manager.

6. What to strive for as you manage your career.

Setting the Stage

Some Get It, Some Don't

For companies and management teams, "They get it" seems to be the ultimate compliment in today's business world. "They don't get it" is the ultimate insult. *Getting it* refers to successfully navigating the "new economy"—usually meaning the successful business use of the Internet. *Not getting it* means either not trying to do business via the Net, or doing it badly.

One company that gets it is Bechtel. One of the biggest construction companies in the world, Bechtel has been part of virtually every important construction project of the 20th century, including the Hoover Dam and the Chunnel. Today, it has its sights set on the Net. It has new contracts to build 26 warehouses for Webvan Group, the online grocer; 30 vehicle certification centers for iMotors.com; and 30 fortified Internet hubs around the world for Equinix. As the new economy magazine *Business 2.0* put it, "If you got the clicks, Bechtel's got the bricks."

A second company that gets it is Boeing, which launched the aviation industry's first Website for ordering and tracking spare parts shipments. Boeing is partnering with several other companies to create a procurement hub for the entire industry, linking more than 37,000 suppliers, hundreds of airlines, and national governments in a Web-based marketplace. A third is General Motors, which has an Internet-linked business "all the way from the foundry to the bank," according to Mark Hogan, president of the new "e GM" unit. "We're using the Net to change the culture in the company because we want to be big and we also want to be fast; in the past, we've been big and slow."

Bechtel has been part of virtually every important construction project of the 20th century, including the Hoover Dam.
[Reed Rahn/Liaison Agency]

Who doesn't get it? One source slams Disney, whose Go.com portal lost $2 billion; Macy's and its parent company Federated Department Stores, which did less than 1 percent of its business online in 1999; and Sears, which went online with its Craftsman tools and Kenmore appliances but not with its clothing lines. All of these companies have plans to do better, though. Alan Lacy of Sears is focusing on networked homes of the future, and intends to capitalize on both technology and Sears's armies of in-store sales advisors and service technicians. "We intend to make Sears the premier clicks-and-mortar retailer in America in the next year or two," he vows.

"Not getting it" is not just about established companies that don't adapt to the Internet era; it goes the other way, too. Josh Harris, founder of the streaming media company Pseudo.com, told *60 Minutes* and CBS, "Our business is to take you guys out. I'm in a race to take CBS out of business . . . That's why we're going to make the big bucks." CBS, of course, is still around, whereas Pseudo.com is not. Many, many dot.com companies have gone under—some analysts estimate that 95 percent of all dot.coms will fail. And many are now trying to find places in the physical world. Gazoontite.com began as an e-tailer but quit the Web entirely after it opened five physical stores that became profitable. WingspanBank.com was strictly virtual but now is tapped into a network of tens of thousands of ATMs. E*Trade is opening outposts in SuperTarget stores, Amazon allies with Toys"R"Us, and other e-tailers are producing print catalogs. *Fortune* calls it a rush to the middle, with virtual companies seeking physicality and physical companies seeking virtualness. The latter is probably much easier to "get."

Sources: S. Bennett, "Wings and a Prayer," Business 2.0, June 13, 2000, pp. 209–11; D. Buss, "Brightest of the Big Three," Business 2.0, June 13, 2000, pp. 221–23; D. Buss, "Not So Magical Kingdom," Business 2.0, June 13, 2000, pp. 227–29; D. Buss, "The Dimmer Side of Sears," Business 2.0, June 13, 2000, pp. 236–38; A. Saracevic, "Bricks for the Clicks," Business 2.0, June 13, 2000, pp. 206–07; R. Tadjer, "Macy's Mahem," Business 2.0, June 13, 2000, pp. 232–34; and J. Useem, "Dot-coms: What Have We Learned?" Fortune, October 30, 2000, pp. 82–104.

Managing in the new era

Today's corporations, like those just described, are at a crossroads. Some say that the old economy is gone, giving way to a new economy. The new economy, they say, plays by different rules. Whether or not that is an overstatement, the Internet and other forces are transforming the country and the world, and especially the business world. As *Business Week* describes it, "The Darwinian struggle of daily business will be won by the people—and the organizations—that adapt most successfully to the new world that is unfolding" (p. 78).[1]

During this transition to the Internet era, your company must not only survive, but also exploit, the changes going on.[2] Today's managers, young or old, cannot construct a business model, or manage effectively, based solely on either the old (Industrial Age) model or on the new Internet model. Both are highly relevant today, and both must be understood and managed appropriately. You and your company must recognize the new opportunities and threats, and reconcile them with fundamental management practices.

What are the key components of the "new world"? Bearing in mind that you will be reading about many vital issues in the chapters to come, here we begin by highlighting four elements that are drastically reshaping the world of management: the rise of the Internet, globalization, the importance of knowledge and ideas, and collaboration across organizational "boundaries."

The Internet

Communication technologies are driving massive change in the world of management. The Internet changes the way management must think and act with regard to everything from devising strategies to leading and motivating employees. Management is still strategic, and still intensely interpersonal and human, but now it also must happen via the Web.[3]

In the future, one of the most important jobs in your company will be that of chief Web officer.[4] Now most commonly called chief information officer (CIO), the chief Web officer of the future will not only oversee information systems and strategies, but also

table 1.1
Web DNA

Web DNA

Following are the six characteristics that Russell Reynolds Associates believes define successful Web executives. Ask yourself, "Am I right for the job?"

CarpeDiem.com: When was the last time that you had a breakthrough in business? When was the last time that you took a risk and failed? Describe a time when your business wasn't meeting the expectations that you had set out to meet. What did you do to change that?

Radiate vision: Are you more evangelical than Matthew, Mark, Luke, or John? What's important to you and to your business? How do you define your success? Your team's success? How do you communicate your company's vision to your team?

80/20 mind-set: Have you freed yourself from analysis paralysis? How do you use resources? How do you figure out what your customers want? When was the last time that you drew from your experience and insights to fill in a blank when faced with incomplete information?

Organizational improvisers: Are you more interested in getting stuff done than in playing by the rules of the org chart? What does an ideal organization look like? How do you use the talents of your employees? How do you plan for future growth?

Learning obsessed: Are you like a sponge when it comes to learning? Do you love to place yourself in the middle of feedback loops? When was the last time that you learned something that led to an "aha" moment? When was the last time that you changed a tightly held point of view?

Get the right stuff done: Do you know what it takes to ruthlessly prioritize? Can you zoom out to see the most important objectives, instead of allowing yourself to be distracted by tangential tasks with little payoff?

Source: http://www.fastcompany.com/disclaimer.html

will create and manage business relationships via the new communications technologies. Through strategic use of the Web, managers forge flexible and essential links between a company and its partners, suppliers, and customers. Web officers—and in fact, people throughout the organization—must be adept at spotting opportunities and exploiting them quickly and more effectively than does the competition. They will need to make strategic decisions, foster a culture of experimentation and change, partner with others outside the company, and train and empower their staff and people throughout the firm to fully exploit opportunity.

In appraising managerial talent, Becky Stein, executive recruiter with the Silicon Valley Internet practice at Russell Reynolds Associates, looks for what she calls "Web DNA": the personal characteristics considered the "right stuff" needed for managers to thrive in the Internet economy.[5] Take a look at Table 1.1, which shows the skills she looks for in Web executives. The list is not validated scientifically, but you can use it to think about yourself and your Web DNA—and also start considering how these skills might apply as well to management more generally.

In the late 1990s, most observers described Internet-driven change as "revolutionary." Now that many dot.coms have failed, more observers talk in terms of significant evolution, not revolution.[6] Whereas a few short months ago many people thought that the dot.coms were the future of business, the shakeout in 2000 made it clear that being a successful company is not simply a matter of being a Web-based dot.com. In the future, some great companies will be dot.coms, but many (most?) will be big corporations that capitalize most fully on the Web's potential for transforming their businesses.

Think back to the beginning of this chapter, and the "rush to the middle" by both traditional corporations and Internet start-ups. Clearly, the distinction between Internet and non-Internet companies is fading. Some stand-alone Internet companies will continue to survive, thrive, and even dominate. But Intel Chairman Andy Grove has declared that

Intel Chairman Andy Grove believes all companies will need to evolve into Internet companies to survive.
[Courtesy Intel Corporation]

soon "there won't be any Internet companies. All companies will be Internet companies, or they will be dead."[7] As *Fortune* put it, the dot.com revolution may be dead, but the Internet revolution is definitely here. And the real wealth creation is yet to come.[8]

Globalization

For U.S. and non–U.S. managers alike, isolationism is a thing of the past.[9] This must be so for organizations to survive worldwide competition in a global marketplace. U.S. companies are no longer the unrivaled stars of the business world. The great companies of the world now include Sony, Honda, Bayer, and Royal Dutch Shell.

Multinational enterprises have offices and production facilities in countries all over the world. Corporations such as Bertelsmann, Citicorp, ASEA Brown Boveri, and Nestlé are "stateless": They operate worldwide without reference to national borders.[10] Here is some hard evidence that makes it clear how important globalization has become to companies: Corporations try to take advantage of their transnational status to operate beyond the control of national governments, including the shifting of income from high-tax to low-tax jurisdictions. A General Accounting Office (GAO) study reported that *most* U.S. corporations pay *zero* U.S. income taxes.[11]

Even small firms that do not operate on a global scale must make important strategic decisions based on international considerations. Many small companies export their goods. Many domestic firms assemble their products in other countries. And organizations are under pressure to improve their products in the face of intense competition from high-quality foreign producers. Firms today must ask themselves, "How can we be the best in the world?"

Knowledge management

Perhaps the most important force for change in management is the growing need for good, new ideas. Because companies in advanced economies have become so efficient at producing physical goods, most workers have been freed up to provide services or "abstract goods" like software, entertainment, data, advertising, and so on. Efficient factories with few workers produce the cereals and cell phones the market demands; meanwhile, more and more workers create software and invent new products and services.[12] As top consultant Gary Hamel puts it, "We have moved from an economy of hands to an economy of heads."[13]

Just as chief Web officer will be an important job in coming years, so will that of knowledge manager.[14] Knowledge management is the set of practices aimed at discovering and harnessing an organization's intellectual resources—fully utilizing the intellects of the organization's people. Knowledge management is about finding, unlocking, sharing, and altogether capitalizing on the most precious resources of an organization: people's expertise, skills, wisdom, and relationships. Knowledge managers find these human assets, help people collaborate and learn, help people generate new ideas, and harness those ideas into successful innovations.

Production of tangible goods remains an essential part of the economy and of effective management, but companies like GE, Dell, Toyota, and ABB owe their success in large part to intellectual capital. Whereas "capital" used to be a purely financial concept, it now has an additional meaning. Intellectual capital is the collective brainpower of the organization.[15] Today, managers must create a work environment that attracts good people, makes them want to stay, and inspires creative ideas from everyone. The ultimate goal is to turn the brainpower of their people into profitable products.

Collaboration across "boundaries"

One of the most important processes of knowledge management is to ensure that people in different parts of the organization collaborate effectively with one another. This requires productive communications among different departments, divisions, or other subunits of the organization. Moreover, companies today must motivate and capitalize on the ideas of people outside the traditional company "boundaries." How can a company best use the services of its consultants, ad agencies, and suppliers? What kinds of partnerships can it create with other companies in the same industry—even companies with which it competes? And how about customers? Companies today still need to focus on delivering a product and making the numbers, but above all they must realize that the need to serve the customer drives everything else.

Best serving the customer can start with involving the customer more in company decisions. Customers now do some of the work that used to be done by employees, such as filling their own gas tanks, pouring their own soft drinks in restaurants, and using ATMs. But now some companies are more effectively capitalizing on customers' brains—not just their hands, but their opinions and ideas.

For example, market research has always measured consumer attitudes. Now, companies like P&G are getting customers to think creatively and talk with one another online to come up with new product and service ideas. P&G's reflect.com allows consumers to create up to 50,000 cosmetic and perfume formulations.[16] WingspanBank.com, an offshoot of Bank One Corp., invites customers to help improve its services. "Our customers have a great desire to improve the bank, and we act on their ideas," says the president.[17] This isn't about the occasional comment from a customer; it's about a strategic, systematic, active approach to achieve better customer service through actively managing customer relationships in such a way that customers contribute their best ideas.

The Internet, globalization, the monumental importance of new ideas, collaboration across disappearing boundaries . . . what are the repercussions of this tidal wave of new forces? The magazine *Fast Company* asked 17 new-economy leaders to comment on the promises and perils of the new economy. Table 1.2 shows some of their comments. The complete comment by an MIT business professor follows the table.

table 1.2
Comments on the
new economy

Comments on the new economy

Tom Peters, author and consultant: "Somebody once asked me what I wanted my epitaph to say. I want it to say, 'He was a player.' It wouldn't mean that I got rich . . . It would mean that I participated fully in these fascinating times . . . whatever this 'new economy' thing is, it is reinventing the world of commerce."

Patricia Seybold, author of customers.com: "A lot of people think the new economy is all about the Internet . . . it's really about customers. Customers are transforming entire industries . . . the customer is at the core of the business."

Caroline Soeborg Ohlsen, CEO of MouseHouse: "It's fantastic to be alive at a time when you can have an idea that, through its realization, can profoundly impact the way that commerce, communication, and society at large work. We can create products, services, or processes that will possibly affect the lives of our children and our grandchildren."

Jonathan Hoenig, founder of capitalistpig asset management: "The most valuable commodity isn't soybeans but service . . . The human touch is what's going to propel our 'commodified' business models into the next century and beyond. I feel terribly privileged to be alive at such an exciting time in history."

Nathan Myhrvold, cofounder and copresident of Intellectual Ventures: "The new economy is about rethinking and reshaping what has already happened. It's about producing fertile ground for radically new ideas. Workers with good ideas, or the ability to generate ideas, can write their own ticket."

Krishna Subramanian, chairwoman and CEO, Kovair Inc.: "Companies used to be structured around individual contribution. Now teamwork—presenting a seamless interface to the customer, across all points of contact and all business functions—is becoming more important . . . What do I worry about? Pace. Everything is so frenzied right now. I'm not sure that we stop—or even slow down—often enough to think about what we're doing, to try to balance our work with our lives."

Pehong Chen, chairman, president and CEO, Broadvision Inc.: "That's what is so awesome about the new economy. You have the ability to do something with your work and to know that you made a difference. You. Not your system. Not your company's policies. You."

What is your reaction to these comments? Many of these issues are discussed in later chapters.

Source: R.F. Maruca, "Voices," *Fast Company*, September 2000, pp. 105–144.

A comment on the new economy

WE HAVE AN OPPORTUNITY TO INVENT A NEW WORLD—collectively. And we can make it better than the existing world, not just in a narrowly economic sense but also in a broader human sense: for ourselves and for our children and for our children's children.

For instance, new information technologies and new ideas about management are bringing us to a place where we can consider radically new ways of organizing work. It may be possible to create companies that give employees a better sense of achievement, of camaraderie, or of autonomy than ever before.

That's tremendously exciting.

What worries me is the possibility that we'll create a world that is much more economically efficient—but that is much less satisfying to live in—than the one that we inhabit today.

Right now, when you hear the words "new economy," you probably think of dotcoms and extraordinary wealth. But you probably don't think of personal satisfaction. I'm worried that we won't bring the personal side of the equation up to the level of the financial side.

I also worry about people who live and work in developing countries. It's clear that the economy is becoming more global. But the jury is still out on whether the developing world will be integrated into the developed world in a thoughtful and fair way, or in a way that exploits and oppresses people.

We have a historical opportunity—perhaps even a historical obligation—to make wise choices about how we move forward.

I just hope we don't blow it.

Thomas W. Malone (malone@mit.edu) is the Patrick J. McGovern Professor of Information Systems at the MIT Sloan School of Management. He is also the founder and director of the MIT Center for Coordination Science and was one of the two founding codirectors of the five-year MIT research initiative "Inventing the Organizations of the 21st Century."

Source: *Fast Company*, September, 2000 p. 142. ●

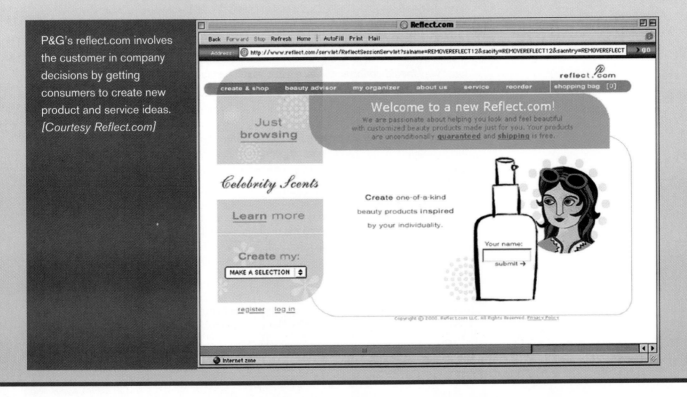

P&G's reflect.com involves the customer in company decisions by getting consumers to create new product and service ideas.
[Courtesy Reflect.com]

Managing for competitive advantage

In the last several years, the rise of the Internet seems to have turned lives upside down. People dropped out of school to join Internet start-ups, or start their own. Managers in big corporations quit their jobs to do the same. Investors salivated, and invested heavily. The risks were often ignored, or downplayed, sometimes tragically.

Consider two earlier industries of similar transforming power: automobiles and aviation. There have been at least 2,000 car makers, but now there are only three car companies left in the United States—and even they have not been great investments. Similarly, hundreds of aircraft manufacturers have gone bankrupt (Continental, twice). And the total amount of money made by all U.S. airline companies is zero. That's right: All of those companies in total have made no money whatsoever.[18]

What is the lesson to be learned from all the failures in these important transformational industries? A key to understanding the success of a company—whether traditional, Internet-based, or a combination of both—is not how much the industry in which it operates will affect society, or how much it will grow. The key is the competitive advantage held by a particular company, and how sustainable or renewable that advantage is.[19] Good managers know that they are in a competitive struggle to survive and win.

To survive and win, you have to gain advantage over your competitors. You gain competitive advantage by being better than your competitors at doing valuable things for your customers. But what does this mean, specifically? What drives success? What must managers deliver? The fundamental success drivers are quality, cost competitiveness, innovation, and speed.

Cost competitiveness

cost competitiveness
Keeping costs low in order to achieve profits and prices that are attractive to consumers.

Cost competitiveness means that your costs are kept low enough so that you can realize profits and price your products (goods or services) at levels that are attractive to consumers. Needless to say, if you can offer a desirable product at a low price, it is more likely to sell. Southwest Airlines is a good example of a company that has a big cost advantage over its rivals.[20]

You can offer low prices by managing your costs and keeping them down. This means being efficient: accomplishing your goals by using your resources wisely and minimizing waste. If your cost structure is competitive (as low as or lower than your competitors'), your success is not guaranteed. But you cannot be successful without a competitive cost structure.[21]

Raw materials, equipment, capital, manufacturing, marketing, delivery, and labor are just some of the costs that need to be managed carefully. One reason so many dot.coms fail is that their huge, up-front advertising costs usually don't translate into big sales; their customer acquisition costs are as much as four times higher than those of offline competitors. Because the cost of customer acquisition is so high, the Net is a great way to communicate with customers but a terrible way to get new customers.[22]

John Chambers, CEO of Cisco Systems, predicts that in the next three years the prices of consumer products in Britain will come down 10 percent to 15 percent, and the price of a new car will come down 30 percent.[23] Why? Because consumers can now easily compare prices on the Net from thousands of competitors. If you can't cut costs, you can't compete.

Quality

A CPA in Michigan says, "People are more aware than ever that you are judged by the quality of your product above all."[24] Larry Harmon, a highly successful plumber in California, wants to start franchising: "I think the nation is ready for a national franchised plumbing company—as long as it is high quality."[25] Brio America, a division of the

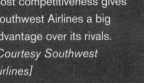

Cost competitiveness gives Southwest Airlines a big advantage over its rivals. *[Courtesy Southwest Airlines]*

Swedish maker of high-quality toys, distributes through small specialty toy stores rather than the huge toy merchants. Why? The specialty stores "sell toys based on what is in the package rather than what is on the package."[26] In other words, they focus on quality products that provide the value customers want.

quality The excellence of a product, including such things as attractiveness, lack of defects, reliability, and long-term dependability.

Quality is the excellence of your product, including its attractiveness, lack of defects, reliability, and long-term dependability. The importance of quality, and standards for acceptable quality, have increased dramatically in recent years. Firms cannot get by offering poor-quality products as they could a few years ago. Customers now demand high quality and value, and will accept nothing less.

Providing world-class quality requires a *thorough* understanding of what quality really is.[27] Quality can be measured in terms of performance, additional features, reliability (failure or breakdowns), conformance to standards, durability, serviceability, and aesthetics. Only by moving beyond broad, generic concepts like "quality," to identifying the more specific elements of quality, can you identify problems, target needs, set performance standards more precisely, and deliver world-class value.

Speed

speed Fast and timely execution, response, and delivery of results.

Speed often separates the winners from the losers in the world of competition. How fast can you develop and get a new product to market? How quickly can you respond to customer requests? You are far better off if you are faster than the competition—and if you can respond quickly to your competitors' actions.

Speed isn't everything—reliability, dependability, quality, costs, and so forth separate winners from losers. But those things being equal, faster companies are more likely to be the winners; slow ones the losers. Even pre-Internet, speed had become a vital requirement in the 1990s. Companies were getting products to market, and in the hands of customers, faster than ever. Now, the speed requirement has increased exponentially. Andy Grove, chairman of Intel Corporation, says the Internet is a tool, and the biggest impact of that tool is speed.[28] Everything, it seems, is on fast-forward.

For executives at established companies who left their world and joined the "great migration" to risky Internet start-ups, one of the biggest shocks was the sheer speed of Internet life. L. Gregory Ballard of MyFamily.com said that in established companies, you should not make any major decisions in your first three months on the job, while you learn the business. But "Internet time doesn't give you three months. It gives you three days"[29] (p. 5).

Innovation

innovation Introduction of new products.

Two Stanford business professors recently completed a study of 18 great companies. Impressed with all the companies, the authors still were able to choose one above them all that they believed would be the most successful over time. That company was 3M, and the reason is its extraordinary ability to innovate.[30]

Innovation is the introduction of new goods and services. Your firm must adapt to changes in consumer demands and to new sources of competition. Products don't sell forever; in fact, they don't sell for nearly as long as they used to, because so many competitors are introducing so many new products all the time. Your firm must innovate, or it will die. Like the other sources of competitive advantage, innovation comes from people; it must be a goal; and it must be managed. You will learn how 3M and other great companies innovate in later chapters.

Delivering all four

Don't assume you can settle for delivering just one of the four competitive advantages: low cost alone, or quality alone, for example. The best managers and companies deliver them all. And small firms that can provide multiple advantages over larger, more powerful companies can seize the competitive edge. For example, in custom software development, big name corporations take a long time and charge big daily fees that can add up seemingly forever. Sapient Corp. was founded on the premise that customers who want new software systems would love to be given a guaranteed delivery date and a fixed price. With this combination of speed and low price, relative to its famous competitors, Sapient got off to a flying start.[31]

Michael Dell started Dell Computer in his dorm room and used a low-cost, direct-sales approach to making his company the driving force in the PC business. Dell says, "We will be the lowest-cost provider, period."[32] But low cost is not the only thing at which Dell excels. Dell builds and ships PCs within 36 hours of receiving an order. All of its suppliers know they must deliver parts to Dell within one hour. At the same time, Dell computers have consistently held some of the highest quality ratings in the industry. Nonetheless, Michael Dell recently became obsessed with improving quality even further.[33] The sensitive hard drive needed to be handled less during assembly, he decided. Revamping the production lines, he reduced the number of touches from more than 30 per drive to fewer than 15. Rejected hard drives fell by 40 percent, and the overall PC failure rate by 20 percent.

From his dorm room, Michael Dell took on giants IBM, Apple, and Compaq. The amazing success of Dell computer is due to its quality, low cost, innovation, and speed.
[Reuters/Toshiyuki Aizawa/Archive Photos]

The functions of management

management The process of working with people and resources to accomplish organizational goals.

Management is the process of working with people and resources to accomplish organizational goals. Good managers do those things both effectively and efficiently. To be *effective* is to achieve organizational goals. To be *efficient* is to achieve goals with minimum waste of resources; that is, to make the best possible use of money, time, materials, and people. Some managers fail on both criteria, or focus on one at the expense of another. The best managers maintain a clear focus on both effectiveness *and* efficiency.

These definitions have been around for a long time. But as you know, business is changing radically. The real issue is what to *do*.[34]

If the new economy is so new, do we need to abandon all of the old management concepts, and start all over?[35] It is true that the context of business and the specifics of doing business are changing. But there are still plenty of timeless principles that make great managers, and great companies, great. While fresh thinking and new approaches are required now more than ever, much of what has already been learned about successful management practices remains relevant, useful, and adaptable, with fresh thinking, to the 21st century business environment.

To use an analogy: Engineering practices evolve continually, but the laws of physics are relatively constant.[36] In the business world today, the great executives not only adapt to changing conditions, but also apply—fanatically, rigorously, consistently, and with discipline—the fundamental management principles. You must understand and adapt to what's happening in the business environment, but your best chance of success lies in knowing and applying the proven fundamentals. These fundamentals include the four traditional functions of management: planning, organizing, leading, and controlling. They remain as relevant as ever, and they still provide the fundamentals that are needed in startups as much as in established corporations. But their form has evolved.

Planning: delivering strategic value

planning The management function of systematically making decisions about the goals and activities that an individual, a group, a work unit, or the overall organization will pursue in the future.

Planning is specifying the goals to be achieved and deciding in advance the appropriate actions taken to achieve those goals. Planning activities include analyzing current situations, anticipating the future, determining objectives, deciding in what types of activities the company will engage, choosing corporate and business strategies, and determining the resources needed to achieve the organization's goals. Plans set the stage for action and for major achievements.

Part 2 of this textbook is dedicated to planning, but the planning function for the new era is more broadly described as *delivering strategic value*. Historically, planning described a top-down approach to establishing business plans that must then be implemented. Now and in the future, delivering strategic value is a dynamic process in which people throughout the organization use their brains and the brains of customers, suppliers, and other stakeholders to identify opportunities to create, seize, strengthen, and sustain competitive advantage. This dynamic process swirls around the objective of creating more and more value for the customer. Effectively creating value requires fully considering a new and changing set of stakeholders and issues, including the government, the natural environment, globalization, and the dynamic economy in which ideas are king and entrepreneurs are both formidable competitors and potential collaborators. You will learn about these and related topics in Chapter 4 (planning and strategic management), Chapter 5 (ethics and corporate social responsibility), Chapter 6 (international management), and Chapter 7 (new ventures).

Organizing: building a dynamic organization

organizing The management function of assembling and coordinating human, financial, physical, informational, and other resources needed to achieve goals.

Organizing is assembling and coordinating the human, financial, physical, informational, and other resources needed to achieve goals. Activities include attracting people to the organization, specifying job responsibilities, grouping jobs into work units, marshalling and allocating resources, and creating conditions so that people and things work together to achieve maximum success.

Part 3 of the book describes the organizing function as *building a dynamic organization*. Historically, organizing involved creating an organization chart by identifying business functions, establishing reporting relationships, and having a personnel department that administered plans, programs, and paperwork. Now and in the future, effective managers will be using new forms of organizing and viewing their people as perhaps their most valuable resources. They will build organizations that are flexible and adaptive, particularly in response to competitive threats and customer needs. Progressive human resource practices that attract and retain the very best of a highly diverse population will be essential aspects of the successful company. You will learn about these topics in Chapter 8 (organization structure), Chapter 9 (responsive organizations), Chapter 10 (human resources management), and Chapter 11 (the diverse workforce).

Leading: mobilizing people

leading The management function that involves the manager's efforts to stimulate high performance by employees.

Leading is stimulating people to be high performers. It is directing, motivating, and communicating with employees, individually and in groups. Leading involves close day-to-day contact with people, helping to guide and inspire them toward achieving team and organizational goals. Leading takes place in teams, departments, and divisions, as well as at the tops of large organizations.

In earlier textbooks, the leading function was about how managers motivate workers to come to work and execute top management's plans by doing their jobs. Today and in the future, managers must be good at *mobilizing people* to contribute their ideas, to use their brains in ways never needed or dreamed of in the past. As described in Part 4, they must rely on a very different kind of leadership (Chapter 12) that empowers and motivates people (Chapter 13). Far more than in the past, great work must be done via great teamwork (Chapter 14), both within work groups and across group boundaries. Ideally, underlying these processes will be effective interpersonal and organizational communication (Chapter 15).

Managers work with people and resources to accomplish organizational goals.
[Walter Hodges/Stone]

Controlling: learning and changing

controlling The management function of monitoring progress and making needed changes.

Planning, organizing, and leading do not guarantee success. The fourth function, **controlling,** monitors progress and implements necessary changes.

When managers implement their plans, they often find that things are not working out as planned. The controlling function makes sure that goals are met. It asks and answers the question, "Are our actual outcomes consistent with our goals?" It makes adjustments as needed.

Successful organizations, large and small, pay close attention to the controlling function. But Part 5 of the book makes it clear that today and for the future, the key managerial challenges are far more dynamic; they involve continually *learning and changing*. Controls must still be in place, as described in Chapter 16. But new technologies and other innovations (Chapter 17) make it possible to achieve controls in more effective ways, and to help everyone throughout the company, and across company boundaries (including customers and suppliers), to use their brains, learn, make a variety of new contributions, and help the organization change in ways that forge a successful future (Chapter 18).

The four management functions apply to you personally, as well. You must find ways to create value, organize for your own personal effectiveness, mobilize your own talents and skills as well as those of others, and constantly learn, develop, and change for the future. As you proceed through this book, and this course, we encourage you to not merely do your "textbook learning" of an impersonal course subject, but to think about these issues from a personal perspective as well, using the ideas for personal development and advantage.

Performing all four management functions

As a manager, your typical day will not be neatly divided into the four functions. You will engage in all of these activities, but usually not independently or sequentially. You will be doing many things more or less simultaneously.[37] Your days will be busy and fractionated, spent dealing with interruptions, meetings, and firefighting. There will be plenty to do that you wish you could be doing but can't seem to get to. These activities will involve all four management functions.

Some managers are particularly interested in, devoted to, or skilled in a couple of the four functions but not in the others. The manager who does not devote adequate attention and resources to *all four* functions will fail. You can be a skilled planner and controller, but if you organize your people improperly or fail to inspire them to perform at high levels, you will not be an effective manager. Likewise, it does no good to be the kind of manager who loves to organize and lead, but who doesn't really understand where to go or how to determine whether you are on the right track. Good managers don't neglect any of the four management functions. Knowing what they are, you can periodically ask yourself if you are devoting adequate attention to *all* of them.

The management process: Effective action, great results

Louise Kitchen, age 29, successfully managed all four management functions at the gas company Enron. Kitchen was head of Enron's 200-person gas-trading business. One day, her boss asked her a simple question: Would she be interested in looking at the risks and rewards of trading gas contracts online? The risks were huge, as the slightest errors or losses could be catastrophic. She was definitely interested, believing that this was the future and that Enron had to get there fast.

She swung into action with all four management functions. Her plan was not just to "look at" Enron's options for online trading. She wanted to create real value by kicking the door wide open to this new way of doing business, developing a great online trading system, and getting Enron on the Net before its competitors. She started working immediately on her action plan.

Kitchen couldn't do it alone; she couldn't do it without lots of help. She needed to build a coalition of talent and support. She began organizing. She met with Enron's "heads of desks," the top traders. The idea sounded crazy to the traders, and "There was total disbelief that we could actually pull this off" (p. 180). But they were impressed with her enthusiasm and commitment.

She kept lobbying, and one by one she talked collaborators into getting on board with her Internet cause. Her new team roughed out a plan for the system. Now they had a plan, the team was organized, and they were motivated. But she needed more help, beyond her team, and cajoled the doubters by saying, "Do you see the world going this way in the next two or three years? If so, shouldn't we be first?" (p. 182). Eventually over 300 people were involved in one way or another.

The importance of effective controls was looming large. Inappropriate pricing information, for example, could cost Enron millions. The traders started experimenting with the system, voiced their concerns, and made suggestions. Kitchen and her team listened to the feedback and made changes. They made the system more precise, entered passwords into the system to be sure they worked, proofread Web pages, and did one final test. The test was successful, and the big launch came on November 29, 1999. EnronOnline was selling U.S. and Canadian gas online.

Just six months after her boss asked the question, Kitchen and her colleagues had revolutionized the energy-trading business, were doing more than $1 billion in trades daily, and had raised Enron's market value by billions of dollars. In *Fortune*'s annual poll measuring corporate reputations, Enron is ranked number one for innovativeness and quality of management.

This is just a short version of a complex process, the process of managing. The rest of the book is dedicated to fleshing out more of the details.

G. Hamel, "Driving Grassroots Growth." *Fortune,* September 4, 2000, pp. 173–87.

Management levels and skills

Different managers emphasize different activities or exhibit different management styles. There are many reasons for these differences, including the managers' training, personalities, and backgrounds. However, you will find that the organizational level at which the manager operates often influences the mixture of important functions and skills. Organizations (particularly large organizations) have multiple levels. In this section, you will learn about the types of managers found at three different levels in large organizations: top-level, middle, and frontline. Figure 1.1 shows the levels these managers occupy within the large organization.

Top-level managers

top-level managers Senior executives responsible for the overall management and effectiveness of the organization.

Top-level managers are the senior executives of an organization and are responsible for its overall management. Typically top-level managers, often referred to as *strategic managers,* focus on long-term issues and emphasize the survival, growth, and overall effectiveness of the organization.

Top managers are concerned not only with the organization as a whole, but also with the interaction between the organization and its external environment. This interaction often requires managers to work extensively with outside individuals and organizations.

The chief executive officer (CEO) is one type of top-level manager found in large corporations. This individual is the primary strategic manager of the firm. Others include

figure 1.1
Management levels

the chief operating officer (COO), company presidents, vice presidents, and members of the top executive committee.

Traditionally, the role of top-level managers has been to set overall direction by formulating strategy and controlling resources. But now, top managers are more commonly called upon to be not only strategic architects but also true organizational leaders. As leaders they must create and articulate a broader corporate purpose with which people can identify, and one to which people will enthusiastically commit. Effective top leaders treat people as valued members of the organization. Thus, Percy Barnevik, one of the most revered business leaders in Europe, strives to create an environment in which people are motivated to work for an organization in which they are proud to belong.

Middle-level managers

middle-level managers
Managers located in the middle layers of the organizational hierarchy, reporting to top-level executives.

As the name implies, **middle-level managers** are located in the organization's hierarchy between top-level management and the frontline managers. Sometimes called *tactical managers,* they are responsible for translating the general goals and plans developed by strategic managers into more specific objectives and activities.

Traditionally, the role of the middle manager is to be an administrative controller who bridges the gap between higher and lower levels. Middle-level managers take corporate objectives and break them down into business unit targets; put together separate business unit plans from the units below them for higher-level corporate review; and serve as linchpins of internal communication, interpreting and broadcasting top management's priorities downward, and channeling and translating information from the front lines, upward.

The evolving role of middle managers now requires them to be not only administrative controllers but also developmental coaches to the people who report to them. They should support the activities of their people, and coach people to become more entrepreneurial and innovative. Paul Guehler of 3M describes his job as "to help develop the people to develop the business."[38] Waldemar Schmidt of ISS, who recently became CEO, constantly contacted his frontline managers to say, "Well done!" and "How can I help?"

Middle managers should ensure that those reporting to them keep long-term strategic objectives and short-term, more immediate operating priorities in balance. For example, Paul Guehler forced one of his frontline managers to make major cuts in his units in order to meet financial objectives, but at the same time fought against attempts to close the unit down and worked to line up support and resources for the manager's proposed development initiatives.

Frontline managers

frontline managers Lower-level managers who supervise the operational activities of the organization.

Frontline managers, or *operational managers,* are lower-level managers who supervise the operations of the organization. These managers often have titles such as supervisor or sales manager. They are directly involved with nonmanagement employees, implementing the specific plans developed with middle managers. This role is critical in the organization, because operational managers are the link between management and nonmanagement personnel. Your first management position probably will fit into this category.

Traditionally, frontline managers have been directed and controlled from above, to make sure that they successfully implement operations in support of company strategy. But in leading companies, the role has expanded. Whereas the operational execution aspect of the role remains vital, in leading companies frontline managers are increasingly called upon to be innovative and entrepreneurial, managing for growth and new business development.

As examples, Andy Wong took over a struggling division at 3M, fought some battles, focused attention on new goals, reenergized a discouraged team of people, introduced new products, and found new markets for old products. His unit became a showcase within 3M—quite an honor in a company known for its innovative and successful business units.[39] When Don Jans managed Westinghouse's relays business unit, he was urged to milk the declining but modestly profitable operations. But when ABB bought Westinghouse's power transmission and distribution business, which included the relays business unit, Jans and his team were able to turn the mature business into one that looked like a new growth company. Export sales skyrocketed, new products were introduced, operating profits doubled, and the foundation was laid for long-term expansion into a major new growth area.[40]

These and other outstanding frontline managers are not only *allowed* to initiate new activities, but are *expected* to by their top- and middle-level managers. And they are given freedom, incentives, and support to find ways to do so.

Table 1.3 elaborates on the changing aspects of different management levels. You will learn about each of these aspects of management throughout this course.

Working leaders with broad responsibilities

You may have noted that several times we have qualified our descriptions of managerial levels by referring to large organizations. These descriptions represent the traditional model for large organizations. But the trend today is toward less hierarchy and more teamwork. Small companies have become more common and important as large corporations lay off people, those people and other entrepreneurs start their own firms, and

table 1.3
Transformation of management roles and tasks

	Frontline managers	Middle-level managers	Top-level managers
Changing roles	• From operational implementers to aggressive entrepreneurs	• From administrative controllers to supportive coaches	• From resource allocaters to institutional leaders
Primary value	• Driving business performance by focusing on productivity, innovation and growth within frontline units	• Providing the support and coordination to bring large company advantage to the independent frontline units	• Creating and embedding a sense of direction, commitment and challenge to people throughout the organization
Key activities	• Creating and pursuing new growth opportunities for the business	• Developing individuals and supporting their activities	• Challenging embedded assumptions while establishing a stretching opportunity horizon and performance standards
	• Attracting and developing resources and competencies	• Linking dispersed knowledge, skills, and best practices across units	• Institutionalizing a set of norms and values to support cooperation and trust
	• Managing continuous performance improvement within the unit	• Managing the tension between short-term performance and long-term ambition	• Creating an overarching corporate purpose and ambition

Source: C. Bartlett and S. Goshal, "The Myth of the Generic Manager: New Personal Competencies for New Management Roles," *California Management Review* Vol. 40, No. 1, Fall 1997, pp. 92–116.

these smaller firms prove themselves capable of beating the giants with specialized products and strategies and the ability to adapt quickly to change.

In these small firms—and in those large companies that have adapted to the times—managers have strategic, tactical, *and* operational responsibilities. They are *complete* businesspeople; they have knowledge of all business functions, are accountable for results, and focus on serving customers both inside and outside their firms. All of this requires the ability to think strategically, translate strategies into specific objectives, coordinate resources, and do real work with lower-level people.

In short, today's best managers can do it all; they are "working leaders."[41] They focus on relationships with other people and on achieving results. They are hands-on, working managers. They don't just make decisions, give orders, wait for others to produce, and then evaluate results. They get dirty, do hard work themselves, solve problems, and produce value.

Management skills

Performing management functions and achieving competitive advantage are the cornerstones of a manager's job. However, understanding this does not ensure success. Managers need a variety of skills to *do* these things *well*. Skills are specific abilities that result from knowledge, information, practice, and aptitude. Although managers need many individual skills, which you will learn about throughout the text, consider three general categories: technical skills, interpersonal and communication skills, and conceptual and decision skills.[42] When the key management functions are performed by managers who have these critical management skills, the result is a high-performance work environment.

technical skill The ability to perform a specialized task involving a particular method or process.

A **technical skill** is the ability to perform a specialized task that involves a certain method or process. Most people develop a set of technical skills to complete the activities that are part of their daily work lives. The technical skills you learn in school will provide you with the opportunity to get an entry-level position; they will also help you as a manager. For example, your basic accounting and finance courses will develop the technical skills you need to understand and manage the financial resources of an organization. Managers may rely less on their basic technical skills as they rise through an organization, but these skills give them the background for their new responsibilities, as well as an appreciation of the activities of others in the firm.

conceptual and decision skills Skills pertaining to a manager's ability to recognize complex and dynamic issues, examine the numerous and conflicting factors such issues involve, and resolve the problems for the benefit of the organization and its members.

Conceptual and decision skills involve the manager's ability to identify problems and resolve problems for the benefit of the organization and everyone concerned. Managers use these skills when they consider the overall objectives and strategy of the firm, the interactions among different parts of the organization, and the role of the business in its external environment. As you acquire greater responsibility, you must exercise your conceptual and decision skills with increasing frequency. You will confront issues that involve all aspects of the organization and must consider a larger and more interrelated set of decision factors. Much of this text is devoted to enhancing your conceptual and decision skills, but remember that experience also plays an important part in their development.

interpersonal and communication skills People skills; the ability to lead, motivate, and communicate effectively with others.

Interpersonal and communication skills influence the manager's ability to work well with people. These skills are often called *people skills*. Managers spend the great majority of their time interacting with people,[43] and they must develop their abilities to lead, motivate, and communicate effectively with those around them.

A recent *Fortune* article decried the lack of communication and other "people" skills among recent MBAs launching their management careers.[44] It is vital to realize the importance of these skills in getting a job, keeping it, and performing well in it. As one expert commented, "In many, many companies, the reason a manager fails is not because he doesn't have the technical skills. It's because he doesn't have the people skills."[45]

While there are still plenty of traditional managers around, concentrating on being the boss, giving orders, and carefully monitoring employees, the manager of today and of the future must focus more on interpersonal skills such as being a team player, sharing

Successful managers, such as amazon.com CEO Jeffrey Bezos, have the ability to work well with people.
[Mark Richards/Photo Edit]

information with others, and teaching and helping people learn. Many high-potential, "fast-track" managers have had their careers "derailed" due to problems in the interpersonal arena.[46]

You and your career

Chances are, you will work for several different organizations during your career. Some observers believe that "career jobs"—in which companies employ people and provide good wages and benefits for the long term—are disappearing.[47] Later in the book you will learn more about temporary and shifting employment relationships.

It is very true that jobs are no longer as secure for managers as they used to be. But currently, the shortage of managerial talent has sent the pendulum back toward development and retention of good people. Although companies no longer "guarantee" jobs permanently, those that provide long-term career benefits like training and profit sharing and some degree of security can improve corporate performance. Employee loyalty and commitment are still important; they improve teamwork, while outsourcing and temporary employment do not generate the high levels of service and quality that create customer satisfaction. Companies offering "employability" to workers, in the form of training and other learning experiences while employees fulfill more important responsibilities, tend to be more successful.[48]

With this in mind, the two models shown in Figure 1.2 illustrate career paths within a single organization. Traditionally, people's careers advanced through promotions up the hierarchy within a single business function or discipline. Now, career progress is more likely to include lateral moves across disciplines. Figure 1.2 depicts traditional, vertical career paths within single functions and the current move toward career paths that include sideways moves providing more general experience and demanding more general skills. Whatever your current interests and expertise, you should assume that you will need to become more of a generalist and to view the business and manage from a broader, strategic, general perspective.

What should you do to forge a successful, gratifying career? You are well-advised to be both a specialist and a generalist, to be self-reliant and connected, to actively manage your relationship with your organization, and to be fully aware of what is required to not only survive, but also to thrive, in today's world.

Be both a specialist and generalist

If you think your career will be as a specialist, think again. Managers are found in each area of an organization. Chances are, you will not want to stay forever in strictly technical jobs with no managerial responsibilities. Accountants are promoted to accounting

figure 1.2
Organizational careers: From vertical to horizontal paths

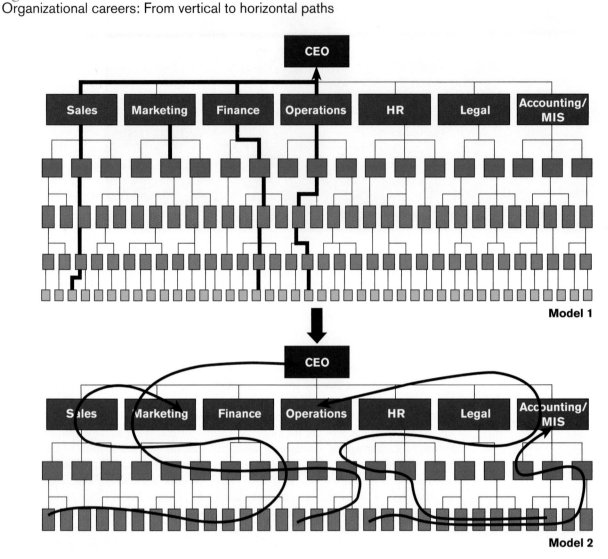

department heads and project team leaders, sales representatives become sales managers, writers become editors, and nurses become nursing directors. As your responsibilities increase, you must deal with more people, understand more about other aspects of the organization, and make bigger and more complex decisions. Beginning to learn now about these managerial challenges may yield benefits sooner than you think.

So, as the preceding discussion suggests, it will help if you can become both a specialist and a generalist.[49] Seek to become a *specialist:* you must be an expert in something. This will give you specific skills that help you provide concrete, identifiable value to your firm and to customers. And over time, you should learn to be a *generalist,* knowing enough about a variety of business or technical disciplines so that you can understand and work with different perspectives.

Be self-reliant

To be self-reliant means to take full responsibility for yourself, your actions, and your career.[50] You cannot count on your boss or your company to take care of you. A useful metaphor is to think of yourself as a business, with you as president and sole employee. Table 1.4 gives some specific advice about what this means in practice.

To make this point in another way: Managers today must be more entrepreneurial than ever. Apply this point directly to yourself. To add value, you must think and act like an entrepreneur. Even in a big corporation, one opportunity to start behaving entrepreneurially could be to create your own job title and responsibilities. What do you think are the meanings of some of these recently spotted job titles:[51] Director of Consumer Delight & Loyalty, Culture Czar, Chief Talent Scout, Director of Privacy, and Sultan of Sound Bites? Internet start-ups have had the most fun identifying new roles for people who want to find creative new ways to contribute. But who knows what job a person can create, even within a big corporation?

We have dedicated a chapter to entrepreneurship, and most of what you will read throughout the book applies to managers in entrepreneurial start-ups as well as to those in big corporations. Regardless of where you work, think and act like an entrepreneur. Don't just do your work and wait for orders; look for opportunities to contribute in new ways, to develop new products and processes, and generate constructive change that strengthens the company and benefits customers and colleagues.

Be connected

Being *connected* means having many good working relationships, and being a team player with strong interpersonal skills.[52] For example, those who want to become partners in professional service organizations like accounting, advertising, and consulting firms, strive constantly to build a network of contacts. Their goal is to work not only with lots of clients but also with a half-dozen or more senior partners, including several from outside their home offices and some from outside their country.

Few would argue against the usefulness of having such a strong network of allies. Just ask Jay Alix, a successful advisor to and acquirer of troubled companies who has helped restructure Wang Laboratories, Unisys, and National Car Rental System. Believing that in his competitive business getting hired is not a function of competence alone, but also of whom you know, Mr. Alix prides himself on his networking prowess. He stays in constant touch with hundreds of people, and calls his network of contacts "the daisy chain."[53]

Look at this another way: All business is a function of human relationships.[54] Building competitive advantage depends not only on you but on other people. Management is personal. Commercial dealings are personal. Purchase decisions, repurchase decisions, and contracts all hinge on relationships. Even the biggest business deals—takeovers—are intensely personal and emotional. Without good work relationships, you are an outsider, not a good manager and leader.

table 1.4
Keys to career
management

> Vicky Farrow of Sun Microsystems gives the following advice to help people assume responsibility for their own careers:
>
> 1. Think of yourself as a business.
>
> 2. Define your product: What is your area of expertise?
>
> 3. Know your target market: To whom are you going to sell this?
>
> 4. Be clear on why your customer buys from you. What is your "value proposition"—what are you offering that causes him to use you?
>
> 5. As in any business, strive for quality and customer satisfaction, even if your customer is just someone else in your organization—like your boss.
>
> 6. Know your profession or field and what's going on there.
>
> 7. Invest in your own growth and development, the way a company invests in research and development. What new products will you be able to provide?
>
> 8. Be willing to consider changing your career.
>
> Source: W. Kiechel III, "A Manager's Career in the New Economy," *Fortune,* April 4, 1994, pp. 68–72. Copyright © 1994 Times, Inc. All rights reserved. Reprinted by permission.

Actively manage your relationship with your organization

Many of the previous comments suggest the importance of taking responsibility for your own actions and your own career. Unless and until you become self-employed and your own boss, one way to do this is to think about the nature of the relationship between you and your employer. Figure 1.3 shows two possible relationships—and you have some control over which relationship you will be in. Relationship #1 is one in which you view yourself as an employee and passively expect your employer to tell you what to do and give you pay and benefits. Your employer, of course, also has the power to withhold these things from you. Your employer is in charge, and you are a passive recipient of its actions. This is a model for just getting by, perhaps for a long time, perhaps just for a while. But your contributions are likely to be minimal—you won't strengthen your organization, and if all organizational members take this perspective, the organization is not likely to be strong for the long run. Personally, you may lose your job, or keep your job in a declining organization, or receive few positive benefits from working there and either quit or become cynical and unhappy in your work.

In contrast, relationship #2 is a two-way exchange relationship in which you and your organization both benefit from one another. The mindset is different: Instead of doing what you are told, you think about how you can contribute—and you act accordingly. To the extent that your organization values your contributions, you are likely to benefit in return by receiving full and fair rewards, support for further personal development, and a more gratifying work environment. If you think in broad terms about how you can help your company, and if others think like this as well, there is likely to be continuous improvement in the company's ability to innovate, cut costs, and deliver quality products quickly to an expanding customer base. As the company's bottom line strengthens, benefits accrue to shareholders as well as to you and other employees.

What is the nature of the contributions you can make? You can do your basic work. This is the standard thing to do. But you can, and should, go further. You can also figure out new ways to add value—by thinking of and implementing new ideas that improve processes and results. You can do this by using your technical knowledge and skills, as in applying a better information system, accounting technique, or sales technique.

You also can contribute with your managerial actions (see Figure 1.4). As dynamic and challenging as today's business world is, you can contribute mightily by effectively executing the essential management functions and delivering competitive advantage. Your managerial actions can strengthen the organization, which in turn benefits you and others. You can deliver strategic value (Part 2 of this book). You can take actions that help build a more dynamic organization (Part 3). You can mobilize people to contribute to their fullest potential (Part 4). And you can learn and change—and help your colleagues and company learn and change—in order to adapt to changing realities and forge a successful future (Part 5).

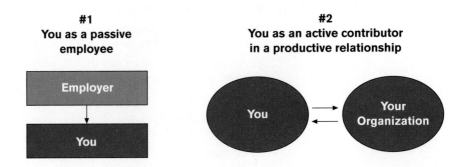

figure 1.3
Two relationships: Which will you choose?

#1
You as a passive employee

Employer

You

#2
You as an active contributor in a productive relationship

You ⇄ Your Organization

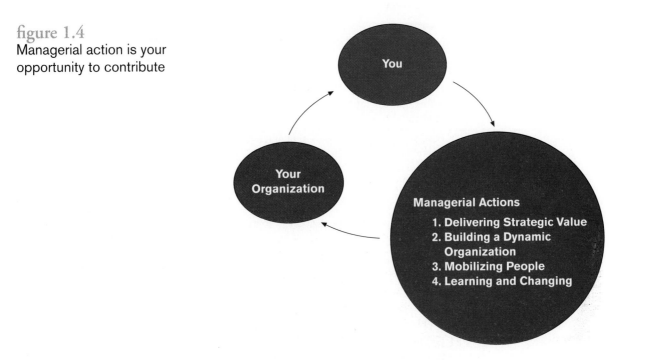

figure 1.4
Managerial action is your
opportunity to contribute

Survive and thrive

Table 1.5 shows a resume that might help a person to not just survive, but to thrive, in
the 21st century.[55] Don't be discouraged if your resume doesn't match this idealized
resume—it's tough to match, especially early in life! But do think about the messages.
It indicates the kinds of skills that companies need now more than ever—and therefore
the skills you might consider working to develop and the experiences you might want
to accumulate.

Management consultant and author Tom Peters points out that now—far more than
ever—you will be accountable for your actions and for results.[56] In the past, people at
many companies could show up, do an OK job, get a decent evaluation, and get a raise
equal to the cost of living and maybe higher. Today, managers must do more, better, and
it will all be far more visible. Managers will have many teammates, all around the globe,
some of whom will know each other personally but many of whom will never meet. You
are likely to move from project to project and from team to team. You will be evaluated
"pass by pass, at-bat by at-bat—for the quality and uniqueness and timeliness and passion" of your contribution.[57] Peters concludes that the minimal skills you will need to
survive and thrive are to be a master at something that the world values (and be able to
state succinctly what it is); to develop a strong network of colleagues who can help (and
whom you will help) with current and future projects; to have entrepreneurial skills that
help you act as if you were running your own business; to love technology; to market
yourself (for example, via a personal Website); and to be willing to constantly improve
and even reinvent yourself.

A recent study of career success led the author to state, "In the current economic environment, people who fear competition, want security, and demand stability are often sink-
ing like rocks in water."[58] Success requires high standards, self-confidence in competitive situations, and a willingness to keep growing and learning new things.[59] You will
need to learn how to think strategically, discern and convey your business vision, make
decisions, and work in teams. You will need to deliver competitive advantage and thrive
on change. These and other topics, essential to your successful career, provide the focus
for the following chapters.

table 1.5
A resume for the
21st century

A resume for the 21st century

Experience

- Multinational Corp—Worked with top-notch mentors in an established company with global operations. Managed a talented and fickle staff and helped tap new markets.

- Foreign Operation LLC—A stint at a subsidiary of a U.S. company, or at a foreign operation in a local market. Exposure to different cultures, conditions, and ways of doing business.

- Startup Inc.—Helped to build a business from the ground up, assisting with everything from product development to market research. Honed entrepreneurial skills.

- Major Competitor Ltd.—Scooped up by the competition and exposed to more than one corporate culture.

Education

- Liberal Arts University—Majored in economics, but took courses in psychology (how to motivate customers and employees), foreign language (the world is a lot bigger than the 50 states), and philosophy (to seek vision and meaning in your work).

- Graduate Studies—The subject almost doesn't matter, so long as you developed your thinking and analytical skills.

Extracurricular

- Debating (where you learned to market ideas and think on your feet).

- Sports (where you learned discipline and team work).

- Volunteer work (where you learned to step outside your own narrow world to help others).

- Travel (where you learned about different cultures).

Source: D. Brady "Wanted: Eclectic Visionary with a Sense of Humor," *Business Week.* August 28, 2000, p. 144.

Key terms

Summary of learning objectives

Now that you have studied Chapter 1, you should know:
The major challenges of managing in the new era.

Managers today must deal with dynamic forces that create greater and more constant change than ever before. Among many forces that are creating a need for managers to rethink their approaches, we highlighted four major waves of change: the Internet, globalization, knowledge management, and collaboration across organizational boundaries.

The drivers of competitive advantage for your company.

Because management is a competitive arena, you need to deliver value to customers in ways that are superior to your competitors. The four pillars of competitive advantage are low cost, quality products, speed, and innovation.

The functions of management and how they are evolving in today's business environment.

Despite massive change, management retains certain foundations that will not disappear. The primary functions of management are planning, organizing, leading, and controlling. Planning is analyzing a situation, determining the goals that will be pursued, and deciding in advance the actions needed to pursue these goals. Organizing is assembling the resources needed to complete the job and grouping and coordinating employees and tasks for maximum success. Leading is motivating people and stimulating high performance. Controlling is monitoring the progress of the organization or the work unit toward goals and then taking corrective action if necessary. In today's business environment, these functions more broadly require creating strategic value, building a dynamic organization, mobilizing people, and learning and changing.

The nature of management at different organizational levels.

Top-level, strategic managers are the senior executives and are responsible for the organization's overall management. Middle-level, tactical managers translate general goals and plans into more specific objectives and activities. Frontline, operational managers are lower-level managers who supervise the operations of the organization.

The skills you need to be an effective manager.

To execute management functions successfully, managers need technical skills, conceptual and decision skills, and interpersonal and communication skills. A technical skill is the ability to perform a specialized task involving a certain method or process. Conceptual and decision skills help the manager recognize complex and dynamic issues, analyze the factors that influence those issues or problems, and make appropriate decisions. Interpersonal and communication skills enable the manager to interact and work well with people.

What to strive for as you manage your career.

To help you succeed in your career, keep in mind several goals: Be both a specialist and a generalist; be self-reliant but also connected; actively manage your relationship with your organization; and continuously improve your skills in order to perform in the ways demanded in the changing work environment.

Discussion questions

1. Identify and describe a great manager. What makes him or her stand out from the crowd?

2. Have you ever seen or worked for an ineffective manager? Describe the causes and the consequences of the ineffectiveness.

3. Describe how the Internet and globalization affect your daily life.

4. Using Table 1.1, how would you describe your "Web DNA," and your interest and ability to successfully pursue a career in the "wired world"—and in management more generally?

5. Identify some examples of how different organizations collaborate "across boundaries."

6. Name a great organization. How do you think management contributes to making it great?

7. Name an ineffective organization. What can management do to improve it?

8. Give examples you have seen of firms that are outstanding and weak on each of the four pillars of competitive advantage. Why do you choose the firms you do?

9. Describe your use of the four management functions in the management of your daily life. Discuss the importance of technical, conceptual, and interpersonal skills at school and in jobs you have held.

10. What are your strengths and weaknesses as you contemplate your career? How do they correlate to the skills and behaviors identified in the chapter? How would you go about improving your managerial skills?

11. Devise a plan for developing yourself and making yourself attractive to potential employers.

Concluding Case
Would you work here?

At Siebel Systems, which sells complicated software packages, sales are up 117 percent. The stock is up 400 percent. The company has 5,200 employees. Some people love it there and are rewarded handsomely, but others don't survive the place for very long.

People say that the founder and CEO, Tom Siebel, is brilliant. They also say he is the most intense, competitive, driven person they know. "Running a business is a fundamentally rational process" says Siebel (p. 132). "We unemotionally put things on the table, look each other straight in the eye, and state the facts." Every six months, Mr. Siebel weeds out the bottom 5 percent of his workers.

Siebel Systems doesn't miss deadlines, like so many other software companies do. It releases new versions of its product every spring, right on schedule. And it is the only enterprise-software company in the United States to zoom past $1 billion in revenues without serious problems along the way. It is growing like crazy, but everything is carefully controlled.

Siebel has rules for everything. Offices must have medium-blue carpeting, off-white walls, gray desktops. There is no eating at desks, no cartoons or posters on doors. An occasional photo of family or friends is OK—but not too many. Men must wear suit and tie, and women must wear pant or skirt suits and pantyhose. It seems old-fashioned; Siebel knows this, but says it impresses customers.

Contrasting the work environment of his company with those of the Silicon Valley stereotype, Siebel says, "We go to work to realize our professional aspirations, not to have a good time. We could be having encounter groups and yoga classes, and I could play the guitar in the rock & roll band at the company picnic. Instead we're just trying to create good products, satisfied customers, and loyal employees. I think we're doing that" (p. 133). He also says "There are people who think I'm God's gift to technology, and people who think I'm the world's biggest S.O.B" (p. 140).

Siebel wants all of his people to focus on the customer, and motivates them by systematically and regularly measuring customer satisfaction with specific departments and individuals. These results determine bonuses and commissions. Moreover, to remind his people who matters most, every conference room is named after a Siebel customer. Says Siebel, "The cornerstone of our corporate culture is that we are committed to do whatever it takes to make sure that each and every one of our customers succeeds" (p. 136).

Siebel believes that if he keeps micromanaging, the company will grind to a halt, so he is trying to loosen up a bit and stop over-controlling. Some people say that he is changing. But the character of the company remains: If you want to succeed there, you must be smart, thorough, fastidious about the details, and perhaps a workaholic. You must also be fast; Siebel sometimes calls on a customer on a Friday and promises a proposal by Monday. One employee says, "That's part of the reason we win so many deals. We turn on a dime" (p. 140).

Questions

1. On a 10-point scale, in which 1 = not at all and 10 = extremely, how attractive is Siebel as a place to work?

2. What are the strengths and weaknesses of the organization and its leader?

3. Based on this profile, do you think Siebel will do well in the long run? How is it doing now?

4. How would you advise Mr. Siebel?

5. If you were interested in working for Siebel, would it see you as an attractive candidate? Why or why not?

6. If you worked for Siebel, how would you contribute to making the company stronger?

Source: M. Warner, "Confessions of a Control Freak," *Fortune,* September 4, 2000, pp. 130–140.

Thomas Siebel, founder and CEO of Siebel Systems, strives to create good products, satisfied customers, and loyal employees.
[AP/WIDE WORLD PHOTOS]

Experiential Exercises

1.1 Effective managers

Objectives

1. To better understand what behaviors contribute to effective management.

2. To conceive a ranking of critical behaviors that you personally believe reflects their importance to your success as a manager.

Instructions

1. Following is a partial list of behaviors in which managers may engage. Rank these items in terms of their importance for effective performance as a manager. Put a 1 next to the item that you think is most important, 2 for the next most important, down to 10 for the least important.

2. Bring your rankings to class. Be prepared to justify your results and rationale. If you can add any behaviors to this list that might lead to success or greater management effectiveness, write them in.

Effective managers worksheet

_____ Communicates and interprets policy so that it is understood by the members of the organization.

_____ Makes prompt and clear decisions.

_____ Assigns subordinates to the jobs for which they are best suited.

_____ Encourages associates to submit ideas and plans.

_____ Stimulates subordinates by means of competition among employees.

_____ Seeks means of improving management capabilities and competence.

_____ Fully supports and carries out company policies.

_____ Participates in community activities as opportunities arise.

_____ Is neat in appearance.

_____ Is honest in all matters pertaining to company property or funds.

Source: Excerpted from Lawrence R. Jauch, Arthur G. Bedeian, Sally A. Coltrin, and William F. Glueck, *The Managerial Experience: Cases, Exercises, and Readings,* 4th ed. Copyright © 1986 by The Dryden Press. Reprinted by permission of the publisher.

1.2 Career Planning

Objectives

1. To explore your career thinking.

2. To visualize your ideal job in terms as concrete as possible.

3. To summarize the state of your career planning, and to become conscious of the main questions you have about it at this point.

Instructions

Read the instructions for each activity, reflect on them, and then write your response. Be as brief or extensive as you like.

Career Planning Worksheet

1. Describe your ideal occupation in terms of responsibilities, skills, and how you would know if you were successful.

_____

_____

_____

_____

_____

_____

_____

2. Identify 10 statements you can make today about your current career planning. Identify 10 questions you need answered for career planning.

10 statements

1. _____

_____

_____

2. _____

_____

_____

3. _____

_____

_____

4. _____

_____

_____

5. _____

_____

_____

6. _____

_____

_____

7. _____

_____

_____

10 questions

1. _____

_____

_____

2. _____

_____

_____

3. _____

_____

_____

4. _____

_____

_____

5. _____

_____

_____

6. _____

_____

_____

7. _____

_____

_____

8. _____   8. _____

_____   _____

_____   _____

9. _____   9. _____

_____   _____

_____   _____

10. _____   10. _____

_____   _____

_____   _____

The 411 on . . .

The evolution of management

For thousands of years, managers have wrestled with the same issues and problems confronting executives today. Around 1100 B.C., the Chinese practiced the four management functions—planning, organizing, leading, and controlling—discussed in Chapter 1. Between 350 and 400 B.C., the Greeks recognized management as a separate art and advocated a scientific approach to work. The Romans decentralized the management of their vast empire before the birth of Christ. During medieval times, the Venetians standardized production through the use of an assembly line, building warehouses and using an inventory system to monitor the contents.[1]

But through out history most managers operated strictly on a trial-and-error basis. The challenges of the industrial revolution changed that. Management emerged as a formal discipline at the turn of the century. The first university programs to offer management and business education, the Wharton School at the University of Pennsylvania and the Amos Tuck School at Dartmouth, were founded in the late 19th century. By 1914, 25 business schools existed.[2]

Thus, the management profession as we know it today is relatively new. This appendix explores the roots of modern management theory. Understanding the origins of management thought will help you grasp the underlying contexts of the ideas and concepts presented in the chapters ahead.

Although this appendix is titled "The Evolution of Management," it might be more appropriately called "The Revolutions of Management," because it documents the wide swings in management approaches over the last 100 years. Out of the great variety of ideas about how to improve management, parts of each approach have survived and been incorporated into modern perspectives on management. Thus, the legacy of past efforts, triumphs, and failures has become our guide to future management practice.

Early management concepts and influences

Communication and transportation constraints hindered the growth of earlier businesses. Therefore, improvements in management techniques did not substantially improve performance. However, the industrial revolution changed that. As companies grew and became more complex, minor improvements in management tactics produced impressive increases in production quantity and quality.[3]

 The emergence of **economies of scale**—reductions in the average cost of a unit of production as the total volume produced increases—drove managers to strive for further growth. The opportunities for mass production created by the industrial revolution spawned intense and systematic thought about management problems and issues—particularly efficiency, production processes, and cost savings.[4]

Figure 1.A.1 provides a timeline depicting the evolution of management thought through the decades. This historical perspective is divided into two major sections: classical approaches and contemporary approaches. Many of these approaches developed simultaneously, and they often had a significant impact on one another. Some approaches were a direct reaction to the perceived deficiencies of previous approaches. Others developed as the needs and issues confronting managers changed over the years. All the approaches attempted to explain the real issues facing managers and provide them with tools to solve future problems.

figure 1.A.1
The evolution of management thought

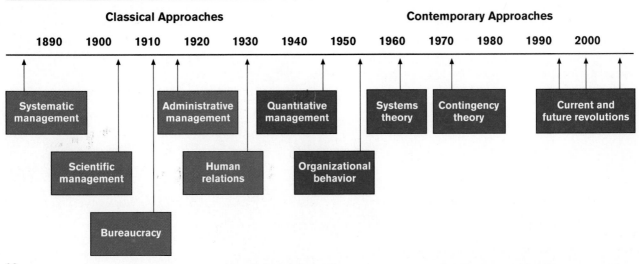

Production costs dropped as mass manufacturing lowered unit costs. Thus economies of scale was born, a
concept that persists in the modern manufacturing era.
[Martin Rogers/Tony Stone Images]

Figure 1.A.1 will reinforce your understanding of the key relationships among the approaches and place each perspective in its
historical context.

Classical approaches

The classical period extended from the mid-19th century through
the early 1950s. The major approaches that emerged during this period were systematic management, scientific management, administrative management, human relations, and bureaucracy.

Systematic management During the 19th century, growth in U.S.
business centered on manufacturing.[5] Early writers such as Adam
Smith believed the management of these firms was chaotic, and
their ideas helped to systematize it. Most organizational tasks were
subdivided and performed by specialized labor. However, poor coordination among subordinates and different levels of management
caused frequent problems and breakdowns of the manufacturing
process.

The **systematic management** approach attempted to build specific procedures and processes into operations to ensure coordination of effort. Systematic management emphasized economical operations, adequate staffing, maintenance of inventories to meet
consumer demand, and organizational control. These goals were
achieved through:

• Careful definition of duties and responsibilities.
• Standardized techniques for performing these duties.
• Specific means of gathering, handling, transmitting, and ana-
  lyzing information.
• Cost accounting, wage, and production control systems to
  facilitate internal coordination and communications.

Systematic management emphasized internal operations because managers were concerned primarily with meeting the explosive growth in demand brought about by the Industrial Revolution.

In addition, managers were free to focus on internal issues of efficiency, in part because the government did not constrain business
practices significantly. Finally, labor was poorly organized. As a result, many managers were oriented more toward things than toward
people.

Table 1.A.1 lists some of the key concepts, contributions, and
limitations of systematic management. Although systematic management did not address all the issues 19th-century managers
faced, it tried to raise managers' awareness about the most pressing
concerns of their job.

Scientific management Systematic management failed to lead to
widespread production efficiency. This shortcoming became apparent to a young engineer named Frederick Taylor who was hired by
Midvale Steel Company in 1878. Taylor discovered that production
and pay were poor, inefficiency and waste were prevalent, and most
companies had tremendous unused potential. He concluded that
management decisions were unsystematic and no research to determine the best means of production existed.

In response, Taylor introduced a second approach to management, known as **scientific management.**[6] This approach advocated
the application of scientific methods to analyze work and to determine how to complete production tasks efficiently. For example,
U.S. Steel's contract with the United Steel Workers of America
specified that sand shovelers should move 12.5 shovelfuls per
minute; shovelfuls should average 15 pounds of river sand composed of 5.5 percent moisture.[7]

Taylor identified four principles of scientific management:

1. Management should develop a precise, scientific approach for
each element of one's work to replace general guidelines.

table 1.A.1
Systematic management

Key concepts
Systematized manufacturing operations.
Coordination of procedures and processes built into internal operations.
Emphasis on economical operations, inventory man-agement, and cost control.

Contributions
Beginning of formal management in the United States.
Promotion of efficient, uninterrupted production.

Limitations
Ignored relationship between an organization and its environment.
Ignored differences in managers' and workers' views.

Frederick Taylor (left) and Dr. Lillian Gilbreth (right) were early experts in managment efficiency.
[Stock Montage, Inc.]

2. Management should scientifically select, train, teach, and develop each worker so that the right person has the right job.

3. Management should cooperate with workers to ensure that jobs match plans and principles.

4. Management should ensure an appropriate division of work and responsibility between managers and workers.

To implement this approach, Taylor used techniques such as time-and-motion studies. With this technique, a task was divided into its basic movements, and different motions were timed to determine the most efficient way to complete the task.

After the "one best way" to perform the job was identified, Taylor stressed the importance of hiring and training the proper worker to do that job. Taylor advocated the standardization of tools, the use of instruction cards to help workers, and breaks to eliminate fatigue.

 Another key element of Taylor's approach was the use of the differential piecerate system. Taylor assumed workers were motivated by receiving money. Therefore, he implemented a pay system in which workers were paid additional wages when they exceeded a standard level of output for each job. Taylor concluded that both workers and management would benefit from such an approach.

Scientific management principles were widely embraced. Other proponents, including Henry Gantt and Frank and Lillian Gilbreth, introduced many refinements and techniques for applying scientific management on the factory floor. One of the most famous examples of the application of scientific management is the factory Henry Ford built to produce the Model T.

 At the turn of the century, automobiles were a luxury that only the wealthy could afford. They were assembled by craftspeople who put an entire car together at one spot on the factory floor. These workers were not specialized, and Henry Ford believed they wasted time and energy bringing the needed parts to the car. Ford took a revolutionary approach to automobile manufacturing by using scientific management principles.

After much study, machines and workers in Ford's new factory were placed in sequence so that an automobile could be assembled without interruption along a moving production line. Mechanical energy and a conveyor belt were used to take the work to the workers.

The manufacture of parts likewise was revolutionized. For example, formerly it had taken one worker 20 minutes to assemble a flywheel magneto. By splitting the job into 29 different operations, putting the product on a mechanical conveyor, and changing the height of the conveyor, Ford cut production time to 5 minutes.

By 1914 chassis assembly time had been trimmed from almost 13 hours to 1½ hours. The new methods of production required complete standardization, new machines, and an adaptable labor force. Costs dropped significantly, the Model T became the first car accessible to the majority of Americans, and Ford dominated the industry for many years.[8]

The legacy of Taylor's scientific management approach is broad and pervasive. Most important, productivity and efficiency in manufacturing improved dramatically. The concepts of scientific methods and research were introduced to manufacturing. The piecerate system gained wide acceptance because it more closely aligned effort and reward. Taylor also emphasized the need for cooperation between management and workers. And, the concept of a management specialist gained prominence.

Despite these gains, not everyone was convinced that scientific management was the best solution to all business problems. First, critics claimed that Taylor ignored many job-related social and psychological factors by emphasizing only money as a worker incentive. Second, production tasks were reduced to a set of routine, machinelike procedures that led to boredom, apathy, and quality control problems. Third, unions strongly opposed scientific management techniques because they believed management might abuse their power to set the standards and the piecerates, thus exploiting workers and diminishing their importance. Finally, although scientific management resulted in intense scrutiny of the internal efficiency of organizations, it did not help managers deal

table 1.A.2
Scientific management

Analyzed work using scientific methods to determine the "one best way" to complete production tasks.

Emphasized study of tasks, selection and training of workers, and cooperation between workers and management.

Improved factory productivity and efficiency.

Introduced scientific analysis to the workplace.

Piecerate system equated worker rewards and performance.

Instilled cooperation between management and workers.

Simplistic motivational assumptions.

Workers viewed as parts of a machine.

Potential for exploitation of labor.

Excluded senior management tasks.

Ignored relationship between the organization and its environment.

with broader external issues such as competitors and government regulations, especially at the senior management level. Table 1.A.2 summarizes some of the key concepts, contributions, and limitations of scientific management.

Administrative management   The **administrative management** approach emphasized the perspective of senior managers within the organization, and argued that management was a profession and could be taught.

An explicit and broad framework for administrative management emerged in 1916, when Henri Fayol, a French mining engineer and executive, published a book summarizing his management experiences. Fayol identified five functions and 14 principles of management. The five functions, which are very similar to the four functions discussed in Chapter 1, include planning, organizing, commanding, coordinating, and controlling. Table 1.A.3 lists and defines the 14 principles. Although some critics claim Fayol treated the principles as universal truths for management, he actually wanted them applied flexibly.[9]

A host of other executives contributed to the administrative management literature. These writers discussed a broad spectrum of management topics, including the social responsibilities of management, the philosophy of management, clarification of business terms and concepts, and organizational principles. Chester Barnard's and Mary Parker Follet's contributions have become classic works in this area.[10]

Barnard, former president of New Jersey Bell Telephone Company, published his landmark book *The Functions of the Executive* in 1938. He outlined the role of the senior executive: formulating the purpose of the organization, hiring key individuals, and main-

taining organizational communications.[11] Mary Parker Follet's 1942 book *Dynamic Organization* extended Barnard's work by emphasizing the continually changing situations that managers face.[12] Two of her key contributions—the notion that managers desire flexibility and the differences between motivating groups and individuals—laid the groundwork for the modern contingency approach discussed later in the chapter.

All the writings in the administrative management area emphasize management as a profession along with fields such as law and medicine. In addition, these authors offered many recommendations based on their personal experiences, which often included managing large corporations. Although these perspectives and recommendations were considered sound, critics noted that they may not work in all settings. Different types of personnel, industry conditions, and technologies may affect the appropriateness of these principles.

Table 1.A.4 summarizes the administrative management approach.

table 1.A.3
Fayol's 14 principles of management

1. *Division of work*—divide work into specialized tasks and assign responsibilities to specific individuals.
2. *Authority*—delegate authority along with responsibility.
3. *Discipline*—make expectations clear and punish violations.
4. *Unity of command*—each employee should be assigned to only one supervisor.
5. *Unity of direction*—employees' efforts should be focused on achieving organizational objectives.
6. *Subordination of individual interest to the general interest*—the general interest must predominate.
7. *Remuneration*—systematically reward efforts that support the organization's direction.
8. *Centralization*—determine the relative importance of superior and subordinate roles.
9. *Scalar chain*—keep communications within the chain of command.
10. *Order*—order jobs and material so they support the organization's direction.
11. *Equity*—fair discipline and order enhance employee commitment.
12. *Stability and tenure of personnel*—promote employee loyalty and longevity.
13. *Initiative*—encourage employees to act on their own in support of the organization's direction.
14. *Esprit de corps*—promote a unity of interests between employees and management.

table 1.A.4
Administrative management

Key concepts
Fayol's five functions and 14 principles of management.
Executives formulate the organization's purpose, secure employees, and maintain communications.
Managers must respond to changing developments.

Contributions
Viewed management as a profession that can be trained and developed.
Emphasized the broad policy aspects of top-level managers.
Offered universal managerial prescriptions.

Limitation
Universal prescriptions need qualifications for environmental, technological, and personnel factors.

Human relations A fourth approach to management, **human relations,** developed during the 1930s. This approach aimed at understanding how psychological and social processes interact with the work situation to influence performance. Human relations was the first major approach to emphasize informal work relationships and worker satisfaction.

This approach owes much to other major schools of thought. For example, many of the ideas of the Gilbreths (scientific management) and Barnard and Follet (administrative management) influenced the development of human relations from 1930 to 1955. In fact, human relations emerged from a research project that began as a scientific management study.

Western Electric Company, a manufacturer of communications equipment, hired a team of Harvard researchers led by Elton Mayo and Fritz Roethlisberger. They were to investigate the influence of physical working conditions on workers' productivity and efficiency in one of the company's factories outside Chicago. This research project, known as the *Hawthorne Studies,* provided some of the most interesting and controversial results in the history of management.[13]

The Hawthorne Studies were a series of experiments conducted from 1924 to 1932. During the first stage of the project (the Illumination Experiments), various working conditions, particularly the lighting in the factory, were altered to determine the effects of these changes on productivity. The researchers found no systematic relationship between the factory lighting and production levels. In some cases, productivity continued to increase even when the illumination was reduced to the level of moonlight. The researchers concluded that the workers performed and reacted differently because the researchers were observing them. This reaction is known as the **Hawthorne Effect.**

This conclusion led the researchers to believe productivity may be affected more by psychological and social factors than by physical or objective influences. With this thought in mind, they initiated the other four stages of the project. During these stages, the researchers performed various work group experiments and had extensive interviews with employees. Mayo and his team eventually concluded that productivity and employee behavior were influenced by the informal work group.

Human relations proponents argued that managers should stress primarily employee welfare, motivation, and communication. They believed social needs had precedence over economic needs. Therefore, management must gain the cooperation of the group and promote job satisfaction and group norms consistent with the goals of the organization.

Another noted contributor to the field of human relations was Abraham Maslow.[14] In 1943, Maslow suggested that humans have five levels of needs. The most basic needs are the physical needs for food, water, and shelter; the most advanced need is for self-actualization, or personal fulfillment. Maslow argued that people try to satisfy their lower-level needs and then progress upward to the higher-level needs. Managers can facilitate this process and achieve organizational goals by removing obstacles and encouraging behaviors that satisfy people's needs and organizational goals simultaneously.

Although the human relations approach generated research into leadership, job attitudes, and group dynamics, it drew heavy criticism.[15] Critics believed that one result of human relations—a belief that a happy worker was a productive worker—was too simplistic. While scientific management overemphasized the economic and formal aspects of the workplace, human relations ignored the more rational side of the worker and the important characteristics of the formal organization. However, human relations was a significant step in the development of management thought, because it prompted managers and researchers to consider the psychological and social factors that influence performance.

Table 1.A.5 summarizes the human relations approach.

Bureaucracy Max Weber, a German sociologist, lawyer, and social historian, showed how management itself could be more efficient and consistent in his book *The Theory of Social and Economic Organizations.*[16] The ideal model for management, according to Weber, is the **bureaucracy** approach.

Weber believed bureaucratic structures can eliminate the variability that results when managers in the same organization have different skills, experiences, and goals. Weber advocated that the jobs themselves be standardized so that personnel changes would not disrupt the organization. He emphasized a structured, formal network of relationships among specialized positions in an organization. Rules and regulations standardize behavior, and authority resides in positions rather than in individuals. As a result, the organization need not rely on a particular individual, but will realize efficiency and success by following the rules in a routine and unbiased manner.

According to Weber, bureaucracies are especially important

table 1.A.5
Human relations

Key concepts

Productivity and employee behavior are influenced by the informal work group.

Cohesion, status, and group norms determine output. Managers should stress employee welfare, motivation, and communication.

Social needs have precedence over economic needs.

Contributions

Psychological and social processes influence performance.

Maslow's hierarchy of needs.

Limitations

Ignored workers' rational side and the formal organization's contribution to productivity.

Research findings later overturned the simplistic belief that happy workers are always more productive.

Quantitative management   Although Taylor introduced the use of science as a management tool early in the 20th century, most organizations did not adopt the use of quantitative techniques for management problems until the 1940s and 1950s.[17] During World War II, military planners began to apply mathematical techniques to defense and logistic problems. After the war, private corporations began assembling teams of quantitative experts to tackle many of the complex issues confronting large organizations. This approach, referred to as **quantitative management,** emphasizes the application of quantitative analysis to management decisions and problems.

Quantitative management helps a manager make a decision by developing formal mathematical models of the problem. Computers have facilitated the development of specific quantitative methods. These include such techniques as statistical decision theory, linear programming, queuing theory, simulation, forecasting, inventory modeling, network modeling, and break-even analysis. Organizations apply these techniques in many areas, including production, quality control, marketing, human resources, finance, distribution, planning, and research and development.

because they allow large organizations to perform the many routine activities necessary for their survival. Also, bureaucratic positions foster specialized skills, eliminating many subjective judgments by managers. In addition, if the rules and controls are established properly, bureaucracies should be unbiased in their treatment of people, both customers and employees.

Many organizations today are bureaucratic. Bureaucracy can be efficient and productive. However, bureaucracy is not the appropriate model for every organization. Organizations or departments that need rapid decision making and flexibility may suffer under a bureaucratic approach. Some people may not perform their best with excessive bureaucratic rules and procedures.

Other shortcomings stem from a faulty execution of bureaucratic principles rather than from the approach itself. Too much authority may be vested in too few people; the procedures may become the ends rather than the means; or managers may ignore appropriate rules and regulations. Finally, one advantage of a bureaucracy—its permanence—can also be a problem. Once a bureaucracy is established, dismantling it is very difficult.

Table 1.A.6 summarizes the key concepts, contributions and limitations of bureaucracy.

Contemporary approaches

The contemporary approaches to management include quantitative management, organizational behavior, systems theory, and the contingency perspective. The contemporary approaches have developed at various times since World War II, and they continue to represent the cornerstones of modern management thought.

table 1.A.6
Bureaucracy

Key concepts

Structured, formal network of relationships among specialized positions in an organization.

Rules and regulations standardize behavior.

Jobs staffed by trained specialists who follow rules.

Hierarchy defines the relationship among jobs.

Contributions

Promotes efficient performance of routine organizational activities.

Eliminates subjective judgment by employees and management.

Emphasizes position rather than the person.

Limitations

Limited organizational flexibility and slow decision making.

Ignores the importance of people and interpersonal relationships.

Accumulation of power can lead to authoritarian management.

Rules may become ends in themselves.

Difficult to dismantle once established.

table 1.A.7
Quantitative management [9]

Key concept
Application of quantitative analysis to management decisions.

Contributions
Developed specific mathematical methods of problem analysis.
Helped managers select the best alternative among a set.

Limitations
Models neglect nonquantifiable factors.
Managers not trained in these techniques and may not trust or understand the techniques' outcomes.
Not suited for nonroutine or unpredictable management decisions.

Despite the promise quantitative management holds, managers do not rely on these methods as the primary approach to decision making. Typically they use these techniques as a supplement or tool in the decision process. Many managers will use results that are consistent with their experience, intuition, and judgment, but they will reject results that contradict their beliefs. Also, managers may use the process to compare alternatives and eliminate weaker options.

Several explanations account for the limited use of quantitative management. Many managers have not been trained in using these techniques. Also, many aspects of a management decision cannot be expressed through mathematical symbols and formulas. Finally, many of the decisions managers face are nonroutine and unpredictable.

Table 1.A.7 summarizes the quantitative management approach.

Organizational behavior During the 1950s, a transition took place in the human relations approach. Scholars began to recognize that worker productivity and organizational success are based on more than the satisfaction of economic or social needs. The revised perspective, known as **organizational behavior,** studies and identifies management activities that promote employee effectiveness through an understanding of the complex nature of individual, group, and organizational processes. Organizational behavior draws from a variety of disciplines, including psychology and sociology, to explain the behavior of people on the job.

During the 1960s, organizational behaviorists heavily influenced the field of management. Douglas McGregor's Theory X and Theory Y marked the transition from human relations.[18] According to McGregor, Theory X managers assume workers are lazy and irresponsible and require constant supervision and external motivation to achieve organizational goals. Theory Y managers assume employees *want* to work and can direct and control themselves. McGregor advocated a Theory Y perspective, suggesting that managers who encourage participation and allow opportunities for individual challenge and initiative would achieve superior performance.

Other major organizational behaviorists include Chris Argyris, who recommended greater autonomy and better jobs for workers,[19] and Rensis Likert, who stressed the value of participative management.[20] Through the years, organizational behavior has consistently emphasized development of the organization's human resources to achieve individual and organizational goals. Like other approaches, it has been criticized for its limited perspective, although more recent contributions have a broader and more situational viewpoint. In the past few years, many of the primary issues addressed by organizational behavior have experienced a rebirth with a greater interest in leadership, employee involvement, and self-management.

Table 1.A.8 summarizes the key concepts, contributions, and limitations of organizational behavior.

Systems theory The classical approaches as a whole were criticized because they (1) ignored the relationship between the organization and its external environment, and (2) usually stressed one aspect of the organization or its employees at the expense of other considerations. In response to these criticisms, management scholars during the 1950s stepped back from the details of the organization to attempt to understand it as a whole system. These efforts were based on a general scientific approach called **systems**

table 1.A.8
Organizational behavior

Key concepts
Promotes employee effectiveness through understanding of individual, group, and organizational processes.
Stresses relationships among employees, managers, and the work they perform for the organization.
Assumes employees want to work and can control themselves (Theory Y).

Contributions
Increased participation, greater autonomy, individual challenge and initiative, and enriched jobs may increase performance.
Recognized the importance of developing human resources.

Limitation
Some approaches ignored situational factors, such as the environment and the organization's technology.

table 1.A.9
Systems theory

Key concepts

Organization is viewed as a managed system.

Management must interact with the environment to gather inputs and return the outputs of its production.

Organizational objectives must encompass both efficiency and effectiveness.

Organizations contain a series of subsystems.

There are many avenues to the same outcome.

Synergies exist where the whole is greater than the sum of the parts.

Contribution

Recognized the importance of the organization's relationship with the external environment.

Limitation

Does not provide specific guidance on the functions and duties of managers.

theory.[21] An organization is a managed system that changes inputs (raw materials, people, and other resources) into outputs (the goods and services that comprise its products).

Table 1.A.9 summarizes systems theory.

Contingency perspective Building on systems theory ideas, the **contingency perspective** refutes universal principles of management by stating that a variety of factors, both internal and external to the firm, may affect the organization's performance.[22] Thus, there is no "one best way" to manage and organize, because circumstances vary. For example, a universal strategy of offering low-cost products would not succeed in a market that is not cost conscious.

Situational characteristics are called **contingencies.** Understanding contingencies helps a manager know which sets of circumstances dictate which management actions. You will learn the recommendations for the major contingencies throughout this text.

The contingencies include

1. Circumstances in the organization's external environment.

2. The internal strengths and weaknesses of the organization.

3. The values, goals, skills, and attitudes of managers and workers in the organization.

4. The types of tasks, resources, and technologies the organization uses.

With an eye to these contingencies, a manager may categorize the situation and then choose the proper competitive strategy, organization structure, or management process for the circumstances.

Researchers continue to identify key contingency variables and their effects on management issues. As you read the topics covered in each chapter, you will notice similarities and differences among management situations and the appropriate responses. This perspective should represent a cornerstone of your own approach to management. Many of the things you will learn about throughout this course apply a contingency perspective.

Table 1.A.10 summarizes the contingency perspective.

table 1.A.10
Contingency perspective

Key concepts

Situational contingencies influence the strategies, structures, and processes that result in high performance.

There is more than one way to reach a goal.

Managers may adapt their organizations to the situation.

Contributions

Identified major contingencies.

Argued against universal principles of management.

Limitations

Not all important contingencies have been identified.

Theory may not be applicable to all managerial issues.

Contemporary approaches

All of these historical perspectives have left legacies that affect contemporary management thought and practice. Their undercurrents continue to flow, even as the context and the specifics change.

But new approaches to management continue to appear, and contribute to an ever-changing management profession. The remaining chapters report on these dynamic, contemporary perspectives. For example, the 1980s brought a new gospel called *quality management,* new perspectives on competition and on business strategy, a focus on excellence, and a renewed interest in people,

including both employees and customers.[23] The 1990s brought theories and practices such as learning organizations, lean manufacturing, knowledge management, and the characteristics of corporate cultures that help to build great, enduring companies.[24] The rest of this book, and perhaps the rest of your career, will be spent enacting the management functions, the drivers of competitive advantage, the enduring aspects of the historical perspectives, and the continually evolving contemporary perspectives on the successful practice of management.

Key terms

administrative management A classical management approach that attempted to identify major principles and functions that managers could use to achieve superior organizational performance, p. 35.

bureaucracy A classical management approach emphasizing a structured, formal network of relationships among specialized positions in the organization, p. 36.

contingencies Factors that determine the appropriateness of managerial actions, p. 39.

contingency perspective An approach to the study of management proposing that the managerial strategies, structures, and processes that result in high performance depend on the characteristics, or important contingencies, or the situation in which they are applied, p. 39.

economies of scale Reductions in the average cost of a unit of production as the total volume produces increases, p. 32.

Hawthorne Effect People's reactions to being observed or studied resulting in superficial rather than meaningful changes in behavior, p. 36.

human relations A classical management approach that attempted to understand and explain how human psychological and social processes interact with the formal aspects of the work situation to influence performance, p. 36.

organizational behavior A contemporary management approach that studies and identifies management activities that promote employee effectiveness by examining the complex and dynamic nature of individual, group, and organizational processes, p. 38.

quantitative management A contemporary management approach that emphasizes the application of quantitative analysis to managerial decisions and problems, p. 37.

scientific management A classical management approach that applied scientific methods to analyze and determine the "one best way" to complete production tasks, p. 33.

systematic management A classical management approach that attempted to build into operations the specific procedures and processes that would ensure coordination of effort to achieve established goals and plans, p. 33.

systems theory A theory stating that an organization is a set of interdependent elements, which in turn are interdependent with the external environment, p. 38.

Discussion questions

1. How does today's business world compare with the one of 40 years ago? What is different about today, and what is not so different?

2. What is scientific management? How might today's organizations use it?

3. Table 1.A.3 lists Fayol's 14 principles of management, first published in 1916. Are they as useful today as they were then? Why or why not? *When* are they most, and least, useful?

4. What are the advantages and disadvantages of a bureaucratic organization?

5. In what situations are quantitative management concepts and tools applicable?

6. Choose any organization and describe its system of inputs and outputs.

7. Why did the contingency perspective become such an important approach to management? Generate a list of contingencies that might affect the decisions you make in your life or as a manager.

8. For each of the management approaches discussed in the chapter, give examples you have seen. How effective or ineffective were they?

Experiential Exercises

1.A.1 Approaches to management

Objectives

1. To help you conceive a wide variety of management approaches.
2. To clarify the appropriateness of different management approaches in different situations.

Instructions

Your instructor will divide your class randomly into groups of four to six people each. Acting as a team, with everyone offering ideas and one person serving as official recorder, each group will be responsible for writing a one-page memo to your present class. Subject matter of your group's memo will be "My advice for managing people today is . . . " The fun part of this exercise (and its creative element) involves writing the memo from the viewpoint of the person assigned to your group by your instructor.

Among the memo viewpoints your instructor may assign are:

- An ancient Egyptian slave master (building the great pyramids)
- Henri Fayol
- Frederick Taylor
- Mary Parker Follett
- Douglas McGregor
- A contingency management theorist
- A Japanese auto company executive
- The chief executive officer of IBM in the year 2030
- Commander of the Starship Enterprise II in the year 3001
- Others, as assigned by your instructor

Use your imagination, make sure everyone participates, and try to be true to any historical facts you've encountered. Attempt to be as specific and realistic as possible. Remember, the idea is to provide advice about managing people from another point in time (or from a particular point of view at the present time).

Make sure you manage your 20-minute time limit carefully. A recommended approach is to spend 2 to 3 minutes putting the exercise into proper perspective. Next, take about 10 to 12 minutes brainstorming ideas for your memo, with your recorder jotting down key ideas and phrases. Have your recorder use the remaining time to write your group's one-page memo, with constructive comments and help from the others. Pick a spokesperson to read your group's memo to the class.

Source: R. Krietner and A. Kinicki, *Organization Behavior,* 3d ed. (Burr Ridge, IL: Richard D. Irwin, 1994), pp. 30–31.

1.A.2 The university grading system analysis

Objectives

1. To learn to identify the components of a complex system.
2. To better understand organizations as systems.
3. To visualize how a change in policy affects the functioning of an organization system.

Instructions

1. Assume that your university has decided to institute a pass–fail system of grading instead of the letter-grade system it presently has. Apply the systems perspective learned from this chapter to understanding this decision.
2. Answer the questions on the Grading System Analysis Worksheet individually, or in small groups, as directed by your instructor.

Discussion Questions

Share your own or your group's responses with the entire class. Then answer the following questions.

1. Did you diagram the system in the same way?
2. Did you identify the same system components?
3. Which subsystems will be affected by the change?
4. How do you explain differences in your responses?

Grading system analysis worksheet

Description

1. What subsystems compose the system (the university)? Diagram the system.

_____

_____

_____

_____

_____

_____

2. Identify in this system: inputs, outputs, transformations.

_____

_____

_____

_____

_____

_____

Diagnosis

3. Which of the subsystems will be affected by the change; that is, what changes are likely to occur throughout the system as a result of the policy change?

_____

_____

_____

_____

_____

_____

_____

Source: J. Gordon, A _Diagnostic Approach to Organizational Behavior_ (Englewood Cliffs, NJ: Prentice Hall, 1983), p. 38. Reprinted with permission of Prentice Hall, Inc., Englewood Cliffs, NJ. ●

Chapter Two
The External Environment

The essence of a business is outside itself.

— Peter Drucker

Chapter Outline

Learning Objectives

After studying Chapter 2, you will know:

1. How environmental forces influence organizations, as well as how organizations can influence their environments.

2. How to make a distinction between the macroenvironment and the competitive environment.

3. Why organizations should attend to economic and social developments in the environment.

4. How to analyze the competitive environment.

5. How organizations respond to environmental uncertainty.

Setting the Stage

The New Landscape for e-Learning

You've signed up for a management course called Managing in a Competitive Environment. Pretty boring topic, right? Let's hope it's not an 8:00 A.M. class. To your surprise, on the first day there's no dry lecture, not even a syllabus. From your laptop, you click to the opening screen and discover you're caught up in a (simulated) business crisis. You're the president of Giga Computers, a company that's getting beat up by Dell, Compaq, and Gateway. What's worse, you're having a difficult time getting the chips you need, at the price and specifications you want. And your distribution agreements with Computer Land have you tied in knots. As Giga's chief executive, you have to make a series of decisions to navigate through this minefield to save your company from the dreaded beasts warring in the digital marketplace.

Welcome to the virtual classroom. Learning over the Net is dramatically changing the environment—and industry—of management education and training. Customers are lining up to take a look at these innovations. Students like you are increasingly comfortable with the technologies and like the flexibility this format offers. Businesses and other customers for web training are finding that this alternative is more flexible, less costly, and more effective than traditional education and training programs. "It's time, not money, that's the precious commodity in business these days," says Jeff Oberlin, vice-president for course development and sourcing at Motorola University. The best online courses are better than (some) classroom teaching. New e-courses can be customized to your own learning style, calling up video clips of noted professors or industry pundits, if that's

Learning over the Net via the virtual classroom is dramatically changing management education and training.
[David Hanover/Stone]

your wish. You can skip parts you already know. And many courses require collaboration among students, which can be handled by e-mail or designated chat rooms.

Who are the competitors in this newly emerging industry? Well, universities for sure, but other businesses are getting into the game. UNext.com, for example, is a new Internet university that brings together talent from five elite schools—Columbia, Stanford, Chicago, Carnegie Mellon, and the London School of Economics. Three Nobel laureates are on the faculty, and investors such as Michael Milken and Oracle's Larry Ellison. Columbia was the first to sign on and the school will get 5 percent of the profits. If UNext flops, Columbia gets $20 million for its trouble. Nice deal. Customers like Bank of America are enrolling pilot groups of employees for classes. UNext is spending $1 million per course to develop not just a made-for-online curriculum, but an entirely new way of teaching over the Net. It will eventually offer MBA and other graduate degrees; the sheepskins will be from Cardean (CAR-dee-an) University. Other competitors include Corpedia (started by management guru Peter Drucker), Ninth House Network, ElementK, MeansBusiness, and SkillSoft.

Despite the excitement, e-learning is not yet a panacea. Some hands-on skills, such as presentation or communications proficiency, require attention to eye contact and body language, talents better mastered in face-to-face encounters. Adds LoriLee Sadler, UNext's technology chief, "What none of us is satisfied with is the social aspect of this." UNext is working with a team from IBM and Lotus Development on still-secret ways of connecting students. One option among many: Mount cameras on each student's computer, and use broadband video to bring everyone together, live, on the computer screen. UNext has other bells and whistles. Instructors won't just sit back and blindly hope that students will collaborate with each other: they'll see spider-web diagrams that show which students are e-mailing others—and who's hanging back.

As the environment shifts, competing universities are scrambling to reposition themselves. Perhaps your university has already entered this arena. Perhaps you have already taken a course via the Web. These changes represent challenges and opportunities—and they redefine the terms of competition in the business of education.

Sources: John McCormick, "The New School," Newsweek, April 24, 2000, vol. 135, no. 17, pp. 60–62; and Larry Armstrong, "The B-School On Your Desk," Business Week, April 3, 2000, issue 3675, p. 154; "Corporate Training," Forbes, September, 2000, pp. 310–311.

external environment All relevant forces outside a firm's boundaries, such as competitors, customers, the government, and the economy.

competitive environment The immediate environment surrounding a firm; includes suppliers, customers, competitors, and the like.

macroenvironment The most general environment; includes governments, economic conditions, and other fundamental factors that generally affect all organizations.

UNext, like other universities, is trying to compete in an environment characterized by intense competition, economic fluctuations, technological advances, government regulations, and other forces that directly influence its success. In this chapter, we will discuss how pressures outside organizations create an external context in which they operate.

As you learned in the first chapter, organizations are open systems that are affected by, and in turn affect, their external environments. By **external environment,** we mean all relevant forces outside the organization's boundaries. By *relevant,* we mean factors to which managers must pay attention to help their organizations compete effectively and survive.

Many of these factors are uncontrollable. Companies large and small are buffeted or battered about by recession, government interference, competitors' actions, and so forth. But their lack of control does not mean that managers can ignore such forces, use them as excuses for poor performance, and try to just get by. Managers must stay abreast of external developments and react accordingly. Moreover, as we will discuss later in the chapter, it sometimes is possible to influence components of the external environment. We will examine ways in which organizations can do just that.

Figure 2.1 shows the external environment of a firm. The firm exists in its **competitive environment,** which is composed of the firm and competitors, suppliers, customers, new entrants, and substitutes. At the more general level is the **macroenvironment,** which

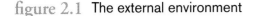

figure 2.1 The external environment

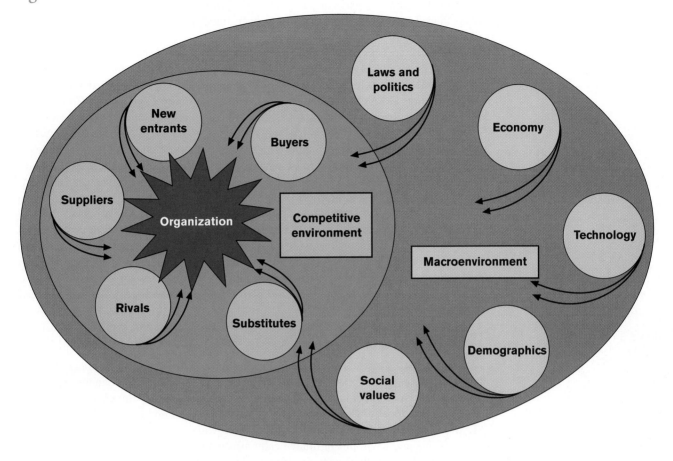

includes legal, political, economic, technological, demographic, and social and natural factors that generally affect all organizations.

A look ahead

In this chapter, we discuss the basic characteristics of an organization's environment and the importance of that environment for strategic management. Later chapters will elaborate on many of the basic environmental forces introduced here. For example, technology will be discussed again in Chapter 17. The global environment gets a thorough treatment in Chapter 6, which is devoted entirely to international management. Other chapters focus on ethics, social responsibility, and the natural environment. Chapter 18 reiterates the theme that recurs throughout this text: Organizations must continually change because environments continually change.

The macroenvironment

All organizations operate in a macroenvironment, which is defined by the most general elements in the external environment that can potentially influence strategic decisions. Although a top executive team may have unique internal strengths and ideas about its goals, it still must consider external factors before taking action.

Laws and regulations

U.S. government policies both impose strategic constraints and provide opportunities. The government can affect business opportunities through tax laws, economic policies, and international trade rulings. One example of restraint on business action is the U.S.

government's standards regarding bribery. In some countries, bribes and kickbacks are common and expected ways of doing business. But for U.S. firms, these are illegal practices. Indeed, some U.S. businesses have been fined for using bribery when competing internationally.

Regulators are specific government organizations in a firm's more immediate task environment. Regulatory agencies such as the Occupational Safety and Health Administration (OSHA), the Interstate Commerce Commission (ICC), the Federal Aviation Administration (FAA), the Equal Employment Opportunity Commission (EEOC), the National Labor Relations Board (NLRB), the Office of Federal Contract Compliance Programs (OFCCP), and the Environmental Protection Agency (EPA) have the power to investigate company practices and take legal action to ensure compliance with the laws.

For example, the Securities and Exchange Commission (SEC) regulates U.S. financial markets; since the insider-trading scandals, the SEC has dramatically changed investment houses' policies and practices. And the Food and Drug Administration (FDA) can prevent a company from selling an unsafe or ineffective product to the public.

The FDA, for example, recently approved mifepristone, or RU486, a controversial abortion pill, for manufacture and sale. However, the FDA intends to impose unusual restrictions on physicians prescribing mifepristone. They would have to register publicly, be admitted to practice at a nearby hospital, and perform follow-up studies of all their abortion patients. Only doctors trained to perform surgical abortions would be permitted to prescribe the drug.[1]

The economy

Although most Americans are used to thinking in terms of the U.S. economy, the economic environment is created by complex interconnections among economies of different countries. Wall Street investment analysts begin their workday thinking not just about what the Dow Jones did yesterday but also about how the London and Tokyo exchanges did overnight. Growth and recessions occur worldwide as well as domestically.

The economic environment dramatically affects companies' ability to function effectively and influences their strategic choices. Interest and inflation rates affect the availability and cost of capital, the ability to expand, prices, costs, and consumer demand for products. Unemployment rates affect labor availability and the wages the firm must pay, as well as product demand.

One important economic influence these days has centered on the stock market. Individuals (and institutions) looking for good returns invest in promising companies, blue chip performers, start-ups, and dot.coms. Over the past decade, technology-based firms, in particular, have offered very good investments. Investors have enjoyed better than 20 percent returns on their money, and these kinds of incentives have brought more investors into the capital markets. However, recently the market for tech stocks has been more volatile, and returns have diminished considerably. Figure 2.2 shows a comparison of three major stock market indices: Nasdaq, Dow Jones Industrials, and the S&P 500.[2]

Economic conditions change over time and are difficult to predict. Bull and bear markets come and go. Periods of dramatic growth may be followed by a recession. Every trend undoubtedly will end—but when? Even when times seem good, budget deficits or other considerations create concern about the future.

Technology

Today, a company cannot succeed without incorporating into its strategy the astonishing technologies that exist and continue to evolve. Technological advances create new products, advanced production techniques, and better ways of managing and communicating. In addition, as technology evolves, new industries, markets, and competitive niches develop. For example, the advent of computers created a huge industry. Early entrants in biotechnology are trying to establish dominant positions, while later entrants work on technological advances that will give them a competitive niche.

New technologies also provide new production techniques. In manufacturing, sophisticated robots perform jobs without suffering fatigue, requiring vacations or weekends

figure 2.2
Twelve-month
comparison of
stock markets

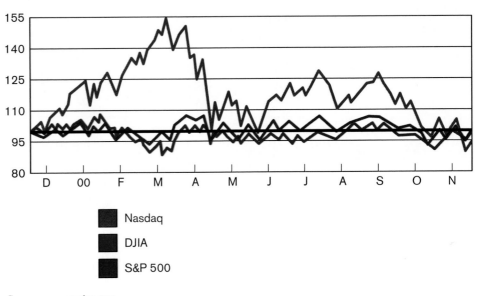

Source: www.nasdaq.com

off, or demanding wage increases. Until the U.S. steel industry began modernizing its plants, its productivity lagged far behind that of the technologically superior Japanese plants.

New technologies also provide new ways to manage and communicate. Computerized management information systems (MIS) make information available when needed. Computers monitor productivity and note performance deficiencies. Telecommunications allow conferences to take place without requiring people to travel to the same location. Consider the following discussion of changes in the field of telecommunications. As you can see, technological advances create innovations in business. Strategies developed around the cutting edge of technological advances create a competitive advantage; strategies that ignore or lag behind competitors in considering technology lead to obsolescence and extinction. This issue is so important that we devote an entire chapter (Chapter 17) to the topic.

From the Pages of BusinessWeek

At the speed of light

Chief Andrew Isaac Health Center in Fairbanks, Alaska, has 30 clinics scattered across a frozen tundra the size of Texas. Some clinics are in villages, such as Fort Yukon, that are more than 100 miles away. Worse yet, most aren't accessible by road. All too often, patients who use the clinics are left biting their nails for days, waiting for X-rays and other medical tests to be mailed to experts in Fairbanks. If the weather is dicey, they may not get critical diagnoses for a week.

All of that is about to change. Thanks to a high-speed, optical-communications network that will soon be completed, the clinics will be linked directly to Fairbanks. Then X-rays, medical tests, and case files can be zipped instantly to doctors—and the analysis is done in minutes. This breakthrough technology transmits data, video, and voice in the form of light over glass, instead of using electrons over copper—the method of choice since the telephone was invented more than 100 years ago. Because light on glass is startlingly more efficient, it is increasing the capacity of the communications systems by staggering amounts. Consider this: With the latest optical technology, a single strand of fiber thinner than a human hair can now carry every phone call, e-mail, and web page used by every person in the world.

Combine that kind of speed with the ubiquity of the Internet, and the implications

Just as the railroad opened the West, optical fiber networks will alter the landscape.
[Ed Lallo]

are profound. Today, downloading a digital movie—say, *The Matrix*—takes more than seven hours over the fastest cable modem. With an optical connection, it could be done in four seconds flat. Simply put: It's business carried out at the speed of light. David R. Huber, the founder and CEO of optical upstart Corvis Corp., estimates that optical equipment has helped drive down the price of moving a bit of information over long distances to 0.006 percent of what it was in 1996. "If BMW could do that, you could buy a new BMW for $2.50," says Huber.

It's the latest disruptive technology. Just as the rise of the personal computer gave Microsoft the opportunity to overthrow IBM for leadership of the computing world, optical technology is turning the $377 billion communications equipment market upside down. A few years ago, Lucent was the runaway leader in telecommunications equipment in the United States. But in late 1996, Canada's Nortel Networks Corp. introduced a new optical system that routes data at 10 gigabits a second. Lucent, convinced that demand for the complex technology would develop slowly, stuck with gear that operates at one-quarter the speed. Nortel has been proven right and Lucent's market share has tumbled.

Surprisingly, the notion of sending information over a beam of light is almost as old as the telephone itself. Alexander Graham Bell experimented with the idea of photonics back in the late 19th century. In 1880, four years after receiving a patent for a telephone that used copper wire, the inventor created what he called a "photophone" that carried voice signals on a beam of light. He used it to talk to his assistant, Sumner Tainter, over a distance of 1,300 feet. Ultimately, though, Bell found that using copper wires was more workable. Photonics has come a long way since then. When the first transcontinental fiber network was installed two decades ago, a single stream of bits flowed along a fiber strand so it could carry 45 megabits of information per second. Today, using prisms to send multiple colors of light down a single fiber—a process called dense wave division multiplexing—a fiber strand can be split into 160 different colors, each capable of carrying its own stream of data. All told, technological improvements have boosted the capacity of a strand of fiber 18,000-fold, to 800 gigabits or more, over the past 20 years.

As optical technology pushes deeper into modern life, it is bound to have a profound impact on the way people live. Just as the railroad opened the West, and the highways gave rise to the suburbs, next generation communication networks will alter the landscape. Telecommuting, now a luxury for workers, will become more commonplace, says Paul Saffo, director of the Institute for the Future, a think tank in Silicon Valley. That will free people from having to live near their jobs, so they can move to more scenic locales such as Santa Fe, New Mexico or Telluride, Colorado. Or even Fort Yukon, Alaska.

Source: John G. Shinal and Timothy J. Mullaney, "At the Speed of Light," *Business Week,* October 9, 2000, pp. 144–52.

Demographics

demographics Measures of various characteristics of the people who comprise groups of other social units.

Demographics are measures of various characteristics of the people comprising groups or other social units. Work groups, organizations, countries, markets, or societies can be described statistically by referring to their members' age, gender, family size, income, education, occupation, and so forth.

Companies must consider workforce demographics in formulating their human resources strategies. Population growth influences the size and composition of the labor force. By 2005, the U.S. civilian labor force, growing at a rate of 1.3 percent annually, is expected to reach approximately 151 million. Fluctuations in the birthrate influence population trends somewhat. In past years, the number of younger workers (16 to 24 years of age) has declined, but now that children of the baby-boom generation are entering the workforce, this age group is expected to grow 16 percent by 2005. At the same time, baby boomers themselves are reaching retirement age, so the number of older workers (55 and above) will also rise to about 15 percent of the labor force. Eventually, declining participation in work of older persons will largely offset the increase in the number of persons in this population group.

Immigration is also a factor that significantly influences the U.S. population and labor force. Over the past decade, immigrants have accounted for approximately 40 percent of the increase in U.S. population growth, a trend that has an important impact on the labor force. Immigrants are frequently of working age but have different educational and occupational backgrounds from the rest of the labor force. By 2005, the labor force will be even more diverse than it is today. White males will constitute approximately 38 percent of the labor force, African-Americans 13 percent, Hispanics 16 percent, and Asians and others nearly 6 percent. Together these groups are expected to account for nearly 65 percent of the growth in the labor force by 2005.

Women continue to join the U.S. labor force in record numbers. In 1970, women made up only about one-third of the labor force. By 2005 women are expected to account for over 47 percent, a trend that provides companies with more talent from which to choose.[3]

A more diverse workforce has its advantages, but managers have to make certain they provide equality for women and minorities with respect to employment, advancement opportunities, and compensation. Strategic plans must be made for recruiting, retaining, training, motivating, and effectively utilizing people of diverse demographical backgrounds with the skills needed to achieve the company's mission. Large numbers of single-parent and two-income families with children led to the creation and success of KinderCare and other day care facilities. These demographic trends also led to policies such as parental leaves, part-time employment, flexible work schedules, job sharing, telecommuting, and child care assistance.

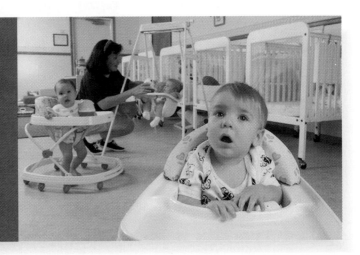

With ever-greater numbers of women entering the workforce, KinderCare centers such as this one in Plano, Texas, are becoming increasingly popular. [Charles Thatcher]

Social issues and the natural environment

Societal trends regarding how people think and behave have major implications for management of the labor force, corporate social actions, and strategic decisions about products and markets.

In the 1990s, it was unfashionable for women pursuing careers to have children; instead, they dedicated themselves to their work, postponing or deciding against having children. During the past decade, having children has become popular again. Today, companies that want to create or maintain a competitive advantage—or that merely hope to stay competitive—are introducing more supportive policies regarding maternal leave (and even paternal leave), flexible working hours, and child care.

A prominent issue in today's press pertains to the social costs of smoking. Forty states have sued the tobacco companies to recoup billions of dollars in health care costs. Recently, tobacco companies were ordered to pay $368.5 billion to settle the decades-long dispute over how to cut tobacco use. Currently there is new legislation that toughens penalties on tobacco companies and gives the Food and Drug Administration (FDA) authority to regulate tobacco advertising, particularly to youths. This particular issue shows how various elements in the macroenvironment can combine to influence an industry.[4]

Another issue of growing concern is the protection of our natural environment. This topic is so important in managerial decision making that we devote the Chapter 5 appendix to it.

The competitive environment

All organizations are affected by the general components of the macroenvironment we have just discussed. Each organization also functions in a closer, more immediate competitive environment. The competitive environment comprises the specific organizations with which the organization interacts. As shown in Figure 2.3, the competitive environment includes rivalry among current competitors, threat of new entrants, threat of substitutes, power of suppliers, and power of customers. This model was originally developed by Michael Porter, a Harvard professor and noted authority on strategic management. According to Porter, successful managers do more than simply react to the environment; they act in ways that actually shape or change the organization's environment. In strategic decision making, Porter's model is an excellent method for analyzing the competitive environment in order to adapt to or influence the nature of competition.

figure 2.3
The competitive
environment

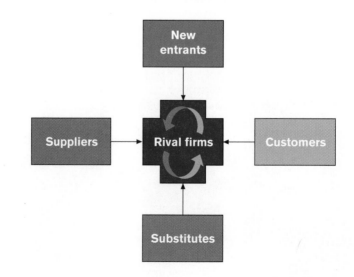

With the closing of many of its stores, Sears Roebuck faced near extinction. After making major managerial changes, this former giant is gradually regaining prominence.
[Mark Richards/DOT]

Competitors

Of the various components of the competitive environment, competitors within the industry must first deal with one another. When organizations compete for the same customers and try to win market share at the others' expense, all must react to and anticipate their competitors' actions.

The first question to consider is: Who is the competition? Sometimes answers are obvious. Coca-Cola and PepsiCo are competitors, as are the Big Three automakers: General Motors, Ford, and Daimler Chrysler. But sometimes organizations focus too exclusively on traditional rivalries and miss the emerging ones. Historically, Sears & Roebuck focused on its competition with J.C. Penney. However, Sears' real competitors are Kmart and Wal-Mart at the low end; Target in the middle; Nordstrom at the high end; and a variety of catalogers, such as Lands' End, L.L. Bean, and Eddie Bauer. Similarly, United Airlines, Delta, American, and U.S.Airways have focused their attention to a battle over long haul and international routes. In the process, they all but ignored smaller carriers such as Southwest, Alaska Air, and America West that have grown and succeeded in regional markets.[5]

Thus, as a first step in understanding their competitive environment, organizations must identify their competitors. Competitors may include (1) small domestic firms, especially their entry into tiny, premium markets; (2) overseas firms, especially their efforts to solidify positions in small niches (a traditional Japanese tactic); (3) big, new domestic companies exploring new markets; (4) strong regional competitors; and (5) unusual entries such as Internet shopping.

Once competitors have been identified, the next step is to analyze how they compete. Competitors use tactics like price reductions, new-product introductions, and advertising campaigns to gain advantage over their rivals. It's essential to understand what competitors are doing when honing your own strategy. Competition is most intense when there are many direct competitors (including foreign contenders), when industry growth is slow, and when the product or service cannot be differentiated in some way.

New, high-growth industries offer enormous opportunities for profits. When an industry matures and growth slows, profits drop. Then, intense competition causes an industry shakeout: Weaker companies are eliminated, and the strong companies survive.[6]

Threat of new entrants

barriers to entry Conditions that prevent new companies from entering an industry.

New entrants into an industry compete with established companies. If many factors prevent new companies from entering the industry, the threat to established firms is less serious. If there are few such **barriers to entry,** the threat of new entrants is more serious. Some major barriers to entry are government policy, capital requirements, brand identification, cost disadvantages, and distribution channels. The government can limit or prevent entry, as when the FDA forbids a new drug entrant. Some industries, such as trucking and liquor retailing, are regulated; more subtle government controls operate in fields such as mining and ski area development. Patents are also entry barriers. When a patent expires (like Polaroid's basic patents on instant photography), other companies (e.g., Kodak) can then enter the market.

Other barriers are less formal but can have the same effect. Capital requirements may be so high that companies won't risk or try to raise such large amounts of money. Brand identification forces new entrants to spend heavily to overcome customer loyalty. The cost advantages established companies hold—due to large size, favorable locations, existing assets, and so forth—also can be formidable entry barriers.

Finally, existing competitors may have such tight distribution channels that new entrants have difficulty getting their products or services to customers. For example, established food products already have supermarket shelf space. New entrants must displace existing products with promotions, price breaks, intensive selling, and other tactics.

Threat of substitutes

Technological advances and economic efficiencies are among the ways that firms can develop substitutes for existing products. For example, although Southwest Airlines has developed strong rivalries with other airlines, it also competes—as a substitute—with bus companies such as Greyhound and rental car companies such as Avis. Southwest has gotten its cost base down to such a low point that it is now cheaper to fly from Los Angeles to Phoenix than it is to take a bus or rent a car. This particular example shows that substitute products or services can limit another industry's revenue potential. Companies in those industries are likely to suffer growth and earnings problems unless they improve quality or launch aggressive marketing campaigns.[7]

In addition to current substitutes, companies need to think about potential substitutes that may be viable in the near future. For example, as alternatives to fossil fuels, experts suggest that nuclear fusion, solar power, and wind energy may prove useful one day. The advantages promised by each of these technologies are many: inexhaustible fuel supplies, electricity "too cheap to meter," zero emissions, universal public acceptance, etc. And yet, while they may look good on paper (and give us a warm, fuzzy feeling inside), they often come up short in terms of economics and/or technical viability. Table 2.1 shows a list of products and potential substitutes.[8]

table 2.1
Potential substitutes
for products

If the product is . . .	The substitute might be . . .
Cotton	Polyester
Coffee	Soft drinks
Fossil fuels	Solar Fusion
Movie theater	Home video
Music CD	Radio, cassette, LP
Automobile	Train, bus, bicycle
Typewriter	Personal computer
Sugar	Nutrasweet
House	Apartment, condo, mobile home
Bricks	Aluminum siding
Trashy magazine	Internet
Local telephone	Cellular phone, pager

Actor Richard Dreyfuss appeared at a rally in New York on the first day of the SAG & AFTRA strike. *[Reuters NewMedia Inc./CORBIS]*

Suppliers

Recall from our discussion of open systems that organizations must acquire resources from their environment and convert those resources into products or services to sell. Suppliers provide the resources needed for production and may come in the form of people (supplied by trade schools and universities), raw materials (supplied by producers, wholesalers, and distributors), information (supplied by researchers and consulting firms), and financial capital (supplied by banks and other sources). But suppliers are important to an organization for reasons beyond the resources they provide. Suppliers can raise their prices or provide poor quality goods and services. Labor unions can go on strike or demand higher wages. Workers may produce defective work. Powerful suppliers, then, can reduce an organization's profits, particularly if the organization cannot pass on price increases to its customers.

One particularly noteworthy set of suppliers to some industries is the international labor unions. Although unionization in the United States has dropped to about 10 percent of the private labor force, labor unions are still particularly powerful in industries such as steel, autos, and transportation. Even the Screen Actors Guild, the union representing workers in the entertainment industry, exerts considerable power on behalf of its members. Recently, Tiger Woods was fined $100,000 for making a nonunion Buick commercial during a strike by the American Federation of Television and Radio Artists. Labor unions represent and protect the interests of their members with respect to hiring, wages, working conditions, job security, and due process appeals. Historically, the relationship between management and labor unions has been adversarial; however, both sides seem to realize that to increase productivity and competitiveness, management and labor work together in collaborative relationships. Troubled labor relations can create higher costs and productivity declines and eventually lead to layoffs.[9]

Organizations are at a disadvantage if they become overly dependent on any powerful supplier. A supplier is powerful if the buyer has few other sources of supply or if the supplier has many other buyers. For example, if computer companies can only go to Microsoft for software or to Intel for microchips, those suppliers can exert a great deal of pressure. In many cases, companies build up switching costs. **Switching costs** are fixed costs buyers face if they change suppliers. For example, once a buyer learns how to operate a supplier's equipment, such as computer software, the buyer faces both economic and psychological costs in changing to a new supplier.[10]

Choosing the right supplier is an important strategic decision. Suppliers can affect manufacturing time, product quality, and inventory levels. The relationship between suppliers and the organization is changing in some companies. The close supplier relationship has become a new model for many organizations, such as Ford Motor, that are using a just-in-time manufacturing approach (discussed in Chapters 16 and 17).

switching costs Fixed costs buyers face when they change suppliers.

From the Pages of

BusinessWeek

Online auctions: Connecting with suppliers

Web technology has had a major impact on the way organizations connect with their suppliers. In many industries, firms have established Internet procurement portals for online auctioning. These auctions can be for purchases that range from cleaning supplies to security systems to office furniture—you name it. The portals themselves are set up as Internet firms and are typically established as joint ventures among partners. The belief is that online auctions will streamline business to business (B2B) transactions and make the whole purchasing process more efficient. To date, more than 70 industry-sponsored exchanges have been created. Here is just a sample:

Automotive: The Big Three automakers—DaimlerChrysler, Ford, and General Motors—have pooled the $240 billion they spend each year on parts in order to create one of the first industry coalitions, when they announced plans to team up on an online supplies exchange. That marketplace alone is expected to involve annual transactions totaling more than $300 billion. The new company now has a name: Covisint (go to www.covisint.com to find out what it means).

Computers: Ehitex.com is the offspring of Hewlett-Packard, Compaq, Gateway, and several other high-tech companies to do online sourcing. Its chief competitor is e2open.com, an exchange set up by IBM and others.

Retail: GlobalNetXchange is a B2B retail marketplace set up by Sears Roebuck, French retailer Carrefour, Kroger, and several others (including software company Oracle). All told, retailers in the exchange account for $175 billion in annual purchases from more than 50,000 suppliers, partners, and distributors worldwide. One competitor is WorldWide Retail Exchange, an online auction established by 22 of the world's largest retailers, such as Royal Ahold and Kmart. Wal-Mart has it own online marketplace that it uses for supplier auctioning. With annual sales of $165 billion, Wal-Mart buys and sells twice as many goods as Sears and Carrefour combined.

Consumer goods: Transora.com is an online supplier exchange established by 49 consumer-goods makers, including Procter & Gamble, Sara Lee, and Coca-Cola.

Oil: Although still in its formative stage, 14 energy and petrochemical companies—including BP Amoco, Royal Dutch/Shell, Unocal, Conoci, and Dow Chemical—have agreed to set up an exchange portal.

Will it work? There are still some questions that need to be answered. Governance remains a prickly issue for many of these exchanges. Can member companies, which usually are competitors, truly cooperate and allow an independent management team to lead the joint venture? Already, many of the industry-led marketplaces have retained Big Five consulting firms to help oversee negotiations during the start-up phase. And yet, the future looks promising: Unlike some risky Net start-ups, there is good reason to believe these industry exchanges will succeed. AMR Research projects that 29 percent of all commercial transactions, worth some $5.7 trillion, will flow through the Internet by 2004. Founders of these trading exchanges "bring so much transaction volume to the table, they are not going to let it fail," says Rory Jones, a PricewaterhouseCoopers partner in its e-markets practice.

Sources: Jennifer Gill, "What Most Big B2B Exchanges Are Missing: A CEO," *Business Week,* July 14, 2000, online); and Michael Arndt, "Sears: Can the Old Retail King Win a B2B Throne?" *Business Week,* February 29, 2000, online.

Customers

final consumer Those who purchase products in their finished form.

intermediate consumer Customers who purchase raw materials or wholesale products before selling them to final customers.

customer service The speed and dependability with which an organization can deliver what customers want.

Customers purchase the products or services the organization offers. Without customers, a company won't survive. You are a **final consumer** when you buy a McDonald's hamburger or a pair of jeans from a retailer at the mall. **Intermediate consumers** buy raw materials or wholesale products and then sell to final consumers. Intermediate customers actually make more purchases than individual final consumers do. Examples of intermediate customers include retailers, who buy clothes from wholesalers and manufacturers' representatives before selling them to their customers, and industrial buyers, who buy raw materials (such as chemicals) before converting them into final products.

Like suppliers, customers are important to organizations for reasons other than the money they provide for goods and services. Customers can demand lower prices, higher quality, unique product specifications, or better service. They can also play competitors against one another, such as when a car customer (or a purchasing agent) collects different offers and negotiates for the best price.

Customer service means giving customers what they want or need, the way they want it, the first time. This usually depends on the speed and dependability with which an organization can deliver its products or services. Actions and attitudes that mean excellent customer service include:

- Speed of filling and delivering normal orders.
- Willingness to meet emergency needs.
- Merchandise delivered in good condition.
- Readiness to take back defective goods and resupply quickly.
- Availability of installation and repair services and parts.
- Service charges (that is, whether services are "free" or priced separately).[11]

In all businesses—services as well as manufacturing—strategies that emphasize good customer service provide a critical competitive advantage. The organization is at a disadvantage if it depends too heavily on powerful customers. Customers are powerful if they make large purchases or if they can easily find alternative places to buy. If you are the largest customer of a firm, and there are other firms from which you can buy, you have power over that firm, and you are likely to be able to negotiate with it successfully. Your firm's biggest customers—especially if they can buy from other sources—will have the greatest negotiating power over you. Customer relationship management is discussed more fully in Chapter 9.

Environmental analysis

environmental uncertainty Lack of information needed to understand or predict the future.

If managers do not understand how the environment affects their organizations, or cannot identify opportunities and threats that are likely to be important, then their ability to make decisions and execute plans will be severely limited. For example, if little is known about customer likes and dislikes, organizations would have a difficult time designing new products, scheduling production, developing marketing plans, and the like. In short, timely and accurate environmental information is critical for running a business.

But information about the environment is not always readily available. **Environmental uncertainty** means that managers do not have enough information about the environment to understand or predict the future. Uncertainty arises from two related factors: (1) complexity and (2) dynamism. Environmental *complexity* refers to the number of issues to which a manager must attend as well as their interconnectedness. For example, industries that have many different firms that compete in vastly different ways tend to be more complex—and uncertain—than industries with only a few key competitors. Similarly, environmental *dynamism* refers to the degree of discontinuous change that occurs within the industry. For example, high-growth industries with products and technologies that change rapidly tend to be more uncertain than stable industries where change is less dramatic and more predictable.[12]

As environmental uncertainty increases, managers must develop techniques and methods for collecting, sorting through, and interpreting information about the environment. By analyzing environmental forces—both in the macro and competitive environments—managers can identify opportunities and threats that might impact the organization.

Environmental scanning

Perhaps the first step in coping with uncertainty in the environment is pinning down what might be of importance. It is frequently the case that organizations (and individuals) act out of ignorance, only to regret those actions in the future. IBM, for example, had the opportunity to purchase the technology behind xerography, but turned it down. Xerox saw the potential, and the rest is history. However, Xerox researchers later developed the technology for the original computer mouse, but not seeing the potential, the company missed an important market opportunity.

environmental scanning
Searching for and sorting through information about the environment.

In order to understand and predict changes, opportunities, and threats, organizations such as Monsanto, Weyerhaeuser, and Union Carbide spend a good deal of time and money monitoring events in the environment. **Environmental scanning** means both searching out information that is unavailable to most people and also sorting through that information in order to interpret what is important and what is not. Managers can ask questions such as

- Who are our current competitors?
- Are there few or many entry barriers to our industry?
- What substitutes exist for our product or service?
- Is the company too dependent on powerful suppliers?
- Is the company too dependent on powerful customers?[13]

competitive intelligence
Information that helps managers determine how to compete better.

Answers to these questions help managers develop **competitive intelligence,** the information necessary to decide how best to manage in the competitive environment they have identified. Porter's competitive analysis, discussed earlier, can guide environmental scanning and help managers evaluate the competitive potential of different environments. Table 2.2 describes two extreme environments: an attractive environment, which gives a firm a competitive advantage, and an unattractive environment, which puts a firm at a competitive disadvantage.[14]

Scenario development

scenario A narrative that describes a particular set of future conditions.

As managers attempt to determine the effect of environmental forces on their organizations, they frequently develop **scenarios** of the future. Scenarios represent alternative combinations of different factors into a total picture of the environment and the firm. For example, as Congress and the president try to work toward a balanced budget, and eventually reduce the federal debt, they have developed several different scenarios about what the economy is likely to do over the next decade or so. Frequently, organizations develop a *best-case scenario* (i.e., if events occur that are favorable to the firm), a *worst-case scenario* (i.e., if events are all unfavorable), and some middle-ground alternatives. The value of scenario development is that it helps managers develop contingency plans for what they might do given different outcomes.[15]

table 2.2
Attractive and unattractive environments

Environmental factor	Unattractive	Attractive
Competitors	Many; low industry growth; equal size; commodity	Few; high industry growth; Unequal size differentiated
Threat of entry	High threat; few entry barriers	Low threat; many barriers
Substitutes	Many	Few
Suppliers	Few; high bargaining power	Many; low bargaining power
Customers	Few; high bargaining power	Many; low bargaining power

Forecasting

Whereas environmental scanning is used to identify important factors and scenario development is used to develop alternative pictures of the future, **forecasting** is used to predict exactly how some variable or variables will change in the future. For example, in making capital investments, firms may try to forecast how interest rates will change. In deciding to expand or downsize a business, firms may try to forecast the demand for goods and services, or forecast the supply and demand of labor they would likely use. Available publications such as *Business Week's Business Outlook* provide forecasts to businesses both large and small.

Although forecasts are designed to help executives make predictions about the future, their accuracy varies from application to application. Because they extrapolate from the past to project the future, forecasts tend to be most accurate when the future ends up looking a lot like the past. Of course, we don't need sophisticated forecasts in those instances. Forecasts are most useful when the future will look radically different than the past. Unfortunately, that is when forecasts tend not to be so accurate. The more things change, the less confidence we tend to have in our forecasts. The best advice for using forecasts might include the following:

- Use multiple forecasts and perhaps average their predictions.
- Remember that accuracy decreases the farther into the future you are trying to predict.
- Forecasts are no better than the data used to construct them.
- Use simple forecasts (rather than complicated ones) where possible.
- Important events often are surprises and represent a departure from predictions.[16]

Benchmarking

In addition to trying to predict changes in the environment, firms can undertake intensive study of the best practices of various firms to understand their sources of competitive advantage. **Benchmarking** means identifying the best-in-class performance by a company in a given area, say product development or customer service, and then comparing your processes to theirs. To accomplish this, a benchmarking team would collect information on its own company's operations and those of the other firm in order to determine gaps. These gaps serve as a point of entry to learn the underlying causes of performance differences. Ultimately, the team would map out a set of best practices that lead to world class performance. We will discuss benchmarking further in Chapter 4.[17]

Collaborative benchmarking: A tool for sharing and cooperation

The National Aeronautics and Space Administration (NASA) leads the world in preparing and launching missions from earth to the frontiers of space. However, an audit for the President's Quality Award suggested that NASA consider benchmarking as a way to progress from incremental improvement to breakthrough improvements.

To improve processes, NASA and its contractors were challenged to begin sharing information—a concept that was initially met with resistance. Because the contractors were essentially competitors, and had closely guarded information and performance levels, they hesitated to work in collaborative benchmarking efforts. Over time, however, reluctance to share information was overcome as participants realized that NASA's objective was to provide an opportunity to learn from contractors and to help them improve their own processes, rather than to force every participant's process into the same mold. Soon the consortium participants learned to work together as a team to facilitate effective benchmarking, optimize efficiencies, and leverage quality improvements across all participating organizations.

Participants were encouraged to share practices and learn more about how each organization achieved its results. As the various practices were discussed, the team began to identify those processes that contributed to performance that was superior to the other organizations. These were identified as best practices; team participants then adapted the best practices to their own organizations. In adapting and implementing these best practices, contractors produced a combined savings of $41,000 and reduced cycle time by 57 percent. These results benefited each participant organization as well as NASA—their common customer.

Consortium benchmarking like that used by NASA can be a cost-effective alternative to conventional benchmarking. By joining forces, the cost to each participant is generally less than it would be for each contractor to conduct a study individually. Continued informal benchmarking among the consortium process owners has a synergistic benefit by creating a culture that values continual improvement and teamwork to achieve excellence. It builds a foundation for continued benchmarking, formal and/or informal, through the use of common terminology, tools, and techniques.

The approach prevents "industrial tourism," or plant visits simply to see what is out there. Benchmarking can provide a wealth of ideas on which to build significant improvement. The commitment of resources to participate in a benchmarking study is typically well worth the effort involved due to the insights that result from learning from others.

Source: Adapted from Denise DeVito and Sara Morrison, "Benchmarking: A Tool for Sharing and Cooperation," *The Journal for Quality and Participation,* Fall 2000, vol. 23 no. 4, pp. 56–61.

Responding to the environment

Organizations have a number of options for responding to the environment. In general, these can be grouped into three categories: (1) adapting to the environment, (2) influencing the environment, and (3) selecting a new environment.

Adapting to the environment: changing yourself

In order to cope with environmental uncertainty, organizations frequently make adjustments in their structures and work processes. In the case of uncertainty arising from environmental complexity, we can say that organizations tend to adapt by *decentralizing* decision making. For example, if a company faces a growing number of competitors in various markets, if different customers want different things, if the characteristics of different products keep increasing, and if production facilities are being built in different regions of the world, then it may be impossible for the chief executive (or a small group of top executives) to keep abreast of all activities and understand all the operational details of a business. In these cases, the top management team is likely to give authority to lower level managers to make decisions that benefit the firm. The term **empowerment** is frequently used today to talk about this type of decentralized authority. We will address empowerment and decision making in more detail in Chapters 3 and 9.

In response to uncertainty caused by change (dynamism) in the environment, organizations tend to establish more flexible structures. In today's business world, it is commonplace for the term *bureaucracy* to take on a bad connotation. Most of us recognize that bureaucratic organizations tend to be formalized and very stable; frequently they are unable to adjust to change or exceptional circumstances that "don't fit the rules." And while bureaucratic organizations may be efficient and controlled if the environment is stable, they tend to be slow moving and plodding when products, technologies, customers, competitors, and the like start changing over time. In these cases, more *organic*

empowerment The process of sharing power with employees, thereby enhancing their confidence in their ability to perform their jobs and their belief that they are influential contributors to the organization.

structures tend to have the flexibility needed to adjust to change. Although we will discuss organic structures in more detail in Chapter 9, suffice it to say here that they are less formal than bureaucratic organizations, so decisions tend to be made more through interaction and mutual adjustment among individuals rather than via a set of predefined rules. Table 2.3 shows four different approaches that organizations can take in adapting to environmental uncertainty.

Adapting at the boundaries

From the standpoint of an open system, organizations create buffers on both the input and output sides of their boundaries with the environment. **Buffering** is one such approach used for adapting to uncertainty. On the input side, organizations establish relationships with employment agencies to hire part-time and temporary help during rush periods when labor demand is difficult to predict. The growth of contingent workers in the U.S. labor force is a good indication of the popularity of this approach to buffering input uncertainties. On the output side of the system, most organizations use some type of ending inventories that allow them to keep merchandise on hand in case a rush of customers decide to buy their products. Auto dealers are a particularly common example of this use of buffers, but we can see similar use of buffer inventories in fast food restaurants, book stores, clothing stores, and even real estate agencies.[18]

In addition to buffering, organizations may try **smoothing** or leveling normal fluctuations at the boundaries of the environment. For example, during winter months (up north) when automobile sales drop off, it is not uncommon for dealers to cut the price of their instock vehicles in order to increase demand. At the end of each clothing season, retailers discount their merchandise to clear it out in order to make room for incoming inventories. These are each examples of smoothing environmental cycles in order to level off fluctuations in demand.

Adapting at the core

While buffering and smoothing work to manage uncertainties at the boundaries of the organization, firms also can establish **flexible processes** that allow for adaptation in their technical core. For example, firms increasingly try to customize their products and services to meet the varied and changing demands of customers. Even in manufacturing, where it is difficult to change basic core processes, firms are adopting techniques of mass customization that help them create flexible factories. Instead of mass-producing large quantities of a "one-size-fits-all" product, mass customization means that organizations can produce individually customized products at an equally low cost. Whereas Henry Ford used to claim that "you could have a Model T in any color you wanted, as long as it was black," auto companies now offer a wide array of colors and trim lines, with different options and accessories. The process of mass customization involves the use of a network of independent operating units that each performs a specific process or task such as making a dashboard assembly on an automobile. When an order comes in, different modules join forces to deliver the product or service as specified by the customer. We will discuss mass customization and flexible factories in more depth in Chapters 9.[19]

buffering Creating supplies of excess resources in case of unpredictable needs.

smoothing Leveling normal fluctuations at the boundaries of the environment.

flexible processes Methods for adapting the technical core to changes in the environment.

table 2.3
Four approaches for managing uncertainty

	Stable	Dynamic
Complex	Decentralized	Decentralized
	Bureaucratic (Standardized skills)	Organic (Mutual adjustment)
Simple	Centralized	Centralized
	Bureaucratic (Standardized work processes)	Organic (Direct supervision)

Influencing your environment

In addition to adapting or reacting to the environment, organizations can develop proactive responses aimed at changing the environment. Two general types of proactive responses include independent action and cooperative action.

independent strategies
Strategies that an organization acting on its own uses to change some aspect of its current environment.

Independent action   A company uses **independent strategies** when it acts on its own to change some aspect of its current environment.[20] Table 2.4 shows the definitions and uses of these strategies. For example, when Southwest Airlines enters a new market, it demonstrates competitive aggression by cutting fares so that other less-efficient airlines must follow it down. In contrast, Kellogg Company typically promotes the cereal industry as a whole, thereby demonstrating competitive pacification. Weyerhaeuser Company advertises its reforestation efforts (public relations). First Boston forgoes its Christmas party and donates thousands of dollars to the poor (voluntary action). Dow Chemical recently sued General Electric for hiring away some of its engineers (legal action). Dow Corning lobbied and recently won the right to put silicon implants back on the market (political action). Each of these examples shows how organizations—on their own—can have an impact on the environment.

cooperative strategies
Strategies used by two or more organizations working together to manage the external environment.

Cooperative action   In some situations, two or more organizations work together using cooperative strategies to influence the environment.[21] Table 2.5 shows several examples of **cooperative strategies.** An example of contracting occurs when suppliers and customers, or managers and labor unions, sign formal agreements about the terms and conditions of their future relationships. These contracts are explicit attempts to make their future relationship predictable. An example of cooptation might occur when universities invite wealthy alumni to join their boards of directors. Finally, an example of *coalition* formation might be when local businesses band together to curb the rise of employee health care costs and when organizations in the same industry form industry

table 2.4 Independent action

Strategy	Definition	Examples
Competitive aggression	Exploiting a distinctive competence or improving internal efficiency for competitive advantage.	Aggressive pricing, comparative advertising (e.g., Advil)
Competitive pacification	Independent action to improve relations with competitors.	Helping competitors find raw materials
Public relations	Establishing and maintaining favorable images in the minds of those making up the environment.	Sponsoring sporting events
Voluntary action	Voluntary commitment to various interest groups, causes, and social problems.	Ronald McDonald Houses
Legal action	Company engages in private legal battle with competition on antitrust deceptive and advertising or other grounds	Blue Mountain Art, Inc.'s lawsuit against Hallmark for allegedly copying its cards
Political action	Efforts to influence elected representatives to create a more favorable business environment or limit competition.	ARCO's corporate constituency programs; issue advertising; lobbying at state and national levels

Source: Reprinted from *Journal of Marketing,* published by the American Marketing Association. C. Zeithaml and V. Zeithaml, "Environmental Management: Revising the Marketing Perspective," Spring 1984.

table 2.5
Cooperative action

Strategy	Definition	Examples
Contraction	Negotiation of an agreement between the organization and another group to exchange goods, services, information, patents, and so on.	Contractual marketing systems
Cooptation	Absorbing new elements into the organization's leadership structure to avert threats to its stability or existence.	Consumer and labor representatives and bankers on boards of directors
Coalition	Two or more groups coalesce and act jointly with respect to some set of issues for some period of time.	Industry associations; political initiatives of the Business Roundtable and the U.S. Chamber of Commerce

Source: Reprinted from *Journal of Marketing*, published by the American Marketing Association. C. Zeithaml and V. Zeithaml, "Environmental Management: Revising the Marketing Perspective," Spring 1984.

associations and special-interest groups. You may have seen cooperative advertising strategies, such as when dairy producers, beef producers, orange growers, and the like jointly pay for television commercials.

At a more organizational level, organizations establish strategic alliances, partnerships, joint ventures, and mergers with competitors to deal with environmental uncertainties. Cooperative strategies such as these make most sense when (1) taking joint action will reduce the organizations' costs and risks and (2) cooperation will increase their power (that is, their ability to successfully accomplish the changes they desire).

strategic maneuvering The organization's conscious efforts to change the boundaries of its task environment.

prospectors Companies that continuously change the boundaries for their task environments by seeking new products and markets, diversifying and merging, or acquiring new enterprises.

Changing the environment you are in

As we noted previously, organizations can cope with environmental uncertainty by changing themselves (environmental adaptation), changing the environment, or changing the environment they are in. We refer to this last category as **strategic maneuvering.** By making a conscious effort to change the boundaries of its competitive environment, firms can maneuver around potential threats and capitalize on arising opportunities.[22] Table 2.6 defines and gives examples of several of these strategies, including domain selection, diversification, merger and acquisition, and divestiture.

Organizations engage in strategic maneuvering when they move into different environments. Some companies, called **prospectors,** are more likely than others to engage in strategic maneuvering.[23] Aggressive companies continuously change the boundaries

Goodyear associates help to build a playground along with United Way.
[Courtesy of The Goodyear Tire and Rubber Company]

table 2.6
Strategic maneuvering

Strategy	Definition	Examples
Domain selection	Entering industries or markets with limited competition or regulation and ample suppliers and customers; entering high growth markets.	IBM's entry into the personal computer market; Miller's entry into the light-beer market
Diversification	Investing in different types of businesses, manufacturing different types of products or geographic expansion to reduce dependence on single market or technology.	General Electric's purchase of RCA and NBC
Merger and acquisition	Combining two or more firms into a single enterprise; gaining possession of an ongoing enterprise.	RJR and Nabisco, Sperry and Burroughs (now Unisys) Boeing and McDonnell Douglas
Divestiture	Selling one or more businesses.	Kodak and Eastman Chemical

Source: Reprinted from *Journal of Marketing,* published by the American Marketing Association. C. Zeithaml and V. Zeithaml, "Environmental Management: Revising the Marketing Perspective," Spring 1984.

defenders Companies that stay within a stable product domain as a strategic maneuver.

of their competitive environments by seeking new products and markets, diversifying, and merging or acquiring new enterprises. In these and other ways, corporations put their competitors on the defensive and force them to react. **Defenders,** on the other hand, stay within a more limited, stable product domain.

Choosing a response approach

Three general considerations help guide management's response to the environment. First, organizations should attempt to *change appropriate elements of the environment.* Environmental responses are most useful when aimed at elements of the environment that (1) cause the company problems; (2) provide it with opportunities; and (3) allow the company to change successfully. Thus, automobile companies faced with intense competition from Japanese automakers successfully lobbied (along with labor) for government-imposed ceilings on Japanese imports. And one charcoal producer, hoping to increase consumers' opportunities to use its product, launched a campaign to increase daylight saving time.

Second, organizations should *choose responses that focus on pertinent elements of the environment.* If a company wants to better manage its competitive environment, competitive aggression and pacification are viable options. Political action influences the legal environment, and contracting helps manage customers and suppliers.

Third, companies should *choose responses that offer the most benefit at the lowest cost.* Return-on-investment calculations should incorporate short-term financial considerations as well as long-term impact. Strategic managers who carefully consider these factors will more effectively guide their organizations to competitive advantage.

Key terms

Summary of learning objectives

Now that you have studied Chapter 2, you should know:

How environmental forces influence organizations, as well as how organizations can influence their environments.

Organizations are open systems that are affected by, and in turn affect, their external environments. Organizations receive financial, human, material, and information resources from the environment; transform these resources into finished goods and services; and then send these outputs back into the environment.

How to make a distinction between the macroenvironment and the competitive environment.

The macroenvironment is composed of international, legal and political, economic, technological, and social forces that influence strategic decisions. The competitive environment is composed of forces closer to the organization, such as current competitors, threat of new entrants, threat of substitutes, suppliers, and customers. Perhaps the simplest distinction between the macroenvironment and the competitive environment is in the amount of control that a firm can exert on external forces. Macroenvironmental forces such as the economy or social trends are much less controllable than forces in the competitive environment such as suppliers and customers.

Why organizations should attend to economic and social developments in the international environment.

Developments in other countries have a profound effect on the way U.S. companies compete. European unification, for example, is creating a formidable buying and selling bloc. The North American Free Trade Agreement opened up trade among the United States, Canada, and Mexico. Managed well, the EU and NAFTA represent opportunities for market growth, joint ventures, and the like. Managed poorly, these free trade agreements may give advantage to more competitive firms and nations.

How to analyze the competitive environment.

Environments can range from favorable to unfavorable. To determine how favorable a competitive environment is, managers should consider the nature of the competitors, potential new entrants, threat of substitutes, suppliers, and customers. Analyzing how these five forces influence the organization provides an indication of potential threats and opportunities. Attractive environments tend to be those that have high industry growth, few competitors, products that can be differentiated, few potential entrants, many barriers to entry, few substitutes, many suppliers (none with much power), and many customers. After identifying and analyzing competitive forces, managers must formulate a strategy that minimizes the power that external forces have over the organization (a topic to be discussed more fully in Chapter 5).

How organizations respond to environmental uncertainty.

Responding effectively to the environment often involves devising proactive strategies to change the environment. Strategic maneuvering, for example, involves changing the boundaries of the competitive environment through domain selection, diversification, mergers, and the like. Independent strategies, on the other hand, do not require moving into a new environment but rather changing some aspect of the current environment through competitive aggression, public relations, legal action, and so on. Finally, cooperative strategies, such as contracting, cooptation, and coalition building, involve the working together of two or more organizations.

Discussion questions

1. This chapter's opening quote by Peter Drucker said, "The essence of a business is outside itself." What do you think this means? Do you agree?

2. What are the most important forces in the macroenvironment facing companies today?

3. Go back to the UNext.com example in "Setting the Stage." What other organizations have faced or are facing similar circumstances in their external environments?

4. What are the main differences between the macroenvironment and the competitive environment?

5. What kinds of changes do companies make in response to environmental uncertainty?

6. We outlined several proactive responses that organizations can make to the environment. What examples have you seen recently of an organization's responding effectively to its environment? Did the effectiveness of the response depend on whether the organization was facing a threat or an opportunity?

Concluding Case
Many new airlines will never grow old

These should be the best of times for young airlines. A robust economy is packing planes and allowing big carriers to jack up airfares. At the same time, poor service and sky-high business fares are sending many travelers in search of alternatives to the major airlines. But against this rosy backdrop, many new entrants are struggling or going out of business. Pro Air Inc., recently grounded by federal regulators over safety concerns, and tiny AccessAir in Iowa have both filed for bankruptcy protection. Vanguard Airlines Inc., hurt by high fuel prices, operational problems, and too-rapid growth, is losing millions of dollars from its Kansas City, Missouri base.

As start-ups have discovered so often in the cutthroat airline business, it's easy to enter the fray but hard to succeed. Yes, the giants have been accused of crushing small fry with predatory tactics, fortress hubs, and big frequent-flier programs. But start-ups often make their own mistakes—from choosing the wrong routes to running sloppy operations. That worries consumer advocates, who want more competition to keep the majors in check. And if consolidation follows on the heels of UAL Corp.'s deal to buy US Airways Group Inc., "you're going to need new entry more than ever," says Kevin P. Mitchell, chairman of the Business Travel Coalition, which represents big corporations.

Certainly, there are success stories. JetBlue Airways, the best-financed start-up in airline history, appears to be off to a phenomenal start since February 2000. The low-fare airline that offers live TV and leather upholstery is filling 72 percent of the seats on its eight new Airbus A320s. It flies to 9 cities, going up to 12 in November, 2000. CEO David Neeleman says the airline, based at New York's John F. Kennedy International Airport, posted a "double-digit" profit margin in August and should be profitable this year. It just raised another $30 million from its investors on top of the $130 million it started with. Neeleman "is the most successful airline entrepreneur of the last 10 years," says Darryl Jenkins, director of the Aviation Institute at George Washington University.

And after a rocky start, six-year-old Frontier Airlines Inc. in Denver seems to be on course. It is benefiting in part from operational and labor woes at UAL's United Airlines. Second-quarter net income doubled, to more than $16 million, as the airline attracted more business passengers and raised fares. Likewise, 10-year-old Spirit Airlines has proven to be a survivor, after shifting its strategy to avoid markets dominated by one major carrier. It even moved its home base last year from Northwest Airline Corp.'s hub in Detroit to Fort Lauderdale.

But for every JetBlue and Frontier, there seems to be a Pro Air. Even before the Federal Aviation Administration revoked Pro Air's operating certificate in September—a move Pro Air is contesting—the airline was ailing. Despite winning contracts from major companies such as General Motors Corp., it failed to offer the frequent flights that business passengers demanded and spread itself too thin, with only three aircraft. What's more, it chose to compete head-on in Detroit with Northwest. "They were lucky to fly as long as they did," says Cameron R. Burr, a partner at the Burr Group, an investment firm. Pro Air insists it was about to raise $70 million right before the FAA shut it down.

Some experts see a smoother ride ahead. Led by United and its recent pilot contract, major carriers are expected to see big increases in labor costs. That probably means higher fares for passengers—and a bigger pricing umbrella for the little guys to work under. And even if the economy softens, "that will refocus [customers] on economic value" instead of frequent-flier benefits, says Stanley L. Pace, head of Bain & Co.'s airline practice. But until then, the new guys in the skies have little room for error.

Questions

1. Which of the five forces of competition seem to be having the greatest impact on the airline industry: buyers, suppliers, rivals, new entrants, or substitutes? How attractive is this industry?

2. Imagine you were running one of these start-up airlines. What response(s) would you suggest given the environmental situation?

3. Do you see any similarities between the airline industry and the education/learning industry discussed at the beginning of the chapter in "Setting the Stage"?

Source: Wendy Zellner and Michael Arndt, "Many New Airlines Will Never Grow Old," *Business Week,* October 23, 2000, p. 104.

CEO David Neeleman's JetBlue Airways appears to be off to a phenomenal start since February 2000.
[Courtesy JetBlue Airways]

Chapter Three

Managerial Decision Making

The business executive is by profession a decision maker. Uncertainty is his opponent. Overcoming it is his mission.

—*John McDonald*

Chapter Outline

Learning Objectives

After studying Chapter 3, you will know:

1. The kinds of decisions you will face as a manager.

2. How to make "rational" decisions.

3. The pitfalls you should avoid when making decisions.

4. The pros and cons of using a group to make decisions.

5. The procedures to use in leading a decision-making group.

6. How to encourage creative decisions.

7. The processes by which decisions are made in organizations.

8. How to make decisions in a crisis.

Setting the Stage

Decision Pressures

Famous companies make big news when their managers make brilliant, bold, foolish, or unethical decisions. In the year 2000 Firestone Tire provided a tragic example of terrible managerial decision making, and you will read more about it later. But most managerial decisions, like the companies at which they are made, are not newsworthy. Here are a few recent examples that you probably haven't heard about despite their importance. Consider what you would have done.

Imagine that you get a report that a folding chair that your company sells collapsed, causing a customer to strain a muscle. What would you do?

Or you manage a different company, one that sells smoke alarms, and a few customers tell you their alarms don't work properly. What actions would you take?

Or you learn that some removable seats on the jogging strollers you sell were not snapped onto the frame. Now what?

Or a hinge on a baby crib's drop gate is defective. What do you do?

In the last case, Baby's Dream furniture notified the Consumer Product Safety Commission (CPSC)—but not until nine injuries were reported, and the company was fined $200,000 for not reporting the defect promptly.

For the jogging strollers, Baby Trend management acted decisively by contacting 120 Babies "R" Us stores, checked 2,250 strollers to make sure the snaps were fastened, and retrieved the strollers already sold.

Reports of product defects do not always make headline news.
[Courtesy U.S. Consumer Product Safety Commission]

For the smoke alarms, Harvey Grossblatt of Universal Security Instruments decided to collect more information, contacted an independent laboratory and the CPSC, and learned that neither could find a problem with the alarms. But whereas so many decision makers would consider the episode to be over, Mr. Grossblatt said, "Let's have an abundance of caution, and let's deal with it," and recalled 34,000 smoke alarms at a cost of $150,000.

What about the folding chair incident? Peter Jenkins of Boston Warehouse Trading Corp. had no idea whether it was a freak accident or a flawed chair. He described it as very stressful because he didn't know whether there really was a problem and he didn't know what to do. Fortunately, he conducted tests in the company's warehouse, discovered a screw that was too small and weakened the chairs, notified the CPSC, and recalled 1,800 chairs. "I wouldn't want my mother sitting on [one]," he said.

This chapter is not about product recalls, or the CPSC, or ethics and social responsibility, which are discussed thoroughly in Chapter 5. It is about decision making, the most basic and constant of managerial activities. Whereas the context and specifics of decisions differ, the examples just described reveal some common aspects of most managerial decisions: They are consequential, and stressful, and ambiguous; it is not always clear that there is a problem at all, or whether a decision is needed; inaction may constitute the wrong decision; different managers apply different criteria in reaching a final choice; and once a decision is made, appropriate action must be taken to implement it.

Source: B. Kwon, "When Bad Things Happen to Good Companies," Fortune Small Business, November 2000, pp. 104–108; J. Mull and N. St. Pierre, "How Will Firestone and Ford Steer Through This Blowout?," Business Week, August 28, 2000, p. 54.

The best managers make decisions constantly, and make them well. At CNN, the president makes critical decisions every minute or two, all day long, while standing eye-to-eye with reporters, editors, and others. Executive producers may make a hundred decisions during a live one-hour show. And these instantaneous decisions have lasting impact. It is no task for the indecisive or squeamish. As CNN's vice chairman said, "Nobody is going to tell you what to do. It's up to you to figure out what to do, then do it. Always take the proactive path. Ask for advice, sure, but don't sit on your hands waiting for an order."[1]

Decisions. If you can't make them, you won't be an effective manager. This chapter discusses the kinds of decisions managers face, how they are made, and how they *should* be made.

Characteristics of managerial decisions

Managers face problems constantly. Some problems that require a decision are relatively simple; others seem overwhelming. Some demand immediate action, while others take months or even years to unfold.

Actually, managers often ignore problems.[2] For several reasons, they avoid taking action.[3] First, managers can't be sure how much time, energy, or trouble lies ahead once they start working on a problem. Second, getting involved is risky; tackling a problem but failing to solve it successfully can hurt the manager's track record. Third, because problems can be so perplexing, it is easier to procrastinate or to get busy with less demanding activities.

figure 3.1
Characteristics of
managerial decisions

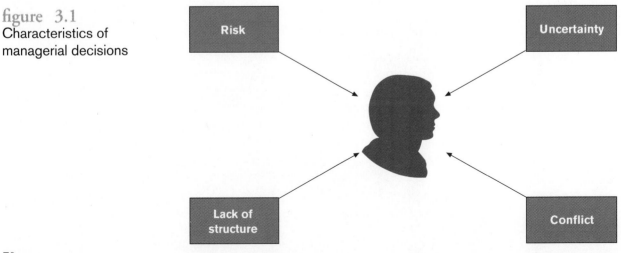

It is important to understand why decision making can be so challenging. Figure 3.1 illustrates several characteristics of managerial decisions that contribute to their difficulty and pressure. Most managerial decisions lack structure and entail risk, uncertainty, and conflict.

Lack of structure

Lack of structure is the usual state of affairs in managerial decision making.[4] Although some decisions are routine and clear-cut, for most there is no automatic procedure to follow. Problems are novel and unstructured, leaving the decision maker uncertain about how to proceed.

A well-known distinction illustrating this point is between programmed and nonprogrammed decisions. **Programmed decisions** have been encountered and made before. They have objectively correct answers and can be solved by using simple rules, policies, or numerical computations. If you face a programmed decision, there exists a clear procedure or structure for arriving at the right decision. For example, if you are a small-business owner and must decide the amounts for your employees' paychecks, you can use a calculator—and if the amounts are wrong, your employees will prove it to you. Table 3.1 gives some other examples.

If most important decisions were programmed, managerial life would be much easier. But managers typically face **nonprogrammed decisions:** new, novel, complex decisions having no certain outcomes. There are a variety of possible solutions, all of which have merits and drawbacks. The decision maker must create or impose a method for making the decision; there is no predetermined structure on which to rely. As Table 3.1 suggests, important, difficult decisions tend to be nonprogrammed, and they demand creative approaches.

programmed decisions
Decisions encountered and made before, having objectively correct answers, and solvable by using simple rules, policies, or numerical computations.

nonprogrammed decisions
New, novel, complex decisions having no proven answers.

table 3.1
Types of decisions

	Programmed decisions	Nonprogrammed decisions
Type of problem	Frequent, repetitive, routine, much certainty regarding cause-and-effect relationships.	Novel, unstructured, much uncertainty regarding cause-and-effect relationships.
Procedure	Dependence on policies, rules, and definite procedures.	Necessity for creativity, intuition, tolerance for ambiguity, creative problem solving.
Examples	Business firm: Periodic reorders of inventory.	Business firm: Diversification into new products and markets.
	University: Necessary grade-point average for good academic standing.	University: Construction of new classroom facilities.
	Health care: Procedure for admitting patients.	Health care: Purchase of experimental equipment.
	Government: Merit system for promotion of state employees.	Government: Reorganization of state government agencies.

Source: J. Gibson, J. Ivancevich, and J. Donnelly, Jr., *Organizations,* 5th ed. (Plano, TX: BPI, 1985).

Uncertainty and risk

certainty The state that exists when decision makers have accurate and comprehensive information.

uncertainty The state that exists when decision makers have insufficient information.

risk The state that exists when the probability of success is less than 100 percent.

If you have all the information you need, and can predict precisely the consequences of your actions, you are operating under a condition of **certainty.**[5] Managers are expressing their preference for certainty when they are not satisfied hearing about what *may have* happened or *might* happen and insist on hearing what *did* or *will* happen.[6] But perfect certainty is rare. For important, nonprogrammed managerial decisions, uncertainty is the rule.

Uncertainty means the manager has insufficient information to know the consequences of different actions. Decision makers may have strong opinions—they may feel sure of themselves—but they are still operating under conditions of uncertainty if they lack pertinent information and cannot estimate the likelihood of different results of their actions.

When you can estimate the likelihood of various consequences, but still do not know with certainty what will happen, you are facing **risk.** Risk exists when the probability of an action being successful is less than 100 percent. If the decision is the wrong one, you may lose money, time, reputation, or other important assets.

Risk, like uncertainty, is a fact of life in managerial decision making. But this is not the same as *taking* a risk. Whereas it sometimes seems as though risk takers are admired, and that entrepreneurs and investors thrive on taking risks, the reality is that good decision makers prefer to *avoid* or *manage* risk. This means that, while they accept the fact that consequential decisions entail risk, they do everything they can to anticipate the risk, minimize it, and control it.

George Conrades, the chairman and CEO of Akamai Technologies, says "We operate in an environment—the Internet—where there's an enormous amount of uncertainty. You can't be sure what's going to happen tomorrow, never mind next year. The danger is that the uncertainty can lead to paralysis. You spend so much time trying to nail down all the possibilities and risks, you never get around to taking action. And if that happens— if you become indecisive—you're dead. Because in the Internet world, if you don't take action, somebody else will" (p. 120).[7]

Conflict

conflict Opposing pressures from different sources. Two levels of conflict are psychological conflict and conflict that arises between individuals or groups.

Important decisions are even more difficult because of the conflict managers face. **Conflict,** which exists when the manager must consider opposing pressures from different sources, occurs at two levels.

First, individual decision makers experience psychological conflict when several options are attractive, or when none of the options is attractive. For instance, a manager may have to decide whom to lay off, when she doesn't want to lay off anyone. Or she may have three promising job applicants for one position—but choosing one means she has to reject the other two.

Second, conflict arises between individuals or groups. The chief financial officer argues in favor of increasing long-term debt to finance an acquisition. The chief executive officer, however, prefers to minimize such debt and find the funds elsewhere. The marketing department wants more product lines to sell to its customers, and engineers want higher-quality products. But production people want to lower costs by having longer production runs of fewer products with no changes. Few decisions are without conflict.

The stages of decision making

Faced with these challenges, how are good decisions made? The ideal decision-making process moves through six stages. At companies that have institutionalized the process, these stages are intended to answer the following questions:[8] What do we want to change? What's preventing us from reaching the "desired state"? How *could* we make the change? What's the *best* way to do it? Are we following the plan? and How well did it work out?

More formally, as Figure 3.2 illustrates, decision makers should (1) identify and diagnose the problem, (2) generate alternative solutions, (3) evaluate alternatives, (4) make the choice, (5) implement the decision, and (6) evaluate the decision.

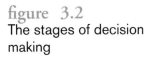

figure 3.2
The stages of decision making

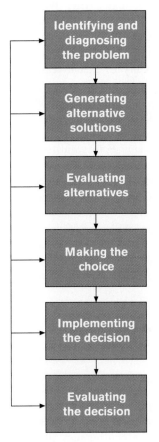

Identifying and diagnosing the problem

Generating alternative solutions

Evaluating alternatives

Making the choice

Implementing the decision

Evaluating the decision

ready-made solutions Ideas that have been seen or tried before.

custom-made solutions The combination of ideas into new, creative solutions.

Identifying and diagnosing the problem

The first stage in the decision-making process is to recognize that a problem exists and must be solved. Typically, a manager realizes some discrepancy between the current state (the way things are) and a desired state (the way things ought to be). Such discrepancies—say, in organizational or departmental performance—may be detected by comparing current performance against (1) *past* performance, (2) the *current* performance of other organizations or departments, or (3) *future* expected performance as determined by plans and forecasts.[9]

Recognizing that a problem exists is only the beginning of this stage. The decision maker also must want to do something about it and must believe that the resources and abilities necessary for solving the problem exist.[10] Then the decision maker must dig in deeper and attempt to *diagnose* the true cause of the problem symptoms that surfaced.

For example, a sales manager knows that sales have dropped drastically. If he is leaving the company soon or believes the decreased sales volume is due to the economy (which he can't do anything about), he won't take further action. But if he does try to solve the problem, he should not automatically reprimand his sales staff, add new people, or increase the advertising budget. He must analyze *why* sales are down and then develop a solution appropriate to his analysis. Asking why, of yourself and others, is essential to understanding the real problem.

Useful questions to ask and answer in this stage include[11]

- Is there a difference between what is actually happening and what should be happening?
- How can you describe the deviation, as specifically as possible?
- What is/are the cause(s) of the deviation?
- What specific goals should be met?
- Which of these goals are absolutely critical to the success of the decision?

Generating alternative solutions

In the second stage, problem diagnosis is linked to the development of alternative courses of action aimed at solving the problem. Managers generate at least some alternative solutions based on past experiences.[12]

Solutions range from ready made to custom made.[13] Decision makers who search for **ready-made solutions** use ideas they have tried before or follow the advice of others who have faced similar problems. **Custom-made solutions,** on the other hand, must be designed for specific problems. This technique requires combining ideas into new, creative solutions. For example, the Sony Walkman was created by combining two existing products: earphones and a tape player.[14] Potentially, custom-made solutions can be devised for any challenge. Later in the chapter, we will discuss how to generate creative ideas.

Importantly, there are potentially many more alternatives available than managers may realize. For example, what would you do if one of your competitors reduced prices? An obvious choice would be to reduce your own prices. But when American Airlines, Northwest Airlines, and other carriers engaged in fare wars in the early 1990s, the result was record volume of air travel and record losses for the industry.[15]

Fortunately, cutting prices in response to a competitor's price cuts is not the only alternative available, although sometimes it is assumed to be. If one of your competitors cuts prices, don't automatically respond with the initial, obvious response. Generate multiple options, and thoroughly forecast the consequences of these different options. Options other than price cuts include nonprice responses such as emphasizing consumer risks to low-priced products, building awareness of your products' features and overall quality, and communicating your cost advantage to your competitors so they realize that they can't win a price war. Winn-Dixie used that last strategy to its advantage against Food Lion, and the stores stopped competing on price. If you do decide to cut your price as a last resort, do it fast—if you do it slowly, your competitors will gain sales in the meantime, and it may embolden them to employ the same tactic again in the future.[16]

Evaluating alternatives

The third stage involves determining the value or adequacy of the alternatives that were generated. Which solution will be the best?

Too often, alternatives are evaluated with little thought or logic. After Walter P. Chrysler died, Chrysler's lawyer sometimes contacted the ghost of Walter P. for advice. The lawyer would excuse himself from the meeting, go into Chrysler's office, close the door and drapes, turn off the lights, and conjure up Chrysler's spirit. Then the lawyer would return to the meeting and reveal his findings, which the Chrysler executives would use to make the final decision.[17]

Obviously, alternatives should be evaluated more carefully than this. Fundamental to this process is to predict the consequences that will occur if the various options are put into effect.

Managers should consider several types of consequences. Of course, they must attempt to predict the effects on financial or other performance measures. But there are other, less clear-cut consequences to address.[18] Decisions set a precedent; will this precedent be a help or a hindrance in the future? Also, the success or failure of the decision will go into the track records of those involved in making it.

Refer again to your original goals, defined in the first stage. Which goals does each alternative meet, and fail to meet? Which alternatives are most acceptable to you and to other important stakeholders? If several alternatives may solve the problem, which can be implemented at the lowest cost? If no alternative achieves all your goals, perhaps you can combine two or more of the best ones.

Key questions here are:[19]

- Is our information about alternatives complete and current? If not, can we get more and better information?
- Does the alternative meet our primary objectives?
- What problems could we have if we implement the alternative?

Of course, results cannot be forecast with perfect accuracy. But sometimes decision makers can build in safeguards against an uncertain future by considering the potential consequences of several different scenarios. Then they generate **contingency plans**— alternative courses of action that can be implemented based on how the future unfolds.

For example, scenario planners making decisions about the future might consider four alternative views of the future state of the U.S. economy:[20] (1) An economic boom with 5 to 6 percent annual growth and the United States much stronger than its global competitors; (2) a moderately strong economy with 2 to 3 percent growth and the United States pulling out of a recession; (3) a pessimistic outlook with no growth, rising unemployment, and recession; or (4) a worse scenario with global depression, massive unemployment, and widespread social unrest.

Some scenarios will seem more likely than others, and some may seem highly improbable. Ultimately, one of the scenarios will prove to be more accurate than the others. The process of considering multiple scenarios raises important "what if?" questions for decision makers and highlights the need for preparedness and contingency plans.

As you read this, what economic scenario is unfolding? What are the important current events and trends? What scenarios could evolve six or eight years from now? How will *you* prepare?

contingency plans Alternative courses of action that can be implemented based on how the future unfolds.

From the Pages of BusinessWeek

Big decisions at Pfizer

Pharmaceutical giant Pfizer spent $116 billion to buy Warner-Lambert. The driver of the decision was one drug: Lipitor, which lowers cholesterol. Pfizer got not only a product poised to be the world's best-selling medication, but also the largest research and development organization in the industry. *Business Week* said "Be careful what you wish for," alluding to the risks associated with the deal, with consequences difficult to forecast.

The acquisition has numerous potential costs and benefits. In the drug industry, bigger research programs are not necessarily better; a study by Boston Consulting Group showed no relationship between R&D budget and productivity. And it is not clear whether anyone can successfully manage a $4.7 billion R&D program, the size of the new operation. John F. Niblack, vice chairman and head of the R&D effort, says "No one has ever operated at this scale before. There's no manual on how to do this" (p. 217).

Adding to the risk is that this big program is the product of a merger of companies with different management structures. Pfizer has a formal, team-oriented decision process; Warner's was faster and more flexible. Pfizer hopes to combine the financial benefits of a huge corporation with the entrepreneurialism of the smaller biotech company, but blending the two cultures may be difficult. Many Warner executives have left the new company. On the other hand, according to Pfizer's Henry A. McKinnell, previous mergers have been done because of slow growth, failing research pipelines, and patent problems. This merger, in contrast, is between two of the fastest-growing companies in the industry.

Another risk: Rising costs in the industry could become a political target, and drug prices could fall through the floor. Pfizer will need to maintain growth via a steady stream of new, blockbuster drugs. Such a product portfolio has evaded other giant pharmaceutical companies, and some Wall Street analysts are skeptical.

Perhaps the biggest uncertainty of all, and the most pervasive source of difficulty in forecasting outcomes of the company's efforts, is nature. The diseases that offer the greatest opportunities in the business are the most complex and difficult to tackle, and therefore entail the greatest risks. For example, Pfizer was hopeful about an experimental compound for the treatment of late-stage prostate cancer and an advanced form of lung cancer that was supposed to shut off the blood supply to tumors. But it failed to stop the cancers, and Pfizer had to halt the trials. Other promising compounds have to be stopped when they lead to unexpected side effects in some patients. By nature, nature is unpredictable.

Pfizer hopes to manage the risk and uncertainty through its massive R&D effort, its partnerships, and a highly aggressive approach to marketing its successful products. It has about 8,000 sales representatives, and spends significantly more than the industry average on sales. It may need to spend more than other companies spend to deal with another major challenge: the competition. For example, Lipitor, the product that made Warner so attractive to Pfizer, is being pressured by a powerful new anticholesterol agent from AstraZeneca. Pfizer's defense includes not just aggressive marketing but also a growing pile of studies and research data about the effectiveness of Lipitor. In the end, the success of Pfizer's decision to acquire Warner, and its decisions surrounding product development, depend on how well it can influence another set of decisions: those made by physicians in treating their patients.

Source: A. Barrett, "Pfizer; How Big is Too Big?", *Business Week*, August 28, 2000, pp. 216–22. ●

Making the choice

Once you have considered the possible consequences of your options, it is time to make your decision. Important concepts here are maximizing, satisficing, and optimizing.[21]

To **maximize** is to make the best possible decision. The maximizing decision realizes the greatest positive consequences and the fewest negative consequences. In other words, maximizing results in the greatest benefit at the lowest cost, with the largest expected total return. Maximizing requires searching thoroughly for a complete range of alternatives, carefully assessing each alternative, comparing one to another, and then choosing or creating the very best.

maximize A decision realizing the best possible outcome.

satisfice To choose an option that is acceptable, although not necessarily the best or perfect.

To **satisfice** is to choose the first option that is minimally acceptable or adequate; the choice appears to meet a targeted goal or criterion. When you satisfice, you compare your choice against your goal, not against other options. Satisficing means a search for alternatives stops at the first one that is okay. Commonly, people do not expend the time or energy to gather complete information. Instead, they make the expedient decision based on readily available information. Satisficing is sometimes a result of laziness; other times, there is no other option because time is short, information is unavailable, or other constraints make it impossible to maximize.

Let's say you are purchasing new equipment and your goal is to avoid spending too much money. You would be maximizing if you checked out all your options and their prices, and then bought the cheapest one that met your performance requirements. But you would be satisficing if you bought the first one you found that was within your budget and failed to look for less expensive options.

optimizing Achieving the best possible balance among several goals.

Optimizing means that you achieve the best possible balance among several goals. Perhaps, in purchasing equipment, you are interested in quality and durability as well as price. So, instead of buying the cheapest piece of equipment that works, you buy the one with the best combination of attributes, even though there may be options that are better on the price criterion and others that are better on the quality and durability criteria.

The same idea applies to achieving business goals: One marketing strategy could maximize sales, while a different strategy might maximize profit. An optimizing strategy is the one that achieves the best balance among multiple goals.

Implementing the decision

The decision-making process does not end once a choice is made. The chosen alternative must be implemented. Sometimes the people involved in making the choice must put it into effect. At other times, they delegate the responsibility for implementation to others, such as when a top management team changes a policy or operating procedure and has operational managers carry out the change.

Those who implement the decision must *understand* the choice and why it was made. They also must be *committed* to its successful implementation. These needs can be met by involving those people in the early stages of the decision process. At Steelcase, the world's largest manufacturer of office furniture, new product ideas are put through simultaneous design, engineering, and marketing scrutiny.[22] This is in contrast to an approach whereby designers design and the concept is later relayed to other departments for implementation. In the latter case, full understanding and total commitment of all departments are less likely.

Managers should plan implementation carefully. Adequate planning requires several steps:[23]

1. Determine how things will look when the decision is fully operational.
2. Chronologically order, perhaps with a flow diagram, the steps necessary to achieve a fully operational decision.
3. List the resources and activities required to implement each step.
4. Estimate the time needed for each step.
5. Assign responsibility for each step to specific individuals.

Decision makers should assume that things will *not* go smoothly during implementation. It is very useful to take a little extra time to *identify potential problems* and *identify potential opportunities*. Then, you can take actions to prevent problems and also be ready to seize on unexpected opportunities. Useful questions are:

- What problems could this action cause?
- What can we do to prevent the problems?
- What unintended benefits or opportunities could arise?
- How can we make sure they happen?
- How can we be ready to act when the opportunities come?

The following example illustrates what happens when potential problems are not explicitly considered.

Worse off than before

Half the decisions made in organizations fail. Most fail because managers make mistakes in the stages of the decision-making model. They may fail to thoroughly forecast consequences of solutions, fail to think carefully about implementation issues, neglect contingency planning, and so on.

Consider this example:

Everybody had agreed on the proposed plan. The mayor had the support of both the citizens and the city council. Because the volume of traffic downtown and the resultant noise and air pollution had become intolerable, the speed limit was lowered to 20 miles per hour and concrete speed bumps were installed to prevent cars from exceeding it.

But the results were hardly what the planners anticipated. The lower speeds forced cars to travel in second rather than third gear, so they were noisier and produced more exhaust. Shopping trips that used to take only 20 minutes now took 30, so the number of cars in the downtown area at any given time increased markedly. A traffic disaster? No—shopping downtown became so nerve-racking that fewer and fewer people went there. So the desired result was achieved after all? Not really, for even though the volume of traffic gradually went back to its original level, the noise and air pollution remained significant. To make matters worse, during the period of increased traffic, word had gotten around that once-a-week shopping expeditions to a nearby mall on the outskirts of a neighboring town were practical and saved time. More and more people started shopping that way. To the distress of the mayor, downtown businesses that had been flourishing now teetered on the verge of bankruptcy. Tax revenues sank drastically. The master plan turned out to be a major blunder, the consequences of which will burden this community for a long time to come.

Sources: From D. Dorner, "Unforeseen Consequences," *Across the Board,* November–December, 1996, pp. 25–28. Reprinted with permission of The Conference Board; and P. Nutt, "Surprising But True: Half the Decisions in Organizations Fail," *Academy of Management Executive,* November 2000, pp. 75–90. ●

Always expect the unexpected. It is better not to learn about unexpected issues in the implementation stage but to do a thorough job thinking through the earlier stages in the decision-making process.

Many of the chapters in this book are concerned with implementation issues: how to implement strategy, allocate resources, organize for results, lead and motivate people, manage change, and so on. View the chapters from that perspective, and learn as much as you can about how to implement properly.

Evaluating the decision

The final stage in the decision-making process is evaluating the decision. This means collecting information on how well the decision is working. Quantifiable goals—a 20 percent increase in sales, a 95 percent reduction in accidents, 100 percent on-time deliveries—can be set before the solution to the problem is implemented. Then objective data can be gathered to accurately determine the success (or failure) of the decision.

Decision evaluation is useful whether the feedback is positive or negative. Feedback that suggests the decision is working implies that the decision should be continued and perhaps applied elsewhere in the organization. Negative feedback, indicating failure, means that either (1) implementation will require more time, resources, effort, or thought; or (2) the decision was a bad one.

If the decision appears inappropriate, it's back to the drawing board. Then the process cycles back to the first stage: (re)definition of the problem. The decision-making process begins anew, preferably with more information, new suggestions, and an approach that attempts to eliminate the mistakes made the first time around.

The best decision

vigilance A process in which a decision maker carefully executes all stages of decision making.

How can managers tell whether they have made the best decision? One approach is to wait until the results are in. But what if the decision has been made but not yet implemented? While nothing can guarantee a "best" decision, managers should at least be confident that they followed proper *procedures* that will yield the best possible decision under the circumstances. This means that the decision makers were appropriately vigilant in making the decision. **Vigilance** occurs when the decision makers carefully and conscientiously execute all six stages of decision making, including making provisions for implementation and evaluation.[24]

Even if managers reflect on these decision-making activities and conclude that they were executed conscientiously, they still will not know whether the decision will work; after all, nothing guarantees a good outcome. But they *will* know that they did their best to make the best possible decision.

Most of the causes of business failures described in the following section are a result of inadequate vigilance. Consider them decision traps; if you find yourself thinking in the following ways, you may be making poor decisions.

Why businesses fail

Why do firms fail? What kills companies is poor decisions at the top. Once entrepreneurs decide to start a business, they put their hearts into it but fail to use their heads. Faulty thought processes by entrepreneurs inculde:

- *I need to make the decisions myself.* Early on, you are responsible for everything. But over time, you need to bring in good people and let go a bit. Stay in touch with what's happening, but you have to delegate more, give other people more responsibility, and let them do what they do best.
- *E-commerce is easy and cheap.* It's easy to construct a Web site that can handle transactions. But most e-commerce efforts have failed, and many big companies have had to try many times before getting it close to right. The strategic, technological, and organizational issues should not be underestimated.
- *We don't need to make a profit.* Yeah, right. Obviously wrong, but the year 2000 was well underway before a lot of people learned the hard way that the new economy didn't mean that all the old rules no longer applied.
- *My forecasts are conservative.* You may think you can make your plan work because you have made cautious predictions. But you'd better have contingency plans in case your forecasts prove wrong. A rule of thumb is that start-ups take twice as long or need three times as much money as their founders predict. Sales projections are almost never met.
- *With this much money to work with, we can't miss.* It's tough to have to pinch pennies. But too much money may make for risky or poorly thought-out decisions, and you will lose control of costs.
- *Fortunately, our biggest customer is General Motors (or Nokia, or IBM).* Traditionally, many managers would have loved to be in such a position. Today they'd better be ready in case they lose their biggest customer—it happens all the time.
- *Actually, our important numbers have never looked better.* Don't ignore signs of trouble; don't assume problems are temporary. Look constantly for trouble signs, and act on them immediately.

Sources: B. G. Posner, "Why Companies Fail," *Inc.,* June 1993, pp. 102–6; R. Balu (Ed.), "Starting your Startup," *Fast Company,* January-February 2000, pp. 81–114; and A. Segars, "The Seven Myths of e-commerce," *Financial Times Mastering Management Review,* January 2000, pp. 28–35. ●

Barriers to effective decision making

Vigilance and full execution of the six-stage decision-making process are the exception rather than the rule in managerial decision making. But research shows that when managers use such rational processes, better decisions result.[25] Managers who make sure they engage in these processes are more effective.

Why don't people automatically invoke such rational processes? It is easy to neglect or improperly execute these processes. The problem may be improperly defined, or goals misidentified. Not enough solutions may be generated, or they may be evaluated incompletely. A satisficing rather than maximizing choice may be made. Implementation may be poorly planned or executed, or monitoring may be inadequate or nonexistent. And decisions are influenced by subjective psychological biases, time pressures, and social realities.

Psychological biases

Decision makers are far from objective in the way they gather, evaluate, and apply information toward making their choices. People have biases that interfere with objective rationality. The examples that follow represent only a few of the many documented subjective biases.[26]

illusion of control People's belief that they can influence events, even when they have no control over what will happen.

The **illusion of control** is a belief that one can influence events even when one has no control over what will happen. Gambling is one example: Some people believe they have the skill to beat the odds even though most people, most of the time, cannot. In business, such overconfidence can lead to failure because decision makers ignore risks and fail to objectively evaluate the odds of success. Relatedly, they may have an unrealistically positive view of themselves or their companies,[27] believe they can do no wrong, or hold a general optimism about the future that can lead them to believe they are immune to risk and failure.[28]

framing effects A psychological bias influenced by the way in which a problem or decision alternative is phrased or presented.

Framing effects refer to how problems or decision alternatives are phrased or perceived, and how these subjective influences can override objective facts. In one example, managers indicated a desire to invest more money in a course of action that was reported to have a 70 percent chance of profit than in one said to have a 30 percent chance of loss.[29] The choices were equivalent in their chances of success; it was the way the options were framed that determined the managers' choices. Thus, framing can exert an undue, irrational influence on people's decisions.

discount the future A bias weighting short-term costs and benefits more heavily than longer-term costs and benefits.

Often decision makers **discount the future.** That is, in their evaluation of alternatives, they weigh short-term costs and benefits more heavily than longer-term costs and benefits. Consider your own decision about whether or not to go for a dental checkup. The choice to go poses short-term financial costs, anxiety, and perhaps physical pain. The choice not to go will inflict even greater costs and more severe pain if dental problems worsen. How do you choose? Many people decide to avoid the short-term costs by not going for regular checkups but end up facing much greater pain in the long run.

Professional gambling establishments count on people's willingness to try to beat the odds. Their illusion of control is a major contributor to the high profits earned by most casinos. *[Jose Fuste Raga/The Stock Market]*

The same bias applies to students who don't study, weight watchers who sneak dessert or skip an exercise routine, and working people who take the afternoon off to play golf when they really need to work. It can also affect managers who hesitate to invest funds in research and development programs that may not pay off until far into the future. In all of these cases, the avoidance of short-term costs or the seeking of short-term rewards results in negative long-term consequences.

When U.S. companies sacrifice present value to invest for the future—such as when Weyerhaeuser incurs enormous costs for its reforestation efforts that won't lead to harvest until 60 years in the future—it seems the exception rather than the rule. Discounting the future partly explains governmental budget deficits, environmental destruction, and decaying urban infrastructure.[30]

Personality and decision making

Individuals differ in their approaches to decision making. One well-known measure that assesses how people differ from one another, the Myers-Briggs Type Indicator (MBTI), has implications for how people make decisions both individually and in groups.

The basis for the MBTI is that people have preferences for one way of doing things over another. This is not about skill or ability, but about what people would do and how they would do it given free choice to exercise their true preferences. If you were to complete the MBTI, your results would indicate your preferences with respect to four basic choices:

1. Which do you prefer: extraversion (E)—attending to the external world of action, people, activities, and things—or introversion (I)—attending to the internal world of reflection, thought, ideas, and concepts?
2. Do you prefer sensing (S)—absorbing detailed, factual information through all the senses, through direct experience—or intuiting (N)—seeing the big picture and learning through reading, discussing, and interpreting?
3. Do you prefer thinking (T)—making decisions based on rational, economic logic and objective, quantitative criteria—or feeling (F)—making decisions also in a logical way but invoking personal values and impact on other people?
4. Do you prefer judging (J)—living a structured, well-planned, organized life, and making decisions quickly in order to reach closure—or perceiving (P)—being flexible and adaptable, going with the flow, and being comfortable with postponing decisions and keeping options open?

Think about your own preferences on these dimensions. What implications do these different types—especially S versus N and T versus F—have for decision making? Which of the types have the most relevance to which stages of the rational model? How might individuals differ in the way they go through the stages? And what are the implications for a group of people making decisions together? For example, what if everyone at the meeting is an E? Or everyone an I? Everyone a T, or everyone an F?

Source: S. K. Hirsh and J. M. Kummerow, *Introduction to Type in Organizations* (Oxford: Oxford Psychologists Press, 1994): and D. Leonard and S. Straus, "Putting Your Company's Whole Brain to Work," *Harvard Business Review*, July–August, 1997, pp. 110–21. ●

Time pressures

In today's rapidly changing business environment, the premium is on acting quickly and keeping pace. The most conscientiously made business decisions can become irrelevant and even disastrous if managers take too long to make them.

How can managers make decisions quickly? Some natural tendencies, at least for North Americans, might be to skimp on analysis (not be too vigilant), suppress conflict, and make decisions on your own without consulting other managers.[31] These strategies might speed up decision making, but they reduce decision *quality.*

Can managers under time pressure make both timely and high-quality decisions? A recent study of decision-making processes in microcomputer firms—a high-tech, fast-paced industry—showed some important differences between fast-acting and slower-acting firms.[32] The fast-acting firms realized significant competitive advantages—and did not sacrifice the quality of their decisions.

What tactics do such companies use? First, instead of relying on old data, long-range planning, and futuristic forecasts, they focus on *real-time information:* current information obtained with little or no time delay. For example, they constantly monitor daily operating measures like work in process rather than checking periodically the traditional accounting-based indicators such as profitability.

Second, they *involve people more effectively and efficiently* in the decision-making process. They rely heavily on trusted experts, which yields both good advice and the confidence to act quickly despite uncertainty. They also take a realistic view of conflict: They value differing opinions, but they know that if disagreements are not resolved, the top executive must make the final choice in the end. Slow-moving firms, in contrast, are stymied by conflict. Like the fast-moving firms they seek consensus, but when disagreements persist they fail to come to a decision.

Social realities

As the description of decision making in the microcomputer industry implies, many decision are made by a group rather than by an individual manager. In the slow-moving firms, interpersonal factors decrease decision-making effectiveness. Even the manager acting alone is accountable to the boss and to others and must consider the preferences and reactions of many people. Important managerial decisions are marked by conflict among interested parties. Therefore, many decisions are the result of intensive social interactions, bargaining, and politicking.

The remainder of this chapter focuses on the social context of decisions, including decision making in groups and the realities of decision making in organizations.

Decision making in groups

Sometimes a manager finds it necessary to convene a group of people for the purpose of making an important decision. Some advise that in today's complex business environment, significant problems should *always* be tackled by teams.[33] Managers therefore must understand how groups and teams operate and how to use them to improve decision making. You will learn much more about how teams work later in the book.

The basic philosophy behind using a group to make decisions is captured by the adage "two heads are better than one." But is this statement really valid? Yes, it is—potentially.

If enough time is available, groups usually make higher-quality decisions than most individuals acting alone. However, groups often are inferior to the best individual.[34] How well the group performs depends on how effectively it capitalizes on the potential advantages and minimizes the potential problems of using a group. Table 3.2 summarizes these issues.

table 3.2
Pros and cons of using a group to make decisions

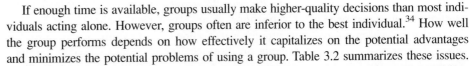

Potential advantages	Potential disadvantages
1. Larger pool of information	1. One person dominates.
2. More perspectives and approaches.	2. Satisficing.
3. Intellectual stimulation.	3. Groupthink.
4. People understand the decision.	4. Goal displacement.
5. People are committed to the decision.	

Potential advantages of using a group

If other people have something to contribute, using groups to make a decision offers at least five potential advantages.[35]

1. More *information* is available when several people are making the decision. If one member doesn't have all the facts or the pertinent expertise, another member might.

2. A greater number of *perspectives* on the issues, or different *approaches* to solving the problem, are available. The problem may be new to one group member but familiar to another. Or the group may need to consider other viewpoints—financial, legal, marketing, human resources, and so on—to achieve an optimal solution.

3. Group discussion provides an opportunity for *intellectual stimulation*. It can get people thinking and unleash their creativity to a far greater extent than would be possible with individual decision making.

These three potential advantages of using a group improve the chance that a more fully informed, higher-quality decision will result. Thus, managers should involve people with different backgrounds, perspectives, and access to information. They should not involve only their cronies who think the same way they do.

4. People who participate in a group discussion are more likely to *understand* why the decision was made. They will have heard the relevant arguments both for the chosen alternative and against the rejected alternatives.

5. Group discussion typically leads to a higher level of *commitment* to the decision. Buying into the proposed solution translates into high motivation to ensure that it is executed effectively.

The last two advantages improve the chances that the decision will be implemented successfully. Therefore, managers should involve the people who will be responsible for implementing the decision as early in the deliberations as possible.

Potential problems of using a group

Things *can* go wrong when groups make decisions. Most of the potential problems concern the process through which group members interact with one another.[36]

1. Sometimes one group member *dominates* the discussion. When this occurs—such as when a strong leader makes his or her preferences clear—the result is the same as if the dominant individual made the decision alone. Individual dominance has two disadvantages. First, the dominant person does not necessarily have the most valid opinions, and may even have the most unsound ideas. Second, even if that person's preference leads to a good decision, convening as a group will have been a waste of everyone else's time.

2. *Satisficing* is more likely with groups. Most people don't like meetings and will do whatever they can to end them. This may include criticizing members who want to continue exploring new and better alternatives. The result is a satisficing rather than an optimizing or maximizing decision.

groupthink A phenomenon that occurs in decision making when group members avoid disagreement as they strive for consensus.

3. *Pressure to avoid disagreement* can lead to a phenomenon called *groupthink*. **Groupthink** occurs when people choose not to disagree or raise objections because they don't want to break up a positive team spirit. Some groups want to think as one, tolerate no dissension, and strive to remain cordial. Such groups are overconfident, complacent, and perhaps too willing to take risks. Pressure to go along with the group's preferred solution stifles creativity and the other behaviors characteristic of vigilant decision making.

goal displacement A condition that occurs when a decision-making group loses sight of its original goal and a new, possibly less important, goal emerges.

4. *Goal displacement* often occurs in groups. The goal of group members should be to come up with the best possible solution to the problem. But when **goal displacement** occurs, new goals emerge to replace the original ones. It is common for two or more group members to have different opinions and present their conflicting cases. Attempts at rational persuasion become heated disagreement. Winning the argument becomes the new goal. Saving face and defeating the other person's idea become more important than solving the problem.

Effective managers pay close attention to the group process; they manage it carefully. The following sections and later chapters provide suggestions for the effective management of group meetings.

Managing group decision making

Figure 3.3 illustrates the requirements for effectively managing group decision making: (1) an appropriate leadership style; (2) the constructive use of disagreement and conflict; and (3) the enhancement of creativity.

Leadership style

The leader of a decision-making body must attempt to minimize process-related problems. The leader should avoid dominating the discussion or allowing another individual to dominate. This means encouraging less vocal group members to air their opinions and suggestions and asking for dissenting viewpoints.

At the same time, the leader should not allow the group to pressure people into conforming. The leader should be alert to the dangers of groupthink and satisficing. Also, she should be attuned to indications that group members are losing sight of the primary objective: to come up with the best possible solution to the problem.

This implies two things. First, don't lose sight of the problem. Second, make a decision! Keep in mind the slow-moving microcomputer firms that were paralyzed when group members couldn't come to an agreement.

Constructive conflict

Total and consistent agreement among group members can be destructive. It can lead to groupthink, uncreative solutions, and a waste of the knowledge and diverse viewpoints that individuals bring to the group. Thus, a certain amount of *constructive* conflict should exist. Some companies, including Sun Microsystems, Compaq, and United Parcel Service, take steps to ensure that conflict and debate are generated within their management teams.[37]

figure 3.3   Managing group decision making

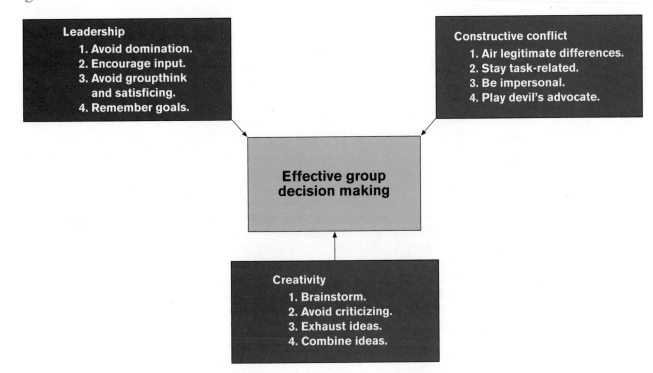

cognitive conflict Issue-based differences in perspectives or judgments.

affective conflict Emotional disagreement directed toward other people.

The most constructive type of conflict is **cognitive conflict,** or differences in perspectives or judgments about issues. In contrast, **affective conflict** is emotional and directed at other people. Affective conflict is likely to be destructive to the group because it can lead to anger, bitterness, goal displacement, and lower-quality decisions. Cognitive conflict, on the other hand, can air legitimate differences of opinion and develop better ideas and problem solutions. Conflict, then, should be task related rather than personal.[38]

Many management teams have too little conflict; their culture is one in which the boss dominates and crushes dissension, or in which people urge one another to be agreeable or not make waves. Such teams are losing the potential benefits of constructive conflict.

Constructive conflict can arise from public disagreement surfacing in an open, participative environment. Managers can increase the likelihood of constructive conflict by assembling teams of different types of people, by creating frequent interactions and active debates, and by encouraging multiple alternatives to be generated from a variety of perspectives.[39]

Conflict also can be generated formally through structured processes.[40] Two techniques that purposely program cognitive conflict into the decision-making process are devil's advocacy and the dialectic method.

devil's advocate A person who has the job of criticizing ideas to ensure that different viewpoints are fully explored.

dialectic A structured debate comparing two conflicting courses of action.

A **devil's advocate** has the job of criticizing ideas. The group leader can formally assign people to play this role. Requiring people to present contrary arguments can lessen inhibitions about disagreeing and make the conflict less personal and emotional.

An alternative to devil's advocacy is the dialectic. The **dialectic** goes a step beyond devil's advocacy by requiring a structured debate between two conflicting courses of action.[41] The philosophy of the dialectic stems from Plato and Aristotle, who advocated synthesizing the conflicting views of a thesis and an antithesis. Structured debates between plans and counterplans can be useful prior to making a strategic decision. For example, one team might present the case for acquiring a firm while another team advocates not making the acquisition.

It is important to remember that generating constructive conflict does not need to be done on such a formal basis, and is not solely the leader's responsibility. Any team member can introduce cognitive conflict by being honest with opinions; by not being afraid to disagree with others; by pushing the group to action if it is taking too long, or making the group slow down if necessary; and by advocating long-term considerations if the group is too focused on short-term results. Introducing constructive conflict is a legitimate and necessary responsibility of all group members interested in improving the group's decision-making effectiveness.

Encouraging creativity

As you've already learned, ready-made solutions to a problem can be inadequate or unavailable. In such cases, custom-made solutions are necessary. This means the group must be creative in generating ideas.

Some say we are in the midst of the next great business revolution: the "creative revolution."[42] Said to transcend the agricultural, industrial, and information revolutions, the most fundamental unit of value in the creativity revolution is ideas. Creativity is more than just an option; it is essential to survival. Allowing people to be creative may be one of the manager's most important and challenging responsibilities.

You might be saying to yourself, "I'm not creative." But even if you are not an artist or a musician, you do have potential to be creative in countless other ways. You are being creative if you (1) bring a new thing into being *(creation)*; (2) join two previously unrelated things *(synthesis)*; or (3) improve something or give it a new application *(modification)*. You don't need to be a genius in school, either—Thomas Edison and Albert Einstein were not particularly good students. Nor does something need to change the world to be creative; the "little things" can always be done in new, creative ways that add value to the product and the customer.

How do you "get" creative?[43] Recognize the almost infinite "little" opportunities to be creative. Assume you can be creative if you give it a try. Obtain sufficient resources, including facilities, equipment, information, and funds. Escape from work once in a

Rolf Smith, formerly of the U.S. Air Force, now leads companies on outdoor "Thinking Expeditions." *[Sam Jones/CORBIS OUTLINE]*

brainstorming A process in which group members generate as many ideas about a problem as they can; criticism is withheld until all ideas have been proposed.

while. Read widely, and try new experiences. Talk to people, constantly, about the issues and ideas with which you are wrestling. And take a course or find a good book about creative thought processes; there are plenty available.

How do you "get" creativity out of other people?[44] Give creative efforts the credit they are due, and don't punish creative failures. If possible, relax pressure for short-term results. Stimulate and challenge people intellectually, and give people some creative freedom. Allow enough time to explore different ideas. Put together teams of people with different styles of thinking and behaving. Get your people in touch with customers, and let them bounce ideas around. Protect them from managers who demand immediate payoffs, who don't understand the importance of creative contributions, or who try to take credit for others' successes. And strive to be creative yourself—you'll set a good example.

A commonly used technique is brainstorming. In **brainstorming,** group members generate as many ideas about a problem as they can. As the ideas are presented, they are posted so that everyone can read them, and people can use the ideas as building blocks. The group is encouraged to say anything that comes to mind, with one exception: No criticism of other people or their ideas is allowed. This rule was violated at the Walt Disney Company when, during a brainstorming session for the design of Euro Disneyland, two architects began shoving each other and almost came to blows.[45]

In the proper brainstorming environment—free of criticism—people are less inhibited and more likely to voice their unusual, creative, or even wild ideas. By the time people have exhausted their ideas, a long list of alternatives has been generated. Only then does the group turn to the evaluation stage. At that point, many different ideas can be considered, modified, or combined into a creative, custom-made solution to the problem.

Although brainstorming is a common practice, some research has shown that face-to-face groups generate fewer independent ideas than the same number of people working alone. This is because in a group: (1) some people, worried about what others might think, are reluctant to express their ideas; (2) people don't always work as hard as if they are alone and accountable for results as individuals; and (3) listening to others takes time that can block people's productivity. But the potential benefits of good brainstorming are clear.[46]

Brainstorming: The Air Force, Play, and IDEO

Rolf Smith, who launched the U.S. Air Force's first Office of Innovation, and now leads companies on outdoor "Thinking Expeditions," says that if you truly pay attention to ideas—even the small, seemingly insignificant ones—then you'll create an environment in which people feel comfortable generating and offering them (p. 162). A playful approach is often effective. "Play" is the name of a small but fast-growing marketing agency gaining attention for its playful work environment and its productive brainstorming sessions for companies including Calvin Klein, PricewaterhouseCooper, Oscar Mayer, and Disney. At a typical recent session, a meeting generated more than 70 ideas for a Weather Channel marketing campaign.

The most carefully studied examples of brainstorming come from IDEO, a firm that has contributed to the design of thousands of products in dozens of industries.

A "brainstormer" at IDEO is a scheduled, face-to-face meeting called to generate ideas. The rules of brainstorming are posted on the wall, and enforced.

Several benefits of brainstorming accrue to IDEO. First, the company is better able to acquire, remember, and use potential solutions to design products. Second, brainstorming adds variety and fun to the job. Third, it helps designers acquire wisdom, to be both confident and humble, as they learn what they know and also what they don't know. Fourth, it encourages people to respect others and work to gain others' respect, so they go out of their way to contribute and to help one another. Fifth, it impresses clients ("We really wow' em!"). Sixth, it provides income. Clients are billed for the brainstorming sessions. And whereas clients in all industries have complaints about their bills, complaints about these charges are rare because clients see the value.

And the design results? Examples are the original Apple computer mouse, Crest toothpaste tubes, bike helmets, an electric guitar, Nike sunglasses, part of the Jaminator toy guitar, an angioplasty device, fishing equipment, Smith ski goggles, and a combination beach chair and cooler. IDEO has won more *Business Week* Design Excellence Awards, for several years running, than any other product design firm.

Sources: C. Dahle, "Mind Games," *Fast Company* January-February 2000, pp. 169–80, and A. Muoio, "Idea Summit," *Fast Company,* January-February 2000, pp. 151–64.

Sources: R. Sutton and A. Hargadon, "Brainstorming Groups in Context: Effectiveness in a Product Design Firm." *Administrative Science Quarterly* 41, (1996), pp. 685–718, and B. Nussbaum, "Winners: The Best Product Designs of the Year," *Business Week,* June 2, 1997, pp. 38–41. ●

Organizational decision making

Individuals and groups make decisions constantly and everywhere throughout organizations. To understand decision making in organizations, a manager must consider a number of additional concepts and processes, including (1) the constraints decision makers face, (2) organizational decision processes, (3) negotiations and politics, (4) decision making during a crisis, and (5) emergent strategies.

Constraints on decision makers

Organizations—or, more accurately, the people who make important decisions—cannot do whatever they wish. They face various constraints—financial, legal, market, human, and organizational—that inhibit certain actions. Capital or product markets may make an expensive new venture impossible. Legal restrictions may restrain the kinds of international business activities in which a firm can participate. Labor unions may successfully defeat a contract proposed by management, contracts may prevent certain managerial actions, and managers and investors may block a takeover attempt.

Suppose you have a great idea that will provide a revolutionary service for your bank's customers. You won't be able to put your idea into action immediately. You will have to sell it to the people who can give you the go-ahead and also to those whose help you will need to carry out the project. You might start by convincing your boss of your idea's merit. Next, the two of you may have to hash it out with a vice president. Then maybe the president has to be sold. At each stage, you must listen to these individuals' opinions and suggestions and often incorporate them into your original concept. Ultimately, you will have to derive a proposal acceptable to everyone.

In addition, ethical and legal considerations must be thought out carefully. You will have plenty of opportunity to think about ethical issues in Chapter 5. Decision makers must consider ethics and the preferences of many constituent groups—the realities of life in organizations.

Models of organizational decision processes

Just as with individuals and groups, organizational decision making historically was described with rational models like the one depicted earlier in Figure 3.2. But Nobel laureate Herbert Simon challenged the rational model and proposed an important alternative called *bounded rationality*. According to Simon's **bounded rationality,** decision makers cannot be truly rational because (1) they have imperfect, incomplete information about alternatives and consequences; (2) the problems they face are so complex; (3) human beings simply cannot process all the information to which they are exposed; (4) there is not enough time to process all relevant information fully; and (5) people, including managers within the same firm, have conflicting goals.

When these conditions hold—and they do, for most consequential managerial decisions—perfect rationality will give way to more biased, subjective, messier decision processes. For example, the **incremental model** of decision making occurs when decision makers make small decisions, take little steps, move cautiously, and move in piece-meal fashion toward a bigger solution. The classic example is the budget process, which traditionally begins with the budget from the previous period and makes incremental decisions from that starting point.

The **coalitional model** of decision making arises when people disagree on goals or compete with one another for resources. The decision process becomes political, as groups of individuals band together and try collectively to influence the decision. Two or more coalitions form, each representing a different preference, and each tries to use power and negotiations to sway the decision.

The **garbage can model** of decision making occurs when people aren't sure of their goals, or disagree about the goals, and likewise are unsure of or in disagreement about what to do. This occurs because some problems are so complex that they are not well understood, and also because decision makers move in and out of the decision process because they have so many other things to attend to as well. This model implies that some decisions are chaotic, and almost random. You can see that this is a dramatic departure from rationality in decision making.

Every one of these processes occurs in every organization. Let's look more closely at a few of the practical realities of organizational life that make it impossible to achieve perfect rationality.

Negotiations and politics

As the coalitional model suggests, decision makers often need to negotiate, bargain, or compromise. Some decisions must be negotiated with parties outside the organization, such as local government, consumer groups, or environmental groups. Even inside the organization, decisions are negotiated among a number of people.

The fact that decisions often must be negotiated implies that they are political; that is, they galvanize the preferences of competing groups and individuals. The decision that is best on objective grounds may lose out because powerful individuals push through their preferred alternatives.

Consider a company that is pursuing a strategy of growth through acquisitions. Such activity constitutes a favorite power game of a powerful coalition of top executives. These executives may prefer to acquire another company even if their own company really needs to focus its efforts on strengthening its internal operations. Other types of decisions, including pay raises, promotions, and budgets, also may be made (and criticized) on the basis of politics.

Organizational politics, in which people try to influence organizational decisions so that their own interests will be served and use power to pursue hidden agendas, can

bounded rationality A less-than-perfect form of rationality in which decision makers cannot conduct a complete, rational analysis because decisions are complex and complete information is unavailable.

incremental model Model of organizational decision making in which major solutions arise through a series of smaller decisions.

coalitional model Model of organizational decision making in which groups with differing preferences use power and negotiations to influence decisions.

garbage can model Model of organizational decision making depicting a chaotic process and seemingly random decisions.

reduce decision-making effectiveness.[47] One of the best ways to reduce such politics, and to make sure that constructive cognitive conflict does not degenerate into affective conflict, is to *create common goals* for members of the team. That is, make the decision-making process a collaborative, rather than a competitive, exercise by establishing a goal around which the group can rally. In one study, top management teams with stated goals like "build the biggest financial war chest" for an upcoming competitive battle, or "create *the* computer firm of the decade," or "build the best damn machine on the market" were less likely to have dysfunctional conflict and politics between members.[48]

Most managers accept political realities and consider them a basic challenge of organizational life.[49] For any important decision that you wish to influence, it is essential that you identify and marshal the support of powerful individuals or interest groups.

Decision making in a crisis

In crisis situations, managers must make decisions under a great deal of pressure.[50] A VIP customer threatens to cancel his contract if your company doesn't get his computers operating within the hour. A strike shuts down your plant. People are killed or injured in a crash of one of your airline's jets or in an explosion in one of your company's mines. What actions will you take? Whatever you decide, you must act quickly.

You have no doubt heard of some of the most famous recent crises: the *Exxon Valdez;* bombings in Oklahoma City and the World Trade Center; Barings Bank's collapse; airline crashes and the Firestone Tire recall (see the concluding case). Union Carbide's gas

table 3.3
Two disasters

Union Carbide	Johnson & Johnson
Failed to identify as a crisis the public perception that the company was a negligent, uncaring killer.	Identified the crisis of public perception that Tylenol was unsafe and J&J was not in control.
No planning before reacting: CEO immediately went to India to inspect damage.	Planned before reacting: CEO picked one executive to head crisis team.
All executives involved.	Rest of company involved only on a need-to-know basis.
Set no goals.	Set goals to: Stop the killings. Find reasons for the killings. Provide assistance to the victims. Restore Tylenol's credibility.
Action: Damage control/stonewalling. Distanced itself. Misrepresented safety conditions. Did not inform spokespeople. Adopted bunker mentality.	Action: Gave complete information. Worked with authorities. Pulled Tylenol from shelves (first-year cost: $150 million). Used strong marketing program. Reissued Tylenol with tamper-proof packaging.
Chronic problems continued: Public confidence low. Costly litigation. No formal crisis plan resulted.	Crisis resolved: Public confidence high. Sales high again. Well-documented crisis management plan.

Companies handle crisis decision making in different ways. Union Carbide's mishandling of the gas leak in Bhopal, India, resulted in the perception that the company was negligent and uncaring. Many years after the tragic accident, people demonstrated vigorously against the company. *[AP/Wide World Photos]*

leak in Bhopal, India, killed thousands of people; several people were killed in the cyanide poisonings of Johnson & Johnson's Tylenol. As outlined in Table 3.3, the two companies handled their crises in very different ways. To this day, J&J is known for its effective handling of the crisis, as outlined in the table.

Commonly a crisis makes effective decision making less likely. Psychological stress and lack of time cause decision makers to think in simplistic terms, to fail to consider an adequate number of alternatives, and to ignore the long-term implications of their actions.

Some crises can be prevented by clarifying the corporation's values and social responsibilities, and monitoring people's behavior and ethical conduct as described in later chapters. For example, at Barings Bank a single employee was allowed to conduct and oversee his own trades. The lack of control systems allowed the trader to increase his activity dramatically, use leverage to an extreme, escalate trade amounts, and greatly increase risk. The resulting crisis brought down the entire bank.

Your organization should be prepared for crises in advance. However, many Fortune 1000 firms have no crisis-management plan at all.[51] Table 3.4 lists some common

table 3.4
Mistaken assumptions: how *not* to handle crisis management

We don't have a crisis.

We can handle a crisis.

Crisis management is a luxury we can't afford.

If a major crisis happens, someone else will rescue us.

Accidents are just a cost of doing business.

Most crises are the fault of bad individuals; therefore, there's not much we can do to prevent them.

Only executives need to be aware of our crisis plans; why scare our employees or members of the community?

We are tough enough to react to a crisis in an objective and rational manner.

The most important thing in crisis management is to protect the good image of the organization through public relations and advertising campaigns.

Source: From C. M. Pearson and I. I. Mitroff. "From Crisis Prone to Crisis Prepared: A Framework for Crisis Management," *The Executive,* February 1993, pp. 48–59. Reprinted by permission of the Academy of Management.

rationalizations that prevent companies from preparing for and managing crises properly. Effective managers do not allow these evasions to prevent them from preparing carefully for crisis.

Crisis management experts have identified several lessons from crises such as airline deaths, the Orange Country bankruptcy, and Intel's defective Pentium chip.[52] First, it is essential to detect the signals that a potential crisis is looming.[53] Second, if a crisis arises, the world will learn all there is to know about your daily operations and crisis preparation and response. You will be thoroughly investigated and publicized immediately. Third, the remedy for one problem can create others, so attention to implementation and monitoring is vital.

Although many companies don't concern themselves with crisis management, it is imperative that it be on management's agenda. An effective plan for crisis management (CM) should include the following elements.[54]

1. *Strategic actions* such as integrating CM into strategic planning and official policies.
2. *Technical and structural actions* such as creating a CM team and dedicating a budget to CM.
3. *Evaluation and diagnostic actions* such as conducting audits of threats and liabilities, conducting environmental impact audits, and establishing tracking systems for early warning signals.
4. *Communication actions* such as providing training for dealing with the media, local communities, and police and government officials.
5. *Psychological and cultural actions* such as showing a strong top management commitment to CM and providing training and psychological support services regarding the human and emotional impacts of crises.

Ultimately, it is imperative that management be able to answer the following questions:[55]

- What kinds of crises could your company face?
- Can your company detect a crisis in its early stages?
- How will it manage a crisis if one occurs?
- How can it benefit from a crisis after it has passed?

The last question makes an important point: A crisis, managed effectively, can have *benefits.* Old as well as new problems can be resolved, new strategies and competitive advantages may appear, and positive change can emerge. And if someone steps in and manages the crisis well, a hero is born.

Emergent strategies

Soon you will learn more about how managers formulate strategies for their firms to pursue. Again, a rational model can describe this process in its ideal form. But once again, the reality of organizational decision making often differs. **Emergent strategy** is the strategy that the organization "ends up" pursuing, based not solely on what was originally planned and attempted, but also on what actually evolves from all the activities engaged in by people throughout the organization.

emergent strategy The strategy that evolves from all the activities engaged in by people throughout the organization.

As shown in Figure 3.4, decision making and strategy emergence are dynamic processes through which people engage in discovery; make decisions; carry out those choices in sometimes tentative, trial-and-error ways; and discover new things and new ways by chance. Discovery is the process of systematically gathering facts and analyzing them. This forms the basis for decision making, which includes generating and selecting goals and courses of action. Action, then, is implementation and evaluation. Discovery continues unabated.

Thus, emergent strategies may start with planning from the top executives, but may also involve trial-and-error, experimenting, learning from mistakes, seizing unexpected

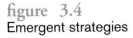
figure 3.4
Emergent strategies

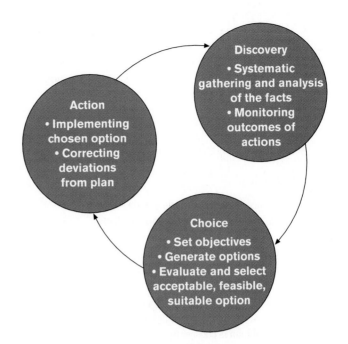

Adapted from: Ralph D. Stacey. *Strategic Management and Organizational Dynamics*. London: Pittman Publishing. 1993, p. 27.

opportunities, and so on. And these activities can occur at any organizational level, in any unit, at any location.

You may notice that all of those processes are constructive and useful. In the coming chapters, we will discuss in more depth the strategy formulation process and its implementation, as well as learning, adapting, and changing in order to thrive in changing circumstances.

Key terms

Summary of learning objectives

Now that you have studied Chapter 3, you should know:

The kinds of decisions you will face as a manager.

Most important managerial decisions are ill structured and characterized by uncertainty, risk, and conflict. Yet managers are expected to make rational decisions in the face of these challenges.

How to make "rational" decisions.

The ideal decision-making process involves six stages. The first, identifying and diagnosing the problem, requires recognizing a discrepancy between the current state and a desired state and then delving below surface symptoms to uncover the underlying causes of the problem. The second stage, generating alternative solutions, requires adopting ready-made or designing custom-made solutions. The third, evaluating alternatives, means predicting the consequences of different alternatives, sometimes through building scenarios of the future. Fourth, a solution is chosen; the solution might maximize, satisfice, or optimize. Fifth, decision makers implement the decision; this stage requires more careful planning than it often receives. Finally, managers should evaluate how well the decision is working. This means gathering objective, valid information about the impact the decision is having. If the evidence suggests the problem is not getting solved, either a better decision or a better implementation plan must be developed.

The pitfalls you should avoid when making decisions.

Situational and human limitations lead most decision makers to satisfice rather than maximize. Psychological biases, time pressures, and the social realities of organizational life may prevent rational execution of the six decision-making stages. But vigilance and an understanding of how to manage decision-making groups and organizational constraints will improve the process and result in better decisions.

The pros and cons of using a group to make decisions.

Advantages include more information, perspectives, and approaches brought to bear on problem solving; intellectual stimulation; greater understanding by all of the final decision; and higher commitment to the decision once it is made. Potential dangers or disadvantages of using groups include individual domination of discussions, satisficing, groupthink, and goal displacement.

The procedures to use in leading a decision-making team.

Effective leaders in decision-making teams or groups avoid dominating the discussion; encourage people's input; avoid groupthink and satisficing; and stay focused on the group's goals. They encourage constructive conflict via devil's advocacy and the dialectic, posing opposite sides of an issue or solutions to a problem. They also encourage creativity through a variety of techniques.

How to encourage creative decisions.

When creative ideas are needed, leaders should set a good example by being creative themselves. They should recognize the almost infinite "little" opportunities for creativity and have confidence in their own creative abilities. They can inspire creativity in others by pushing for creative freedom, rewarding creativity, and not punishing creative failures. They should encourage interaction with customers, stimulate discussion, and protect people from managers who might squelch the creative processes. Brainstorming is one of the most popular techniques for generating creative ideas.

The processes by which decisions are made in organizations.

Decision making in organizations is often a highly complex process. Individuals and groups are constrained by a variety of factors and constituencies. In practice, decision makers are boundedly rational rather than purely rational. Some decisions are made on an incremental basis. Coalitions form to represent different preferences. The process is often chaotic, as depicted in the garbage can model. Politics enter the process, decisions are negotiated, crises arise, and strategies emerge and evolve.

How to make decisions in a crisis.

Crisis conditions make sound, effective decision making more difficult. However, it is possible for crises to be managed well. A strategy for crisis management can be developed beforehand, and the mechanisms put into readiness, so that if crises do arise, decision makers are prepared.

Discussion questions

1. Refer back to "Setting the Stage." If you didn't know the conclusions to those incidents, what would you have done? What do you think of the decisions those managers made?

2. Identify some risky decisions you have made. Why did you take the risks? How did they work out? Looking back, what did you learn?

3. Identify a decision you made that had important unintended consequences. Were the consequences good, bad, or both? Should you, and could you, have done anything differently in making the decision?

4. What do you think is your Myers-Briggs type? What are the personal implications?

5. Recall a recent decision that you had difficulty making. Describe it in terms of the characteristics of managerial decisions.

6. What do you think are some advantages and disadvantages to using computer technology in decision making?

7. Do you think that when managers make decisions they follow the decision-making steps as presented in this chapter? Which steps are apt to be overlooked or given inadequate attention? What can people do to make sure they do a more thorough job?

8. Discuss the potential advantages and disadvantages of using a group to make decisions. Give examples in your experience.

9. Suppose you are the CEO of a major corporation and one of your company's oil tanks has erupted, spilling thousands of gallons of oil into a river that empties into the ocean. What should you do to handle the crisis?

10. Look at the mistaken assumptions described in Table 3.4. Why do such assumptions arise, and what can be done to overcome these biases?

11. Identify some problems you want to solve. Brainstorm with others a variety of creative solutions.

Concluding Case

Crisis at Ford and Firestone

Put yourself in the shoes of Jac Nasser, CEO of Ford. A crisis strikes from out of the blue. How you handle the crisis will determine whether you keep your job, and will affect your reputation forever.

Nasser became CEO in late 1998, and promised not to behave like others in the auto industry who had made so many big mistakes and lost the faith of the public. By now you probably are aware of the subsequent tragedy: Reports of fatal accidents due to faulty tires on Ford Explorer sport utilities and Ranger pickup trucks began appearing, and eventually more than 88 deaths and over 1,400 accidents were attributed to the tires peeling off under pressure. The U.S. government began investigating, and the Venezuelan government threatened criminal charges against Firestone, the tire manufacturer, and Ford, which bought the tires and sold the vehicles.

Nasser did not cause the problems. But as CEO, they became his responsibility.

What to do? Nasser was briefed about the tire failures in early July 2000, and created a war room (actually, several rooms) on the 11th floor of Ford's world headquarters in Dearborn, Michigan. Daily task force meetings included manufacturing, engineering, finance, public affairs, and legal and regulatory executives. The public-affairs unit monitored media coverage, and reviewed devel-

The recall of 6.5 million Firestone tires created a huge logistical challenge for Ford.
[AFP/CORBIS]

opments each morning in a global conference call. Work on the crisis went on night and day, every day, and involved 500 people directly and thousands more indirectly.

Adding greatly to the decision-making and public relations challenges was that Ford had to coordinate its actions with Bridgestone/Firestone, the producer of the defective tires. Bridgestone/Firestone is a Japanese-owned company with very different cultural norms, including norms about making information available to the public. Communications between Ford and Firestone were difficult. Ford did not want to get into a public dispute with its supplier, but did want to distance itself from the tire defects. Ford communicated with everyone—customers, dealers, the media, the government, other suppliers—about what it was doing. But it tried to avoid quibbling about whose fault it was and who would have to pay for it. Rather, the concern was to get a handle on the problem as quickly as possible.

Ford was in an awkward position. Car manufacturers warrant all components—except tires. Therefore, they don't collect tire data. Ford immediately started gathering as much valid data as it could, and made the data publicly available. Ford also wanted to learn where the problem tires were located, so it could get new tire supplies to those locations as quickly as possible. Said Nasser,"Yes, these are Firestone tires, but our customers are driving on them" (p. 124). Statisticians and research engineers looked at large quantities of data by region, product, and tire size—according to Nasser, it was "like trying to boil the ocean" (p. 124). But the company wanted its decisions to be based on data and science, not on "I-think, you-think opinion" (p. 124).

Ford collected and analyzed accident data from four continents. The company engaged in an exhaustive effort to gather, analyze, and disseminate relevant information. It then recalled 6.5 million Firestone tires. This was a huge logistical challenge. Ford had to obtain replacement tires from competing manufacturers. Other needs were less obvious. For example, it had to find enough service bays to change all those tires.

Nasser closed three assembly plants and used their 70,000 new tires as replacements for consumers. Think about the repercussions of that decision. These plants are the mainstay of the auto industry. Closing one plant is extremely tough, both financially and operationally. The company had to mothball machinery, secure partially assembled cars, and stop the supply of parts. And whereas lost production means lost revenues, costs didn't change much because workers received most of their base pay. One company official called Nasser's decision to close the plants "the most courageous decision I've seen since I've been at Ford"(p. 124).

Ford's public relations challenge was enormous. Historically, auto companies often tried to hide problems from the public, and Ford's handling of the exploding Pintos in the 1970s was a notorious example. But when Nasser met with the lead technical person in charge of light trucks, he advised him to be completely open, share any and all data and incidents, and to hold back no information whatsoever. Nasser also advised him not to be constrained by product-liability concerns. "If you are mesmerized by that, you will not ultimately do what's right for the customer"(p. 126).

Nasser did many things well, but criticisms and tough questions ensued. Why didn't the company act sooner to identify the defects? Why wasn't Chairman Bill Ford, Jr. used as a spokesman during the crisis? Why did't he go directly to the scene of the crisis and personally demonstrate his concern for the people involved? Why

were there temporary shortages of replacement tires? And how will Nasser perform during the investigations and lawsuits?

Meanwhile, in October 2000, John Lampe was named the new chairman of Bridgestone/Firestone. He has been extremely busy tackling what he calls "challenges" and "opportunities" rather than problems. He and the company are dedicated to keeping the Firestone name, which he says has a tremendous heritage and loyal following. When a reporter asked if he would agree to a "customer satisfaction" campaign to replace any tires not named in the recall if customers asked for replacements, he replied "No, ma'am" (p. E10). But he is committed to recalling all problem tires specified in the recall, ahead of schedule.

Ford acknowledged that it knew about tire failures in Venezuela in 1998. When Ford first notified Firestone of a potential problem, Firestone failed to act.

Despite Ford's intentions, the two companies were fighting publicly, pointing fingers, and providing an incoherent story. It appeared to the public as if neither company had been completely forthcoming. Members of Congress were upset that the two companies weren't working well together, presented confusing stories, and dragged their feet. They not only were not explaining the problems, they were failing to find solutions.

Questions

1. What do you think of how Nasser and Ford handled the crisis? What could they have done differently?

2. What is Ford's status now from this crisis? Moving forward, what else should it do? What should it *not* do?

3. How damaged is the Firestone brand? The Explorer brand? The Ford brand?

4. Should Firestone agree to replace any tires that customers request, including tires not named in the recall?

Sources: A. Taylor, III., "Jac Nasser's Biggest Test," *Fortune,* September 18, 2000, pp. 123–28, C.E. Mayer, "Hot situation, Cool Head: Firestone's New Chief Undaunted by Recall," *The Washington Post,* November 17, 2000, pp. E1, E10. J. Muller and J. Green, with N. St. Pierre and P. Moore,"Firestone and Ford: The Ride Gets Bumpier," *Business Week,* September 11, 2000, p. 42. ●

Experiential Exercises

3.1 Competitive escalation: The dollar auction

Objective

To explore the effects of competition on decision making.

Instructions

Step 1: 5 Minutes. The instructor will play the role of auctioneer. In this auction, the instructor will auction off $1 bills (the instructor will inform you whether this money is real or imaginary). All members of the class may participate in the auction at the same time.

The rules for this auction are slightly different from those of a normal auction. In this version, *both the highest bidder and the next highest bidder will play their last bids* even though the dollar is only awarded to the highest bidder. For example, if Bidder A bids 15 cents for the dollar and Bidder B bids 10 cents, and there is no further bidding, then A pays 15 cents for the dollar and receives the dollar, while B pays 10 cents and receives nothing. The auctioneer would lose 75 cents on the dollar just sold.

Bids must be made in multiples of 5 cents. The dollar will be sold when there is no further bidding. If two individuals bid the same amount at the same time, ties are resolved in favor of the bidder located physically closest to the auctioneer. *During each round, there is to be no talking except for making bids.*

Step 2: 15 Minutes. The instructor (auctioneer) will auction off five individual dollars to the class. Any student may bid in an effort to win the dollar. A record sheet of the bidding and winners can be kept in the worksheet the follows.

Discussion questions

1. Who made the most money in this exercise—one of the bidders or the auctioneer? Why?
2. As the auction proceeded, did bidders become more competitive or more cooperative? Why?
3. Did two bidders ever pay more for the money being auctioned than the value of the money itself? Explain how and why this happened.
4. Did you become involved in the bidding? Why?
   a. If you became involved, what were your motivations? Did you accomplish your objectives?
   b. If not, why didn't you become involved? What did you think were the goals and objectives of those who did become involved?
5. Did people say things to one another during the bidding to influence their actions? What was said, and how was it influential?

Dollar auction worksheet

	Amount paid by winning bidder	Amount paid by second bidder	Total paid for this dollar
First dollar			
Second dollar			
Third dollar			
Fourth dollar			
Fifth dollar			

Source: Excerpted from R. Lewicki, *Experiences in Management and Organizational Behavior* (New York: John Wiley and Sons, 1991), pp. 91–92, 27–28, and 225–27. Reprinted by permission of John Wiley and Sons, Inc.

3.2 Group problem-solving meeting at the community agency

Objective

To understand the interactions in group decision making through role playing a meeting between a chairman and his subordinates.

Instructions

1. Gather role sheets for each character and instructions for observers.
2. Set up a table in front of the room with five chairs around it arranged in such a way that participants can talk comfortably and have their faces visible to observers.
3. Read the introduction and cast of characters.
4. Five members from the class are selected to role play the five characters. All other members act as observers. The participants study the roles. All should play their roles without referring to the role sheets.
5. The observers read the instructions for observers.
6. When everyone is ready, John Cabot enters his office, joins the others at the table, and the scene begins. Allow 20 minutes to complete the meeting. The meeting is carried to the point of completion unless an argument develops and no progress is evident after 10 or 15 minutes of conflict.

Discussion Questions

1. Describe the group's behavior. What did each member say? Do?
2. Evaluate the effectiveness of the group's decision making.
3. Did any problems exist in leadership, power, motivation, communication, or perception?
4. How could the group's effectiveness be increased?

Introduction

The Community Agency is a role-play exercise of a meeting between the chairman of the board of a social service agency and four of his subordinates. Each character's role is designed to recreate the reality of a business meeting. Each character comes to the meeting with a unique perspective on a major problem facing the agency as well as some personal impressions of the other characters developed over several years of business and social associations.

The Cast of Characters

John Cabot, the Chairman, was the principal force behind the formation of the Community Agency, a multiservice agency. The agency employs 50 people, and during its 19 years of operations has enjoyed better client relations, a better service record, and a better reputation than other local agencies because of a reputation for high-quality service at a moderate cost to funding agencies. Recently, however, competitors have begun to overtake the Community Agency, resulting in declining contracts. John Cabot is expending every possible effort to keep his agency comfortably at the top.

Ron Smith, Director of the Agency, reports directly to Cabot. He has held this position since he helped Cabot establish the agency 19 years ago.

Joan Sweet, Head of Client Services, reports to Smith. She has been with the Agency 12 years, having worked before that for HEW as a contracting officer.

Tom Lynch, Head Community Liaison, reports to Joan Sweet. He came to the Community Agency at Sweet's request, having worked with Sweet previously at HEW.

Jane Cox, Head Case Worker, also works for Joan Sweet. Cox was promoted to this position two years ago. Prior to that time, Jane had gone through a year's training program after receiving an MSW from a large urban university.

Today's meeting

John Cabot has called the meeting with these four managers in order to solve some problems that have developed in meeting service schedules and contract requirements. Cabot must catch a plane to Washington in half an hour; he has an appointment to negotiate a key contract that means a great deal to the future of the Community Agency. He has only 20 minutes to meet with his managers and still catch the plane. Cabot feels that getting the Washington contract is absolutely crucial to the future of the agency.

Source: J. Gordon, *A Diagnostic Approach to Organizational Behavior* (Englewood Cliffs, N.J.: Prentice-Hall, 1983), pp. 340–41. Reprinted by permission of Prentice-Hall, Inc., Englewood Cliffs, NJ ●

Integrating Case
SSS Software In-Basket Exercise

One way to assess your own strengths and weaknesses in management skills is to engage in an actual managerial work experience. The following exercise gives you a realistic glimpse of the tasks faced regularly by practicing managers. Complete the exercise, and then compare your own decisions and actions with those of classmates.

SSS Software designs and develops customized software for businesses. It also integrates this software with the customer's existing systems and provides system maintenance. SSS Software has customers in the following industries: airlines, automotive, finance/banking, health/hospital, consumer products, electronics, and government. The company has also begun to generate important international clients. These include the European Airbus consortium and a consortium of banks and financial firms based in Kenya.

SSS Software has grown rapidly since its inception just over a decade ago. Its revenue, net income, and earnings per share have all been above the industry average for the past several years. However, competition in this technologically sophisticated field has grown very rapidly. Recently, it has become more difficult to compete for major contracts. Moreover, although SSS Software's revenue and net income continue to grow, the rate of growth declined during the last fiscal year.

SSS Software's 250 employees are divided into several operating divisions with employees at four levels: nonmanagement, technical/professional, managerial, and executive. Nonmanagement employees take care of the clerical and facilities support functions. The technical/professional staff perform the core technical work for the firm. Most managerial employees are group managers who supervise a team of technical/professional employees working on a project for a particular customer. Staff who work in specialized areas such as finance, accounting, human resources, nursing, and law are also considered managerial employees. The executive level includes the 12 highest-ranking employees at SSS Software. There is an organization chart in Figure A that illustrates SSS Software's structure. There is also an Employee Classification Report that lists the number of employees at each level of the organization.

In this exercise, you will play the role of Chris Perillo, Vice President of Operations for Health and Financial Services. You learned last Wednesday, October 13, that your predecessor,

Michael Grant, has resigned and gone to Universal Business Solutions, Inc. You were offered his former job, and you accepted it. Previously, you were the Group Manager for a team of 15 software developers assigned to work on the Airbus consortium project in the Airline Services Division. You spent all of Thursday, Friday, and most of the weekend finishing up parts of the project, briefing your successor, and preparing for an interim report you will deliver in Paris on October 21.

It is now 7 A.M. Monday and you are in your new office. You have arrived at work early so you can spend the next two hours reviewing material in your in-basket (including some memos and messages to Michael Grant), as well as your voice mail and e-mail. Your daily planning book indicates that you have no appointments today or tomorrow but will have to catch a plane for Paris early Wednesday morning. You have a full schedule for the remainder of the week and all of next week.

Assignment

During the next two hours, review all the material in your in-basket, as well as your voice mail and e-mail. Take only two hours. Use the following response form as a model, indicate how you want to respond to each item (that is, via letter/memo, e-mail, phone/voice mail, or personal meeting). If you decide not to respond to an item, check "no response" on the response form. All of your responses must be written on the response forms. Write your precise, detailed response (do not merely jot down a few notes). For example, you might draft a memo or write out a message that you will deliver via phone/voice mail. You may also decide to meet with an individual (or individuals) during the limited time available on your calendar today or tomorrow. If so, prepare an agenda for a personal meeting and list your goals for the meeting. As you read through the items, you may occasionally observe some information that you think is relevant and want to remember (or attend to in the future) but that you decide not to include in any of your responses to employees. Write down such information on a sheet of paper titled "note to self."

Source: D. Whetten and K. Cameron, *Developing Management Skills*, 3e, New York: Harper Collins, 1995 ●

figure A   Partial organization chart of health and financial services division

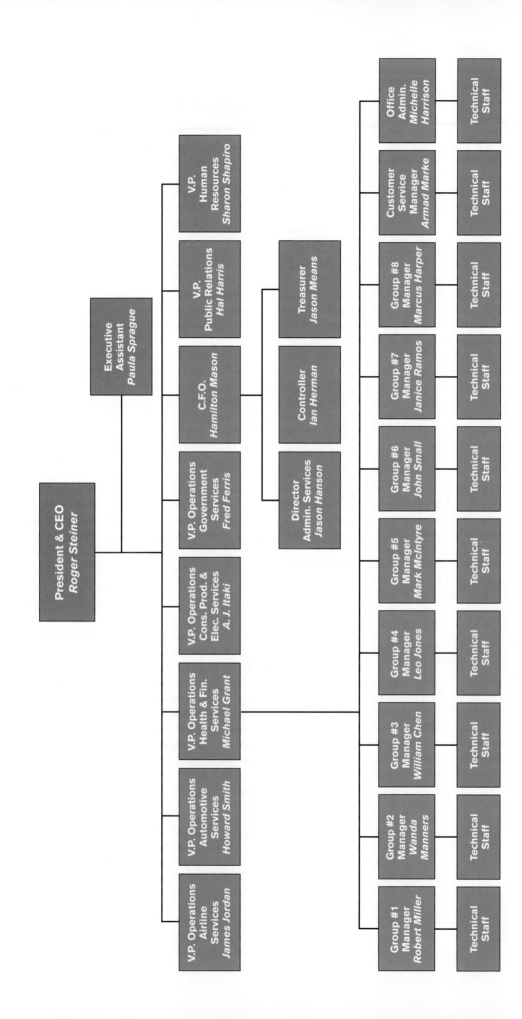

Sample Response Form

Relates To:

Memo # _____   E-mail # _____   Voice mail # _____

Response form:

_____ Letter/Memo   _____ Meet with person (when, where)

_____ E-mail   _____ Note to self

_____ Phone call/Voice mail   _____ No response

ITEM 1 Memo

TO: All Employees

FROM: Roger Steiner, Chief Executive Officer

DATE: October 15

I am pleased to announce that Chris Perillo has been appointed as Vice President of Operations for Health and Financial Services. Chris will immediately assume responsibility for all operations previously managed by Michael Grant. Chris will have end-to-end responsibility for the design, development, integration, and maintenance of custom software for the health and finance/banking industries. This responsibility includes all technical, financial, and staffing issues. Chris will also manage our program of software support and integration for the recently announced merger of three large health maintenance organizations (HMOs). Chris will be responsible for our recently announced project with a consortium of banks and financial firms operating in Kenya. This project represents an exciting opportunity for us, and Chris's background seems ideally suited to the task.

Chris comes to this position with an undergraduate degree in Computer Science from the California Institute of Technology and an M.B.A. from the University of Virginia. Chris began as a member of our technical/professional staff six years ago and has most recently served for three years as a Group Manager supporting domestic and international projects for our airlines industry group, including our recent work for the European Airbus consortium.

I am sure you all join me in offering congratulations to Chris for this promotion.

ITEM 2 Memo

TO: All Managers

FROM: Hal Harris, Vice President, Community and Public Relations

DATE: October 15

For your information, the following article appeared on the front page of the business section of Thursday's *Los Angeles Times.*

In a move that may create problems for SSS Software, Michael Grant and Janice Ramos have left SSS Software and moved to Universal Business Solutions Inc. Industry analysts see the move as another victory for Universal Business Solutions Inc. in their battle with SSS Software for share of the growing software development and integration business. Both Grant and Ramos had been with SSS Software for over 7 years. Grant was most recently Vice President of Operations for all SSS Software's work in two industries: health and hospitals, and finance and banking. Ramos brings to Universal Business Solutions Inc. her special expertise in the growing area of international software development and integration.

Hillary Collins, an industry analyst with Merrill Lynch, said "the loss of key staff to a competitor can often create serious problems for a firm such as SSS Software. Grant and Ramos have an insider's understanding of SSS Software's strategic and technical limitations. It will be interesting to see if they can exploit this knowledge to the advantage of Universal Business Solutions Inc."

ITEM 10 Voice Mail

> *Chris, this is Bob Miller. Just thought you'd like to know that John's joke during our planning meeting has disturbed a few of the women in my group. Frankly I think the thing's being blown out of proportion, especially since we all know this is a good place for both men and women to work. Give me a call if you want to chat about this.*

ITEM 11 Voice Mail

> *Hello. This is Lorraine Adams from Westside Hospital. I read in today's Los Angeles Times that you will be taking over from Michael Grant. We haven't met yet, but your division has recently finished two large million dollar projects for Westside. Michael Grant and I had some discussion about a small conversion of a piece of existing software to be compatible with the new systems. The original vendor had said that they would do the work, but has been stalling and I need to move quickly. Can you see if Harris Wilson, Chu Hung Woo, and Elise Soto are available to do this work as soon as possible? They were on the original project and work well with our people. You can call me at 213-555-3456.*
>
> *Um . . . (long pause) I guess I should tell you that I got a call from Michael offering to do this work. But I think I should stick with SSS Software. Give me a call.*

ITEM 12 Voice Mail

> *Hi Chris, This is Roosevelt Moore calling. I'm a member of your technical/professional staff. I used to report to Janice Ramos, but since she left the firm, I thought I'd bring my concerns directly to you. I'd like to arrange some time to talk with you about my experience since returning from six weeks of paternity leave. Some of my major responsibilities have been turned over to others. I seem to be out of the loop and wonder if my career is at risk. Also, I am afraid that I won't be supported or seriously considered for the opening created by Janice's departure. Frankly, I feel I'm being screwed for taking my leave. I'd like to talk with you this week.*

ITEM 13 E-mail

> To: Michael Grant
>
> From: Jose Martinez, Group 1 Technical Staff
>
> Date: October 12
>
> I would like to set up a meeting with you as soon as possible. I suspect that you will get a call from Jim Bishop of United Hospitals and want to be sure that you hear my side of the story first. I have been working on a customized system design for quality assurance for them using a variation of the J-3 product we developed several years ago. They had a number of special requirements and some quirks in their accounting systems, so I have had to put in especially long hours. I've worked hard to meet their demands, but they keep changing the ground rules. I keep thinking, this is just another J-3 I'm working on, but they have been interfering with an elegant design I have developed. It seems I'm not getting anywhere on this project. Then Mr. Bishop asked me if the system was running yet. I was worn out from dealing with the Controller, and I made a sarcastic comment to Mr. Bishop. He gave me a funny look and just walked out of the room.
>
> I would like to talk with you about this situation at your earliest convenience.

ITEM 14 E-mail

> TO: Chris Perillo
>
> FROM: John Small, Group 6 Manager
>
> DATE: October 15
>
> Welcome aboard, Chris. I look forward to meeting with you. I just wanted to put a bug in your ear about finding a replacement for Janice Ramos. One of my technical staff, Mala Abendano, has the ability and drive to make an excellent group manager. I have encouraged her to apply for the position. I'd be happy to talk with you further about this, at your convenience.

ITEM 15 E-mail

> TO: Chris Perillo
>
> FROM: Paula Spague, Executive Assistant to Roger Steiner
>
> DATE: October 15
>
> Roger asked me to let you know about the large contract we have gotten in Kenya. It means that a team of four managers will be making a short trip to determine current needs. They will assign their technical staff the task of developing a system and software here over the next six months, and then the managers and possibly some team members will be spending about 10 months on site in Kenya to handle the implementation. Roger would appreciate an E-mail of your thoughts about the issues to be discussed at this meeting, additional considerations about sending people to Kenya, and about how you will put together an effective team to work on this project. The October 15 memo I sent to you will provide you with some information you'll need to start making these decisions.

ITEM 16 E-mail

> TO: Chris Perillo
>
> FROM: Sharon Shapiro, V. P. of Human Resources
>
> DATE: October 15
>
> RE: Upcoming meeting
>
> I want to update you on the rippling effect of John Small's sexual joke at last week's planning meeting. Quite a few woman have been very upset and have met informally to talk about it. They have decided to call a meeting of all the people concerned about this kind of behavior throughout the firm. I plan to attend, so I'll keep you posted.

Item 17 E-mail

TO: All SSS-Software Managers
FROM: Sharon Shapiro, Vice President, Human Resources
DATE: October 14
RE: Promotions and External Hires

Year-to-date (January through September) promotions and external hires

| | | | Race | | | | Sex | | |
Level	White	Black	Asian	Hispanic	Native American	M	F	Total
Hires into Executive Level	0 (0%)	0 (0%)	0 (0%)	0 (0%)	0 (0%)	0 (0%)	0 (0%)	0
Promotions to Executive Level	0 (0%)	0 (0%)	0 (0%)	0 (0%)	0 (0%)	0 (0%)	0 (0%)	0
Hires into Management Level	2 (67%)	1 (33%)	0 (0%)	0 (0%)	0 (0%)	2 (67%)	1 (33%)	3
Promotions to Management Level	7 (88%)	0 (0%)	1 (12%)	0 (0%)	0 (0%)	7 (88%)	1 (12%)	8
Hires into Technical/ Professional Level	10 (36%)	6 (21%)	10 (36%)	2 (7%)	0 (0%)	14 (50%)	14 (50%)	28
Promotions to Technical/ Professional Level	0 (0%)	0 (0%)	0 (0%)	0 (0%)	0 (0%)	0 (0%)	0 (0%)	0
Hires into Non-Management Level	4 (20%)	10 (50%)	2 (10%)	4 (20%)	0 (0%)	6 (30%)	14 (70%)	20
Promotions to Non-Management Level	NA	NA	NA	NA	NA	NA	NA	NA

SSS Software employee (EEO) classification report as of June 30

| | | | Race | | | | Sex | | |
Level	White	Black	Asian	Hispanic	Native American	M	F	Total
Executive Level	11 (92%)	0 (0%)	1 (8%)	0 (0%)	0 (0%)	11 (92%)	1 (8%)	12
Management Level	43 (90%)	2 (4%)	2 (4%)	1 (2%)	0 (0%)	38 (79%)	10 (21%)	48
Technical/ Professional Level	58 (45%)	20 (15%)	37 (28%)	14 (11%)	1 (1%)	80 (62%)	50 (38%)	130
Non-Management Level	29 (48%)	22 (37%)	4 (7%)	4 (7%)	1 (2%)	12 (20%)	48 (80%)	60
Total	141 (56%)	44 (18%)	44 (18%)	19 (8%)	2 (1%)	141 (56%)	109 (44%)	250

Critical Incidents

Employee raiding

Litson Cotton Yarn Manufacturing Company, located in Murray, New Jersey, decided as a result of increasing labor costs to relocate its plant in Fairlee, a southern community of 4,200. Plant construction was started, and a human resources office was opened in the state employment office, located in Fairlee.

Because of ineffective HR practices in the other three textile mills located within a 50-mile radius of Fairlee, Litson was receiving applications from some of the most highly skilled and trained textile operators in the state. After receiving applications from approximately 500 people, employment was offered to 260 male and female applicants. These employees would be placed immediately on the payroll with instructions to await final installation of machinery, which was expected within the following six weeks.

The managers of the three other textile companies, faced with resignations from their most efficient and best-trained employees, approached the Litson managers with the complaint that their labor force was being "raided." They registered a strong protest to cease such practices and demanded an immediate cancellation of the employment of the 260 people hired by Litson.

Litson managers discussed the ethical and moral considerations involved in offering employment to the 260 people. Litson clearly faced a tight labor market in Fairlee, and management thought that if the 260 employees were discharged, the company would face cancellation of its plans and large construction losses. Litson management also felt obligated to the 260 employees who had resigned from their previous employment in favor of Litson.

The dilemma was compounded when the manager of one community plant reminded Litson that his plant was part of a nationwide chain supplied with cotton yarn from Litson. He implied that Litson's attempts to continue operations in Fairlee could result in cancellation of orders and the possible loss of approximately 18 percent market share. It was also suggested to Litson managers that actions taken by the nationwide textile chain could result in cancellation of orders from other textile companies. Litson's president held an urgent meeting of his top subordinates to (1) decide what to do about the situation in Fairlee, (2) formulate a written policy statement indicating Litson's position regarding employee raiding, and (3) develop a plan for implementing the policy.

Source: J. Champion and J. James, *Critical Incidents in Management: Decision and Policy Issues,* 6th ed. (Burr Ridge, IL: Richard D. Irwin, 1989).

Effective management

Dr. Sam Perkins, a graduate of the Harvard University College of Medicine, had a private practice in internal medicine for 12 years. Fourteen months ago, he was persuaded by the Massachusetts governor to give up private practice to be director of the State Division of Human Services.

After one year as director, Perkins recognized he had made little progress in reducing the considerable inefficiency in the division. Employee morale and effectiveness seemed even lower than when he had assumed the position. He realized his past training and experiences were of a clinical nature with little exposure to effective management techniques. Perkins decided to research literature on the subject of management available to him at a local university.

Perkins soon realized that management scholars are divided on the question of what constitutes effective management. Some believe people are born with certain identifiable personality traits that make them effective managers. Others believe a manager can learn to be effective by treating subordinates with a personal and considerate approach and by giving particular attention to their need for favorable working conditions. Still others emphasize the importance of developing a management style characterized by either authoritarian, democratic, or laissez-faire approaches. Perkins was further confused when he learned that a growing number of scholars advocate that effective management is contingent on the situation.

Since a state university was located nearby, Perkins contacted the dean of its college of business administration. The dean referred him to the director of the college's management center, Professor Joel McCann. Discussions between Perkins and McCann resulted in a tentative agreement that the management center would organize a series of management training sessions for the State Division of Human Services. Before agreeing on the price tag for the management conference, Perkins asked McCann to prepare a proposal reflecting his thoughts on the following questions:

1. How will the question of what constitutes effective management be answered during the conference?
2. What will be the specific subject content of the conference?
3. Who will the instructors be?
4. What will be conference's duration?
5. How can the conference's effectiveness be evaluated?
6. What policies should the State Division of Human Services adopt regarding who the conference participants should be and how they should be selected? How can these policies be best implemented?

Source: J. Champion and J. James, *Critical Incidents in Management: Decision and Policy Issues*, 6th ed. (Burr Ridge, IL: Richard D. Irwin, 1989). ●

Part Two

Planning and Strategy

Foundations of Management

Managing
The External Environment
Managerial Decision Making

**Planning:
Delivering Strategic Value**

Planning and Strategic Management
Ethics and Corporate Responsibility
International Management
New Ventures

Strategy Implementation

**Organizing: Building
a Dynamic Organization**

Organization Structure
The Responsive Organization
Human Resources Management
Managing the Diverse Workforce

**Leading:
Mobilizing People**

Leadership
Motivating for Performance
Managing Teams
Communicating

**Controlling:
Learning and Changing**

Managerial Control
Managing Technology and Innovation
Creating and Managing Change

Part II introduces key concepts of planning and strategy. The topics emphasize the decisions made by top managers and their implications for the entire organization. Chapter 4 presents a summary of the planning process and an overview of how senior executives manage strategically. The next three chapters treat subjects that have recently emerged as vital considerations for modern managers. Chapter 5 examines the impact of ethical concerns and social and political factors on major decisions. Chapter 6 addresses the pressing reality of managing in a global competitive environment. Finally, Chapter 7 describes entrepreneurs and the new ventures they create. These chapters will provide you with a clear understanding of the strategic directions that effective organizations pursue.

Chapter Four

Planning and Strategic Management

Manage your destiny, or someone else will.

—Jack Welch, CEO, General Electric

Chapter Outline

Learning Objectives

After studying Chapter 4, you will know:

1. How to proceed through the basic steps in any planning process.

2. How strategic planning differs from tactical and operational planning.

3. Why it is important to analyze both the external environment and internal resources of the firm before formulating a strategy.

4. The choices available for corporate strategy.

5. How companies can achieve competitive advantage through business strategy.

6. How core competencies provide the foundation for business strategy.

7. The keys to effective strategy implementation.

Setting the Stage

A New Groove at Hard Rock Café

Hard Rock Café unplugged? Not anymore. To pump up the volume, the Orlando-based company—which oversees 105 locations in 38 countries—has developed a "three-part, music-centric strategy to reinvent the 30-year-old brand" for its rock-and-roll-themed restaurants, hotels, and casinos. The bill for all of these changes is nearly $50 million.

In addition to redesigning its restaurants, Hard Rock's plans include more late-night live musical acts, which it intends to stream into its other venues via the Web. Will it work? Maybe. Hard Rock still has some hurdles to clear. But for the first time since launching its Website at the end of 1998, the company has a definitive Net strategy. "We'll use the Web to create a forum for up-and-coming artists and to bring national bands that play our large concert venues into the smaller location," says Scott Little, chief financial officer and head of strategic planning for Hard Rock. The company has been working with Microsoft to build a state-of-the-art network to handle e-commerce and the digital streaming of live events in real time. Hard Rock is also in talks with all five major record labels and expects to ink a revenue-sharing deal with a leading online CD distributor. The Website's traffic of 100,000 unique monthly visitors before the redesign has already climbed to 500,000, and it's expected to draw 1 million within a year.

Meanwhile, Hard Rock recently announced a partnership with the online auctioneer eBay to create its own branded section within the site. The section will feature Hard Rock Café commemorative items and collectibles once displayed in various Hard Rock locations, as well as some 2,500 to 5,000 listings posted by independent traders. Hard Rock has also partnered with Music Choice, a digital-music programmer

To get its groove back, Hard Rock is focusing more on today's music rather than only nostalgia.
[John Warden/Stone]

that reaches 28 million cable households, to jointly produce and distribute concerts from the Hard Rock Orlando and Chicago locations for the Internet and television.

These moves come after nearly a decade of waning growth and revenues in an industry that has suffered from too-rapid expansion. When former Hard Rock President Robert Earl left the company in 1990 to launch Planet Hollywood, he opened 50 locations—twice the number of Hard Rock Cafés—in four years. A slew of other theme competitors soon followed: Rainforest Café, Fashion Café, and Harley-Davidson Café. But by 1999, the overcrowded industry was stagnant, and sales plummeted. In November of 2000, Planet Hollywood buckled and filed for bankruptcy.

To get its groove back in the niche it invented, Hard Rock is focusing more on today's music rather than only nostalgia. In addition, the company is diversifying a bit and partnering a lot. The risk the company takes with its new strategy is losing its focus on food and the restaurant business. James Scurlock, publisher of *Restaurant Investor,* questions Hard Rock's growing emphasis on entertainment. "Hard Rock has built an extraordinary brand, but I'm not sure how well they will do as music entrepreneurs. One is a business of selling food and T-shirts, and the other is one of entertaining people with hip content."

Source: Stefani Eads, "Hard Rock Café Lays Down a New Groove," Business Week, September 20, 2000.

Trying to sort out the plans of a company such as Hard Rock Café can be mind-boggling. Yet there are a few key ideas that are fundamental to the planning process that most companies—including Hard Rock—use to figure out how to succeed. In this chapter, we examine the most important concepts and processes involved in planning and strategic management. By learning these concepts, and reviewing the steps outlined, you will be on your way to understanding the current approaches to the strategic management of today's organizations.

An overview of planning fundamentals

Planning is the conscious, systematic process of making decisions about goals and activities that an individual, group, work unit, or organization will pursue in the future. Planning is not an informal or haphazard response to a crisis; it is a purposeful effort, directed and controlled by managers, often drawing on the knowledge and experience of employees throughout the organization. Planning provides individuals and work units with a clear map to follow in their future activities; at the same time this map may allow for individual circumstances and changing conditions.

The importance of formal planning in organizations has grown dramatically. During the first half of this century, most planning was unstructured and fragmented, and formal planning was restricted to a few large corporations. Although management pioneers such as Alfred Sloan of General Motors instituted formal planning processes, planning became a widespread management function only during the last 30 years. While larger organizations adopted formal planning initially, even small firms operated by aggressive, opportunistic entrepreneurs now engage in formal planning.[1]

The basic planning process

Because planning is a decision process, the important steps followed during formal planning are similar to the basic decision-making steps discussed in Chapter 4. Figure 4.1 shows these formal planning steps and their decision process counterparts.

Step one: situational analysis
As the contingency approach advocates, planning begins with a **situational analysis.** Within their time and resource constraints, planners should gather, interpret, and summarize all information relevant to the planning issue in question. A thorough situational analysis studies past events, examines current conditions, and attempts to forecast future trends. It focuses on the internal forces at work in the organization or work unit and, consistent with the open-systems approach, examines influences from the external environment. The outcome of this step is the identification and diagnosis of planning assumptions, issues, and problems.

A recent situational analysis conducted by a major medical center gathered extensive information from external groups such as consumers, physicians, government and

situational analysis A process planners use, within time and resource constraints, to gather, interpret, and summarize all information relevant to the planning issue under consideration.

figure 4.1
Decision-making stages
(Chapter 3) and formal
planning steps
(Chapter 4)

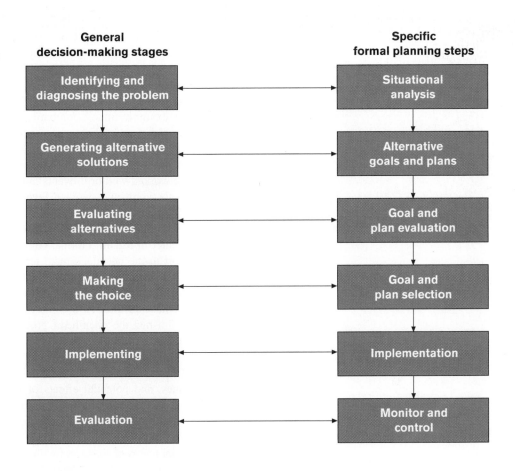

figure 4.1
Decision-making stages (Chapter 3) and formal planning steps (Chapter 4)

regulatory agencies, insurance companies, and other hospitals. The analysis included information from all departments in these organizations. Historical trends in financial data and the use of various hospital services were examined, and projections were developed based on assumptions about the future. The situational analysis took 10 months, and the information was summarized in a 250-page planning document. To give you an idea of the importance of this step to the planning process, the remaining steps took only three months, and the final set of goals and plans was only 50 pages long!

Step two: alternative goals and plans
Based on the situational analysis, the planning process should generate alternative goals that may be pursued in the future and the alternative plans that may be used to achieve those goals. This step in the process should stress creativity and encourage managers and employees to assume a broad perspective about their jobs. Evaluation of the merits of these alternative goals and plans should be delayed until a range of alternatives has been developed.

goal A target or end that management desires to reach.

Goals are the targets or ends the manager wants to reach. Goals should be specific, challenging, and realistic. Jack Welch's goal of making General Electric first or at least second in all its markets is specific and challenging. When appropriate, goals should also be quantified and linked to a time frame. They should be acceptable to the managers and employees charged with achieving them, and they should be consistent both within and among work units.

plans The actions or means that managers intend to use to achieve organizational goals.

Plans are the actions or means the manager intends to use to achieve goals. At a minimum, this step should outline alternative actions that may lead to the attainment of each goal, the resources required to reach the goal through those means, and the obstacles that may develop. Aramark's plan to become the premier provider of corporate services outlines the company's activities designed to expand business in catering, food services, and uniform services, as well as health and education. This plan is focused on the company's goals of 10 percent annual growth in sales and profitability.[2]

In this chapter we will talk about various types of plans. Some plans, called *single-use plans,* are designed to achieve a set of goals that are not likely to be repeated in the future. For example, city planners might prepare for an upcoming sesquicentennial celebration by putting in place a plan for parades, festivities, speeches, and the like. Other plans, called *standing plans,* focus on ongoing activities designed to achieve an enduring set of goals. For example, many companies have standing plans for their efforts to recruit minorities and women. Frequently, standing plans become more permanent policies and rules for running the organization. Finally, *contingency plans* might be referred to as "what if" plans. They include sets of actions to be taken when a company's initial plans have not worked well or if events in the external environment require a sudden change. For example, companies worked feverishly at the end of 1999 to prevent Y2K problems. At the same time, they also made preparations—contingency plans—for how they would continue if the systems failed. This planning paid off at the Veterans Affairs Medical Center in Miami, Florida. On the night of November 23, 1999, a power surge caused a short in the hospital's main electrical panel. Power was lost to all passenger elevators in the main building and the lights were out in most places. Meanwhile, doctors were in the midst of an open-heart surgery procedure. Luckily, an emergency plan had been rehearsed through months of preparation for potential Y2K-related disasters. Surgeons finished the open-heart procedure using flashlights (and the patient's prognosis was bright).[3]

Step three: goal and plan evaluation

Next, decision makers must evaluate the advantages, disadvantages, and potential effects of each alternative goal and plan. Decision makers must prioritize those goals or even eliminate some from further consideration. At the same time, the manager needs to consider the implications of alternative plans designed to meet high-priority goals.

In some companies, special teams of managers with diverse backgrounds conduct this evaluation. During major planning efforts at Atlantic Richfield Company (ARCO), senior executives meet with planning groups from strategic planning, public and government affairs, operations, marketing, and other areas. Often the different perspectives and ideas such groups generate lead to a more balanced and comprehensive review of company goals and plans. This approach often identifies new alternatives or refines existing ones.

Step four: goal and plan selection

The planner is now in a position to select the most appropriate and feasible goals and plans. The evaluation process should identify the priorities and trade-offs among goals and plans and leave the final choice to the decision maker. Experienced judgment always plays an important role. However, as you will discover later in the chapter, relying on judgment alone may not be the best way to proceed.

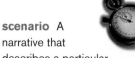

scenario A narrative that describes a particular set of future conditions.

Typically, a formal planning process leads to a written set of goals and plans that are appropriate and feasible within a predicted set of circumstances. In some organizations, the alternative generation, evaluation, and selection steps generate planning **scenarios,** as discussed in Chapter 2. A different contingency plan is attached to each scenario. The manager pursues the goals and implements the plans associated with the most likely scenario. However, the work unit is prepared to switch to another set of plans if the situational contingencies change and another scenario becomes relevant. This approach helps avoid crises and allows greater flexibility and responsiveness.

Step five: implementation

Once managers have selected the goals and plans, they must implement the plans designed to achieve the goals. The best plans are useless unless they are implemented properly. Managers and employees must understand the plan, have the resources necessary to implement it, and be motivated to do so. If both managers and employees have participated in the previous steps of the planning process, the implementation phase probably will be more effective and efficient. Employees usually are better informed, more committed, and more highly motivated when a goal or plan is one that they helped develop.

Finally, successful implementation requires that the plan be linked to other systems in the organization, particularly the budget and reward systems. If the budget does not provide the manager with sufficient financial resources to execute the plan, the plan is probably doomed. Similarly, goal achievement must be linked to the organization's reward system. Many organizations use incentive programs to encourage employees to achieve goals and to implement plans properly. Commissions, salaries, promotions, bonuses, and other rewards are based on successful performance.

Step six: monitor and control   Although it is sometimes ignored, the final step in the formal planning process—monitor and control—is essential. Because planning is an ongoing, repetitive process, managers must continually monitor the actual performance of their work units according to the unit's goals and plans. Also, they must develop control systems that allow the organization to take corrective action when the plans are implemented improperly or when the situation changes. You will study control systems in greater detail later in this chapter and in Chapter 16.

Levels of planning

In Chapter 1, you learned about the three major types of managers: top-level (*strategic* managers), middle-level (*tactical* managers), and frontline (*operational* managers). Because planning is an important management function, managers at all three levels use it. However, the scope and activities of the planning process at each level of the organization often differ.

Strategic planning

Strategic planning involves making decisions about the organization's long-term goals and strategies. Strategic plans have a strong external orientation and cover major portions of the organization. Senior executives are responsible for the development and execution of the strategic plan, although they usually do not personally formulate or implement the entire plan.

Strategic goals are major targets or end results that relate to the long-term survival, value, and growth of the organization. Strategic managers—top-level managers—usually establish goals that reflect both effectiveness (providing appropriate outputs) and efficiency (a high ratio of outputs to inputs). Typical strategic goals include various measures of return to shareholders, profitability, quantity and quality of outputs, market share, productivity, and contribution to society.

A **strategy** is a pattern of actions and resource allocations designed to achieve the goals of the organization. The strategy an organization implements is an attempt to match the skills and resources of the organization to the opportunities found in the external environment; that is, every organization has certain strengths and weaknesses. The actions, or strategies, the organization implements should be directed toward building strengths in areas that satisfy the wants and needs of consumers and other key factors in the organization's external environment. Also, some organizations may implement strategies that change or influence the external environment, as discussed in Chapter 2.

Tactical and operational planning

Once the organization's strategic goals and plans are identified, they become the basis of planning done by middle-level and frontline managers. Goals and plans become more specific and involve shorter periods of time as planning moves from the strategic level to the operational level. **Tactical planning** translates broad strategic goals and plans into specific goals and plans that are relevant to a definite portion of the organization, often a functional area like marketing or human resources. Tactical plans focus on the major actions that a unit must take to fulfill its part of the strategic plan. **Operational planning** identifies the specific procedures and processes required at lower levels of the organization. Frontline managers usually develop plans for very short periods of time

strategic planning A set of procedures for making decisions about the organization's long-term goals and strategies.

strategic goals Major targets or end results relating to the organization's long-term survival, value, and growth.

strategy A pattern of actions and resource allocations designed to achieve the organization's goals.

tactical planning A set of procedures for translating broad strategic goals and plans into specific goals and plans that are relevant to a distinct portion of the organization, such as a functional area like marketing.

operational planning The process of identifying the specific procedures and processes required at lower levels of the organization.

Starbucks investment in extensive employee training and programs results in good service and a healthy bottom line.
[AP Photo/Don Ryan/Wide World Photos]

and focus on routine tasks such as production runs, delivery schedules, and human resources requirements.

The organization's strategic, tactical, and operational goals and plans must be consistent and mutually supportive. Starbucks, for example, has built its strategy of growth and profitability around the notion of excellent service and ambience. No longer is coffee just a morning ritual; it has evolved into something with a far more existential quality. "We are trying to create a *'third place'* for our customers," says CEO Howard Schultz. "A *'third place'* is a place between home and work where people can come to get their own personal time out, their respite, meet with friends, have a sense of gathering."

A key tactical planning issue for Starbucks is linking its obsession with service and quality to a healthy bottom line. Excellent service attracts new customers and keeps loyal customers coming back. Excellent service and quality depend upon highly efficient processes for brewing coffee and terrific customer relations. These processes in turn are carried out by a dedicated and well-trained workforce. According to Schultz, "We've never viewed coffee as a commodity. And we've never viewed our people as commodities. I think the foundation of our success is the passionate commitment we have to the quality of coffee that we buy and roast, and making sure that the people in our company are not simply a line item. We view our people as business partners. The company's "Bean Stock" program gives all employees the opportunity to own stock in the company, and the company's commitment to training and benefits has established Starbucks as the employer of choice in the industry (its turnover rate is one-fifth that of others in the industry).

One method for linking strategic and operational planning at Starbucks is the balanced scorecard. Figure 4.2 shows how the balanced scorecard works. There are four primary cells: financial, customer, process, and people/learning. In each cell, Starbucks would identify the key drivers that help translate strategic goals to operational issues. Each of those goals would also have a set of metrics. For example, under customer metrics, Starbucks might look at percentage of repeat customers, number of new customers, growth rate, and the like. Under people/learning, managers might measure the number of suggestions provided by employees, participation in the Bean Stock program, employee turnover, training hours spent, and the like.

figure 4.2
Applying the balanced scorecard for Starbucks

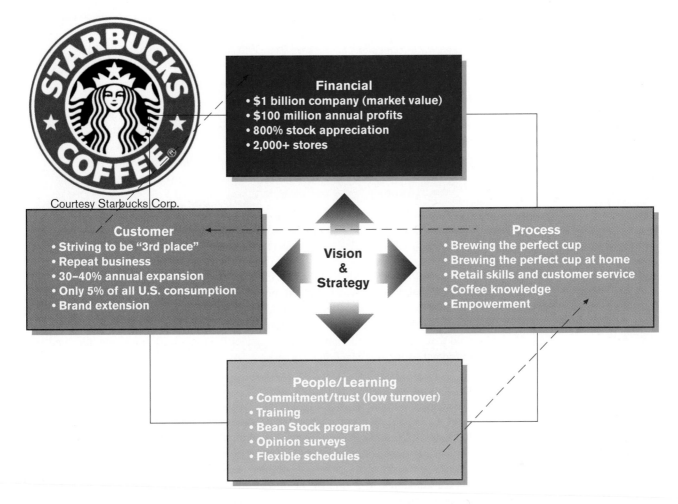

Courtesy Starbucks Corp.

Each of these cells links vertically. People management issues such as rewards, training, suggestions, and the like can be linked to efficient processes (brewing the perfect cup, customer service, etc.). These processes then lead to better customer loyalty and growth. Growth and customer loyalty in turn lead to higher profitability and market value. As shown in Table 4.1, the balanced scorecard can be used to develop measures and standards for each of these operational areas. And when implemented in this way, it helps translate strategic and tactical issues into operational criteria.[4]

Using this overview of planning as background, we will devote the remainder of this chapter to strategic issues, concepts, and processes. Strategic decision making is one of the most exciting and controversial topics in management today. In fact, many organizations currently are changing the ways they develop and execute their strategic plans.

Strategic planning: yesterday and today

Traditionally, strategic planning has emphasized a top-down approach. That is, senior executives and specialized planning units were given the responsibility of developing goals and plans for the entire organization. Tactical and operational managers often received goals and plans from staff members, and their own planning activities were limited to specific procedures and budgets for the units.

Over the years, managers and consulting firms innovated a variety of analytical techniques and planning approaches, many of which have been critical for analyzing complex business situations and competitive issues. However, it is fair to state that—in many

table 4.1

Using the balanced scorecard for planning

1. *Clarify the vision:* Executive team and middle managers use the balanced scorecard to translate a generic vision into a strategy that is understood and communicated.

2. *Develop business unit scorecards:* Each business unit develops its own scorecard that translates strategic goals into tactical and operational goals.

3. *Review business unit scorecards:* The CEO and executive team review the business unit scorecards. This review identifies cross-business issues that are used to revise the strategic plan.

4. *Communicate the scorecard to the entire company:* Managers and employees develop individual scorecards that link strategic and tactical plans to operational issues relevant to them. Individual objectives and rewards are linked to these scorecards.

5. *Conduct annual strategy reviews:* Previous year's performance is reviewed and strategies are updated. Each business unit is asked to develop a position on each issue as a prelude to strategic planning.

Source: Adapted from R. S. Kaplan and D. Norton, "Using the Balanced Scorecard as a Strategic Management System," *Harvard Business Review,* January-February 1996, pp. 75–85.

strategic management A process that involves managers from all parts of the organization in the formulation and implementation of strategic goals and strategies.

instances—senior executives spent too much time with their planning specialists to the exclusion of line managers in the rest of the organization. A gap often developed between strategic managers and tactical and operational managers. Unfortunately, executives discovered that managers and employees throughout the organization became alienated and uncommitted to the organization's success.[5]

Today, however, senior executives increasingly are involving managers throughout the organization in the strategy formation process.[6] The problems just described and the rapidly changing environment of the 1980s and 1990s have forced executives to look to all levels of the organization for ideas and innovations to make their firms more competitive. Although the CEO and other top managers continue to furnish the strategic direction, or "vision" of the organization, tactical and even operational managers often provide valuable inputs to the organization's strategic plan. In some cases, these managers also have substantial autonomy to formulate or change their own plans. This increases flexibility and responsiveness, critical requirements of success in the modern organization.

Because of this trend, a new term for the strategic planning process has emerged: *strategic management.* **Strategic management** involves managers from all parts of the organization in the formulation and implementation of strategic goals and strategies. It integrates strategic planning and management into a single process. Strategic planning becomes an ongoing activity in which all managers are encouraged to think strategically

McDonald's tactical planning efforts have resulted in a menu that now includes everything from the renowned Big Mac to pizza, tacos, and egg rolls.
[Michael Abramson]

figure 4.3
The strategic management process

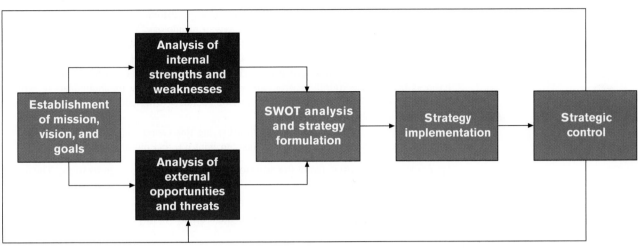

and to focus on long-term, externally oriented issues as well as short-term tactical and operational issues.

Figure 4.3 shows the six major components of the strategic management process: (1) establishment of mission, vision, and goals; (2) analysis of external opportunities and threats; (3) analysis of internal strengths and weaknesses; (4) SWOT (strengths, weaknesses, opportunities and threats) analysis and strategy formulations; (5) strategy implementation; and (6) strategic control. Because this process is a planning and decision process, it is similar to the planning framework discussed earlier. Although organizations may use different terms or emphasize different parts of the process, the components and concepts described in this section are found either explicitly or implicitly in every organization.

Step 1: Establishment of mission, vision, and goals

mission An organization's basic purpose and scope of operations.

The first step in strategic planning is establishing a mission, vision, and goals for the organization. The **mission** is the basic purpose and values of the organization, as well as its scope of operations. It is a statement of the organization's reason to exist. The mission often is written in terms of the general clients it serves. Depending on the scope of the organization, the mission may be broad or narrow. For example, the mission of Kellogg Company is to be the world's leading producer of ready-to-eat cereal products and to manufacture frozen pies and waffles, toaster pastries, soups, and other convenience foods. On the other hand, the local bar found next to most campuses has the implicit mission of selling large quantities of inexpensive beer to college students.

strategic vision The long-term direction and strategic intent of a company.

The **strategic vision** moves beyond the mission statement to provide a perspective on where the company is headed and what the organization can become. Although the terms *mission* and *vision* often are used interchangeably, the vision statement ideally clarifies the long-term direction of the company and its *strategic intent*. Shell Oil, for example, has a stated vision of becoming the "premier U.S. company." As described below, this vision conveys Shell's dedication to technology development, customer service, employee development, and community involvement.[7]

Shell Oil Company's Mission and Vision

Mission:
Shell Oil Company is in business to excel in the oil, gas, petrochemical, and related businesses in the United States and where we add value internationally. In doing so, our mission is to maximize long-term shareholder value by being the best at meeting the expectations of customers, employees, suppliers, and the public.

We are an independently managed company within the Royal Dutch/Shell Group that benefits from and contributes to the Group's worldwide knowledge and technology base.

Vision:

Our vision is to the premier U.S. company with sustained world-class performance in all aspects of our business.

We will be a dynamic characterized by our integrity, customer focus, profitable growth, the value placed on people, and superior applications of technology. We will be the best at generating and applying new ideas and learning faster than other organizations.

Customers will prefer us because of our unsurpassed responsiveness and our ability to provide value. People will be proud to work for shell because we consistently attain superior business results, offer fulfilling work, and provide the opportunity for individuals to achieve their full potential. The communities in which we operate will welcome us because of our sensitivity and involvement.

We, the people of Shell, are the key to achieving this vision and will be distinguished by our professionalism, energy, sense of urgency to improve, and our shared core values.

Strategic goals evolve from the mission and vision of the organization. The chief executive officer of the organization, with the input and approval of the board of directors, establishes the mission, vision, and major strategic goals. These three statements need to be communicated to everyone who has contact with the organization.

table 4.2
Environmental analysis

Industry and market analysis

- *Industry profile:* major product lines and significant market segments in the industry.
- *Industry growth:* growth rates for the entire industry, growth rates for key market segments, projected changes in patterns of growth, and the determinants of growth.
- *Industry forces:* threat of new industry entrants, threat of substitutes, economic power of buyers, economic power of suppliers, and internal industry rivalry (recall Chapter 2).

Competitor analysis

- *Competitor profile:* major competitors and their market shares.
- *Competitor analysis:* goals, strategies, strengths, and weaknesses of each major competitor.
- *Competitor advantages:* the degree to which industry competitors have differentiated their products or services or achieved cost leadership.

Political and regulatory analysis

- *Legislation and regulatory activities* and their effects on the industry.
- *Political activity:* the level of political activity that organizations and associations within the industry undertake (see Chapter 5).

Social analysis

- *Social issues:* current and potential social issues and their effects on the industry.
- *Social interest groups:* consumer, environmental, and similar activist groups that attempt to influence the industry (see Chapters 5 and 6).

Human resources analysis

- *Labor issues:* key labor needs, shortages, opportunities, and problems confronting the industry (see Chapters 10 and 11).

Macroeconomic analysis

- *Macroeconomic conditions:* economic factors that affect supply, demand, growth, competition, and profitability within the industry.

Technological analysis

- *Technological factors:* scientific or technical methods that affect the industry, particularly recent and potential innovations (see Chapter 17).

Step 2: Analysis of external opportunities and threats

The mission and vision drive the second component of the strategic management process: analysis of the external environment. Successful strategic management depends on an accurate and thorough evaluation of the environment. The various components of the environment were introduced in Chapter 2.

Table 4.2 lists some of the important activities in an environmental analysis. The analysis begins with an examination of the industry. Next, organizational stakeholders are examined. **Stakeholders** are groups and individuals who affect and are affected by the achievement of the organization's mission, goals, and strategies. They include buyers, suppliers, competitors, government and regulatory agencies, unions and employee groups, the financial community, owners and shareholders, and trade associations. The environmental analysis provides a map of these stakeholders and the ways they influence the organization.[8]

The environmental analysis should also examine other forces in the environment, such as macroeconomic conditions and technological factors. One critical task in environments analysis is forecasting future trends. As noted in Chapter 2, forecasting techniques range from simple judgment to complex mathematical models that examine systematic relationships among many variables. Even simple quantitative techniques outperform the intuitive assessments of experts. Judgment is susceptible to bias, and managers have a limited ability to process information. Managers should use subjective judgments as inputs to quantitative models or when they confront new situations.

The following example of Toys 'R' Us shows the power of understanding the external environment, and correctly forecasting future trends in the industry.

stakeholders Groups and individuals who affect and are affected by the achievement of the organization's mission, goals, and strategies.

From the Pages of BusinessWeek

Planning at Toys 'R' Us is not child's play

John H. Eyler, Jr. is the latest chief executive of long-troubled Toys 'R' Us, Inc. He's making a lot of changes in order to bring a bit of the magic back to the company. The hope is that by showing shoppers a friendlier, more helpful face and lining shelves with great toys not available elsewhere, Toys 'R' Us can break out of the low-price supermarket approach that hyperefficient Wal-Mart does much better. Two years ago, Wal-Mart overtook toys 'R' Us as the no. 1 U.S. toy seller.

Eyler is the third Toys 'R' Us CEO to try to stop the onslaught of the discounters since founder Charles Lazarus retired in 1994. And his store overhaul is the company's third since 1996. Toys 'R' Us has found that offering the widest selection 12 months a year just isn't enough to keep customers happy. "When I started, if you had good selection and good prices, that was the key," says Lazarus, now 77 and still a member of the board of directors. "Today, our competition is very good, and we have to be better." Although Toys 'R' Us had a 6 percent increase in sales in 2000, it trailed the 10 percent increase for the toy industry.

The chain has struggled so hard trying to figure out how to beat the latest challenge—online toy stores—that it finally joined them instead, linking up with Amazon.com to create a joint Website. The move should make the Toys 'R' Us site profitable more quickly than it would be on its own. Overall, retailers seem more sanguine about a shift to online sales, partly because online toy sales are not expected to exceed 10 percent to 15 percent of the industry total in the long term. After several sites closed down, it now seems less likely that the internet will be the threat to toy stores that it may be to music- and booksellers.

If customers respond to the changes at Toys 'R' Us, Eyler will have gone a long way toward proving that he has figured out how to make a 1980s-style, big-box retailer attractive to today's shopper. But he faces stiff headwinds. Retailers have already begun wringing their hands, worried about the gloomy shadow that a jittery stock market, higher gas prices, and a slowing economy might cast upon consumers. Normally consistent specialty merchants such as Gap, Inc. and Home Depot, Inc. have recently been performing less well.

But competitors are only part of the challenge. Eyler wants to begin mending fences with Hasbro (maker of Tonka trucks) and Mattel (home of Barbie) so that he has a steady supply of inventory when it is needed. His answer: more systematic stocking of the top 1,500 toys that make up two-thirds of the chain's sales. Toys 'R' Us, like every other retailer, knows it can't be sure it won't run out of the hot toys—the Pokemons and Tickle Me Elmos—the week before Christmas. But it can ensure that standbys such as Monopoly will be in stores 90 percent of the time. Eyler says that a one-season wonder might make $75 million in a year—sizable, but still only 1 percent of U.S. sales. "We can't make a consistently profitable business on the back of a hot toy," he insists.

But if Toys 'R' Us can reestablish relations with suppliers, it will take a lot longer to bring customers around. Their animosity goes much deeper than not finding enough of the right toys. A recent Sanford C. Bernstein study of U.S. shoppers' opinions of 15 big retailers found that Toys 'R' Us ranked near the bottom of the list on measures such as service—only Kmart, Inc. ranked lower—and value for the dollar. Overall, shoppers ranked the chain 10th out of the 15 retailers.

With stiff competition from Wal-Mart, Target Corp., and others, there's little room for mistakes. "What Toys 'R' Us has lost is their uniqueness, and that they will not be able to recapture," says retail consultant Kurt Barnard. Eyler's out to prove the naysayers wrong. But this isn't child's play.

Source: Condensed from Nanette Byrnes, "Can CEO John Eyler Fix the Chain?," *Business Week,* December 4, 2000, 3710, no. 128, online. ●

The Toys 'R' Us example illustrates how organizations must develop a clear sense of market opportunities by analyzing the external environment. In the same way, executives can identify potential threats as well.

Frequently, the difference between an opportunity and a threat depends upon how a company positions itself strategically. For example, Southwest Airline's original base of operations at Love Field (outside of Dallas, Texas) was originally seen as a problem for the company. Other major competitors were permitted to fly into the larger and state-of-the-art Dallas–Fort Worth Airport, but Southwest was not. However, given this apparent threat, Southwest built its strategy around point-to-point flights into smaller airports that catered to business travelers. Other airlines soon found that they could not compete with Southwest in its niche. So what was originally seen as a threat turned into an opportunity for Southwest.[9]

Step 3: Analysis of internal strengths and weaknesses

At the same time external analysis is conducted, the strengths and weaknesses of major functional areas within the organization are assessed. Internal analysis provides strategic decision makers with an inventory of the organization's skills and resources as well as its overall and functional performance levels. Many of your other business courses will prepare you to conduct internal analysis. Table 4.3 lists some of the major components of the internal resource analysis.

Resources and core competencies   Without question, strategic planning has been strongly influenced in recent years by a focus on internal resources. **Resources** are inputs to production (recall systems theory) that can be accumulated over time to enhance the performance of a firm. Resources can take many forms, but tend to fall into two

Resources Inputs to a system that can enhance performance.

table 4.3
Internal resource analysis

Financial analysis

Examines financial strengths and weaknesses through financial statements such as a balance sheet and an income statement and compares trends to historical and industry figures (see Chapter 18).

Human resources assessment

Examines strengths and weaknesses of all levels of management and employees and focuses on key human resources activities, including recruitment, selection, placement, training, labor (union) relationships, compensation, promotion, appraisal, quality of work life, and human resources planning (see Chapters 10 and 11).

Marketing audit

Examines strengths and weaknesses of major marketing activities and identifies markets, key market segments, and the competitive position (market share) of the organization within key markets.

Operations analysis

Examines the strengths and weaknesses of the manufacturing, production, or service delivery activities of the organization (see Chapters 9, 16, and 17).

Other internal resource analyses

Examine, as necessary and appropriate, the strengths and weaknesses of other organizational activities, such as research and development (product and process), management information systems, engineering, and purchasing.

broad categories: (1) *tangible assets* such as real estate, production facilities, raw materials, and so on, and (2) *intangible assets* such as company reputation, culture, technical knowledge, patents, as well as accumulated learning and experience. The Walt Disney Company, for example, has developed its strategic plan on combinations of tangible assets (e.g., hotels and theme parks) as well as intangible assets (brand recognition, talented craftspeople, culture focused on customer service).[10]

Effective internal analysis provides a clearer understanding of how a company can compete through its resources. Resources are a source of competitive advantage only under certain circumstances. First, if the resource is instrumental for creating customer *value*—that is, if it increases the benefits customers derive from a product or service relative to the costs they incur—then the resource can lead to a competitive advantage. For example, Wal-Mart's computerized inventory control system mentioned previously helps make certain that products are on the shelves and that inventory costs are minimized. In this case, Wal-Mart's information technology is clearly a valuable resource.

Second, resources are a source of advantage if they are *rare* and not equally available to all competitors. Even for extremely valuable resources, if all competitors have equal access, the resource cannot provide a source of competitive advantage. For example, when long-distance telephone service was deregulated, AT&T no longer had exclusive use of its telecommunications infrastructure. For companies such as Merck, DuPont, Dow Chemical, and others, patented formulas represent important resources that are both rare and valuable.

Third, if resources are *difficult to imitate,* they provide a source of competitive advantage. Xerox, for example, believed for many years that no one could duplicate its reprographic capabilities. Kodak and Canon soon proved Xerox wrong. McDonald's brand name recognition, on the other hand, has been extremely difficult for competitors such as Burger King, Wendy's, and others to duplicate.[11]

Finally, resources can enhance a firm's competitive advantage when they are well *organized.* For example, as strategies are changed and organizations are restructured, many companies lay off long-time employees and lose as well their potentially valuable skills. To avoid this problem and maintain its flexibility, AT&T has developed its own internal employment agency—called Resource Link—to reassign "at-risk" employees to other jobs within the company rather than laying them off. Resource Link employs AT&T

figure 4.4
Resources and core
competence

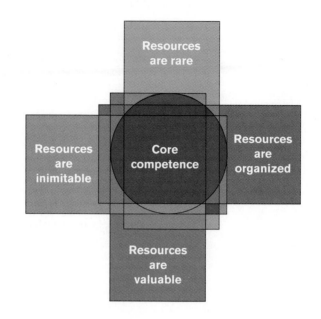

figure 4.4
Resources and core
competence

people full-time and contracts them out to various AT&T businesses on a part-time basis. Resource Link provides AT&T a great deal of flexibility, helps manage the flow of people throughout the organization, and ensures that the company makes the most of its valuable human resources.[12]

As shown in Figure 4.4, when resources are valuable, rare, inimitable, and organized, they can be viewed as a company's core competencies. Simply stated, a **core competence** is something a company does especially well relative to its competitors. Honda, for example, has a core competence in small engine design and manufacturing; Sony has a core competence in miniaturization; Federal Express has a core competence in logistics and customer service. Typically, a core competence refers to a set of skills or expertise in some activity, rather than physical or financial assets. For example, among U.S. automobile manufacturers, General Motors has traditionally been viewed as having a core competence in marketing, while Ford has established quality as its number one strength. Recently Chrysler redefined its core competence around design and engineering.

core competencies The unique skills or knowledge an organization possesses that give it an edge over competitors.

Benchmarking
Benchmarking is the process of assessing how well one company's basic functions and skills compare to those of some other company or set of companies. The goal of benchmarking is to thoroughly understand the "best practices" of other firms, and to undertake actions to achieve both better performance and lower costs. For example, Xerox Corporation, a pioneer in benchmarking, established a program to study 67 of its key work processes against "world class" companies. Many of these companies were not in the copier business. For example, in an effort to improve its order fulfillment process, Xerox studied L. L. Bean, the clothing mail-order company. Benchmarking programs have helped Xerox and a myriad of other companies such as Ford, Corning, Hewlett-Packard, and Anheuser-Busch make great strides in eliminating inefficiencies and improving competitiveness. Perhaps the only downside of benchmarking is that it only helps a company perform as well as its competitors; strategic management ultimately is about surpassing those companies.[13]

Step 4: SWOT analysis and strategy formulation

After analyzing the external environment and internal resources, strategic decision makers have the information they need to formulate corporate, business, and functional strategies of the organization. A comparison of strengths, weaknesses, opportunities, and threats is normally referred to as a **SWOT analysis.** SWOT analysis helps executives summarize the major facts and forecasts derived from the external and internal analyses. From this, executives can derive a series of statements that identify the primary and

SWOT analysis A comparison of strengths, weaknesses, opportunities, and threats that helps executives formulate strategy.

corporate strategy The set of businesses, markets, or industries in which an organization competes and the distribution of resources among those entities.

concentration A strategy employed for an organization that operates a single business and competes in a single industry.

vertical integration
The acquisition or development of new businesses that produce parts or components of the organization's product.

concentric diversification
A strategy used to add new businesses that produce related products or are involved in related markets and activities.

conglomerate diversification A strategy used to add new businesses that produce unrelated products or are involved in unrelated markets and activities.

secondary strategic issues confronting the organization. Strategy formulation builds on SWOT analysis to utilize strengths of the organization in order to capitalize on opportunities, counteract threats, and alleviate internal weaknesses. In short, strategy formulation moves from simply analysis to devising a coherent course of action.

Corporate strategy   **Corporate strategy** identifies the set of businesses, markets, or industries in which the organization competes and the distribution of resources among those businesses. Figure 4.5 shows four basic corporate strategy alternatives, ranging from very specialized to highly diverse. A **concentration** strategy focuses on a single business competing in a single industry. In the food-retailing industry, Kroger, Safeway, and A&P all pursue concentration strategies. Frequently companies pursue concentration strategies to gain entry into an industry, when industry growth is good, or when the company has a narrow range of competencies.

A **vertical integration** strategy involves expanding the domain of the organization into supply channels or to distributors. At one time, Henry Ford had fully integrated his company from the ore mines needed to make steel all the way to the showrooms where his cars were sold. Vertical integration is generally used to eliminate uncertainties and reduce costs associated with suppliers or distributors. A strategy of **concentric diversification** involves moving into new businesses that are related to the company's original core business. William Marriott expanded his original restaurant business outside Washington, D.C., by moving into airline catering, hotels, and fast food. Each of these businesses within the hospitality industry is related in terms of the services they provide, the skills necessary for success, and the customers they attract. Often companies such as Marriott pursue a strategy of concentric diversification to take advantage of their strengths in one business to gain advantage in another. Because the businesses are related, the products, markets, technologies, or capabilities used in one business can be transferred to another.

In contrast to concentric diversification, **conglomerate diversification** is a corporate strategy that involves expansion into unrelated businesses. Union Pacific Corporation has diversified from its original base in railroads to such wide-ranging industries as oil and gas exploration, mining, microwave and fiber optic systems, hazardous waste disposal, trucking, and real estate. Typically, companies pursue a conglomerate diversification strategy to minimize risks due to market fluctuations in one industry. The corporate strategy of an organization is sometimes called its business portfolio. One of the most popular techniques for analyzing and communicating corporate strategy has been the BCG matrix.

figure 4.5
Summary of corporate strategies

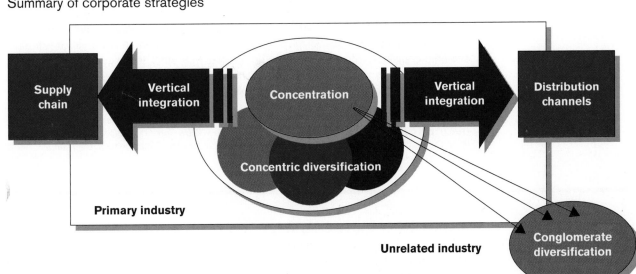

The BCG matrix

In response to senior executives' needs to understand and manage complex, modern organizations, the Boston Consulting Group (BCG) introduced the growth/share matrix. The BCG matrix is shown in Figure 4.6. Each business in the corporation is plotted on the matrix based on the growth rate of its market and the relative strength of its competitive position in that market (market share). The business is represented by a circle whose size depends on the business's contribution to corporate revenues.

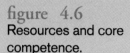

figure 4.6
Resources and core competence.

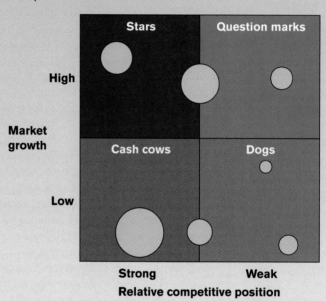

High-growth, weak-competitive-position businesses are called *question marks*. They require substantial investment to improve their position; otherwise, divestiture is recommended. High-growth, strong-competitive-position businesses are called *stars*. These businesses require heavy investment, but their strong position allows them to generate the needed revenues. Low-growth, strong-competitive-position businesses are called *cash cows*. These businesses generate revenues in excess of their investment needs and therefore fund other businesses. Finally, low-growth, weak-competitive-position businesses are called *dogs*. The remaining revenues from these businesses are realized, and then the businesses are divested.

The BCG matrix and similar tools can help both the corporation and the businesses if they are used as vehicles for discussion rather than as bases for major strategic decisions. The matrix should be applied with other techniques, and strategic managers must emphasize the development of long-term competitive advantages for all businesses. No single technique is a substitute for creativity, insight, or leadership.

Sources: P. Haspeslagh, "Portfolio Planning: Uses and Limits," *Harvard Business Review* 60, no. 1 (1982). pp. 58–67; R. Hamermesh, *Making Strategy Work* (New York: John Wiley & Sons, 1986); and R. A. Proctor. "Toward a New Model for Product Portfolio Analysis," *Management Decision* 28, no. 3 (1990), pp. 14–17. ●

Trends in corporate strategy   In recent years, corporate America has been swept by a wave of mergers and acquisitions such as Chrysler and Mercedes Benz, and Bell Atlantic and GTE (to create Verizon). Such mergers and acquisitions often influence the organization's corporate strategy, either by concentrating in one industry or by diversifying its portfolio.

The value of implementing a diversified corporate strategy depends on individual circumstances. Many critics have argued that unrelated diversification hurts a company more often than it helps it. In recent years, a number of diversified companies have sold their peripheral businesses so they could concentrate on a more focused portfolio. For example, Merck & Company sold its consumer products business to focus on the application of biotechnology in the pharmaceutical industry. Sears sold Allstate Insurance to concentrate more on the core business of retail merchandising. Kodak sold off Eastman Chemical to boost profitability and concentrate more on its imaging business.[14]

On the other hand, the diversification efforts of an organization competing in a slow-growth, mature, or threatened industry often are applauded. Many recent bank mergers, such as the creation of Citigroup from Travelers and Citicorp, were designed to yield greater efficiencies and increased market share in the banking industry.

Although the merits of diversification are an issue for continued study, most observers agree that organizations usually perform better if they implement a more concentric diversification strategy in which businesses are somehow related or similar to one another. Disney, for example, spent $19 billion to merge with ABC/Cap Cities. While the two companies are somewhat different, their businesses are complementary. Disney's success in movies and videos is matched by ABC's network TV as well as its production capabilities in Cap Cities. Though Disney has a cable channel (The Disney Channel), its ability to reach millions of viewers has been enhanced by ABC's presence in network television.[15]

Business strategy

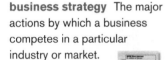

business strategy The major actions by which a business competes in a particular industry or market.

low-cost strategy A strategy an organization uses to build competitive advantage by being efficient and offering a standard, no-frills product.

differentiation strategy A strategy an organization uses to build competitive advantage by being unique in its industry or market segment along one or more dimensions.

functional strategies Strategies implemented by each functional area of the organization to support the organization's business strategy.

Business strategy   After the top management team and board make the corporate strategic decisions, executives must determine how they will compete in each business area. **Business strategy** defines the major actions by which an organization builds and strengthens its competitive position in the marketplace. A competitive advantage typically results from one of two generic business strategies introduced here and elaborated in Chapter 7.[16]

First, organizations such as Wal-Mart and Southwest Airlines (mentioned earlier) pursue competitive advantage through **low-cost strategies.** Businesses using a low-cost strategy attempt to be efficient and offer a standard, no-frills product. They often are large and try to take advantage of economies of scale in production or distribution. In many cases, the large size allows them to sell their products and services at a lower price, which leads to higher market share, volume, and, ultimately, profits. To succeed, an organization using this strategy often must be the cost leader in its industry or market segment. However, even a cost leader must offer a product that is acceptable to customers when compared to competitors' products. As Gordon Bethune, CEO of Continental Airlines, has said, "You can make a pizza so cheap that no-one will buy it." In the end, organizations need to use a cost strategy to increase value to customers, rather than take it away.[17]

Second, an organization may pursue a **differentiation strategy.** With a differentiation strategy, a company attempts to be unique in its industry or market segment along some dimensions that customers value. This unique or differentiated position within the industry often is based on high product quality, excellent marketing and distribution, or superior service. Nordstrom's commitment to quality and customer service in the retail apparel industry is an excellent example of a differentiation strategy. While perhaps not as fancy as competitors such as Saks Fifth Avenue and Neiman Marcus, Nordstrom's strategy focuses on providing a full assortment of clothing and accessories to customers and ensuring their personal attention. The company's personal shopper program has become a hit in all of the company's 84 stores. Customers can come in and enjoy a refreshing beverage in a private room while a tireless assistant brings them endless wardrobe options. Nordstrom's personal shoppers reinforce efficiency, speed, and individual service. Better still for the customer, there is absolutely no charge for the service. So in an otherwise impersonal and at times overwhelming department store, Nordstrom's differentiates itself by returning to the days when service was more genteel and individualized.[18]

Functional strategy

Functional strategy   The final step in strategy formulation is to establish the major functional strategies. **Functional strategies** are implemented by each functional area of the organization to support the business strategy. The typical functional areas include production, human resources, marketing, research and development, finance, and distribution. For example, the human resource strategy at GTE supports the firm's strategy through the creation of its own balanced scorecard.

GTE's people strategy

Garrett Walker, GTE's director of HR planning, and seven other HR specialists created the HR Balanced Scorecard.
[Cornell University Center for Advanced Human Resource Studies (CAHRS)]

Not long ago, Garrett Walker, GTE's director of HR planning, and seven other HR specialists, were given a mission: to create and implement a tool that would measure HR's contribution to the business. To do this, they had to fold HR's vision and strategy into GTE's business objectives, integrate them into all of the company's work units, and then measure their effectiveness. It wasn't going to be easy. They couldn't find an overall model that quantitatively measured the bottom-line impact of HR services, so they began to construct one of their own.

"Our senior HR leaders understood from the business strategy that we needed to deliver a lot of new skill sets to help our employees become more competitive in the current environment," said Walker. That drove HR strategies. "Once those were defined and we knew what our actions were going to be, we needed to know, quantitatively, if HR was delivering on the strategy. We needed a state-of-the-art way of measuring the effectiveness of HR." They ultimately came up with the HR Balanced Scorecard. The HR Balanced Scorecard would allow managers to react to the data, predicting problems, and focusing their energy on solutions for those problems rather than symptoms. Another benefit of this system is that it underscored the culture change within GTE, in which functions were no longer working within silos, to an environment where they were sharing information across the organization to improve productivity.

All of this was becoming increasingly important because the world in which GTE operates was changing dramatically. Since the Telecom Act, the industry had been deregulated, and there were increased pressures from investors as well as competitors. Accelerating technology had brought about vast changes in the services that telecommunications companies could offer, global expansion offered new opportunities, and customers had become very savvy, wanting more choices and expecting outstanding quality. Finally, the workforce had also changed. All of these factors created an eagerness to excel and to be able to use hard information to make sure the company was meeting its goals.

To establish an HR strategy, the planning team met with upper HR management to develop key questions that would become the framework of a measurement model. "We've taken general business strategy and translated that to HR strategy. Then we created an instrument to use hard quantitative measures to translate that into basic actionable metrics," says Walker. The team had five targets to measure:

- *Managing talent:* Grow the talent pool, invest in our people, provide growth opportunities, leverage diversity, build an environment that fosters creativity and innovation.
- *Developing world-class leadership:* Invest in leadership growth, define leadership competencies, structure rewards to foster leadership behavior.
- *Customer service and support:* Create an environment that supports employee engagement, build service capability.
- *Organizational integration:* Leverage total GTE capabilities, partner with our unions, foster business unit teaming, structure rewards to foster integration.
- *HR capability:* Invest in our own growth development, organize to deliver excellent service, enhance our technological capabilities.

Then came the process of interviewing dozens and dozens of individuals in HR to collect data. "It was a grueling process," says Walker. "Data collection is always a challenge in a company, especially one as large as GTE. But we wanted to challenge our colleagues to think through the measures that would be most valuable to them and then work backwards to see how to go about finding the information." Ultimately, the HR Balanced Scorecard team linked the measurement system to performance criteria for the broad-based incentive pay program, which was followed quickly by a phased communication to explain the process throughout the HR organization.

The results from all of this have been quite effective. Every quarter, the group publishes the results, not only to the 2,000-plus HR staff, but to GTE's business leaders as well. The results are a fundamental way to see how the company is performing against its strategic objectives.

Source: Condensed from Charlene Marmer Solomon, "Putting HR on the Score Card," *Workforce,* March 2000, 79, no. 3, pp. 94–98. ●

Functional strategies such as those described at GTE are typically put together by functional area executives with the input and approval of the executives responsible for business strategy. Senior strategic decision makers review the functional strategies to ensure that each major department is operating in a manner consistent with the business strategies of the organization.

Step 5: Strategy implementation

As with any plan, formulating the appropriate strategy is not enough. Strategic managers also must ensure that the new strategies are implemented effectively and efficiently. Recently corporations and strategy consultants have been paying more attention to implementation. They realize that clever techniques and a good plan do not guarantee success. This greater appreciation is reflected in two major trends.

First, organizations are adopting a more comprehensive view of implementation. The strategy must be supported by decisions regarding the appropriate organization structure, technology, human resources, reward systems, information systems, organization culture, and leadership style. Just as the strategy of the organization must be matched to the external environment, it also must fit the multiple factors responsible for its implementation. The remainder of this text discusses these factors and the ways they can be used to implement strategy.

Second, many organizations are extending the more participative strategic management process to implementation. Managers at all levels are involved with strategy formulation and the identification and execution of the means to implement the new strategies. Senior executives still may orchestrate the overall implementation process, but they place much greater responsibility and authority in the hands of others in the organization.

In general, strategy implementation involves four related steps:

- *Step 1: Define strategic tasks.*   Articulate in simple language what must be done in a particular business to create or sustain a competitive advantage. Define strategic tasks in order to help employees understand how they contribute to the organization. This can also redefine relationships among the parts of the organization.
- *Step 2: Assess organization capabilities.*   Evaluate the organization's ability to implement the strategic tasks. A task force (typically) interviews employees and managers to identify specific issues that help or hinder effective implementation. Results are summarized for top management.
- *Step 3: Develop implementation agenda:*   Management decides how it will change its management pattern, how critical interdependencies will be managed, what skills and individuals are needed in key roles, and what structures, measures, information, and rewards might ultimately support specified behavior. A philosophy statement, communicated in value terms, is the natural outcome of this process.

figure 4.7

Attacking the six barriers to strategy implementation

Change starts with the leader

The Silent Killers	Principles for Engaging and Changing the Silent Killers
Top-down or laissez-faire senior management style	With the top team and lower levels, the CEO/general manager creates a partnership built around the development of a compelling business direction, the creation of an enabling organizational context, and the delegation of authority to clearly accountable individuals and teams.
Unclear strategy and conflicting priorites	The top team, as a group, develops a statement of strategy, and priorities that members are willing to stand behind are developed.
An ineffective senior management team	The top team, as a group, is involved in all steps in the change process so that its effectiveness is tested and developed.
Poor vertical communication	An honest, fact-based dialogue is established with lower levels about the new strategy and the barriers to implementing it.
Poor coordination across functions, businesses, or borders	A set of business-wide initiatives and new organizational roles and responsibilities are defined that require "the right people to work together on the right things in the right way" to implement the strategy.
Inadequate down-the-line leadership skills and development	Lower-level managers develop skills through newly created opportunities to lead change and to drive key business initiatives. They are supported with just-in-time coaching, training, and targeted recruitment. Those who still are not able to make the grade must be replaced.

Source: M. Beer and R. A. Eisenstat, "The Silent Killers of Strategy Implementation and Learning," *Sloan Management Review* (Summer 2000), 4 (4), pp. 29–40.

- *Step 4: Implementation plan:*   The top management team, the employee task force, and others develop the implementation plan. The top management team monitors progress. The employee task force is charged with providing feedback about how others in the organization are responding to the changes.

This process, though straightforward, does not always go smoothly. Figure 4.7 shows six different barriers to strategy implementation and provides a description of some key principles for overcoming these "silent killers." By paying closer attention to the processes by which strategies are implemented, executives, managers, and employees can play an important role in making sure that strategic plans are actually carried out.[19]

Step 6: Strategic control

strategic control system

A system designed to support managers in evaluating the organization's progress regarding its strategy and, when discrepancies exist, taking corrective action.

The final component of the strategic management process is strategic control. A **strategic control system** is designed to support managers in evaluating the organization's progress with its strategy and, when discrepancies exist, in taking corrective action. The system must encourage efficient operations that are consistent with the plan while allowing the flexibility to adapt to changing conditions. As with all control systems, the organization must develop performance indicators, an information system, and specific mechanisms to monitor progress.

Most strategic control systems include some type of budget to monitor and control major financial expenditures. The dual responsibilities of a control system—efficiency and flexibility—often seem contradictory with respect to budgets. The budget usually establishes limits on spending, but changing conditions or innovation may require different financial commitments during the budgetary period. To solve this dilemma, some companies have responded with two separate budgets: strategic and operational. For example, managers at Texas Instruments Incorporated control two budgets under the OST (objectives-strategies-tactics) system. The strategic budget is used to create and maintain long-term effectiveness, and the operational budget is tightly monitored to achieve short-term efficiency. The topic of control in general, and budget in particular, will be discussed in more detail in Chapter 16.

Key terms

Business strategy, p. 127
Concentration, p. 125
Concentric diversification, p. 125
Conglomerate diversification, p. 125
Core competencies, p. 124
Corporate strategy, p. 125
Differentiation strategy, p. 127
Functional strategies, p. 127
Goals, p. 113
Low-cost strategy, p. 127
Mission, p. 119
Operational planning, p. 115
Plans, p. 113

Resources, p. 122
Scenario, p. 114
Situational analysis, p. 112
Stakeholders, p. 120
Strategic control system, p. 130
Strategic goals, p. 115
Strategic management, p. 118
Strategic planning, p. 115
Strategic vision, p. 119
Strategy, p. 115
SWOT analysis, p. 124
Tactical planning, p. 115
Vertical integration, p. 125

Summary of learning objectives

Now that you have studied Chapter 4, you should know:

How to proceed through the basic steps in any planning process.

The planning process begins with a situation analysis of the external and internal forces affecting the organization. This will help identify and diagnose issues and problems, and may surface alternative goals and plans for the firm. Next the advantages and disadvantages of these goals and plans should be evaluated against one another. Once a set of goals and a plan have been selected, implementation involves communicating the plan to employees, allocating resources, and making certain that other systems such as rewards and budgets are supporting the plan. Finally, planning requires that control systems are put in place to monitor progress toward the goals.

How strategic planning differs from tactical and operational planning.

Strategic planning is different from operational planning in that it involves making long-term decisions about the entire organization. Tactical planning translates broad goals and strategies into specific actions to be taken within parts of the organization. Operational planning identifies the specific short-term procedures and processes required at lower levels of the organization.

Why it is important to analyze both the external environment and internal resources of the firm before formulating a strategy.

Strategic planning is designed to leverage the strengths of a firm while minimizing the effects of its weaknesses. It is difficult to know the potential advantage a firm may have unless external analysis is done well. For example, a company may have a talented marketing department or an efficient production system. However, there is no way to determine whether these internal characteristics are sources of competitive advantage until something is known about how well the competitors stack up in these areas.

The choices available for corporate strategy.

Corporate strategy identifies the breadth of a firm's competitive domain. Corporate strategy can be kept narrow, as in a concentration strategy, or can move to suppliers and buyers via vertical integration. Corporate strategy can also broaden a firm's domain via concentric (related) diversification or conglomerate (unrelated) diversification.

How companies can achieve competitive advantage through business strategy.

Companies gain competitive advantage in two primary ways. They can attempt to be unique in some way by pursuing a differentiation strategy, or they can focus on efficiency and price by pursuing a low-cost strategy.

How core competencies provide the foundation for business strategy.

A core competence is something a company does especially well relative to its competitors. When this competence, say in engineer-

ing or marketing, is in some area important to market success, it becomes the foundation for developing a competitive advantage.

The keys to effective strategy implementation.

Many good plans are doomed to failure because they are not implemented correctly. Strategy must be supported by structure, technology, human resources, rewards, information systems, culture, leadership, and so on. Ultimately the success of a plan depends on how well employees at low levels are able and willing to implement it. Participative management is one of the more popular approaches used by executives to gain employees' input and ensure their commitment to strategy implementation.

Discussion questions

1. This chapter opened with a quote by GE's Jack Welch: "Manage your destiny, or someone else will." What does this mean for strategic management? What does it mean when Welch adds, ". . . or someone else will"?

2. How do strategic, operational, and tactical planning differ? How might the three levels complement one another in an organization?

3. What accounts for the shift from strategic planning to strategic management? In which industries would you be most likely to observe these trends?

4. In your opinion, what are the core competencies of companies in the auto industry such as General Motors, Ford, and Chrysler? How do these competencies help them compete against foreign competitors such as Honda, Toyota, Nissan, Mercedes Benz, BMW, and others?

5. What are the key challenges in strategy implementation? What barriers might prevent strategy implementation?

Concluding Case
What lies ahead

What if you could predict today which industries are fated to flourish or fail in the 21st century? What if, a decade past, you could have imagined the impact of the Internet? And what if, five years ago, you had foreseen today's supertight labor market or soaring health care costs? Then maybe you could hang out your shingle as a futurist and charge corporate clients or the federal government big bucks to help them prepare for the vagaries that lie ahead.

Prediction 1: Labor

Forecast: If you're waiting for a rising unemployment rate to ease your labor woes, you'll be waiting a long time. Assuming that the economy doesn't take a nosedive, you've got at least eight more

years of a tight labor supply, predicts Roger E. Herman, a futurist who looks at the workplace. And don't get your hopes up too high after that, cautions Edie Weiner, president of Weiner, Edrich, Brown, Inc. in Manhattan. Entry-level talent will become more plentiful in the next few years with the maturing of Generation Y, but the shortage of senior managers won't let up for years. There are 76 million baby boomers moving through the labor market, but only 44 million Gen-Xers, the first of whom will turn 40 in 2004.

Implications: Recruitment and retention efforts will become more important than ever, particularly with senior managers. "If you don't have a stable workforce, you are at a competitive disadvantage," warns Herman. You might take some comfort in the fact that your rivals will be just as hard-pressed, although that means they'll be gunning for your employees. You'll want to keep your successful strategies close to the vest. Your rivals certainly will.

Job fairs offer small companies an opportunity to market themselves.
[Mark Richards/PhotoEdit]

Prediction 2: Real Estate

Forecast: Small companies will relocate in record numbers during the next decade, as they get squeezed by two powerful forces—a tight labor market and rising rents, according to real estate futurist Roulac. Employees in their twenties and thirties, who will be in short supply over the next five years, move around at twice the rate of older people.

To attract these mobile workers, small companies will be forced to create strong images for themselves and spend more time and money marketing themselves. The right location will be crucial, says Roulac, who conducts an analysis he calls a "geostrategy" of cultural, economic, and other factors that help companies determine the best locale for their business.

Implications: You'll want to choose the kind of hometown base your target employees want, one with a high quality of life, strong education, public transportation, and recreation and entertainment amenities. "If you're not in a place where people choose to be, you may not be able to attract employees," says Roulac. As more companies seek new homes and demand keeps pushing commercial rents skyward, more companies will seek to buy their own office space. Alternatively, they will scale down their current space and move some employees to less expensive outlying areas accessible by public transportation, says Christopher Ireland, CEO of Cheskin Research, a Redwood Shores (California) forecasting firm. (In fact, she did just that with her own company earlier this year.) That means small companies may lose the classic advantage of having a flexible, cohesive workforce all under one roof. They will increasingly be faced with managing employees in multiple locations. That will require more logistical coordination and technology, so that everyone will stay on the same page. Ireland says she now manages employees at five different locations, making communications and office culture issues more important than ever.

Prediction 3: Customer Relations

Forecast: The current pace of corporate mergers and acquisitions will continue over the coming decade, so small businesses are in for a rough ride as their trusty major accounts vanish, predicts Jennifer Jarratt, futurist at Coates & Jarratt, Inc., based in Washington, D.C. A total of $520 billion in domestic mergers and acquisitions was announced in the third quarter of 2000 alone. That's the third-highest transaction volume in history, according to *Mergers & Acquisitions Report*. "You just don't have the continuity that you had several years ago," says Weiner.

Implications: To cope with customer churn, more small companies will be forced to step up their marketing and rethink their business strategies. Rather than focus so heavily on big corporate clients, they will pursue more stable small-to midsize ones, predicts Jarratt. Companies will also attempt to cope by narrowing their focus to serve a more select group of customers and give them superior service. That strategy could potentially help small businesses retain their clients that merge or are acquired.

While some small companies with desirable businesses will undoubtedly get gobbled up as mergers escalate, Weiner doesn't foresee a future without small business. To the contrary, as giant mergers take place, big corporations will abandon some market niches, leaving new opportunities for smaller businesses, she says. "As merged companies try to find efficiencies they create demand for outsourcing, which spurs growth in medium and smaller businesses," says Weiner.

Prediction 4: Wealth Transactions

Forecast: In what is expected to be one of the largest wealth transfers in history, baby boomers will inherit thousands of family businesses and billions of dollars from their parents over the next two decades, says futurist Johnson.

Implications: Some small businesses will profit from an infusion of new blood and leadership that will help them grow. Others will be acquired, leaving heirs with money to invest in other ventures. Baby boomers, who will begin to face age discrimination in the workplace, will also use their inheritances to start new businesses or buy existing businesses that are coming up for sale, says futurist Weiner.

As small-business growth is spurred, business consulting opportunities will abound to provide these newly minted entrepreneurs with everything from succession planning to financial services, says Weiner. For example, Weiner has studied the trend and sees a future for her own company. She says she is already planning to expand her future consulting services to serve more small companies. Other businesses may want to consider a similar move. A five-year projection done in 1997 by Arthur Andersen/Mass Mutual found that 28 percent of small family-owned businesses expected their owners to retire by 2002. An additional 14 percent said their CEO would retire in that period.

Prediction 5: Technology

Forecast: The next 50 years will see the evolution of what David Smith of Technology Futures, Inc. calls the Age of Bio. Biological science will be applied to manufacturing, information processing, and other fields. As computing power surpasses the abilities of the human mind by 2040, artificial intelligence will become a reality.

Implications: The field of "bioinformatics" will explode. Someday, you may trade in your computer monitor for a "retinal display" or use a DNA computer. "Instead of having to dig in the ground for specialty chemicals we'll be able to grow them," says Smith. These changes will breed new business opportunities. All of this new technology will require more energy resources. But rising prices for oil and diminishing natural resources will trigger the growth of so-called green industries that use alternative energy, says Jarratt. Running your business could get easier, too. Artificial intelligence might let you turn over to computers an ever-growing array of tasks, says Smith. But since computers still don't have feelings, more consultants will be needed to handle the human issues that arise in the workplace.

Source: Alison Stein Wellner, "What Comes Next," *Business Week,* December 4, 2000, 3710, p. F24. ●

Questions:

1. How would these forecasts affect the planning process in organizations?

2. Is the impact different for small firms versus large firms?

3. What other forcasts might you make if you had a "crystal ball," and how would these affect businesses?

Experiential Exercises

4.1 Strategic planning

Objective

To study the strategic planning of a corporation recently in the news.

Instructions

Business Week magazine has frequent articles on the strategies of various corporations. Find a recent article on a corporation in an industry of interest to you. Read the article and answer the questions below.

Strategic planning worksheet

1. Has the firm clearly identified what business it is in and how it is different from its competitors? Explain.

_____

_____

_____

_____

_____

_____

2. What are the key assumptions about the future that have shaped the firm's new strategy?

_____

_____

_____

_____

_____

3. What key strengths and weaknesses of the firm influenced the selection of the new strategy?

_____

_____

_____

_____

_____

4. What specific objectives has the firm set in conjunction with the new strategy?

_____

_____

_____

_____

_____

_____

Source: R. R. McGrath, Jr., _Exercises in Management Fundamentals_ (Englewood Cliffs, NJ: Prentice Hall, 1985), p. 15. Reprinted by permission of Prentice-Hall, Inc.

4.2 Formulating business strategy

Objectives

1. To illustrate the complex interrelationships central to business strategy formulation.
2. To demonstrate the use of SWOT (Strengths-Weaknesses-Opportunities-Threats) analysis in a business situation.

Instructions

1. Your instructor will divide the class into small groups and assign each group with a well-known organization for analysis.
2. Each group will
   a. Study the SWOT Introduction and the SWOT Worksheet to understand the work needed to complete the assignment.
   b. Obtain the needed information about the organization under study through library research, interviews, and so on.
   c. Complete the SWOT Worksheet.
   d. Prepare group responses to the discussion questions
3. After the class reconvenes, group spokespersons present group findings.

Discussion Questions

1. Why would most organizations not develop strategies for matches between opportunities and strengths?
2. Why would most organizations not develop strategies for matches between opportunities and weaknesses?
3. Why do most organizations want to deal from strength?

SWOT introduction

One of the more commonly used strategy tools is SWOT (Strengths-Weaknesses-Opportunities-Threats) analysis, which is accomplished in four steps:

Step 1: Analyze the organization's internal environment, identifying its strengths and weaknesses.

Step 2: Analyze the organization's external environment, identifying its opportunities and threats.

Step 3: Match (1) strengths with opportunities, (2) weaknesses with threats, (3) strengths with threats, and (4) weaknesses with opportunities.

Step 4: Develop strategies for those matches that appear to be of greatest importance to the organization. Most organizations give top priority to strategies that involve the matching of strengths with opportunities and second priority to strategies that involve the matching of weaknesses with threats. The key is to exploit opportunities where the organization has a strength and to defend against threats where the organization has a weakness.

SWOT worksheet

Organization being analyzed: _____

Internal Analysis	External Analysis
Strengths	Opportunities
_____	_____
_____	_____
_____	_____
_____	_____
_____	_____
_____	_____
_____	_____
_____	_____
_____	_____
_____	_____
_____	_____
Weaknesses	Threats
_____	_____
_____	_____
_____	_____
_____	_____
_____	_____
_____	_____
_____	_____
_____	_____
_____	_____
_____	_____

Strategies that match strengths with opportunities	Strategies that match weaknesses with threats

Chapter Five
Ethics and Corporate Responsibility

It is truly enough said that a corporation has no conscience; but a corporation of conscientious men is a corporation with a conscience.

—Henry David Thoreau

Chapter Outline

Ethics
    Ethical Systems
    Business Ethics
    The Ethics Environment
    Ethical Decision Making
Corporate Social Responsibility
    Contrasting Views
    Reconciliation
    Corporate Social Responsiveness
    Strategic Voluntarism
The Political Environment
    Competitive Advantage
    Corporate Legitimacy
    Strategies for Influencing the Political
       Environment
The Natural Environment
    A Risk Society
    Ecocentric Management
    Environmental Agenda for the Future

Learning Objectives

After studying Chapter 5, you will know:

1. How different ethical perspectives guide decision making.

2. How companies influence the ethics environment.

3. The options you have when confronting ethical issues.

4. The important issues surrounding corporate social responsibility.

5. How the political and social environment affects your firm's competitive position and legitimacy.

6. The strategies corporations use to manage the political and social environment.

7. The role of managers in our natural environment.

Setting the Stage

Corporate America Is Both Hero and Villain

Two-thirds of Americans give corporate America credit for the prosperity of recent years. At the same time, nearly three-quarters believe that business is too powerful, and controls too many aspects of their lives. Slightly less than half think that what's good for business is good for most Americans. And two-thirds think that big profits are more important to big companies than safe, reliable products. These results come from a *Business Week*/Harris Poll released on August 31, 2000.

What explains the discontent? This chapter discusses some recent incidents and issues in business news. But to set the context for later specifics, consider some broader explanations:

• With Americans' material needs so well satisfied, they have the luxury of focusing on other things that affect their quality of life.

• Many individuals and families are feeling overworked but not getting their fair share of the rewards. Relatedly, most people perceive a growing gap between society's "haves and have-nots," both in the United States and globally.

• Highlighted by Senator John McCain's push for campaign finance reform, companies are seen as unfairly buying their way into government.

• Big business is not as accountable as it was in the past. Big government and strong unions have lost clout, and the power imbalance causes resentment. As *Business Week* put it, "For two decades market deregulation has fostered competition and lowered many prices. But the pendulum may have swung too far for many citizens, who now take the gains for granted and want to dampen the extremes that can come with unfettered capitalism" (p. 146).

• Cultural norms have shifted. It is becoming fashionable to be anticorporate. The sudden prevalence of dot.com companies with their casual atmospheres led many professionals to turn against the traditional culture of corporate America.

Two thirds of Americans give corporate America credit for the prosperity of recent years. *[VCG/FPG International LLC]*

• A generation ago, antibusiness attitudes were found mostly among young people. Today, they cut across generations, geography, and income levels. Moreover, the Net makes negative information and commentaries more readily available, and provides, to those who care about the issues, additional power to have an impact.

Pollster Daniel Yankelovich states that, "There's an increased readiness to believe negative things about corporations today, which makes it a dangerous time for companies. Executives haven't had to worry about social issues for a generation, but there's a yellow light flashing now, and they better pay attention" (p. 147).

Business Week stated that it is primarily the "incredible success of the economy that allows companies to wield enormous power in American society today. With that power, however, comes added responsibility. Corporate executives would be wise to deal with the burden—and take care to avoid the hubris that so often accompanies heady success. If they don't, a growing number of Americans stand ready to call them to account" (p. 158).[1]

Source: A. Bernstein, "Too Much Corporate Power?," Business Week, September 11, 2000, pp. 145–58.

This chapter will help you understand the complex issues associated with business ethics and corporate social responsibility. Business is in the center of a controversy; although most agree that corporations should avoid illegal actions and decisions that significantly harm society, there is disagreement about the impact of their activities and the extent of their responsibilities.

Ethics

The aim of ethics is to identify both the rules that should govern people's behavior and the "goods" that are worth seeking. Ethical decisions are guided by the underlying values of the individual. Values are principles of conduct such as caring, honesty, keeping of promises, pursuit of excellence, loyalty, fairness, integrity, respect for others, and responsible citizenship.[2]

Most people would agree that all of these values are admirable guidelines for behavior. However, ethics becomes a more complicated issue when a situation dictates that one value overrule others. **Ethics** is the system of rules that governs the ordering of values.

An **ethical issue** is a situation, problem, or opportunity in which an individual must choose among several actions that must be evaluated as right or wrong.[3] Ethical issues arise in every facet of life; we concern ourselves here with business ethics in particular. **Business ethics** comprises the moral principles and standards that guide behavior in the world of business.[4]

Ethical systems

Moral philosophy refers to the principles, rules, and values people use in deciding what is right or wrong. This is a simple definition, in the abstract, but often terribly complex and difficult when facing real choices. How do you decide what is right and wrong? Do you know what criteria you apply, and how you apply them?

Ethics scholars point to various major ethical systems as guides.[5] The first ethical system, **universalism,** states that individuals should uphold certain values, such as honesty, regardless of the immediate result. The important values are those that society needs to function. For instance, people should always be honest because otherwise communication would break down.

But rarely are things so simple. Before we describe other ethical systems, consider the following example, and think about how you or others would resolve it. Remember, what you would do is not necessarily what others would do. And what people say, hope, or think they would do is often different from what they *really* would do, faced with the demands and pressures of the real situation.

ethics The system of rules governing the ordering of values.

ethical issue Situation, problem, or opportunity in which an individual must choose among several actions that must be evaluated as right or wrong.

business ethics The moral principles and standards that guide behavior in the world of business.

moral philosophy Principles, rules, and values people use in deciding what is right or wrong.

universalism The ethical system upholding certain values regardless of immediate result.

An example

Suppose that Sam Colt, a sales representative, is preparing a sales presentation for his firm, Midwest Hardware, which manufactures nuts and bolts. Colt hopes to obtain a large sale from a construction firm that is building a bridge across the Missouri River near St. Louis. The bolts manufactured by Midwest Hardware have a 3 percent defect rate, which, although acceptable in the industry, makes them unsuitable for use in certain types of projects, such as those that might be subject to sudden, severe stress. The new bridge will be located near the New Madrid Fault line, the source of the United States' greatest earthquake in 1811. The epicenter of that earthquake, which caused extensive damage and altered the flow of the Missouri, is less than 200 miles from the new bridge site.

Bridge construction in the area is not regulated by earthquake codes. If Colt wins the sale, he will earn a commission of $25,000 on top of his regular salary. But if he tells the contractors about the defect rate, Midwest may lose the sale to a competitor whose bolts are more reliable. Thus, Colt's ethical issue is whether to point out to the bridge contractor that in the event of an earthquake, Midwest bolts could fail, possibly resulting in the collapse of the bridge and the death of anyone driving across it at the time.

Source: O. C. Farrell and J. Fraedrich, *Business Ethics: Ethical Decision Making and Cases,* 3rd ed. Copyright © 1997 by Houghton Mifflin Company. Used with permission.   ●

Not everyone would behave the same in this scenario. Different individuals would apply different moral philosophies. Consider each of the following moral philosophies and the actions to which they might lead in the preceding case.[6]

teleology Considers an act to be morally right or acceptable if it produces a desired result.

Teleology

Teleology considers an act to be morally right or acceptable if it produces a desired result. The result can be anything desired by the person, including pleasure, personal growth, money, knowledge, or other self-interest. The key criterion is the consequences of the act, so teleology is sometimes referred to as consequentialism.

egoism An ethical system defining acceptable behavior as that which maximizes consequences for the individual.

Two types of teleology are *egoism* and *utilitarianism*. **Egoism** defines acceptable behavior as that which maximizes consequences for the individual. "Doing the right thing," the focus of moral philosophy, is defined by egoism as "do the act that promotes the greatest good for oneself." If everyone follows this system, the well-being of society

In the movie "Amistad," what type of ethical system do you think was portrayed? [© 1997 Dream Works/ Wide World/Photo by Lorey Sebastian/Motion Picture & TV]

as a whole should increase. This notion is similar to Adam Smith's concept of the invisible hand in business. Smith argued that if every organization follows its own economic self-interest, the total wealth of society will be maximized.

Utilitarianism is also concerned with consequences, and as such is a teleological philosophy. But unlike egoism, utilitarianism seeks the greatest good for the greatest number of people. A utilitarian approach seeks to maximize total utility, achieving the greatest benefit for people affected by a decision.

Deontology

Deontology focuses on the rights of individuals. Attention to individual rights ensures that equal respect is given to all persons. In this way, actions that maximize utility for many parties will be rejected if they do serious injustice to just one party. In contrast, utilitarianism might allow such an action in the spirit of maximizing overall consequences. Utilitarianism concentrates more on ends, and deontology more on means.

What criteria do *you* use? You may or may not be able by this point to choose the perspective that you use or would use in making tough decisions. But it should be clear that ethical issues can and are evaluated from many different perspectives, that each perspective has a different basis for deciding right and wrong, and that people will disagree about what is and is not ethical because they are assessing ethics by different ethical standards.

Relativism

Perhaps it seems clear to this point that the individual makes ethical choices on a personal basis, applying personal perspectives. But this is not necessarily the case. **Relativism** defines ethical behavior based on the opinions and behaviors of relevant other people. This perspective acknowledges the existence of different ethical viewpoints, and turns to other people for advice, input, and opinions. Professional bodies provide guidelines to follow, and decision makers can convene a group to share perspectives and derive conclusions. Group consensus is sought; a positive consensus signifies that an action is right, ethical, and acceptable.

Virtue ethics

The moral philosophies just described apply different types of rules and reasoning. **Virtue ethics** is a perspective that goes beyond the conventional rules of society by suggesting that what is moral must also come from what a mature person with "good" moral character would deem right. Society's rules provide a moral minimum, and then moral individuals can transcend rules by applying their personal virtues such as faith, honesty, and integrity.

Individuals differ in this regard. **Kohlberg's model of cognitive moral development** classifies people into one of three categories based on their level of moral judgment.[7] People in the *preconventional* stage make decisions based on concrete rewards and punishments and immediate self-interest. People in the *conventional* stage conform to the expectations of ethical behavior held by groups or institutions such as society, family, or peers. People in the *principled* stage take a broader perspective in which they see beyond authority, laws, and norms and follow their self-chosen ethical principles.[8] Some people forever reside in the preconventional stage, some move into the conventional stage, and some develop further yet into the principled stage. Over time, and through education and experience, people may change their values and ethical behavior.

Returning to the bolts-in-the-bridge example, *egoism* would result in keeping quiet about the bolts' defect rate. *Utilitarianism* would dictate a more thorough cost–benefit analysis and possibly the conclusion that the probability of a bridge collapse is so low compared to the utility of jobs, economic growth, and company growth that the defect rate is not worth mentioning. *Deontology* would likely create an obligation to tell because of the potential danger. The *relativist* perspective might prompt the salesperson to look at company policy and general industry practice, and to seek opinions from colleagues and perhaps trade journals and ethics codes. Whatever is then perceived to be a consensus

---

utilitarianism An ethical system stating that the greatest good for the greatest number should be the overriding concern of decision makers.

deontology focuses on rights of individuals.

relativism bases ethical behavior on the opinions and behaviors of relevant other people.

virtue ethics A perspective that what is moral comes from what a mature person with "good" moral character would deem right.

Kohlberg's model of cognitive moral development classifies people into one of three categories based on their level of moral judgment.

or normal practice would dictate action. And finally, *virtue ethics,* applied by people in the principled stage of moral development, would likely lead to full disclosure about the product and risks, and perhaps suggestions for alternatives that would reduce the risk.[9]

These major ethical systems underlie personal moral choices and ethical decisions in business.

Business ethics

Questions of ethics in business have been prominent in the news in recent years. Insider trading, illegal campaign contributions, bribery, and other scandals have created a perception that business leaders use illegal means to gain competitive advantage, increase profits, or improve their personal positions. In a survey of 200 professionals, 35 percent admitted lying to customers and colleagues. In another recent survey, of 158 experienced businesspeople, 65 percent agreed that mid- to upper-level managers believe that profits are more important than product safety. Shareholders tend to ignore fraudulent financial reporting, believing it is routine, as long as profits and market share don't suffer.[10] By the way, you might find it interesting that surveys suggest that males are more likely to behave unethically than females.[11]

Neither young managers[12] nor consumers[13] believe top executives are doing a good job of establishing high ethical standards. Some even joke that *business ethics* has become a contradiction in terms.

Most business leaders believe they uphold ethical standards in business practices.[14] But many managers and their organizations must deal frequently with ethical dilemmas, and the issues are becoming increasingly complex. Tables 5.1 and 5.2 show some important examples.

<table>
<tr><td>table 5.1

Some current ethical issues</td><td>

ARTISTIC CONTROL Rock musicians, independent filmmakers, and other artists are rebelling against control by big media and retail companies.

BRANDS In-your-face marketing campaigns have sparked antibrand attitudes among students.

CEO PAY Nearly three-fourths of Americans see executive pay packages as excessive.

COMMERCIALISM IN SCHOOLS Parent groups have mounted battles in hundreds of communities against advertising in the public schools.

CONSUMERISM Anger and frustration are mounting over high gasoline and drug prices, poor airline service, and HMOs that override doctors' decisions. The latest fiasco: faulty auto tires.

FRANKENFOODS Europeans' skepticism about genetically modified food is taking hold in the U.S., making targets of companies such as Monsanto.

GLOBALIZATION Environmentalists, students, and unionists charge that global trade and economic bodies operate in the interests of multinational companies.

POLITICS Public revulsion over the corporate bankrolling of politicians has energized campaign-finance reform activists.

SWEATSHOPS Anti-sweatshop groups have sprung up on college campuses; they routinely picket clothing manufacturers, toymakers, and retailers.

URBAN SPRAWL Groups in more than 100 cities have blocked big-box superstores by Wal-Mart and other chains.

WAGES Some 56% of workers feel they are underpaid, especially as wages since 1992 have topped inflation by 7.6%, while productivity is up 17.9%.

Source: A. Bernstein, 2000. "Too Much Corporate Power?," *Business Week*, September 11, 2000, pp. 146–47.

</td></tr>
</table>

table 5.2
Ethical decision making in the international context

What would you do in each of these true-life situations, and why?

- You are a sales representative for a construction company in the Middle East. Your company wants very much to land a particular project. The cousin of the minister who will award the contract informs you that the minister wants $20,000 in addition to the standard fees. If you do not make this payment, your competition certainly will—and will get the contract.

- You are international vice president of a multinational chemical corporation. Your company is the sole producer of an insecticide that will effectively combat a recent infestation of West African crops. The minister of agriculture in a small, developing African country has put in a large order for your product. Your insecticide is highly toxic and is banned in the United States. You inform the minister of the risks of using your product, but he insists on using it and claims it will be used "intelligently." The president of your company believes you should fill the order, but the decision ultimately is yours.

- You are a new marketing manager for a large automobile tire manufacturer. Your company's advertising agency has just presented plans for introducing a new tire into the Southeast Asia market. Your tire is a truly good product, but the proposed advertising is deceptive. For example, the "reduced price" was reduced from a hypothetical amount that was established only so it could be "reduced," and claims that the tire was tested under the "most adverse" conditions ignore the fact that it was not tested in prolonged tropical heat and humidity. Your superiors are not concerned about deceptive advertising, and they are counting on you to see that the tire does extremely well in the new market. Will you approve the ad plan?

Source: N. Adler, *International Dimensions of Organizational Behavior,* 2nd ed. (Boston: Kent, 1997).

Think about this: Just how ethical are businesspeople? Opinions differ.

Differences of opinion

Are businesspeople ethical? The following statements are taken from a recent article in *Across the Board,* an influential magazine for American executives:

- Business "is a game with different rules from those that apply to the rest of society." (p. 17)
- "Most large firms . . . suffer from a surfeit of ethics. They have their high ethics . . . ethics as it is preached. Then they also have an ethics as it is practiced." (p. 18)
- MBA students "won't necessarily cheat or lie more than other people, but they . . . are more willing to accept the unethicalness of others, because they expect it as normal." (p. 18)
- "Is there something about large business organizations in particular that leads people astray? The answer seems to be: just about everything." (p. 18)
- "The essence of business is competition, making business still a game where winning matters more than how the game is played." (p. 21)
- "In most of the infamous cases of corporate wrongdoing—the exploding Pinto is a famous example—it was not just one person who did wrong but sometimes dozens." (p. 21)
- "Everyone agrees that lying is unethical, but misrepresentation during a purchase negotiation is widely considered not to be lying, because if all parties know that everyone is lying there is no deception and thus no sin." (p. 22)

On the other hand, this article generated outrage from many readers, who wrote in a subsequent issue of the magazine:

- "[I and others] would strongly debate the notion that business ethics is different from everyday ethics." (p. 48)
- "For every unethical or amoral manager, there is at least another manager trying to do the right thing for the right reasons." (p. 48)

In today's business environment, managers face ethical dilemas daily.
[Kaluzny/Thatcher/Tony Stone Images]

- "People can make the difference. They can set the tone of ethical behavior . . . it's imperative. It will make the difference for the future. Because a sale is nice, but the future is the future." (p. 49)
- "There are certainly many companies—even hierarchical ones operating in highly competitive environments with enormous sums of money at stake—whose managers do behave responsibly, indeed sometimes even courageously." (p. 49)
- "Business will (must) act in such a way that its market approves. Thank goodness that today's societal market demands accountability and checks ethical behavior." (p. 50)
- "At the heart of business success . . . is customer or client trust and loyalty. This trust and loyalty is [sic] built by product or service credibility, reliability, and performance, which is [sic] reinforced by ethical standards and behavior. Attempting to define business interests and ethical interests as separate, or antithetical, ignores this fundamental fact of how business survives and prospers." (p. 50)

Sources: J. Krohe Jr., "Ethics Are Nice, but Business Is Business," *Across the Board,* April 1997, pp. 16–22; and D. Driscoll, M. Rion, M. Roth, D. Vogel, L. Pincus, and D. Orlov, "Who Says Ethics Are 'Nice'"? *Across the Board,* June 1997, pp. 47–50. Reprinted with permission of the Conference Board. ●

The ethics environment

ethical climate of an organization refers to the processes by which decisions are evaluated and made on the basis of right and wrong.

Ethics are not shaped only by society and by individual development and virtue. They also may be influenced by the company's work environment. The **ethical climate** of an organization refers to the processes by which decisions are evaluated and made on the basis of right and wrong.[15]

When people make decisions that are judged by ethical criteria, these questions always seem to get asked: Why did she do it? Good motives or bad ones? His responsibility or someone else's? Who gets the credit, or the blame? So often, responsibility for unethical acts is placed squarely on the individual who commits them. But the environment has a profound influence, as well.

Consider the question of responsibility in the cases of illegal, unethical actions at Kidder Peabody and at Sears, Roebuck. A securities trader at Kidder Peabody allegedly created about $350 million in phony profits for the firm. By engaging in these illegalities, he made $9 million in salary and bonuses. (By playing it straight and honest, he would have made $2 or $3 million.)

How could the scandal have happened? Was it just a renegade trader? The trader's immediate boss claimed he could not monitor the records of all 750 traders in his department. Kidder's CEO said the same thing could have happened anywhere on Wall Street. Supporters said that in a company as big as GE (Kidder's parent corporation), there are bound to be some bad apples. And Kidder top executives, according to GE's Jack Welch, were open and candid and worked hard to get at the truth once the scandal was uncovered.[16] But the profits the trader claimed were outrageous; $5 million to $10 million per month on government bonds seemed impossible. Kidder executives consistently ignored, evaded, or answered incorrectly questions about his profits. Critics cannot understand why it took so long to uncover the misdeeds, and maintained that the trader could not have pulled it off if management had been paying attention.

In another example of joint responsibility, Sears, Roebuck did not set out to defraud its automotive service customers in the early 1990s. Nor did employees necessarily intend to cheat consumers. But when the company instituted high-pressure, unrealistic quotas and incentives, people's judgment was affected. Management did not make clear the distinction between unnecessary service and legitimate preventive maintenance. Moreover, customers were often ignorant or oblivious. A vast gray area of repair options was exaggerated, overinterpreted, and misrepresented. The company may not have intended to deceive customers, but the result of the work environment was that consumers and attorneys general in more than 40 states accused the company of fraud. The total cost of the settlement was an estimated $60 million.[17]

As illustrated by the Kidder Peabody and Sears examples, unethical corporate behavior may be the responsibility of an unethical individual; but it often also reveals a company culture that is ethically lax.[18] Likewise, ethical individuals are likely to behave ethically, but all the more so in organizations that infuse a sense of ethics into their people.

Corporate ethical standards
People often give in to what they perceive to be the pressures or preferences of powerful others. States Professor Arthur Brief of Tulane University, "If the boss says, 'Achieve a specific sales or profit target, period,' I think people will do their very best to achieve those directions even if it means sacrificing their own values. They may not like it, but they define it as part of the job."[19]

Because individuals have differing personal ethical codes, organizations must be explicit regarding their corporate ethical standards and expectations. Some companies advocate the "golden rule": Do unto others as you would have them do unto you. However, others argue that current or accepted business practice should govern behavior. Their motto is "Everyone else does it." A more extreme attitude is that organizations should seek every possible advantage without regard for traditional social laws and customs—a "might equals right" philosophy. Finally, some believe that ethics should be determined by intuition, that is, by doing whatever "feels right."

IBM uses a guideline for business conduct that asks employees to determine whether under the "full glare of examination by associates, friends, and family, they would remain comfortable with their decisions." One suggestion is to imagine how you would feel if you saw your decision and its consequences on the front page of the newspaper.[20] This "light of day" or "sunshine" ethical framework is extremely powerful.[21]

Such fear of exposure compels people more strongly in some cultures than in others. In Asia, anxiety about losing face often makes Asian executives resign immediately if they are caught in ethical transgressions, or if their companies are embarrassed by revelations in the press. By contrast, in the United States, exposed executives might respond with indignation, intransigence, stonewalling, and an everyone-else-does-it self-defense, or by not admitting wrongdoing and giving no sign that resignation ever crossed their minds. Partly because of legal tradition, the attitude often is: Never explain, never apologize, do not resign, even if the entire world knows exactly what happened. Don't admit the mistake and accept the consequences.[22]

Danger signs
In organizations, it is an ongoing challenge to maintain consistent ethical behavior by all employees. What are some danger signs that an organization may be allowing or even encouraging unethical behavior among its people? Many factors create a climate conducive to unethical behavior, including (1) excessive emphasis on short-term revenues over longer-term considerations; (2) failure to establish a written code of ethics; (3) a desire for simple, "quick fix" solutions to ethical problems; (4) an unwillingness to take an ethical stand that may impose financial costs; (5) consideration of ethics solely as a legal issue or a public relations tool; (6) lack of clear procedures for

handling ethical problems; and (7) response to the demands of shareholders at the expense of other constituencies.[23]

Ethics codes   One of the most visible signs of possible corporate commitment to ethical behavior is a written code of ethics. Often, the statements are just for show, but when implemented well they can change a company's ethical climate for the better and truly encourage ethical behavior.

Ethics codes must be carefully written and tailored to individual companies' philosophies. Aetna Life & Casualty believes that tending to the broader needs of society is essential to fulfilling its economic role. Johnson & Johnson has one of the most famous ethics codes (see Table 5.3). J&J consistently receives high rankings for community and social responsibility in *Fortune*'s annual survey of corporate reputations.

Most ethics codes address subjects such as employee conduct, community and environment, shareholders, customers, suppliers and contractors, political activity, and technology. Often the codes are drawn up by the organizations' legal departments and begin with research into other companies' codes. The Ethics Resource Center in Washington assists companies interested in establishing a corporate code of ethics.[24]

To make an ethics code effective, do the following:[25] (1) involve everyone who has to live with it in writing the statement; (2) have a corporate statement, but also allow separate statements by different units throughout the organization; (3) keep it short and therefore easily understood and remembered; (4) don't make it too corny—make it something important, that people really believe in; and (5) set the tone at the top, having executives talk about and live up to the statement. When reality differs from the statement—as when a motto says people are our most precious asset or a product is the finest in the world, but in fact people are treated poorly or product quality is weak—the statement becomes a joke to employees rather than a guiding light.

Ethics programs   Corporate ethics programs commonly include formal ethics codes articulating the company's expectations regarding ethics; ethics committees that

table 5.3
Johnson & Johnson's ethics code

We believe our first responsibility is to the doctors, nurses, and patients, to mothers and all others who use our products and services. In meeting their needs everything we do must be of high quality. We must constantly strive to reduce our costs in order to maintain reasonable prices. Customers' orders must be serviced promptly and accurately. Our suppliers and distributors must have an opportunity to make a fair profit.

We are responsible to our employees: the men and women who work with us throughout the world. Everyone must be considered as an individual. We must respect their dignity and recognize their merit. They must have a sense of security in their jobs. Compensation must be fair and adequate, and working conditions clean, orderly, and safe. Employees must feel free to make suggestions and complaints. There must be equal opportunity for employment, development, and advancement for those qualified. We must provide competent management, and their actions must be just and ethical.

We are responsible to the communities in which we live and work and to the world community as well.

We must be good citizens—support good works and charities and bear our fair share of taxes. We must encourage civic improvements and better health and education.

We must maintain in good order the property we are privileged to use, protecting the environment and natural resources.

Our final responsibility is to our stockholders. Business must make a sound profit. We must experiment with new ideas. Research must be carried on, innovative programs developed, and mistakes paid for. New equipment must be purchased, new facilities provided, and new products launched. Reserves must be created to provide for adverse times.

When we operate according to these principles, the stockholders should realize a fair return.

Source: Reprinted with permission of Johnson & Johnson.

compliance-based ethics programs Company mechanisms typically designed by corporate counsel to prevent, detect, and punish legal violations.

develop policies, evaluate actions, and investigate violations; ethics communication systems giving employees a means of reporting problems or getting guidance; ethics officers or ombudspersons who investigate allegations and provide education; ethics training programs; and disciplinary processes for addressing unethical behavior.[26]

Ethics programs can range from compliance-based to integrity-based.[27] **Compliance-based ethics programs** are designed by corporate counsel to prevent, detect, and punish legal violations. Compliance-based programs increase surveillance and controls on people and impose punishments on wrongdoers. Program elements include establishing and communicating legal standards and procedures, assigning high-level managers to oversee compliance, auditing and monitoring compliance, reporting criminal misconduct, punishing wrongdoers, and taking steps to prevent offenses in the future.

Such programs should reduce illegal behavior and help the company stay out of court. But they do not create a moral commitment to ethical conduct; they merely ensure moral mediocrity. As Richard Breeden, former chairman of the SEC, said, "It is not an adequate ethical standard to aspire to get through the day without being indicted."[28]

integrity-based ethics programs Company mechanisms designed to instill in people a personal responsibility for ethical behavior.

Integrity-based ethics programs go beyond the mere avoidance of illegality; they are concerned with the law but also with instilling in people a personal responsibility for ethical behavior. With such a program, companies and people govern themselves through a set of guiding principles that they embrace.

For example, the Americans with Disabilities Act (ADA) requires companies to change the physical work environment so it will allow people with disabilities to function on the job. Mere compliance would involve making the necessary changes to avoid legal problems. Integrity-based programs would go further, by training people to understand and perhaps change attitudes toward people with disabilities, and sending clear signals that people with disabilities also have valued abilities. This goes far beyond taking action to stay out of trouble with the law.

When top management has more personal commitment to responsible ethical behavior, programs tend to be better integrated into operations, thinking, and behavior. For example,[29] at a meeting of about 25 middle managers at a major financial services firm, every one of them told the company's general counsel that they had never seen or heard of the company's ethics policy document. The policies existed but were not a part of the everyday thinking of managers. In contrast, one health care products company bases one-third of managers' annual pay raises on how well they carry out the company's ethical ideals. Their ethical behavior is assessed by superiors, peers, and subordinates—making ethics a thoroughly integrated aspect of the way the company and its people do business.

The elements of an integrity strategy include:

1. The guiding values are shared and clearly understood by everyone.
2. Company leaders are personally committed to the values and willing to take action on them.
3. The values are considered in decision making and reflected in all important activities.
4. Information systems, reporting relationships, and performance appraisals support and reinforce the values. At some companies, like Levi Strauss, people's raises depend in part on the ethics of their decisions.
5. People at all levels have the skills and knowledge to make ethically sound decisions on a daily basis.

Integrity-based programs go beyond mere compliance with a law.
[David Young Wolff/Tony Stone Images]

Companies with strong integrity-based programs include Martin Marietta, NovaCare (a provider of rehabilitation services to hospitals and nursing homes), and Wetherill Associates (a supplier of electrical parts to the automotive market). These companies believe that their programs contribute to competitiveness, higher morale, and sustainable relationships with key stakeholders.[30]

Ethical decision making

Good people sometimes commit unethical acts because they do not carefully think through the consequences and implications of their actions.[31] Corporate policies can help ensure ethical decision making. In addition, some guidelines for decision making may help you avoid inadvertent breaches of ethics.[32]

First, *define the issue clearly.* What is the context of the issue? Who are the affected stakeholders? Talk to various stakeholders to ensure that all the facts are considered. Often a decision maker omits this step, assuming she or he already understands the problem without stopping to consider all of its components.

Second, *identify the relevant values in the situation.* Any ethical dilemma involves multiple values: the various consequences of your choices, what you care about the most, and what others care about the most. Clearly stating these values focuses attention on the ethical component of the decision.

Third, *weigh the conflicting values and choose an option that balances them,* with greatest emphasis on the most important values. At this stage, the decision maker must decide which values are more important than others. Companies that have clearly defined their values through a code of ethics and other actions already have clarified the value priorities. In organizations in which values are unclear or inconsistent, balancing the values is a more difficult challenge.

Fourth, *implement the decision.* This step may require justifying your actions. Because the short- and long-term ethical consequences already have been assessed, you can more effectively defend the decision to stakeholders.

What can you do if you see managers in your company behaving in ways that go against your ethical principles? Your options include the following, among others:[33] (1) Don't think about it; (2) go along with it to avoid conflict; (3) object, verbally or via memo; (4) quit; (5) privately or publicly blow the whistle—that is, inform others inside or outside the organization about what you have observed; or (6) negotiate and build a consensus for changing the unethical behavior. What are the advantages and disadvantages of each of these options? What other options can you think of? What do you think determines which option a person chooses?

Recalling Chapter 3, ethical dilemmas are ill-structured problems made under conditions of uncertainty. As such, there are no formulas, and no clear right or wrong answers. Mistakes will be made. But also recalling Chapter 3, the more you engage in vigilance and procedural rationality—and the better you understand your own moral philosophy and criteria—the better chance you have of making the most ethical decisions possible. Importantly, the stronger your intentions to behave in an ethical manner, consistently over time, the better chance you have of making decisions with which you and others can live. While mistakes still may be made—recalling also the likelihood of unintended consequences—good intentions, and vigilant decision processes, followed by actions that are consistent with ethical judgments, will reduce guilt and raise the overall level of positive consequences for decision makers, for organizations, and for society.

Corporate social responsibility

Should business be responsible for social concerns lying beyond its own economic well-being? Do social concerns affect a corporation's financial performance? The extent of business's responsibility for noneconomic concerns has been hotly debated. In the 1960s and 1970s, the political and social environment became more important to U.S. corporations as society turned its attention to issues like equal opportunity, pollution control, energy and natural resource conservation, and consumer and worker protection.[34] Public debate addressed these issues and how business should respond to them. This controversy focused on the concept of corporate social responsibility.

corporate social responsibility Obligation toward society assumed by business.

Corporate social responsibility is the obligation toward society assumed by business. The socially responsible business maximizes its positive effects on society and minimizes its negative effects.[35]

economic responsibilities are to produce goods and services that society wants at a price that perpetuates the business and satisfies its obligations to investors.

Social responsibilities can be categorized more specifically,[36] as shown in Figure 5.1. The **economic responsibilities** of business are to produce goods and services that society wants at a price that perpetuates the business and satisfies its obligations to investors.

figure 5.1
The pyramid of corporate
social responsibility

**Voluntary
responsibilities**

Be a good corporate citizen.
**Contribute resources
to the community;
improve quality of life.**

**Ethical
responsibilities**

Be ethical.
**Obligation to do what is right,
just, and fair. Avoid harm.**

**Legal
responsibilities**

Obey the law.
**Law is society's codification of right
and wrong. Play by the rules of the game.**

**Economic
responsibilities**

Be profitable.
The foundation upon which all others rest.

Source: Archie B. Carroll, "The Pyramid of Corporate Responsibility: Toward the Moral Management of Organizational Stakeholders," adaptation of Figure 3, p. 42. Reprinted from *Business Horizons,* July/August 1991. Copyright 1991 by the Foundation for the School of Business at Indiana University. Used with permission.

legal responsibilities To obey local, state, federal, and relevant international laws.

ethical responsibilities Meeting other social expectations, not written as law.

voluntary responsibilities Additional behaviors and activities that society finds desirable and that the values of the business support.

Legal responsibilities are, at the very least, to obey local, state, federal, and relevant international laws. **Ethical responsibilities** include meeting other societal expectations, not written as law. As such, ethics is one dimension of social responsibility. Finally, **voluntary responsibilities** are additional behaviors and activities that society finds desirable and that the values of the business support. Examples include supporting community projects and making charitable contributions.

Although criteria and standards for determining these responsibilities vary among organizations and countries, some efforts have been made to establish sets of global or universal ethical principles. For example, it is widely agreed that all people are morally obligated to adhere to core principles such as avoid harm to others, respect the autonomy of others, avoid lying, and honor agreements.[37] Appendix A shows the international ethics code created by the Caux Roundtable in Switzerland, collaborating with business leaders from Europe, Japan, and the United States.

Contrasting views

Two basic and contrasting views about which principles should guide managerial responsibility are common. The first is critical of the broad domain of corporate social responsibility; it holds that managers act as agents for shareholders and, as such, are obligated to maximize the present value of the firm. This tenet of capitalism is widely associated with the early writings of Adam Smith in *The Wealth of Nations,* and more recently by Milton Friedman, the Nobel Prize–winning economist of the University of

Chicago. With his now-famous dictum "The social responsibility of business is to increase profits," Friedman contended that organizations may help improve the quality of life as long as such actions are directed at increasing profits.

These critics argue that in a capitalistic society, economic performance is an organization's primary social responsibility. If corporations do not serve shareholders first, they will fail to serve society. Society relies on the profit incentive to motivate organizations to create jobs and make investments. Without investments, economic growth is impossible.

Some considered Friedman to be "the enemy of business ethics," but his position was ethical: He believed that it was unethical for unelected business leaders to decide what was best for society, and unethical for them to spend shareholders' money on projects unconnected to key business interests.[38]

business judgment rule
allows management wide latitude in policy if the policy can be justified.

Management's duty to pursue profits is not absolute. The **business judgment rule** allows management wide latitude in policy if the policy can be justified. The goal of shareholder wealth is legally qualified by the American Law Institute's (ALI) Principles of Corporate Governance, which state that the corporation "may take into account ethical considerations that are reasonably regarded as appropriate to the responsible conduct of the business."[39]

Some people disagree with the qualifier "may."[40] They see ethical actions as not optional, but mandatory.[41] This is the second perspective, different from the profit maximization perspective: that managers should be motivated by principled moral reasoning. Followers of Friedman and *The Wealth of Nations* might sneer at such soft-headed propaganda. But it is argued that Adam Smith wrote about a different world from the one we are in now, driven in the 18th century by the self-interest of small owner-operated farms and craft shops trying to generate a living income for themselves and their families. This self-interest was quite different from that of top executives of modern corporations.[42] It is interesting to note that Adam Smith also wrote *A Theory of Moral Sentiments,* in which he argued that "sympathy," defined as a proper regard for others, was the basis of a civilized society.[43]

Advocates of corporate social responsibility argue that organizations have a wider range of responsibilities that extend beyond the production of goods and services at a profit. As members of society, organizations should actively and responsibly participate in the community and in the larger environment.

How would these perspectives apply to the following example?

American cigarettes, overseas and at home

Some people argue that U.S. tobacco companies should not promote tobacco abroad. The tobacco companies disagree. The Chinese already manufacture and consume well over 1 trillion cigarettes annually (90 percent of Chinese males and 63 percent of Japanese males smoke), and the U.S. tobacco industry wants part of that market. U.S. tobacco companies argue that Asians complain about the menace of American cigarette conglomerates but do little in terms of requiring warning labels, prohibiting sales to minors, or banning smoking. Taiwan has a cigarette brand called "Long Life," and Japan's tepid health warning reads, "Please don't smoke too much." Smoking-related deaths have overtaken communicable diseases as Asia's top health risk.

Fewer than 10 percent of Asian women and adolescents smoke, and U.S. companies have promised not to court those markets. Nevertheless, a Taiwanese official complained that U.S. manufacturers handed out cigarettes to 12-year-olds at amusement parks. Critics claim that saturation marketing, depicting smoking as glamorous, rugged, and very Western, is designed to entice the enormous, untapped market of Asian women and teens.

In Europe, member countries of the European Union are working to ban tobacco advertising in sport, but U.K. Prime Minister Tony Blair voted to exclude

Formula One auto racing from the ban. Formula One claims to be the third biggest sport worldwide in television audience, after the Olympic Games and the World Cup. And tobacco is easily the largest sponsor. Former racing great Jackie Stewart, whose team refuses tobacco ads because its sponsors (Ford and Hewlett-Packard) are nonsmoking companies, estimates his team is 25–30 percent poorer as a result.

Tobacco companies have no place else to advertise on television. Recent studies show that young male Formula One fans are four times more likely to become smokers. A ban would greatly reduce the sport's income, and some fear it would leave Europe and move elsewhere, perhaps East Asia.

Antismoking activists maintain that an unbridled pursuit of profit is fueling an anti-American backlash and hostility toward other U.S. exports. Tobacco interests counter that taxes on their products go directly into the coffers of very poor countries.

Meanwhile, in the United States, the big news in the industry was the Big Tobacco trial in Miami. The punitive-damage judgment against the industry was $144.8 *billion*. The foreman of the jury that delivered the judgment said that jurors intended to "put the companies on notice—not just tobacco companies, all companies—concerning fraud or misrepresentation of the American public" (p. 148).

Sources: M. Levin, "U.S. Tobacco Firms Push Eagerly into the Asian Market," *Marketing News,* January 21, 1991, pp. 2. 14; P. Schmeiser, "Pushing Cigarettes Overseas," *New York Times Magazine.* July 10, 1988, pp. 16 ff; M. Jacques, "Can Formula One Give Up the Tobacco Habit?" *The European,* November 13–19, 1997, pp. 9–13; and A. Bernstein, "Too Much Corporate Power?," *Business Week,* September 11, 2000, pp. 145–58. ●

Reconciliation

It used to be that these views were regarded as antagonistic, leading to opposing policies. But now, in a more "ethicized" business climate, the two views can converge.[44] As the contemporary British economist and management scholar Charles Handy put it, "Markets, for wealth and efficiency, need to be balanced by sympathy [as Adam Smith defined it], for civilization."[45] Even supporters of the wealth maximization view now often explicitly consider important legal, ethical, and social issues. The argument that ethical behavior is both right and more profitable is more common today than in the "greed decade" of the 1980s.[46]

Earlier attention to corporate social responsibility focused on alleged wrongdoing and how to control it. More recently, attention has been on the possible competitive advantage of socially responsible actions, including financial success and consumer purchase decisions. A recent study showed that corporate social responsibility enhances company reputations, which in turn makes them more attractive employers, and they attract more applicants.[47] Thus corporate social responsibility can provide competitive advantage by helping to attract and perhaps retain superior employees.

Socially responsible actions can have other long-term advantages for organizations. Organizations can avoid unnecessary and costly regulation if they are perceived as socially responsible. Honesty and fairness—including admitting mistakes; apologizing genuinely, quickly, and sincerely; and making up for the mistake—may pay great dividends to the conscience, to the personal reputation, to the public image of the company, and to the market response.[48] In addition, society's problems can offer business opportunities, and profits can be made from systematic and vigorous efforts to solve these problems. In other words, it can pay to be good.[49]

Merck, for example, states in its internal management guide, "We are in the business of improving human life. All of our actions must be measured by our success in achieving this goal." And the company means it. For example, Merck developed a drug called Mectizan to cure "river blindness," a disease that infected over a million people. That's

table 5.4
Approaches to corporate social responsiveness

Approach	Posture of strategy	Performance
1. Reactive	Deny responsibility	Do less than required
2. Defensive	Admit responsibility but fight it	Do the least that is required
3. Accommodative	Accept responsibility	Do all that is required
4. Proactive	Anticipate responsibility	Do more than required

Source: M. B. E. Clarkson, "A Stakeholder Framework for Analyzing and Evaluating Corporate Social Performance," *Academy of Management Review* 20 (1995), pp. 92–117.

a big potential market, except that the victims could not afford the product. Merck hoped that someone else would help pay for the cure, but the company gave the drug away for free, and invested in costly distribution efforts to make sure the people who needed it were able to get it.[50]

Asked why Merck did this, then-CEO Roy Vagelos said to not do so would have been to violate the reason the company was in business and would demoralize its scientists. He also cited an earlier example: After World War II, Merck brought streptomycin to Japan to cure tuberculosis, which was devastating Japan. Merck made no money but did tremendous good. And today Merck has a tremendous reputation and presence in Japan.[51]

Corporate social responsiveness

corporate social responsiveness The process companies follow and the actions they take in the domain of corporate social responsibility.

How companies respond to the corporate social responsibility debate is called **corporate social responsiveness**.[52] The two are sometimes distinguished by the acronyms CSR1 and CSR2. Whereas CSR1 (corporate social responsibility) refers to principles, philosophies, and beliefs, CSR2 (corporate social responsiveness) refers to the processes companies follow and the actions they take. These processes and strategies are reactive, defensive, accommodative, and proactive. Table 5.4 summarizes these responses.

Both corporate social responsibility and corporate social responsiveness have their critics, in both academia and business.[53] Critics say these ideas came from outside the business world and are value laden, poorly defined, and vague. To many, they are not as

Hanna Anderson receives awards for its community commitment, including a program called Hanna-downs that donates customers' outgrown clothing to local charities and disaster relief.
[Robbie McClaran]

meaningful as stakeholder management. Managers do not manage relationships with society, they say, but with stakeholders. As such, stakeholder management is much more directly relevant, real, and manageable.

Stakeholder management considers key stakeholders and the specific issues relevant to each.[54] For any manager, stakeholders would include the company, employees, shareholders, customers, suppliers, and public stakeholders.[55] *Company issues* include economic performance, organizational mission or purpose, the competitive environment, and corporate codes. *Employee issues* include compensation and rewards, health and assistance programs, leaves of absence, dismissals and appeals, terminations and layoffs, discrimination, family accommodation, safety, career planning, and others. *Shareholder issues* include shareholder rights, advocacy, communications, and complaints. *Customer issues* include communications, complaints, product safety, services, and others. *Supplier issues* include relative power, treatment, and other issues. *Public issues* include public health and safety, energy conservation, public policy, environmental issues, involvement in public policy, social donations, and community relations.

Many of these managerially relevant issues are discussed in other parts of this book. After describing some ethical and social issues surrounding the Internet, we will turn our attention to three issues in particular: strategic voluntarism, the political environment, and the natural environment.

Ethical and social issues with the Internet

Recall Setting the Stage, about the power of corporations and the perception that they hold too much control over people's lives. Some say that corporations can gain complete control over individuals via the Internet. The issues include intellectual capital, free speech, and privacy.

Regarding *intellectual capital,* some view the Internet as a copying machine run amok, in which anyone can make perfect copies of anything, regardless of copyright. Many believe that this is a dire threat to the entertainment and publishing industries. But the opposite threat may be more serious, as copyright holders may eventually be able to monitor and charge users for every single use. Intellectual property rights traditionally are intended to balance the interests of producers with those of society; with the Net, it remains to be seen whether and how such a balance will emerge.

Regarding *free speech,* cyberspace can promote free and open communications, or it may control our lives in ways unimaginable and undesired. Right now it is not clear in which direction we're headed. Design decisions can permit or prohibit anonymity on the Net, and include or exclude certain types of speech. Sometimes, messages can be sent anonymously; in other systems, in which individuals must register before they can access e-mail, messages identify senders. America Online (AOL) allows multiple pseudonyms, apparently facilitating freer speech, but AOL managers can easily trace messages that appear to be anonymous.

In the early Net, it was almost impossible to filter material, but now it is much easier. Some fear that the government or commercial forces will censor Internet content. Blocking or filtering can be done upstream by Internet service providers, portals, or employers, and users may be unaware. Others think that censorship is unlikely, and that Internet surfers or parents will make their own choices and block what they don't like. Many prefer that organizations be required to disclose their filtering policies, believing that this will make censorship less likely.

Privacy needs to be a concern of every company that does business on the Net. Some fear that cyberspace may eliminate all of our privacy, as vendors gain access to people's Internet shopping and buying patterns. DoubleClick sells clickstream data, E-Loan is struggling to keep customers' highly confidential financial data completely secure, and people are beginning to worry that employers will purchase such data on job applicants. Think about it: How would you feel if any-one could purchase data showing everything you read, every Web site you vis-ited, every file you downloaded, every message you sent or received, and every purchase you made?

Source: C. Shapiro, "Will E-commerce Erode Liberty?," *Harvard Business Review,* May–June 2000, pp. 189–99; and L. Lessig, *Code and Other Laws of Cyberspace* (New York: Basic Books, 2000).   ●

Strategic voluntarism

Community service by corporate executives traditionally was a matter of giving some time and money to civic organizations, and going to luncheons and charity balls. Such activities generated political connections, goodwill, and marketing benefits. The biggest charitable givers locally are those with the highest local visibility, such as banks, retail-ers, and insurance companies. States a banker, "Community service helps us cultivate customers. We will have no customers unless the community is vital."[56]

Companies today are engaging in philanthropic activities more strategically and actively than the traditional cocktail circuit, seeking more focus and impact. BankBoston's senior vice president for government and community affairs said, "We want to make a difference, not just play a part. We were giving to too many causes at too modest a level. It didn't make much difference . . . now we want to leverage our investments."[57] Bank-Boston and other strategic philanthropists strive to do things that matter, to get recogni-tion for their contribution, and to support causes that both capitalize on and serve their businesses.

Thus, a book publisher sponsors literacy programs, and donates books and cash to a children's library at a hospital. Wellfleet Communications and AT&T donated technology, training, and engineering support to the New England Shelter for Homeless veterans, and thus developed demonstration sites while connecting homeless shelters nationwide. And Lotus assisted black communities with information technology projects, and offered internships to black programming trainees, as it entered the South African software market.[58]

Community service is increasingly an employee benefit, as well. Employees sometimes are given a say in their companies' philanthropic activities. Their communities benefit, and they develop pride in their company.

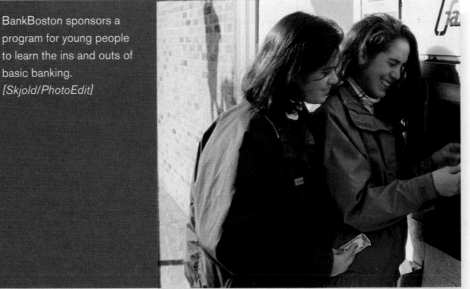

BankBoston sponsors a program for young people to learn the ins and outs of basic banking.
[Skjold/PhotoEdit]

Volunteer work: Good or bad for your career?

Don't do too much volunteer community service, because it could harm your career.

This was the message of an article in *The Wall Street Journal*. A few years ago, many companies urged people to get involved in volunteer work. But currently, said the article, companies want more than 40 hours of work per week out of you, and want your extra hours spent working for them, not others.

To some bosses, if you are doing a lot of volunteer work, you must not be spending enough time on your paid job. Said one consultant, "If I were a manager today and had an employee who was extraordinarily task-oriented and another who was a mediocre performer but a great citizen in the community, I'd promote the person getting the important things done in the company. Who's kidding whom? The very survival of the corporation is at stake."

Some companies, like Schnucks Supermarkets in St. Louis and General Mills in Minneapolis, consider community involvement in performance reviews and pay raises. But this is uncommon. Community service can help you meet business contacts, acquire leadership experience, and develop other skills. But some experts say it's not worth the risk if your company doesn't value outside activities.

However, volunteering is an essential part of the lives of most executives in the United States. They find it personally satisfying, and it gives them the opportunity to practice business skills. In other words, they extend their leadership beyond their companies to the larger problems of the world.

Executives say they volunteer because they believe in it and they have a sense of community responsibility. To get the most out of volunteer work, executives say you should choose activities wisely, based on your interests, goals, competencies, and situations. Don't overload yourself; turn down some invitations, perhaps passing them along to a colleague. Apply to this work your same business standards for rigorous, objective decision making. And manage your activities as a portfolio; this means occasionally adding new ones, divesting old ones, and devoting more time and energy to some than to others, in order to achieve the right balance for your goals.

What do you think? How should you make decisions about your own volunteer activities?

Sources: T. D. Schellhardt, "Fewer Good Deeds Go Unpunished in 90s Corporate Climate," *The Wall Street Journal,* October 6, 1993, p. B1; and J. A. Ross, "Community Service: More Rewarding Than You Think," *Harvard Business Review,* July–August 1997, p. 14. ●

The political environment

The explosive growth of regulation in the late 1960s and early 1970s imposed a vast body of laws and public policy on organizations. Through this regulation, government decision makers exerted increasing control over key areas of managerial decision making—areas where managers often did not want to lose control. While managers use public policy to define their social responsibilities, they also may recognize the need to influence the laws and regulations that constitute public policy. Therefore, organizations attempt to influence the political environment to achieve two principal goals within their ethical structures: competitive advantage and corporate legitimacy.

Competitive advantage

In many cases, the corporate community sees government as an adversary. However, many progressive organizations realize that government may be the source of competitive advantages for an individual company or an entire industry.[59] For example, public policy may prevent or limit entry into an industry by new foreign or domestic competitors. Government may subsidize failing companies or provide tax breaks to some. Federal patents may be used to protect innovative products or production process technologies. Legislation may be passed to support industry prices, thereby guaranteeing profits or survival. Finally, regulation may favor competitors in one region of the country.

Specific examples of public policy beneficial to business are numerous. Government loan guarantees saved Chrysler Corporation from probable bankruptcy and gave it the opportunity to become a viable, profitable corporation. The utility industry entered into the nuclear power business only after the government provided insurance through the Price-Anderson Act. Since the Great Depression, farmers have been the beneficiaries of government aid and subsidies. Several airlines received help from the government or employed various regulatory and legal maneuvers to promote their survival.

Corporate legitimacy

corporate legitimacy A motive for organizational involvement in the public policy process. The assumption is that organizations are legitimate to the extent that their goals, purposes, and methods are consistent with those of society.

The second motive for corporate involvement in the public process is to increase **corporate legitimacy.**[60] Corporations are legitimate to the extent that their goals, purposes, and methods are consistent with those of society. Because the broader social system is the source of corporate support and allows organizations to pursue their goals, corporations must be sensitive to the expectations and values society establishes. These expectations, in the form of social norms, laws, and regulations, act as controls on the company's behavior. Gross or frequent violations of these expectations will cause the corporation to lose its support and will limit its discretion.

domain defense Activities intended to counter challenges to the organization's legitimacy.

Corporations sometimes face threats that challenge the legitimacy of their existence or their actions. They may be criticized for their efforts to gain competitive advantage, or questions regarding their social responsibility or ethical behavior may be raised. Activity intended to counter challenges to the organization's legitimacy is called **domain defense.**[61] It is designed to strengthen the corporation's right to exist and to operate freely. Domain defense occurs when corporations, acting in their own self-interest, use socially responsible and ethical behavior to maintain and enhance their legitimacy.

From the Pages of BusinessWeek

Money and Olympic Ideals

The International Olympic Committee (IOC) has transformed a bankrupt, amateurishly managed operation into a tremendously successful global marketing machine. In 15 years, the Olympic movement's revenues have multiplied fortyfold, to an annual average of about $1 billion.

Critics say the raw pursuit of money is a betrayal of the Olympic ideal of amateur athletics for its own sake. Defenders say the powerful new Olympic "brand" has saved the Games. IOC President Juan Antonio Samaranch says in response to the criticism, "Society changes. So does sport and the Olympic movement. We have adapted our organization to a new reality."

Samaranch is a highly controversial leader. The president hand-picks most of the 112 IOC members, and most are named for life. Many are long-time communists, and many have close links to deposed or current dictators. Samaranch was a faithful supporter of Spanish dictator Francisco Franco. States one author, "It's an authoritarian club run by an old Francoist who doesn't believe democracy works." Samaranch says he must include officials named by governments even if he doesn't like their politics. He is proud of the record number of countries that now participate, and the unity he has forged.

Critics also allege bribery of committee members by host cities, and drug abuse cover-ups. The IOC says it does more about drugs than other sports organizations.

Samaranch is said to run the IOC in an authoritarian fashion, pushing relentlessly for greater control and even more money. The IOC releases no official financial statements. It says it will open its books in the near future, but doesn't say when.

The IOC has implemented its own reforms, but the bad news continues with drug scandals in Sydney and a federal bribery case pending in Salt Lake City. Nonetheless, corporate sponsors keep signing on, the TV money grows, and the 2008 summer games in Beijing represent a huge marketing opportunity. Critics say there still is no transparency, the IOC continues to try to fool the world, and Congress may become more actively involved. The Olympic commitment to integrity remains under a dark cloud of suspicion.

Business Week concluded that the IOC is an increasingly powerful multinational "accountable only to itself. That makes it like no other multinational on the planet."

Discussion Questions

1. Discuss the International Olympic Committee, using concepts in this chapter.

2. Based on current news and your own research, how is the IOC operating now, and what are the current controversies and opinions?

Source: W. Echikson, "Making the Games Run On Time," *Business Week,* February 9, 1998, pp. 58–59; J. Weiner, "The Olympics: Still Poised on a Pedestal," *Business Week,* October 16, 2000, p. 109; and "W. Echikson with W. C. Symonds and S. Brull, "The Olympics: Not Exactly World-class House Cleaning," *Business Week,* December 13, 2000, pp. 138–40. ●

Strategies for influencing the political environment

public affairs department A department that monitors key events and trends in the organization's political and social environments, analyzes their effects on the organization, recommends organizational responses, and implements political strategies.

Managers have an array of strategic options for dealing with the political environment. Many corporations have specialized units for managing these activities. The **public affairs department** of a corporation monitors key events and trends in the political and social environment, analyzes their effects on the organization, recommends the appropriate corporate responses, and implements political strategies. A successful public affairs program enhances an organization's credibility, facilitates a timely and appropriate response to issues, and has a positive financial impact (although this impact may be difficult to measure accurately).[62]

Depending on the needs of an industry or of an individual campaign, the public affairs department performs a variety of important activities.[63]

- *Issues management.* It identifies important social, political, economic, and technological developments and integrates this information into strategic planning.
- *Government relations (federal, state, and local).* It monitors legislative and regulatory developments, assesses their implications, and tries to affect the course of public policy.
- *Public relations.* It communicates information about the organization to the media.
- *International relations.* It promotes company interests in foreign capitals and in international forums.
- *Investor and stockholder relations.* It is often in charge of company communications with investors, brokerage houses, and other financial institutions.
- *Corporate contributions.* It frequently coordinates company contributions to the community.
- *Institutional advertising.* To heighten public awareness, it often engages in image building through nonproduct advertising.

Some specific strategies and vehicles used for managing the political environment are lobbying, PACs, corporate constituency programs, coalition building, stonewalling, and strategic retreat.[64]

Lobbying

Lobbying is the most traditional form of influencing the political environment. Lobbying involves efforts by political professionals or company executives to establish communication channels with regulatory bodies, legislators, and their staffs. It is designed to monitor legislation, provide issues papers and other information on the anticipated effects of proposed legislation, convey the company's sentiments on legislative issues to elected officials and their staffs, and attempt to influence the decisions of legislators and key advisers.

Political action committees (PACs)

political action committees (PACs) Political action groups that represent an organization and make donations to candidates for political office.

In recent years, many business have created corporate **political action committees (PACs).** PACs make donations to candidates for political office. Under reforms in federal election laws passed after the Watergate scandal, companies are allowed to ask their employees and shareholders for contributions for political candidates, subject to a set of limitations.

The PAC system has received much criticism. Some opponents complain that it gives large donors an unfair advantage both in an election and when their interests are brought before the elected legislator. Others claim PAC contributions are not an effective or efficient way for corporations to influence the legislative process. Because political candidates often accept contributions from many diverse and even opposing interests, the impact of any specific contribution is offset by other donations. As a result, the PAC contribution may be "protection money"—a corporation may donate funds to a candidate to ensure that it does not start at a disadvantage during the legislative process. Because of such criticisms, major reforms are now being discussed.

Corporate constituency programs

corporate constituency programs Organizational efforts to identify, educate, and motivate individuals to take political action that could benefit the organization.

In the 1980s, many organizations started political action programs called **corporate constituency programs.** Constituency programs encourage interested stakeholders to engage in grassroots political activity on behalf of the corporation.[65] These actions may include writing a letter to a congressperson or local politician, signing a petition, marching in a demonstration, or expressing an opinion on a television or radio talk show. Some companies spend a great amount of time and money identifying interested stakeholders and educating them on the issues.

Of the common political strategies, a comprehensive corporate constituency program probably requires the greatest commitment of organizational resources. However, many experts believe this strategy may have the most significant long-term potential to influence the political environment. Instead of providing money to politicians, constituency programs may deliver something even more valuable to elected officials: votes!

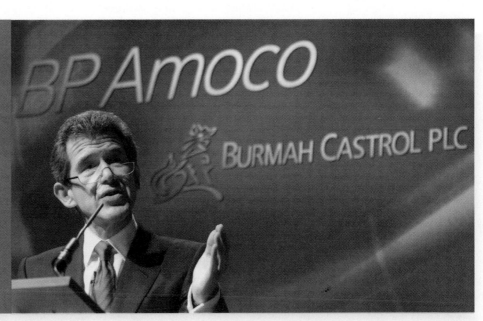

John Brown, CEO of BP Amoco, has led the oil industry to adopt more pro-environmental attitudes. *[Reuters NewMedia/CORBIS]*

coalition building Finding other organizations or groups of voters that share political interests on a particular legislative issue.

Coalition building

Many corporations and senior executives participate in cooperative efforts to manage the political and social environment. **Coalition building** involves efforts to find other organizations or groups of voters who share interest in a particular legislative issue and attempt to influence the environment through combined effort and power.

stonewalling The use of public relations, legal action, and administrative processes to prevent or delay the introduction of legislation and regulation that may have an adverse impact on the organization.

Stonewalling

The final two political strategies—stonewalling and strategic retreat—are less opportunistic and proactive than the strategies just discussed, but they are viable options for managing the political and social environment. **Stonewalling** is the use of public relations, legal action, and administrative processes to delay legislation and regulation that may have an adverse impact on the organization. Legal suits or campaigns that improve the company's public image may help protect the organization against threat.

However, stonewalling has disadvantages. Although it may prevent certain problems, it rarely changes the conditions that led to the adverse law or regulation. The organization may constantly be in court or waging a continuous, losing battle for favorable public opinion. This strategy does not create opportunities for the company. Stonewalling often consumes considerable time and money that could be spent on activities leading to long-term positive outcomes. In fact, it often boomerangs, generating more criticism, damaging brand images and sales, and hurting the stock price.[66]

strategic retreat Efforts to adapt products and processes to changes in the political and social environments while minimizing the negative effects of those changes.

Strategic retreat

In some situations, top management and public affairs executives decide the organization will be better served by accepting legislative or regulatory changes even if the changes may hurt the company. **Strategic retreat** involves an organization's efforts to adapt its products and processes to changes in the political and social environment while minimizing the negative effects of these changes. Senior managers may realize that the new law or regulation has support in most segments of society. Political action or stonewalling to oppose the change could have more negative consequences for the company, particularly in the long term, than would adapting to the environment or implementing more proactive strategies.[67]

Global warming

Global climate change is a controversial business issue. How convincing is the evidence on global warming? ExxonMobil is one company that maintains that the global warming evidence is inconclusive. If the company can postpone regulation of carbon dioxide emissions, it can protect short-term asset values. It may even be able to convince the public that global warming is a smaller threat than government regulation. But the number of companies with this perspective is dwindling. Most (not all) scientists fear serious consequences of global warming. And consider this: According to business leaders at the World Economic Forum in Davos, Switzerland, global warming is the most pressing issue facing the business world today.

Shifts in global climate present risks and also business opportunity. Managers who care will work to influence regulations, make efforts to reduce the problems associated with climate change, and inform the public about those efforts.

Many industries and companies are directly affected by the weather; planning now for the potential consequences of climate change is essential. For example, insurance companies need to adapt their predictive models regarding financial losses. Realtors need to learn flood patterns. The tourism industry should anticipate how new storm patterns will change demand for different vacation locations, including depressed demands for affected tropical areas and ski resorts. Agricultural companies may need to abandon investments in regions that become too warm, and invest heavily in new areas where farming becomes more viable. Timber operations may need to spend more money on fire management.

Environmental shifts create business opportunities as well. Seed-sellers can develop crops that deliver higher yields in drier conditions. ABB and Honeywell are investing in sophisticated thermostats and other products whose value will increase as energy costs increase. Ford and GM view global warming as an opportunity to gain advantage over rivals that are less advanced technologically. Both are investing in cars that do not produce carbon dioxide (a greenhouse gas), and may be able to dominate a new market.

BP Amoco has been a real leader in working to reduce global warming. In 1997, CEO Sir John Brown became the first oilman to declare the serious possibility of global warming, and clashed with others in the industry. He pledged voluntary reductions of carbon dioxide emissions, and he has led the industry to adopt more pro-environmental altitudes on other issues, including wastewater disposal.

Sir John has other environmental concerns as well. He considers air pollution to be the industry's main environmental issue. "If you go anywhere in China or India and ask about global warming, the intelligentsia will say, 'Absolutely, I want to talk to you about that, but first could we just talk about what we could do to clean up the air around our major cities and how to get good drinking water and to make sure industry doesn't pollute our rivers?'" (p. F-87).

Sources: K. O'Neill Packard and F. Reinhardt, "What Every Executive Needs to Know about Global Warming," *Harvard Business Review*, July–August, 2000, pp. 129–35; and "A Big-oil Man Gets Religion," *Fortune*, March 6, 2000, pp. F87–F89. ●

The natural environment

Most large corporations developed in an era of abundant raw materials, cheap energy, and unconstrained waste disposal.[68] Many of the technologies developed during this era are contributing to the destruction of ecological ecosystems. James Post, professor of management and public policy at Boston University, states, "[E]nvironmental issues will be . . . a force of such power as to literally transform the way managers manage their businesses and think about the relationship of the firm to its internal and external stakeholders."[69]

The range of environmental issues is broad, and the impact huge. Effectively managing with the environment in mind requires attention to efficiency, effectiveness, and long-term goals. Environmental management must consider a mix of technical, ethical, social, and competitive issues.[70]

A McKinsey survey found that 92 percent of CEOs and board members stated the environment should be one of the top three management priorities; 85 percent said one of their major goals should be integrating environment into strategy, but only 37 percent said they do so successfully.[71] Richard A. Clarke, CEO of Pacific Gas and Electric Company, put it this way: "A strong global economy is sustained only if it integrates economic, social, and environmental well-being.[72]

Business used to look at environmental issues as a no-win situation: You either help the environment and hurt your business, or help your business only at a cost to the environment. Fortunately, things have changed. "When Americans first demanded a cleanup of the environment during the early 1970s, corporations threw a tantrum. Their response ran the psychological gamut from denial to hostility, defiance, obstinacy, and fear. But today, when it comes to green issues, many U.S. companies have turned from rebellious underachievers to active problem solvers."[73]

A risk society

We live in a risk society. That is, the creation and distribution of wealth generate byproducts that can cause injury, loss, or danger to people and the environment. The fundamental sources of risk in modern society are the excessive production of hazards and ecologically unsustainable consumption of natural resources.[74] Risk has proliferated through population explosion, industrial pollution, and environmental degradation.[75]

Industrial pollution risks include air pollution, smog, global warming, ozone depletion, acid rain, toxic waste sites, nuclear hazards, obsolete weapons arsenals, industrial accidents, and hazardous products. Over 30,000 uncontrolled toxic waste sites have been documented in the United States alone, and the number is increasing by perhaps 2,500 per year. The situation is far worse in other parts of the world. The pattern, for toxic waste and many other risks, is one of accumulating risks and inadequate remedies. The institutions that create environmental and technological risk (corporations and government agencies) also are in charge of controlling and managing the risks.[76]

Ecocentric management

ecocentric management
has as its goal the creation of
sustainable economic development and improvement of quality of life worldwide for all
organizational stakeholders.

Ecocentric management has as its goal the creation of sustainable economic development and improvement of quality of life worldwide for all organizational stakeholders.[77] Management decisions seek to minimize negative environmental impact through all aspects of the organization. Ecocentric management encourages low energy use, smaller resource quantities, environmentally appropriate production technologies, and products with ecofriendly packaging and recyclable materials. It minimizes waste and pollution and tries to renew natural resources.[78] You can read more specifics about this approach in Appendix B at the end of this chapter.

**design for environment
(DFE)** A tool for creating
products that are easy to
recover, reuse, or recycle.

With ecocentric management, each business function operates with the ecology in mind. An important example is **design for environment (DFE),** a tool for creating products that are easier to recover, reuse, or recycle. All environmental effects of a product are examined during the design phase. The analysis is cradle-to-grave: full assessment of all inputs, through a detailed analysis of how customers use and dispose of it.

Profitability need not suffer, and may in time be positively affected by ecocentric philosophies and practices. Some, but not all, research has indicated a positive relationship between corporate environmental performance and profitability.[79]

In Sweden, an organization called The Natural Step works with business leaders to create operational strategies with both environmental and economic benefits.[80] The Natural Step works with scientists to create sustainability guidelines and has a board of governors that includes nine business leaders. Its methods are collaborative rather than adversarial. Swedish companies that have worked with The Natural Step include IKEA International, Scandic Hotels, and Electrolux International. At least 20 U.S.-based organizations are now working with The Natural Step. Ray Anderson, CEO of Interface, a $1 billion carpet manufacturer based in Atlanta that works with The Natural Step principles, said his realization of the importance of sustainability came "as a spear in the chest for me, and I determined almost in an instant to change my company . . . it began in the heart . . . that's where the next industrial revolution has to begin—in the hearts of people—to do the right thing" (p. 72).

The most admired company in Britain, British Petroleum, ranks No. 1 in the country in environmental responsibility. For example, BP spent about $80 million adding environmental safeguards to a facility in Scotland. CEO John Browne said, "Unlike in the U.S., there was no regulatory pressure at all to do that in Scotland, but we did it voluntarily. It's our way of saying to people, we're here to stay."[81]

Environmental agenda for the future

Business strategies and tactics for greening have up to now been primarily technical and operational, as in the pollution-prevention programs that have saved companies billions of dollars. Now, however, some executives are realizing how environmental opportunities can create revenue growth. In the past, companies were oblivious to their negative environmental impact; more recently, many have begun striving for low impact. Now, some strive for positive impact, and to sell solutions to the world's problems.

Environmental problems are traced to explosive population growth and rapid economic development. These issues are beyond the ability and mandate of a single company to solve. But corporations are the only organizations with the resources, technology, and global power to help create a sustainable world.

Individual companies do not need to act alone. Webs of companies with a common ecological vision can combine their efforts into high-leverage, impactful action.[82] In Kalundborg, Denmark, such a collaborative alliance exists among an electric power generating plant, an oil refiner, a biotech production plant, a plasterboard factory, cement producers, heating utilities, a sulfuric acid producer, and local agriculture and horticulture. Chemicals, energy (for both heating and cooling), water, and organic materials flow among companies. Resources are conserved, "waste" materials generate revenues, and water, air, and ground pollution all are reduced.

Companies not only have the *ability* to solve environmental problems; they are coming to see and acquire the *motivation* as well. Many industries are now turning their attention to pursuing what some see as one of the biggest opportunities in the history of commerce.[83]

Key terms

Summary of learning objectives

Now that you have studied Chapter 5, you should know:

How different ethical perspectives guide decision making.

The purpose of ethics is to identify the rules that govern human behavior and the "goods" that are worth seeking. Ethical decisions are guided by the individual's values, or principles of conduct such as honesty, fairness, integrity, respect for others, and responsible citizenship. Different ethical systems include universalism; teleology, including egoism and utilitarianism; deontology; relativism; and

virtue ethics. These philosophical systems, as practiced by different individuals according to their level of cognitive moral development and other factors, underlie the ethical stances of individuals and organizations.

How companies influence the ethics environment.

Different organizations apply different ethical perspectives and standards. Ethical codes sometimes are helpful, although they must be implemented properly. Ethics programs can range from compliance-based to integrity-based. An increasing number of organizations are adopting ethics codes. Such codes address employee conduct, community and environment, shareholders, customers, suppliers and contractors, political activity, and technology.

The options you have when confronting ethical issues.

Individuals have a variety of options when they witness unethical behavior. Their choice of action will depend on both their beliefs about the action's likely outcomes and their own moral judgment. When faced with ethical dilemmas, you should define the issue clearly, identify relevant values, weigh conflicting values and choose an appropriate option, and implement your decision.

The important issues surrounding corporate social responsibility.

Corporate social responsibility is the extension of the corporate role beyond economic pursuits. It includes not only economic but also legal, ethical, and voluntary responsibilities. Advocates believe managers should consider societal and human needs in their business decisions because corporations are members of society and carry a wide range of responsibilities. Critics of corporate responsibility believe managers' first responsibility is to increase profits for the shareholders who own the corporation. The two perspectives are potentially reconcilable. Whereas corporate social responsibility (CSR1) refers to principles, philosophies, and beliefs surrounding these issues, corporate social responsiveness (CSR2) is the processes companies actually use and the actions they take.

How the political and social environment affects your firm's competitive position and legitimacy.

Corporations have two goals within their ethical structures: competitive advantage and corporate legitimacy. Progressive organizations realize that the government can be an ally and a source of competitive advantage rather than just an adversary. Corporate legitimacy comes from goals, purposes, and methods that are consistent with those of society. Thus, organizations must be sensitive to the expectations and values of society.

The strategies corporations use to manage the political and social environment.

The public affairs department monitors the political and social environment, analyzes its impact on the organization, and implements political strategies. Strategies include lobbying, political action committees, corporate constituency programs, coalition building, stonewalling, and strategic retreat. Generally, strategies that adapt to or change the environment are most effective in the long run.

The role of managers in our natural environment.

Organizations have contributed risk to society and have some responsibility for reducing risk to the environment. They also have the capability to help solve environmental problems. Ecocentric management attempts to minimize negative environmental impact, create sustainable economic development, and improve the quality of life worldwide. Some companies now are moving beyond pollution prevention programs and zero-impact efforts to interorganizational alliances and strategic initiatives that pursue positive opportunities and revenue growth.

Discussion questions

1. Assess the possible explanations for people's cynicism toward business outlined in Setting the Stage. Do you agree that people are as negative as the *Business Week*/Harris Poll survey suggests? Support your arguments.

2. Consider the various ethical systems described early in the chapter. Identify concrete examples from your own past decisions or the decisions of others you have seen or read about.

3. Choose one or more topics from Table 5.1 and discuss the ethical issues surrounding them.

4. What would you do in each of the scenarios described in Table 5.2, "Ethical Decision Making in the International Context"?

5. Identify and discuss illegal, unethical, and socially responsible business actions in the current news.

6. Does your school have a code of ethics? If so, what does it say? Is it effective? Why or why not?

7. You have a job you like at which you work 40 to 45 hours per week. How much off-the-job volunteer work would you do? What kinds of volunteer work? How will you react if your boss makes it clear he or she wants you to cut back on the outside activities and devote more hours to your job?

8. What are the arguments for and against the concept of corporate social responsibility? Where do you stand, and why? Give your opinions, specifically, with respect to the text discussions of American cigarettes and the International Olympic Committee.

9. How can the political and social environment both constrain and help the corporation in its pursuit of competitive advantage? Give examples.

10. Under what conditions might stonewalling and strategic retreat be the most appropriate political strategies? Have you seen these tactics work?

11. A company in England slaughters 70,000 baby ostrich chicks each year for their meat. It told a teen magazine that it would stop if it received enough complaints. Analyze this policy, practice, and public statement using the concepts discussed in the chapter.

12. A Nike ad in the U.S. magazine *Seventeen* shows a picture of a girl, aged perhaps 8 or 9. The ad reads,

> If you let me play. . .
>
> I will like myself more.
>
> I will have more self-confidence.
>
> I will suffer less depression.
>
> I will be 60% less likely to get breast cancer.
>
> I will be more likely to leave a man who beats me.
>
> I will be less likely to get pregnant before I want to.
>
> I will learn what it means to be strong.
>
> If you let me play sports.

Assess this ad in terms of chapter concepts surrounding ethics and social responsibility. What questions would you ask in doing this analysis?

Concluding Case

Nike controversies

"A company that ignores its social responsibility is playing with fire," states one critic of Nike. Another condemns Nike for glorifying violence and bad taste, and for doing "nothing to promote values, especially among impressionable youngsters." International soccer barons fume that Nike is infecting futbol with the American disease of money-will-get-you-everything. Human rights groups accuse Nike contractors of operating their factories like prison camps, hiring 13-year-old children and treating workers "little better than slaves." Nike denies such charges, but also is changing its ways.

Nike has always prided itself on its radical, rebellious, antiestablishment image. Its brashness has paid off big-time in the United States. But Nike believes that its future lies in the international arena. The company wants to generate more than half of its revenues overseas. But as its marketing efforts expand into the international arena, many of the company's decisions are decried as irresponsible.

For example, a Nike ad in *Soccer America* magazine crowed, "Europe, Asia, and Latin America: Barricade your stadiums. Hide your trophies. Invest in some deodorant. As Asia and Latin America have been crushed, so shall Europe . . . the world has been warned." The deodorant line did not amuse, and Nike was seen by many as the ugly American trashing hallowed traditions.

A TV commercial featured a Manchester United player explaining how spitting at a fan and insulting a coach won him a Nike contract. A Nike advertising campaign at the Atlanta Olympic Games employed the slogan, "You don't win silver, you lose gold." Olympic committees from several countries were incensed; The slogan was said to denigrate the Olympic spirit of competition, and belittled all the athletes who failed to win gold.

Several years ago it was reported that in Vietnam, Nike paid its workers a daily wage less than the cost of three meals of rice, vegetables, and tofu. American businessman Thuyen Nguyen interviewed 35 Vietnamese workers and concluded that 32 had lost weight, and that they were subjected to humiliations including having stiffly-enforced limits of two drinks of water and one bathroom break in an eight-hour shift; being hit over the head for poor workmanship; being forced to kneel with their hands in the air for up to 25 minutes; having their mouths taped for talking; and being "sun-dried"—forced to stand in the hot sun for lengthy periods writing their mistakes over and over. Nike was criticized in *Doonesbury* for

Nike has designs on untapped market share in the international arena, but must overcome controversies such as the accusation by human rights groups that their factories are like prison camps.
[Reuters/Keith B. Richburg/Archive Photos]

the factory conditions in Vietnam, although even Nike critics concede that Nike is not the only, or the worst, corporate offender.

Many people would consider the Vietnam factory conditions as highly unethical. But in a *Fortune* article titled "The Case for Sweatshops," David R. Henderson of the Hoover Institution and the Naval Postgraduate School argues that critics must not lose sight of what happens when low-wage child laborers lose their jobs. "They are worse off," Henderson writes. "You don't make someone better off by taking away the best of their bad options . . . sweatshops, in short, are a path from poverty to greater wealth." (p. 22)

People like Mao Genhe agree—they believe that they and their families are much better off since Nike came to China. Mr. Genhe earns $150 a month working in a factory that supplies makers of Nike and Adidas shoes. He sends most of it to his family, bought a new plow for his parents' rice fields, built his parents a new house (adding a 21-inch color TV), and is saving money to open a store with his wife. Thanks primarily to foreign investment and exports, urban per capita income in China has grown tenfold since 1978. Much of the income growth has come from thousands of shoe, garment, toy, and electronics factories.

In late 1997, Nike announced at its shareholder meeting that it would sever ties with four Indonesian factories for violating labor standards. Such violations are exceptions, though, said the chairman. But in mid-1998, Nike chairman Phil Knight publicly acknowledged how much damage the criticism had done to his company's image, and announced that it would raise the minimum wage for its workers and impose American air quality standards on its overseas plants.

Nike now states that it wants consumers to hold it accountable for the conditions in the factories where Nike products are made. Nike invited 16 students to monitor 32 of its partner factories,

and published their uncensored findings on its Web site, www.nikebiz.com. It is releasing other auditing reports as well. Others in the industry have refused to make such audits public, and Nike's announcement that it was doing so was both a coup for anti-sweatshop activists and probably a spur to other companies in the industry to do the same.

Questions

1. Nike's success in the United States is inarguable. What about its strategies and tactics? What do you think of the actions described above? Are they just business decisions that generated some criticism? Or are they also irresponsible, unethical?

2. If some of Nike's decisions are unethical, which are the most unethical, and which least? How did you reach these judgments?

3. What do you think of the Nike response to the criticism?

4. What else, if anything, should Nike do about the issues raised in the case?

Sources: "Nike Sanctions 3 Firms for Labor Abuses," *International Herald Tribune,* September 24, 1997, p. 19; B. Herbert, "Making Billions on the Backs of Hungry Women," *International Herald Tribune,* April 1, 1997, p. 9; R. Thurow, "In Global Push, Nike Finds Its Brash Ways Don't Always Pay Off," *The Wall Street Journal,* May 6, 1997, pp. 1, 6; D. R. Henderson, "The Case for Sweatshops," *Fortune,* October 28, 1996, pp. 20, 22; E. J. Dionne, Jr. "Swoosh! Shaming Net Results," *International Herald Tribune,* May 15, 1998, p. 11; A. Bernstein, "Too Much Corporate Power?" *Business Week,* September 11, 2000, pp. 145–58; L. Lee and A. Bernstein, "Commentary: Who Says Student Protests Don't Matter?" *Business Week,* June 12, 2000, pp. 94–96; and M. L. Clifford and P. Engardio with E. Malkin, D. Roberts, and W. Echikson, "Up the Ladder, Global Trade: Can All Nations Benefit?" *Business Week,* November 6, 2000, pp. 78–84.

Experiential Exercises
5.1 Measuring your ethical work behavior

Objectives

1. To explore a range of ethically perplexing situations.
2. To understand your own ethical attitudes.

Instructions

Make decisions in the situations described in the Ethical Behavior Worksheet. You will not have all the background information on each situation, and, instead, you should

make whatever assumptions you feel you would make if you were actually confronted with the decision choices described. Select the decision choice that most closely represents the decision you feel you would make personally. You should choose decision options even though you can envision other creative solutions that were not included in the exercise.

Ethical behavior worksheet

Situation 1. You are taking a very difficult chemistry course, which you must pass to maintain your scholarship and to avoid damaging your application for graduate school. Chemistry is not your strong suit, and, because of a just-below-failing average in the course, you will have to receive a grade of 90 or better on the final exam, which is two days away. A janitor, who is aware of your plight, informs you that he has found the master stencil for the chemistry final in a trash barrel and saved it. He will make it available to you for a price, which is high, but which you could afford. What would you do?

_____ (a) I would tell the janitor thanks, but no thanks.

_____ (b) I would report the janitor to the proper officials.

_____ (c) I would buy the exam and keep it to myself.

_____ (d) I would not buy the exam myself, but I would let some of my friends, who are also flunking the course, know that it is available.

Situation 2. You have been working on some financial projections manually for two days now. It seems that each time you think you have them completed your boss shows up with a new assumption or another "what-if" question. If you only had a copy of a spreadsheet software program for your personal computer, you could plug in the new assumptions and revise the estimates with ease. Then, a colleague offers to let you make a copy of some software that is copyrighted. What would you do?

_____ (a) I would accept my friend's generous offer and make a copy of the software.

_____ (b) I would decline to copy it and plug away manually on the numbers.

_____ (c) I would decide to go buy a copy of the software myself, for $300, and hope I would be reimbursed by the company in a month or two.

_____ (d) I would request another extension on an already overdue project date.

Situation 3. Your small manufacturing company is in serious financial difficulty. A large order of your products is ready to be delivered to a key customer when you discover that the product is simply not right. It will not meet all performance specifications, will cause problems for your customer, and will require rework in the field; but this, you know, will not become evident until after the customer has received and paid for the order. If you do not ship the order and receive the payment as expected, your business may be forced into

bankruptcy. And if you delay the shipment or inform the customer of these problems, you may lose the order and also go bankrupt. What would you do?

_____ (a) I would not ship the order and place my firm in voluntary bankruptcy.

_____ (b) I would inform the customer and declare voluntary bankruptcy.

_____ (c) I would ship the order and inform the customer, after I received payment.

_____ (d) I would ship the order and not inform the customer.

Situation 4. You are the cofounder and president of a new venture, manufacturing products for the recreational market. Five months after launching the business, one of your suppliers informs you it can no longer supply you with a critical raw material since you are not a large-quantity user. Without the raw material, the business cannot continue. What would you do?

_____ (a) I would grossly overstate my requirements to another supplier to make the supplier think I am a much larger potential customer in order to secure the raw material from that supplier, even though this would mean the supplier will no longer be able to supply another, non-competing small manufacturer who may thus be forced out of business.

_____ (b) I would steal raw material from another firm (noncompeting) where I am aware of a sizable stockpile.

_____ (c) I would pay off the supplier, since I have reason to believe that the supplier could be "persuaded" to meet my needs with a sizable "under the table" payoff that my company could afford.

_____ (d) I would declare voluntary bankruptcy.

Situation 5. You are on a marketing trip for your new venture for the purpose of calling on the purchasing agent of a major prospective client. Your company is manufacturing an electronic system that you hope the purchasing agent will buy. During the course of your conversation, you notice on the cluttered desk of the purchasing agent several copies of a cost proposal for a system from one of your direct competitors. This purchasing agent has previously reported mislaying several of your own company's proposals and has asked for additional copies. The purchasing agent leaves the room momentarily to get you a cup of coffee, leaving you alone with your competitor's proposals less than an arm's length away. What would you do?

_____ (a) I would do nothing but await the man's return.

_____ (b) I would sneak a quick peek at the proposal, looking for bottom-line numbers.

_____ (c) I would put the copy of the proposal in my briefcase.

_____ (d) I would wait until the man returns and ask his permission to see the copy.

Source: Jeffrey A. Timmons, *New Venture Creation,* 3rd ed. (Burr Ridge, IL: Richard D. Irwin, 1994), pp. 285–86. ●

5.2 Social responsibility

Objectives

1. To have a look at a socially responsible undertaking of a firm.
2. To examine the pros and cons of firms taking on the role of trying to solve social ills.

Instructions

There are many arguments for and against firms taking a role in trying to alleviate community or social ills. Find an example of a business acting in a manner that is clearly socially responsible, such as providing job training programs for the unemployed or providing financial support for urban renewal. You may be able to find your own example of this locally, or in articles in business periodicals.

Ethical behavior worksheet

1. Briefly describe the firm and its program(s).

_____

_____

_____

_____

_____

2. What is the rationale the firm uses to support this program? _____

_____

_____

_____

_____

3. What is the response from those affected by the program? _____

_____

_____

_____

4. What is the response, if any, from those who oppose the program? _____

_____

_____

_____

_____

5. Do you think the company is benefiting from the program to the extent of the program's cost?

_____

_____

_____

_____

_____

Source: R. R. McGrath Jr., *Exercises in Management Fundamentals* (Englewood Cliffs, NJ: Prentice Hall, 1985), p. 192. Reprinted by permission of Prentice Hall, Inc. ●

5.3 Strategy for dealing with toxic waste in the river

Objectives

1. To examine your attitude toward managing in our natural environment.
2. To explore new strategies for dealing with a natural-environment challenge.

Instructions

1. Read the following scenario about discovery of a toxic effluent by a firm's chemist.
2. You are the manager and must decide how to respond to the discovery of the unsuspected toxic by-product.

Discovery of a toxic by-product

You are the plant manager of a small chemical plant north of St. Louis. For years your firm dumped its untreated effluents into the Mississippi as a matter of everyday business. Recently, Environmental Protection Agency standards have required you to install a treatment system to minimize the level of several specific contaminants. Your firm has abided by the ruling; only treated sewage is being dumped into the river. However, you have just received a report from your head chemist, who has discovered that a by-product of a new chemical being produced by the firm is highly toxic. Moreover, the present filtration system utterly fails to filter out the toxic substance. It is all headed downstream toward St. Louis.

Strategy worksheet

Now that you have this report, what do you plan to do? Consider your alternatives and develop a strategy. If part of your strategy is to get in touch with your boss at company headquarters in Chicago, state what recommendation you intend to make.

_____

_____

_____

_____

_____

_____

_____

_____

_____

_____

_____

_____

_____

Source: Excerpted from Robert B. Carson, _Enterprise: An Introduction to Business_ (Orlando, FL: Harcourt Brace, 1985), p. 51. Copyright © 1985 by Harcourt Brace and Company. Reprinted by permission of the publisher. ●

5.4 An environmental protection code of ethics

Objectives

1. To further clarify the role business plays in environmental pollution.
2. To identify codes of ethics that businesses adopt to minimize the potential adverse impact of their activities on the environment.

Instructions

1. Your instructor will divide the class into small groups and assign each group one or more environmental problems to investigate.

2. For each environmental problem assigned, the groups will complete the Environmental Code of Ethics Worksheet by investigating the things business does that affect the environment and developing "code of ethics" statements by which businesses can deal with the problems in a positive, socially responsible manner.
3. After the class reconvenes, group spokespersons present group findings.
4. The class may proceed to the development of an overall Environmental Code of Ethics for businesses.

The environmental code of ethics worksheet

In the space provided, identify business activities that contribute to the environmental problem(s) assigned by your instructor and develop code of ethics statements that can be adopted to deal with the problem(s).

Environmental Pollution Problem: _____

Business activity	Corresponding code of ethics statement

The 411 on . . .

The Caux Round Table Business Principles of Ethics

Principle 1. the responsibilities of businesses: beyond shareholders toward stakeholders

The value of a business to society is the wealth and employment it creates and the marketable products and services it provides to consumers at a reasonable price commensurate with quality. To create such value, a business must maintain its own economic health and viability, but survival is not a sufficient goal.

Businesses have a role to play in improving the lives of all their customers, employees, and shareholders by sharing with them the wealth they have created. Suppliers and competitors as well should expect businesses to honor their obligations in a spirit of honesty and fairness. As responsible citizens of the local, national, regional, and global communities in which they operate, businesses share a part in shaping the future of those communities.

Principle 2. the economic and social impact of business: toward innovation, justice, and world community

Businesses established in foreign countries to develop, produce, or sell should also contribute to the social advancement of those countries by creating productive employment and helping to raise the purchasing power of their citizens. Businesses also should contribute to human rights, education, welfare, and vitalization of the countries in which they operate.

Businesses should contribute to economic and social development not only in the countries in which they operate, but also in the world community at large, through effective and prudent use of resources, free and fair competition, and emphasis upon innovation in technology, production, methods, marketing, and communications.

Principle 3. business behavior: beyond the letter of law toward a spirit of trust

While accepting the legitimacy of trade secrets, businesses should recognize that sincerity, candor, truthfulness, the keeping of promises, and transparency contribute not only to their own credibility and stability but also to the smoothness and efficiency of business transactions, particularly on the international level.

Principle 4. respect for rules

To avoid trade friction and to promote freer trade, equal conditions for competition, and fair and equitable treatment for all participants, businesses should respect international and domestic rules. In addition, they should recognize that some behavior, although legal, may still have adverse consequences.

Principle 5. support for multilateral trade

Businesses should support the multilateral trade systems of GATT/World Trade Organization and similar international agreements. They should cooperate in efforts to promote the progressive and judicious liberalization of trade, and to relax those domestic measures that unreasonably hinder global commerce, while giving due respect to national policy objectives.

Principle 6. respect for the environment

A business should protect and, where possible, improve the environment, promote sustainable development, and prevent the wasteful use of natural resources.

Principle 7. avoidance of illicit operations

A business should not participate in or condone bribery, money laundering, or other corrupt practices; indeed, it should seek cooperation with others to eliminate them. It should not trade in arms or other materials used for terrorist activities, drug traffic, or other organized crime.

Principle 8. customers

We believe in treating all customers with dignity, irrespective of whether they purchase our products and services directly from us or otherwise acquire them in the market. We therefore have a responsibility to:
- provide our customers with the highest quality products and services consistent with their requirements;
- treat our customers fairly in all respects of our business transactions, including a high level of service and remedies for their dissatisfaction;
- make every effort to ensure that the health and safety of our customers, as well as the quality of their environment, will be sustained or enhanced by our products and services;
- assure respect for human dignity in products offered, marketing, and advertising; and respect the integrity of the culture of our customers.

Principle 9. employees

We believe in the dignity of every employee and in taking employee interests seriously. We therefore have a responsibility to:
- provide jobs and compensation that improve worker's living conditions;
- provide work conditions that respect each employee's health and dignity;
- be honest in communications with employees and open in

173

sharing information, limited only by legal and competitive restraint;

- listen to and, where possible, act on employee suggestions, ideas, requests, and complaints;
- engage in good faith negotiations when conflict arises;
- avoid discriminatory practices and guarantee equal treatment and opportunity in areas such as gender, age, race, and religion;
- promote in the business itself the employment of differently abled people in places of work where they can be genuinely useful;
- protect employees from avoidable injury and illness in the workplace;
- encourage and assist employees in developing relevant and transferable skills and knowledge; and
- be sensitive to serious unemployment problems frequently associated with business decisions, and work with the government, employee groups, other agencies and each other in addressing these dislocations.

Principle 10. owners/investors

We believe in honoring the trust our investors place in us. We therefore have a responsibility to:

- apply professional and diligent management in order to secure a fair and competitive return on our owners' investment;
- disclose relevant information to owners/investors subject only to legal requirements and competitive constraints;
- conserve, protect, and increase the owners/investors' assets; and
- respect owners/investors' requests, suggestions, complaints, and formal resolutions.

Principle 11. suppliers

Our relationship with suppliers and subcontractors must be based on mutual respect. We therefore have a responsibility to:

- seek fairness and truthfulness in all of our activities, including pricing, licensing, and rights to sell;
- ensure that business activities are free from coercion and unnecessary litigation;
- foster long-term stability in the supplier relationship in return for value, quality, competitiveness, and liability;
- share information with suppliers and integrate them into our planning processes;
- pay suppliers on time and in accordance with agreed terms of trade;

- seek, encourage, and prefer suppliers and subcontractors whose employment practices respect human dignity.

Principle 12. competitors

We believe that fair economic competition is one of the basic requirements for increasing the wealth of the nations and, ultimately, for making possible the just distribution of goods and services. We therefore have a responsibility to:

- foster open markets for trade and investments;
- promote competitive behavior that is socially and environmentally beneficial and demonstrates mutual respect among competitors;
- refrain from either seeking or participating in questionable payments of favors to secure competitive advantages;
- respect both tangible and intellectual property rights; and
- refuse to acquire commercial information by dishonest or unethical means, such as industrial espionage.

Principle 13. communities

We believe that as global corporate citizens, we can contribute to such forces of reform and human rights as are at work in the communities in which we operate. We therefore have a responsibility in those communities to:

- respect human rights and democratic institutions, and promote them wherever practicable;
- recognize government's legitimate obligation to the society at large and support public policies and practices that promote human development through harmonious relations between business and other segments;
- collaborate with those forces in the community dedicated to raising standards of health, education, workplace safety, and economic well-being;
- promote and stimulate sustainable development and play a leading role in preserving and enhancing the physical environment and conserving the earth's resources;
- support peace, security, diversity, and social integration;
- respect the integrity of local cultures; and
- be a good corporate citizen through charitable donations, educational and cultural contributions, and employee participation in community and civic affairs.

Source: Caux Round Table in Switzerland, "Principles for Business," special advertising supplement contributed as a public service by Canon, *Business Ethics,* May–June 1995, p. 35. ●

The 411 on . . .

Managing in our natural environment

Business and the Environment: Conflicting Views

Some people believe everyone wins when business tackles environmental issues.[1] Others disagree.

The win-win mentality

Business used to look at environmental issues as a no-win situation: You either help the environment and hurt your business, or help your business only at a cost to the environment. Fortunately, things have changed. As stated in the chapter, "When Americans first demanded a cleanup of the environment during the early 1970s, corporations threw a tantrum. Their response ran the psychological gamut from denial to hostility, defiance, obstinacy, and fear. But today, when it comes to green issues, many U.S. companies have turned from rebellious underachievers to active problem solvers."[2]

The Earth Summit in Rio in 1992 helped increase awareness of environmental issues. This led to the Kyoto Protocol, an international effort to control global warming that included an unsuccessful meeting in the Hague in November 2000.[3] "There has been an evolution of most groups—whether industry, governments, or nongovernmental organizations—toward a recognition that everyone plays a part in reaching a solution."[4]

Being "green" is potentially a catalyst for innovation, new market opportunities, and wealth creation. Advocates believe that this is truly a win-win situation; actions can be taken that benefit both business and the environment. For example, Procter & Gamble in a span of five years reduced disposable wastes by over 50 percent while increasing sales by 25 percent.[5] Only win-win companies will survive; they will come out ahead of those companies that have an us-versus-them, we-can't-afford-to-protect-the-environment mentality. Table 5.B.1 gives just a few examples of things U.S. corporations are doing to help solve environmental problems.

Is the easy part over?[6] Companies have found a lot of easy-to-harvest, "low-hanging fruit"—that is, overly costly practices that were made environmentally friendlier and that saved money at the same time. Many big companies have made these easy changes, and reaped benefits from them. Many small companies still have such low-hanging fruit to harvest,[7] and plenty remains to be done.

The dissenting view

The critics of environmentalism in business are vocal. Some economists maintain that not a single empirical analysis supports the "free lunch view" that spending money on environmental problems provides full payback to the firm.[8] Skepticism should continue, they say; the belief that everyone will come out a winner is naive.

What really upsets many businesspeople is the financial cost of complying with environmental regulations.[9] Consider a few examples:

- GM spent $1.3 billion to comply with California requirements that 10 percent of the cars sold there be emission-free.

table 5.B.1
What companies are doing to enhance the environment

- Interface Corporation's new Shanghai carpet factory circulates liquid through a standard pumping loop like those used in most industries. But simply by using fatter pipes and short, straight pipes instead of long and crooked pipes, it cut the power requirements by 92 percent.

- Scandic uses employee suggestions about the environment, including the recommendations of chambermaids, to educate patrons to make informed choices about reusing their towels and linens.

- Oticon, the Danish hearing-aid maker, cut paper use by 30 percent by redesigning its decision-making processes so decisions are made faster. AT&T cut paper costs by 15 percent by setting defaults on copies and printers to double-sided mode.

- Electrolux uses more environmentally friendly water-based and powder paints instead of solvent-based paints, and introduced the first refrigerators and freezers free of chloroflourocarbons.

- Many chemical and pharmaceutical companies, including Novo Nordisk and Empresas La Moderna, are exploring "green chemistry" and seeking biological substitutes for synthetic materials.

- Anheuser-Busch just saved 21 million pounds of metal a year by reducing its beer-can rims by 1/8 of an inch (without reducing its contents).

- Nissan enlisted a group of ecologists, energy experts, and science writers to brainstorm about how an environmentally responsible car company might behave. Among the ideas: to produce automobiles that snap together into electrically powered trains for long trips and then detach for the dispersion to final destinations.

Sources: C. Garfield, *Second to None: How Our Smartest Companies Put People First* (Burr Ridge, IL; Business One-Irwin, 1992); H. Bradbury and J. A. Clair, "Promoting Sustainable Organizations with Sweden's Natural Step," *Academy of Management Executive*, November 1999, pp. 63–74; A. Loving, L. Hunter Lovins, and P. Hawken, "A Road Map for Natural Capitalism," *Harvard Business Review*, May–June 1999, pp. 145–58; P. Hawken, A. Lovings, and L. Hunter Lovins, *Natural Capitalism* (Boston: Little Brown, 1999); S. L. Hart and M. B. Milstein, "Global Sustainability and the Creatine Destruction of Industries." *Sloan Management Review*, Fall 1999, 23–32

European automakers spent $7 billion to install pollution-control equipment in all new cars during a five-year period.

- At Bayer, 20 percent of manufacturing costs are for the environment. This is approximately the same amount spent for labor.
- The Clean Air Act alone was expected to cost U.S. petroleum refiners $37 billion, more than the book value of the entire industry.
- California's tough laws are a major reason why manufacturers move to Arkansas or Nevada.

In industries like chemicals and petroleum, the ability to respond to environmental regulations was once considered a threat to their very survival.[10]

Balance   A more balanced view is that business must weigh the environmental benefits of an action against value destruction. The advice here is, don't obstruct progress, but pick your environmental initiatives carefully. J. Ladd Greeno of Arthur D. Little believes that compliance and remediation efforts will protect, but not increase, shareholder value.[11] And it is shareholder value, rather than compliance, emissions, or costs, that should be the focus of objective cost/benefit analyses. Such an approach is environmentally sound but also hardheaded in a business sense, and is the one approach that is truly sustainable over the long term.

Johan Piet maintains, "Only win-win companies will survive, but that does not mean that all win-win ideas will be successful."[12] In other words, rigorous analysis is essential. Thus, Polaroid maintains continuous improvement in environmental performance, but funds only projects that meet financial objectives.

Most people understand that business has the resources and the competence to bring about constructive change, and that this creates great opportunity—if well managed—for both business and the environment.

Why Manage with the Environment in Mind?

Business is turning its full attention to environmental issues for many reasons, including legal compliance, cost effectiveness, competitive advantage, public opinion, and long-term thinking.

Legal Compliance   Table 5.B.2 shows just some of the most important U.S. environmental laws. Government regulations and liability for damages provide strong economic incentives to comply with environmental guidelines. Most industries already have made environmental protection regulation and liability an integral part of their business planning.[13] The U.S. Justice Department has handed out tough prison sentences to executives whose companies violate hazardous-waste requirements.

Many businesspeople consider the regulations to be too rigid, inflexible, and unfair. In response to this concern, regulatory reform may become more creative. The Aspen Institute Series on the Environment in the Twenty-First Century is trying to increase the cost-effectiveness of compliance measures through more flexibility in meeting standards and relying on market-based incentives. Such mechanisms, including tradable permits, pollution charges, and

table 5.B.2
Some U.S. environmental laws

Superfund [Comprehensive Environmental Response, Compensation, and Liability Act (CERCLA)]: Establishes potential liability for any person or organization responsible for creating an environmental health hazard. Individuals may be prosecuted, fined, or taxed to fund cleanup.

Clean Water Act [Federal Water Pollution Control Act]: Regulates all discharges into surface waters, and affects the construction and performance of sewer systems. The Safe Drinking Water Act similarly protects groundwaters.

Clean Air Act: Regulates the emission into the air of any substance that affects air quality, including nitrous oxides, sulfur dioxide, and carbon dioxide.

Community Response and Right-to-Know Act: Mandates that all facilities producing, transporting, storing, using, or releasing hazardous substances provide full information to local and state authorities and maintain emergency-action plans.

Federal Hazardous Substances Act: Regulates hazards to health and safety associated with consumer products. The Consumer Product Safety Commission has the right to recall hazardous products.

Hazardous Materials Transportation Act: Regulates the packaging, marketing, and labeling of shipments of flammable, toxic, and radioactive materials.

Resource Conservation and Recovery Act: Extends to small-quantity generators the laws regulating generation, treatment, and disposal of solid and hazardous wastes.

Surface Mining Control and Reclamation Act: Establishes environmental standards for all surface-mining operations.

Toxic Substances Control Act: Addresses the manufacture, processing, distribution, use, and disposal of dangerous chemical substances and mixtures.

Source: Dennis C. Kinlaw, *Competitive and Green: Sustainable Performance in the Environmental Age* (Amsterdam: Pfeiffer & Co., 1993). Reprinted by permission of the author.

deposit refund systems, provide positive financial incentives for good environmental performance.[14]

Cost effectiveness   Environmentally conscious strategies can be cost effective.[15] In the short run, company after company is realizing cost savings from repackaging, recycling, and other approaches. Union Carbide, for instance, faced costs of $30 a ton for disposal of solid wastes and $2,000 a ton for disposal of hazardous wastes. By recycling, reclaiming, or selling its waste, it avoided $8.5 million in costs *and* generated $3.5 million in income during a six-month period. Dow Chemical launched in 1996 a 10-year program to improve its environmental, health, and safety performance worldwide. Dow projects that the environmental improvements will save $1.8 billion over the 10-year period.[16]

Environmentally conscious strategies offer long-run cost advantages as well. Companies that are functioning barely within legal limits today may incur big costs—being forced to pay damages or upgrade technologies and practices—when laws change down the road.

A few of the other cost savings include fines, cleanups, and litigation; lower raw materials costs; reduced energy use; less-expensive waste handling and disposal; lower insurance rates; and possibly higher interest rates.

Competitive advantage
Corporations gain a competitive advantage by channeling their environmental concerns into entrepreneurial opportunities and by producing higher-quality products that meet consumer demand. Business opportunities abound in pollution protection equipment and processes, waste cleanup, low-water-use plumbing, new light bulb technology, and marketing of environmentally safe products like biodegradable plastics. With new pools of venture capital, government funding, and specialized investment funds available, environmental technology becomes a major sector of the venture-capital industry.[17]

In addition, companies that fail to innovate in this area will be at a competitive *disadvantage*. Environmental protection is not only a universal need; it is also a major export industry. U.S. trade has suffered as other countries—notably Germany—have taken the lead in patenting and exporting anti–air pollution and other environmental technologies. If the United States does not produce innovative, competitive new technologies, it will forsake a growth industry and see most of its domestic spending for environmental protection go to imports.[18]

In short, competitive advantage can be gained by maintaining market share with old customers, and by creating new products for new market opportunities. And, if you are an environmental leader, you may set the standards for future regulations—regulations that you are prepared to meet, while your competitors are not.

Public opinion
The majority of the U.S. population believes business must clean up; few people think it is doing its job well. Gallup surveys show that more than 80 percent of U.S. consumers consider environmentalism in making purchases. An international survey of 22 countries found that majorities in 20 countries gave priority to environmental protection even at the risk of slowing economic growth. Consumers seem to have reached the point of routinely expecting companies to come up with environmentally friendly alternatives to current products and practices.[19]

Companies also receive pressure from local communities and from their own employees. Sometimes the pressure is informal and low key, but much pressure is exerted by environmental organizations, aroused citizen groups, societies and associations, international codes of conduct, and environmentally conscious investors.[20]

Another important reason for paying attention to environmental impact is TRI, the Toxic Release Inventory.[21] Starting in 1986, the EPA required all the plants of approximately 10,000 U.S. manufacturers to report annual releases of 317 toxic chemicals into the air, ground, and water. The substances include freon, PCBs, asbestos, and lead compounds. Hundreds of others have been added to the list. The releases are not necessarily illegal, but they provide the public with an annual environmental benchmark. TRI provides a powerful incentive to reduce emissions.

Finally, it is useful to remember that companies recover very slowly in public opinion from the impact of an environmental disaster. Adverse public opinion may affect sales as well as the firm's ability to attract and retain talented people. You can see why companies like P&G consider concern for the environment a consumer need, making it a basic and critical business issue.

Long-term thinking
Long-term thinking about resources helps business leaders understand the nature of their responsibilities with regard to environmental concerns. Economic arguments, sustainable growth, and the tragedy of the commons highlight the need for long-term thinking.

Economic arguments   In Chapter 3, we discussed long-term versus short-term decision making. We stated that it is common for managers to succumb to short-term pressure for profits and to avoid spending now when the potential payoff is years down the road. In addition, some economists maintain that it is the responsibility of management to maximize returns for shareholders, implying the preeminence of the short-term profit goal.

But other economists argue that such a strategy caters to immediate profit maximization for stock speculators and neglects serious investors who are with the company for the long haul. Attention to environmental issues enhances the organization's long-term viability because the goal is the long-term creation of wealth for the patient, serious investors in the company[22]—not to mention the future state of our planet and the new generations who will inhabit it.

Sustainable growth   Today many companies are moving beyond the law to be truly environmentalist in their philosophies and practices. Their aim is to jointly achieve the goals of economic growth and environmental quality in the long run by striving for sustainable growth. **Sustainable growth** is economic growth and development that meets the organization's present needs without harming the ability of future generations to meet their needs.[23] Sustainability is fully compatible with the natural ecosystems that generate and preserve life.

Some believe that the concept of sustainable growth offers[24] (1) a framework for organizations to use in communicating to all stakeholders, (2) a planning and strategy guide, and (3) a tool for evaluating and improving the ability to compete. The principle can begin at the highest organizational levels and be made explicit in performance appraisals and reward systems.

The tragedy of the commons   In a classic article in *Science*, Garrett Hardin described a situation that applies to all business decisions and social concerns regarding scarce resources like clean water, air, and land.[25] Throughout human history, a commons was a tract of land shared by communities of people on which they grazed their animals. A commons has limited **carrying capacity,** or the ability to sustain a population, because it is a finite resource. For individual herders, short-term interest lies in adding as many animals to the commons as they can. But problems develop as more herders add more animals to graze the commons. This leads to tragedy: As each herder acts in his short-term interest, the long-run impact is the destruction of the commons. The only solution is to make choices according to long-run rather than short-run consequences.

In many ways, we are witnessing this **tragedy of the commons.** Carrying capacities are shrinking as precious resources, water chief among them, become scarcer. Inevitably, conflict arises—and solutions are urgently needed.

The environmental movement

The 1990s were labeled the "earth decade" when a "new environmentalism" with new features emerged.[26] For example, proponents of the new environmentalism asked companies to reduce their wastes, use resources prudently, market safe products, and take responsibility for past damages. These requests were formalized in the CERES principles (see Table 5.B.3).

The new environmentalism combined many diverse viewpoints, but initially it did not blend easily with traditional business values. Some of the key aspects of this philosophy are noted in the following discussion of the history of the movement.[27]

Conservation and environmentalism

A strand of environmental philosophy that is not at odds with business management is **conservation**. The conservation movement is anthropocentric (human centered), technologically optimistic, and concerned chiefly with the efficient use of resources. The movement seeks to avoid waste, promote the rational and efficient use of natural resources, and maximize long-term yields, especially of renewable resources.

The **environmental movement**, in contrast, historically has posed dilemmas for business management. Following the lead of early thinkers like George Perkins Marsh (1801–1882), it has shown that the unintended negative effects of human economic activities on the environment often are greater than the benefits. For example, there are links between forest cutting and soil erosion and between the draining of marshes and lakes and the decline of animal life.

Other early environmentalists, such as John Muir (1838–1914) and Aldo Leopold (1886–1948), argued that humans are not above nature but a part of it. Nature is not for humans to subdue but is sacred and should be preserved not simply for economic use but for its own sake—and for what people can learn from it.

Science and the environment

Rachel Carson's 1962 best-selling book *The Silent Spring* helped ignite the modern environmental movement by alerting the public to the dangers of unre-

table 5.B.3
The CERES principles

- **Protection of the biosphere:** Minimize the release of pollutants that may cause environmental damage.

- **Sustainable use of natural resources:** Conserve nonrenewable resources through efficient use and careful planning.

- **Reduction and disposal of waste:** Minimize the creation of waste, especially hazardous waste, and dispose of such materials in a safe, responsible manner.

- **Wise use of energy:** Make every effort to use environmentally safe and sustainable energy sources to meet operating requirements.

- **Risk reduction:** Diminish environmental, health, and safety risks to employees.

- **Marketing of safe products and services:** Sell products that minimize adverse environmental impact and are safe for consumers.

- **Damage compensation:** Accept responsibility for any harm the company causes the environment; conduct bioremediation; and compensate affected parties.

- **Disclosure of environmental incidents:** Public dissemination of accidents relating to operations that harm the environment or pose health or safety risks.

- **Environmental directors:** Appoint at least one board member who is qualified to represent environmental interests; create a position of vice president for environmental affairs.

- **Assessment and annual audit:** Produce and publicize each year a self-evaluation of progress toward implementing the principles and meeting all applicable laws and regulations worldwide. Environmental audits will also be produced annually and distributed to the public.

Sources: *Chemical Week*, September 20, 1989, copyright permission granted by *Chemical Week* magazine. *CERES Coalition Handbook.*

stricted pesticide use.[28] Carson brought together the findings of toxicology, ecology, and epidemiology in a form accessible to the public. Blending scientific, moral, and political arguments, she connected environmental politics and values with scientific knowledge.

Barry Commoner's *Science and Survival* (1963) continued in this vein. Commoner expanded the scope of ecology to include everything in the physical, chemical, biological, social, political, economic, and philosophical worlds.[29] He argued that all of these elements fit together, and have to be understood as a whole. According to Commoner, the symptoms of environmental problems are in the biological world, but their source lies in economic and political organizations.

Economics and the environment   Economists promote growth for many reasons: to restore the balance of payments, to make the nation more competitive, to create jobs, to reduce the deficit, to provide for the elderly and the sick, and to reduce poverty. Environmentalists criticize economics for its notions of efficiency and its emphasis on economic growth.[30] For example, environmentalists argue that economists do not adequately consider the unintended side effects of efficiency. Environmentalists hold that economists need to supplement estimates of the economic costs and benefits of growth with estimates of other factors that historically were not measured in economic terms.[31]

Economists and public policy analysts argue that the benefits of eliminating risk to the environment and to people must be balanced against the costs. Reducing risk involves determining how effective the proposed methods of reduction are likely to be and how much they will cost. There are many ways to consider cost factors. Analysts can perform cost effectiveness analyses, in which they attempt to figure out how to achieve a given goal with limited resources, or they can conduct more formal risk-benefit and cost-benefit analyses, in which they quantify both the benefits and the costs of risk reduction.[32]

Qualitative judgments in cost–benefit analysis
Formal, quantitative approaches to balancing costs and benefits do not eliminate the need for qualitative judgments. For example, how does one assess the value of a magnificent vista obscured by air pollution? What is the loss to society if a particular genetic strain of grass or animal species becomes extinct? How does one assess the lost opportunity costs of spending vast amounts of money on air pollution that could have been spent on productivity enhancement and global competitiveness?

Fairness cannot be ignored when doing cost-benefit analysis.[33] For example, the costs of air pollution reduction may have to be borne disproportionately by the poor in the form of higher gasoline and automobile prices. Intergenerational fairness also plays a role.[34] Future generations have no representatives in the current market and political processes. To what extent should the current generation hold back on its own consumption for the sake of posterity? This question is particularly poignant because few people in the world today are well off. To ask the poor to reduce their life's chances for the sake of a generation yet to come is asking for a great sacrifice.

International perspectives   Environmental problems present a different face in various countries and regions of the world. The United States and Great Britain lag behind Germany and Japan in mandated emissions standards.[35] In Europe, the Dutch, the Germans, and the Danes are among the most environmentally conscious. Italy, Ireland, Spain, Portugal, and Greece are in the early stages of developing environmental policies. Poland, Hungary, the Czech Republic, and former East Germany are the most polluted of the world's industrialized nations.[36]

The environmental movement is a worldwide phenomenon. The "Greens," pictured here demonstrating in LePuy, France, are a growing European political party. [Maillac/REA–SABA]

U.S. companies need to realize that there is a large growth market in Western Europe for environmentally "friendly" products. U.S. managers also need to be fully aware of the environmental movement in Western Europe. Environmentalists in Europe have been successful in halting many projects.[37] China has been paying a high ecological price for its rapid economic growth. But the government has begun recognizing the problem and is creating some antipollution laws.[38] It is now impossible to plan a large-scale project in Western Europe without considering an adverse reaction by the Green party.

Industries that pollute or make polluting products will have to adjust to the new reality, and companies selling products in certain parts of the world must take into account a growing consumer consciousness about environmental protection. Manufacturers may even be legally required to take products and packaging back from customers after use, to recycle or dispose of. In order to meet these requirements in Germany, and be prepared for similar demands in other countries, Hewlett-Packard redesigned its office-machine packaging worldwide.

What Managers Can Do

To be truly "green"—that is, a cutting-edge company with respect to environmental concerns—legal compliance is not enough. Progressive companies stay abreast *and* ahead of the laws by going beyond marginal compliance and anticipating future requirements and needs.[39] But companies can go further still by experimenting continually with innovations that protect the environment. McDonald's, for example, conducted tests and pilot projects in composting food scraps and in offering refillable coffee mugs and starch-based (biodegradable) cutlery.[40]

Systems thinking   The first thing managers can do to better understand environmental issues in their companies is to engage in systems thinking. Environmental considerations relate to the organization's inputs, processes, and outputs.[41] *Inputs* include raw materials and energy. Environmental pressures are causing prices of some raw materials, such as metals, to rise. This greatly increases the costs of production. Higher energy costs are causing firms to switch to more fuel-efficient sources.

Firms are considering new *processes* or methods of production that will reduce water pollution, air pollution, noise and vibration, and waste. They are incorporating technologies that sample and monitor (control) these by-products of business processes. Some chemical plants have a computerized system that flashes warnings when a maximum allowable pollution level is soon to be reached. Many companies keep only minimal stocks of hazardous materials, making serious accidents less likely.

Outputs have environmental impact, whether the products themselves or the waste or by-products of processes. To reduce the impact of its outputs, Herman Miller recycles or reuses nearly all waste from the manufacturing process. It sells fabric scraps to the auto industry, leather trim to luggage makers, and vinyl to stereo and auto manufacturers. It buys back its old furniture, refurbishes it, and resells it. Its corporatewide goal is to send zero waste to landfills. Environmental manager Paul Murray says, "There is never an acceptable level of waste at Miller. There are always new things we can learn."[42]

Strategic integration   Systems thinking reveals that environmental issues permeate the firm, and therefore should be addressed in a comprehensive, integrative fashion. Perhaps the first step is to create the proper mindset. Does your firm see environmental concerns merely in terms of a business versus environment trade-off, or does it see in it a potential source of competitive advantage and an important part of a strategy for long-term survival and effectiveness? The latter attitude, of course, is more likely to set the stage for the following strategic actions.

These ideas help to strategically integrate environmental considerations into the firm's ongoing activities:[43]

1. *Develop a mission statement and strong values supporting environmental advocacy.* Table 5.B.4 shows Procter & Gamble's environmental quality policy.

table 5.B.4
Procter & Gamble's environmental quality policy

Procter & Gamble is committed to providing products of superior quality and value that best fill the needs of the world's consumers. As part of this, Procter & Gamble continually strives to improve the environmental quality of its products, packaging, and operations around the world. To carry out this commitment, it is Procter & Gamble's policy to:

• Ensure our products, packaging, and operations are safe for our employees, consumers, and the environment.

• Reduce or prevent the environmental impact of our products and packaging in their design, manufacture, distribution, use, and disposal whenever possible.

• Meet or exceed the requirements of all environmental laws and regulations.

• Continually assess our environmental technology and programs, and monitor programs toward environmental goals.

• Provide our consumers, customers, employees, communities, public interest groups, and others with relevant and appropriate factual information about the environmental quality of P&G products, packaging, and operations.

• Ensure every employee understands and is responsible and accountable for incorporating environmental quality considerations in daily business activities.

• Have operating policies, programs, and resources in place to implement our environmental quality policy.

Source: K. Dechant and B. Altman, "Environmental Leadership: From Compliance to Competitive Advantage," *The Academy of Management Executive*, August 1994, p. 10. Reprinted by permission.

2. *Establish a framework for managing environmental initiatives.* Some industries have created voluntary codes of environmental practice, for example the chemical industry's Responsible Care Initiative. Not all standard practices are adopted by all companies, however.[44] At J&J,[45] Environmental Regulatory Affairs uses external audit teams to conduct environmental audits. The Community Environmental Responsibility Program includes strategy and planning, and the development of products and processes with neutral environmental impact.

3. *Engage in "green" process and product design.* The core concept of total quality management is that products will cost more to fix after manufacture than if the defects are prevented in the first place. With respect to the environment, a similar concept

is pollution prevention as opposed to "end-of-pipe" cleanup strategies. Such programs strive for zero emissions or at least continuous improvement toward that goal.

4. *Establish environmentally focused stakeholder relationships.* Many firms work closely with the FDA and receive technical assistance to help convert to more energy-efficient facilities. And to defray costs as well as develop new ideas, small companies like WHYCO Chromium Company establish environmental management partnerships with firms like IBM and GM.[46]

5. *Provide internal and external education.* Engage employees in environmental actions. Dow's WRAP program has cut millions of pounds of hazardous and solid waste and emissions, and achieved annual cost savings of over $10 million, all through employee suggestions.[47] At the same time, inform the public of your firm's environmental initiatives. For example, eco-labeling can urge consumers to recycle and communicate the environmental friendliness of your product.

Life cycle analysis
Increasingly, firms are paying attention to the pollution caused by their manufacturing processes in the context of the total environmental impact throughout the entire life cycle of their products.[48] **Life-cycle analysis (LCA)** is a process of analyzing all inputs and outputs to determine the total environmental impact of the production and use of a product. LCA quantifies the total use of resources, and the releases into the air, water, and land. For example, Xerox is using product life-cycle analysis in its design-for-environment tool kit in its efforts to make research and technology investment decisions to improve environmental performance.[49]

Green design considers the extraction of raw materials, product packaging, transportation, and disposal. Consider packaging alone. Goods make the journey from manufacturer to wholesaler to retailer to customer, and are then recycled back to the manufacturer. They may be packaged and repackaged several times, from bulk transport to large crates to cardboard boxes to individual consumer sizes. Repackaging not only creates waste—it costs *time*. The design of initial packaging in sizes and formats adaptable to the final customer can minimize the need for repackaging, cut waste, and realize many benefits.

Implementation
How can companies implement "greening" strategies? A fundamental requirement for effective environmentalism is a commitment by top management. Specific actions could include commissioning an environmental audit in which an outside company checks for environmental hazards, drafting (or reviewing) the organization's environmental policy, communicating the policy and making it highly visible throughout the organization, having environmental professionals within the company report directly to the president or CEO, allocating sufficient resources to support the environmental effort, and building bridges between the organization and other companies, governments, environmentalists, and local communities.

Ultimately, it is essential to make employees accountable for any of their actions that have environmental impact.[50] Texaco, Du Pont, and other companies evaluate managers on their ideas for minimizing pollution and for new, environment-friendly products. Kodak ties some managers' compensation to the prevention of chemical spills; the company attributes to this policy a dramatic reduction in accidents.[51]

Companies can employ all areas of the organization to meet the challenges posed by pollution and environmental challenges. A variety of companies have responded creatively to these challenges[52] and may serve as models for other organizations. The following sections describe more specific actions companies can take to address environmental issues.

Strategy   Actions companies can take in the area of strategy include the following:

1. *Cut back on environmentally unsafe businesses.* Du Pont, the leading producer of CFCs, announced it would voluntarily pull out of this $750 million business.[53]

2. *Carry out R&D on environmentally safe activities.* Du Pont claims it is spending up to $1 billion on the best replacements for CFCs. Shell is investing in solar and renewable energy.[54]

3. *Develop and expand environmental cleanup services.* Building on the expertise gained in cleaning up its own plants, Du Pont formed a safety and environmental resources division to help industrial customers clean up their toxic wastes.[55]

4. *Compensate for environmentally risky projects.* AES has a long-standing policy of planting trees to offset its power plants' carbon emission.[56]

5. *Make your company accountable to others.* Royal Dutch Shell and Bristol-Meyers Squibb are trendsetters in green reporting.[57] Danish health care and enzymes company Novo Nordisk purposely asked for feedback from environmentalists, regulators, and other interested bodies from around Europe. Its reputation has been enhanced, its people have learned a lot, and new market opportunities have been identified.[58]

6. *Make every new product environmentally better than the last.* This is IBM's goal. IBM aims to use recyclable materials, reduce hazardous materials, reduce emissions, and use natural energy and resources in packaging.[59]

Public Affairs   In the area of public affairs, companies can take a variety of actions:

1. *Attempt to gain environmental legitimacy and credibility.* The cosponsors of Earth Day included Apple Computer, Hewlett-Packard, and the Chemical Manufacturers Association. McDonald's has tried to become a corporate environmental "educator." Ethel M. Chocolates, in public tours of its Las Vegas factory, showcases effective handling of its industrial wastes.[60]

2. *Try to avoid losses caused by insensitivity to environmental issues.* As a result of Exxon's apparent lack of concern after the

Valdez oil spill, 41 percent of Americans polled said they would consider boycotting the company.[61] MacMillan Bloedel lost a big chunk of sales almost overnight when it was targeted publicly as a clear-cutter and chlorine user. [62]

3. *Collaborate with environmentalists.* Executives at Pacific Gas & Electric seek discussions and joint projects with any willing environmental group, and ARCO has prominent enviromentalists on its board of directors.

The legal area   Actions companies can take in the legal area include the following:

1. *Try to avoid confrontation with state or federal pollution control agencies.* W. R. Grace faced expensive and time-consuming lawsuits as a result of its toxic dumps. Browning-Ferris, Waste Management Inc., and Louisiana-Pacific were charged with pollution control violations, damaging their reputations.

2. *Comply early.* Because compliance costs only increase over time, the first companies to act will have lower costs. This will enable them to increase their market share and profits and win competitive advantage. 3M's goal was to meet government requirements to replace or improve underground storage tanks five years ahead of the legally mandated year.

3. *Take advantage of innovative compliance programs.* Instead of source-by-source reduction, the EPA's bubble policy allowed factories to reduce pollution at different sources by different amounts, provided the overall result is equivalent. Therefore, 3M has installed equipment on only certain production lines at its tape-manufacturing facility in Pennsylvania, thereby lowering its compliance costs.[63] Today, there is greater use of economic instruments like tradable pollution permits, charges, and taxes to encourage improvements.[64] *Joint implementation* (or *activities implemented jointly*) involves companies in industrialized nations working with businesses in developing countries to help them reduce greenhouse gas emissions. The company lending a hand then receives credit toward fulfilling its environmental obligations at home. The developing country receives investment, technology, and jobs; the company giving a lending hand receives environmental credits; and the world gets cleaner air.[65]

4. *Don't deal with fly-by-night subcontractors for waste disposal.* They are more likely to cut corners, break laws, and do a poor job. Moreover, the result for you could be bad publicity and legal problems.[66]

Operations   The actions companies can take in the area of operations include the following:

1. *Promote new manufacturing technologies.* Louisville Gas and Electric took the lead in installing smokestack scrubbers, Consolidated Natural Gas pioneered the use of clean-burning technologies, and Nucor developed state-of-the-art steel mills. Pacific Gas & Electric agreed to rely on combinations of smaller-scale generating facilities like windmills or cogeneration plants alongside aggressive conservation efforts.

2. *Aim for zero waste or zero discharge.* This may be unachievable, but it is a useful target. It imposes discipline and encourages continuous improvement.

3. *Encourage technological advances that reduce pollution from products and manufacturing processes.* 3M's "Pollution Prevention Pays" program is based on the premise that it is too costly for companies to employ add-on technology and instead they should attempt to eliminate pollution at the source.[67] Pollution prevention, more than pollution control, is related to both better environmental performance and better manufacturing performance, including cost and speed.[68]

4. *Develop new product formulations.* Weyerhaeuser, recognizing the decreasing supply of timber and growing demand, is working to produce high-quality wood on fewer, continuously regenerated acres.[69] Electrolux has developed a sun-powered lawnmower and a chainsaw that runs on vegetable oil.[70] Many companies are developing green pesticides.

5. *Eliminate manufacturing wastes.* With fewer wastes, add-on equipment becomes less necessary. 3M's philosophy is to invest in reducing the number of materials that can trigger regulation. For example, it replaced volatile solvents with water-based ones, thereby eliminating the need for costly air pollution control equipment. BPAmoco and Polaroid have implemented similar programs.

6. *Find alternative uses for wastes.* When Du Pont halted ocean dumping of acid iron salts, it discovered that the salts could be sold to water treatment plants at a profit.

7. *Insist that your suppliers have strong environmental performance.* IBM, British Telecom, Wal-Mart, British supermarkets, and many others do this. Scott Paper discovered that many of its environmental problems were "imported" through the supply chain. Initially focusing on pulp suppliers, the company sent questionnaires asking for figures on air, water, and land releases, energy consumption, and energy sources. Scott was astonished at the variance. For example, carbon dioxide emissions varied by a factor of 17 among different suppliers. Scott dropped the worst performers and announced that the best performers would in the future receive preference in its purchasing decisions.[71]

8. *Assemble products with the environment in mind.* Make them easy to snap apart, sort, and recycle, and avoid glues and screws.

Marketing   Companies can also take actions in the marketing area:

1. *Cast products in an environment-friendly light.* Most Americans believe a company's environmental reputation influences what they buy.[72] Companies such as Procter & Gamble, Colgate-Palmolive, Lever Brothers, 3M, and Sunoco try to act on the basis of this finding. Wal-Mart has made efforts to provide customers with recycled or recyclable products.

2. *Avoid attacks by environmentalists for unsubstantiated or inappropriate claims.* A few years ago, British Petroleum claimed

that a new brand of unleaded gasoline caused no pollution, a claim that it had to withdraw after suffering much embarrassment. The degradable-plastics controversy should serve as another warning to consumers about the perils of unsubstantiated or inappropriate claims. Companies should be honest with their employees and the public and educate them continuously.

3. *Differentiate your product via environmental services.* ICI takes back and disposes of customers' waste as a customer service. Disposal is costly, but the service differentiates the firm's products. Teach customers how to use and dispose of products; for instance, farmers inadvertently abuse pesticides. Make education a part of a firm's after-sales service.

Accounting   Actions companies can take in the accounting area include the following:

1. *Collect useful data.* The best current reporters of environmental information include Dow Europe, Danish Steel Works, BSO/Origin, 3M, and Monsanto. BSO/Origin has begun to explore a system for corporate environmental accounting.[73]

2. *Make polluters pay.* CIBA-GEIGY has a "polluter pays principle" throughout the firm, so managers have the incentive to combat pollution at the sources they can influence.[74]

3. *Demonstrate that antipollution programs pay off.* 3M's Pollution Prevention Pays program is based on the premise that only if the program pays will there be the motivation to carry it out. Every company needs to be cost effective in its pollution reduction efforts.

4. *Use an advanced waste accounting system.* Do this in addition to standard management accounting, which can hinder investment in new technologies. Waste accounting makes sure all costs are identified and better decisions can be made.

5. *Adopt full cost accounting.* This approach, called for by Frank Popoff, Dow's chairman, ensures that the price of a product reflects its full environmental cost.[75]

6. *Show the overall impact of the pollution reduction program.* Companies have an obligation to account for the costs and benefits of their pollution reduction programs. 3M claims half a *billion* dollars in savings from pollution prevention efforts.[76]

Finance   In the area of finance, companies can do the following:

1. *Gain the respect of the socially responsible investment community.* Many investment funds in the United States and Europe take environmental criteria into account. A study by ICF Kaiser concluded that environmental improvements could lead to significant reduction in the perceived risk of a firm, with a possible 5 percent increase in stock.[77] Socially responsible rating services and investment funds try to help people invest with a "clean conscience."[78]

2. *Recognize true liability.* Investment houses often employ environmental analysts who search for companies' true environmental liability in evaluating their potential performance. Bankers look at environmental risks and environmental market opportunities when evaluating a company's credit rating.[79] The Securities and Exchange Commission in New York requires some companies to report certain environmental costs. The Swiss Bank Corp. has specialized Environmental Performance Rating Units to include environmental criteria in order to improve the quality of financial analysis.[80]

3. *Fund and then assist green companies.* Ann Winblad of Hummer Winblad Venture Partners was one of the first venture capitalists to coach green entrepreneurs to increase their business skills and chances of success.[81]

4. *Recognize financial opportunities.* Worldwide, one of these great opportunities is water. Water must be purified and delivered reliably to everyone worldwide. Three billion people lack sanitary sewage facilities, and 1 billion have poor access to drinking water. Infrastructures in big cities, including those in the United States, are seriously deteriorating. Supplying clean water to people and companies is a $400 billion-a-year industry—one-third larger than the global pharmaceutical industry. Companies like Thames of Britain, Enron of the United States, and Suez and Vivendi are aggressively pursuing this market. They are betting that water in the 21st century will be like oil in the 20th century. A Bear Stearns analyst calls water the best sector for the next century.[82]

Key terms

Carrying capacity   The ability of a finite resource to sustain a population. p. 178

Conservation   An environmental philosophy that seeks to avoid waste, promote the rational and efficient use of natural resources, and maximize long-term yields, especially of renewable resources. p. 178

Environmental movement   An environmental philosophy postulating that the unintended negative effects of human economic activities on the environment are often greater than the benefits, and that nature should be preserved. p. 178

Life-cycle analysis (LCA)   A process of evaluating all inputs and outputs to determine the total environmental impact of the production and use of a product. p. 181

Sustainable growth   Economic growth and development that meet the organization's present needs without harming the ability of future generations to meet their needs. p. 177

Tragedy of the commons   A term describing the environmental destruction that results as individuals and businesses consume finite resources (i.e., the "commons") to serve their short-term interests without regard for the long-term consequences. p. 178

Discussion questions

1. To what extent can we rely on government to solve environmental problems? What are some of government's limitations? Take a stand on the role and usefulness of government regulations on business activities.

2. To what extent should managers today be responsible for cleaning up mistakes from years past that have hurt the environment?

3. How would you characterize the environmental movement in Western Europe? How does it differ from the United States movement? What difference will this make to a multinational company that wants to produce and market goods in many countries?

4. What business opportunities can you see in meeting environmental challenges? Be specific.

5. You are appointed environmental manager of XYZ Company. Describe some actions you will take to address environmental challenges. Discuss obstacles you are likely to encounter in the company and how you will manage them.

6. Interview a businessperson about environmental regulations and report your findings to the class. How would you characterize his or her attitude? How constructive is his or her attitude?

7. Interview a businessperson about actions he or she has taken that have helped the environment. Report your findings to the class and discuss.

8. Identify and discuss some examples of the tragedy of the commons. How can the tragedies be avoided?

9. Discuss the status of recycling efforts in your community, your perspectives on it as a consumer, and what business opportunities could be available.

10. What companies currently come to mind as having the best and worst reputations with respect to the environment? Why do they have these reputations?

11. Choose one product and discuss its environmental impact through its entire life cycle.

12. What are you, your college or university, and your community doing about the environment? What would you recommend doing?

Chapter Six
International Management

It was once said that the sun never sets on the British Empire. Today, the sun does set on the British Empire, but not on the scores of global empires, including those of IBM, Unilever, Volkswagen, and Hitachi.

—Lester Brown

Chapter Outline

Learning Objectives

After studying Chapter 6, you will know:

1. Why the world economy is becoming more integrated than ever before.

2. What integration of the global economy means for individual companies and for their managers.

3. The strategies organizations use to compete in the global marketplace.

4. The various entry modes organizations use to enter overseas markets.

5. How companies can approach the task of staffing overseas operations.

6. The skills and knowledge managers need to manage globally.

7. Why cultural differences across countries influence management.

Setting the Stage

A Bumpy Ride at DaimlerChrysler

It was the deal heard 'round the world. In May 1998, a stunning $36 billion merger was announced by Daimler Benz and Chrysler Corporation. The marriage promised to rock the global auto industry and provide a blueprint for international consolidation on an epic scale. But the union didn't turn out to be a merger made in heaven. Daimler chief Jurgen E. Schrempp grabbed the wheel of DaimlerChrysler (DCX). His co-chairman from Chrysler, Robert J. Eaton, took a backseat. And Thomas T. Stallkamp, Chrysler's president, got caught in between.

The lofty expectations would be dashed in DaimlerChrysler's first year. At the first meeting of the global management team, the officers ate, drank, mixed, and matched for two days; Germans joined Americans in discussion groups, with a member of the board of management—the company's top executives—heading up each table. After the breakout sessions and dinner, the hotel turned into a giant, free-form cocktail party. A Chrysler finance exec, Thomas F. Gilman, began playing piano in the bar, and Americans

Cultural differences as well as a gap in pay scales have strained the merger between Daimler Benz and Chrysler.
[AP/WIDE WORLD PHOTOS]

and Germans alike joined in to sing. Schrempp and the group bellowed song after song until the wee hours. The German co-chairman led one final chorus of "Bye, Bye, Miss American Pie." Then, with a wild gleam in his eye, Schrempp grabbed his ever-present assistant, Lydia Deininger, picked her up, and threw her over his shoulder. Schrempp snatched a bottle of champagne in his free hand, raised it in the air, and yelled out with a grin: "See you later, boys!" Then he carried her off, not to be seen for the rest of the night. Executives in Auburn Hills just weren't accustomed to a married CEO openly carrying on a relationship with his attractive assistant. "It's odd," Stallkamp said. "Some people say it's Continental, but it's not appropriate business behavior."

It was only the tip of the cultural iceberg. The Germans smoked, drank wine with lunch, and worked late hours, sending out for pizza and beer at their desks. The old Chrysler banned smoking and alcohol in its facilities. The Americans worked around the clock on deadlines but didn't stay late as a routine. The yawning gap in pay scales fueled an undercurrent of tension. The Americans earned two, three, and, in some cases, four times as much as their German counterparts. But the expenses of U.S. workers were tightly controlled compared with those of the German system. Daimler-side employees thought nothing of flying to Paris or New York for a half-day meeting, then capping the visit with a fancy dinner and a night in an expensive hotel. The Americans blanched at the extravagance.

The Germans and Americans simply did business differently. The six-hour time difference didn't help. By the time the Americans started their day, the Germans had already had lunch. Stuttgart always seemed to have a head start on Auburn Hills. German management-board members had executive assistants who prepared detailed position papers on any number of issues. The Americans didn't have assigned aides and formulated their decisions by talking directly to engineers or other specialists. A German decision worked its way through the bureaucracy for final approval at the top. Then it was set in stone. The Americans allowed midlevel employees to proceed on their own initiative, sometimes without waiting for executive-level approval.

The Americans, to their dismay, saw their worst fear become reality. Eaton slowly but surely withdrew, grew detached, and didn't contribute. Schrempp didn't exactly intimidate Eaton. He overwhelmed him. Eaton didn't cower. He abdicated. For his part, Eaton saw himself as a team builder: "I think my legacy is the cultural change and building the strong team. It wouldn't have happened if I wasn't there." But some of his own execs could not get past the barriers Eaton had erected. Stallkamp had hoped the Chrysler side could use Eaton as a "silver bullet" to be fired at crucial times to tip an issue its way. But that couldn't happen if Eaton wasn't up for it.

The public view of DaimlerChrysler as a "merger of equals" had begun to crack. U.S. investors fled from the stock because the company wasn't incorporated in America. High-profile defections of Chrysler execs fed the image of German control. Two vice-presidents quit to join Ford Motor Co. On September 24, after a tense meeting in Frankfurt, the supervisory board dropped the bomb. The management board would shrink from 17 members to 13, with 8 Germans and 5 Americans. A new business structure was put in place, with three equal automotive pillars: Mercedes-Benz cars, Chrysler, and heavy trucks. Today, DaimlerChrysler still hasn't made money for its shareholders.

Source: Condensed from Bill Vlasic and Bradley A. Stertz, "Taken for a Ride," Business Week Online, June 5, 2000.

As the DaimlerChrysler story shows, today's manager must constantly make decisions about whether and how to pursue global opportunities. Of course, these opportunities need to be evaluated carefully, not just from a competitive or financial standpoint, but from a cultural and managerial standpoint as well. It is often the case that global opportunities look good on paper, but don't pan out if managers are unable to work in a different international context.

In this chapter, we review the reasons for the globalization of competition, examine why international management differs from domestic management, consider how companies expand globally, and see how companies can develop individuals to manage across borders.

The global environment

The global economy is becoming more integrated than ever before. For example, in January 1995, the World Trade Organization (WTO) was formed and now includes 125 member countries (the International Monetary Fund, set up by the United Nations, serves a similar purpose and includes 182 countries). WTO rules apply to over 90 percent of international trade. Recently the WTO has become controversial, as its role has expanded from reducing tariffs to eliminating nontariff barriers. The controversy stems from the fact that the WTO can be used to challenge environmental, health, and other regulations. These regulations often serve legitimate social goals, but may be regarded as impediments to international trade. You can see the importance—and stickiness—of this issue at http://www.wto.org/.

In addition to the WTO, there are other economic influences that operate on a global scale. Three areas, typically referred to as the triad of North America, Europe, and Asia, are most dominant. However, other developing countries and regions represent important areas for economic growth as well.

European unification

Europe is integrating economically to form the biggest market in the world. In concept, the European Union (EU) will allow goods, services, capital, and human resources to flow freely across national borders. Figure 6.1 shows a map of participating countries in the EU. The goal of unification is to strengthen Europe's position as the third economic superpower, right behind the United States and Japan.[1]

figure 6.1
The nations of the European Union

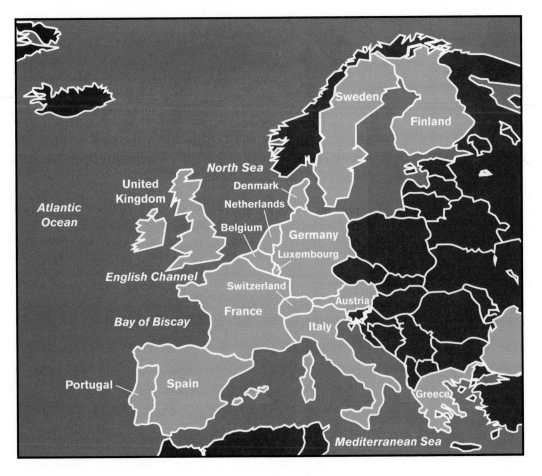

Siemens Microelectronics Inc. of Cupertino, California, is one of more than 30 Siemens companies located in the United States. *[Courtesy of Siemens Microelectronics, Inc.]*

Under the Maastricht Treaty, member countries have agreed to adopt a common European currency called the Euro. However, the pace of unification has been slower than anticipated. There are structural issues within Europe that need to be corrected for the EU to function effectively. In particular, Western Europeans on average work fewer hours, earn more pay, take longer vacations, and enjoy far more social entitlements than their counterparts in North America and Asia. To be competitive in a global economy, Europeans must increase their level of productivity. In the past, powerful trade unions have fiercely defended social benefits, and local governments have regulated the labor markets. Both of these actions have encouraged companies such as Siemens and ABB Asea Brown Boveri Ltd. to move operations abroad. Now it appears that labor markets are being deregulated and there are more incentives to create jobs.[2]

Unification will create a more competitive Europe. The EU's share of the world's top 100 industrial firms is rising. The community is pursuing an active industrial policy to enhance its competitiveness in information technology. It is making fast gains in semiconductors and is restructuring in defense and aerospace.

The impact is hard to predict, but there are many possibilities. U.S. exports to Europe could be replaced by the goods of European producers; European exports could replace U.S. products in other markets; U.S. capital could flow into Europe to the detriment of capital formation and productivity growth in the United States. Another possibility is a "Fortress Europe" that restricts trade with countries outside EU walls.

The consensus among U.S. observers is that the United States must remain vigilant to ensure that a Fortress Europe does not close itself to U.S. goods and services. Management and labor must work cooperatively to achieve high levels of quality that will make U.S. products and services attractive to consumers in Europe and other markets across the world. The United States needs not only managers who will stay on top of worldwide developments and manage high-quality, efficient organizations, but a well-educated, well-trained, and continually *retrained* labor force to remain competitive with the Europeans, the Japanese, and other formidable competitors.[3]

The Pacific Rim

Among the Pacific Rim countries, Japan dominated world attention during much of the last decade. But Japan is hardly the only important global player from the Pacific region. China is developing and becoming more prosperous. Even Japan is concerned about the countries known as the "four tigers," or the "four dragons": South Korea, Taiwan, Singapore, and Hong Kong. Korea is foremost among them; its immediate goal is to become one of the world's 10 most technologically advanced nations. Already the four dragons, along with other Asian growth nations like Thailand, Malaysia, and the Philippines, account for more trade with the United States than Japan does.[4]

For the past several years, the 18 member countries of the Asia-Pacific Economic Cooperation (APEC) have been working to reduce trade barriers and establish general rules for investment and policies that encourage international commerce. Recent volatility in global financial markets has been linked directly to economic uncertainties in the Pacific Rim. The U.S. government has been working with APEC countries to stabilize the economic environment and facilitate more open-trade agreements. Although the United States has been trading with member countries such as Australia, Singapore, Malaysia, Japan, Indonesia, China, and South Korea, APEC holds much the same promise as NAFTA and the EU in facilitating and strengthening international business relationships. Member countries represent 40 percent of the world's population and 50 percent of the world's economic output.[5]

North America

North American Free Trade Agreement (NAFTA) An economic pact that combined the economies of the United States, Canada, and Mexico into the world's largest trading block.

The **North American Free Trade Agreement (NAFTA)** combined the economies of the United States, Canada, and Mexico into the world's largest trading bloc with more than 370 million customers and approximately $6.5 trillion in total GNP. Within the next 10 years, virtually all United States industrial exports into Mexico and Canada will be duty free. Although the United States has had a longer-standing agreement with Canada, Mexico has quickly emerged as the United States' third-largest trading partner as a result of NAFTA. U.S. industries that have benefited in the short run include capital-goods suppliers, manufacturers of consumer durables, grain producers and distributors, construction equipment manufacturers, the auto industry, as well as the financial industry, which now has privileged access into a previously protected market.

Despite the potential benefits of NAFTA, Mexico will need to bolster its infrastructure and take care of troubling environmental issues in order to support its economic growth. Mexico has recently established a comprehensive statute for environmental regulation to address issues such as air pollution, hazardous waste, water pollution, and noise pollution. Surprisingly, Mexico has very strict laws protecting natural resources, many of which were fashioned after U.S. laws. However, there has not been sufficient enforcement of those laws. Mexico has some way to go in developing a strong environmental services industry to handle environmental protection and cleanup. Both the United States and Mexico are committing up to $8 billion for environmental protection.[6]

The Border Environment Cooperation Commission (BECC) is working with close to 100 communities throughout the Mexico–U.S. border region to address their environmental concerns. To date, the BECC has certified 42 water, wastewater, and municipal solid waste infrastructure projects. These projects will represent a total estimated investment of $963 million (see http://www.nadbank.org/).

The rest of the world

We can't begin to fully discuss all of the important developments, markets, and competitors shaping the global environment. But we can convey the immense potential for other major developments and new competitive threats and opportunities. For example, globalization so far has left out three huge, high-potential regions of the world: the Middle East, Africa, and Latin America.[7] Together these regions comprise a major share of the world's natural resources and are among the fastest-growing economies. Their potential has not begun to be realized.[8]

Consequences of a global economy

The increasing integration of the global economy has had many consequences. First, over the last decade the volume of world trade has grown at a faster rate than the volume of world output. Over the past few decades, world output has grown by approximately 30 percent while world trade has grown by over 50 percent.[9] Years of emphasis on international commerce by major industrial countries, as well as recent liberalized trading brought about by NAFTA, EU, and APEC, have resulted in lowering the barriers to the free flow of goods, services, and capital among nation-states. The impact of these trends is staggering. The dollar value of international trade (merchandise exports and commercial

figure 6.2
Direct investment
positions on a historical-
cost basis, 1982–1999

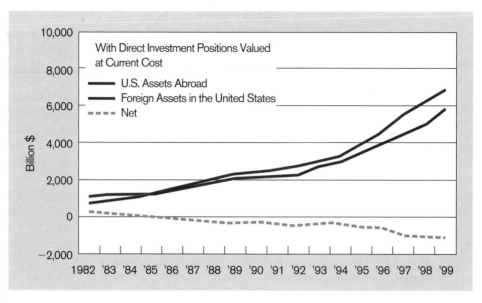

Source: Russell B. Scholl, "The International Investment Position of the United States at Yearend 1999," *Survey of Current Business,* July 2000, 80, no. 7, p. 46.

services) is approximately $6.82 trillion. Most experts expect competition to increase as trade is liberalized, and as is so often the case, the more efficient players will survive. To succeed in this industrial climate, managers need to study opportunities in existing markets, as well as work to enhance the competitiveness of their firms. Second, *foreign direct investment (FDI)* is playing an ever-increasing role in the global economy as companies of all sizes invest in overseas operations (see Figure 6.2). As shown in Table 6.1, foreign direct investments are matched closely on a regional basis by U.S. investments abroad. The major investments have been among the United States, Europe, and Japan. These figures support the idea of the economic triad mentioned earlier.[10]

A third consequence of an increasingly integrated global economy is that imports are penetrating deeper into the world's largest economies. For the first time, manufactured goods rather than raw materials account for more than half of Japan's imports.[11] The growth of imports is a natural by-product of the growth of world trade and the trend toward the manufacture of component parts, or even entire products, overseas before shipping them back home for final sale.

Finally, the growth of world trade, foreign direct investment, and imports implies that companies around the globe are finding their home markets under attack from foreign competitors. This is true in Japan, where Kodak has taken market share in the photographic film industry away from Fuji; in the United States, where Japanese automakers

table 6.1
U.S. and foreign direct
investments (1995)

	United States investment abroad	Foreign direct investment in United States
Canada	$ 81,387	$ 46,005
Europe	363,527	360,762
Latin America	122,765	22,716
Africa	347	936
Middle East	7,982	5,053
Asia and Pacific	125,968	124,615

Source: Jeffrey H. Lowe and Sylvia E. Bargas, "Direct Investment Positions on a Historical-Cost Basis," *Survey of Currrent Business,* July 1996, pp. 45–55.

have captured market share from GM, Ford, and DaimlerChrysler; and in Western Europe, where the once-dominant Dutch company Philips N. V. has lost market share in the consumer electronics industry to Japan's JVC, Matsushita, and Sony.

What does all of this mean for the manager? Compared with only a few years ago, *opportunities are greater* because the movement toward free trade has opened up many formerly protected national markets. The potential for export, and for making direct investments overseas, is greater today than ever before. *The environment is more complex* because today's manager often has to deal with the challenges of doing business in countries with radically different cultures and of coordinating globally dispersed operations. *The environment is more competitive* because in addition to domestic competitors, the manager must deal with cost-efficient overseas competitors.

Companies both large and small now view the world, rather than a single country, as their marketplace. As Table 6.2 shows, the United States has no monopoly on international business. Nearly half of the top 50 corporations in the world are based in countries outside the United States. Also, companies have dispersed their manufacturing, marketing, and research facilities to those locations around the globe where cost and skill conditions are most favorable. This trend is now so pervasive in industries such as automobiles, aerospace, and electronics that it is becoming increasingly irrelevant to talk about "American products" or "British products" or "Japanese products." Consider how Ford went about designing and manufacturing its Contour/Mystique line.

So is the Ford Contour an "American product"? Not really—but neither is it a "British

table 6.2
The top 50 global companies

The Business Week Global 1000			
Rank			**Market value**
1999	**1998**		**Billions of U.S. dollars**
1	2	MICROSOFT	U.S. 407.22
2	1	GENERAL ELECTRIC	U.S. 333.05
3	13	INTERNATIONAL BUSINESS MACHINES	U.S. 214.81
4	5	EXXON	U.S. 193.92
5	3	ROYAL DUTCH/SHELL GROUP	Neth./Britain 191.32
6	9	WAL-MART STORES	U.S. 189.55
7	16	AT&T	U.S. 186.14
8	10	INTEL	U.S. 180.24
9	30	CISCO SYSTEMS	U.S. 174.09
10	26	BP AMOCO	Britain 173.87
11	4	COCA-COLA	U.S. 168.99
12	6	MERCK	U.S. 159.80
13	8	NIPPON TELEGRAPH & TELEPHONE	Japan 156.77
14	71	MCI WORLDCOM	U.S. 152.24
15	36	CITIGROUP	U.S. 150.94
16	19	LUCENT TECHNOLOGIES	U.S. 150.34
17	25	AMERICAN INTERNATIONAL GROUP	U.S. 141.62
18	7	PFIZER	U.S. 138.37
19	14	BRISTOL-MYERS SQUIBB	U.S. 136.53
20	229	AMERICA ONLINE	U.S. 129.07
21	20	JOHNSON & JOHNSON	U.S. 124.64
22	12	PROCTER & GAMBLE	U.S. 124.05

(continued)

(continued)

23	32	DEUTSCHE TELEKOM	Germany 115.02
24	33	BANK OF AMERICA	U.S. 112.87
25	22	BERKSHIRE HATHAWAY	U.S. 109.37
26	40	BRITISH TELECOMMUNICATIONS	Britain 107.14
27	NR	NTT DOCOMO	Japan 106.14
28	15	ROCHE HOLDING	Switzerland 103.72
29	11	NOVARTIS	Switzerland 101.63
30	17	GLAXO WELLCOME	Britain 101.53
31	34	SBC COMMUNICATIONS	U.S. 100.32
32	18	TOYOTA MOTOR	Japan 99.83
33	42	HEWLETT-PACKARD	U.S. 95.73
34	39	HSBC HOLDINGS	Britain 93.69
35	21	PHILIP MORRIS	U.S. 93.55
36	44	BELLSOUTH	U.S. 89.38
37	63	DELL COMPUTER	U.S. 87.34
38	87	NOKIA	Finland 87.20
39	66	DAIMLERCHRYSLER	Germany 86.87
40	35	BELL ATLANTIC	U.S. 84.99
41	54	HOME DEPOT	U.S. 83.64
42	76	TIME WARNER	U.S. 81.19
43	59	FRANCE TELECOM	France 79.93
44	49	MOBIL	U.S. 79.29
45	37	ELI LILLY	U.S. 78.67
46	45	AMERICAN HOME PRODUCTS	U.S. 75.95
47	23	DUPONT	U.S. 73.74
48	50	SMITHKLINE BEECHAM	Britain 72.92
49	73	AMERITECH	U.S. 72.33
50	28	LLOYDS TSB GROUP	Britain 71.95

Source: Adapted from *The Wall Street Journal, Business Week,* and other company documents.

product," a "German product," a "Belgian product," a "French product," an "Italian product," a "Mexican product," and so on. You get the idea. Like an increasing number of the products we buy today, it is an international product.

Internationalization is not limited to large corporations like Ford. An increasing number of medium-size and small firms also engage in international trade. Some companies have limited their involvement to exporting, while others have taken the process a step further by setting up production facilities overseas. Consider Lubricating Systems, Inc. of Kent, Washington. The company manufactures lubricating fluids for machine tools. The company is hardly an industrial giant, yet approximately one-third of its total sales are generated by exports to countries such as Japan, Israel, and the United Arab Emirates. Moreover, Lubricating Systems is now setting up a joint venture with a German company to serve the European market. Even a tiny company such as SpringHill Greenhouses in Lodi, Ohio, operates internationally. With only a half dozen employees, SpringHill works with wholesale growers in the Netherlands (for tulips and lilies) and Colombia (for roses) to get the best value for flowers. Then, working through global associations such as FTD and Teleflora, SpringHill networks with other florists to send and receive orders virtually anywhere around the world.[12]

Ford's $6 billion world car

Its code name is CDW27. We know it better as the Ford Contour or Mercury Mystique. In Europe it's called the Ford Mondeo. It took 11 years to develop and cost over $6 billion to launch, but CDW27 is more than a car; it is a platform for how Ford is competing globally. Most experts agree that national borders mean less and less in the world auto industry, and that building a world car—one that can be made and marketed around the world—can provide the ultimate in economies of scale.

To organize the design and manufacture of CDW27, Ford had four design studios, in Italy, California, Germany, and Michigan, work on the project. Engineers

Ford Motor Company's "global" car, the Ford Mondeo, has become a leader in the mid-sized segment of the European market. Its U.S. versions (Contour and Mystique) are doing well, too. *[Courtesy of Ford Motor Company]*

in Detroit designed the all-new 2.5-liter V-6 engine, the automatic transmission, and the heating and air-conditioning units. A team in Dunton, England, contributed the interior, the steering, the suspension, the electronics, the manual transmission, and the new four-cylinder engine. Employees in Cologne, Germany, did the basic structural engineering and also designed three sheet-metal bodies for the car tailored to different markets. In addition to design, renovations and retooling were done at nine factories, including engine parts in Wales, Cologne, Cleveland, and Chihuahua, Mexico. To ensure quality, Ford airlifted 150 engineers from England and Germany to mobile offices outside the production plant in Genk, Belgium. The executive in charge of CDW27, John Oldfield, was British and based in Cologne, Germany. But final responsibility for the program rested at Ford's world headquarters in Dearborn, Michigan.

With all the obstacles that had to be overcome, why did Ford create CDW27? Ford executives point to the economics of the project as a primary rationale. By designing and manufacturing the car for both Europe and the United States, Ford was able to allocate people and facilities to other projects. By using identical production tools at both Genk and Kansas City, Ford saved an estimated 25 percent on custom-built factory items. In the end, Ford saved $150 per car. Spread over 700,000 units, the total savings is $100 million a year. A second reason for CDW27 was that it was a learning experience. CDW27 is the nucleus for a decade's worth of products, all built from a common design and with great economies of scale. For $6 billion the company got three new models, two new engines, two new transmissions, and nine new or revamped factories.

Sources: David Welch and Christine Tierney, "Can the Mondeo Get Ford Back into the Race?," *Business Week Online,* October 16, 2000; Jack Ewing, "Europe: Where Ford Needs to Step on the Gas," *Business Week Online,* October 11, 1999; "Long-Term Update: Ford Contour SE," *Ward's Auto World* 32, no. 2. February 1996, p. 60; Wade A. Hoyt, "Chevrolet Lumina and Ford Contour: Going Head-to-Head against Popular Japanese Sedans," *Medical Economics* 72, no. 4. February 27, 1995, pp. 44–53; and Ken Korane, "Mercury Mystique: Look Out, Imports," *Machine Design* 67, no. 6. March 23, 1995, pp. 102–3. ●

figure 6.3
Organizational models

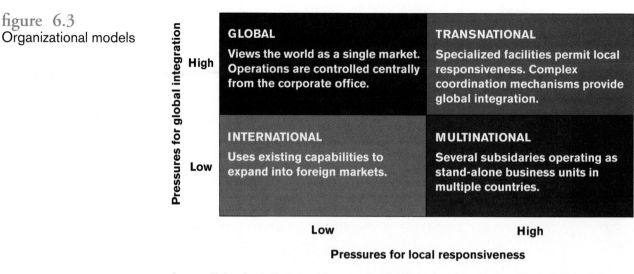

Sources: Christopher A. Bartlett and Sumantra Ghoshal, *Managing across Borders: The Transnational Solution* (Boston: Harvard Business School Press, 1991); and Anne-Wil Harzing, "An Empirical Analysis and Extension of the Bartlett and Goshal Typology of Multinational Companies," *Journal of International Business Studies* (2000), 31, no. 1, pp. 101–20.

Global strategy

One of the critical tasks an international manager faces is to identify the best strategy for competing in a global marketplace. To approach this issue, it is helpful to plot a company's position on an integration–responsiveness grid (see Figure 6.3). The vertical axis measures pressures for *global integration,* and the horizontal axis measures pressures for local responsiveness.

Pressures for global integration

Universal needs create strong pressure for a global strategy. Universal needs exist when the tastes and preferences of consumers in different countries with regard to a product are similar. Products that serve universal needs require little adaptation across national markets; thus, global integration is facilitated. This is the case in many industrial markets. Electronic products such as capacitors, resistors, and semiconductor chips are products that meet universal needs.

Competitive *pressures to reduce costs* may force a company to globally integrate manufacturing. This can be particularly important in industries in which price is the main competitive weapon and competition is intense (for example, hand-held calculators and semiconductor chips). It is also important in industries in which key international competitors are based in countries with low factor costs (e.g., low labor and energy costs).

The presence of competitors engaged in *global strategic coordination* is another factor that creates pressure for global integration. Reacting to global competitive threats calls for global strategic coordination, which creates pressure to centralize decisions regarding the competitive strategies of different national subsidiaries at corporate headquarters. Thus, once one multinational company in an industry adopts global strategic coordination, its competitors may be forced to respond in kind.

Pressures for local responsiveness

In some circumstances, companies must be able to adapt to different needs in different locations. Strong pressures for local responsiveness emerge when *consumer tastes and preferences differ significantly* among countries. In such cases, product and/or marketing messages have to be customized.

In the automobile industry, for example, demand by United States consumers for pickup trucks is strong. This is particularly true in the South and West, where many families have a pickup truck as a second or third car. In contrast, in Europe pickup trucks are viewed as utility vehicles and are purchased primarily by companies rather than by individuals. As a result, automakers must tailor their marketing messages to the differences in consumer demand.

Pressures for local responsiveness also emerge when there are *differences in traditional practices* among countries. For example, in Great Britain people drive on the left side of the road, creating a demand for right-hand-drive cars, whereas in neighboring France people drive on the right side of the road. Obviously automobiles must be customized to accommodate this difference in traditional practices.

Differences in distribution channels and sales practices among countries may also create pressures for local responsiveness. In the pharmaceutical industry, the Japanese distribution system differs radically from the U.S. system. Japanese doctors will respond unfavorably to an American-style, high-pressure sales force. Thus, pharmaceutical companies have to adopt different marketing practices in Japan (soft versus hard sell).

Finally, *economic and political demands* imposed by host country governments may necessitate a degree of local responsiveness. Most important, threats of protectionism, economic nationalism, and local content rules (rules requiring that a certain percentage of a product be manufactured locally) dictate that international companies manufacture locally.

Choosing a global strategy

Figure 6.3 shows the integration-responsiveness grid, implying the existence of four approaches to international competition: the international model, the multinational model, the global model, and the transnational model. Each of these types of organizations differs in terms of its approach to strategy as well as the structure and systems that drive operations.

international organization model An organization model that is composed of a company's overseas subsidiaries and characterized by greater control by the parent company over the research function and local product and marketing strategies than is the case in the multinational model.

The international model   The **international organization model** is designed to help companies exploit their existing core capabilities to expand into foreign markets. The international model uses subsidiaries in each country in which the company does business, with ultimate control exercised by the parent company. In particular, while subsidiaries may have some latitude to adapt products to local conditions, core functions such as research and development tend to be centralized in the parent company. Consequently, subsidiary dependence on the parent company for new products, processes, and ideas requires a great deal of coordination and control by the parent company.

The advantage of this model is that it facilitates the transfer of skills and know-how from the parent company to subsidiaries around the globe. For example, IBM, Xerox, and Kodak all profited from the transfer of their core skills in technology and R&D overseas. The overseas successes of Kellogg, Coca-Cola, Heinz, and Procter & Gamble are

Heinz is especially skilled at overseas marketing. This prominent billboard is displayed in Guangdong, China.
[Greg Girard/Contact Press Images]

based more on marketing know-how than on technological expertise. During the 1970s and 1980s, many Japanese companies, including Toyota and Honda, successfully penetrated U.S. markets with their core competencies in manufacturing relative to local competitors. Still others have based their competitive advantage on general management skills. These factors explain the growth of international hotel chains such as Hilton International, Intercontinental, and Sheraton.

One disadvantage of the international model is that it does not provide maximum latitude for responding to local conditions. In addition, it frequently does not provide the opportunity to achieve a low-cost position via scale economics.

multinational organization model An organization model that consists of the subsidiaries in each country in which a company does business, with ultimate control exercised by the parent company.

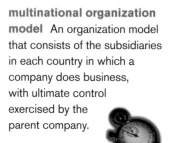

The multinational model

In contrast to the international model, the **multinational organization model** uses subsidiaries (i.e., independent companies) in each country in which the company does business, and provides a great deal of discretion to those subsidiaries to respond to local conditions. Each local subsidiary is a self-contained unit with all the functions required for operating in the host market. Thus, each subsidiary has its own manufacturing, marketing, research, and human resources functions. Because of this autonomy, each multinational subsidiary can customize its products and strategies according to the tastes and preferences of local consumers; the competitive conditions; and political, legal, and social structures.

The multinational model was widespread among many of the early European corporations such as Unilever and Royal Dutch Shell. One advantage of allowing local responsiveness is that there is less need for coordination and direction from corporate headquarters. Since each subsidiary is a self-contained unit, few transfers of goods and services occur among subsidiaries, thus alleviating problems with transfer pricing and the like.

A major disadvantage of the multinational form is higher manufacturing costs and duplication of effort. Although a multinational can transfer core skills among its international operations, it cannot realize scale economies from centralizing manufacturing facilities and offering a standardized product to the global marketplace. Moreover, because a multinational approach tends to decentralize strategy decisions (discussed further in Chapters 8 and 9), it is difficult to launch coordinated global attacks against competitors. This can be a significant disadvantage when competitors have this ability.

global organization model An organization model consisting of a company's overseas subsidiaries and characterized by centralized decision making and tight control by the parent company over most aspects of worldwide operations. Typically adopted by organizations that base their global competitive strategy on low cost.

The global model

The **global organization model** is designed to enable a company to market a standardized product in the global marketplace and to manufacture that product in a limited number of locations where the mix of costs and skills is most favorable. The global model has been adopted by companies that view the world as one market and assume that there are no tangible differences among countries with regard to consumer tastes and preferences. Procter & Gamble, for example, has been successful in Europe against Unilever because it has approached the entire continent as a unified whole.

Companies that adopt the global model tend to become the low-cost players in any industry. These companies construct global-scale manufacturing facilities in a few selected low-cost locations so that they can realize scale economies. These scale economies come from spreading the fixed costs of investments in new-product development, plant and equipment, and the like over worldwide sales. By using centralized manufacturing facilities and global marketing strategies, Sony was able to push down its unit costs to the point where it became the low-cost player in the global television market. This enabled Sony to take market share away from Philips, RCA, and Zenith, all of which traditionally based manufacturing operations in each major national market (a characteristic of the multinational approach). Because operations are centralized, subsidiaries usually are limited to marketing and service functions.

On the downside, because a company pursuing a purely global approach tries to standardize its products and services, it may be less responsive to consumer tastes and demands in different countries. Attempts to lower costs through global product standardization may result in a product that fails to satisfy anyone. For example, while Procter & Gamble has been quite successful using a global approach, the company experienced problems when it tried to market Cheer laundry detergent in Japan. Unfortunately for P&G, the product did not "suds up" as promoted in Japan because the Japanese use a great deal of fabric softener, which suppresses suds. Moreover, the claim that Cheer worked in all water temperatures was irrelevant in Japan, where most washing is done in cold water.

Companies pursuing a pure global approach to strategy require increased coordination and paperwork and additional staff. Moreover, such companies must decide how to price transfers of goods and services among parts of the company based in different countries. Transfer-pricing problems are difficult enough to resolve within just one country; in a global company, transfer pricing can be further complicated by volatile exchange rates.

The transnational model

In today's global economy, achieving a competitive advantage often requires the *simultaneous* pursuit of gains from local responsiveness, transfer of know-how, and cost economies.[13] This raises the question of whether it is possible to design an organization that enables a company to simultaneously reap all the benefits of global expansion. Recently a number of companies, including Unilever, Caterpillar, and Philips, have been experimenting with a new organization model—the transnational organization model—that is designed to do just that.

transnational organization model An organization model characterized by centralization of certain functions in locations that best achieve cost economies; basing of other functions in the company's national subsidiaries to facilitate greater local responsiveness; and fostering of communication among subsidiaries to permit transfer of technological expertise and skills.

In companies that adopt the **transnational organization model,** certain functions, particularly research, tend to be centralized at home. Other functions are also centralized, but not necessarily in the home country. To achieve cost economies, companies may base global-scale production plants for labor-intensive products in low-wage countries such as Mexico or Singapore and locate production plants that require a skilled workforce in high-skill countries such as Germany or Japan.

Other functions, particularly marketing, service, and final-assembly functions, tend to be based in the national subsidiaries to facilitate greater local responsiveness. Thus, major components may be manufactured in centralized production plants to realize scale economies and then shipped to local plants, where the final product is assembled and customized to fit local needs.

Caterpillar Tractor is a transnational company.[14] The need to compete with low-cost competitors such as Komatsu has forced Caterpillar to look for greater cost economies by centralizing global production at locations where the factor cost/skill mix is most favorable. At the same time, variations in construction practices and government regulations across countries mean that Caterpillar must be responsive to local needs. On the integration–responsiveness grid in Figure 6.3, therefore, Caterpillar is situated toward the top right-hand corner.

To deal with these simultaneous demands, Caterpillar has designed its products to use many identical components and invested in a few large-scale component manufacturing facilities to fill global demand and realize scale economies. But while the company manufactures components centrally, it has assembly plants in each of its major markets. At these plants Caterpillar adds local product features, tailoring the finished product to local needs. Thus, Caterpillar is able to realize many of the benefits of global manufacturing while managing pressure for local responsiveness by differentiating its product among national markets.

Perhaps the most important distinguishing characteristic of the transnational organization is the fostering of communications among subsidiaries. National subsidiaries communicate better with one another so that they can transfer technological expertise and skills among themselves to their mutual benefit. At the same time, centralized manufacturing plants coordinate their production with local assembly plants, thereby facilitating the smooth operation of an integrated, worldwide production system.

Achieving such communications across subsidiaries requires elaborate formal mechanisms, such as transnational committees staffed by people from the various subsidiaries who are responsible for monitoring coordination among subsidiaries. Equally important is to transfer managers among subsidiaries on a regular basis. This enables international managers to establish a global network of personal contacts in different subsidiaries with whom they can share information as the need arises. Finally, achieving coordination among subsidiaries requires that the head office play a proactive role in coordinating their activities.

table 6.3
Comparison of entry modes

Exporting	Licensing	Franchising	Joint venture	Wholly owned subsidiary
Advantages				
Scale economies	Lower development costs	Lower development costs	Local knowledge	Maintains control over technology
Consistent with pure global strategy	Lower political risk	Lower political risk	Shared costs and risk	Maintains control over operations
			May be the only option	
Disadvantages				
No low-cost sites	Loss of control over technology	Loss of control over quality	Loss of control over technology	High cost
High transportation costs			Conflict between partners	High risk
Tariff barriers				

Entry mode

When considering global expansion, international managers must decide on the best means of entering an overseas market. There are five basic ways to expand overseas: exporting, licensing, franchising, entering into a joint venture with a host country company, and setting up a wholly owned subsidiary in the host country.[15] Table 6.3 compares the entry modes.

Exporting

Most manufacturing companies begin global expansion as exporters and later switch to one of the other modes for serving an overseas market. The advantages of exporting are that it (1) provides scale economies by avoiding the costs of manufacturing in other countries and (2) is consistent with a pure global strategy. By manufacturing the product in a centralized location and then exporting it to other national markets, the company may be able to realize substantial scale economies from its global sales volume.

On the other hand, exporting has a number of drawbacks. First, exporting from the company's home base may be inappropriate if other countries offer lower-cost locations for manufacturing the product. An alternative is to manufacture in a location where the mix of factor costs and skills is most favorable and then export from that location to other markets to achieve scale economies. Several U.S. electronics companies have moved some manufacturing operations to the Far East, where low-cost, high-skill labor is available, then export from that location to other countries, including the United States.

A second drawback of exporting is that high transportation costs can make it uneconomical, particularly in the case of bulk products. Chemical companies get around this by manufacturing their products on a regional basis, serving several countries in a region from one facility.

A third drawback is that host countries can impose (or threaten to impose) tariff barriers. As noted earlier, Japanese automakers reduced this risk by setting up manufacturing plants in the United States.

Licensing

International licensing is an arrangement whereby a licensee in another country buys the rights to manufacture a company's product in its own country for a negotiated fee (typically, royalty payments on the number of units sold). The licensee then puts up most of the capital necessary to get the overseas operation going. The advantage of licensing is that the company need not bear the costs and risks of opening up an overseas market.

On the other hand, a problem arises when a company licenses its technological expertise to overseas companies. Technological know-how is the basis of the competitive advantage of many multinational companies. But RCA Corporation lost control over its color TV technology by licensing it to a number of Japanese companies. The Japanese companies quickly assimilated RCA's technology and then used it to enter the U.S. market. Now the Japanese have a bigger share of the U.S. market than the RCA brand does.

Pokemon—Gotta catch 'em all

Pika-who? Try Pikachu, a character you may not know by name, but certainly by its association with the game Pokemon. From an import perspective, the Pokemon products, which range from video games, TV shows, and toys, to the highly popular trading card game, are hot items. Granted, the dynamics that surround the toy industry are unique from those of other industries, yet the reasons behind Pokemon's success in the United States can provide valuable insight for U.S. traders.

Pokemon crossed the ocean from Japan and arrived in North America in September 1998 as a TV show and video game. Although many were skeptical that the Japanese craze would be repeated with American kids, Nintendo took a gamble and hit the mother lode. Sales for Nintendo and its licensees have already surpassed U.S. $1 billion. Video game giant Nintendo makes the Pokemon Red, Blue, and Yellow cartridges for its palm-sized Game Boy. Silver and Gold versions arrived recently, along with more Pokemon species to add to the existing 150 characters.

The Pokemon craze skyrocketed with the introduction of the trading card game by Renton, Washington-based Wizards of the Coast. The company unveiled the trading cards in January 1999, and sales have climbed steadily since. Carole Pucik, Pokemon brand manager for Wizards of the Coast, says that cultivating "brand awareness" is a key component for successful marketing. Indeed, American kids are being bombarded by Pokemon, from Burger King giveaways to General Mills candy strips called Pokemon rolls, and Quaker Cereal's promotions involving Cap'n Crunch and Life cereals and the company's chewy granola bars. *Pokemon: The First Movie* raked in a record-setting $50.8 million during its first five days in release even though many, kids included, considered the film a dud. The second and third Pokemon movies have subsequently been released. And, of course, don't forget the Pokemon.com Website.

Japenese import Pokemon has taken North America by storm since its introduction in September 1998. *[AP/WIDE WORLD PHOTOS]*

Overall, Pokemon underwent few changes in preparation for its debut in America. The developer of the Cabbage Patch doll was hired by Nintendo of America and its Japanese partner to assist with toy merchandising, and a few modifications were made to the original Japanese show. For instance, some names like Satoshi and Shigeru were Westernized to become Ash and Gary. However, careful attention to the successes and failures of other "unique" toy products, and a carefully scripted product launch (the movie, for example, had been completed well before its release and licensed merchandise was not sold until the trading card craze was already well under way), appear to have helped keep Pokemon fever alive.

Source: Condensed from Lara L Sowinski, "Exporting American know-how," *World Trade*, April 2000, 13, no. 4, pp. 42–51. ●

Franchising

In many respects, franchising is similar to licensing. However, whereas licensing is a strategy pursued primarily by manufacturing companies, franchising is used primarily by service companies. McDonald's, Hilton International, and many other companies have expanded overseas by franchising.

In franchising, the company sells limited rights to use its brand name to franchisees in return for a lump-sum payment and a share of the franchisee's profits. However, unlike most licensing agreements, the franchisee has to agree to abide by strict rules as to how it does business. Thus, when McDonald's enters into a franchising agreement with an overseas company, it expects the franchisee to run its restaurants in a manner identical to those run under the McDonald's name elsewhere in the world.

The advantages of franchising as an entry mode are similar to those of licensing. The most significant disadvantage concerns quality control. The company's brand name guarantees consistency in the company's product. Thus, a business traveler booking into a Hilton International hotel in Hong Kong can reasonably expect the same quality of room, food, and service that he or she would receive in New York. But if overseas franchisees are less concerned about quality than they should be, the impact can go beyond lost sales in the local market to a decline in the company's reputation worldwide. If a business traveler has an unpleasant experience at the Hilton in Hong Kong, she or he may decide never to go to another Hilton hotel—and urge colleagues to do likewise. To make matters worse, the geographical distance between the franchisor and its overseas franchisees makes poor quality difficult to detect.

Joint ventures

Establishing a joint venture (a formal business agreement discussed in more detail in Chapter 11) with a company in another country has long been a popular means for entering a new market. Joint ventures benefit a company through (1) the local partner's knowledge of the host country's competitive conditions, culture, language, political systems, and business systems; and (2) the sharing of development costs and/or risks with the local partner. In addition, many countries' political considerations make joint ventures the only feasible entry mode. As the following discussion shows, many U.S. companies are finding this to be the case in China.

Good fortune in China

A number of U.S. companies are making inroads to China via joint ventures and other forms of partnerships:

- Eastman Kodak has established a joint venture with China Lucky Film Corporation in order to gain a stronger foothold in the country's $250 million market for film. Kodak's investment not only will help China Lucky's financial per-

Joint ventures enable companies like DaimlerChrysler to gain better access to foreign markets. *[Jeffrey Aaronsen/ Network Aspen]*

formance (which has been poor of late) but will allow Kodak to avoid the 60 percent duty on imported film. This venture remains caught in a national debate about whether China should bolster its domestic producers or allow foreign investment.

- AT&T is forming a joint venture with Shanghai Telecom and Shanghai Information Investment, Inc. to provide broadband IP value-added services to the enterprise sector. AT&T's $25 million investment will give it a 25 percent stake in the venture, Shanghai Symphony Telecommunications. STC will own 60 percent of the company, and SII will own 15 percent. Executives and members of the board of directors will come from the three founding companies. For China, allowing entry by AT&T into its markets is a move toward membership in the World Trade Organization.
- DuPont and Teijin recently integrated their polyester film operations. The joint venture, called DuPont Teigjin, has operations in seven countries, and has a total global capacity for film of roughly 300,000 tons per year.
- Volvo, part of Ford Motor Company, recently established a $97 million joint venture with a local airplane maker in Xian to make easy-handling city and commuter buses in Shanghai. Others making full-sized buses in China include DaimlerChrysler, Daewoo, and Isuzu.
- Maytag has invested approximately $70 million in a series of joint ventures in laundry and refrigeration with the Hefei Rongshida Group. To extend its marketing reach, Maytag recently acquired a Chinese domestic washing machine maker, Three Gorge Co.

Sources: Toby Weber, "The Great Wall Comes Down," *Telephony,* December 11, 2000, 239, no. 24, p. 10; "DuPont Teijin Films to Expand Its Films Operations in China," *Chemical Market Reporter,* November 27, 2000, 258, no. 22, p. 7; Bruce Gilley, ``Goodbye to the Bone Shakers,'' *Far Eastern Economic Review,* November 16, 2000, 163, no. 46, p. 46; Jack Robertson, "IBM Micro Building $300 Million Facility in China," *Electronic Buyers' News,* October 30, 2000, 1235, p. 8; Robert L. Holding and Joe Jancsurak, "Globalization: The Second Decade," *Appliance Manufacturer,* May 1999, 47, no. 5, pp. 34, 37. ●

Despite the advantages of joint ventures such as these, they also have two possible disadvantages. First, as in the case of licensing, a company runs the risk of losing control over its technology to its venture partner. Second, because control is shared with the partner, the company may lose control over its subsidiaries. Indeed, conflict over who controls what within a joint venture is a primary reason many joint ventures fail.

Wholly owned subsidiaries

Establishing a wholly owned subsidiary, that is, an independent company owned by the parent corporation, is the most costly method of serving an overseas market. Companies that use this approach must bear the full costs and risks associated with setting up overseas operations (as opposed to joint ventures, in which the costs and risks are shared, or licensing, in which the licensee bears most of the costs and risks).

Nevertheless, setting up a wholly owned subsidiary offers two clear advantages. First, when a company's competitive advantage is based on technology, a wholly owned subsidiary normally will be the preferred entry mode because it reduces the risk of losing control over the technology. This was the case for 3M, who was the first to set up a wholly owned subsidiary in China.[16] Wholly owned subsidiaries tend to be the favored entry mode in the semiconductor, electronics, and pharmaceutical industries.

Second, a wholly owned subsidiary gives a company tight control over operations in other countries, which is necessary if it chooses to pursue a global strategy. Establishing a global manufacturing system requires world headquarters to have a high degree of control over the operations of national affiliates. Unlike licensees or joint venture partners, wholly owned subsidiaries usually accept centrally determined decisions about how to produce, how much to produce, and how to price output for transfer among operations.

Managing across borders

expatriates Parent-company nationals who are sent to work at a foreign subsidiary.

host-country nationals Natives of the country where an overseas subsidiary is located.

third-country nationals Natives of a country other than the home country or the host country of an overseas subsidiary.

When establishing operations overseas, headquarter executives have a choice among sending **expatriates** (individuals from the parent country), using **host-country nationals** (natives of the host country), or deploying **third-country nationals** (natives of a country other than the home country or the host country). While most corporations use some combination of all three types of employees, there are advantages and disadvantages of each. Colgate-Palmolive, for example, uses expatriates in an effort to shorten the delivery time of products-to-market, while AT&T uses expatriates to help transfer the company's culture. On the other hand, companies such as Chevron and Texas Instruments make more limited use of expatriates. Chevron typically sends a management team to review the skills of local employees, and sends expatriates only if their technical skills are needed. If expatriates are sent, it is expected that operational control will be passed over to local employees. Texas Instruments uses very few expatriates, but relies on phone, fax, and computers to facilitate communication. However, TI frequently sends people on extended travel so they meet their cohorts around the world.[17]

Working internationally can be very stressful, even for experienced "globalites." Table 6.4 shows some of the primary stressors for expatriates at different stages of their assignments. It also shows ways for executives to cope with stress as well as some of the things that companies can do to help with the adjustment.

Developing a valuable pool of expatriates is important. However, as shown in Figure 6.4, companies tend to make more use of host-country nationals over time. Local employees are more available, tend to have familiarity with the culture and language, and usually cost less because they do not have to be displaced. In addition, local governments often provide incentives to companies that create good jobs for their citizens (or they may place restrictions on the use of expatriates). For these reasons, executives at Allen Bradley, a division of Rockwell International, believe that building a strong local workforce is critical to their success overseas, and they transport key host-country nationals to the United States for skills training. The trend away from using expatriates in top management positions is especially apparent in companies that truly want to create a multinational culture. In Honeywell's European division, for example, many of the top executive positions are held by non-Americans.[18]

Over the years, U.S.–based companies, in particular, have tended to use more third-country nationals to work in a country different from their own, and different from the parent company's. When Eastman Kodak assembled a management team to devise a launch strategy for its Photo-CD line in Europe, the team members were based in London, but the leader was from Belgium. Because third-country nationals can soften the political tensions between the parent country and the host country, they often represent a convenient compromise.[19]

table 6.4

Stressors and coping responses in the developmental stages of expatriate executives

Stage	Primary stressors	Executive coping response	Employer coping response
Expatriate selection	Cross-cultural unreadiness.	Engage in self-evaluation.	Encourage expatriate's self- and family evaluation. Perform an assessment of potential and interests.
Assignment acceptance	Unrealistic evaluation of stressors to come. Hurried time frame.	Think of assignment as a growth opportunity rather than an instrument to vertical promotion.	Do not make hard-to-keep promises. Clarify expectations.
Pre- and post-arrival training	Ignorance of cultural differences.	Do not make unwarranted assumptions of cultural competence and cultural rules.	Provide pre-, during, and post-assignment training. Encourage support-seeking behavior.
Arrival	Cultural shock. Stressor re-evaluation. Feelings of lack of fit and differential treatment.	Do not construe identification with the host and parent cultures as mutually exclusive. Seek social support.	Provide post-arrival training. Facilitate integration in expatriate network.
Novice	Cultural blunders or inadequacy of coping responses. Ambiguity owing to inability to decipher meaning of situations.	Observe and study functional value of coping responses among locals. Do not simply replicate responses that worked at home.	Provide follow-up training. Seek advice from locals and expatriate network.
Transitional	Rejection of host or parent culture.	Form and maintain attachments with both cultures.	Promote culturally sensitive policies at host country. Provide Internet access to family and friends at home. Maintain constant communication and periodic visits to parent organization.
Mastery	Frustration with inability to perform boundary spanning role. Bothered by living with a cultural paradox.	Internalize and enjoy identification with both cultures and walking between two cultures.	Reinforce rather than punish dual identification by defining common goals.
Repatriation	Disappointment with unfulfilled expectations. Sense of isolation. Loss of autonomy.	Realistically reevaluate assignment as a personal and professional growth opportunity.	Arrange pre-repatriation briefings and interviews. Schedule post-repatriation support meetings.

Source: J. Sanchez, P. Spector, and C. Cooper, "Adapting to a Boundaryless World: A Developmental Expatriate Model," *The Academy of Management Executive*, May 2000, 14, no. 2, pp. 96–106.

figure 6.4

Evolution of a foreign subsidiary

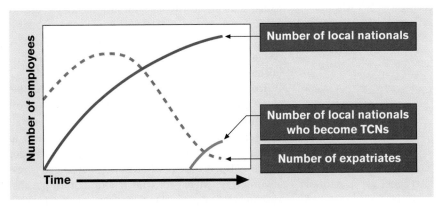

Source: Calvin Reynolds, "Strategic Employment of Third Country Nationals," *Human Resource Planning* v20, nl, 1997, pp. 33–93. Reprinted by permission of Organization Resources Counselors, Inc.

Skills of the global manager

It is estimated that nearly 15 percent of all employee transfers are to an international location. However, a recent survey of 1,500 senior executives showed that there is a critical shortage of U.S. managers equipped to run global businesses.[20] Indicative of this fact is the **failure rate** among expatriates (defined as those who come home early), which has been estimated to range from 25 to 50 percent. The average cost of each of these failed assignments ranges from $40,000 to $250,000.[21] Typically the causes for failure overseas extend beyond technical capability, and include personal and social issues as well. Interestingly, one of the biggest problems is a spouse's inability to adjust to his or her new surroundings. For both the expatriate and the spouse, adjustment requires flexibility, emotional stability, empathy for the culture, communication skills, resourcefulness, initiative, and diplomatic skills.[22]

Interestingly, while many U.S. companies have hesitated to send women abroad—believing that women either do not want international assignments or that other cultures would not welcome women—their success rate has been estimated at 97 percent (far greater than for their male counterparts).[23] Ironically, for a country that had been viewed as not welcoming foreign women, in Japan U.S. women are first viewed as foreigners (*gaijin* in Japanese) and only second as women. And because it is unusual for women to be sent on foreign assignments, their distinctiveness and visibility tend to increase their chances for success.[24]

Companies such as Levi-Strauss, Bechtel, Monsanto, Whirlpool, and Dow Chemical have worked to identify the characteristics of individuals that will predict their success abroad. Figure 6.5 shows skills that can be used to identify candidates who are likely to succeed in a global environment. Interestingly, in addition to such things as cultural sensitivity, technical expertise, and business knowledge, an individual's success abroad may depend greatly on his or her ability to learn from experience.[25]

Companies such as Amoco, Mercedes Benz, Hyatt, British Petroleum, and others with large international staffs have extensive training programs to prepare employees for international assignments. Table 6.5 suggests ways to improve their likelihood of success. Other organizations such as Coca-Cola, Motorola, Chevron, and Mattel have extended this training to include employees who may be located in the United States but who nevertheless deal in international markets. These programs focus on areas such as language, culture, and career development.

Understanding cultural issues

In many ways, cultural issues represent the most elusive aspect of international business. In an era when modern transportation and communication technologies have created a "global village," it is easy to forget how deep and enduring the differences among nations actually can be. The fact that people everywhere drink Coke, wear blue jeans, and drive Toyotas doesn't mean we are all becoming alike. Each country is unique for reasons rooted in history, culture, language, geography, social conditions, race, and religion. These differences complicate any international activities, and represent the fundamental issues that inform and guide how a company should conduct business across borders.

Ironically, while most of us would guess that the trick to working abroad is learning about the foreign culture, in reality our problems often stem from our being oblivious to our own cultural conditioning. Most of us pay no attention to how culture influences our everyday behavior, and because of this we tend to adapt poorly to situations that are unique or foreign to us. This is one reason why people traveling abroad frequently experience **culture shock**—the disorientation and stress associated with being in a foreign environment. Managers who ignore culture put their organizations at a great disadvantage in the global marketplace. Because each culture has its own norms, customs, and expectations for behavior, success in an international environment depends on one's ability to understand one's own and the other culture and to recognize that abrupt changes will be met with resistance.[26]

figure 6.5
Identifying international
executives

End-state dimensions	Sample items
1. Sensitivity to cultural differences	When working with people from other cultures, works hard to understand their perspective.
2. Business knowledge	Has a solid understanding of the company's products and services.
3. Courage to take a stand	Is willing to take a stand on issues.
4. Brings out the best in people	Has a special talent for dealing with people
5. Acts with integrity	Can be depended on to tell the truth regardless of circumstances.
6. Is insightful	Is good at identifying the most important part of a complex problem.
7. Is committed to success	Clearly demonstrates commitment to seeing the organization succeed.
8. Takes risks	Takes personal as well as business risks.

Learning-oriented dimensions	Sample items
1. Uses feedback	Has changed as a result of feedback.
2. Is culturally adventurous	Enjoys the challenge of working in countries other than his/her own.
3. Seeks opportunities to learn	Takes advantage of opportunities to do new things.
4. Is open to criticism	Appears brittle—as if criticism might cause him/her to break.
5. Seeks feedback	Pursues feedback even when others are reluctant to give it.
6. Is flexible	Doesn't get so invested in things that he/she cannot change when something doesn't work.

Source: Gretchen M. Sprietzer, Morgan W. McCall, and Joan D. Mahoney, "Early Identification of International Executive Potential," *Journal of Applied Psychology* 82, no. 1 (1997), pp. 6–29.

A wealth of cross-cultural research has been conducted on the differences and similarities among various countries. Geert Hofstede, for example, has identified four dimensions along which managers in multinational corporations tend to view cultural differences:

table 6.5
How to prevent failed
assignments

Structure assignments clearly: Develop clear reporting relationships and job responsibilities.

Create clear job objectives.

Develop performance measurements based on objectives.

Use effective, validated selection and screening criteria (both personal and technical attributes).

Prepare expatriates and families for assignments (briefings, training, support).

Create a vehicle for ongoing communication with expatriate.

Anticipate repatriation to facilitate reentry when they come back home.

Consider developing a mentor program that will help monitor and intervene in case of trouble.

- *Power distance:* the extent to which a society accepts the fact that power in organizations is distributed unequally.
- *Individualism/collectivism:* the extent to which people act on their own or as a part of a group.
- *Uncertainty avoidance:* the extent to which people in a society feel threatened by uncertain and ambiguous situations.
- *Masculinity/femininity:* the extent to which a society values quantity of life (e.g., accomplishment, money) over quality of life (e.g., compassion, beauty).

Figure 6.6 offers a graphic depiction of how 40 different nations differ on the dimensions of individualism/collectivism and power distance. Clearly, cultures such as the United States that emphasize "rugged individualism" differ significantly from collectivistic cultures such as those of Pakistan, Taiwan, and Colombia. In order to be effective in cultures that exhibit a greater power distance, managers often must behave more autocratically, perhaps being less participative in decision making. Conversely, in Scandinavian cultures, in Sweden, for instance, where power distance is low, the very idea that management has the prerogative to make decisions on their own may be called into question. Here, managers tend to work more toward creating processes that reflect an "industrial democracy."

Cross-cultural management extends beyond U.S. employees going abroad. As the Mazda case exemplifies, international workers also have a difficult time adjusting to the United States.

Amazed at Mazda

The Japanese management team that went to Flat Rock, Michigan, to launch the first Mazda manufacturing plant on U.S. soil had been warned that working with American autoworkers would be different than managing their counterparts back in Japan. The rumor circulating among the Japanese expatriate community was that Americans lacked dedicated work habits.

Even so forewarned, the Mazda managers were amazed at what they found. By the first fall, the plant was closing in on its targeted first-year production numbers, the Americans having proved able workers and the start-up having gone as well as could be expected. Then November rolled around and production slowed to a crawl as half the plant's line workers and supervisors requested time off. Why so many? And why now? The answer: Deer season.

Welcome to America, land of the bottom line and the blaze-orange vest. The fact that Americans hunt was hardly new information to the Japanese. The idea that Americans would think nothing of sacrificing the operation of an automobile plant for the opening of deer season came as quite a shock.

Source: From "Welcome to America" by David Stamps. Reprinted with permission from the November 1996 issue of *Training Magazine.* Lakewood Publications, Minneapolis, MN. All rights reserved. Not for resale.   ●

This example from Mazda shows that culture shock works both ways. U.S. employees going abroad must adjust. But international workers must adjust as well. But despite the difficulties, there are a number of things that can be done to ease the adjustment of international workers coming to the United States. A few basic categories include the following:

- *Meetings:* Americans may dislike meetings, but they tend to have a fairly specific view of the purpose for them and how much time can be wasted. International workers, on the other hand, may have different preconceptions about how time is supposed to be spent in meetings and whether or not it is being wasted.

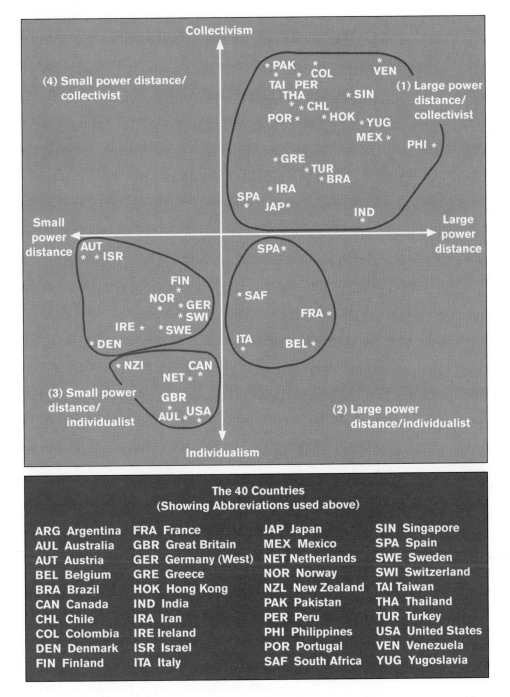

figure 6.6

The position of the 40 countries on the power distance and individualism scales

Source: Geert Hofstede, "Motivation, Leadership, and Organization: Do American Theories Apply Abroad?," *Organizational Dynamics* 9, no. 1 (Summer 1980), pp. 42–63. Reprinted by permission.

- *Work(aholic) schedules:* Workers from other countries can work long hours, but may be puzzled how U.S. workers can survive with only two or three weeks of vacation. Europeans in particular may balk at the idea of working on weekends.
- *E-mail:* Most of the world has not embraced e-mail and voice mail the way U.S. workers have. Most others would prefer to communicate face-to-face.
- *Fast-trackers:* Although U.S. companies may take a young MBA student and put him or her on the fast track to management, most other cultures (Germany and Japan in particular) still see no substitute for the wisdom gained through experience.
- *Feedback:* A manager's use of excessive positive feedback tends to be less prevalent in other cultures than in the United States.[27]

Cultural differences can often affect management expectations and styles.
[Loren Santow/Tony Stone Images]

Ethical issues in international management

If managers are to function effectively in a foreign setting, they must understand how culture influences both how they are perceived as well as how others behave. One of the most sensitive issues in this regard is understanding how culture plays out in terms of ethical behavior.[28] Issues of right and wrong get blurred as we move from one culture to another, and actions that may be normal and customary in one setting may be unethical—even illegal—in another. The use of bribes, for example, is an accepted part of commercial transactions in many Asian, African, Latin American, and Middle Eastern cultures. In the United States, of course, such behavior is illegal, but what should a U.S. businessperson do when working abroad? Estimates are that bribery and corruption cost U.S. firms over $64 billion in lost business each year.[29]

Though most Americans prefer to conduct business in a way consistent with prevailing U.S. laws, many people feel that we should not impose our cultural values on others. As a consequence, opinions differ widely on what is acceptable behavior when confronted with certain ethical dilemmas. Figure 6.7 shows the results of a survey that asked managers about the ethicality of payments to foreign officials. Surprisingly, less than half of the respondents said that the bribes were never acceptable, and in many cases managers suggested that such behavior would be acceptable if it was the local custom. In reality, these particular views are somewhat naive—while giving and receiving business gifts may be acceptable, the Foreign Corrupt Practices Act (1977) strictly prohibits U.S. employees from providing payments to foreign officials. While small "grease payments" to lower-level figures are permissible under the act, if the dollar amount of the payments is significant and would influence the outcome of negotiations, the transaction would be illegal.

Without an understanding of local customs, ethical standards, and applicable laws, an expatriate might be woefully unprepared to work internationally. To safeguard against these and other ethical problems, companies such as Caterpillar Tractor, General Dynamics, and United Technologies have established codes of conduct for international business. The codes lay out precisely what kinds of actions are permissible, and provide procedures and support systems that individuals can use in ambiguous situations. Four steps for establishing and reinforcing these codes might include the following:

- *Clearly articulate the company's values.* For example, Digital Equipment's Code of Business Conduct contains 27 pages of practices the company expects employees to use as well as suggestions for dealing with gray areas such as gifts given and received.

figure 6.7
Is this ethical?

Ethical dilemma: A company paid a $350,000 "consulting" fee to an official of a foreign country. In return, the official promised assistance in obtaining a contract that should produce a $10 million profit for the contracting company.

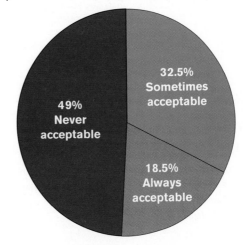

Percentage of respondents who said the payments were:

49.0% "never acceptable"
32.5% "sometimes acceptable"
18.5% "always acceptable"

Source: J. G. Longenecker, J. A. McKinney, and C. W. Moore, "The Ethical Issues of International Bribery: A Study of Attitudes among U.S. Business Professionals," *Journal of Business Ethics* 7 (1988), pp. 341–46. Reprinted with kind permission from Kluwer Academic Publishers.

- *Train employees to apply the values.* Levi-Strauss has a three-day ethics course (called the Principled Reasoning Approach) that teaches employees how to logically evaluate situations and figure out how ethical values translate into behavior.
- *Let business partners know the standards.* Levi-Strauss has established a set of global sourcing and operating guidelines that address workplace issues for all of its partners. The terms of engagement detail everything from environmental requirements to health and safety issues.
- *Translate ethics into performance appraisal.* H. B. Fuller ties compensation to performance evaluation (which includes an ethical component). It also conducts audits of key people who are in positions that could be subjected to difficult moral decisions.[30]

Interestingly, despite some obvious differences across cultures, research suggests that there are actually a set of five core values that most people embrace regardless of nationality or religion: *compassion, fairness, honesty, responsibility,* and *respect for others.* These values lie at the heart of human rights issues and seem to transcend more superficial differences among Americans, Europeans, and Asians. Finding shared values such as these allows companies to build more effective partnerships and alliances, especially across cultures. It may be the case that as long as people understand that there is a set of core values, they can permit all kinds of differences in strategy and tactics.[31]

To a large extent, the challenge of managing across borders comes down to the philosophies and systems used to manage people. In moving from domestic to international management, managers need to develop a wide portfolio of behaviors along with the capacity to adjust their behavior for a particular situation. This adjustment, however, should not compromise the values, integrity, and strengths of their home country. When managers can transcend national borders, and move among different cultures, then they will finally be in a position to leverage the strategic capabilities of the organization and take advantage of the opportunities that our global economy has to offer.

Key terms

Summary of learning objectives

Now that you have studied Chapter 6, you should know: Why the world economy is becoming more integrated than ever before.

The gradual lowering of barriers to free trade is making the world economy more integrated. This means that the modern manager operates in an environment that offers more opportunities but is also more complex and competitive than that faced by the manager of a generation ago.

What integration of the global economy means for individual companies and for their managers.

In recent years, rapid growth in world trade, foreign direct investment, and imports has occurred. One consequence is that companies around the globe are now finding their home markets under attack from international competitors. The global competitive environment is becoming a much tougher place in which to do business. However, companies now have access to markets that were previously denied to them.

The strategies organizations use to compete in the global marketplace.

The international corporation builds on its existing core capabilities in R&D, marketing, manufacturing, and so on, to penetrate overseas markets. A multinational is a more complex form that usually has fully autonomous units operating in multiple countries. Subsidiaries are given latitude to address local issues such as consumer preferences, political pressures, or economic trends in different regions of the world. The global organization pulls control of overseas operations back into the headquarters and tends to approach the world market as a "unified whole" by combining activities in each country to maximize efficiency on a global scale. A transnational attempts to achieve both local responsiveness and global integration by utilizing a network structure that coordinates specialized facilities positioned around the world.

The various entry modes organizations use to enter overseas markets.

There are five ways to enter an overseas market: exporting, licensing, franchising, entering into a joint venture, and setting up a wholly owned subsidiary. Each mode has advantages and disadvantages.

How companies can approach the task of staffing overseas operations.

Most executives use a combination of expatriates, host-country nationals, or third-country nationals. Expatriates are sometimes used to quickly establish new country operations, transfer the company's culture, and bring in a specific technical skill. Host-country nationals have the advantages that they are familiar with local customs and culture, may cost less, and are viewed more favorably by local governments. Third-country nationals are often used as a compromise in politically touchy situations or when home-country expatriates are not available.

The skills and knowledge managers need to manage globally.

The causes for failure overseas extend beyond technical capability, and include personal and social issues as well. Success depends on a manager's core skills, such as having a multidimensional perspective; having proficiency in line management and decision making; and having resourcefulness, cultural adaptability, sensitivity, team-building skills, and mental maturity. In addition, helpful augmented skills include computer literacy, negotiating skills, strategic vision, and ability to delegate.

Why cultural differences across countries influence management.

Culture influences our actions and perceptions as well as the actions and perceptions of others. Unfortunately, we are often unaware of how culture influences us, and this can cause problems. Today, managers must be able to change their behavior to match the needs and customs of local cultures. For example, in various cultures, employees expect a manager to be either more or less autocratic or participative. By recognizing their cultural differences, people can find it easier to work together collaboratively and benefit from the exchange.

Discussion questions

1. Why is the world economy becoming more integrated? What are the implications of this integration for international managers?

2. Imagine you were the CEO of a major company. What approach to global competition would you choose for your firm: international, multinational, global, or transnational? Why?

3. Why have franchises been so popular as a method of international expansion in the fast-food industry? Contrast this with high-tech manufacturing where joint ventures and partnerships have been more popular. What accounts for the differences across industries?

4. What are the pros and cons of using expatriates, host-country nationals, and third-country nationals to run overseas operations? If you were expanding your business, what approach would you use?

5. If you had entered into a joint venture with a foreign company, but knew that women were not treated fairly in that culture, would you consider sending a female expatriate to handle the start-up? Why or why not?

6. What are the biggest cultural obstacles that we must overcome if we are to work effectively in Mexico? Are there different obstacles in France? Japan?

Concluding Case

The big (Procter &) Gamble

Battered by disappointing revenue growth and demanding retail customers, Procter & Gamble is a company in a bind. In 1998, its executives boldly declared that the consumer-products giant would double its net sales by 2006, to $70 billion. P&G has consistently missed its growth targets ever since. And global economic turmoil is crimping overseas operations. The behemoth so used to leading the pack is looking lost. So P&G has set itself on a remarkably outward-looking self-improvement plan. It is undergoing a structural shift prompted at least in part by its big chain-store customers. And it is already rolling out an aggressive global marketing blitz.

But even as the giant revs its engines, critics wonder if it can overcome both economic turmoil around the world and cultural turmoil within its own ranks. "This is a very big deal, for Procter and for all the companies that watch Procter's moves," says Watts Wacker, chairman of consulting firm FirstMatter in Westport, Connecticut. "But great plans often come with great obstacles."

This new global vision has already had an accidental test run. Last year, P&G introduced an extension of its Pantene shampoo line. The ad campaign for the product was almost entirely visual, with images of beautiful women and their lustrous hair, and had a very limited script. That meant the campaign was easily translated and shipped to P&G markets around the world without the usual months of testing and tinkering. The result: P&G was able to introduce the brand extension in 14 countries in six months, versus the two years it took to get the original shampoo into stores abroad. "It's a success story that gets quite a bit of talk internally," says Chris T. Allen, a marketing professor at the University of Cincinnati. "I see the reorganization as an attempt to do more Pantenes on a regular basis."

P&G didn't come to this global focus entirely on its own. Its biggest chain-store customers, such as Wal-Mart Stores, Inc. and French-owned Carrefour, have been agitating for just such a pro-

Procter & Gamble's ad campaign for an extension of Pantene shampoo line was almost entirely visual.
[Bill Aron/PHOTO EDIT]

gram to mirror their own global expansion. While P&G craves an international image for its products, retailers want something more tangible: a global price. As it stands, prices are negotiable on a country or regional basis. What an international retailer pays for Crest in the United States could be considerably less than what it costs the chain in Europe or Latin America. A consistent global price gives big chains more power to plan efficiently and save money. Wal-Mart Chief Executive David D. Glass describes his company's goal as "global sourcing," which includes worldwide relationships on pricing and distribution. Moving P&G products from regional to global management is pointing "somewhat in that direction," Glass says.

In addition to marketing and pricing, global business units will supervise new-product development. P&G will move away from its long-used "sequential" method, which tested products first in midsize U.S. cities and then gradually rolled them out to the world. An example: Swiffer, a new disposable mop designed by P&G, is being tested simultaneously in Cedar Rapids, Iowa; Pittsfield, Massachusetts; and Sens, France, in hopes of sculpting a globally popular product right out of the box.

New CEO Dirk I. Jager concedes that it won't be a quick fix. Even if P&G could implement its strategy more quickly, it would still run into the ugly realities of global economic markets. For its extra $35 billion in revenues through 2006, Procter is counting on about $8 billion from emerging markets in Eastern Europe, China, and Latin America, says Clayton C. Daley, Jr., P&G's treasurer, who recently became chief financial officer. Yet Asian emerging markets are likely to remain mired in deep economic slumps for at least two more years. Recent turmoil in Russia, which was a bright prospect for Procter just a year ago, has gotten so bad that the company has temporarily halted shipments there.

Procter has additional obstacles closer to home. How, for example, will tradition-bound P&G managers react to the new hierarchy? "You're going from 144 chiefs to 8. That's a lot of ex-chiefs," says consultant Wacker. And everyone will be affected by the change in tone that is sure to come from the corner office. CEO Jager has a reputation for aggressive moves and abrasiveness. In the 1980s, he turned around Procter's failing Japanese business with such a fury that his Japanese managers called him "Crazy Man Dirk" behind his back. Crazy or not, Jager is sticking to the 2006 target date. He's wasting no time stepping into his new role as champion of the global focus: Already, even before taking on the official title of CEO, he has started preaching the new structure to P&G managers. After all, the clock is ticking.

Questions

1. How would you describe P&G's posture (international, global, transnational, multinational)?

2. What are the biggest strategic challenges for this company now?

3. How does P&G's global position influence the way it does business?

Source: Condensed from Peter Galuszka, Ellen Neuborne, and Wendy Zellner, "P&G's Hottest New Product," *Business Week Online*, October 5, 1998.

Experiential Exercises
6.1 Understanding multinational corporations

Objective

To gain a more thorough picture of how a multinational corporation operates.

Instructions

Perhaps the best way to gain an understanding of multinational corporations is to study a specific organization and how it operates throughout the world. Select a multinational corporation and find several articles on that company and answer the questions on the Multinational Worksheet.

Multinational worksheet

1. What is the primary business of this organization?

_____

_____

_____

_____

2. To what extent does the company engage in multinational operations? For example, does it only market its products/services in other countries or does it have manufacturing facilities? What portion of the firm's operating income comes from overseas operations?

_____

_____

_____

_____

3. What percentage of the managers in international activities are American (or from the country the corporation considers home)? Are these managers given any special training prior to their international assignment?

_____

_____

_____

_____

4. What characteristics of the organization have contributed to its success or lack of success in the international marketplace?

_____

_____

_____

_____

Source: R. R. McGrath, Jr., *Exercises in Management Fundamentals* (Englewood Cliffs, NJ: Prentice Hall, 1985), p. 177. Reprinted by permission of Prentice-Hall, Inc.

6.2 Expatriates versus locals

Objectives

1. To help you understand the various advantages and disadvantages of using expatriates and locals as managers and professional staffers.
2. To broaden your understanding of the difficult human resources management problems the multinational enterprise faces.

Instructions

1. Working alone, read the Expatriates versus Locals Situation.
2. Go to the library and research the pros and cons of using expatriates versus locals.
3. Complete the Expatriates versus Locals Worksheet.
4. When the class reconvenes, your instructor can organize a debate on the expatriates versus locals issue.

Expatriates versus locals situation

Your company is planning to open a number of manufacturing and distribution centers in other countries to become a true multinational enterprise. There has been considerable controversy among top management as to how to staff the overseas operations. It's agreed that for nonmanagerial and nonprofessional staff positions, locals should be hired and trained whenever possible. However, for managerial and professional staff positions, there is considerable and sometimes emotional disagreement. You are to investigate the various advantages and disadvantages of using expatriates versus locals in overseas operations.

Expatriates versus locals worksheet

Advantages of using expatriates	Advantages of using locals

Chapter Seven
New Ventures

A man is known by the company he organizes.

—*Ambrose Bierce*

Chapter Outline

Independent Entrepreneurs
    Why Become an Independent Entrepreneur?
    The Role of the Economic Environment
    What Business Should You Start?
    What Does It Take to Be Successful?
    Planning
    Entrepreneurial Hazards
    Global Start-Ups
Spin-Offs
    Why Spin-Offs Occur
    The Spin-Off Process
    Changes in Industry Structure
Intrapreneurship
    Building Support for Your Idea
    Building Intrapreneurship
    Organizing New Corporate Ventures
    Hazards in Intrapreneurship
    Entrepreneurial Orientation
    3M—A Prototype

Learning Objectives

After studying Chapter 7, you will know:

1. The activities of entrepreneurship.

2. How to find and evaluate ideas for new business ventures.

3. What it takes to be a successful entrepreneur.

4. How to write a great business plan.

5. The important management skills, resources, and strategies needed to avoid failure and achieve success.

6. Key criteria for deciding whether your start-up should be global from the outset.

7. The process of spinning off new ventures.

8. How to foster intrapreneurship and an entrepreneurial orientation in large companies.

Setting the Stage

Starting from Scratch

Some heads of *Inc.* 500 companies began their entrepreneurial careers in their college dorm rooms. Many other successful businesspeople have equally humble beginnings.

• Ron Vos started with $125 and couldn't pay people to work for him in his efforts to market alternative rock for major labels. But he recruited unpaid interns on college campuses across the country. In return for experience in the industry, contacts, free CDs, and backstage passes, students handed out free samples on campus and persuaded local radio stations and clubs to play Vos's clients' songs. Today, Hi Frequency Marketing has projected revenues of $2 million, and its clients include Everclear, Radiohead, and Squirrel Nut Zippers.

• Thomas First and Thomas Scott spent summers doing odd jobs on Nantucket Island, then started making and selling fruit juices off their 19-foot motorboat and out of an icehouse at Nantucket Harbor. At $1 per bottle, they sold 2,000 bottles in the first summer. They then expanded to Boston-area college football games. Then, to Georgetown and Washington, D.C. A few years later, Nantucker Nectars sold 28 varieties of juice and had $30 million in sales.

Abby Margalith and her brother started their Starving Students moving company with one 50-year-old truck. After two years their sales reached $15 million.
[Rocky Thies]

• Abby Margalith was waiting tables, and her brother Ethan had just finished high school and needed a summer job. He borrowed a truck and hauled a few items, made some cash, and realized he had his summer job. Abby joined him in the moving business. Their first real moving truck was a 1944 weapons carrier they dug out of a mud slide. After painting "Starving Students" and their phone number on the side, they parked it at a Beverly Hills street corner. The phone rang off the hook. After a couple of years, Starving Students had 14 locations in five states, and sales had reached $15 million.

• Jason Olim was a student at Brown University when he got his entrepreneurial idea: selling hard-to-find CDs. He didn't have the money to open a real store, so he opened his on the Internet. He and his parents invested $20,000 for a Macintosh, a Unix server, software licenses, fees for engineers to help with programming problems, graphic designers, print advertisements, and a public relations contract. In its first month, his company brought in $387 in revenues. A modest start before things got rolling for CDnow.

New-business start-up worksheet

1. *Product*

   What customer need will we satisfy?

   How can our product be unique?

2. *Customer*

   Who are our customers? What are their profiles?

   Where do they live/work/play?

   What are their buying habits?

   What are their needs?

3. *Competition*

   Who/where is the competition?

   What are their strengths and weaknesses?

   How might they respond to us?

4. *Suppliers*

   Who/where are our suppliers?

   What are their business practices?

   What relationships can we expect?

5. Location

   Where are our customers/competitors/suppliers?

   What are the location costs?

   What are the legal limitations to location?

6. *Physical Facilities/Equipment*

   Rent/own/build/refurbish facilities?

   Rent/lease/purchase equipment?

   Maintenance?

7. *Human Resources*

   Availability?

   Training?

   Costs?

8. *Legal/Regulatory Environment*

   Licenses/permits/certifications?

   Government agencies?

   Liability?

9. *Cultural/Social Environment*

   Cultural issues?

   Social issues?

10. *International Environment*

    International issues?

11. *Other*

The 411 on . . .

Information for entrepreneurs

If you are interested in starting or managing a small business, you have access to many sources of information.

The **Small Business Administration (SBA)** is an agency of the federal government charged with promoting the growth of small businesses. It provides financial, educational, and lobbying services. The SBA defines a small business as a business that has fewer than 500 employees or lacks dominant market power.

The SBA's most visible services are its direct loans and loan guarantees. Under the direct loan program, the SBA acts as a lender of last resort to small businesses. In recent years, these loans generally have been used for special target populations. Under the loan guarantee program, the SBA protects the lender in the event the loan holder defaults. Each loan program is designed to improve the environment for small business by expanding the sources of capital. Many states offer similar lending programs to encourage investment in certain industries or geographic areas.

The SBA sponsors and delivers training programs and provides a wide range of booklets and brochures on small-business management. Many SBA training programs are delivered through community colleges and universities. Some of these programs, such as the Small Business Institute and Small Business Development Centers, involve students and faculty in special consulting projects designed to help specific clients. In addition to its college-based programs, the SBA uses SCORE (Service Corps of Retired Executives) to provide services for struggling new businesses. Most of these services are free; for others, a small fee is charged.

Several publications are produced specifically for the entrepreneurial audience. *Inc.* publishes articles about the management problems of growing businesses. *Business Week (Frontier)* and *Fortune (FSB)* now also target small businesses. *Venture Capital Journal* caters to entrepreneurs and the venture capital industry at large. Pratt's *Guide to Venture Capital* is a "must-have" for any entrepreneur: it covers not only the how-to's of starting a business and obtaining venture capital but also profiles every major venture capital organization in the country.

Still other sources of help are available. The entrepreneurs center (www.ecenteronline.org) is a collaborative effort among private industry, nonprofits, and the public sector that provides entrepreneurs with resources, information, and tools. Private groups, universities, and government agencies supply technical and managerial assistance to entrepreneurs. For example. several organizations in various parts of the country offer the services of a board of directors for an evening. One such program, the MIT Forum, is offered by volunteers in cities nationwide. At each meeting of the Forum, a businessperson presents a plan to an audience and preselected panelists provide feedback on the plan. Then the audience reacts to both the plan and the panelists. Most presenters find they obtain more advice than they could purchase on the open market.

In addition, several major accounting firms have groups specifically geared to the needs of smaller, emerging companies. Most publish guides to new-business formation and management as a service to their current and prospective clientele. These companies can provide professional consulting and financial services and also make critical introductions within the financial community. One screened introduction can save months of effort and thousands of dollars in lost opportunities.

Small-business ownership or management can provide a challenging and rewarding career. The interested student should start looking in the local community for sources of ideas and assistance. Plenty of resources are available, and planning can't begin too soon! ●

Part Three

Organizing: Building a Dynamic Organization

Foundations of Management

Managing
The External Environment
Managerial Decision Making

**Planning:
Delivering Strategic Value**

Planning and Strategic Management
Ethics and Corporate Responsibility
International Management
New Ventures

Strategy Implementation

**Organizing: Building
a Dynamic Organization**

Organization Structure
The Responsive Organization
Human Resources Management
Managing the Diverse Workforce

**Leading:
Mobilizing People**

Leadership
Motivating for Performance
Managing Teams
Communicating

**Controlling:
Learning and Changing**

Managerial Control
Managing Technology and Innovation
Creating and Managing Change

Now that you know about planning and strategy, the remaining three parts
correspond to the other three functions of management: organizing, leading, and controlling. Parts 3, 4, and 5 discuss issues pertaining to *implementing* strategic plans. In Part 3, we describe how to organize and staff
for maximum effectiveness. Chapter 8 introduces you to different organization structures and explains how to group and delegate tasks. Chapter 9
builds on those basic concepts by describing more complex organization
designs. This chapter discusses how firms can adapt quickly to rapidly
changing environments and how "corporate America" is restructuring.
Chapter 10 addresses the management of human resources. Its focus is on
staffing the firm with capable employees and the issues surrounding
employee reward systems. Finally, Chapter 11 discusses the challenge of
managing today's workforce, one composed of diverse groups of people.
Chapters 12 and 13 set the stage for Part 4, which further elaborates on
how to manage people.

Chapter Eight
Organization Structure

Take my assets—but leave me my organization and in five years I'll have it all back.

—*Alfred P. Sloan, Jr.*

Chapter Outline

Learning Objectives

After studying Chapter 8, you will know:

1. How differentiation and integration influence your organization's structure.

2. How authority operates.

3. The roles of the board of directors and the chief executive officer.

4. How span of control affects structure and managerial effectiveness.

5. How to delegate work effectively.

6. The difference between centralized and decentralized organizations.

7. How to allocate jobs to work units.

8. How to manage the unique challenges of the matrix organization.

9. The nature of important integrative mechanisms.

Setting the Stage

Adidas Enters a Three-Legged Race

Faced with sagging sales in North America as well as tough competition in Europe, Adidas has been reevaluating its game plan and getting its structure in shape. By trimming the fat of duplicated functions and integrating its U.S. organization into the company's global structure, Adidas is expected to return to the industry's "A-team."

The company has a redesigned, three-divisional approach that veers from the traditional "footwear and apparel" structure of most other sporting goods companies. Each of the three divisions will produce its own footwear and apparel lines in order to address the needs of consumers in a targeted way:

• The Forever Sport Division—which currently accounts for 90 percent of Adidas's overall business—will feature performance products that will also appeal to the lifestyle sector. It will use the Adidas Performance logo and focus on the training, running, tennis, soccer, and basketball categories.

• The Original Division will leverage the company's sports heritage by offering sport-inspired leisure products under the classic Trefoil logo. Its mission is to compete against traditional athletic brands as well as such fashion labels as Polo Sport, Abercrombie & Fitch, and the Gap. In the long term, this division should account for 25 to 30 percent of the total business, and will log double-digit annual growth beginning in 2001.

• The Equipment Division focuses on multifunctional products and will be the bridge between the Forever Sport and Original lines. The category will use the new Adidas Equipment logo and will eventually account for 5 to 10 percent of the overall business.

With its new organization structure, Adidas is expected to return to the industry's "A-team." [David Stoecklein/The Stock Market]

Herbert Hainer, Adidas-Salomon COO and deputy chairman of the board, concluded, "Our new . . . organizational structure will revolutionize the way Adidas does business. It will provide us with the dynamic framework that we need to aggressively expand our business and will enable us to deliver significant growth rates in the coming years."

Source: Jeffrey Lacap, "Adidas Embraces New Global Strategy," Sporting Goods Business, November 10, 2000, 33, no. 16, p. 8; Judy Leand, "The SGB Interview: Ross McMullin," Sporting Goods Business, November 10, 2000, 33, no. 16, p. 44; and Roxanna Guilford, "Adidas-Salomon: Apparel, Taxes and Domestic Sales Slow Adidas-Salomon Growth," Apparel Industry Magazine

Adidas is a company that pretty much all of us know, but the little excerpt in "Setting the Stage" gives us some insight into its struggles and plans for the future. Although a quick story such as this doesn't provide all the details about Adidas's strategy and structure, it does highlight a few important issues that we want to cover in this chapter. Make no mistake: How a company organizes itself is as important as—if not more important than—its strategy. And Adidas, like many other companies, is working hard to make certain that its strategy and structure are aligned with each other.

In this chapter, we focus on the vertical and horizontal dimensions of organization structure. We begin this chapter by covering basic principles of *differentiation* and *integration*. Next, we discuss the vertical structure, which includes issues of *authority,* hierarchy, delegation, and decentralization. We continue on to describe the horizontal structure, which includes functional, divisional, and matrix forms. Finally, we illustrate the ways that organizations can integrate their structures: coordination by standardization, coordination by plan, and coordination by mutual adjustment.

In the next chapter, we continue on with the topic of organization structure, but take a different perspective. In that chapter we will focus on the flexibility and responsiveness of an organization; that is, how capable it is of changing its form and adapting to strategy, technology, the environment, and so on.

Fundamentals of organizing

organization chart The reporting structure and division of labor in an organization.

To get going, let's start simple. We often begin to describe a firm's structure by looking at its organization chart. The **organization chart** depicts the positions in the firm and how they are arranged. The chart provides a picture of the reporting structure (who reports to whom) and the various activities that are carried out by different individuals. Most companies have official organization charts drawn up to give people this information.

Figure 8.1 shows the traditional organization chart. Note the various kinds of information that are conveyed in a very simple way:

1. The boxes represent different work.
2. The titles in the boxes show the work performed by each unit.
3. Reporting and authority relationships are indicated by solid lines showing superior–subordinate connections.
4. Levels of management are indicated by the number of horizontal layers in the chart. All persons or units that are of the same rank and report to the same person are on one level.

Although the organization chart presents some clearly important structural features, there are other design issues related to structure that—while not so obvious—are no less important. Two fundamental concepts around which organizations are structured are differentiation and integration. **Differentiation** means that the organization is comprised of many different units that work on different kinds of tasks, using different skills and work methods. **Integration,** on the other hand, means that these differentiated units are put back together so that work is coordinated into an overall product.[1]

differentiation An aspect of the organization's internal environment created by job specialization and the division of labor.

integration The degree to which differentiated work units work together and coordinate their efforts.

division of labor The assignment of different tasks to different people or groups.

specialization A process in which different individuals and units perform different tasks.

Differentiation

Several related concepts underlie the idea of structural differentiation. For example, differentiation is created through division of labor and job specialization. **Division of labor** means that the work of the organization is subdivided into smaller tasks. Various individuals and units throughout the organization perform different tasks. **Specialization,** in turn, refers to the fact that different people or groups often perform specific parts of the entire task. The two concepts are, of course, closely related. Secretaries and accountants specialize in, and perform, different jobs; similarly, marketing, finance, and human resources tasks are divided among those respective departments. The numerous tasks that must be carried out in an organization make specialization and division of labor necessities. Otherwise the complexity of the overall work of the organization would be too much for any individual.[2]

figure 8.1
A conventional
organizational chart

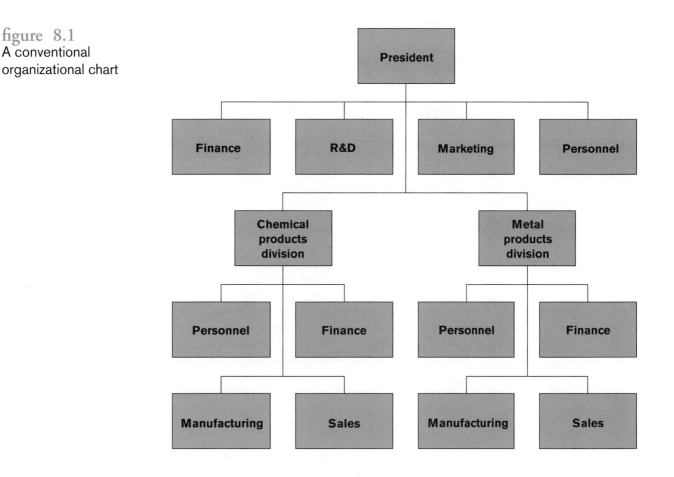

Differentiation is high when there are many subunits and many kinds of specialists who think differently. Harvard professors Lawrence and Lorsch found that organizations in complex, dynamic environments (plastics firms, in their study) developed a high degree of differentiation in order to cope with the complex challenges. Companies in simple, stable environments (container companies) had low levels of differentiation. Companies in intermediate environments (food companies) had intermediate differentiation.[3]

Integration

As organizations differentiate their structures, managers must simultaneously consider issues of integration. All of the specialized tasks in an organization cannot be performed completely independently. Because the different units are part of the larger organization, some degree of communication and cooperation must exist among them. Integration and its related concept, **coordination,** refer to the procedures that link the various parts of the organization to achieve the organization's overall mission.

coordination The procedures that link the various parts of the organization for the purpose of achieving the organization's overall mission.

Integration is achieved through structural mechanisms that enhance collaboration and coordination. Any job activity that links different work units performs an integrative function. Remember, the more highly differentiated your firm, the greater the need for integration among the different units. Lawrence and Lorsch found that highly differentiated firms were successful if they also had high levels of integration. Organizations are more likely to fail if they exist in complex environments and are highly differentiated, but fail to adequately integrate their activities.[4]

These concepts permeate the rest of the chapter. First we will discuss *vertical differentiation* within organization structure. This includes issues pertaining to authority within an organization, the board of directors, the chief executive officer, and hierarchical levels, as well as issues pertaining to delegation and decentralization. Next, we will discuss *horizontal differentiation* in an organization's structure including issues of departmentalization that create functional, divisional, and matrix organizations. Finally, we will discuss issues pertaining to structural integration including coordination, organizational roles, interdependence, and boundary spanning.

The vertical structure

In order to understand issues such as reporting relationships, authority, responsibility, and the like, we need to begin with the vertical dimension of a firm's structure.

Authority in organizations

authority The legitimate right to make decisions and to tell other people what to do.

Authority, the legitimate right to make decisions and to tell other people what to do, is fundamental to the functioning of every organization. For example, a boss has the authority to give an order to a subordinate.

Authority resides in *positions* rather than in people. Thus, the job of vice president of a particular division has authority over that division, regardless of how many people come and go in that position and who presently holds it.

In private business enterprises, the owners have ultimate authority. In most small, simply structured companies, the owner also acts as manager. Sometimes the owner hires another person to manage the business and its employees. The owner gives this manager some authority to oversee the operations, but the manager is accountable to—that is, reports and defers to—the owner. Thus, the owner still has the ultimate authority.

Traditionally authority has been the primary means of running an organization. An order that a boss gives to a lower-level employee is usually carried out. As this occurs throughout the organization day after day, the organization can move forward toward achieving its goals.[5]

We will discuss the authority structure of organizations from the top down, beginning with the board of directors.

The board of directors

In corporations, the owners are the stockholders. But because there are numerous stockholders, and these individuals generally lack timely information, few are directly involved in managing the organization. Stockholders elect a board of directors to oversee the organization. The board, led by the chair, makes major decisions affecting the organization, subject to corporate charter and bylaw provisions. Boards perform at least three major sets of duties: (1) selecting, assessing, rewarding, and perhaps replacing the CEO; (2) determining the firm's strategic direction and reviewing financial performance; and (3) assuring ethical, socially responsible, and legal conduct.[6]

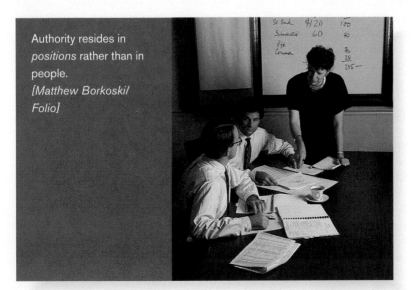

Authority resides in *positions* rather than in people.
[Matthew Borkoski/ Folio]

Some top executives are likely to sit on the board (they are called *inside directors*). Outside members of the board tend to be executives at other companies. The trend in recent years has been toward reducing the number of insiders and increasing the number of outsiders. Today, most companies have a majority of outside directors. Boards made up of strong, independent outsiders are more likely to provide different information and perspectives and to prevent big mistakes. Table 8.1 shows the results of a recent *Business Week* poll of the best and worst boards. Successful boards tend to be those that are active, critical participants in determining company strategies. Campbell Soup's board, for example, took control over selecting a new CEO and routinely conducts performance evaluations on board members to make certain they are active contributors.[7]

The chief executive officer   The authority officially vested in the board of directors is assigned to a chief executive officer, who occupies the top of the organizational pyramid. The chief executive is personally accountable to the board and to the owners for the organization's performance.

It is estimated that in 15 percent of *Fortune 500* corporations, one person holds all three positions of CEO, chair of the board of directors, and president.[8] More commonly, however, one person holds two of those positions, with the CEO serving also as either the chair of the board or the president of the organization. When the CEO is president, the chair may be honorary and may do little more than conduct meetings. In other cases, the chair may be the CEO and the president is second in command.

The top management team   Increasingly, CEOs share their authority with other key members of the top management team. Top management teams are typically comprised of the CEO, president, chief operating officer, chief financial officer, and other key executives. Rather than make critical decisions on their own, CEOs at companies such as Shell, Honeywell, and Merck regularly meet with their top management teams to make decisions as a unit.[9]

Hierarchical levels

hierarchy The authority levels of the organizational pyramid.

In Chapter 1, we discussed the three broad levels of the organizational pyramid, commonly called the **hierarchy.** The CEO occupies the top position and is the senior member of top management. The top managerial level also includes presidents and vice presidents. These are the strategic managers in charge of the entire organization. The second broad level is middle management. At this level, managers are in charge of plants or departments. The lowest level is made up of lower management and workers. It includes office managers, sales managers, supervisors, and other first-line managers, as well as the employees who report directly to them. This level is also called the *operational level* of the organization.

An authority structure is the glue that holds these levels together. Generally (but not always), people at higher levels have the authority to make decisions and to tell lower-level people what to do. For example, middle managers can give orders to first-line supervisors; first-line supervisors, in turn, direct operative-level workers.

subunits Subdivisions of an organization.

A powerful trend for U.S. businesses over the past few decades has been to reduce the number of hierarchical layers. General Electric used to have 29 levels; today, following a major reorganization, it has only 5. Most executives today believe that fewer layers create a more efficient, fast-acting, and cost-effective organization. This also holds true for the **subunits** of major corporations. A study of 234 branches of a financial services company found that branches with fewer layers tended to have higher operating efficiency than branches with more layers.[10]

Span of control

span of control The number of subordinates who report directly to an executive or supervisor.

The number of people under a manager is an important feature of an organization's structure. The number of subordinates who report directly to an executive or supervisor is called the **span of control.** The implications of differences in the span of control for the shape of an organization are straightforward. Holding size constant, narrow spans build a *tall* organization that has many reporting levels. Wide spans create a *flat* organization with fewer

table 8.1
The best and worst
boards of directors

The best boards of directors	
BW Rank	**Details**
1. GENERAL ELECTRIC	Outside directors average $6.6 million in GE stock. New recruits diversify a board of heavyweights.
2. JOHNSON & JOHNSON	Prestige board gets high marks for independence and accountability.
3. CAMPBELL SOUP	A first? Board reduced its pay this year. Mandates stockholdings for directors and all execs.
4. COMPAQ	Wins high marks from governance advocates despite recent poor performance.
5. APRIA HEALTHCARE	Governance activists create model board and execute turnaround of health-care firm.
6. INTEL	Boasts lead director to organize outside board members without management.
7. TEXAS INSTRUMENTS	Outside directors well invested in company; highly independent board.
8. HOME DEPOT	Requires directors to visit at least 20 stores a year, yet four of 10 are insiders on board.
9. IBM	High-powered board gains high marks for performance and independence.
10. LUCENT TECHNOLOGIES	Strong board got investor endorsement before recent surprise earnings drop.
The Worst Boards of Directors	
1. DISNEY	Board reforms viewed as token gestures as Disney performance lags.
2. RITE AID	Audit panel met just twice last year; interim chairman missed 37% of meetings.
3. FIRST UNION	Unwieldy board of 27 members rife with potential conflicts.
4. CENDANT	Board gets blame for accounting meltdown and stock repricing.
5. DILLARDS	Dillards family dominates board of poorly performing retailer.
6. STARWOOD HOTEL	Board loaded with insiders and friends of founder CEO.
7. WARNACO	Small clubby board dominated by CEO in poorly performing company.
8. WASTE MANAGEMENT	Insider trading charges hurt board that has adopted many best practices.
9. ARCHER DANIELS MIDLAND	Dubious distinction: Board makes worst list for third time in a row.
10. BANKAMERICA	Big merger still leaves big board with lots of ties to CEO McColl.

The highest possible score in this ranking is 100, with half the points coming from *Business Week*'s survey of money managers and governance experts and half from an analysis of the makeup of each board. For each individual category, the maximum score is 10.

Source: John Byrne, "The Best & Worst Boards," *Business Week,* January 24, 2000, pp. 142–52.

table 8.1

The best and worst boards of directors

reporting levels. The span of control can be too narrow or too wide. The optimal span of control maximizes effectiveness because it is (1) narrow enough to permit managers to maintain control over subordinates, but (2) not so narrow that it leads to overcontrol and an excessive number of managers who oversee a small number of subordinates.

What is the optimal number of subordinates? Five, according to Napoleon.[11] Some managers today still consider five a good number. At one Japanese bank, in contrast, several hundred branch managers report to the same boss.

Actually, the optimal span of control depends on a number of factors. The span should be wider when (1) the work is clearly defined and unambiguous, (2) subordinates are highly trained and have access to information, (3) the manager is highly capable and supportive, (4) jobs are similar and performance measures are comparable, and (5) subordinates prefer autonomy to close supervisory control. If the opposite conditions exist, a narrow span of control may be more appropriate.[12]

Delegation

delegation The assignment of new or additional responsibilities to a subordinate.

As we look at organizations, and recognize that authority is spread out over various levels and spans of control, the issue of delegation becomes paramount. Specifically, **delegation** is the assignment of authority and responsibility to a subordinate at a lower level. It requires that the subordinate report back to his or her boss as to how effectively the assignment was carried out. Delegation is perhaps the most fundamental feature of management, because it entails getting work done through others. Thus, delegation is important at all hierarchical levels. The process can occur between any two individuals in any type of structure with regard to any task.

Some managers are comfortable delegating to subordinates; others are not. Consider the differences between the two office managers and the ways they gave out the same assignment in the following example.

Are both of these examples of delegation?

Manager A: "Call Tom Burton at Nittany Office Equipment. Ask him to give you the price list on an upgrade for our personal computers. I want to move up to a Pentium III with 256 megs of RAM and at least a 40-gigabyte hard drive. Ask them to give you a demonstration of Windows 2000 and Office 2000. I want to be able to establish a LAN for the entire group. Invite Cochran and Snow to the demonstration and let them try it out. Have them write up a summary of their needs and the potential applications they see for the new systems. Then prepare me a report with the costs and specifications of the upgrade for the entire department. Oh yes, be sure to ask for information on service costs."

Manager B: "I'd like to do something about our personal computer system. I've been getting some complaints that the current systems are too slow, can't run current software, and don't allow for networking. Could you evaluate our options and give me a recommendation on what we should do? Our budget is probably around $3,500 per person, but I'd like to stay under that if we can. Feel free to talk to some of the managers to get their input, but we need to have this done as soon as possible." ●

Responsibility, authority, and accountability   When delegating work, it is helpful to keep in mind the important distinctions among the concepts of authority, responsibility, and accountability.

responsibility The assignment of a task that an employee is supposed to carry out.

Responsibility means that a person is assigned a task that he or she is supposed to carry out. When delegating work responsibilities, the manager should also delegate to the subordinate enough authority to get the job done. *Authority,* recall, means that the person has the power and the right to make decisions, give orders, draw upon resources, and do whatever else is necessary to fulfill the responsibility. Ironically, it is quite common for people to have more responsibility than authority; they must perform as best they can through informal influence tactics instead of relying purely on authority. More will be said about informal power and how to use it in Chapter 12.

As the manager delegates responsibilities, subordinates are held accountable for achieving results. **Accountability** means that the subordinate's manager has the right to expect the subordinate to perform the job, and the right to take corrective action in the event the subordinate fails to do so. The subordinate must report upward on the status and quality of his or her performance of the task.

On the other hand, the ultimate responsibility—accountability to higher-ups—lies with the manager doing the delegating. Managers remain responsible and accountable not only for their own actions but for the actions of their subordinates. Thus, managers should not resort to delegation to others as a means of escaping their own responsibilities. In many cases, however, managers refuse to accept responsibility for subordinates' actions. Managers often "pass the buck" or take other evasive action to ensure they are not held accountable for mistakes.[13]

accountability The expectation that employees perform a job, take corrective action when necessary, and report upward on the status and quality of their performance.

Advantages of delegation

Delegating work offers important advantages. The manager saves time by giving some of his or her own responsibilities to someone else. Then the manager is free to devote energy to important, higher-level activities like planning, setting objectives, and monitoring performance.

Delegation essentially gives the subordinate a more important job. The subordinate acquires an opportunity to develop new skills and to demonstrate potential for additional responsibilities and perhaps promotion. In essence, the subordinate receives a vital form of on-the-job training that could pay off in the future.

The organization also receives payoffs. Allowing managers to devote more time to important managerial functions while lower-level employees carry out assignments means that jobs are done in a more efficient and cost-effective manner.

How should managers delegate?

To achieve the advantages just discussed, delegation must be done properly. As Figure 8.2 shows, effective delegation proceeds through several steps.[14]

The first step in the delegation process, defining the goal, requires that the manager have a clear understanding of the outcome he or she wants. Then the manager should select a person who is capable of performing the task.

The person who gets the assignment should be given the authority, time, and resources needed to successfully carry out the task. Throughout the delegation process, the manager and the subordinate must work together and communicate about the project. The manager should know the subordinate's ideas at the beginning and should inquire about progress or problems at periodic meetings and review sessions. Thus, even though the subordinate performs the assignment, the manager is available and aware of its current status.

Some tasks, such as disciplining subordinates and conducting performance reviews, should not be delegated. But when managers err, it usually is because they delegated too little rather than too much. The manager who wants to learn how to delegate more effectively should remember this distinction: If you are not delegating, you are merely *doing* things; but the more you delegate, the more you are truly *building* and *managing* an organization.[15]

Decentralization

centralized organization An organization in which high-level executives make most decisions and pass them down to lower levels for implementation.

decentralized organization An organization in which lower-level managers make important decisions.

The delegation of responsibility and authority *decentralizes* decision making. In a **centralized organization,** important decisions usually are made at the top. In **decentralized organizations,** more decisions are made at lower levels. Ideally, decision making occurs at the level of the people who are most directly affected and have the most intimate knowledge about the problem. This is particularly important when the business environment is fast-changing and decisions must be made quickly and well. Consider the changes at Harley-Davidson.

figure 8.2
The steps in effective
delegation

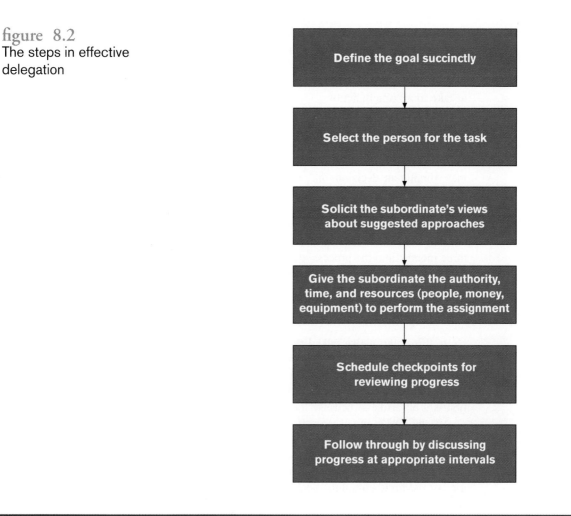

Define the goal succinctly

Select the person for the task

Solicit the subordinate's views about suggested approaches

Give the subordinate the authority, time, and resources (people, money, equipment) to perform the assignment

Schedule checkpoints for reviewing progress

Follow through by discussing progress at appropriate intervals

Harley-Davidson: Re-born to be wild?

In the 1980s, Harley-Davidson faced tough competition from Honda, Suzuki, and Yamaha. The company was able to survive under the direction of a very strong hierarchical, centralized leadership group. The key structural concerns at that time were reining in control, getting a firm grasp on manufacturing costs, and producing a quality product at a reasonable price.

Today, that approach alone probably won't work. According to CEO Richard F. Teerlink, the days of controlling leaders and dependent followers are long gone. Over the past three years, Harley-Davidson has been making the transition to a flatter, more empowered organization that decentralizes decision making. In order to support individual growth and excellence, Teerlink has been recreating Harley-Davidson to replace hierarchy with collaborative leadership. The changes are built on a philosophy that includes employee empowerment and accountability, mutual trust and respect through education and training, open communications, commitment, and problem solving through consensus. As a consequence of pushing down authority, managers are finding that trust replaces fear-based power. Ultimately the goal is to establish a much more innovative organization that taps into the creativity and resourcefulness of its employees. This is believed to be the type of organization needed to address today's complex business challenges.

Source: Clyde Fessler, "Rotating Leadership at Harley-Davidson: From Hierarchy to Interdependence," *Strategy & Leadership* 25, no. 4 (July/August 1997), pp. 42–43; and Jeffrey Young and Kenneth L. Murrell, "Harley-Davidson Motor Company Organizational Design: The Road to High Performance," *Organization Development Journal*, Spring 1998, 16, no. 1, p. 65. ●

Most American executives today understand the advantages of pushing decision-making authority down to the point of the action. The level that deals directly with problems and opportunities has the most relevant information and can best foresee the consequences of decisions. They also see how the decentralized approach allows people to take more timely action.[16]

At AES, the world's largest global power company (with revenues in excess of $3 billion), all decisions are pushed down to the lowest levels in the organization. Teams in plants have total responsibility for operations and maintenance. According to CEO Dennis Bakke and Chairman Roger Sant, giving people the power and responsibility to make important decisions has multiple benefits. It leads to better and faster decisions because decisions are made where the action is. Also, it gives employees a chance to learn and get engaged in the business—turning them into "mini-CEOs." An extreme example of this decentralized approach occurred when the plant executives let the maintenance staff take a stab at investing the $12 million cash reserve held at the plant. By three months into the process, the team was actually beating the returns of the people in the home office who were investing money for the company's treasury![17]

The horizontal structure

Up to this point, we've talked primarily about vertical aspects of organization structure. Issues of authority, span of control, delegation, and decentralization are important in that they give us an idea of how managers and employees relate to one another at different levels. At the same time, separating vertical differentiation from horizontal differentiation is a bit artificial because the elements work simultaneously.

As the tasks of organizations become increasingly complex, the organization inevitably must be subdivided—that is, *departmentalized*—into smaller units or departments. One of the first places this can be seen is in the distinction between line and staff departments. **Line departments** are those that have responsibility for the principal activities of the firm. Line units deal directly with the organization's primary goods or services; they make things, sell things, or provide customer service. At General Motors, for example, line departments would include such areas as product design, fabrication, assembly, distribution, and the like. Line managers typically have much authority and power in the organization. They have the ultimate responsibility for making major operating decisions. They also are accountable for the "bottom-line" results of their decisions.

line departments Units that deal directly with the organization's primary goods and services.

Staff departments are those that provide specialized or professional skills that support line departments. These would include research, legal, accounting, public relations, and human resources departments. Each of these specialized units often has its own vice president. And some are vested with a great deal of authority, as when accounting or finance groups approve and monitor budgetary activities. But while staff units formerly focused on monitoring and controlling performance, today most staff units are moving toward a new role focused on strategic support and expert advice.[18]

staff departments Units that support line departments.

As organizations divide work into different units, we can detect patterns in the way departments are clustered and arranged. The three basic approaches to **departmentalization** include functional, divisional, and matrix. We will talk about each and highlight some of their similarities and differences.

departmentalization Subdividing an organization into smaller subunits.

The functional organization

In a **functional organization,** jobs (and departments) are specialized and grouped according to *business functions* and the skills they require: production, marketing, human resources, research and development, finance, accounting, and so forth. At perhaps the most basic level, we can think about a functional structure being organized around a firm's value chain. A **value chain** depicts the relationships among separate activities that are performed to create a product or service. Figure 8.3(a) shows a generic value chain and Figure 8.3(b) shows how it might be translated into an organization's functional structure.[19]

functional organization Departmentalization around specialized activities, such as production, marketing, human resources, etc.

value chain Sequence of activities that flow from raw materials to the delivery of a product or service.

figure 8.3 Generic value chain and functional structure

a. Generic value chain

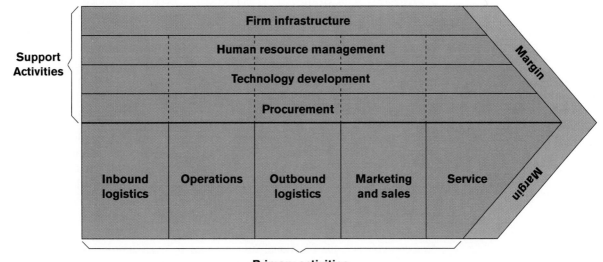

Source: Michael Porter, *Competitive Advantage: Creating and Sustaining Superior Performance* (New York: Free Press, 1985).

b. Functional structure

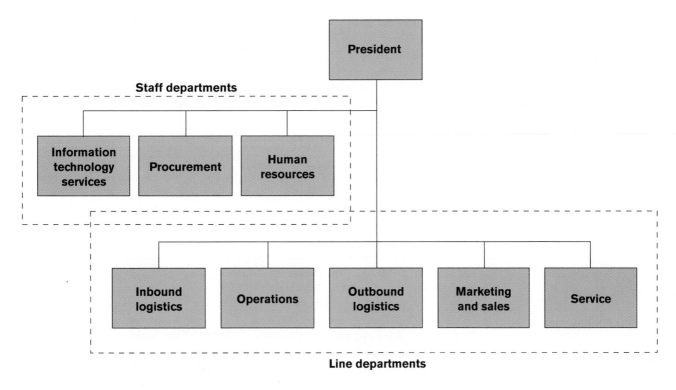

Functional departmentalization is common in both large and small organizations. Large companies may organize along several different functional groupings, including groupings unique to their business. For example, Carmike Cinema has vice presidents of finance, real estate, operations, advertising, information systems, technical, and concessions and a vice president who is the head film buyer.

The traditional functional approach to departmentalization has a number of potential advantages for an organization:[20]

1. *Economies of scale can be realized.* When people with similar skills are grouped, more efficient equipment can be purchased, and discounts for large purchases can be used.
2. *Monitoring of the environment* is more effective. Each functional group is more closely attuned to developments in its own field and therefore can adapt more readily.
3. *Performance standards* are better maintained. People with similar training and interests may develop a shared concern for performance in their jobs.
4. People have greater opportunity for *specialized training* and *in-depth skill development.*
5. Technical specialists are relatively *free of administrative work.*
6. *Decision making* and *lines of communication* are simple and clearly understood.

The functional form has disadvantages as well as advantages. People may care more about their own function than about the company as a whole, and their attention to functional tasks may make them lose focus on overall product quality and customer satisfaction. Managers develop functional expertise but do not acquire knowledge of the other areas of the business; they become specialists, but not generalists. Between functions, conflicts arise, and communication and coordination fall off. In short, while functional differentiation may exist, *functional integration* may not.

As a consequence, the functional structure may be most appropriate in rather simple, stable environments. If the organization becomes fragmented (or *dis*-integrated), it may be difficult to develop and bring new products to market, and difficult to respond quickly to customer demands and other changes. Particularly when companies are growing and business environments changing, the need arises to integrate work areas more effectively so that the organization can be more flexible and responsive. Other forms of departmentalization can be more flexible and responsive than the functional structure.

Demands for total quality, customer service, innovation, and speed have made clear the shortcomings of the functional form for some firms. Functional organizations are highly differentiated and create barriers to coordination across functions. Cross-functional coordination is essential for total quality, customer service, innovations, and speed. The functional organization will not disappear, in part because functional specialists will always be needed, but functional managers will make fewer decisions. The more important units will be cross-functional teams that have integrative responsibilities for products, processes, or customers.[21]

The divisional organization

divisional organization Departmentalization that groups units around products, customers, or geographic regions.

The discussion of a functional structure's weaknesses leads us to the **divisional structure.** As organizations grow and become increasingly diversified, they find that functional departments have difficulty managing a wide variety of products, customers, and geographic regions. In this case, organizations may restructure in order to group all functions into a single division, and duplicate each of the functions across all of the divisions. Division A has its own operations and marketing department, Division B has its own operations and marketing department, and so on. In this regard, separate divisions may act almost as separate businesses or profit centers and work autonomously to accomplish the goals of the entire enterprise. Table 8.2 presents examples of how the same tasks would be organized under functional and divisional structures.

There are several ways to create a divisional structure. It can be created around products, customers, or geographic regions. Each of these is described in the following sections.

Product divisions
In the product organization, all functions that contribute to a given product are organized under one manager. Figure 8.4 shows a product structure. In the product organization, managers in charge of functions for a particular product report to a product manager. Johnson & Johnson is one example of this form. J&J has 168 independent divisions in 33 groups, each responsible for a handful of products worldwide. Another example is The Limited (see Figure 8.4), which has 17 divisions organized under apparel, intimate brands, and support businesses.

table 8.2
Examples of functional
and divisional organization

Functional organization	Divisional organization
A typing pool.	Each typist is assigned to one boss.
A central purchasing department.	Each division has its own purchasing unit.
Separate companywide marketing, production, design, and engineering departments.	Each product group has experts in marketing, design, production, and engineering.
A central-city health department.	The school district and the prison have their own health units.
Plantwide inspection, maintenance, and supply departments.	Production Team Y does its own inspection, maintenance, and supply.
A university statistics department teaches statistics for the entire university.	Each department hires statisticians to teach its own students.

Source: George Strauss and Leonard R. Sayles, *Strauss and Sayles's Behavioral Strategies for Managers,* © 1980, p. 221. Reprinted by permission of Prentice-Hall, Inc., Englewood Cliffs, New Jersey.

The product approach to departmentalization offers a number of advantages:[22]

1. *Information needs are managed more easily.* Less information is required, because people work closely on one product and need not worry about other products.
2. *People have a full-time commitment to a particular product line.* They develop a greater awareness of how their jobs fit into the broader scheme.
3. *Task responsibilities are clear.* When things go wrong in a functional organization, functional managers can "pass the buck" ("that other department is messing up, making it harder for us to do our jobs"). In a product structure, managers are more independent and accountable because they usually have the resources they need to perform their tasks. Also, the performances of different divisions can be compared by contrasting their profits and other measures.

figure 8.4
Product divisions at The
Limited, Inc.

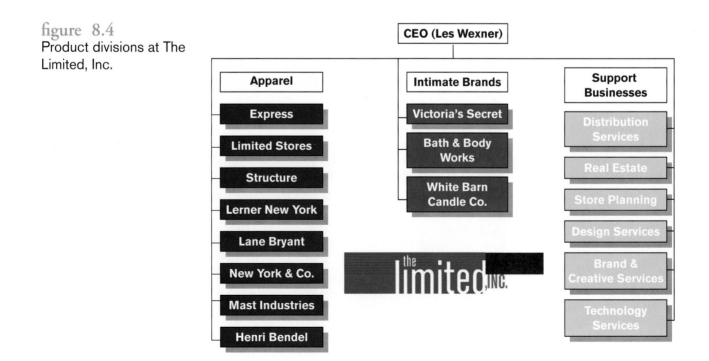

4. *People receive broader training.* General managers develop a wide variety of skills, and they learn to be judged by results. Many top executives received crucial early experience in product structures.

Because the product structure is more flexible than the functional structure, it is best suited for unstable environments, when an ability to rapidly adapt to change is important. But the product structure also has disadvantages. It is difficult to coordinate across product lines and divisions. And, although managers learn to become generalists, they may not acquire the depth of functional expertise that develops in the functional structure.

Furthermore, functions are not centralized at headquarters where they can be done for all product lines or divisions. Such duplication of effort is expensive. Also, decision making is decentralized in this structure, so top management can lose some control over decisions made in the divisions. Proper management of all the issues surrounding decentralization and delegation, as discussed earlier, is essential for this structure to be effective.[23]

Customer and geographical divisions   Some companies build divisions around groups of customers or around geographical distinctions. Adidas, mentioned in "Setting the Stage," is organized into *customer* divisions. Similarly, a hospital may organize its services around child, adult, psychiatric, and emergency cases. Bank loan departments commonly allocate assignments based on whether customers are requesting consumer, mortgage, small-business, corporate, or agricultural loans.

In contrast to customers, divisions can be structured around geographic regions. Sears, for example, was a pioneer in creating *geographic divisions*. Geographical distinctions include district, territory, region, and country. In companies like the industrial wholesaler diagrammed in Figure 8.5, different managers are in charge of the Southwest, Pacific, Midwest, Northeast, and Southeast regions. Seagram International is one of many companies that assign managers to Europe, the Far East, and Latin America.

The primary advantage of both the product and customer/regional approaches to departmentalization is the ability to focus on customer needs and provide faster, better service. But again, duplication of activities across many customer groups and geographic areas is expensive.

figure 8.5
Geographical divisions

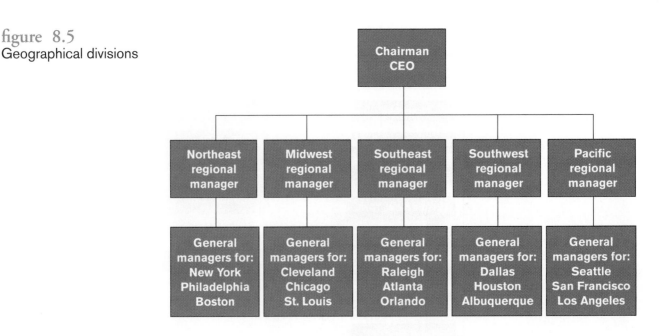

The matrix organization

NASA successfully used the matrix organization to organize and implement the launch of the Mercury astronauts in the late 1950s.
[Courtesy of NASA]

matrix organization An organization composed of dual reporting relationships in which some managers report to two superiors—a functional manager and a divisional manager.

unity-of-command principle A structure in which each worker reports to one boss, who in turn reports to one boss.

A **matrix organization** is a hybrid form of organization in which functional and divisional forms overlap. Managers and staff personnel report to two bosses—a functional manager and a divisional manager. Thus, matrix organizations have a dual rather than a single line of command. Figure 8.6 illustrates the basic matrix structure.

The matrix form originated in the aerospace industry, first with TRW in 1959 and then with NASA. Applications now occur in hospitals and health care agencies, entrepreneurial organizations, government laboratories, financial institutions, and multinational corporations.[24] Companies that have used or presently use the matrix form include IBM, Boeing, General Electric, Dow Chemical, Xerox, Shell Oil, Texas Instruments, Bechtel, Phillips Petroleum, and Dow Corning.

Pros and cons of the matrix form   Like other organization structures, matrix has both strengths and weaknesses. Table 8.3 summarizes the advantages of using a matrix structure. The major potential advantage is a higher degree of flexibility and adaptability.

Table 8.4 summarizes the potential shortcomings of the matrix form. Many of the disadvantages stem from the matrix's inherent violation of the **unity-of-command principle,** which states that a person should have only one boss. Reporting to two superiors can create confusion and a difficult interpersonal situation.

Matrix survival skills   To a large degree, problems can be avoided if the key managers in the matrix learn the behavioral skills demanded in the matrix structure.[25] These skills vary depending on the job in the four-person diamond structure shown in Figure 8.7.

figure 8.6
Matrix organizational structure

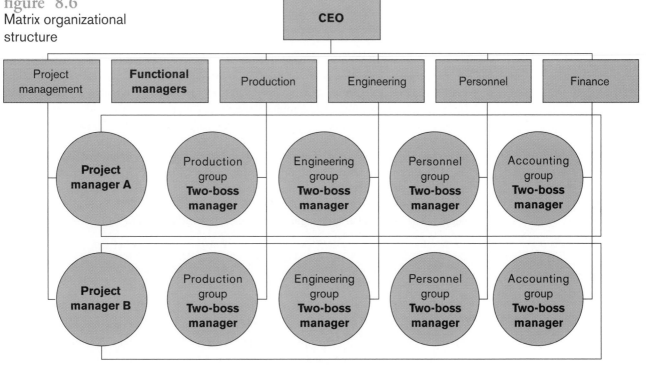

Source: D. Robey and C. Sales, *Designing Organizations,* 4th ed. (Burr Ridge, IL: Richard D. Irwin, 1994), p. 222. Reprinted by permission.

table 8.3
Advantages of the
matrix design

- Decision making is decentralized to a level where information is processed properly and relevant knowledge is applied.
- Extensive communications networks help process large amounts of information.
- With decisions delegated to appropriate levels, higher management levels are not overloaded with operational decisions.
- Resource utilization is efficient because key resources are shared across several important programs or products at the same time.
- Employees learn the collaborative skills needed to function in an environment characterized by frequent meetings and more informal interactions.
- Dual career ladders are elaborated as more career options become available on both sides of the organization.

Source: H. Kolodny, "Managing in a Matrix," *Business Horizons,* March–April 1981, pp. 17–24.

The *top executive,* who heads the matrix, must learn to balance power and emphasis between the product and functional orientations. *Product or division managers* and *functional managers* must learn to collaborate and manage their conflicts constructively. Finally, the *two-boss managers* or employees at the bottom of the diamond must learn how to be responsible to two superiors. This means prioritizing multiple demands and sometimes even reconciling conflicting orders. Some people function poorly under this ambiguous, conflictual circumstance; sometimes this signals the end of their careers with the company. Others learn to be proactive, communicate effectively with both superiors, rise above the difficulties, and manage these work relationships constructively.

The matrix form today   The popularity of the matrix form waned during the end of the 1980s when many companies had difficulty implementing it. But lately, it has come back strong. Reasons for this resurgence include pressures to consolidate costs and be faster to market, creating a need for better coordination across functions in the business units, and a need for coordination across countries for firms with global business strategies. Many of the challenges created by the matrix are particularly acute in an international context.[26]

The structure of the matrix hasn't changed, but our understanding of it has. The key to managing today's matrix is not the formal structure itself but the realization that the matrix is a *process.* Companies that have had trouble adopting the matrix form may have been correct in creating such a multidimensional structure to cope with environmental complexity, but they needed to go further than trying to construct a flexible organization simply by changing the structure. The formal structure is merely the organization's anatomy. Executives must also attend to its physiology—the relationships that allow information to flow through the organization—and its psychology—the norms, values, and attitudes that shape how people think and behave.[27] We will address these issues in the next chapter and in Part 4 of the text, which focuses on how to lead and manage people. The issues also arise again in Chapter 16 on control and culture.

table 8.4
Disadvantages of
the matrix design

- Confusion can arise because people do not have a single superior to whom they feel primary responsibility.
- The design encourages managers who share subordinates to jockey for power.
- The mistaken belief can arise that matrix management is the same thing as group decision making—in other words, everyone must be consulted for every decision.
- Too much democracy can lead to not enough action.

Source: H. Kolodny, "Managing in a Matrix," *Business Horizons,* March–April 1981, pp. 17–24.

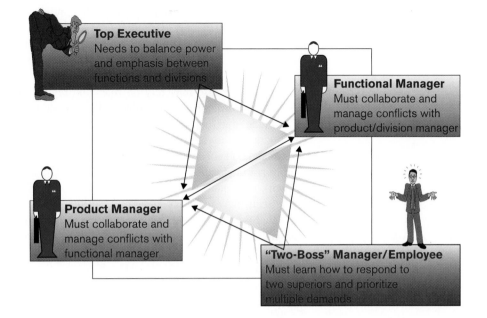

figure 8.7
The matrix diamond

Organizational integration

Although we have covered both the vertical and horizontal dimensions of organizational structure, we have really only focused on structural *differentiation*. At the outset we noted that as organizations differentiate their structures, they also need to be concerned about *integration* and *coordination*. Because of specialization and the division of labor, different groups of managers and employees develop different orientations. Depending on whether employees are in a functional department or in a divisional group, are line or staff, and so on, they will think and act in ways that are geared toward their particular work units. In short, people working in separate functions, divisions, and business units literally tend to forget about one another. When this happens, it is difficult for managers to combine all of their activities into an integrated whole.

There are a variety of approaches available to managers to help them make certain that interdependent units and individuals will work together to achieve a common purpose. Coordination methods include standardization, plans, and mutual adjustment.[28]

Coordination by standardization

When organizations coordinate activities by establishing routines and standard operating procedures that remain in place over time, we say that work has been standardized.

Would you believe all of these people worked on putting this textbook together, not including the authors who wrote it!

standardization Establishing common rules and procedures that apply uniformly to everyone.

Standardization constrains actions and integrates various units by regulating what people do. People oftentimes know how to act—and know how to interact—because there are standard operating procedures that spell out what they should do. Employee manuals and policies, for example, may explain what actions a manager should take to discipline an employee or deal with an unhappy customer.

Organizations also may rely on rules and regulations to govern how people interact (we call this *formalization*). Simple policies regarding attendance, dress, and decorum, for example, may help eliminate a good deal of uncertainty at work. But an important assumption underlying both standardization and formalization is that the rules and procedures should apply to most (if not all) situations. These approaches, therefore, are most appropriate in situations that are relatively stable and unchanging. In some cases, when the work environment requires flexibility, coordination by standardization may not be very effective. Who hasn't experienced a time when rules and procedures—frequently associated with a slow bureaucracy—prevented timely action to address a problem? In these instances, we often refer to rules and regulations as "red tape."[29]

Coordination by plan

coordination by plan Interdependent units are required to meet deadlines and objectives that contribute to a common goal.

If it is difficult to lay out the exact rules and procedures by which work should be integrated, organizations may provide more latitude by establishing goals and schedules for interdependent units. **Coordination by plan** does not require the same high degree of stability and routinization required for coordination by standardization. Interdependent units are free to modify and adapt their actions, as long as they meet the deadlines and targets required for working with others.

In writing this textbook, for example, we (the authors) sat down with the publication team that included the editors, the marketing staff, the production group, and support staff. Together we ironed out a schedule for developing this book that covered approximately a two-year period. That development plan included dates and "deliverables" that specified what was to be accomplished and forwarded to the others in the organization. The plan allowed for a good deal of flexibility on each subunit's part, and the overall approach allowed us to work together effectively.

Coordination by mutual adjustment

coordination by mutual adjustment Units interact with one another to make accommodations so as to achieve flexible coordination.

Ironically, the simplest and most flexible approach to coordination may just be to have interdependent parties to talk to one another. **Coordination by mutual adjustment** involves feedback and discussions to jointly figure out how to approach problems and devise solutions that are agreeable to everyone. The popularity of teams today is in part due to the fact that they allow for flexible coordination; teams can operate under the principle of mutual adjustment.

But the flexibility of mutual adjustment as a coordination device does not come without some cost. "Hashing out" every issue takes a good deal of time and may not be the most expedient approach for organizing work. Imagine how long it would take to accomplish even the most basic tasks if subunits had to talk through every situation. At the same time, mutual adjustment can be very effective when problems are novel and cannot be programmed in advance with rules, procedures, or plans. Particularly in crisis situations in which rules and procedures don't apply, mutual adjustment is likely to be the most effective approach to coordination.

Bill Gates on reorganization: A necessary art

In the corporate world, the word "reorganization" can be chilling. "Did something go wrong?" people ask, "Did somebody lose or win?" Corporate reorganizations may be prompted by failures, but often they are essential elements of success. Done properly, reorganization can move people into new areas where they can be

Bill Gates, founder of Microsoft, believes corporate reorganizations are essential elements of success.
[David Strick/Corbis Outline]

more creative and effective. People often hit plateaus, get too comfortable in their jobs, and no longer come up with new approaches. A realignment presents them with fresh challenges. Great results can happen when people who have worked in product areas get closer to customers, and when people who have been working with customers join the product-development cycle. This mixing helps customer-driven companies conceive and deliver better products.

Whatever the impetus, reorganizations are a lot of work, and they carry risks. For example, if you elect to broaden the experience of an executive by moving him or her from one important job to another, you run the risk that neither job will be performed as well as it was. The new structure may not work as well as the old one. Still, a company unwilling to ever reorganize is rather calcified in terms of how it responds to the marketplace. That is a risk, too. Today any company can find itself driven out of business if it is not adaptive. Sometimes it takes several years for a company to recognize it should have changed, and by then it may be too late.

About every two years, Microsoft undertakes a major reorganization. Even though reorganizations are expected, they still create anxiety for almost everyone, including me. My concern is always whether or not we are making the right decisions, and whether key employees will be enthusiastic about their new roles. I gain confidence about a reorganization when I see that it makes clear what every group is to do, minimizes the dependencies and overlap between groups, and offers developing employees larger responsibilities.

Employees worry about how their careers will be shaped by the new corporate structure. Managers become overly concerned about how their titles or the number of people reporting to them will change. At Microsoft we try to keep titles from carrying too much meaning, simply because descriptive titles encourage inflexibility among people during reorganizations. For example, many people here have the title "product manager." We give these people significant marketing responsibilities, but some report to others who have the same title. Some of our best people don't have anyone working for them. Some run large groups, but others are asked to take on a small but important project or even work alone. You must have great people in every corner.

In designing a new structure, you must strike a balance between keeping it logical and keeping executives happy and effective by giving them assignments they want and will handle well. During our most recent change, we asked: What are our goals? How can we move them into practice? What does this imply for our structure? Will our people be excited about their new roles? Over two months our thinking evolved.

How you communicate the news of a reorganization is significant. I'm a big believer in electronic mail, but describing the details of a reorganization to employees is more effective in person. We gathered thousands of employees together, put key executives on stage, and allocated one hour for questions and answers. We welcomed tough questions, and wanted employees to see first-hand how we responded. We wanted to know what employees were thinking.

In any reorganization, some people distinguish themselves by making it succeed. Other people show inflexibility and inability to rise above their views and interests. A few managers choose not to fit into the new structure or actually don't fit in. It's okay to lose some managers, but high turnover is damaging. The company must show managers a long-term career plan. Employees who don't understand how the company values their skills or where those skills can take them, are bound to be restless. And that can mean an unhappy, ineffective organization—whether reorganized or not.

Source: Excerpt from Bill Gates, "Reorganization: A Necessary Art," Executive Excellence, December 2000, 17, no. 12, p. 3. ●

Looking ahead

The organization chart, differentiation, integration, authority, delegation, coordination, and the like convey fundamental information about an organization's structure. However, the information so far has provided only a snapshot. The real organization is more like a motion picture—it moves! More flexible and innovative—even virtual—forms of organizations are evolving.

No organization is merely a set of static work relationships. Because organizations are composed of people, they are hotbeds of social relationships. Networks of individuals cutting across departmental boundaries interact with one another. Various friendship groups or cliques band together to form *coalitions*—members of the organization who jointly support a particular issue and try to ensure that their viewpoints determine the outcome of policy decisions.[30]

Thus, the formal organization structure does not describe all about how the company really works. Even if you know departments and authority relationships, there is still much to understand. How do things really get done? Who influences whom, and how? Which managers are the most powerful? How effective is the top leadership? Which groups are most and which are least effective? What is the nature of communication patterns throughout the organization? These issues are discussed throughout the rest of the book.

Now you are familiar with the basic organizing concepts discussed in this chapter. In the next chapter, we will discuss the current challenges of designing the modern organization with which the modern executive constantly grapples.

Key terms

Accountability, p. 262
Authority, p. 258
Centralized organization, p. 263
Coordination, p. 257
Coordination by mutual adjustment, p. 272
Coordination by plan, p. 272
Decentralized organizations, p. 263
Delegation, p. 261
Departmentalization, p. 264
Differentiation, p. 256
Division of labor, p. 256
Divisional organization, p. 266
Functional organization, p. 264

Hierarchy, p. 260
Integration, p. 256
Line departments, p. 264
Matrix organization, p. 268
Organization chart, p. 256
Responsibility, p. 261
Span of control, p. 260
Specialization, p. 256
Staff departments, p. 264
Standardization, p. 271
Subunits, p. 260
Unity-of-command principle, p. 269
Value chain, p. 264

Summary of learning objectives

Now that you have studied Chapter 8, you should know:

How differentiation and integration influence your organization's structure.

Differentiation means that organizations have many parts. Specialization means that various individuals and units throughout the organization perform different tasks. The assignment of tasks to different people or groups is often referred to as the division of labor. But the specialized tasks in an organization cannot all be performed independently of one another. Coordination links the various tasks in order to achieve the organization's overall mission. When there are many different specialized tasks and work units, the organization is highly differentiated; the more differentiated the organization, the more integration or coordination is required.

How authority operates.

Authority is the legitimate right to make decisions and tell other people what to do. Authority is exercised throughout the hierarchy, as bosses have the authority to give orders to subordinates. Through the day-to-day operation of authority, the organization proceeds toward achieving its goals. Owners or stockholders have ultimate authority.

The roles of the board of directors and the chief executive officer.

Boards of directors report to stockholders. The board of directors controls or advises management, considers the firm's legal and other interests, and protects stockholders' rights. The chief executive officer reports to the board and is accountable for the organization's performance.

How span of control affects structure and managerial effectiveness.

Span of control is the number of people who report directly to a manager. Narrow spans create tall organizations, and wide spans create flat ones. No single span of control is always appropriate; the optimal span is determined by characteristics of the work, the subordinates, the manager, and the organization.

How to delegate work effectively.

Delegation is the assignment of tasks and responsibilities. Delegation has many potential advantages for the manager, the subordinate, and the organization. But to be effective, the process must be managed carefully. The manager should define the goal, select the person, solicit opinions, provide resources, schedule checkpoints, and discuss progress periodically.

The difference between centralized and decentralized organizations.

In centralized organizations, most important decisions are made by top managers. In decentralized organizations, many decisions are delegated to lower levels.

How to allocate jobs to work units.

Jobs can be departmentalized on the basis of function, product, customers, or geography. Most organizations use several different types of departmentalization.

How to manage the unique challenges of the matrix organization.

The matrix is a complex structure with a dual authority structure. A well-managed matrix enables organizations to adapt to change. But it can also create confusion and interpersonal difficulties. People in all positions in the matrix—top executives, product and function managers, and two-boss managers—must acquire unique survival skills.

The nature of important integrating mechanisms.

Managers can coordinate interdependent units through standardization, plans, and mutual adjustment. Standardization occurs when routines and standard operating procedures are put in place. They are typically accompanied by formalized rules. Coordination by plan is more flexible and allows more freedom in how tasks are carried out, but keeps interdependent units focused on schedules and joint goals. Mutual adjustment involves feedback and discussions among related parties to accommodate each others' needs. It is at once the most flexible and simple to administer, but it is time-consuming.

Discussion questions

1. Using the concepts in the chapter, discuss the advantages and disadvantages of the organization structure approaches described in "Setting the Stage."

2. What are some advantages and disadvantages of being in the CEO position?

3. Would you like to sit on a board of directors? Why or why not? If you did serve on a board, what kind of organization would you prefer? As a board member, in what kinds of activities do you think you would most actively engage?

4. Interview a member of a board of directors and discuss the member's perspectives on his or her role.

5. Pick a job you have held and describe it in terms of span of control, delegation, responsibility, authority, and accountability.

6. Why do you think managers have difficulty delegating? What can be done to overcome these difficulties?

7. Consider an organization in which you have worked, draw its organization chart, and describe it using terms in this chapter. How did you like working there, and why?

8. Would you rather work in a functional or divisional organization? Why?

9. If you learned that a company had a matrix structure, would you be more or less interested in working there? Explain your answer. How would you prepare yourself to work effectively in a matrix?

10. Brainstorm a list of methods for integrating interdependent work units. Discuss the activities that need to be undertaken and the pros and cons of each approach.

Concluding Case
Lucent: Clean Break, Clean Slate?

The company that could seemingly do no wrong in the first three years after it was spun off from AT&T in 1996 seriously lost its way in 2000. Worst of all, it has been completely bested by archrival Nortel Networks Corp. in the key market for optical-fiber telephone switches (see Chapter 2, "At the Speed of Light").

The contrast with Nortel is what stings Lucent execs the most. It was only a few years ago that Nortel was the industry dog. But today, Nortel has 45 percent of the exploding optical-transmission-switch market. That compares with just 15 percent for Lucent, which decided in 1996 to develop a slower switch precisely because its customers weren't asking for anything faster. Lucent now rues the decision to settle for less transmission speed. And CEO Henry Schacht is quick to acknowledge that he is as much at fault as former CEO Richard McGinn. Schacht says he is planning one-on-one meetings with Lucent's customers and is reviewing all the processes now in place with an eye to streamlining Lucent's cumbersome structure.

Under McGinn, Lucent embarked on an organizational overhaul in September 2000. To head up key divisions, it has appointed some aggressive new outsiders who are not mired in the company's bureaucratic mindset. One of those, CFO Deborah C. Hopkins, is putting in place a companywide standard for evaluating a product's profitability, replacing the piecemeal, business-by-business standard used before. The company is also chopping away at management layers, more closely tying compensation to performance, and trying to better integrate its vaunted Bell Labs with product-development teams. But the world's largest telecom-equipment maker actually has a more cosmic task: It must remake itself into a company that can be quick to respond to needs, quick to deliver new technology, and far less bureaucratic. And it has to do all of this while suffering from a 20 percent turnover rate that is siphoning off top talent.

Granted, such an overhaul has been prescribed for just about every lumbering old economy behemoth. Lucent is determined to pull itself apace with that market. And it may have a secret weapon: In September, Lucent named Jeong Kim to head its optical-networks business. Clearly different from the Lucent lifers around him, Kim has reorganized the group into 17 small divisions based on product lines, with managers closely matched to customers and compensation tied to performance. His goal: to improve time to delivery by 30 percent. "I have a 100-day plan," he says.

Kim's entrepreneurial spirit is sorely needed at Lucent, and he is convinced he already has had a positive effect on morale. He recently visited a Lucent plant in North Andover, Massachusetts, and found general managers there very involved in suggesting ways the operation could be improved. "They were really taking ownership of their operation. And morale was running really high. I was very encouraged."

Lucent must also start regaining the trust of its employees if it wants to stem the flood of talent that started rushing out the door as soon as executives' pre-IPO options vested on October 1, 1999. And it hasn't done any better at hanging on to the employees who came on board with its many acquisitions. Adopted employees who have headed for the doors regularly complain that they found themselves stifled by Lucent's many-layered management. "There are a lot of top-level people trying to get out of Lucent right now," one Silicon Valley headhunter says.

Lucent's executives are sounding all of the right turnaround noises. William T. O'Shea, vice president for corporate strategy and business development, is in charge of a massive effort that kicked off this past summer to streamline Lucent's businesses. The goal: to encourage entrepreneurship. "We are putting new people in charge and organizing groups to focus their energy in small teams," he says, rather than structuring the company in large, often uncommunicative, divisions. And the company is including Bell Lab researchers in these teams, to make sure that their inventions are properly promoted. "We are bringing a much broader collection of people to the table internally to make strategic decisions," he says.

Questions:

1. How would you characterize the changes in Lucent's vertical and horizontal structures?

2. What are the strategic reasons behind these changes in strategy?

3. What other management issues do you see in this case? How do they combine with issues of structure?

Source: Condensed from Catherine Arnst, Roger O. Crockett, Andy Reinhardt and John Shinal, "Lucent: Clean Break, Clean Slate?", *Business Week Online*, October 26, 2000. ●

CEO Henry Schacht has been behind Lucent's determination to pull itself apace within its market.
[Courtesy Lucent Technologies, Inc.]

Experiential Exercises

8.1 The Business School Organization Chart

Objectives

1. To clarify the factors that determine organization structure.
2. To provide insight into the workings of an organization.
3. To examine the working relationships within an organization.

Instructions

1. Draw an organization chart for your school of business. Be sure to identify all the staff and line positions in the school. Specify the chain of command and the levels of administration. Note the different spans of control. Are there any advisory groups, task forces, or committees to consider?

2. Review the chapter material on organization structure to help identify both strong and weak points in your school's organization. Now draw another organization chart for the school, incorporating any changes that you believe would improve the quality of the school. Support the second chart with a list of recommended changes and reasons for their inclusion.

Discussion Questions

1. Is your business school well organized? Why or why not?
2. Is your school's organization organic or mechanistic? In what ways?
3. In what ways is the school's structure designed to suit the needs of students, faculty, staff, the administration, and the business community?

8.2 Mechanistic and Organic Structures

Objectives

1. To think about your own preferences when it comes to working in a particular organizational structure.

2. To examine aspects of organizations using as an example this class you are a member of.

Instructions

1. Complete the Mechanistic and Organic Worksheet below.

2. Meet in groups of four to six persons. Share your data from parts 1 and 2 of the worksheet. Discuss the reasons for your responses, and analyze the factors that probably encouraged your instructor to choose the type of structure that now exists.

Mechanistic and Organic Worksheet

1. Indicate your general preference for working in one of these two organizational structures by circling the appropriate response:

Mechanistic	1	2	3	4	5	6	7	8	9	10	Organic

2. Indicate your perception of the form of organization that is used in this class by circling the appropriate response for each item:

A. Task-role definition

Rigid	1	2	3	4	5	6	7	8	9	10	Flexible

B. Communication

Vertical	1	2	3	4	5	6	7	8	9	10	Multidirectional

C. Decision making

Centralized	1	2	3	4	5	6	7	8	9	10	Decentralized

D. Sensitivity to the environment

Closed	1	2	3	4	5	6	7	8	9	10	Open

Source: Keith Davis and John. W. Newstrom, *Human Behavior at Work*, 9th ed. (New York: McGraw-Hill, 1993), p. 358. Reprinted by permission of McGraw-Hill, Inc. ●

Chapter Nine

The Responsive Organization

Bureaucracy defends the status quo long past the time when the quo has lost its status.

—Laurence J. Peter

Chapter Outline

Learning Objectives

After studying Chapter 9, you will know:

1. The market imperatives a firm must meet to survive.

2. The potential advantages of creating an organic form of organization.

3. How a firm can "be" both small and big.

4. How to manage information-processing demands.

5. How firms organize to meet customer requirements.

6. How firms organize around different types of technology.

7. The new types of dynamic organizational concepts and forms that are being used for strategic responsiveness.

Setting the Stage

Few Rules, Fast Responses

Ask Michael E. Marks about his company's procedures for making a big capital investment, and he is likely to refer you to the Flextronics International Corporate Policy Manual. It has 80 pages—all of them blank. Although Marks is Flextronics's chairman and CEO, he says he sometimes lets subordinates do multimillion-dollar acquisitions without showing him the paperwork. He disdains staff meetings at his San Jose, California headquarters, and he refuses to draw up an organization chart delineating his managers' responsibilities.

One might think Marks's style is too casual for a fast-growing conglomerate. This is a giant that owns dozens of factories scattered over four continents and has big contracts with some of the most demanding corporate customers on earth, from Cisco Systems, Inc. to Siemens. What's more, Flextronics seems to be announcing a breakthrough deal a month. In the year 2000 alone, the company spent $5.5 billion to acquire electronics manufacturing plants, design firms, and component makers in the United States, Europe, and Asia. It also has landed huge manufacturing contracts with Motorola, Inc. and Microsoft Corp.

As Marks sees it, the business of global contract manufacturing is all about speed. The time it takes to get a prototype into mass production and onto retail shelves across the globe can determine whether a leading-edge digital gadget succeeds or flops. And with the Internet and corporate makeovers rapidly reconfiguring entire industries, Marks thinks it's a bigger sin to miss important opportunities than to make a mistake or two. So he doesn't want to tie down his top managers with bureaucracy. One of Marks's

Michael Marks, Chairman of the Board and CEO of Flextronics, thinks it's a bigger sin to miss important opportunities than to make a mistake or two. *[Courtesy Flextronics]*

favorite dictums: "It's not the big who eat the small. It's the fast who eat the slow."

So far, Marks has managed to craft the right balance. In seven years, sales have soared from $93 million toward $10.5 billion this year. Its stock has soared from under $10 in 1998 to the mid-$70s currently. This year, Flextronics is poised to become the world's second-largest contract manufacturer, after Solectron Corp.

The basketball hoop hanging in Marks's modest, somewhat disheveled office seems to sum up his self-image. Marks is a passionate player—and in the business world, Marks seems determined to prove a point. One way or another, he's convinced he can retain the agile management style of a start-up, while making Flextronics a global enterprise that can play in the big leagues.

Source: Pete Engardio, "Flextronics: Few Rules, Fast Response," Business Week, October 23, 2000, p.148F.

As you can guess from reading Setting the Stage, some pretty successful companies are "breaking the rules" about how organizations should be run. Or at least they are *changing* the rules—opening up their game—to use an analogy from sports.

Chapter 8 described the formal structure of organizations. The ideas we discussed there are traditional and basic, and fundamental to understanding organizations. But a firm's formal structure is only part of the story. There are other subtle aspects of organizing that really distinguish how firms operate for maximum effectiveness. Organizations are not static structures, but complex systems in which many people do many different things at the same time. The overall behavior of organizations does not just pop out of a chart, but emerges out of other processes, systems, and relationships among interrelated parties. In today's modern firm, new approaches to organizing are emerging. The emphasis in this chapter is not on the formal organization, but on organizing for *action*.

Today's imperatives

The formal structure is put in place to *control* people, decisions, and actions. But in today's fast-changing business environment, *responsiveness*—quickness, agility, the ability to adapt to changing demands—is more vital than ever to a firm's survival.[1]

Progressive companies place a premium on being able to act, and act fast. They want to act in accord with customer needs and other outside pressures. They want to take actions to correct past mistakes, and also to prepare for an uncertain future. They want to be able to respond to threats and opportunities. To do these things, they try to operate organically, manage size effectively, process huge amounts of information, and adopt new forms of organization.

mechanistic organization A form of organization that seeks to maximize internal efficiency.

organic structure An organizational form that emphasizes flexibility.

Many years after Max Weber wrote about the concept of bureaucracy, two British management scholars (Burns and Stalker) described what they called the **mechanistic organization**.[2] The common mechanistic structure they described was similar to Weber's bureaucracy. But they went on to suggest that in the modern corporation, the mechanistic structure is not the only option. The **organic structure** (introduced in Chapter 2) stands in stark contrast to the mechanistic organization. It is much less rigid and, in fact, emphasizes flexibility. The organic structure can be described as follows:

1. Jobholders have broader responsibilities that change as the need arises.
2. Communication occurs through advice and information rather than through orders and instructions.
3. Decision making and influence are more decentralized and informal.
4. Expertise is highly valued.
5. Jobholders rely more heavily on judgment than on rules.
6. Obedience to authority is less important than commitment to the organization's goals.
7. Employees depend more on one another and relate more informally and personally.

Figure 9.1 contrasts the formal structure of an organization—epitomized by the organization chart—to the informal structure, which is much more organic. Astute managers are keenly aware of the network of interactions among the organization's members, and structure around this to increase agility. People in organic organizations work more as teammates than as subordinates who take orders from the boss, thus breaking away from the traditional bureaucratic form.[3]

We rely on the ideas underlying the organic structure and networks as a foundation for discussing the newer forms of organization described in this chapter. The more organic a firm is, the more responsive it will be to changing competitive demands and market realities. For the remainder of this chapter, we summarize some of the most important issues that require organizations to adopt organic structures. These include organizing for optimal size, organizing for environmental response, organizing for technological response, and organizing for strategic response.

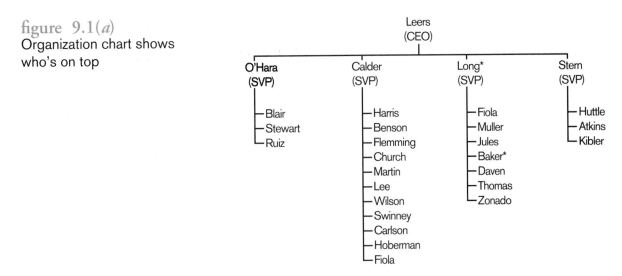

figure 9.1(a)
Organization chart shows who's on top

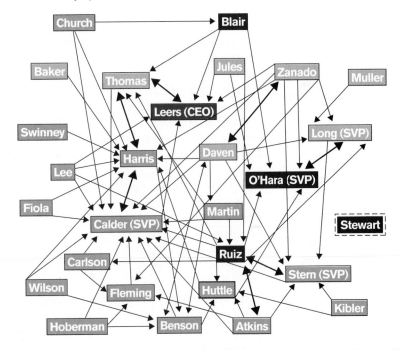

figure 9.1(b)
Advice network reveals knowledge flow

Source: Krackhardt and Hanson, "Information Networks: The Company Behind the Chart," *Harvard Business Review,* July-August 1993, pp. 104–11.

Organizing for optimal size

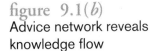

One of the most important characteristics of an organization is its size. Large organizations are typically less organic and more bureaucratic. For example, at Hewlett-Packard, before the recent reduction of its stifling bureaucracy, it took over 90 people on nine committees more than seven months to decide what to name some new software.[4]

In large organizations, jobs become more specialized. More distinct groups of specialists get created because large organizations can add a new specialty at lower proportional expense. The complexity these numerous specialties create makes the organization harder to control. Therefore, in the past management added more levels to keep spans of control from becoming too large. To cope with complexity, large companies tend to become more bureaucratic. Rules, procedures, and paperwork are introduced.

Thus, with size comes greater complexity, and complexity brings a need for increased control. In response, organizations adopt bureaucratic strategies of control. The conventional wisdom is that bureaucratization increases efficiency but decreases a company's ability to innovate. So is large size a good thing or a bad thing? Let's see.

The case for big

Bigger was better after World War II, when foreign competition was limited and growth seemed limitless. To meet high demand for its products, U.S. industry embraced high-volume, low-cost manufacturing methods. IBM, GM, and Sears all grew into behemoths during these decades.

Alfred Chandler, a pioneer in strategic management, noted that big companies were the engine of economic growth throughout the 20th century.[5] Size creates *scale economies,* that is, lower costs per unit of production. And size can offer specific advantages like lowered operating costs, greater purchasing power, and easier access to capital. For example, Microsoft spends nearly $4 billion each year on research and development, far more than its rivals can afford.[6] Size also creates **economies of scope;** materials and processes employed in one product can be used to make other, related products. With such advantages, huge companies with lots of money may be the best at taking on large foreign rivals in huge global markets.

economies of scope
Economies in which materials and processes employed in one product can be used to make other, related products.

The case for small

But a huge, complex organization can find it hard to manage relationships with customers and among its own units. Bureaucracy can run rampant. Too much success can breed complacency, and the resulting inertia hinders change. Experts suggest that this is a surefire formula for being "left in the dust" by hungry competitors. As consumers demand a more diverse array of high-quality, customized products supported by excellent service, giant companies have begun to stumble. There is some evidence, for example, that as firms get larger and their market share grows, customers begin to view their products as having lower quality. Larger companies are more difficult to coordinate and control. So while size may enhance some efficiency by spreading fixed costs out over more units, it may also create administrative difficulties that inhibit efficient performance. A new term has entered business vocabulary: *diseconomies of scale,* or the costs of being too big. "Small is beautiful" has become a favorite phrase of entrepreneurial business managers.[7]

Smaller companies can move fast, can provide quality goods and services to targeted market niches, and can inspire greater involvement from their people. Nimble, small firms frequently outmaneuver big bureaucracies. They introduce new and better products, and they steal market share. The premium now is on flexibility and responsiveness—the unique potential strengths of the small firm. For example, Ultra Pac, Inc. produces recyclable plastic food containers.[8] It has only 300 employees, but competes against Mobil Corp. and Tenneco, Inc. The smaller company turns out 500 different kinds of packaging and ships within three days of an order, in contrast to over a week at the larger companies.

Being big and small

Small *is* beautiful for unleashing energy and speed. But in buying and selling, size offers market power. The challenge then is to be both big and small to capitalize on the advantages of each.

Independent Distributors, Inc. (IDI) is an alliance of 70 industrial distributors in Canada that join forces to give themselves collective buying power. This buying group has 140 distribution branches that stretch from Victoria, British Columbia to St. John's, Newfoundland. Still, while IDI looks very much like a large corporation on the outside, inside it is a network of 70 independent distributors, all committed to serving their local marketplaces. In essence, IDI is trying to combine the best of both worlds—creating small, entrepreneurial companies with the buying power and reach of a national corporation.

From a different angle, companies like Southwest Airlines, AES (mentioned in Chapter 8), Starbucks, and Motorola are large companies that work hard to act small. Each is considered among the best-managed companies in the world. To avoid problems of growth and size, they decentralize decision making and organize around small, adaptive, team-based work units.

Downsizing is the planned elimination of jobs. The fact that layoffs are planned doesn't mean people aren't frightened and angry when they lose their jobs, as evidenced by these placard-carrying ex-employees.
[Tom McKitterick/Impact Visuals]

downsizing The planned elimination of positions or jobs.

rightsizing A successful effort to achieve an appropriate size at which the company performs most effectively.

survivor's syndrome Loss of productivity and morale in employees who remain after a downsizing.

Downsizing   As large companies attempt to regain the responsiveness of small, they often face the dilemma of downsizing. **Downsizing** (or **rightsizing**) is the planned elimination of positions or jobs. Common approaches to downsizing include eliminating functions, hierarchical levels, or units.[9] It is hard to pick up a newspaper without seeing announcements of another company downsizing; likewise, it is hard to name a major corporation that has not downsized in recent years. The list includes IBM, Citicorp, AT&T, Kodak, Goodyear, Exxon, Xerox, TRW, General Motors, and so on.

Historically, layoffs tended to affect manufacturing firms, and operative level workers in particular. But given that the most recent cycle of downsizing has focused on delayering and eliminating bureaucratic structures, "white collar" middle managers have been those chiefly affected.

What can be done to manage downsizing effectively—to help make it a more effective "rightsizing"? First of all, firms should avoid excessive (cyclical) hiring to help reduce the need to engage in major or multiple downsizings. But beyond that, firms must avoid common mistakes such as making slow, small, frequent layoffs; implementing voluntary early retirement programs that entice the best people to leave; or laying off so many people that the company's work can no longer be performed. Instead, firms can engage in a number of positive practices to ease the pain of downsizing:

- Choose positions to be eliminated based on careful analysis and strategic thinking.
- Train people to cope with the new situation.
- Identify and protect talented people.
- Give special attention and help to those who have lost their jobs.
- Communicate constantly with people about the process.
- Emphasize a positive future and people's new roles in attaining it.[10]

Interestingly, the people who lose their jobs because of downsizing are not the only ones deeply affected. Those who survive the process—who keep their jobs—tend to exhibit what has become known as **survivor's syndrome**.[11] They struggle with heavier workloads, wonder who will be next to go, try to figure out how to survive, lose commitment to the company and faith in their bosses, and become narrow-minded, self-absorbed, and risk averse. As a consequence, morale and productivity usually drop.

You will learn more about some of these ideas in later chapters on human resources management, leadership, motivation, communication, and managing change.

The following story shows an example of how one small company dealt with a business downturn, maneuvered quickly, took advantage of Web technologies and the possibilities of e-commerce, developed alliances with outside partners, and became very successful as a new-economy company.

From the Pages of
BusinessWeek

Digital brokers on the Net

Bruce Yoxsimer owned a travel agency for 13 years before events forced him into a bold, new strategy. The seven-employee company in Palo Alto, California, was doing nicely. Annual bookings came to nearly $4 million. But when the airlines capped commissions on ticket sales in 1994, the agency's largest source of revenue was suddenly under siege. To adapt, Yoxsimer took a farsighted approach: He set up shop all over again—this time on the World Wide Web.

Yoxsimer teamed up with a pair of software experts to launch the Internet Travel Network (www.itn.net), now called GetThere.com. In 1995, it became one of the first companies to book trips over the Web. Despite the far greater sales volume of competing airline Websites, the company has secured a place in the Web ticketing business by being there early and building a name. With just 50 employees, it is processing up to 1,000 reservations a day, a rate that is growing by about 10 percent a month, thanks to word-of-mouth referrals, advertising, and Internet search engines—not to mention businesses that have signed ITN as their exclusive on-line agent.

ITN is a sterling example of how rapidly the Web is forcing change on small businesses. From real estate, travel, and insurance agents to car dealers and recruitment firms, many businesses are finding fresh opportunities on the Web. Virtually all, though, will have to change how they do business. That may mean providing a level of customer service that a computer cannot deliver. Or teaming up with an Internet partner. Or converting the business to a Website. As the new digital brokers gobble up market share, giving customers more options than ever, middlemen of all stripes need to develop survival strategies.

However, those who broker products and information without adding value— beware. If your business merely sells access to a database—such as airline schedules, real estate listings, insurance rates, and stock exchanges—watch out. Realistically, you won't be able to beat the Web at its own game: Offering fast access to databases and interactive information tailored to individual consumers. Even businesses that do add some value will have to rethink their business models, says Jeffrey F. Rayport, an assistant professor at the Harvard business school. "It's a wholesale conversion to a better, faster, cheaper, more flexible way of doing business," he says.

As Yoxsimer's success shows, the Web is a superbly efficient way to sell airline tickets. A growing portion of domestic tickets is now sold online, according to the American Society of Travel Agents, and Forrester Research Inc. forecasts that volume will quadruple over the next year or so. That's why Phil Davidoff, 57, owner and co-founder of Bel-air/Empress Travel, a small agency in Bowie, Maryland, has deemphasized airline ticket sales. He says that commission caps may have started the free-fall, but online competition—which emboldened the airlines to slash commissions—accelerated the plunge. In the past few years, airline ticket commissions dropped from 62 percent of his revenues to less than 30 percent. In response, Davidoff is now doing what computers can't—getting to know customers so well that he can advise them on cruises that he books. Other agencies are focusing on specialties such as adventure trips, senior citizen travel, or eco-tourism.

It appears that digital brokers are rapidly changing the face of some businesses. They surface wherever there's a demand for convenient—and often more efficient —services. But if you don't want to go the way of the milkman or become an online broker yourself, what choice remains? Everyone is learning to adapt, and being responsive to customer needs has never been more important.

Source: Evan I. Schwartz, "How Middlemen Can Come Out On Top," *Business Week,* February 9, 1998.

Discussion questions

1. How does network brokering lead to better customer responsiveness?
2. What other businesses might be good prospects for online brokering?
3. What types of organizational adaptation would be required to compete with networking businesses? ●

Organizing for environmental response

Apart from organizing for optimal size, organizations also have to adapt to external environments. In a sense, this is the crux of creating a responsive organization. In Chapter 2, we introduced various approaches organizations might take to respond to the environment. They included *adapting* to the environment, *influencing* the environment, and *selecting* a new environment. In this section, we want to delve more deeply into how organizations organize for environmental response.

Organizing to manage information

Today's environments tend to be complex, dynamic, and (therefore) uncertain. Huge amounts of information flow from the external environment to the organization and back to the environment. To cope, organizations must acquire, process, and respond to that information. Doing so has direct implications for how firms organize. To function effectively, organizations need to develop structures for processing information.

Figure 9.2 shows two general strategies that can help managers cope with high uncertainty and heavy information demands. First, management can act to reduce the need for information. Second, it can increase its capacity to handle more information.[12]

Option one: Reducing the need for information

Managers can reduce the need for information in two ways: (a) creating slack resources and (b) creating self-contained tasks. *Slack resources* are simply extra resources on which organizations can rely "in a pinch" so that if they get caught off guard, they can still adjust. Inventory, for example, is a type of slack resource that provides extra stock on hand in case it is needed. With extra inventory, an organization does not have to have as much information about sales demand, lead-time, and the like. Employees can also be a type of slack resource. For example, Walden Paddlers, a manufacturer of Kayaks, has only eight full-time employees. However, the company has contacts with a crew of 14 part-time employees who come aboard during busy seasons. These part-timers represent a type of slack resource for Walden Paddlers in that the company does not have to perfectly forecast sales peaks, but can rely on supplementary workers to handle irregularities.[13]

Like slack resources, creating *self-contained tasks* allow organizations to reduce the need for some information. *Creating self-contained tasks* refers to changing from a functional organization to a product or project organization and giving each unit the resources it needs to perform its task. Information-processing problems are reduced because each unit has its own full complement of specialties instead of functional specialties having to share their expertise among a number of different product teams. Communications then flow within each team rather than among a complex array of interdependent groups.

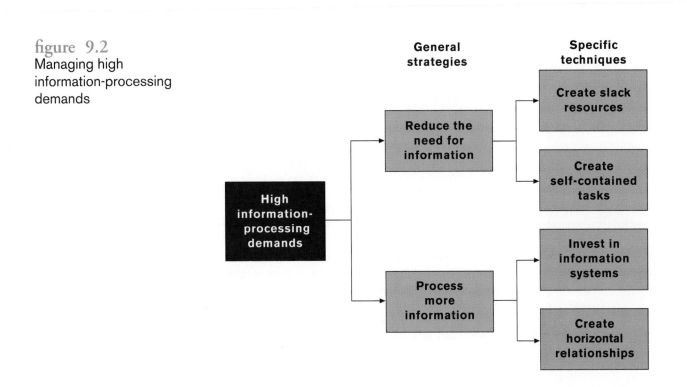

figure 9.2
Managing high
information-processing
demands

Option two: Increasing information processing capability   Instead of reducing the need for information, organizations may take the approach of increasing its information-processing capability. They can *invest in information systems,* which usually means employing or expanding computer systems. And they can create horizontal relationships to foster coordination across different units. Such horizontal relationships are effective because they increase integration (recall Chapter 8), which Lawrence and Lorsch suggest is necessary for managing complex environments. As uncertainty increases, the following horizontal processes may be used, ranging from the simplest to the most complex:[14]

1. Direct contact (mutual adjustment) among managers who share a problem. In a university, for example, a residence hall adviser might call a meeting to resolve differences between two feuding students who live in adjacent rooms.

2. *Liaison roles,* or specialized jobs to handle communications between two departments. A fraternity representative is a liaison between the fraternity and the interfraternity council, the university, or the local community.

3. *Task forces,* or groups of representatives from different departments, brought together temporarily to solve a common problem. For example, students, faculty, and administrators may be members of a task force charged with bringing distinguished speakers to campus for a current-events seminar.

4. *Teams,* or permanent interdepartmental decision-making groups. An executive council made up of department heads might meet regularly to make decisions affecting a college of engineering or liberal arts.

5. *Product, program, or project managers* who direct interdisciplinary groups with a common task to perform. In a college of business administration, a faculty administrator might head an executive education program of professors from several disciplines.

6. *Matrix organizations,* composed of dual relationships in which some managers report to two superiors (recall Chapter 8). Your instructors, for example, may report to department heads in their respective disciplines and also to a director of undergraduate or graduate programs.

Several of these processes are discussed further in Chapter 14, where we examine managing teams and intergroup relations.

Organizing for customer responsiveness

Although it is valuable to discuss environmental uncertainty in general, at this point we hope to move to a more concrete set of circumstances. From Chapter 2 recall that the environment is composed of many different parts (e.g., government, suppliers, competitors and the like). Perhaps no other aspect of the environment has had a more profound impact on organizing in recent years than a focus on *customers.* Dr. Kenichi Ohmae points out that any business unit must take into account three key players: the *company* itself, the *competition,* and the *customer.* These components form what Ohmae refers to as the *strategic triangle,* as shown in Figure 9.3. Managers need to balance the strategic triangle, and successful organizations use their strengths to create value by meeting customer requirements better than competitors do.

customer relationship management A multifaceted process focusing on creating two-way exchanges with customers to foster intimate knowledge of their needs, wants, and buying patterns.

Customer relationship management (CRM)   **Customer relationship management** is a multifaceted process, typically mediated by a set of information technologies, that focuses on creating two-way exchanges with customers so that firms have an intimate knowledge of their needs, wants, and buying patterns. In this way, CRM helps companies understand, as well as anticipate, the needs of current and potential customers. And in that way, it is part of a business strategy for managing customers to maximize their long-term value to an enterprise.[15]

As discussed throughout this book, customers want quality goods and service, low cost, innovative products, and speed. Traditional thinking considered these basic customer wants as a set of potential trade-offs. For instance, customers wanted high quality or low costs passed along in the form of low prices. But world-class companies today know that the "trade-off" mentality no longer applies. Customers want it *all,* and they are learning that somewhere an organization exists that will provide it all.

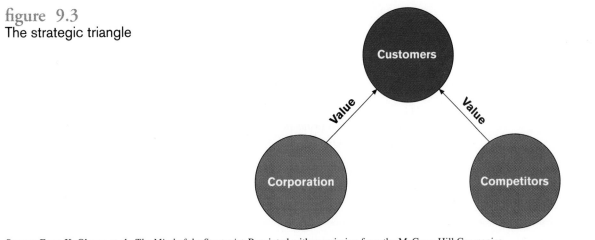

figure 9.3
The strategic triangle

Source: From K. Ohmae et al., *The Mind of the Strategist*. Reprinted with permission from the McGraw-Hill Companies.

But if all companies seek to satisfy customers, how can a company realize a competitive advantage? World-class companies have learned that most any advantage is temporary, for competitors will strive to catch up. Simply stated—though obviously not simply done—a company attains and retains competitive advantage by continuing to improve. This concept—*kaizen,* or continuous improvement—is an integral part of Japanese operations strategy. Motorola, a winner of the Malcolm Baldrige National Quality Award, operates with the philosophy that "the company that is satisfied with its progress will soon find that its customers are not."

As organizations focus on responding to customer needs, they soon find that traditional meaning of customer expands to include "internal customers." The word *customer* now refers to the *next process,* or *wherever the work goes next.*[16] This highlights the idea of interdependence among related functions and means that all functions of the organization—not just marketing people—have to be concerned with customer satisfaction. All recipients of a person's work, whether co-worker, boss, subordinate, or external party, come to be viewed as the customer.

total quality management
An integrative approach to management that supports the attainment of customer satisfaction through a wide variety of tools and techniques that result in high-quality goods and services.

Total quality management (TQM)   **Total quality management** is a way of managing in which everyone is committed to continuous improvement of their part of the operation. In business, success depends on having quality products. As described in Chapter 1 and throughout the book, TQM is a comprehensive approach to improving product quality and thereby customer satisfaction. It is characterized by a strong orientation toward customers (external and internal) and has become an umbrella theme for organizing work. TQM reorients managers toward involving people across departments in improving all aspects of the business. Continuous improvement requires integrative mechanisms that facilitate group problem solving, information sharing, and cooperation across business functions. As a consequence, the walls that separate stages and functions of work tend to come down, and the organization operates more in a team-oriented manner.[17]

W. Edwards Deming was one of the founders of the quality management movement. His "14 points" of quality emphasized a holistic approach to management that demands intimate understanding of the process—the delicate interaction of materials, machines, and people that determines productivity, quality, and competitive advantage:

1. Create constancy of purpose—strive for long-term improvement rather than short-term profit.
2. Adopt the new philosophy—don't tolerate delays and mistakes.
3. Cease dependence on mass inspection—build quality into the process on the front end.
4. End the practice of awarding business on price tag alone—build long-term relationships.
5. Improve constantly and forever the system of production and service—at each stage.
6. Institute training and retraining—continual updating of methods and thinking.

7. Institute leadership—provide resources needed for effectiveness.
8. Drive out fear—people must believe it is safe to report problems or ask for help.
9. Break down barriers among departments—promote teamwork.
10. Eliminate slogans, exhortations, and arbitrary targets—supply methods, not buzzwords.
11. Eliminate numerical quotas—they are contrary to the idea of continuous improvement.
12. Remove barriers to pride in workmanship—allow autonomy and spontaneity.
13. Institute a vigorous program of education and retraining—people are assets, not commodities.
14. Take action to accomplish the transformation—provide a structure that enables quality.

From the Pages of BusinessWeek

The war for better quality is far from won

Executives today are obsessed with reaching new markets at warp speed. But whatever happened to the hoopla surrounding quality control? Has the war against big-time defects been won? Or could corporate America be deluding itself into thinking that quality no longer is the huge problem it once was? It was only a decade ago that CEOs from Motorola, Ford, Xerox, and other U.S. companies undertook a Herculean effort to improve their products in the face of such formidable Japanese competitors as Toyota, Canon, and NEC. Quality gurus such as W. Edwards Deming achieved star status. And with great fanfare, the U.S. Commerce Department established the prestigious Malcolm Baldrige National Quality Award.

Little of this excitement remains. John Yochelson, president of the CEO-laden Council on Competitiveness, explains why. He says his members no longer look at quality as a competitive differentiator because they now understand it is merely the price of entry. Roger G. Ackerman, chairman and CEO of Corning, Inc. believes that we hear less now about quality because it has become deeply embedded in most companies' processes. Ray Stata, chairman of Analog Devices, Inc. and a founder of the Center for Quality of Management in Cambridge, Massachusetts, provides another perspective. He says that because most of the technical problems of manufacturing have been solved, the emphasis has shifted to the quality of management and organization. Harry S. Hertz, who administers the Baldrige Award, agrees. But surely it's too soon to say that the manufacturing sector is in great shape. Just think about recent events: the Firestone tire fiasco, new investigations into Goodyear, crashing servers at Sun Microsystems, recalls of circuit boards by Intel. Consider Federal Aviation Administration charges of systemic manufacturing control problems at Boeing Co., or the nearly 10 percent of cars on the road regularly being recalled.

As we enter the Internet Age, there is as yet no rigorous analytical framework for the new range of quality problems relating to e-business. What are we to make of the high rate of product-delivery failures from e-tailers for Christmas 2000 (16 percent by some accounts)? When it comes to new business-to-business auction markets for supplies, how will buyers ensure the highest quality when the products they purchase are often designed and made by companies that do not have established track records and with whom they have never dealt?

Source: Jeffrey E. Garten and John S. Abbott, "The War for Better Quality Is Far from Won," *Business Week*, December 18, 2000, p. 32. ●

The Baldrige criteria and TQM in the United States

As you know, the Baldrige Award is the prestigious award given to U.S. companies that achieve quality excellence. The award is granted on the basis of the seven following criteria. Included are brief descriptions of the strengths of companies that have applied for the Baldrige Award, and some guidelines for further improvement:

1. *Leadership.* Senior managers in the best companies are committed to quality, have communicated quality values throughout their companies, and have instilled a strong customer orientation. They need to make certain that they balance financial performance with operational issues as well.

2. *Information and analysis.* The very best TQM companies have excellent information systems. Companies need to make certain that information is well organized to support quality management.

3. *Strategic quality planning.* The best TQM companies have written quality plans and quality goals (often stretch goals). In addition, companies need to make certain that they communicate these plans to people so that everyone knows how their activities and objectives relate to the overall plans.

4. *Human resource development and management.* Teams focus on quality improvement projects, all employees receive basic quality training, and plenty of resources are devoted to safety. Beyond this, companies have to make certain that teams are managed effectively, and that management truly empowers these teams to make decisions. The performance evaluation system should be aligned with the quality management system.

5. *Management of process quality.* Most companies use statistical process control, have quality programs in conjunction with their suppliers, have greatly improved the development of new goods and services, and have developed measures of the service production process. Areas for improvement include limited new-product development activity (particularly services), slow and inadequate feedback from customers, and the lack of quality systems audits.

6. *Quality and operational results.* The best Baldrige companies demonstrate the quality of their products and their sustained year-to-year improvement with objective data.

7. *Customer focus and satisfaction.* The better Baldrige companies use surveys and focus groups to assess customer satisfaction, train their customer service representatives well, establish service standards, give more authority to service representatives to solve customer problems, and work hard to provide easy access and quick response times to customers. In addition, companies have to clearly understand customer needs and expectations. Customer data needs to be used in new-product development, and companies need to pay attention to lost customers, new customers, and competitors' customers.[18]

As you can see, total quality requires a thorough, extensive, integrated approach to organizing. Looking carefully at the strengths and improvement needs of good U.S. companies on the Baldrige criteria, you can see that quality comes from the issues and practices discussed throughout this course.

ISO 9000 A series of quality standards developed by a committee working under the International Organization for Standardization to improve total quality in all businesses for the benefit of both producers and consumers.

ISO 9000

The influence of total quality management on the organizing process has become even more acute with the emergence of ISO 9000. **ISO 9000** is a series of quality standards developed by a committee working under the International Organization for Standardization. The purpose of the standards is to improve total quality in all businesses for the benefit of producers and consumers alike. ISO 9000 was originally designed for manufacturing; however, most of the standards can also be readily applied to services operations.

U.S. companies first became interested in ISO 9000 because overseas customers, particularly the European Community (EC), embraced it. Companies that comply with the quality guidelines of ISO 9000 can apply for official certification; some countries and companies demand certification as an acknowledgment of compliance before they will do business. Now, some U.S. customers as well are making the same demand.[19]

BEFORE OUR DESIGNERS CREATE A CAR THEY TALK TO OUTSIDE *EXPERTS.*

BUCKLE UP–TOGETHER WE CAN SAVE LIVES.

SEVERAL times a year we invite people to come and brainstorm with Ford Motor Company designers and engineers. We talk about cars, sure. But often we talk about NON-CAR THINGS: computers, appliances, music, the environment, quality in very general terms. We know that to design cars and trucks with relevance and appeal, you have to LISTEN to your customers. It's part of the learning process that leads us to quality.

INCOLN • MERCURY •

QUALITY IS JOB 1.

Reengineering   Extending from TQM and a focus on organizing around customer needs, organizations have also embraced the notion of reengineering (introduced in Chapter 1). The principal idea of reengineering is to revolutionize key organizational systems and processes to answer the question: "If you were the customer, how would you like us to operate?" The answer to this question forms a vision for how the organization should run, and then decisions are made and actions are taken to make the organization operate like the vision. Processes such as product development, order fulfillment, customer service, inventory management, billing, production, and the like are redesigned from scratch just as if the organization were brand new and just starting out.

For example: Procter & Gamble learned that the average family buying its products rather than private-label or low-priced brands pays an extra $725 per year. That figure, P&G realized, was far too high, and a signal that the company's high prices could drive the company to extinction. Other data also signaled the need for P&G to change. Market shares of famous brands such as Comet, Mr. Clean, and Ivory had been dropping for 25 years. P&G was making 55 price changes *daily* on about 80 brands, and inaccurate billings were common. Its plants were inefficient, and the company had the highest overhead in the business. It was clear that it had to cut prices, and to do that it had to cut costs.

In response, P&G reengineered. The company tore down and rebuilt nearly every activity that contributed to its high costs. It redesigned the way it develops, manufactures, distributes, prices, markets, and sells products. The reengineering was difficult, time-consuming, and expensive. But now, after the changes, price changes are rare, factories are far more efficient, inventory is way down, and sales and profits are up. And P&G brands are now priced comparably to store brands. P&G may have reinvented itself as a leader in the industry once again, and created for itself a long-term competitive advantage that others are scrambling to match.[20]

As you can see, reengineering is not about making minor organizational changes here and there. It is about completely overhauling the operation, in revolutionary ways, in order to achieve the greatest possible benefits to the customer and to the organization.

Organizing for technological response

technology The systematic application of scientific knowledge to a new product, process, or service.

Broadly speaking, **technology** can be viewed as the methods, processes, systems, and skills used to transform resources (inputs) into products (outputs). Although we will discuss technology—and innovation—more fully in Chapter 17, in this chapter we want to highlight some of the important influences technology has on organizational design.

Types of technology configurations

Research by Joan Woodward laid the foundation for understanding technology and structure. According to Woodward, there are three basic technologies that characterize how work is done: small batch, large batch, and continuous process technologies. These three classifications are equally useful for describing either service or manufacturing technologies. Each differs in terms of volume produced and variety of products/services offered. Each also has a different influence on organizing[21]

small batches Technologies that produce goods and services in low volume.

Small batch technologies
When goods or services are provided in very low volume or **small batches,** a company that does such work is called a *job shop.* An example is John Thomas, a specialty printer in Lansing, Michigan, that manufactures printed material for the florist and garden industry. A service example is the doctor's office, which provides a high variety of low-volume, customized services.

In a small batch organization, structure tends to be very organic. There tend not to be a lot of rules and formal procedures, and decision making tends to be decentralized. The emphasis is on mutual adjustment among people.

large batch Technologies that produce goods and services in high volume.

Large batch technologies
As volume increases, product variety usually decreases. Companies with higher volumes and lower varieties than a job shop tend to be characterized as **large batch,** or mass production technologies. Examples of large batch technologies include auto assembly operations of General Motors, Ford, and Chrysler. In the service sector, McDonald's and Burger King might be good examples. Their production runs tend to be more standardized and all customers receive similar (if not identical) products. Machines tend to replace people in the physical execution of work. People run the machines.

With a large batch technology, structure tends to be more mechanistic. There tend not to be many more rules and formal procedures; and decision making tends to be centralized with higher spans of control. Communication tends to be more formal where hierarchical authority is more prominent.

continuous process A process that is highly automated and has a continuous production flow.

Continuous process technologies
At the very-high-volume end of the scale are companies that use **continuous process** technologies, technologies that do not stop and start. Domino Sugar and Shell Chemical, for example, use continuous process technologies where there are a very limited number of products to be produced. People are completely removed from the work itself. It is entirely done by machines and/or computers. In some cases, it may be that people run the computers that run the machines.

Ironically, with continuous process technology, structure can return to a more organic form because less monitoring and supervision are needed. Communication tends to be more informal where fewer rules and regulations are established.

mass customization The production of varied, individually customized products at the low cost of standardized, mass-produced products.

Organizing for flexible manufacturing

Although issues of volume and variety often have been seen as trade-offs in a technological sense, today organizations are trying to produce both high-volume and high-variety products at the same time. This is referred to as **mass customization.**[22]

Automobiles, clothes, computers, and other products are increasingly being manufactured to match each customer's taste, specifications, and budget. While this seemed like only a fantasy a few years ago, mass customization is quickly becoming more prevalent among leading firms. Levi's has been testing mass customization in its women's line. Companies like Motorola, Bell Atlantic, and Hallmark are achieving great success with mass customization.

How do companies organize to pull off this kind of customization at such low cost? As shown in Table 9.1, they organize around a dynamic network of relatively independent operating units.[23] Each unit performs a specific process or task—called a *module*—like making a component, performing a credit check, or performing a particular welding method. Some modules may be performed by outside suppliers or vendors. Different modules join forces to make the good or provide a service. How and when the various modules interact with one another are dictated by the unique requests of each

table 9.1

Key features in mass customization

Mass customization	
Products	High variety and customization
Product design	Collaborative design; significant input from customers
	Short product development cycles
	Constant innovation
Operations and processes	Flexible processes
	Business process reengineering (BPR)
	Use of modules
	Continuous improvement (CI)
	Reduced setup and changeover times
	Reduced lead times
	JIT delivery and processing of materials and components
	Production to order
	Shorter cycle times
	Use of information technology (IT)
Quality management	Quality measured in customer delight
	Defects treated as capability failures
Organizational structure	Dynamic network of relatively autonomous operating units
	Learning relationships
	Integration of the value chain
	Team-based structure
Workforce management	Empowerment of employees
	High value on knowledge, information, and diversity of employee capabilities
	New product teams
	Broad job descriptions
Emphasis	Low-cost production of high-quality, customized products

Source: Reprinted with permission of APICS—The Educational Society for Resource Management, *Production and Inventory Management*, Volume 41, Number 1, 2000, pp. 56–65.

Levis has been successful in using mass customization to better serve its female customers.
[Ryder Photography]

customer. The manager's responsibility is to make it easier and less costly for modules to come together, complete their tasks, and then recombine to meet the next customer demand. The ultimate goal of mass customization is a never-ending campaign to expand the number of ways a company can satisfy customers.

There are a variety of other ways that organizations are attempting to gain more flexibility in their manufacturing operations.

Computer-integrated manufacturing

computer-integrated manufacturing The use of computer-aided design and computer-aided manufacturing to sequence and optimize a number of production processes.

Computer-integrated manufacturing (CIM) encompasses a host of computerized production efforts linked together. Two examples are computer-aided design and computer-aided manufacturing, which offer the ultimate in computerized process technologies. For example, a manufacturer's engineering function may contain a large variety of software applications used in both electronic and mechanical design. Using CIM, different design team members can work on the network from remote sites, often their homes. These systems provide maximum process flexibility with lowest costs of production. They produce high-variety and high-volume products at the same time.[24]

CIM potentially affords greater control and predictability of production processes, reduced waste, faster throughput times, and higher quality. But a company cannot "buy" its way out of competitive trouble simply by investing in superior hardware (technology) alone. It must also ensure that it has strategic and "people" strengths, and a well-designed plan for implementing the technological changes.

Flexible factories

flexible factories Manufacturing plants that have short production runs, are organized around products, and use decentralized scheduling.

As the name implies, **flexible factories** provide more production options and a greater variety of products. They differ from traditional factories in three primary ways: lot size, flow patterns, and scheduling.[25]

First, the traditional factory has long production runs, generating high volumes of a standardized product. Flexible factories have much shorter production runs, with many different products. Second, traditional factories move parts down the line from one location in the production sequence to the next. Flexible factories are organized around products, in work cells or teams, so that people work closely together and parts move shorter distances with shorter or no delays. Third, traditional factories use centralized scheduling, which is time-consuming, inaccurate, and slow to adapt to changes. Flexible factories use local or decentralized scheduling, in which decisions are made on the shop floor by the people doing the work.

lean manufacturing An operation that strives to achieve the highest possible productivity and total quality, cost effectively, by eliminating unnecessary steps in the production process and continually strives for improvement.

Lean manufacturing   **Lean manufacturing** means an operation that is both efficient and effective; it strives to achieve the highest possible productivity and total quality, cost effectively, by eliminating unnecessary steps in the production process and continually striving for improvement. Rejects are unacceptable, and staff, overhead, and inventory are considered wasteful. In a lean operation, the emphasis is on quality, speed, and flexibility more than on cost, efficiency, and hierarchy. But with a well-managed lean production process—like the operations at Toyota and Chrysler—a company can develop, produce, and distribute products with half or less of the human effort, space, tools, time, and overall cost.[26]

For the lean approach to result in more effective operations, the following conditions must be met:[27]

- People are broadly trained rather than specialized.
- Communication is informal and horizontal among line workers.
- Equipment is general purpose.
- Work is organized in teams, or cells, that produce a group of similar products.
- Supplier relationships are long-term and cooperative.
- Product development is concurrent, not sequential, and done by cross-functional teams.

In recent years, many companies have tried to become more lean by cutting overhead costs, laying off operative-level workers, eliminating layers of management, and utilizing capital equipment more efficiently. But if the move to lean manufacturing is simply a harsh, haphazard cost-cutting approach, the result will be chaos, overworked people, and low morale.

Organizing for speed: Time-based competition

Companies worldwide have devoted so much energy to improving product quality that high quality is now the standard attained by all top competitors. Competition has driven quality to such heights that quality products no longer are enough to distinguish one company from another. *Time* is emerging as the key competitive advantage that can separate market leaders from also-rans.[28]

time-based competition (TBC) Strategies aimed at reducing the total time it takes to deliver a product or service.

Companies today must learn what the customer needs and meet those needs as quickly as possible. **Time-based competition (TBC)** refers to strategies aimed at reducing the total time it takes to deliver the product or service. There are several key organizational elements to TBC: logistics, just-in-time (JIT), and simultaneous engineering. JIT production systems reduce the time it takes to manufacture products. Logistics speeds the delivery of products to customers. Both are essential steps toward bringing products to customers in the shortest time possible. In today's world, speed is essential.

logistics The movement of the right goods in the right amount to the right place at the right time.

Logistics   **Logistics** is the movement of resources into the organization (inbound) and products from the organization to its customers (outbound). As an extension of the organization's technology configuration, organizing the logistics function is often critical to an organization's responsiveness and competitive advantage.

Logistics is a great mass of parts, materials, and products moving via trucks, trains, planes, and ships. An average box of breakfast cereal spends 104 days getting from the factory to the supermarket, moving through the warehouses of wholesalers, distributors, brokers, and others! If the grocery industry streamlined logistics, it could save an estimated $30 billion annually.[29] Depending on the product, the duplication and inefficiency in distribution can cost far more than making the product itself.

By contrast, Saturn's distribution system is world class. GM has contracted with both Ryder System and Penske Global Automotive to perform inbound logistics and distribution management for Saturn. Suppliers, factories, and dealers are linked so tightly and efficiently that Saturn barely has any parts inventory.[30]

just-in-time (JIT) A system that calls for subassemblies and components to be manufactured in very small lots and delivered to the next stage of the production process just as they are needed.

Just-in-time operations

An additional element of TBC involves **just-in-time (JIT)** operations. JIT calls for subassemblies and components to be manufactured in very small lots and delivered to the next stage in the process precisely at the time needed, or "just in time." A customer order triggers a factory order and the production process. The supplying work centers do not produce the next lot of product until the consuming work center requires it. Even external suppliers deliver to the company just-in-time.

Just-in-time is a companywide philosophy oriented toward eliminating waste throughout all operations and improving materials throughout. In this way, excess inventory is eliminated and costs are reduced. The ultimate goal of JIT is to better serve the customer by providing higher levels of quality and service.[31]

JIT represents a number of key production concepts. The system, which originated in Japan's Toyota Motor Corporation, includes the following concepts:

• *Elimination of waste.* Eliminate all waste from the production process, including waste of time, people, machinery, space, and materials.

• *Perfect quality.* Produce perfect parts even when lot sizes are reduced, and produce the product exactly when it is needed in the exact quantities that are needed.

• *Reduced cycle times.* Accomplish the entire manufacturing process more rapidly. Reduce setup times for equipment, move parts only short distances (machinery is placed in closer proximity), and eliminate all delays. The goal is to reduce action to the time spent working on the parts. For most manufacturers today, the percentage of time parts are worked on is about 5 percent of the total production time. JIT seeks to eliminate the other 95 percent; that is, to reduce to zero the time spent not working on the parts.

• *Employee involvement.* In JIT, employee involvement is central to success. The workers are responsible for production decisions. Managers and supervisors are coaches. Top management pledges that there will never be layoffs due to improved productivity.

• *Value-added manufacturing.* Do only those things (actions, work, etc.) that add value to the finished product. If it doesn't add value, don't do it. For example, inspection does not add value to the finished product, so make the product correctly the first time and inspection will not be necessary.

• *Discovery of problems and prevention of recurrence.* Foolproofing, or failsafing, is a key component of JIT. To prevent problems from arising, their cause(s) must be known and acted on. Thus, in JIT operations, people try to find the "weak link in the chain" by forcing problem areas to the surface so that preventive measures may be determined and implemented.

With the selection of Ryder System and Penske Global Automotive, GM put together a world class logistics and distribution system for Saturn.
[Courtesy Ryder System]

Many believe that only a fraction of JIT's potential has been realized, and that its impact will grow as it is applied to other processes such as service, distribution, and new-product development.[32]

simultaneous engineering
A design approach in which all relevant functions cooperate jointly and continually in a maximum effort aimed at producing high-quality products that meet customers' needs.

Simultaneous engineering   JIT is a vital component of TBC, but JIT concentrates on reducing time in only one function: manufacturing. TBC attempts to deliver speed in *all* functions—product development, manufacturing, logistics, and customer service. Customers will not be impressed if you manufacture quickly, but it takes weeks for them to receive their products or get a problem solved.

Many companies are turning to simultaneous engineering as the cornerstone of their TBC strategy. **Simultaneous engineering**—also an important component of total quality management—is a major departure from the old development process in which tasks were assigned to various functions in sequence. When R&D completed its part of the project, the work was "passed over the wall" to engineering, which completed its task and passed it over the wall to manufacturing, and so on. This process was highly inefficient, and errors took a long time to correct.

In contrast, simultaneous engineering incorporates the issues and perspectives of all the functions—and customers and suppliers—from the beginning of the process. This team-based approach results in a higher-quality product that is designed for efficient manufacturing *and* customer needs.[33]

Some managers resist the idea of simultaneous engineering. Why should marketing, product planning and design, and R&D "allow" manufacturing to get involved in "their" work? The answer is: because the decisions made during the early, product-concept stage determine most of the manufacturing cost and quality. Furthermore, manufacturing can offer ideas about the product because of its experience with the prior generation of the product and with direct customer feedback. Also, the other functions must know early on what manufacturing can and cannot do. Finally, when manufacturing is in from the start, it is a full and true partner and will be more committed to decisions it helped make.

From the Pages of BusinessWeek

Honda really moves its assembly

In a market where manufacturing advantages are increasingly short-lived, Honda Motor Company has managed to stay ahead of the game, in part by making better cars more cheaply than its big competitors. The new Civic, for example, is the culmination of Honda's efforts to introduce flexible manufacturing systems and to roll out the model simultaneously across 12 factory sites around the globe. Taken together, Honda expects these changes will shave $1 billion off its bottom line.

Honda's earliest efforts to streamline the introduction of the 2001 Civic started years ago, at the Honda New Model Center (HNMC) in Takanezawa, Japan. Starting in 1997, more than 200 personnel from the 12 plants that build the Civic worldwide began to meet regularly to ensure that the process that works in high-tech facilities in Japan and the United States would also work in low-tech sites in Taiwan or Brazil. It wasn't easy. But the rewards are already promising. The HNMC study resulted in less complex welding processes and caught early manufacturing bottlenecks. More importantly, it will enable Honda's fastest-ever global production launch for a new vehicle. In 1996, when Honda last redesigned the Civic, it was six months before the major plants outside Japan were all building the new model. This time it took two.

Flexible systems are the second element of Honda's push boost quality. It promises not only to speed up future product launches but also to improve the company's ability to make different vehicles on a single production line—the two Holy Grails of the auto trade. The old way was expensive. In traditional auto plants, parts are welded and assembled on a model-specific template, or "jig." Parts are placed on the jigs and welded to other panels to form the primary auto body. Typically, these expensive jigs are discarded with each new model. And if a line is used to make more than one model, jigs are switched in and out accordingly. For the 2001 Civic, Honda simply eliminated the jigs in favor of robotic attachments that can be reprogrammed quickly and cheaply to perform welds for each model. "It's about reteaching, not retooling," explains Koki Hirashima, president of Honda Manufacturing of America. Also, the Honda-designed robot servo heads, which grasp parts and apply welds, are more nimble. So machines—not workers—can place parts in the welding bays more accurately than ever. Indeed, the flexibility of the new system made it possible for workers to install some of the machines several months before the model changeover. Ultimately, the automaker shut the line overnight to switch tooling for the 2001 model. U.S. carmakers typically shut down for two weeks. Even for Honda, renowned for its smooth model changeovers, the speedy changeover was unprecedented, says Poland. The company won't say how much it spent to retool the East Liberty plant with new flexible welding robots. But executives brag that the man- ufacturing development costs were 40 percent cheaper than similar, previous efforts.

Says Ron Harbour, an author of the Harbour Report, "Honda is already a leader in flexibility, and now they're going to get more flexible? That has to be scary to the competition." It probably is. Relative to Nissan and Toyota, the earli- est adopters of flexible systems, Honda is deploying the technology later in the game. Even so, Honda has been competitive without flexibility, says East Liberty Plant Manager Tom Shoupe. "The new system will take an already efficient system and make it better," he says. Honda officials estimate that, once completed, the global rollout and the new flexible line technologies will save the company $1 billion per year. Better yet, flexible factory lines mean Honda can make and sell a more diverse line of products. Where the likes of GM, Ford, and Toyota plan and produce models over years, sometimes missing market trends in the process, Honda has been able to fire off new models into niche markets relatively quickly. "The key is how quickly we can get new product to the customer," Shoupe says.

Source: Condensed from Jeff Green, "Honda's Independent Streak," *Business Week*, October 2, 2000, pp. 152B–152H. ●

Organizing for strategic response

As our discussions thus far have focused on organizing in ways that improve respon- siveness, they have been, in a sense, about competitive advantage and strategy. Organi- zational size, environmental adaptation, technology decisions, and the like are all ele- ments of strategic management, as you know. And they all influence the design of organizations.

At the same time, there are issues directly pertaining to other aspects of strategy that influence how an organization is structured and managed. These include core compe- tencies, network organizations, strategic alliances, learning organizations, and high- involvement organizations.

Organizing around core competencies

A recent, different, and important perspective on strategy, organization, and competition hinges on the concept of *core competence*.[34] Companies compete not just with their prod- ucts, but also on the basis of their core strengths and expertise.

As you learned in Chapter 4, a core competence is the capability—knowledge, exper- tise, skill—that underlies a company's ability to be a leader in providing a range of spe- cific goods or services. A core competence gives value to customers, makes the com- pany's products different from (and better than) those of competitors, and can be used in creating new products. Think of core competencies as the roots of competitiveness, and products as the fruits.

What are some concrete examples of core competencies? And how can they be used to make firms more responsive and competitive?

Core competencies: Examples

Sharp and Toshiba committed years ago to being the world's best creators of flat-screen displays. They wanted to monopolize the markets for flat screens, although they didn't yet know all the potential product applications. A business case could not be made for each application; in fact, all applications couldn't even be envisioned. But the companies knew that this would be an important technology of the future.

The applications began with calculators. Over time, flat-screen displays were needed in pocket diaries, laptop computers, miniature televisions, LCD projection televisions, and video telephones. By committing early to a *competence,* these companies were ready for new and future *products* and *markets.*

As another example, SKF is the world's largest manufacturer of roller bearings. Are roller bearings its core competence? No, this would limit it is products and market access. SKF's core competencies are antifriction, precision engineering, and making perfectly spherical devices. Perhaps it could manufacture other products, for example, the round, high-precision rolling heads that go inside a VCR or the tiny balls in roller-ball pens.

Some other examples of companies with special competencies, which feed many specific products, are Hewlett-Packard (measurement computing, communications); Sony (miniaturization); Rubbermaid (low-tech plastics); Lotus (enterprise computing or "groupware"); 3M (adhesives and advanced materials); EDS (systems integration); and Motorola (wireless communications).

Sources: G. Hamel and C. K. Prahalad, *Competing for the Future* (Boston: Harvard Business School Press, 1994); M. Loeb, "How to Grow a New Product Every Day," *Fortune,* November 14, 1994, pp. 269—70; L. Hays, S. Lipin, and W. Bulkeley, "Software Landscape Shifts as IBM Makes Hostile Bid for Lotus," *The Wall Street Journal,* June 6, 1995, pp. A1, A10. ●

Successfully developing a world-class core competence opens the door to a variety of future opportunities; failure means being foreclosed from many markets. Thus, a well-understood, well-developed core competence can enhance a company's responsiveness and competitiveness. Strategically, this means that companies should commit to excellence and leadership in competencies before they commit to winning market share for specific products. Organizationally, this means that the corporation should be viewed as a portfolio of competencies, not just a portfolio of specific businesses. Companies should strive for core competence leadership, not just product leadership.

Managers who want to strengthen their firms' competitiveness via core competencies need to focus on several related issues:

- Identify existing core competencies.
- Acquire or build core competencies that will be important for the future.
- Keep investing in competencies so the firm remains world-class and better than competitors.
- Extend competencies to find new applications and opportunities for the markets of tomorrow.[35]

The network organization

The notion of core competencies takes us right into a discussion of network organizations. In contrast to the traditional, hierarchical firm performing all the business functions, the network organization is a collection of independent, mostly single-function firms. As depicted in Figure 9.4, the **network organization** describes not one organization but the web of interrelationships among many firms. Network organizations are flexible arrangements among designers, suppliers, producers, distributors, and customers where

network organization A collection of independent, mostly single-function firms.

figure 9.4
A dynamic network

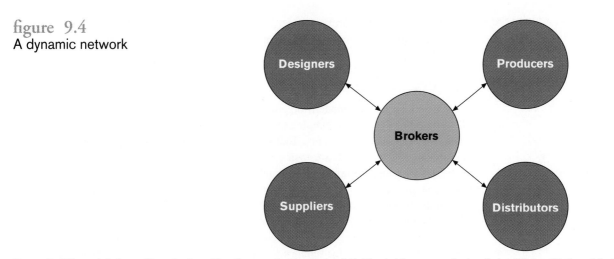

each firm is able to pursue its own distinctive competence. The network as a whole, then, can display the technical specialization of the functional structure, the market responsiveness of the product structure, and the balance and flexibility of the matrix.[36]

The **dynamic network**—also called the *modular* or *virtual* corporation—is comprised of temporary arrangements among members that can be assembled and reassembled to meet a changing competitive environment. The members of the network are held together by contracts that stipulate results expected (market mechanisms) rather than by hierarchy and authority. Poorly performing firms can be removed and replaced.

Such arrangements are common in the electronics, toy, and apparel industries, each of which creates and sells trendy products at a fast pace. For example, Reebok owns no plants; it designs and markets, but does not produce. Nike owns only one small factory that makes sneaker parts. Other examples include the Bombay Company, Louis Galoob Toys, Brooks Brothers, and the Registry (which markets the services of independent software engineers, programmers, and technical writers). In biotechnology, smaller firms do research and manufacture, and the drug giants market the products.[37]

Successful networks potentially offer flexibility, innovation, quick responses to threats and opportunities, and reduced costs and risk. But for these arrangements to be successful, several things must occur:

- The firm must choose the right specialty. This must be something (product or service) that the market needs and for which the firm is better at providing than other firms.
- The firm must choose collaborators that also are excellent at what they do and that provide complementary strengths.
- The firm must make certain that all parties fully understand the strategic goals of the partnership.
- Each party must be able to trust all of the others with strategic information and also trust that each collaborator will deliver quality products, even if the business grows quickly and makes heavy demands.

The role of managers shifts in a network from that of command and control to more like that of a **broker.** Broker/managers serve several important boundary roles that aid network integration and coordination:

- *Designer role.* The broker serves as a network architect who envisions a set of groups or firms whose collective expertise could be focused on a particular product or service.
- *Process engineering role.* The broker serves as a *network co-operator* who takes the initiative to lay out the flow of resources and relationships and makes certain that everyone shares the same goals, standards, payments, and the like.

dynamic network Temporary arrangements among partners that can be assembled and reassembled to adapt to the environment.

broker A person who assembles and coordinates participants in a network.

- *Nurturing role.* The broker serves as a network developer that nurtures and enhances the network (like team building) to make certain the relationships are healthy and mutually beneficial.[38]

Strategic alliances

As discussed earlier, the modern organization has a variety of links with other organizations. These links are more complex than the standard relationships with traditional stakeholders like suppliers and clients. Today even fierce *competitors* are working together at unprecedented levels to achieve their strategic goals. For example, GM, Ford, and DaimlerChrysler have been doing joint research and development. The Partnership for a New Generation of Vehicles (PNGV) is a cooperative research and development program between the federal government and the U.S. Council for Automotive Research (members include DaimlerChrysler, Ford, and General Motors). A goal of the alliance is to develop technologies for a new generation of vehicles able to go 80 miles on a gallon of fuel. In addition to fuel economy, the alliance is also focused on reducing fuel emissions.[39]

strategic alliance
A formal relationship created among independent organizations with the purpose of joint pursuit of mutual goals.

A **strategic alliance** is a formal relationship created with the purpose of joint pursuit of mutual goals. In a strategic alliance, individual organizations share administrative authority, form social links, and accept joint ownership. Such alliances are blurring firms' boundaries. They occur between companies and their competitors, governments, and universities. Such partnering often crosses national and cultural boundaries. Companies form strategic alliances to develop new technologies, enter new markets, and reduce manufacturing costs. Alliances are often the fastest, most efficient way to achieve objectives. Moreover, strategic alliances can pay off not only through the immediate deal, but through creating additional, unforeseen opportunities and opening new doors to the future.[40]

Managers typically devote plenty of time to screening potential partners in financial terms. But for the alliance to work, managers must also foster and develop the human relationships in the partnership. Asian companies seem to be the most comfortable with the nonfinancial, "people" side of alliances; European companies the next so; and U.S. companies the least. So, U.S. companies may need to pay extra attention to the human side of alliances. Table 9.2 shows some recommendations for how to do this. In fact, most of the ideas apply not only to strategic alliances but to any type of relationship.[41]

The learning organization

Being responsive requires continually changing and learning new ways to act. Some experts have stated that the only sustainable advantage is learning faster than the competition. This has led to a new term that is now part of the vocabulary of most managers:

table 9.2
How I's can
become we's

The best alliances are true partnerships that meet these criteria:

1. *Individual excellence:* Both partners add value, and their motives are positive (pursue opportunity) rather than negative (mask weaknesses).

2. *Importance:* Both partners want the relationship to work because it helps them meet long-term strategic objectives.

3. *Interdependence:* The partners need each other; each helps the other reach its goal.

4. *Investment:* The partners devote financial and other resources to the relationship.

5. *Information:* The partners communicate openly about goals, technical data, problems and changing situations.

6. *Integration:* The partners develop shared ways of operating; they teach each other and learn from each other.

7. *Institutionalization:* The relationship has formal status with clear responsibilities.

8. *Integrity:* Both partners are trustworthy and honorable.

Source: R. M. Kanter, "Collaborative Advantage: The Art of Alliances," *Harvard Business Review,* July–August 1994, pp. 96–108.

learning organization An organization skilled at creating, acquiring, and transferring knowledge, and at modifying its behavior to reflect new knowledge and insights.

the learning organization.[42] A **learning organization** is "an organization skilled at creating, acquiring, and transferring knowledge, and at modifying its behavior to reflect new knowledge and insights.[43]

GE, Corning, and Honda are good examples of learning organizations. Such organizations are skilled at solving problems, experimenting with new approaches, learning from their own experiences, learning from other organizations, and spreading knowledge quickly and efficiently.

How do firms become true learning organizations? There are a few important ingredients.[44]

1. Their people must engage in disciplined thinking and attention to details, making decisions based on data and evidence rather than guesswork and assumptions.
2. They search constantly for new knowledge, looking for expanding horizons and opportunities rather than quick fixes to current problems.
3. They carefully review both successes and failures, looking for lessons and deeper understanding.
4. Learning organizations benchmark—they identify and implement the best business practices of other organizations, stealing ideas shamelessly.
5. They share ideas throughout the organization via reports, information systems, informal discussions, site visits, education, and training.

The high-involvement organization

Participative management is becoming increasingly popular as a way to create a competitive advantage. Particularly in high-technology companies facing stiff international competition, such as Microsystems and Compaq Computer, the aim is to generate high levels of commitment and involvement as employees and managers work together to achieve organizational goals.

high-involvement organization A type of organization in which top management ensures that there is consensus about the direction in which the business is heading.

In the **high-involvement organization,** top management ensures that there is a consensus about the direction in which the business is heading. The leader seeks input from his or her top management team and from lower levels of the company. Task forces, study groups, and other techniques are used to foster participation in decisions that affect the entire organization. Also fundamental to the high-involvement organization is continual feedback to participants regarding how they are doing compared to the competition and how effectively they are meeting the strategic agenda.

Structurally, this usually means that even lower-level employees have a direct relationship with a customer or supplier and thus they receive feedback and are held accountable for a product or service delivery. The organizational form is a flat, decentralized structure built around customer, product, or service. Employee involvement is particularly powerful when the environment changes rapidly, work is creative, complex activities require coordination, and firms need major breakthroughs in innovation and speed—in other words, when companies need to be more responsive.[45]

Final thoughts about responsive organizations

As organizations strive to maximize responsiveness, they have to balance their needs for efficiency and effectiveness. We have pointed out throughout this chapter (and the one before) that *any* approach to organizing has its strengths and limitations. And we have noted that advantages gained by a firm through innovative structures and systems are likely to be short-lived. Competitors catch up.

Today's advantages are tomorrow's "table stakes"; requirements that need to be met if a firm expects to be a major player in an industry. Increasingly we hear executives embrace the ideals of GE's Jack Welch, who say that his goal is to create a *boundary-less organization*-capable of doing anything, anytime, anywhere around the world. This is, of course, a lofty goal and one that requires organizations to transcend the limits of their existing structures, technologies, and systems.[46]

Key terms

Summary of learning objectives

Now that you have studied Chapter 9, you should know:

The market imperatives your firm must meet to survive.

Organizations have a formal structure to help control what goes on within them. But to survive today, firms need more than control—they need responsiveness. They must act quickly and adapt to fast-changing demands.

The potential advantages of creating an organic form of organization.

The organic form emphasizes flexibility. Organic organizations are decentralized, informal, and dependent on the judgment and expertise of people with broad responsibilities. The organic form is not a single formal structure, but a concept that underlies all the new forms discussed in this chapter.

How your firm can "be" both small and big.

Historically, large organizations have had important advantages over small. Today, small size has advantages, including the ability to act quickly, respond to customer demands, and serve small niches. The ideal firm today combines the advantages of both. It creates many small, flexible units, while the corporate levels adds value by taking advantage of its size and power.

How to manage information-processing demands.

Integrative mechanisms help coordinate the efforts of differentiated subunits. Slack resources and self-contained tasks reduce the need to process information. Information systems and horizontal relationships help the organization process information.

How firms organize to meet customer requirements.

Firms have embraced principles of continuous improvement and total quality management to respond to customer needs. Baldrige criteria and ISO 9000 standards help firms organize to meet better quality specifications. Extending these, reengineering efforts are directed at completely overhauling processes to provide world-class customer service.

How firms organize around different types of technology.

Organizations tend to move from organic structures to mechanistic structures and back to organic structures as they transition from small batch to large batch and continuous process technologies. To organize for flexible manufacturing, organizations pursue mass customization via computer-integrated manufacturing and lean manufacturing. To organize for time-based competition firms emphasize their logistics operations, just-in-time operations, and simultaneous engineering.

The new types of dynamic organizational concepts and forms that are being used for strategic responsiveness.

New and emerging organizational concepts and forms include core competencies, network organizations, strategic alliances learning organizations, and high-involvement organizations.

Discussion questions

1. Discuss evidence you have seen of the imperatives for change, flexibility, and responsiveness faced by today's firms.

2. Describe large, bureaucratic organizations with which you

have had contact that have not responded flexibly to customer demands. Also describe examples of satisfactory responsiveness. What do you think accounts for the differences between the responsive and nonresponsive organizations?

3. Considering the potential advantages of large and small size, would you describe the "feel" of your college or university as big, small, or small-within-big? Why? What might make it feel different?

4. What is a core competence? Generate some examples of companies with distinctive competencies, identifying what those competencies are. Brainstorm some creative new products and markets to which these competencies could be applied.

5. If you were going into business for yourself, what would be your core competencies? What competencies do you have now, and what competencies are you going to develop? Describe what

your role would be in a network organization, and the competencies and roles of other firms you would want in your network.

6. Identify some recently formed alliances between competitors. What are the goals of the alliance? What brought them together? What have they done to ensure success? How are they doing now?

7. What skills will you need to work effectively in (1) a network organization; (2) a learning organization; and (3) a high-involvement organization? Be specific, generating long lists. Would you enjoy working in these environments? Why or why not? What can you do to prepare yourself for these eventualities?

Concluding Case
Peapod Sprouts a New Strategy

Marc van Gelder is chief executive of Peapod, the online grocer. For a while, Peapod seemed destined to become one of an ever-growing list of ailing e-commerce contenders. But Peapod found itself a fairy godmother in the guise of Royal Ahold NV, a Netherlands-based food and grocery retailer. The company announced a rescue plan that included pouring about $73 million into Peapod for a 51 percent stake and a commitment to extend the online grocery service a $20 million line of credit. In addition to the cash it needed to continue operations, Peapod also got two other things from Royal Ahold: a tie into Ahold's five U.S. supermarket chains encompassing more than 1,000 supermarkets and serving more than 20 million customers along the eastern seaboard—and van Gelder.

Though he's been on the job for just a short time, van Gelder is devising a strategic plan for Peapod. That plan involves utilizing Ahold's existing five supermarket chains in the United States and its 1,063 stores to help build Peapod's distribution capabilities. Peapod was founded as a premium "store picking" service: After customer orders were placed using the company's then-proprietary software, Peapod's staff of personal shoppers would traverse local grocery stores, hand-pick the requested items, and deliver them to customers. In the past three years, Peapod recognized the limitations of its process and began forming alliances with regional supermarket chains—including Ahold's Stop & Shop stores in the Boston metropolitan area and its Edwards chain in New York—as well as establishing its own distribution centers.

The new plan, says van Gelder, calls for a "clicks-and-mortar strategy" in which former mezzanine storage areas at Ahold's U.S. stores will be converted into "fast pick" fulfillment centers to handle the online orders of local Peapod customers. Dry goods can be stored and picked from the back-room fulfillment centers, while perishables can be plucked from the grocery store shelves. Van

Gelder says six such centers are already up and running and serving Web customers, with more than 50 centers expected to be opened within the next few years. "Big companies like Ahold really rationalize the supply chains," says van Gelder. "What happens with a lot of Ahold operations on the East Coast is that logistics get more and more efficient. You have just-in-time inventory already in place in the stores and there are already big storage areas in the stores. . . . You're leveraging the store for the perishable side and outfitting sometimes empty space with a racking system for fast picking."

But that's not all Ahold brings, he says. Ahold's buying power translates into a reduced cost for goods that it says its competitors in the online grocery space can't easily match. "Webvan might be a giant in market capitalization, but not in buying power," he says of Peapod's Foster City, California-based competitor, which currently only serves customers in the San Francisco Bay area.

Van Gelder also points to Ahold's 20 million brick-and-mortar customers in the United States, and the opportunity Peapod now has to reach them through in-store promotions and marketing. Currently, Peapod serves more than 130,000 Web shoppers in eight major markets, including Boston, Dallas, and its home base of Chicago. Given its new link to the eastern seaboard through Ahold, it's no surprise van Gelder says Peapod will focus its early energies on the East Coast. But it hasn't abandoned plans to conquer the West Coast, where it already serves customers in San Francisco and San Jose. "When you put together the buying power of Ahold, the ability to leverage some of the real estate of Ahold and the assets of customers, there are lots of opportunities for a national brand," he says.

It's a good time to be in the online grocery business. Based on its survey of 5,000 online shoppers in April, The NPD Group predicts that the online grocery market will see the greatest gains in customers and sales in the coming months. The research firm estimates online grocery sales reached nearly $260 million during the three months ending in April, and that about 9 percent of all consumers who bought anything over the Web bought groceries on-line during that period. NPD also found that online grocery buyers are frequent customers: Among online grocery purchasers in the past three months, 40 percent bought two to three times, and 20 percent four or more times.

But while today's market for online groceries is promising, it is also more competitive than when Andrew and Thomas Parkinson co-founded Peapod in 1989 (Andrew remains chairman of the company). Today, Peapod faces a host of competitors, including Webvan; HomeGrocer.com, which is backed by online shopping powerhouse Amazon.com; nationwide provider NetGrocer; Streamline; and Dallas-based Grocery Works.com, which recently signed a deal to become the online grocery channel for Safeway, one of North America's largest food and drug retailers.

Like many other dot.com retailers, it's too soon to say whether Peapod will turn into an online Cinderella story. "The grocery business is a business that goes through immense change," says van Gelder, explaining why Peapod will remain an independent e-commerce company. "The kinds of people who work for Peapod are different kinds of people than those who work for Ahold. To have an agile organization, to really make fast decisions, you have to think in Internet time."

Questions

1. What are the key elements of Peapod's flexibility strategy?

2. What are Peapod's most serious threats in the future?

3. What similarities and differences do you recognize between Peapod and Flextronics (in Setting the Stage)?

Source: Condensed from Cohnnie Guglielmo, "Web Grocer Weathers Storm," *Upside,* August 2000, 12, no. 8, p. 96.

Storage areas at Ahold's stores will be converted into "fast pick" fulfillment centers to handle the orders of Peapod customers.
[Tim Boyle/Newsmakers]

Experiential Exercises
9.1 Decentralization: Pros and cons

Objective

To explore the reasons for, as well as the pros and cons of, decentralizing.

Instructions

The following Decentralization Worksheet contains some observations on decentralization. As you review each of the statements, provide an example that illustrates why this statement is important and related problems and benefits of the situation or condition indicated in the statement.

Decentralization worksheet

A large number of factors determine the extent to which a manager should decentralize. Clearly, anything that increases a manager's workload creates a pressure for decentralization because there is only a finite level of work that can be accomplished by a single person. As with many facets of management, there are advantages and disadvantages to decentralization.

1. The greater the diversity of products, the greater the decentralization.

_____

_____

_____

_____

_____

_____

2. The larger the size of the organization, the more the decentralization.

_____

_____

_____

_____

_____

_____

3. The more rapidly changing the organization's environment, the more decentralization.

_____

_____

_____

_____

_____

4. Developing adequate, timely controls is the essence of decentralizing.

_____

_____

_____

_____

5. Managers should delegate those decisions that involve large amounts of time but minimal erosions of their power and control.

_____

_____

_____

_____

_____

6. Decentralizing involves delegating authority, and therefore, the principles of delegation apply to decentralization. (List the principles of delegation before you start your discussion.)

_____

_____

_____

_____

_____

_____

Source: R. R. McGrath, Jr., *Exercises in Management Fundamentals* (Englewood Cliffs, N.J.: Prentice-Hall, 1985) pp. 59–60. Reprinted by permission of Prentice-Hall, Inc.

9.2 The university culture

Objectives

1. To measure the culture at your university.

2. To study the nature of organization culture.

3. To understand how a culture can be changed.

Instructions

1. Working alone, complete and score the University Culture Survey.

2. In small groups, exchange survey scores and develop responses to the discussion questions.

3. Group spokespersons report group findings to the class.

Discussion Questions

1. In what respects did students agree or disagree on survey test items?

2. What might account for differences in students' experiences and attitudes with respect to the university culture?

3. How can the survey results be put to constructive use?

Chapter Ten

Human Resources Management

You can get capital and erect buildings, but it takes people to build a business.

— Thomas J. Watson, Founder, IBM

Chapter Outline

Learning Objectives

After studying Chapter 10, you will know:

1. How companies use human resources management to gain competitive advantage.

2. Why companies recruit both internally and externally for new hires.

3. The various methods available for selecting new employees.

4. Why companies spend so much on training and development.

5. How to determine who should appraise an employee's performance.

6. How to analyze the fundamental aspects of a reward system.

7. How unions influence human resources management.

8. How the legal system influences human resources management.

Setting the Stage

The Dash for Talent

Roopa Foley came up with a well-reasoned analysis during her job interview with e-commerce outfit Dash, Inc. That's one reason why she's now vice president for product development. To make the hiring decision, Dash used the time-honored approach of using probing questions, getting Foley to solve puzzles and react to real-world situations.

But companies use a variety of techniques—some of them quite sophisticated—to size up potential new hires. Take Task Masters, a New York City-based time- and space-management company. Owner Julie Morgenstern likes to find out if candidates are capable of quickly picking up on the company's strategy. So she routinely asks them to describe the mission and key goals of their last two employers. A deft description shows Morgenstern that a possible recruit will most likely "be tuned into the way we do business," she says. Howard D. Leifman, human resources chief at career-advice site Vault.com, relies on a method that's increasingly popular with recruiters: behavioral-based interviewing. Leifman asks candidates to discuss past job achievements and problems—how they produced a large increase in sales or handled a disagreement with the boss—and take him step-by-step through their behavior at the time. "You keep drilling down to what they did and how did they do it. And that will be an indication of future performance," he says.

Companies use a variety of techniques—some of them quite sophisticated—to size up potential new hires.
[Michael Newman/PhotoEdit]

Other employers zero in on what candidates inadvertently disclose about their work attitudes. Interviewees at goRefer.com can kiss the opportunity goodbye if they jab their former employers harshly. That's a flag to hiring managers that candidates "are looking at us only because they are unhappy somewhere else," says PR Manager Kenneth D. Madigan. GoRefer also measures candidates by a more unusual yardstick—their SAT scores. A candidate with stellar results doesn't necessarily get the job, but good scores are a bonus, according to Madigan. "We feel that a smart person can learn quickly," he says.

Roopa Foley didn't have to reveal her SAT scores. But during a four-hour interview at Dash that followed routine resume queries, she did have to answer questions seeking to determine how she deals with tough problems. At the e-commerce outfit, candidates for senior positions are evaluated in good measure on their ability to think on their feet. Depending on the job they are applying for, applicants might be handed a two-men-on-opposite-shores/one-boat-between-them-type brainteaser or asked the approximate number of gasoline stations in the United States, with an explanation of the method used to arrive at the figure. (One possible solution: Start with the U.S. population of about 250 million, estimate the number of gas stations per 10,000 Americans and do the math.) Dash COO Jason S. Priest says interviewers aren't looking for a correct answer so much as a glimpse into how candidates think and react to a challenge under pressure. Do they get flustered? Or are they stimulated and willing to ask their own questions? "What we want to see is how they struggle through a problem," he says.

Foley, 30, didn't flinch when she was asked a typical Dash question: What effect will the Internet have on the U.S. Postal Service's business? "My initial reaction was: Hmmm. That's a good question," she says. In her response, she hit on the major points. She speculated that e-mail would significantly reduce snail-mail traffic but that the post office could benefit from an increase in parcel deliveries as more people ordered goods online—a job-snagging answer.

Source: Pamela Mendels, "Asking the Right Questions," Business Week Online, October 13, 2000.

human resources management (HRM) Formal systems for the management of people within the organization.

Human resources management (HRM), historically known as personnel management, deals with formal systems for managing people at work. We begin this chapter by describing HRM as it relates to strategic management. The quote by Thomas Watson, founder of IBM, summarizes our view of the importance of people to any organization. We also discuss more of the "nuts and bolts" of HRM: staffing, training, performance appraisal, rewards, and labor relations. Throughout the chapter, we discuss legal issues that influence each aspect of HRM. In the next chapter, we expand this focus to address related issues of managing a diverse workforce.

Strategic human resources management

HRM has assumed a vital strategic role in recent years as organizations attempt to compete through people. Recall from Chapter 4, "Planning and Strategic Management," that firms can create a competitive advantage when they possess or develop resources that are valuable, rare, inimitable, and organized. We can use these same criteria to talk about the strategic impact of human resources:

1. **Creates value.** People can increase value through their efforts to decrease costs or provide something unique to customers, or some combination of the two. Empowerment programs, total quality initiatives, and continuous improvement efforts at companies such as Corning, Xerox, and Saturn are intentionally designed to increase the value that employees have on the bottom line.

2. **Is rare.** People are a source of competitive advantage when their skills, knowledge, and abilities are not equally available to all competitors. As the Setting the Stage examples demonstrate, top companies invest a great deal to hire and train the best and the brightest employees in order to gain advantage over their competitors. Recently, Dow Chemical went to court to stop General Electric from hiring away its engineers. This case shows that some companies recognize both the value and rareness of certain employees.

3. **Is difficult to imitate.** People are a source of competitive advantage when their capabilities and contributions cannot be copied by others. Disney, Southwest Airlines, and Mirage Resorts are known for creating unique cultures that get the most from employees (through teamwork) and are difficult to imitate.

4. **Is organized.** People are a source of competitive advantage when their talents can be combined together and rapidly deployed to work on new assignments at a moment's notice. Teamwork and cooperation are two pervasive methods for ensuring an organized workforce. But companies such as Spyglass (a software company) and AT&T have invested in information technology to help allocate and track employee assignments to temporary projects.

These four criteria highlight the importance of people and show the closeness of HRM to strategic management. In a recent survey by *USA Today* and Deloitte & Touche, nearly 80 percent of corporate executives said the importance of HRM in their firms has grown substantially over the past 10 years, and two-thirds said that HR expenditures are now viewed as a strategic investment rather than simply a cost to be minimized.[1] Because employee skills, knowledge, and abilities are among the most distinctive and renewable resources upon which a company can draw, their strategic management is more important than ever. Increasingly organizations are recognizing that their success depends on what people know; that is, their knowledge and skills. The term **human capital** (or more broadly, *intellectual capital*) is often used today to describe the strategic value of employee skills and knowledge.

human capital The knowledge, skills, and abilities of employees that have economic value.

But while concepts such as sustainable competitive advantage and human capital are certainly important, they remain only ideas for action. On a day-to-day basis, HR managers have many concerns regarding their workers and the entire personnel puzzle. These concerns include managing layoffs; addressing employee loyalty issues; managing diversity; creating a well-trained, highly motivated workforce; containing health care costs; and the like. Balancing these issues is a difficult task, and the best approach is likely to vary depending on the circumstances of the organization. A steel producer facing a cutback in business may need human resources activities to assist with layoffs, whereas a semiconductor company may need more staff to produce enough microchips to meet the demands of the burgeoning personal computer market. The emphasis on different HR activities depends on whether the organization is growing, declining, or standing still. This leads to the practical issues involved in HR planning.

The HR planning process

"Get me the right kind and the right number of people at the right time." It sounds simple enough, but meeting the organization's staffing needs requires strategic human resources planning: an activity with a strategic purpose derived from the organization's plans.

The HR planning process occurs in three stages: planning, programming, and evaluating. First, HR managers need to know the organization's business plans to ensure that the right number and types of people are available—where the company is headed, in what businesses it plans to be, what future growth is expected, and so forth. Few things are more damaging to morale than having to lay off recently hired college graduates because of inadequate planning for future needs. Second, the organization conducts programming of specific human resources activities, such as recruitment, training, or layoffs. In this stage, the company's plans are implemented. Third, human resources activities are evaluated to determine whether they are producing the results needed to contribute to the organization's business plans. Figure 10.1 illustrates the components of the human resources planning process. In this chapter, we focus on human resources planning and programming. Many of the other factors listed in Figure 10.1 are discussed in future chapters.

Demand forecasts   Perhaps the most difficult part of human resources planning is conducting *demand* forecasts; that is, determining how many and what type of people are needed. Demand forecasts for people needs are derived from organizational plans. For example, now that a pharmaceutical company Merck has developed Propecia, a new drug to cure baldness, managers must estimate the future size of this market based on demographic projections. Based on current sales and projected future sales growth, managers estimate the plant capacity needed to meet future demand, the sales force

figure 10.1
An overview of the HR planning process

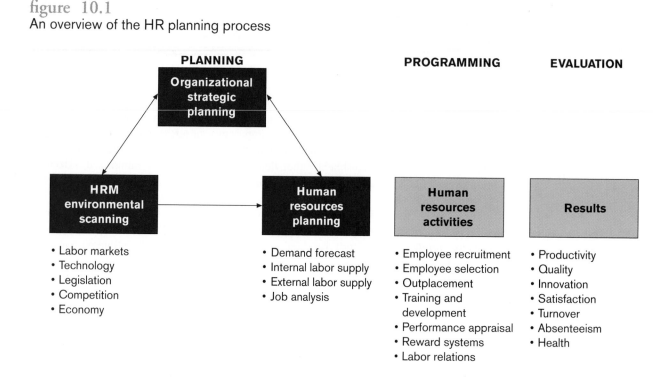

PLANNING   **PROGRAMMING**   **EVALUATION**

Organizational strategic planning			
HRM environmental scanning	**Human resources planning**	**Human resources activities**	**Results**

HRM environmental scanning	Human resources planning	Human resources activities	Results
• Labor markets • Technology • Legislation • Competition • Economy	• Demand forecast • Internal labor supply • External labor supply • Job analysis	• Employee recruitment • Employee selection • Outplacement • Training and development • Performance appraisal • Reward systems • Labor relations	• Productivity • Quality • Innovation • Satisfaction • Turnover • Absenteeism • Health

required, the support staff needed, and so forth. At this point, the number of labor-hours required to operate a plant, sell the product, distribute it, service customers, and so forth can be calculated. These estimates are used to determine the demand for different types of workers.

Labor supply forecasts   In concert with demand forecasts, the *supply of labor* must also be forecast; that is, estimates of how many and what types of employees the organization actually will have. In performing a supply analysis, the organization estimates the number and quality of its current employees as well as the available external supply of workers. To estimate internal supply, the company typically relies on past experiences with turnover, terminations, retirements, or promotions and transfers. A computerized human resources information system assists greatly in supply forecasting.

One of Marriott's HRM programs involves training and employing people with disabilities. Here, Laurie Axtell (left) coaches Jill Durbin. *[© 1991 Dennis Brack/Black Star]*

Externally, organizations have to look at workforce trends to make projections. World-wide, there is a growing gap between the world's supply of labor and the demand for labor.[2] Most of the well-paid jobs are generated in the cities of the industrialized world, but many skilled and unskilled human resources are in the developing nations. This gap is leading to massive relocation (including immigrants, temporary workers, and retirees) and a reduction of protectionist immigration policies (as countries come to rely on and compete for foreign workers).

Forecasts of a diverse workforce have become fact. The business world is no longer the exclusive domain of white males. Minorities, women, immigrants, older and disabled workers, and other groups have made the management of diversity a fundamental activity of the modern manager. Because of the importance of managing the "new workforce," the next chapter is devoted entirely to this topic.

Reconciling supply and demand   Once managers have a good idea of both the supply and demand for various types of employees, they can start developing approaches for reconciling the two. In some cases, organizations find that they need more people than they currently have (i.e., a labor deficit). In such cases, organizations can hire new employees, promote current employees to new positions, or train other employees to move in from other areas in the organization. In other cases, organizations may find that they have more people than they need (i.e., a labor surplus). If this is detected far enough in advance, organizations can use attrition—the normal turnover of employees—to reduce the surplus. In other instances, the organization may lay off employees or transfer them to other areas. The give and take of supply and demand is now playing out on the Internet as discussed next.

From the Pages of
BusinessWeek

And now, the just-in-time employee

A decade ago, human resource heads never dreamed that the employees they were axing from the rolls would one day return as hot commodities, even earning a snappy new name to go with their new status: free agents. The revenge scenario couldn't have been scripted better. In the latter half of the 20th century, power flowed to corporations, where bodies were as replaceable as light bulbs. Today, with the transition to a knowledge-based economy and global connectivity, the power is shifting to those with skills.

Supplies of the talent needed to fuel the new economy are expected to remain scarce for the next 20 years. At the same time, corporations are finding it beneficial to have fluid, nimble workforces that can grow and shrink according to the demands of the global marketplace. That's why, in place of the 20th century labor model, something new is emerging. Think of it as the *human capital exchange* (HCE). Just as Nasdaq and the New York Stock Exchange were the locus of much of the last century's wealth creation, a market for skills and talent will fit the bill in the 21st century. Here, in the HCE, the value of free agents is determined by the open market. The legions who keep their resumes permanently posted on Monster.com represent only the first sign of the shift toward skilled, new economy workers day-trading their careers. More and more companies—from job-posting sites to bounty-paying referral services—are popping up on the Web, creating a kind of labor auction where everyone from screenwriters to scientists can sell their skills to the highest bidder.

Andy Abramson, a 40-year-old sports marketing consultant, figures he makes 75 percent more as a gun-for-hire than he would as a traditional head of marketing. The constant influx of new projects keeps work interesting and offers equity stakes in a variety of companies. But there is a dark side to free agency. Many feel crushed by the law of the jungle and the pressure of hunting for every gig. James Baron, a professor at the Stanford Business School, thinks the reverse trend—stronger attachments to employers—could remerge. "In Silicon Valley, intense labor market competition has already caused some firms like Sun Microsystems to begin thinking about offering not just jobs and stock options, but careers," says Baron. These jobs will look different, he adds, consisting of a series of projects rather than a static job.

Still, the ranks of free agents are growing, from 22 percent of the workforce in 1998 to 26 percent in 2001, according to a poll by Lansing (Michigan) market research firm EPIC/MRA. And by 2010, 41 percent of the workforce will be working on a contract basis, the firm predicts. Career experts believe that, like actors or athletes, talented business superstars will have agents. Groups of workers will come together to tackle projects only to disband when the task is finished, a model already common in Silicon Valley.

Increasingly, companies will keep their most prized employees on site and outsource everything else. When the U.S. computer display unit of Nokia Corp. entered the U.S. market, it did so with only five key employees. Sales, marketing, logistics, and technical support were farmed out.

And just because an employee is on staff doesn't mean she isn't thinking like a free agent. A typical 32-year-old, for example, has already held nine jobs, according to the Labor Department. Experts predict that these same workers will have as many as 20 different positions in their lifetimes. Unlike those with a lifer ethos, these MVPs will constantly bargain for better deals within their organizations (new projects, Thursdays off, an August sabbatical).

Many human resource heads view free agents as the enemy. But they shouldn't. "The only way employers can get the staffing crisis under control is to abandon the old-fashioned idea of an employee," says Bruce Tulgan, author of *Winning the Talent Wars*. Organizations will adopt a revolving-door mentality in which former "turncoats" are viewed as "alumni" or "boomerangers" who are asked—and welcomed—back.

Source: Condensed from Michelle Conlin, "And Now, the Just-in-Time Employee," *Business Week Online*, August 28, 2000. ●

---

job analysis A tool for determining what is done on a given job and what should be done on that job.

Job analysis   While issues of supply and demand are fairly "macro" activities that are conducted at an organizational level, HR planning also has a "micro" side called *job analysis*. **Job analysis** does two things.[3] First, it tells the HR manager about the job itself: the essential tasks, duties, and responsibilities involved in performing the job. This information is called a *job description*. Second, job analysis describes the skills, knowledge, abilities, and other characteristics needed to perform the job. This is called the *job specification*.

Job analysis provides the information that virtually every human resources activity requires. It assists with the essential HR programs: recruitment, training, selection, appraisal, and reward systems. For example, a thorough job analysis helps organizations successfully defend themselves in lawsuits involving employment practices.[4] Ultimately, job analysis helps to increase the value added by employees to the organization because it clarifies what is really required to perform effectively.

Staffing the organization

Once HR planning is completed, managers can focus on staffing the organization. The staffing function consists of three related activities: recruitment, selection, and outplacement.

Recruitment

recruitment The development of a pool of applicants for jobs in the organization.

Recruitment activities help to increase the pool of candidates that might be selected for a job. Recruitment may be internal to the organization (considering current employees for promotions and transfers) or external. Each approach has advantages and disadvantages.[5]

Internal recruiting   The advantages of internal recruiting are that employers know their employees, and employees know their organization. External candidates who are unfamiliar with the organization may find they don't like working there. Also, the opportunity to move up within the organization may encourage employees to remain with the company, work hard, and succeed. Recruiting from outside the company can be demoralizing to employees. Many companies, such as Sears Roebuck and Eli Lilly, prefer internal over external recruiting for these reasons.

Internal staffing has some drawbacks. If existing employees lack skills or talent, internal recruitment yields a limited applicant pool, leading to poor selection decisions. Also, an internal recruitment policy can inhibit a company that wants to change the nature or goals of the business by bringing in outside candidates. In changing from a rapidly growing, entrepreneurial organization to a mature business with more stable growth, Dell Computer went outside the organization to hire managers who better fit those needs.

Many companies that rely heavily on internal recruiting use a job-posting system. A *job-posting system* is a mechanism for advertising open positions, typically on a bulletin board. Texas Instruments uses job-posting. Employees complete a request form indicating interest in a posted job. The posted job description includes a list of duties and the minimum skills and experience required.

External recruiting   External recruiting brings in "new blood" to a company and can inspire innovation. Among the most frequently used sources of outside applicants are newspaper advertisements, employee referrals, and college campus recruiting.

Newspaper advertisements are the most popular recruiting source for many occupations, because they are inexpensive and can generate a large number of responses. Employee referral is another frequently used source of applicants;[6] some companies actively encourage employees to refer their friends by offering cash rewards. The advantages of campus recruiting include a large pool of people from which to draw, applicants with up-to-date training, and a source of innovative ideas.[7]

It is becoming increasingly common for organizations such as Cisco Systems to use the Internet to advertise job openings and to gather applicant information. E-Span, for example, is an online service that lists professional and managerial positions. Federal Job Opportunity Board is a similar service that lists openings in the federal government.

The popularity of various recruiting methods notwithstanding, Figure 10.2 shows how 201 HR executives rated the effectiveness of nine different recruiting sources.

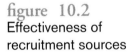

figure 10.2
Effectiveness of recruitment sources

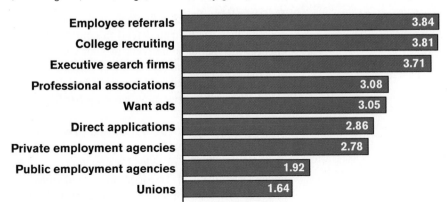

The average rating for nine recruitment sources on a 5-point scale
(1 = not good, 3 = average, 5 = extremely good):

Employee referrals	3.84
College recruiting	3.81
Executive search firms	3.71
Professional associations	3.08
Want ads	3.05
Direct applications	2.86
Private employment agencies	2.78
Public employment agencies	1.92
Unions	1.64

Source: David E. Terpstra, "The Search for Effective Methods," *HRFocus,* May 1996, pp. 16–17. Reprinted by permission of the publisher, from *HRFocus,* May 1996, © 1996. American Management Association, New York. http://www.amanet.org. All rights reserved. Arthur Sherman, George Bohlander, and Scott Snell, *Managing Human Resources,* 11th ed. (Cincinnati, OH: Southwestern Publishing, 1998).

Selection

Selection builds on recruiting and involves decisions about whom to hire. As important as these decisions are, they are—unfortunately—at times made in very careless or cavalier ways. In this section we describe a number of selection instruments to which you may soon be exposed in your own careers.

Applications and résumés
Application blanks and résumés provide basic information to prospective employers. In order to make a first cut through candidates, employers review the profiles and backgrounds of various job applicants. Applications and résumés typically include information about the applicant's name, educational background, citizenship, work experiences, certifications, and the like. While providing important information, applications and résumés tend not to be extremely useful for making final selection decisions.

Interviews
Interviews are the most popular selection tool, and every company uses some type of interview. However, employment interviewers must be careful about what they ask and how they ask it. Questions that are not job related are prohibited. In an unstructured (or nondirective) interview, the interviewer asks different interviewees different questions. As noted in Setting the Stage, the interviewer may also use probes; that is, ask follow-up questions to learn more about the candidate.[8]

In a **structured interview,** the interviewer conducts the same interview with each applicant. There are two basic types of structured interview. The first approach—called the *situational interview*—focuses on hypothetical situations. Zale Corporation, a major jewelry chain, uses this type of structured interview to select sales clerks. A sample question is: "A customer comes into the store to pick up a watch he had left for repair. The watch is not back yet from the repair shop, and the customer becomes angry. How would you handle the situation?" The second approach—called the *behavioral description interview*—explores what candidates have actually done in the past. In selecting college students for an officer training program, the U.S. army asks the following question to assess a candidate's ability to influence others: "What was the best idea you ever sold to a supervisor, teacher, peer, or subordinate?"

Reference checks
Reference checks are another commonly used screening device. Virtually all organizations use either a reference or an employment and education record check. Although reference checking makes sense, reference information is becoming increasingly difficult to obtain as a result of several highly publicized lawsuits. In one case, an applicant sued a former boss on the grounds that the boss told prospective employers the applicant was a "thief and a crook." The jury awarded the applicant $80,000.[9]

Personality tests
Personality tests are less popular for employee selection, largely because they are hard to defend in court.[10] However, they are regaining popularity, and chances are that at some point in your career you will complete some personality tests. A number of well-known paper-and-pencil inventories measure personality traits such as sociability, adjustment, and energy. Typical questions are "Do you like to socialize with people?" and "Do you enjoy working hard?"

Drug testing
Drug testing and *genetic testing* are among the most controversial screening instruments. Since the passage of the Drug-Free Workplace Act of 1988, applicants and employees of federal contractors, Department of Defense contractors, and those under Department of Transportation regulations are subject to testing for illegal drugs. According to a recent survey, 81 percent of *Fortune 500* firms conducted urine tests on their employees to test for the presence of illegal drugs. A genetic test tries to identify the likelihood of contracting a disease (such as emphysema) based on genetic makeup. While genetic screening is far less common than drug testing, its popularity may increase as the technique is perfected.[11]

Cognitive ability tests   *Cognitive ability tests* are among the oldest employment selection devices. These tests measure a range of intellectual abilities, including verbal comprehension (vocabulary, reading) and numerical aptitude (mathematical calculations). About 20 percent of U.S. companies use cognitive ability tests for selection purposes.[12] Figure 10.3 shows some examples of cognitive ability test questions.

Performance tests   *Performance tests* are procedures in which the test taker performs a sample of the job. Most companies use some type of performance test, typically for secretarial and clerical positions. The most widely used performance test is the typing test. However, performance tests have been developed for almost every occupation, including managerial positions. Assessment centers are the most notable offshoot of the managerial performance test.[13]

assessment center A managerial performance test in which candidates participate in a variety of exercises and situations.

Assessment centers originated during World War II. A typical **assessment center** consists of 10 to 12 candidates who participate in a variety of exercises or situations; some of the exercises involve group interactions, and others are performed individually. Each

figure 10.3
Sample measures of cognitive ability

Verbal

1. What is the meaning of the word surreptitious?
   - a. covert
   - b. winding
   - c. lively
   - d. sweet

2. How is the noun clause used in the following sentence:
   "I hope that I can learn this game."
   - a. subject
   - b. predicate nominative
   - c. direct object
   - d. object of the preposition

Quantitative

3. Divide 50 by .5 and add 5. What is the result?
   - a. 25
   - b. 30
   - c. 95
   - d. 105

4. What is the value of 144^2?
   - a. 12
   - b. 72
   - c. 288
   - d. 20736

Reasoning

5. ____ is to boat as snow is to ____
   - a. sail, ski
   - b. water, winter
   - c. water, ski
   - d. engine, water

6. Two women played 5 games of chess. Each woman won the same number of games, yet there were no ties. How can this be so?
   - a. There was a forfeit.
   - b. One player cheated.
   - c. They played different people.
   - d. One game was still in progress.

Mechanical

7. If gear A and gear C are both turning counter-clockwise, what is happening to gear B?
   - a. It is turning counter-clockwise.
   - b. It is turning clockwise.
   - c. It remains stationary.
   - d. The whole system will jam.

A   B   C

Answers: 1a, 2c, 3d, 4d, 5c, 6c, 7b.

Source: George Bohlander, Scott Snell, and Arthur Sherman, *Managing Human Resources,* 12th ed. Copyright © 2001. Reprinted by permission of South-Western College Publishing, a division of International Thomson Publishing, Inc., Cincinnati, Ohio 45227.

exercise taps a number of critical managerial dimensions, such as leadership, decision-making skills, and communication ability. Assessors, generally line managers from the organization, observe and record information about the candidates' performance in each exercise. AT&T was the first organization to use assessment centers. Since then, a number of large organizations have used or currently are using the assessment center technique, including Bristol-Myers, the FBI, and Sears.

Integrity tests   *Integrity tests* are used to assess a job candidate's honesty. Two forms of integrity tests are polygraphs and paper-and-pencil honesty tests. Polygraphs, or lie detector tests, have been banned for most employment purposes.[14] Paper-and-pencil honesty tests are more recent instruments for measuring integrity. These tests include questions such as whether a person has ever thought about stealing and whether he or she believes other people steal ("What percentage of people take more than $1 from their employer?"). Payless ShoeSource, based in Topeka, Kansas, has used an honesty test to reduce employee theft. Within only a year of implementing the program, inventory losses dropped by 20 percent, to less than 1 percent of sales. Despite compelling evidence such as this, the accuracy of these tests is still debatable.[15]

Reliability and validity   Regardless of the method used to select employees, two crucial issues that need to be addressed are a test's reliability and validity. **Reliability** refers to the consistency of test scores over time and across alternative measurements. For example, if three different interviewers talked to the same job candidate, but drew very different conclusions about the candidate's abilities, we might suspect that there were problems with the reliability of one or more of the selection tests or interview procedures.

  Validity moves beyond reliability to assess the accuracy of the selection test. The most common form of validity, *criterion-related validity,* refers to the degree to which a test actually predicts or correlates with job performance. Figure 10.4 shows scatterplots of the correlations between two different tests and job performance. Each of the dots on the scatterplots corresponds to an individual's test score relative to his or her job performance. Dots in the bottom-left corner of each scatterplot show individuals who scored poorly on the test and performed poorly on the job. Individuals in the top-right corner are those who scored well on the selection test and also performed well on the job. By plotting many individual scores, the points begin to reveal a pattern in the relationship between test scores and job performance. This pattern can be captured statistically with a correlation coefficient (i.e., a validity coefficient) that ranges from −1.0 (a perfect negative correlation) to 1.0 (a perfect positive correlation). In reality, most validity coefficients fall somewhere in between these extremes. In Figure 10.4, for example, Test A has a validity coefficient of zero (0.0), indicating that there is no relationship between test scores and job success. Test B, however, has a validity coefficient of .75,

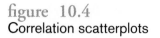

reliability The consistency of test scores over time and across alternative measurements.

validity The degree to which a selection test predicts or correlates with job performance.

figure 10.4
Correlation scatterplots

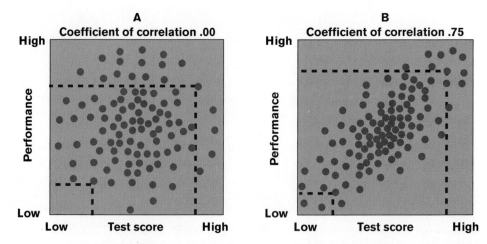

indicating that high test scores tend to be strongly predictive of good performance. Managers would not want to use Test A—it is not valid—but would be wise to use Test B for selecting employees because it has high criterion-related validity.

Another form of validity, *content validity,* concerns the degree to which selection tests measure a representative sample of the knowledge, skills, and abilities required for the job. The best-known example of a content-valid test is a typing test for secretaries, because typing is a task a secretary almost always performs. However, to be completely content valid, the selection process should also measure other skills the secretary would be likely to perform, such as answering the telephone, duplicating and faxing documents, and dealing with the public. Content validity is more subjective (less statistical) than evaluations of criterion-related validity, but is no less important, particularly when defending employment decisions in court.

Workforce reductions

Unfortunately, staffing decisions do not simply focus on hiring employees. As organizations evolve and markets change, the demand for certain employees rises and falls. Also, some employees simply do not perform at a level required to justify continued employment. For these reasons, managers must make sometimes difficult decisions to terminate their employment.

Layoffs
As a result of the massive restructuring of American industry brought about by mergers and acquisitions, divestiture, and increased competition, organizations have been *downsizing*—laying off large numbers of managerial and other employees. Dismissing any employee is tough, but when a company lays off a substantial portion of its workforce, the results can rock the foundations of the organization.[16] The victims of restructuring face all the difficulties of being let go—loss of self-esteem, demoralizing job searches, and the stigma of being out of work. **Outplacement** is the process of helping people who have been dismissed from the company to regain employment elsewhere. This can help to some extent, but the impact of layoffs goes even further than the employees who leave. For many of the employees who remain with the company, disenchantment, distrust, and lethargy overshadow the comfort of still having a job. In many respects, how management deals with dismissals will affect the productivity and satisfaction of those who remain. A well-thought-out dismissal process eases tensions and helps remaining employees adjust to the new work situation.

Organizations with strong performance evaluation systems benefit because the survivors are less likely to believe the decision was arbitrary. Further, if care is taken during the actual layoff process—that is, if workers are offered severance pay and help in finding a new job—remaining workers will be comforted. Companies should also avoid stringing out layoffs; that is, dismissing a few workers at a time.

outplacement The process of helping people who have been dismissed from the company to regain employment elsewhere.

Termination
People sometimes "get fired" for poor performance or other reasons. Should an employer have the right to fire a worker? In 1884, a Tennessee court ruled: "All may dismiss their employee(s) at will for good cause, for no cause, or even for cause morally wrong." The concept that an employee may be fired for any reason is known as *employment-at-will* or *termination-at-will* and was upheld in a 1908 Supreme Court ruling.[17] The logic is that if the employee may quit at any time, the employer is free to dismiss at any time.

Since the mid-1970s, courts in most states have made exceptions to this doctrine. For example, public policy is a policy or ruling designed to protect the public from harm. One exception to the employment-at-will concept under public policy is employee whistle-blowing. For example, if a worker reports an environmental violation to the regulatory agency and the company fires him or her, the courts may argue that the firing was unfair because the employee acted for the good of the community. Another example is that employees may not be fired for serving jury duty.

Employers can avoid the pitfalls associated with dismissal by developing progressive and positive disciplinary procedures.[18] By *progressive,* we mean that a manager takes graduated steps in attempting to correct a workplace behavior. For example, an employee who has been absent receives a verbal reprimand for the first offense. A second offense invokes a written reprimand. A third offense results in employee counseling and probation, and a fourth results in a paid-leave day to think over the consequences of future rule infractions. The employer is signaling to the employee that this is the "last straw." Arbitrators are more likely to side with the employer that fires someone when they believe the company has made sincere efforts to help the person correct his or her behavior.

termination interview A discussion between a manager and an employee about the employee's dismissal.

The **termination interview,** in which the manager discusses the company's position with the employee, is a stressful situation for both parties. Most experts believe that the immediate superior should be the one to deliver the bad news to employees. However, it is often good to have a third party, such as the HR manager, present to serve as a witness, to provide support for an anxious manager, or to diffuse anger by pulling the employee's attention away from the manager. In addition, some suggest that the best time to let someone go is Friday afternoon. However, the research evidence does not support this completely. Finally, it may be a good idea to conduct the termination interview in a neutral location, such as a conference room, so that the manager and employee can exit gracefully afterward. Table 10.1 provides some other guidelines for conducting a termination interview.[19]

Legal issues and equal employment opportunity   In 1964, Congress passed the *Civil Rights Act,* which prohibits discrimination in employment based on race, sex, color, national origin, and religion. Title VII of the act specifically forbids discrimination in employment decisions such as recruitment, hiring, discharge, layoff, discipline, promotion, compensation, and access to training.[20] In 1972, the act was amended to allow the Equal Employment Opportunity Commission (EEOC) to take employers to court. The amendments also expanded the scope of the act to cover private and public employers with 15 or more employees, labor organizations, and public and private employment agencies.

Nevertheless, employment discrimination remains a controversial and costly issue for both organizations and individuals. Opponents of the 1991 *Civil Rights Act* argued that the act would force companies to hire based on mandated quotas rather than on the most

table 10.1
Advice on termination

Do's	Don'ts
• Give as much warning as possible for mass layoffs.	• Don't leave room for confusion when firing. Tell the individual in the first sentence that he or she is terminated.
• Sit down one on one with the individual, in a private office.	• Don't allow time for debate during a termination session.
• Complete a termination session within 15 minutes.	• Don't make personal comments when firing someone; keep the conversation professional.
• Provide written explanations of severance benefits.	• Don't rush a fired employee offsite unless security is an issue.
• Provide outplacement services away from company headquarters.	• Don't fire people on significant dates, like the 25th anniversary of their employment or the day their mother died.
• Be sure the employee hears about his or her termination from a manager, not a colleague.	• Don't fire employees when they are on vacation or have just returned.
• Express appreciation for what the employee has contributed, if appropriate.	

Source: S. Alexander, "Firms Get Plenty of Practice at Layoffs, but They Often Bungle the Firing Process," *The Wall Street Journal,* November 14, 1991, p. 31.

qualified candidates. But the new bill provides protection for many groups. The 1991 *Civil Rights Act* also provides for punitive damages to workers who sue under the *Americans with Disabilities Act.* The latter act, passed in 1990, prohibits employment discrimination against people with disabilities. Recovering alcoholics or drug abusers, cancer patients in remission, and AIDS victims are covered by this legislation.

Thousands of court cases have challenged employment decisions and practices. Today, one common reason why employers are sued is *adverse impact,* in which an apparently neutral employment practice adversely affects a *group* of individuals protected by the *Civil Rights Act.*[21] Discrimination issues provide a means for both minority groups as well as individuals to seek Title VII protection from employment discrimination. Today, the "Uniform Guidelines on Employee Selection Procedures" deal specifically with how to develop employment practices that comply with the law.[22]

Many other important staffing laws affect employment practices. The *Rehabilitation Act* of 1973 and the *Americans with Disabilities Act* of 1990 prohibit discrimination against persons with physical and mental disabilities. The *Age Discrimination in Employment Act (ADEA)* of 1967 and amendments in 1978 and 1986 prohibit discrimination against people age 40 and over. The *Immigration Act* of 1990 was designed to allow immigrants into the country based on what they can contribute to the economy. This legislation nearly tripled the cap on immigrant visas to 140,000 but limited non-immigrant or temporary visas to 90,000 (the latter category previously was unrestricted). This new law complicates the hiring process for non-U.S. professionals under temporary visas such as investment bankers, scientists, and engineers. Finally, the *Worker Adjustment and Retraining Notification Act* of 1989, commonly known as the *WARN Act* or *Plant Closing Bill,* requires covered employers to give affected employees 60 days' written notice of plant closings or mass layoffs. Table 10.2 summarizes many of these major equal employment laws.

Developing the workforce

The skills and performance of employees and managers must be upgraded continually. Meeting this requirement involves training and development activities and appraising performance for the purposes of giving feedback and motivating people to perform at their best.

Training and development

Annual spending by employers on formal training is over $54 billion. Add informal educational and development experiences to that and the number balloons to $200 billion—slightly more than annual public and private spending on elementary and secondary education.[23]

General Motors has invested more than $2 billion over the past decade on education and training, making it the largest privately funded educational institution in the United States. IBM's annual training cost of $1.5 billion exceeds Harvard University's annual operating expenses of $951.7 million. Although these amounts sound like a lot of money (they are), the American Society for Training and Development (ASTD) argues that as a percentage of total payroll, the average organizational investment in training is too small.[24] This is of great concern given that jobs today are requiring more education, but the education level of U.S. workers is not keeping pace.

training Teaching lower-level employees how to perform their present jobs.

development Teaching managers and professional employees broad skills needed for their present and future jobs.

needs assessment An analysis identifying the jobs, people, and departments for which training is necessary.

Overview of the training process   Although we use the general term *training* here, training is sometimes distinguished from development. **Training** usually refers to teaching lower-level employees how to perform their present jobs, while **development** involves teaching managers and professional employees broader skills needed for their present and future jobs. *Phase one* of training should include a **needs assessment.** An analysis should be conducted to identify the jobs, people, and departments for which training is necessary. Job analysis and performance measurements are useful for this purpose.

table 10.2

U.S. equal employment laws

Act	Major provisions	Enforcement and remedies
Equal Pay Act (1963)	Prohibits gender-based pay discrimination between two jobs substantially similar in skill, effort, responsibility, and working conditions.	Fines up to $10,000, imprisonment up to 6 months, or both; enforced by Equal Employment Opportunity Commission (EEOC); private actions for double damages up to 3 years' wages, liquidated damages, reinstatement, or promotion.
Title VII of Civil Rights Act (1964)	Prohibits discrimination based on race, sex, color, religion, or national origin in employment decisions: hiring, pay, working conditions, promotion, discipline, or discharge.	Enforced by EEOC; private actions, back pay, front pay, reinstatement, restoration of seniority and pension benefits, attorneys' fees and costs.
Executive Orders 11246 and 11375 (1965)	Requires equal opportunity clauses in federal contracts; prohibits employment discrimination by federal contractors based on race, color, religion, sex, or national origin.	Established Office of Federal Contract Compliance Programs (OFCCP) to investigate violations; empowered to terminate violator's federal contracts.
Age Discrimination in Employment Act (1967)	Prohibits employment discrimination based on age for persons over 40 years; restricts mandatory retirement.	EEOC enforcement; private actions for reinstatement, back pay, front pay, restoration of seniority and pension benefits; double unpaid wages for willful violations; attorneys' fees and costs.
Vocational Rehabilitation Act (1973)	Requires affirmative action by all federal contractors for persons with disabilities; defines disabilities as physical or mental impairments that substantially limit life activities.	Federal contractors must consider hiring disabled persons capable of performance after reasonable accommodations.
Americans with Disabilities Act (1990)	Extends affirmative action provisions of Vocational Rehabilitation Act to private employers; requires workplace modifications to facilitate disabled employees; prohibits discrimination against disabled.	EEOC enforcement; private actions for Title VII remedies.
Civil Rights Act (1991)	Clarifies Title VII requirements: disparate treatment impact suits, business necessity, job relatedness; shifts burden of proof to employer; permits punitive damages and jury trials.	Punitive damages limited to sliding scale only in intentional discrimination based on sex, religion, and disabilities.
Family and Medical Leave Act (1991)	Requires 12 weeks' unpaid leave for medical or family needs: paternity, family member illness.	Private actions for lost wages and other expenses, reinstatement.

Phase two involves the design of training programs. Based on needs assessment, training objectives and content can be established. *Phase three* involves decisions about the training methods to be used (see Table 10.3). A basic decision for selecting a training method is whether to provide on-the-job or off-the-job training. Examples of training methods include lectures, role playing, programmed learning, case discussion, business simulation, behavior modeling (watching a videotape and imitating what is observed), assigned readings, conferences, job rotation, vestibule training (practice in a simulated job environment), and apprenticeship training. Finally, *phase four* of training should evaluate the program's effectiveness in terms of employee reactions, learning, behavior transferred to the job, and bottom-line results.

table 10.3
Instructional methods

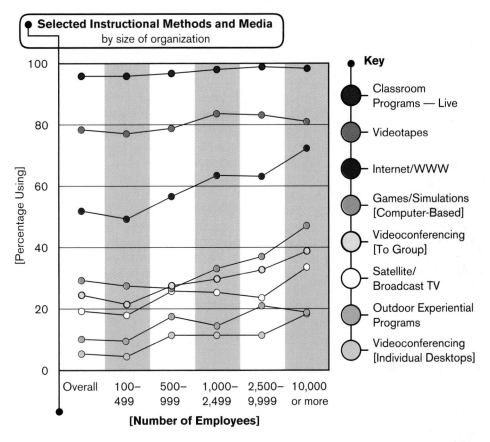

Source: Reprinted with permission from the October 2000 issue of *Training* magazine. Copyright October 2000. Bill Communications, Minneapolis, MN. All rights reserved. Not for resale.

From the Pages of
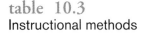

Can G.I. Joe go Hollywood?

The U.S. Army recently signed a five-year, $45 million contract with the Institute of Creative Technology at the University of Southern California to build cutting-edge combat simulations. With the deal, the military hopes to tap into Hollywood's "power of entertainment" in its training—using not only computer wizardry but also compelling human stories with unique characters similar to those in Hollywood dramas, says Jim Blake, senior scientist at the Army Simulation, Training & Instrumentation Command in Orlando, which oversees the project. Blake and the rest of the brass believe such living and breathing scenarios will better simulate the true emotional feel of combat and enable better decision making when bullets really do fly.

But can a bunch of Tinseltown twinkies teach G.I. Joe how to drive a tank? Well, that's the idea. And ICT has already enlisted an A-Team of Hollywood directors, writers, and special-effects experts who have worked on such films as *Apollo 13* and *Star Wars.* Onboard at ICT are *Grease* director Randal Kleiser; Andre Bormanis, chief science adviser for some of the *Star Trek* TV spin-offs; and *Star Wars* vehicle designer Ron Cobb. ICT has also added John Milius, screenwriter of *Clear and Present Danger* and *Apocalypse Now,* as a consultant. "What simulations create are those environments that allow you to learn with consequences but no damage." Use of high-tech combat simulations is nothing new to the military. The U.S. Marines have used a modified version of the popular multiplayer shoot-'em-up computer game *Doom* to train their troops for firefights. And military pilots regularly spend long hours on simulators to hone their skills in an environment where crashing has no consequences. More recently, the military has contracted with Sony to adapt the PlayStation2 game console for virtual training. And Paramount Pictures as signed a deal to deliver simulation training that develops the problem-solving skills of recruits over the Internet.

But the ICT effort for the Army will bring together a unique combination of university computer scientists and movie-industry bigwigs in a grand experiment. The goal is to perfect virtual-reality training by melding artificial intelligence, smells, and sounds with the special effects developed for movies. But unlike standard video games or linear feature films, participants will make complex decisions with seemingly real consequences in a totally immersive environment. Says Michael Murguia of computer-game designer New Pencil, "The ultimate goal is to create a new prototype game in real-time 3-D." And *Ultimat,* which did special-effects work on *Titanic,* has been assigned to come up with new graphic technologies. Says Blake: "The military would like to see a training experience achieve the highest possible level of fidelity." If the success of *Titanic* is any indicator, Blake could have a big hit with the troops on his hands. It sure beats boot camp.

Source: Dennis Blank, "Can Tinseltown's War Games Train G.I. Joe?," *Business Week Online,* January 3, 2001. ●

---

orientation training Training designed to introduce new employees to the company and familiarize them with policies, procedures, culture, and the like.

team training Training that provides employees with the skills and perspectives they need to work in collaboration with others.

diversity training Programs that focus on identifying and reducing hidden biases against people with differences and developing the skills needed to effectively manage a diversified workforce.

Types of training   Companies invest in training to enhance individual performance and organizational productivity. The most popular areas include computer applications, management skills/development and supervisory skills, technical skills, and communication skills. In addition to these, several topics are particularly noteworthy.

Orientation training is typically used to familiarize new employees with their new jobs, work units, and the organization in general. Done well, orientation training has a number of reputed benefits including lower employee turnover, increased morale, better productivity, lower recruiting and training costs, and the like.

Team training has taken on more importance as organizations reorganize to facilitate individuals working together. Team training teaches employees the skills they need to work together and also facilitates their interaction. Coca-Cola's Fountain Manufacturing Operation recently developed a team training program that focused on technical, interpersonal, and team interaction skills.[25]

Diversity training is now offered in over 50 percent of all U.S. organizations. The programs focus on building awareness of diversity issues as well as providing the skills employees need to work with others who are different from them. This topic is so important that the next chapter is devoted solely to managing diversity.

Performance appraisal

performance appraisal (PA) Assessment of an employee's job performance.

Performance appraisal (PA) is the assessment of an employee's job performance. Performance appraisal has two basic purposes. First, appraisal serves an *administrative* purpose. It provides information for making salary, promotion, and layoff decisions, as well as providing documentation that can justify these decisions in court. Second, and perhaps more importantly, performance appraisal serves a *developmental* purpose. The information can be used to diagnose training needs, career planning, and the like. Feedback and coaching based on appraisal information provide the basis for improving day-to-day performance.

What do you appraise?

Performance measures fall into one of three basic categories: traits, behaviors, and results. *Trait appraisals* involve subjective judgments about employee performance. They contain dimensions such as initiative, leadership, and attitude, and ask raters to indicate how much of each trait the employee possesses. Because trait scales tend to be ambiguous (as well as subjective), they often lead to personal bias and may not be suitable for obtaining useful feedback. So while this approach is extremely common—trait scales are easy to develop and implement—they unfortunately are often not valid.

management by objectives (MBO) A process in which objectives set by a subordinate and supervisor must be reached within a given time period.

Behavioral appraisals, while still subjective, focus more on observable aspects of performance. They were actually developed in response to the problems of trait appraisals. These scales focus on specific, prescribed behaviors, which can help ensure that all parties understand what the ratings are really measuring. Because they are less ambiguous, they also can help provide useful feedback. Figure 10.5 contains an example of a behaviorally anchored rating scale (BARS) for evaluating quality.

Results appraisals tend to be more objective and can focus on production data such as sales volume (for a salesperson), units produced (for a line worker), or profits (for a manager). One approach to results appraisals—called **management by objectives (MBO)**—involves a subordinate and a supervisor agreeing on specific performance goals

figure 10.5
Example of BARS used for evaluating quality

Performance Dimension: Total Quality Management. This area of performance concerns the extent to which a person is aware of, endorses, and develops proactive procedures to enhance product quality, ensure early disclosure of discrepancies, and integrate quality assessments with cost and schedule performance measurement reports to maximize client's satisfaction with overall performance.

OUTSTANDING	7	Uses measures of quality and well-defined processes to achieve project goals. Defines quality from the client's perspective.
	6	Look for/identifies ways to continually improve the process.
	5	Clearly communicates quality management to others. Develops a plan that defines how the team will participate in quality.
		Appreciates TQM as an investment.
AVERAGE	4	Has measures of quality that define tolerance levels.
	3	Views quality as costly. Legislates quality.
	2	Focuses his/her concerns only on outputs and deliverables, ignoring the underlying processes.
POOR	1	Blames others for absence of quality. Gives lip service only to quality concerns.

(objectives). They then develop a plan that describes the time frame and criteria for determining whether the objectives have been reached. The aim is to agree on a set of objectives that are clear, specific, and reachable. For example, an objective for a salesperson might be to increase sales 25 percent during the following year. An objective for a computer programmer might be to complete two projects within the next six months. MBO has several advantages and can be useful when managers want to empower employees to adapt their behavior as they deem necessary in order to achieve desired results. Although MBO helps focus employees on reaching specific goals and encourages planning and development, it often focuses too much on short-term achievement and ignores long-term goals.

None of these performance appraisal systems is easy to conduct properly; and all have drawbacks that must be guarded against. In choosing an appraisal method, the following guidelines may prove helpful:

1. Always take legal considerations into account.
2. Base performance standards on job analysis.
3. Communicate performance standards to employees.
4. Evaluate employees on specific performance-related behaviors rather than on a single global or overall measure.
5. Document the PA process carefully.
6. If possible, use more than one rater (discussed in the next section).
7. Develop a formal appeal process.[26]

Who should do the appraisal?

Just as there are multiple methods for gathering performance appraisal information, there are several different sources who can provide PA information. *Managers* and *supervisors* are the traditional source of appraisal information because they are often in the best position to observe an employee's performance. However, companies such as Coors, General Foods, and Digital are turning to peers and team members to provide input to the performance appraisal. *Peers* and *team member*s often see different dimensions of performance, and are often best at identifying leadership potential and interpersonal skills.

One increasingly popular source of appraisal is the person's subordinates. Appraisal by *subordinates* has been used by companies such as Xerox and IBM to give superiors feedback on how their employees view them. However, because this process gives employees power over their bosses, it is normally only used for developmental purposes. *Internal and external customers* are also used as sources of performance appraisal information, particularly for companies such as Ford and Honda that are focused on total quality management. External customers have been used for some time to appraise restaurant employees, but internal customers can include anyone inside the organization who depends upon an employee's work output. Finally, it is usually a good idea for employees to evaluate their own performance. Although *self-appraisals* may be biased upward, the process of self-evaluation helps increase the employee's involvement in the review process, and is a starting point for establishing future goals.

Because each source of PA information has some limitations, and different people may see different aspects of performance, companies such as Westinghouse and Eastman Kodak have taken to using multiple-rater approaches that involve more than one source for appraisal information. By combining different sources—in a process referred to as **360 degree appraisal**—it is possible to obtain a more complete assessment of an employee's performance.

360 degree appraisal
Process of using multiple sources of appraisal to gain a comprehensive perspective of one's performance.

How do you give employees feedback?

Giving PA feedback can be a stressful task for both managers and subordinates. The purposes of PA conflict to some degree. Providing growth and development requires understanding and support; however, the manager must be impersonal and be able to make tough decisions. Employees want to know how they are doing, but typically they are uncomfortable about getting feedback. Finally, the organization's need to make HR decisions conflicts with the individual employee's need to maintain a positive image.[27] These conflicts often make the PA interview difficult; therefore, managers should conduct such interviews thoughtfully.

There is no one "best" way to do a PA interview. The most difficult interviews are those with employees who are performing poorly. Here is a useful PA interview format to use when an employee is performing below acceptable standards:

1. Summarize the employee's specific performance. Describe the performance in behavioral or outcome terms, such as sales or absenteeism. Don't say the employee has a poor attitude; rather, explain which employee behaviors indicate a poor attitude.
2. Describe the expectations and standards, and be specific.
3. Determine the causes for the low performance; get the employee's input.
4. Discuss solutions to the problem, and have the employee play a major role in the process.
5. Agree to a solution. As a supervisor, you have input into the solution. Raise issues and questions, but also provide support.
6. Agree to a timetable for improvement.
7. Document the meeting.

Follow-up meetings may be needed. Here are some guidelines for giving feedback to an average employee:

1. Summarize the employee's performance, and be specific.
2. Explain why the employee's work is important to the organization.
3. Thank the employee for doing the job.
4. Raise any relevant issues, such as areas for improvement.
5. Express confidence in the employee's future good performance.

Designing reward systems

Reward systems are another major set of HRM activities. Most of this section will be devoted to monetary rewards such as pay and fringe benefits. Although traditionally pay has been of primary interest, benefits have received increased attention in recent years. Benefits presently make up a far greater percentage of the total payroll than they did in past decades.[28] The typical employer today pays nearly 40 percent of payroll costs in benefits. Accordingly, employers are trying to find ways to reduce these costs. Another reason for the growing interest in benefits is increased complexity. Many new types of benefits are now available, and tax laws affect myriad fringe benefits, such as health insurance and pension plans.

Pay decisions

Reward systems can serve the strategic purposes of attracting, motivating, and retaining people. The wages paid to employees are based on a complex set of forces. Beyond the body of laws governing compensation, a number of basic decisions must be made in choosing the appropriate pay plan. Figure 10.6 illustrates some of the factors that influence the wage mix.

Three types of decisions are crucial for designing an effective pay plan: pay level, pay structure, and individual pay.

Pay level refers to the choice of whether to be a high-, average-, or low-paying company. Compensation is a major cost for any organization, so low wages can be justified on a short-term financial basis. But being the high-wage employer—the highest-paying company in the region—ensures that the company will attract many applicants. Being a wage leader may be important during times of low unemployment or intense competition.

figure 10.6
Factors affecting the wage mix

Source: George Bohlander, Scott Snell, and Arthur Sherman, *Managing Human Resources,* 12th ed. Copyright © 2001. Reprinted by permission of South-Western College Publishing, a division of International Thomson Publishing, Inc., Cincinnati, Ohio 45227.

The *pay structure* decision is the choice of how to price different jobs within the organization. Jobs that are similar in worth usually are grouped together into job families. A pay grade, with a floor and a ceiling, is established for each job family. Figure 10.7 illustrates a hypothetical pay structure.

Finally, *individual pay decisions* concern different pay rates for jobs of similar worth within the same family. Differences in pay within job families are decided in two ways. First, some jobs are occupied by individuals with more seniority than others. Second, some people may be better performers who are therefore deserving of a higher level of pay.

figure 10.7
Pay structure

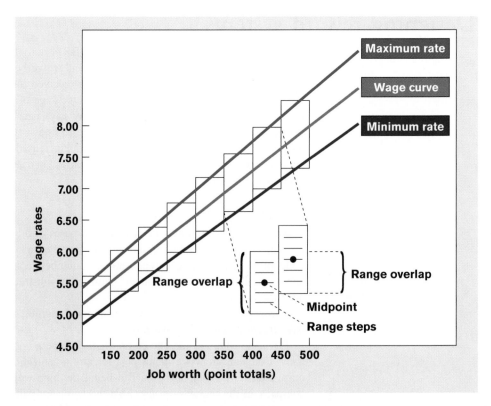

Source: *Effective Personal Management,* 3rd ed., by Randall S. Schuler, Nicholas J. Bentell and Stuart A. Youngblood. Copyright © 1989 by West Publishing Company.

Incentive systems and variable pay

A number of incentive systems have been devised to encourage and motivate employees to be more productive.[29] (See Chapter 13 for more discussion of rewarding performance.) *Individual incentive plans* are the most common type of incentive plan. An individual incentive system consists of an objective standard against which a worker's performance is compared. Pay is determined by the employee's performance. Individual incentive plans are frequently used in sales jobs. If effectively designed, individual incentive plans can be highly motivating.

There are several types of group incentive plans in which pay is based on group performance. *Gainsharing plans* concentrate on saving money.[30] The best known is the Scanlon plan, which is based on a function of the ratio between labor costs and sales value of production. An additional feature of the Scanlon plan is the use of employee committees to evaluate workers' suggestions for improving productivity.

Profit-sharing plans give employee incentives based on unit, department, plant, or company productivity. Nucor Steel, one of the nation's most profitable steel companies, relies heavily on a group-oriented profit-sharing plan. The entire company—4,000 employees—is broken down into bonus groups. For instance, each mill consists of groups of 25 to 35 employees who perform a complete task (e.g., melting and casting the steel or rolling the steel). Each group has a production standard and is paid for the amount of production over the specified level.[31]

When objective performance measures are not available but the company still wants to base pay on performance, it uses a *merit pay system*. Individuals' pay raises and bonuses are based on the judgmental merit rating they receive from their boss. Over the years, Lincoln Electric Company has been noted as having a particularly effective merit pay plan.[32]

Employee benefits

Like pay systems, employee benefit plans are subject to regulation. Employee benefits are divided into those required by law and those optional for an employer.

The three basic required benefits are workers' compensation, social security, and unemployment insurance. *Workers' compensation* provides financial support to employees suffering a work-related injury or illness. *Social security,* as established in the Social Security Act of 1935, provides financial support to retirees; in subsequent amendments, the act was expanded to cover disabled employees. The funds come from payments made by employers, employees, and self-employed workers. *Unemployment insurance* provides financial support to employees who are laid off for reasons they cannot control. Companies that have terminated fewer employees pay less into the unemployment insurance fund; thus, organizations have an incentive to keep terminations at a minimum.

A large number of benefits are not required to be employer provided. The most common are pension plans and medical and hospital insurance. Other optional employee benefits include dental insurance, life insurance, and vacation time. Because of the wide variety of possible benefits and the considerable differences in employee preferences and needs, companies often use **cafeteria** or **flexible benefit programs.** In this type of program, employees are given credits that they "spend" on benefits they desire. FinPac Corporation, a small computer software company, provides each employee with a required amount of life and disability insurance. Then employees use their credits toward individualized packages of additional benefits, including medical and dental insurance, dependent care, extra life insurance, or cash.

Legal issues in compensation and benefits

A number of laws affect employee compensation and benefits. *The Fair Labor Standards Act (FLSA)* of 1938 set minimum wages, maximum hours, child labor standards, and overtime pay provisions. The Department of Labor monitors and enforces the FLSA. *Nonexempt* employees are entitled to premium pay for overtime (e.g., time-and-one-half). *Exempt* employees (e.g., executives, administrators, and professionals) are not subject to the overtime and minimum wage provisions.[33]

cafeteria benefit program
Employee benefit programs in which employees choose from a menu of options to create a benefit package tailored to their needs.

flexible benefit programs
Benefit programs in which employees are given credits to spend on benefits that fit their unique needs.

The *Equal Pay Act (EPA)* of 1963, now enforced by the EEOC, prohibits unequal pay for men and women who perform equal work. Equal work means jobs that require equal skill, effort, and responsibility and are performed under similar working conditions. The law does permit exceptions where the difference in pay is due to a seniority system, a merit system, an incentive system based on quantity or quality of production, or any other factor other than sex, such as market demand. Although equal pay for equal work may sound like common sense, many employers have fallen victim to this law by rationalizing that men, traditionally the "breadwinners," deserve more pay than women or by giving equal jobs different titles (senior assistant versus office manager) as the sole basis for pay differences.

One controversy concerns male and female pay differences within the same company. **Comparable worth** doctrine implies that women who perform *different* jobs of *equal* worth as those performed by men should be paid the same wage.[34] In contrast to the equal-pay-for-equal-work notion, comparable worth suggests that the jobs need *not* be the same to require the same pay. For example, nurses (predominantly female) were found to be paid considerably less than skilled craftworkers (predominantly male), even though the two jobs were found to be of equal value or worth.[35] Under the Equal Pay Act, this would not constitute pay discrimination because the jobs are very different. But under the comparable-worth concept, these findings would indicate discrimination because the jobs are of equal worth.

comparable worth Principle of equal pay for different jobs of equal worth.

To date, no federal law requires comparable worth, and the Supreme Court has made no decisive rulings about it. However, some states have considered developing comparable-worth laws, and others already have implemented comparable-worth changes, raising the wages of female-dominated jobs. For example, Minnesota passed a comparable-worth law for public-sector employees after finding that women on average were paid 25 percent less than men. Several other states have comparable-worth laws for public-sector employees, including Iowa, Idaho, New Mexico, Washington, and South Dakota.[36]

Some laws influence mostly benefit practices. The *Pregnancy Discrimination Act* of 1978 states that pregnancy is a disability and qualifies a woman to receive the same benefits that she would with any other disability. The *Employee Retirement Income Security Act (ERISA)* of 1974 protects private pension programs from mismanagement. ERISA requires that retirement benefits be paid to those who vest or earn a right to draw benefits and ensures retirement benefits for employees whose companies go bankrupt or who otherwise cannot meet their pension obligations.

Health and safety

The *Occupational Safety and Health Act (OSHA)* of 1970 requires employers to pursue workplace safety. Employers must maintain records of injuries and deaths caused by workplace accidents and submit to on-site inspections. Large-scale industrial accidents, such as the Union Carbide gas leak in Bhopal, India, and nuclear power plant accidents worldwide, have focused attention on the importance of workplace safety.

One of many examples of the importance of this issue is the coal-mining industry. Coal miners spend their workdays in 3-foot-high spaces wading in mud and water. Nearly every coal miner can name a friend or family member who has been killed, maimed, or stricken with black lung disease. "You die quick or you die slow," reports one mine worker. However, according to the federal Mine Safety and Health Administration, mines are safer now, and catastrophic cave-ins are largely a thing of the past.[37]

Labor relations

labor relations The system of relations between workers and management.

Labor relations is the system of relations between workers and management. Labor unions recruit members, collect dues, and ensure that employees are treated fairly with respect to wages, working conditions, and other issues. When workers organize for the purpose of negotiating with management to improve their wages, hours, or working conditions, two processes are involved: unionization and collective bargaining. These processes have evolved over a 50-year period in the United States to provide important employee rights.[38]

Labor laws

Try to imagine what life would be like with unemployment at 25 percent. Pretty grim, you would say. Legislators in 1935 felt that way too. Therefore, organized labor received its Magna Carta with the passage of the National Labor Relations Act.

The *National Labor Relations Act* (also called the *Wagner Act* after its legislative sponsor) ushered in an era of rapid unionization by (1) declaring labor organizations legal, (2) establishing five unfair employer labor practices, and (3) creating the National Labor Relations Board (NLRB). Today, the NLRB conducts unionization elections, hears unfair labor practices complaints, and issues injunctions against offending employers. The Wagner Act greatly assisted the growth of unions by enabling workers to use the law and the courts to legally organize and collectively bargain for better wages, hours, and working conditions.

Public policy began on the side of organized labor in 1935, but over the next 25 years the pendulum swung toward the side of management. The *Labor-Management Relations Act,* or *Taft-Hartley Act* (1947), protected employers' free-speech rights, defined unfair labor practices by unions, and permitted workers to decertify (reject) a union as their representative.

Finally, the *Labor-Management Reporting and Disclosure Act,* or *Landrum-Griffin Act* (1959) swung the public policy pendulum midway between organized labor and management. By declaring a bill of rights for union members, establishing control over union dues increases, and imposing reporting requirements for unions, Landrum-Griffin was designed to curb abuses by union leadership and rid unions of corruption.

Unionization

How do workers join unions? Through a union organizer or local union representative, workers learn what benefits they may receive by joining.[39] The union representative distributes authorization cards that permit workers to indicate whether or not they want an election to be held to certify the union to represent them. The National Labor Relations Board will conduct a certification election if at least 30 percent of the employees sign authorization cards. Management has several choices at this stage: to recognize the union without an election, to consent to an election, or to contest the number of cards signed and resist an election.

If an election is warranted, an NLRB representative will conduct the election by secret ballot. A simple majority of those voting determines the winner. Thus, apathetic workers who do not show up to vote in effect support the union. If the union wins the election, it is certified as the bargaining unit representative.

During the campaign preceding the election, efforts are made by both management and the union to persuade the workers how to vote. Most workers, though, are somewhat resistant to campaign efforts, having made up their minds well before the NLRB appears on the scene. If the union wins the election, management and the union are legally required to bargain in good faith to obtain a collective bargaining agreement or contract.

Why do workers vote for a union? Four factors play a significant role (see Figure 10.8).[40] First, economic factors are important, especially for workers in low-paying jobs; unions attempt to raise the average wage rate for their members. Second, job dissatisfaction encourages workers to seek out a union. Poor supervisory practices, favoritism, lack of communication, and perceived unfair or arbitrary discipline and discharge are specific triggers of job dissatisfaction. Third, the belief that the union can obtain desired benefits can generate a pro-union vote. Finally, the image of the union can determine whether a dissatisfied worker will seek out the union. Headline stories of union corruption and dishonesty can discourage workers from unionization.

Collective bargaining

In the United States, management and unions engage in a periodic ritual (typically every three years) of negotiating an agreement over wages, hours, and working conditions. Two types of disputes can arise during this process. First, before an agreement is reached, the

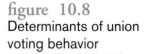

figure 10.8
Determinants of union
voting behavior

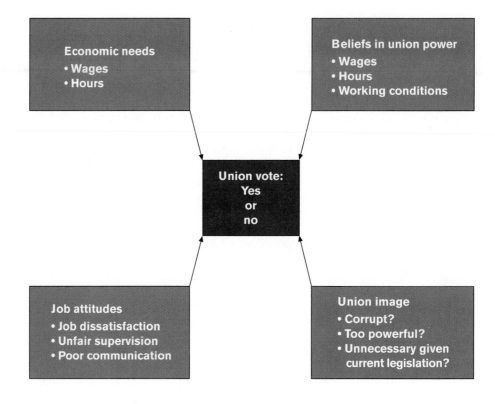

arbitration The use of a
neutral third party to resolve
a labor dispute.

union shop An organization
with a union and union security
clause specifying that workers
must join the union after a set
period of time.

right-to-work Legislation
that allows employees to work
without having to join a union.

workers may go on strike to compel agreement on their terms. Such an action is known
as an *economic strike* and is permitted by law. Once the agreement is signed, however,
management and the union can still disagree over *interpretation* of the agreement. Usually they settle their disputes through arbitration. **Arbitration** is the use of a neutral third
party, typically jointly selected, to resolve the dispute. The United States uses arbitration
while an agreement is in effect to avoid *wildcat strikes* (in which workers walk off the
job in violation of the contract) or unplanned work stoppages.

What does a collective bargaining agreement contain? In a **union shop,** a union security
clause specifies that workers must join the union after a set period of time. **Right-to-work**
states, through restrictive legislation, do not permit union shops; that is, workers have the
right to work without being forced to join a union. The southern United States has many
right-to-work states. The wage component of the contract spells out rates of pay, including
premium pay for overtime and paid holidays. Individual rights usually are specified in terms
of the use of seniority to determine pay increases, job bidding, and order of layoffs.

A feature of any contract is the grievance procedure. Unions perform a vital service
for their membership in this regard by giving workers a voice in what goes on during
both contract negotiations and administration through the grievance procedure.[41] In about
50 percent of discharge cases that go to arbitration, the arbitrator overturns management's
decision and reinstates the worker.[42] Unions have a legal duty of fair representation,
which means they must represent all workers in the bargaining unit and ensure that workers' rights are protected.

What does the future hold?

In recent years, union membership has declined to less than 12 percent of the U.S. labor
force as a consequence of changing laws concerning employee rights, global competition, decreased demand for the products of traditionally unionized industries, the rise of
the service economy (which is difficult to unionize), and changing expectations of the
new workforce. Some people applaud unions' apparent decline. Others hope for an eventual reemergence based on the potential power of management–union cooperation to help
U.S. businesses in the global economy. Unions may play a different role in the future,
one that is less adversarial and more cooperative with management. Unions are adapting

UAW Local 696 President Joe Hasenjager talks with striking workers outside the General Motors corporate plant in Dayton, Ohio. *[AP/Pat Sullivan/Wide World photos]*

to changing workforce demographics; they are paying more attention to women, older workers, and people who work at home. Elimination of inefficient work rules, the introduction of profit sharing, and a guarantee of no layoffs were seen as a big step toward a fundamentally different, cooperative long-term relationship. What seems clear is that when companies recognize that their success depends on the talents and energies of employees, the interests of unions and managers begin to converge. Rather than one side exploiting the other, unions and managers find common ground based on developing, valuing, and involving employees. Particularly in knowledge-based companies, the balance of power is shifting toward employees. Individuals, not companies, own their own human capital. And these employees are free, within limits, to leave the organization, taking their human capital with them. This leaves organizations in a particularly vulnerable position if they manage poorly. To establish competitive capability, organizations are searching for ways to obtain, retain, and engage their most valuable resources: human resources.

Key terms

Summary of learning objectives

Now that you have studied Chapter 10, you should know:

How companies use human resources management to gain competitive advantage.

To succeed, companies must align their human resources to their strategy. Effective planning is necessary to make certain that the right number and kind of employees are available to implement a company's strategic plan. For example, in the "Setting the Stage" it is clear that hiring the most competent people is a very involved process. Companies that compete on cost, quality, service, and so on should also use their staffing, training, appraisal, and reward systems to elicit and reinforce the kinds of behaviors that underlie their strategies.

Why companies recruit both internally and externally for new hires.

Some companies prefer to recruit internally to make certain that employees are familiar with organizational policies and values. AT&T's Resource Link is an example of a company trying very hard to make certain that available work goes to internal candidates before looking externally. In other instances, companies prefer to recruit externally to find individuals with new ideas and fresh perspectives.

The various methods available for selecting new employees.

There are a myriad of selection techniques from which to choose. Interviews and reference checks are most common. Personality tests and cognitive ability tests measure an individual's aptitude and potential to do well on the job. Other selection techniques include assessment centers and integrity tests. Regardless of the approach used, any test should be able to demonstrate reliability (consistency across time and different interview situations) and validity (accuracy in predicting job performance).

Why companies spend so much on training and development.

People cannot depend on a set of skills for all of their working lives. In today's changing, competitive world, old skills quickly become obsolete and new ones become essential for success. Refreshing or updating an individual's skills requires a great deal of continuous training. Companies such as Mirage Resorts understand that gaining a competitive edge in quality of service depends on having the most talented, flexible workers in the industry.

How to determine who should appraise an employee's performance.

Many companies are using multiple sources of appraisal because different people see different sides of an employee's performance. Typically, a superior is expected to evaluate an employee, but peers and team members are often in a good position to see aspects of

performance that a superior misses. Even an employee's subordinates are being asked more often today to give their input in order to get yet another perspective on the evaluation. Particularly in companies concerned about quality, internal and external customers are also surveyed. Finally, employees should evaluate their own performance, if only to get them thinking about their own performance, as well as to engage them in the appraisal process.

How to analyze the fundamental aspects of a reward system.

Reward systems are broken down into three basic components: pay level, pay structure, and individual pay determination. To achieve an advantage over competitors, executives may want to generally pay a higher wage to their company's employees, but this decision must be weighed against the need to control costs (pay-level decisions are often tied to strategic concerns such as these). To achieve internal equity (paying people what they are worth relative to their peers within the company), managers must look at the pay structure, making certain that pay differentials are based on knowledge, effort, responsibility, working conditions, seniority, and so on. Individual pay determination is often based on merit or the different contributions of individuals. In these cases it is important to make certain that men and women receive equal pay for equal work, and managers may wish to base pay decisions on the idea of comparable worth (equal pay for equal contribution).

How unions influence human resources management.

Labor relations involve the interactions between workers and management. One mechanism by which this relationship is conducted is unions. Unions seek to present a collective voice for workers, to make their needs and wishes known to management. Unions negotiate agreements with management regarding a range of issues such as wages, hours, working conditions, job security, and health care. One important tool that unions can use is the grievance procedure established through collective bargaining. This gives employees a way to seek redress for wrongful action on the part of management. In this way, unions make certain that the rights of all employees are protected.

How the legal system influences human resources management.

The legal system influences managers by placing constraints on the ways potential and actual employees are treated. Equal opportunity laws ensure that companies do not discriminate in their hiring and training practices. The Fair Labor Standards Act and the Equal Pay Act ensure that people earn fair compensation for the contribution they make to the organization. The Occupational Safety and Health Act (OSHA) ensures that employees have a safe and healthy work environment. Labor laws seek to protect the rights of both employees and managers so that their relationship can be productive and agreeable.

Discussion questions

1. How will changes in the labor force affect HRM practices for the year 2005?

2. Describe the major regulations governing HRM practices.

3. Define job analysis. Why is job analysis relevant to each of the six key HRM activities discussed in the chapter (i.e., planning, staffing, training, performance appraisal, reward systems, labor relations)?

4. What are the various methods for recruiting employees? Why are some better than others? In what sense are they better?

5. What is a "test"? Give some examples of tests used by employers.

6. What purpose does performance appraisal serve? Why are there so many different methods of appraisal?

7. What are some key ideas to remember when conducting a performance interview?

8. How would you define an effective reward system? What role do benefits serve in a reward system?

9. Why do workers join unions? What implications would this have for the organization that wishes to remain nonunion?

10. Discuss the advantages and disadvantages of collective bargaining for the employer and the employee.

Concluding Case

Boomerang recruiting

R. David Woolf was not looking forward to his scheduled exit interview last year after he announced plans to leave video-projector manufacturer InFocus and take a new job with a high-tech company. Woolf, then a senior production manager, became uneasy when he learned that instead of attending a perfunctory session in the personnel office, he would be meeting with the company's CEO and the head of human resources. He feared a dressing down: "How the heck could you leave? What are you, a traitor?" Instead, Woolf was floored by what he actually heard. "They were absolutely adamant about telling me there was an open door," he recalls. "They said: 'We really like you, and we would really like to hire you back. If next week you don't like it, call us.'"

Woolf needn't have been so surprised. What he experienced is a growing trend known as boomerang recruiting—the wooing of high-performing former employees. In Woolf's case, the tactic worked. Nine months and two jobs after leaving Wilsonville (Oregon)-based InFocus, Woolf decided that his new company was a disappointment and was welcomed back to his old one.

Spurred by a low unemployment rate that has left labor pools dry, more companies are trying to entice former staff back into the fold. "How do we win the war for talent?" asks Erik J. Van Slyke, a Deloitte and Touche senior manager in human-capital consulting. "An obvious quick hit is to get rid of a policy of being reluctant to hire former employees." Some companies—Deloitte is one of them—have long kept the welcome mat out, but Van Slyke and other human-resources experts began to notice more joining the crowd about three years ago, especially when it comes to filling technology jobs. Today, less than 20 percent of large companies have made the boomerang strategy a routine part of recruiting for technology and e-commerce jobs, says Diane Tunick Morello, a Gartner Group consultant. But she expects that figure to jump to perhaps 60 percent in coming years.

The labor crunch is not the only reason boomeranging is gaining popularity, says John Putzier, president of FirStep, a human-resources consulting company in Prospect, Pennsylvania. As companies have abandoned the once-sacred practice of lifetime employment, they have also learned to forget about such concepts as employee loyalty and tolerate more job switching, he says. In addition, managers at established companies who have watched good talent join the exodus to Internet start-ups are betting that some of the prodigal children will regret the decision once confronted with the fragility of the new enterprises. Jennifer W. Christensen, director of alumni relations at McKinsey & Co., says the consulting powerhouse has "opened the door a crack" to taking back defectors in part because of the dot.com phenomenon.

Some companies are making special efforts to keep track of and stay in touch with prized former staff. Valued former technology workers of Fannie Mae, the government-sponsored mortgage company, have found themselves being courted via e-mail, letters, and phone calls from former bosses. "We will check with them periodically to see if they are happy, and if they will consider coming back," says Maureen E. Conte, technology recruiter at the Washington (D.C.) company.

Fannie Mae has never banished its exes, Conte says, but the labor shortage has led to more rehiring than in the past. One big advantage of boomerang recruitment, she says, is that the boss gets a person who already knows the lay of the land, so less time, effort, and money are needed to get a newbie up to speed. Sometimes, there's an added bonus: The employee may have picked up valuable skills at the new job. "They come back ready to roll," Conte says.

Some human-resources consultants recommend that employers adopt policies that make clear that returning is possible. Putzier suggests what he calls "bridge service": If an employee returns within one year, the company not only restores all benefits accrued until the time of the worker's departure, but offers whatever additional benefits would have accumulated during the hiatus.

Still, employers have to watch out for one problem in boomerang recruitment—sending a message to the workforce that the best way to get a raise and a promotion is to leave and return the conquering hero. One way to avoid this is to make sure that rehires are not elevated to a much higher rank than they would have achieved had they remained on the job, says Peter Freire, executive director of the Corporate Leadership Council, a Washington (D.C.) company that does research for large companies on human-resources issues.

Pitfalls notwithstanding, some companies are going to great lengths to stay on good terms with potential second-time-arounders. Van Slyke has heard of employers who send fruit baskets or trinkets such as fancy key rings to ex-employees on special occasions.

InFocus has just such a "no-hard-feelings" approach, says Susan L. Thompson, the human-resources chief who met with Woolf at his exit interview. The company has sent valued exes flowers on their first day at the new job, she notes. And, as a matter of course, her company tries to keep the relationship going through e-mail, phone calls, cards, and even occasional dinners. In a typ-

ical year, the strategy helps the company win back about 10 percent of its former workers in areas such as marketing, sales, engineering, and administration.

Woolf is one of this year's re-recruits. Even though he was making more money, he was bored six months after leaving InFocus and missed its swifter pace and creativity. Neither he nor Thompson recalls the exact chain of events, but somehow Woolf got word back to the company. Thompson was soon on the phone, and Woolf was invited back with a new title. He received more pay than he was receiving when he left, but not as much as he had been making outside InFocus. No matter, Woolf asserts. He is thrilled to be back. "When you go to work," he says, "you've got to like it."

Questions

1. Why is boomerang recruiting becoming so popular?

2 What are some of the benefits and costs of such a policy?

3. Would such an approach help or hurt a company in the long run?

Source: Pamela Mendels, "How 'Boomerang Recruiting' Brings Valued Execs Back," *Business Week Online,* July 26, 2000.

Spurred by a low unemployment rate that has left labor pools dry, more companies are practicing boomerang recruiting.
[Corbis Stock Market/Chris Collins]

Experiential Exercises
10.1 The "legal" interview

Objectives

1. To introduce you to the complexities of employment law.

2. To identify interview practices that might lead to discrimination in employment.

Instructions

1. Working alone, review the text material on interviewing and discrimination in employment.

2. In small groups, complete the "Legal" Interview Worksheet.

3. After the class reconvenes, group spokespersons present group findings.

"Legal" interview worksheet

The employment interview is one of the most critical steps in the employment selection process. It may also be an occasion for discriminating against individual employment candidates. The following represents questions that interviewers often ask job applicants. Identify the legality of each question by circling *L* (legal) or *I* (illegal) and briefly explain your decision.

Interview question	Legality	Explanation
1. Could you provide us with a photo for our files?	L I	_____
2. Have you ever used another name (previous married name or alias)?	L I	_____
3. What was your maiden name?	L I	_____
4. What was your wife's maiden name?	L I	_____
5. What was your mother's maiden name?	L I	_____
6. What is your current address?	L I	_____
7. What was your previous address?	L I	_____
8. What is your social security number?	L I	_____
9. Where was your place of birth?	L I	_____
10. Where were your parents born?	L I	_____
11. What is your national origin?	L I	_____
12. Are you a naturalized citizen?	L I	_____
13. What languages do you speak?	L I	_____
14. What is your religious/church affiliation?	L I	_____
15. What is your racial classification?	L I	_____
16. How many dependents do you have?	L I	_____
17. What are the ages of your dependent children?	L I	_____
18. What is your marital status?	L I	_____
19. How old are you?	L I	_____
20. Do you have proof of your age (birth certificate or baptismal record)?	L I	_____

21. Whom do we notify in case of an emergency?	L	I	_____
22. What is your height and weight?	L	I	_____
23 Have you ever been arrested?	L	I	_____
24. Do you own your own car?	L	I	_____
25. Do you own your own house?	L	I	_____
26. Do you have any charge accounts?	L	I	_____
27. Have you ever had your salary garnished?	L	I	_____
28. To what organizations do you belong?	L	I	_____
29. Are you available to work on Saturdays and Sundays?	L	I	_____
30. Do you have any form of disability?	L	I	_____

10.2 The pay raise

Objectives

1. To further your understanding of salary administration.

2. To examine the many facets of performance criteria, performance criteria weighting, performance evaluation, and rewards.

Instructions

1. Working in small groups, complete the Pay Raise Worksheet.

2. After the class reconvenes, group spokespersons present group findings.

Pay raise worksheet

April Knepper is the new supervisor of an assembly team. It is time for her to make pay raise allocations for her subordinates. She has been budgeted $30,000 to allocate among her seven subordinates as pay raises. There have been some ugly grievances in other work teams over past allocations, so April has been advised to base the allocations on objective criteria that can be quantified, weighted, and computed in numerical terms. After she makes her allocations, April must be prepared to justify her decisions. All of the evaluative criteria available to April are summarized as follows:

| Employee | EEO status | Seniority | Output rating* | Absent rate | Supervisory ratings | | | |
					Skills	Initiative	Attitude	Personal
David Bruce	Caucasian Male	15 yrs.	0.58	0.5%	Good	Poor	Poor	Nearing retirement. Wife just passed away. Having adjustment problems.
Eric Cattalini	Caucasian Male	12 yrs.	0.86	2.0	Excellent	Good	Excellent	Going to night school to finish his BA degree.
Chua Li	Asian Male	7 yrs.	0.80	3.5	Good	Excellent	Excellent	Legally deaf.

(Continued)

Marilee Miller	Black Female	1 yr.	0.50	10.0	Poor	Poor	Poor	Single parent with three children.
Victor Munoz	Hispanic Male	3 yrs.	0.62	2.5	Poor	Average	Good	Has six dependents. Speaks little English.
Derek Thompson	Caucasian Male	11 yrs.	0.64	8.0	Excellent	Average	Average	Married to rich wife. Personal problems.
Sarah Vickers	Caucasian Female	8 yrs.	0.76	7.0	Good	Poor	Poor	Women's activist. Wants to create a union.

*Output rating determined by production rate less errors and quality problem.

Chapter Eleven
Managing the Diverse Workforce

"e pluribus unum"

Chapter Outline

Learning Objectives

After studying Chapter 11, you will know:

1. How changes in the U.S. workforce make diversity a critical organizational and managerial issue.

2. The distinction between affirmative action and managing diversity.

3. How companies can gain a competitive edge by effectively managing diversity.

4. What challenges a company is likely to encounter with a diverse workforce.

5. How an organization can take steps to cultivate diversity.

Setting the Stage

Cisco Beats a Path to Disabled Workers

Students at the Rochester Institute for the Deaf might have a Cisco Systems career in their future. The high-tech juggernaut is looking to set up a recruiting relationship with the technical training departments of the school as part of an ongoing push to hire more disabled employees. Sounds like a nice press release. But this initiative is hardly a token effort. Cisco, the company that makes the computer routers that direct traffic on the Internet, also recruits disabled employees through disability organizations, including regional groups such as Project Hired, TransAccess, Sensory Access, and national groups such as the National Disability Business Council. In fact, the company recently took the extra step of developing and implementing its own curriculum for teaching disability etiquette and outreach techniques to Cisco recruiters. The aim was to increase their ability to communicate effectively and comfortably with disabled potential hires. Bottom line? Cisco gets it when it comes to working with the disabled.

Cisco's logic here is simple. Employees with disabilities are good for business. They add diversity to a workforce, something that Cisco CEO John Chambers has long trumpeted as a factor in improved productivity and creativity. Furthermore, some of the company's customers have disabled employees. So acclimating Cisco's workers to professional contact with disabled workers inside the company has the added benefit of enabling them to work productively with Cisco clients. "We have employees with disabilities, and we have customers with employees with disabilities whose information needs must be met. As a result, we do our best to accommodate their communications needs," says Nancy Cruz, who oversees Cisco's disability policies and recruiting efforts.

Cisco CEO John Chambers has long trumpeted that diversity in a workforce improves productivity and creativity.
[Courtesy of Cisco Systems, Inc.]

That's a nice sound bite. But the truth is, Cisco really practices what it preaches. For example, the company maintains a pool of TDD (text teletype) devices for use on an on-call basis by its deaf and hearing-impaired employees. That's a solid proactive step to ensure that these employees can work in any part of the company and still find a key communications tool at their fingertips. These extra efforts do make a difference. Just ask Lee Mudrock. A hearing-impaired electrical engineer at Cisco, Mudrock claims the company provides him with everything he needs, including a TDD and other assistive-tech tools. "Having been here several years, I know Cisco is really interested in my abilities. I have everything I need for my job," he says.

Diversity training

As you learned in Chapter 10, employees can be developed in a variety of ways. *Diversity training programs* attempt to identify and reduce hidden biases and develop the skills needed to effectively manage a diversified workforce. Traditionally, most management training has been based on the assumption that "managing" means managing a homogeneous, often white-male, full-time workforce. But gender, race, culture, and other differences create an additional layer of complexity.[23]

More than 50 percent of all U.S. organizations sponsor some sort of diversity training. Typically, diversity training has two components: awareness building and skill building.

Awareness building   *Awareness building* is designed to increase awareness of the meaning and importance of valuing diversity.[24] Its aim is not to teach specific skills but to sensitize employees to the assumptions they make about others and how these assumptions affect their behaviors, decisions, and judgment.

To build awareness, people are taught to become familiar with myths, stereotypes, and cultural differences as well as the organizational barriers that inhibit the full contributions of all employees. They develop a better understanding of corporate culture, requirements for success, and career choices that affect opportunities for advancement.

In most companies, the "rules" for success are ambiguous, unwritten, and perhaps inconsistent with written policy. A common problem for women and minorities is that they are unaware of many of the rules that are obvious to people in the mainstream. Valuing diversity means teaching the unwritten "rules" or cultural values to those who need to know them and changing the rules when necessary to benefit employees and hence the organization. It also requires inviting "outsiders" in and giving them access to information and meaningful relationships with people in power.

Skill building   *Skill building* is designed to allow all employees and managers to develop the skills they need to deal effectively with one another and with customers in a diverse environment. Most of the skills taught are interpersonal, such as active listening, coaching, and giving feedback. Hewlett-Packard and Wisconsin Power and Light provide both awareness and skill building. These companies attempt to transfer the training to the job by asking managers to develop personal action plans before they leave the program. For example, a manager may recognize from training that his record of retaining African-American sales representatives is poor and plans to spend more time coaching these salespeople.[25]

Experiential exercises and videotapes often are used in the training programs to help expose stereotypes and encourage employees to discuss fears, biases, and problems. One widely used training tool is a series of seven 30-minute videotapes titled *Valuing Diversity,* produced by Copeland-Griggs with funding from 50 corporations, including Hewlett-Packard, Xerox, U.S. West, and Procter & Gamble. Table 11.7 provides a set of guidelines for designing effective diversity training.

Retaining employees

As replacing qualified and experienced workers becomes more difficult and costly, retaining good workers will become much more important. Aetna estimates its annual turnover expense at more than $100 million—largely money spent on training new employees and the costs of their lower productivity during the learning period. When Deloitte & Touche had problems retaining minorities and women, top executives moved quickly. The firm not only ameliorated its problems, it created a more positive environment for all employees. A number of policies and strategies, like the following, can be used to increase retention of all employees, especially those who are "different" from the norm.[26]

Support groups   Companies can help form minority networks and other support groups to promote information exchange and social support. Support groups provide

table 11.7
Guidelines for
diversity training

1. **Position training in your broad diversity strategy.** Training is one important element of managing diversity, but on its own it will probably fail. Culture change means altering underlying assumptions and systems that guide organizational behavior. Training programs must be internally consistent with, and complement, other initiatives focused on culture change.

2. **Do a thorough needs analysis.** Do not start training prematurely. As with any training program, eagerness to "do something" may backfire unless you have assessed what specific aspects of diversity need attention first. Focus groups help identify what employees view as priority issues.

3. **Distinguish between education and training.** Education helps build awareness and understanding but does not teach usable skills. Training involves activities that enhance skills in areas such as coaching, conducting performance appraisals, and adapting communications styles. Education and training are both important but they're not the same.

4. **Use a participative design process.** Tap a multitude of parties to ensure that the content and tone of the program are suitable to everyone involved. Outsider consultants often provide fresh perspectives, and have credibility. Insiders have specific company knowledge, sensitivity to local issues, and long-standing relationships with company members. Balance these various sources.

5. **Test the training thoroughly before rollout.** Given the sensitivity, even volatility, of diversity issues, use diversity councils and advocacy groups to pilot the programs. Build in ample feedback time to allow these groups to address sensitive concerns, and refine the training.

6. **Incorporate diversity programs into the core training curriculum.** One-time programs do not have a lasting impact. Blend the program's content into other training programs such as performance appraisal, coaching, and so on.

Source: Reprinted with permission from January 1993 issue of *Training* magazine. Copyright 1993. Lakewood Publications, Minneapolis, MN. All rights reserved. Not for resale.

emotional and career support for members who traditionally have not been included in the majority's informal groups. They also can help diverse employees understand work norms and the corporate culture.

At Apple headquarters in Cupertino, California, support groups include a Jewish cultural group, a gay/lesbian group, an African-American group, and a technical women's group. Avon encourages employees to organize into African-American, Hispanic, and Asian networks by granting them official recognition and providing a senior manager to provide advice. These groups help new employees adjust and provide direct feedback to management on problems that concern the groups. Avon once had a women's network, but that group disbanded years ago. With women holding 79 percent of management positions, female employees at Avon believed the group was no longer necessary.

Mentoring

Many people have been puzzled at the inability of women and minorities to move up beyond a certain point on the corporate ladder (the glass ceiling). To help these groups enter the informal network that provides exposure to top management and access to information about organizational politics, many companies have implemented formal mentoring programs. **Mentors** are higher-level managers who help ensure that high-potential people are introduced to top management and socialized into the norms and values of the organization.

Procter & Gamble's "Mentor Up" program has been working very successfully. The number of women at the general manager/vice-president level has more than tripled in the last decade. Today women account for over 30 percent of the vice-president/senior management positions in the organization.[27]

mentors Higher level managers who help ensure that high-potential people are introduced to top management and socialized into the norms and values of the organization.

Career development and promotions
Because they are hitting a glass ceiling, many of the most talented women and minority group members are leaving their organizations in search of better opportunities elsewhere. In response, companies such as Mobil Oil and Honeywell have established teams to evaluate the career progress of women, minorities, and employees with disabilities and to devise ways to move them up through the ranks.

Systems accommodation
Organizations can support diversity by recognizing cultural and religious holidays, differing modes of dress, and dietary restrictions, as well as accommodating the needs of individuals with disabilities. One important disabling condition is AIDS. Under the ADA, organizations must accommodate AIDS sufferers as it would persons with any other disability, permitting and even encouraging them to continue working for as long as they are able and, if warranted, allowing flexible scheduling. AIDS sufferers also are eligible for corporate health and disability benefits.

Accountability
For diversity efforts to succeed, managers must be held accountable for workforce development. Organizations must ensure that their performance appraisal and reward systems reinforce the importance of effective diversity management. Baxter Health Care, Coca-Cola, and Merck (as well as Prudential and Kodak mentioned earlier) all tie compensation to managers' performance in diversity efforts.[28]

For 25 years, U.S. corporations were striving to integrate their workforces because of regulatory and social responsibility pressures. Today globalization, changing demographics, and the expansion of ethnic markets at home have made managing a diverse workforce a bottom-line issue. Labor shortages are causing companies to compete with one another in hiring, developing, and retaining women, minorities, and others who differ from the norm in age, appearance, physical ability, and lifestyle. Companies now realize that to remain competitive in the coming years, they will have to make managing diversity a strategic priority.

Key terms

Glass ceiling, p. 345

Managing diversity, p. 342

Mentors, p. 363

Monolithic organization, p. 357

Multicultural organization, p. 358

Plural organization, p. 358

Sexual harassment, p. 345

Summary of learning objectives

Now that you have studied Chapter 11, you should know:

How changes in the U.S. workforce are making diversity a critical organizational and managerial issue.

The labor force is getting older, more ethnic, with a higher proportion of women. And while the absolute number of workers is increasing, the growth in jobs is outpacing the numerical growth of workers. In addition, the jobs that are being created frequently require higher skills than the typical worker can provide—thus, we are seeing a growing skills gap. To be competitive, organizations can no longer take the traditional approach of depending on white males to form the core of the workforce. Today, managers must look broadly to make use of talent wherever it can be found. As the labor market changes, organizations that can recruit, develop, motivate, and retain a diverse workforce will have a competitive advantage.

The distinction between affirmative action and managing diversity.

Affirmative action is designed to correct past exclusion of women and minorities from U.S. organizations. But despite the accomplishments of affirmative action, it has not resulted in eliminating barriers that prevent individuals from reaching their full potential. Managing diversity goes beyond hiring people who are different from the norm and seems to support, nurture, and use employee difference to the organization's advantage.

How companies can gain a competitive edge by effectively managing diversity.

Managing diversity is a bottom-line issue. If managers are effective at managing diversity, they will have an easier time attracting, retaining, and motivating the best employees. They will be more effective at marketing to diverse consumer groups in the United States and globally. They will enjoy a workforce that is more creative, more innovative, and better able to solve problems. In addition, they are likely to increase the flexibility and responsiveness of the organization to environmental change.

What challenges a company is likely to encounter with a diverse workforce.

The challenges for managers created by a diverse workforce include decreased group cohesiveness, communication problems, mistrust and tension, and stereotyping. These challenges can be turned into advantages by training and effective management.

How an organization can take steps to cultivate diversity.

To be successful, organizational efforts to manage diversity must have top management support and commitment. Organizations should first undertake a thorough assessment of their cultures, policies, and practices, as well as the demographics of their labor pools and customer bases. Only after this diagnosis has been completed is the company in position to initiate programs designed to attract, develop, motivate, and retain a diverse workforce.

Discussion questions

1. What opportunities do you see as a result of changes in our nation's workforce?

2. Is prejudice declining in our society? In our organizations? Why or why not?

3. What distinctions can you make between affirmative action and managing diversity?

4. How can we overcome obstacles to diversity such as mistrust and tension, stereotyping, and communication problems?

5. How can organizations meet the special needs of different groups (e.g., work and family issues) without appearing to show favoritism to those particular sets of employees?

6. How can diversity give a company a competitive edge? Can diversity really make a difference in the bottom line? How?

Concluding Case

Diversity is in good hands at Allstate

In today's competitive environment, companies continue to look for ways to improve their performance and achieve corporate objectives. The task is not easy, but the team of HR executives at Allstate Corp. has found that its diversity strategy has become one of the company's most potent competitive weapons. It has long been Allstate's position that diversity is neither about political mandates nor legal obligation. Rather, the company's vision is that: "Diversity is Allstate's strategy for leveraging differences in order to create a competitive advantage." This strategy has two major points: one internally focused, and the other externally focused.

According to Joan Crockett, VP of human resources, the internal diversity focus is about "unlocking the potential for excellence in all workers by providing them the tools, resources, and opportunities to succeed." The external focus of diversity is about making certain that the workforce matches the experiences, backgrounds, and sensitivities as the markets it serves. In this context, Allstate managers view diversity not as a goal, but as a process that is integrated into the daily life of the company.

In the early days, Allstate's commitment to diversity didn't always link recruitment, development, and retention strategies to business performance. The company focused more on affirmative action and diversity awareness through education and training. And while these initiatives were considered innovative in their day, they had no articulated business outcome. Carlton Yearwood, director of diversity management, notes that the key question has become: "How do you take this workforce of differences and bring them together in a more powerful way so that it can impact business results?" Allstate has taken four specific steps:

Step One: Succession Planning. A diverse slate of candidates is identified and developed for each key position. Allstate's integrated process enables it to track and measure key drivers of career development and career opportunities, ensuring the company's future workforce will be diverse at all levels. Allstate's succession planning has made a difference that is easy to measure. Employment of women and minorities has grown at a rate far surpassing national averages. Today, 40 percent of Allstate's executives and managers are women, while 21 percent are minorities.

Step Two: Development. Through the company's employee

It has long been Allstate's position that diversity is neither about political mandates nor legal obligations. *[Courtesy of Allstate Insurance Company]*

development process, all employees receive an assessment of their current job skills and a road map for developing the critical skills necessary for advancement. Options include education, coaching and mentoring, classroom training, and the like. Leaders are provided employee feedback upon which they can base future development plans. In addition, all of Allstate's nonagent employees with service of more than 1 year have completed diversity training courses, which represent an investment in excess of 640,000 hours in classroom time.

Step Three: Measurement. Twice a year the company takes a snapshot of all 53,000 employees through a survey called the Diversity Index. As part of a larger on-line employee survey and feedback process called the Quarterly Leadership Measurement System (QLMS), the Diversity Index taps the following questions:

1. To what extent does our company deliver quality service to customers regardless of their ethnic background, gender, age, etc.?
2. To what extent are you treated with respect and dignity at work? To what extent does your immediate manager/team leader seek out and utilize the different backgrounds and perspectives of all employees in your work group?
3. How often do you observe insensitive behavior at work; e.g., inappropriate comments or jokes about ethnic background, gender, age, etc.?
4. To what extent do you work in an environment of trust where employees/agents are free to offer different opinions?

Management communicates the results of this survey and actively solicits feedback from employees on creating action plans to solve problems and improve work processes.

Step Four: Accountability and Reward. To link compensation to the company's diversity goals, 25 percent of each manager's merit pay is based on the diversity index and the QLMS. Karleen Zuzich, assistant vice president of HR, says that this sharpens the focus on the initiative. "What you measure is what people focus on. This really sends a clear signal that management of people and doing that well is really important."

Allstate has received considerable recognition for its diversity efforts. Most recently, the company was among the first companies to be ranked by *Fortune* as one of the "50 Best Companies for Asians, Blacks and Hispanics." *Minority MBA Magazine* included Allstate on its list of "Top Ten Companies for Minority Managers." *Working Mother, Vista,* and *Hispanic* likewise have cited Allstate. Although accolades such as these are nice, Allstate views them as an opportunity to improve further. According to Crockett, "Through the process of applying for awards and citations like these, we can gain the feedback needed to continually improve our results. We are convinced that the outstanding results Allstate employees deliver every day for shareholders and policyholders are, in part, the fruits of our diversity strategy. And we expect the steps we have taken to embrace diversity as a business strategy to continue paying off in the years to come."

Questions

1. What competitive advantages is Allstate likely to gain from a diversity strategy?

2. Should competitiveness be the major issue, or is social responsibility more important?

3. What other diversity initiatives would you suggest the company undertake?

Sources: Joan Crockett, "Diversity: Winning Competitive Advantage through a Diverse Workforce," *HR Focus,* 76, no. 5 (May 1999), pp. 9–10; Joan Crockett, "Diversity As a Business Strategy," *Management Review,* 88, no. 5 (May 1999), p. 62; Louisa Wah, "Diversity at Allstate: A Competitive Weapon," *Management Review,* 88, no. 7 (July-August 1999), pp. 24–30.

Experiential Exercises
11.1 Being different

Objectives

1. To increase your awareness of the feeling of "being different."
2. To better understand the context of "being different."

Instructions

1. Working alone, complete the Being Different Worksheet.
2. In small groups, compare worksheets and prepare answers to the discussion questions.

3. After the class reconvenes, group spokespersons present group findings.

Discussion questions

1. Were there students who experienced being different in situations that surprised you?
2. How would you define "being different"?
3. How can this exercise be used to good advantage?

Being different worksheet

Think back to a recent situation in which you experienced "being different," and answer the following questions:

1. Describe the situation in which you experienced "being different."

_____

_____

_____

_____

2. Explain how you felt.

_____

_____

_____

_____

_____

3. What did you do as a result of "being different"? (That is, in what way was your behavior changed by the feeling of "being different"?)

_____

_____

_____

_____

_____

4. What did others in the situation do? How do you think they felt about the situation?

_____

_____

_____

_____

5. How did the situation turn out in the end?

_____

_____

_____

_____

6. As a result of that event, how will you probably behave differently in the future? In what way has the situation changed you?

_____

_____

_____

_____

11.2 He works, she works

Instructions

1. Complete the He Works, She Works Worksheet. In the appropriate spaces, write what you think the stereotyped responses would be. Do not spend too much time considering any one item. Rather, respond quickly and let your first impression or thought guide your answer.

2. Compare your individual responses with those of other class members or participants. It is interesting to identify and discuss the most frequently used stereotypes.

He works, she works worksheet

The family picture is on *his* desk: *He's a solid, responsible family man.*

His desk is cluttered:_____

_____

_____

He's talking with co-workers: _____

_____

_____

He's not at his desk: _____

_____

_____

The family picture is on *her* desk: *Her family will come before her career.*

Her desk is cluttered:_____

_____

_____

She's talking with co-workers: _____

_____

_____

She's not at her desk: _____

_____

_____

The family picture is on *his* desk: *He's a solid, responsible family man.*

He's not in the office: _____

_____

_____

He's having lunch with the boss: _____

_____

The boss criticized *him*: _____

_____

He got an unfair deal: _____

_____

He's getting married: _____

_____

He's going on a business trip: _____

_____

He's leaving for a better job: _____

_____

_____

The family picture is on *her* desk: *Her family will come before her career.*

She's not in the office: _____

_____

_____

She's having lunch with the boss: _____

_____

The boss criticized *her*: _____

_____

She got an unfair deal: _____

_____

She's getting married: _____

_____

She's going on a business trip: _____

_____

She's leaving for a better job: _____

_____

_____

Source: F. Luthans, *Organizational Behavior* (New York: McGraw-Hill, 1989), pp. 224–25. ●

Integrating Case

The merger of Federal Express and the Flying Tigers Line

It was January 1990. Thomas R. Oliver, senior vice president of International Operations for Federal Express Corporation, was on his way to meet with the members of his "Tigerclaws" Committee. The operational merger of Flying Tigers with Federal Express was supposed to have been concluded last August. Yet anticipated and unanticipated problems kept surfacing. International operations were draining financial resources, and there were other problems that had to be immediately resolved.

Several days ago, Mr. Oliver had met with Mr. Fred Smith, the company founder and CEO, and had been assigned the job of heading a special task force whose purpose was to direct the Flying Tigers' merger efforts and resolve the resulting problems. Mr. Oliver requested, and got, representatives of senior executives from every department of the company to form what he named the Tigerclaws Committee (see exhibit "The Tigerclaws Committee"). This committee had the power to cut across departmental bureaucratic lines. It had the resources of all the departments behind it to reach fast-track solutions to any problems in existence. Even with

such commitments, Mr. Oliver realized what a formidable task he and his committee were facing.

Express and Freight Forwarding Industries

In 1990, sending documents or packages by priority mail was viewed as a necessary convenience, rather than a luxury. The domestic market was led by Federal Express Corporation with 53 percent of the market, followed by United Parcel Service at 19 percent. The U.S. Postal Service had 3 to 4 percent of the market.[1] The overnight letter traffic was characterized by slow growth because of the increased use of facsimile machines.

The increasing competition between express delivery services and the traditional air freight industry was changing the face of international cargo transportation. Many independent freight carriers complained that big couriers and integrated carriers were poaching on their market niches. Others ignored the competition, believing that the more personalized relationships provided by the traditional air freight companies would keep clients coming back. Still, such companies as Federal Express were having a big effect on the air freight industry. Express couriers were building their nondocument business by 25 to 30 percent a year.

Express Services in the United States

Federal Express, United Parcel Service (UPS), Airborne Express, and the U.S. Postal Service were quickly introducing services that promised to translate the fundamentals of speed and information into a powerful competitive edge. They were stressing good service at lower costs. For example, UPS had started offering discounts to its bigger customers and shippers that shipped over 250 pieces weekly. In addition, UPS was building an $80 million computer and telecommunications center to provide support for all operations worldwide. Airborne's chief advantage was that it operated its own airport and had begun operating a "commerce park" around its hub in Wilmington, Ohio.

Europe

The international document and parcel express delivery business was one of the fastest-growing sectors in Europe. Although the express business would become more important in the single European market, none of the four principal players in Europe was European. DHL, Federal Express, and UPS were United States companies while TNT was Australian. Europe was not expected to produce a challenger because the "Big Four" were buying smaller rivals at such a fast pace that the odds seemed to be heavily against a comparable competitor emerging.[2]

The Tigerclaws Committee

Departments that are represented

Memphis SuperHub

Business Application

Airfreight Systems

Q.A. Audits

Planning and Administration

International Clearance

Communications

Ramp Plans/Program

Hub Operations

Personnel Services

International Operations

Central Support Services

Customer Support

COSMOS/Pulsar System Division

COO/Quality Improvement

Pacific Rim

The Asia-Pacific air express market was expanding by 20 to 30 percent annually, and the world's major air express and air freight companies had launched massive infrastructure buildups to take advantage of this growth. Industry leader DHL strengthened its access to air service by agreeing to eventually sell 57.5 percent of the equity of its international operation to Japan Air Lines, Lufthansa, and Nissho Iwai trading company. TNT Skypak's strength was in providing niche services, and its ability to tap into the emerging Asian–East European route with its European air hub. Two new U.S. entrants, Federal Express and UPS, were engaged in an undeclared price war. Willing to lose millions of dollars annually to carve out a greater market share, Federal Express already had captured about 10 percent of Pacific express business and 15 percent of freight. UPS's strategy was to control costs and to offer no-frills service at low rates. All four companies were seeking to expand the proportion of parcels, which would yield about twice the profits of the express documents business.[3]

Major Airlines

Since the common adaptation of wide-body jets, major international airlines had extra cargo space in their planes. Japan Air Lines and Lufthansa were two of the worldwide players, with most national airlines providing regional services.

Airlines were expanding and automating their cargo services to meet the challenges presented by fast-growing integrated carriers. Two strategies were being employed: (1) the development of new products to fill the gap between the demand for next-day service and traditional air cargo service and (2) computerization of internal passenger and cargo operations.[4]

The Merging Organizations: Federal Express Corporation

Frederick W. Smith, founder of Federal Express Corporation, went to Yale University, where he was awarded a now infamous "C" on an economics paper that outlined his idea for an overnight delivery service.[5] After college and military service, Smith began selling corporate jets in Little Rock, Arkansas. In 1973, he tapped his $4 million inheritance, rounded up $70 million in venture capital, and launched Federal Express, testing his college paper's thesis. The company turned profitable after three years.

Federal Express always had taken pride in its people-oriented approach and its emphasis on service to its customers. Mr. Smith believed that, in the service industry, it is the employees that make the business.[6] The philosophy of Smith and his managing staff was manifested in many ways, including: (1) extensive orientation programs, (2) training and communications programs, (3) promotion of employees from within, and (4) a tuition reimbursement program. Federal Express's "open door policy" for the expression of employee concerns also illustrated the commitment of top management to resolve problems.[7]

As to services, Federal Express stressed the importance of on-time delivery and established a 100 percent on-time delivery goal. It has achieved a record 95 percent on-time delivery. In 1990, Federal Express was one of the five U.S. firms to win the Malcolm Baldrige National Quality Award. This award was given by the U.S. government to promote quality awareness and to recognize the quality achievements of U.S. companies.

Frederick W. Smith had a vision for the overnight express delivery business. Although Federal Express was the No. 1 express firm in the United States, Mr. Smith firmly believed that globalization was the future for the express business.[8] From 1986 to 1988, Federal struggled to become a major player in international deliveries. The company ran head-on into entrenched overseas rivals, such as DHL, and onerous foreign regulations.[9]

Frustrated with the legal processes in negotiating for landing rights that were restricted by bilateral aviation treaties,[10] Mr. Smith reversed his promise to build only from within and started on a series of acquisitions. From 1987 to 1988, Federal purchased 15 minor delivery companies, mostly in Europe. In December 1988, Mr. Smith announced the merger of Tiger International, Inc., best known for its Flying Tigers airfreight service. On paper, the merger of Federal Express and Tiger International seemed to be a marriage made in heaven. As one Federal Express executive pointed out: "If we lay a route map of Flying Tigers over that of Federal Express, there is almost a perfect match. There are only one or two minor overlaps. The Flying Tigers' routes are all over the world, with highest concentration in the Pacific Rim countries, while Federal Express's routes are mostly in domestic U.S.A." As a result of the merger, Federal Express's world routes were completed. For example, the acquisition of Flying Tigers brought with it the unrestricted cargo landing rights at three Japanese airports that Federal Express had been unsuccessful in acquiring for the last three years.[11]

One high-level Federal Express employee commented that the merger brought other benefits besides routes. He said: "We got a level of expertise with the people we brought in and a number of years of experiences in the company in handling air freight . . . You have to look at this acquisition also as a defensive move. If we hadn't bought Flying Tigers, UPS might have bought Flying Tigers."

The Merging Organizations: Tiger International, Inc.

Tiger International, Inc., better known for The Flying Tigers Line, Inc., freight service, or Flying Tigers, was founded 40 years ago by Robert Prescott. Over the years, the company became modestly profitable. But in 1977, Smith won his crusade for air-cargo deregulation over the strident objection of Prescott. Heightened competition, troubled acquisitions, and steep labor costs led to big losses at Tigers. In 1986, Stephen M. Wolf, the former chairman of Republic Airline Inc., came on board at Tigers and managed to get all employees, including those represented by unions, to accept wage cuts. As Tigers rebounded financially, it was ripe to be taken over by one of the major delivery service companies. In 1988, Federal Express announced the acquisition of Tigers to the pleasure of some and dismay of others. At the announcement, some Tigers' employees shouted, "TGIF—Thank God It's Federal" or "It's purple [Federal Express] not brown [UPS]—thank goodness." In contrast, Robert Sigafoos, who wrote a corporate history of Federal Express, commented, "Prescott must be turning over in his grave."[12]

Flying Tigers always had a distinctive culture, one that partly developed from the military image of its founders. Tigers' employees stressed "Tiger Spirit" or teamwork. Since Mr. Wolf took over as the chairman and CEO at an extremely difficult time, the general orientation of Flying Tigers was to keep the company flying.

The Merger

Federal Express announced the acquisition of Flying Tigers in December 1988. However, because of government regulations, the actual operational merging of the two companies did not occur until August 1989.

One top-level Federal Express executive, with considerable expertise in mergers, described the process in the following way: "I think that after any merger you go through three phases. You come in and you have euphoria. Everybody's happy. The second phase is the transition phase. In that phase, the primary qualification that every employee must have is sadomasochistic tendencies, because you kill yourself going through it . . . And then you start coming out of that into the regeneration and regrowth phase, where you clean up all this hazy area without knowing exactly what you are going to do or thinking this works and trying it out . . . In the meantime, going through all that turmoil creates a number of problems . . . People's morale starts to dip. People start to question all the leadership. You start to see the company reorganizing, you know, trying to figure out, well, what's the best thing to do here or there or whatever and, all of a sudden, all of the confidence that ever existed in the whole world starts to diminish."

Although the two companies were supposed to now become one, problems from the merger kept surfacing. Some of these problems were to be anticipated with the merger of two companies of these sizes. However, many problems were not anticipated and had become very costly to the company.

Human Resources Management Problems

There were union questions. Federal Express traditionally had been a nonunion shop, while the Flying Tigers' employees were predominately unionized. During the merger, the National Mediation Board could not determine a majority among the pilots at Federal Express and Flying Tigers. The board requires a majority to decide the union status at any firm. Because a majority could not be determined, the mediation board decided to allow the temporary mix of union and nonunion employees until the fall of 1989, when elections would determine if there would be union representation. The ruling had created ambiguities in employee status and raised some important financial and legal issues for Federal Express, unions, and employees.[13]

An executive in the international division described Federal Express's feelings on unions: "They [Flying Tigers] had a lot of unions. Tigers was a traditional company . . . and we [Federal Express] don't dislike unions . . . Our feelings about unions is [sic] that if you get a union, you deserve it, because you have not managed your business well. We would like to think that we could keep that old family [feeling]. We realize that we can't keep the old family. It's very difficult to keep the family spirit corporatewide [after a merger]."

Tiger people had a variety of attitudes to job offers after the merger. The employees of Federal Express believed that Federal Express was a great place to work, mainly because of its people-oriented policies. Because of this belief, most of the managers thought that the Flying Tigers' employees would "welcome the merger with open arms." A communications official said: "We tried to position Federal Express as a great place to work, a wonderful place to be—cutting edge technology, a great aircraft fleet, a great employee group, good management—all those types of things."

Flying Tigers had a rich and long history. Tiger employees prided themselves on their team spirit and their willingness to take pay cuts for the good of The Flying Tiger Line, Inc., during the lean years. Employees proudly displayed items with the Tiger logo on them.

A long-time Tiger employee and member of one of the pre-merger Tiger committees remarked on the job offers: "For the employees, it [the merger] was a spectrum, we've got all of them on a line. Up in front, we've got those employees for whom the merger was the best thing that ever happened to them. In the back, you've got the employees where it was the worst thing that ever happened—because of personal things, they decided to leave the company. And then there's the group of employees in the middle, which really composed the majority of Flying Tigers' employees, that it really didn't matter one way or the other since they never moved. All they did was change their uniforms from Friday to Monday. They're basically doing the same jobs in the same locations." A member of his family and many friends refused to accept a job with Federal Express. He explained their refusal, by saying: "Because [Federal Express was] taking the name away. You were taking the history of the Flying Tiger line away . . . because we were a small company, we were like a close-knit family." Another middle-level former Tiger said, "Although a lot of merger information was provided to people at headquarters in L.A., people at other locations, like Boston, received less information." She said that some Tigers refused the job offer for the following reason: "They left, I think, just because of the attitude that . . . you're taking Flying Tigers away and I don't want to go with you." Some Tigers hoped that Federal Express would permit them to keep the Flying Tiger name or change the company name to Federal Tigers.

There were cultural differences. A Federal Express executive on the Tigerclaws Committee commented on cultural differences by saying: "The difference was astounding. Absolutely astounding. Federal Express's employees, typically, they seem to be younger, we're all in uniforms, enthusiastic about the company. You can walk around Federal Express and everybody can tell you what the corporate philosophy is . . . I remember standing in the Los Angeles airport facility . . . it's typical Federal Express. And you go over to the Tiger facility and here are all of these much older guys standing around. None of them in any type of uniform, clothes were all over the mat, there was [sic] no apparent standards, whatsoever. You know, kicking some of the packages, tossing them, throwing. It was just . . . just terrible. I couldn't believe it. But that was part of the way they did business. They referred to a lot of the cargo that they carried as big, ugly freight. And to us . . . we go around thinking every customer's package is the most important thing we carry."

A former Tiger employee shared her perspective on the differences: "Most of the employees that you dealt with you had known for a lot of years. We used to work together side by side very closely for 20 years. And this company, Federal Express, isn't even 20 years old. You walk into a meeting or classroom or something . . . Federal Express people are introducing themselves to other Federal Express people. Tiger people found that really hard to believe—that you didn't know everybody at Federal Express."

During the announcement of the merger, Mr. Smith made a job offer to all the employees of Flying Tigers. Almost 90 percent of the 6,600 former Tiger employees took the offer. In a two-week period, from July 15 to 31, over 4,000 new jobs were to be created and Tiger employees transferred to these jobs. Many employees had to be relocated, because the old Tiger hub in Columbus, Ohio, was phased out, and primarily only freight and maintenance personnel were kept at the hub in Los Angeles. Some job placements were troublesome, because the human resources department had difficulty obtaining job descriptions and pay scales from Flying Tigers. During the haste, there were quite a number of mismatches of jobs and employees.

One of Federal Express's personnel officers remarked: "I was concerned about being able to meet employee's expectations. A lot of times people coming in from outside of Federal Express have this—I mean it's a great place, but they have this picture that it's a fairy tale place, and that there aren't any real problems and that everybody gets his own way. So I was concerned about the expectations that people brought, both positive and negative. How are we going to make people feel real good about the company?"

To help former Flying Tigers' employees determine whether to accept Federal Express's job offers, Federal Express provided the employees with detailed information about the company. Videotapes introducing Federal Express and explaining the benefits of working for the company were mailed to the homes of Tiger employees. Additionally, many Tiger employees were flown into Federal Express's headquarters in Memphis and given the "grand tour." "Express Teams," groups of four to five employees, visited Flying Tigers' locations and gave them previews of what it was like to work for Federal Express.

Regarding expectations, one long-time Tiger remarked: "There's still a lot of unhappy people in Memphis that came out of L.A., because I think they expected an awful lot. They had the option of saying no to a job and being out on the street looking for something else, or they could come to Memphis and have Federal Express be their employer. And there are a lot of people that still take offense at the fact that Federal Express bought Flying Tigers. But those people have an attitude that they have to deal with." Another former Tiger remarked: "And I honestly thought that by going from a small company to a large company, I was just going to be another number. But . . . it's also their attention to people. All of the hype and promotion they did before T-day [merger day] to Flying Tiger people that they were people oriented . . . we really didn't [know] what that meant and what it would mean to us individually until we became employees."

Summary

Since 1985, Federal Express's international business had lost approximately $74 million and given company executives a lifetime supply of headaches.[14] To improve Federal Express's competitive position with its overseas rivals and overcome the foreign regulations regarding landing rights, Frederick Smith announced in December 1988 the acquisition of Tiger International, Inc. Although the combined companies would have $2.1 billion in debt, Flying Tigers was expected to provide Federal Express with desperately needed international delivery routes. The Tiger acquisition would allow Federal Express to use its own planes for overseas package delivery where Federal Express used to contract other carriers. In addition, Tigers' sizable long-range fleet could be used to achieve dominance in the international heavy-freight business that Federal Express had yet to crack.

Suppose you had been in Thomas Oliver's shoes and were the head of the Tigerclaws Committee. What were the major problems and opportunities facing Federal Express? What should be the priorities of the Tigerclaws Committee? How would you solve or reduce the problems and exploit the opportunities?

Source: A case study by Howard S. Tu, Fogelman College of Business and Economics, Memphis State University; and Sherry E. Sullivan, Bowling Green State University. ●

Case Incidents

Questionable purchasing practices

Motton Electronics was widely respected in the industry as being fair, dependable, and progressive. Cy Bennett, founder of the company, was chair of the board and majority stockholder. One of the company's progressive practices was to employ professional managers as members of top management. Each carefully selected manager received an excellent salary for performing his or her job. None of the top management group served on the board.

One month ago, Bennett reported to the board that he had facts proving that the director of purchasing for the company, Russell Hale, was giving preferential treatment to certain vendors and, in turn, was receiving merchandise and money. After the chair presented the evidence, the board formally condemned such purchasing practices by unanimous vote.

Immediately following this action, a vocal board member asserted that he believed the chief executive officer was responsible for all employee behavior on the job, that such administrative negligence should not be tolerated, and that the board needed a policy on the issue. This statement triggered an extensive discussion among the directors on topics such as shared responsibility for subordinates' actions, relevant duties of the board of directors, and related policy implications.

The meeting ended with a motion, unanimously supported, that Bennett (1) decide on appropriate measures regarding the errant director of purchasing and (2) develop and implement a policy on shared responsibility.

Bennett believed his prompt action on these matters would be critical to managerial performance, to the firm's profitability, and to the value of his majority block of company stock.

Source: J. Champion and J. Hames, *Critical Incidents in Management: Decision and Policy Issues,* 6th ed. (Burr Ridge, IL: Richard D. Irwin, 1989). ●

Workforce reduction policy

Five years ago Wireweave, Inc., moved to a rural area 25 miles outside a large southern city. The company, formerly situated in a midwestern industrial city, chose this location primarily because of the lower wage rates paid in the community, a nonunion tradition in the region, and a favorable tax situation.

Wireweave, a manufacturer of wire products, has two major high-volume product lines: aluminum wire screen and dish racks. The dish racks are supplied to several appliance manufacturers for use in automatic dishwashers.

Because of intense industry competition, Wireweave's management realized several years ago that if Wireweave was to continue manufacturing aluminum wire screen and dish racks—and even stay in business—it would have to procure up-to-date equipment, become more automated and computerized, and even use robots for some of the hottest and dustiest jobs. After a two-year evaluation of production needs and an analysis of technologically advanced manufacturing equipment (including robots), Wireweave purchased equipment that would modernize production and replace 65 employees, representing about 33 percent of the total labor force. Significant labor costs would be saved by this employment reduction. As a result, Steve Jackson, president

of Wireweave, expected the company to regain its competitiveness and profitability.

The following spring, shortly after installing the new equipment, Jackson called in Muriel Fincher, human resources director, and told her that the company could no longer afford to employ the unneeded workers. He requested that she decide on an acceptable plan for reducing company employment by 65 persons, and the sooner the better in terms of company profitability. Jackson also asked that she recommend a specific operating policy covering future workforce reductions.

Fincher had successfully handled some tough challenges as human resources director, but the latest assignments from Jackson were the most difficult ones she had faced. As Fincher considered relevant options and constraints, her deliberations were dominated by three factors: (1) the company's economic and ethical responsibilities to terminated employees, (2) the potential moral problems for employees who would be retained, and (3) the pressure from Jackson for prompt decision and action.

Source: J. Champion and J. James, *Critical Incidents in Management: Decision and Policy Issues,* 6th ed. (Burr Ridge, IL: Richard D. Irwin. 1989). ●

Part Four
Leading: Mobilizing People

Foundations of Management

Managing
The External Environment
Managerial Decision Making

Planning:
Delivering Strategic Value

Planning and Strategic Management
Ethics and Corporate Responsibility
International Management
New Ventures

Strategy Implementation

Organizing: Building
a Dynamic Organization

Organization Structure
The Responsive Organization
Human Resources Management
Managing the Diverse Workforce

Leading:
Mobilizing People

Leadership
Motivating for Performance
Managing Teams
Communicating

Controlling:
Learning and Changing

Managerial Control
Managing Technology and Innovation
Creating and Managing Change

Now that you know about organizing and staffing, Part 4 further elaborates on managing people by discussing the third function of management: leading. Effective managers know how to lead others toward unit and organizational success. Chapter 12 explores the essential components of leadership, including the use of power in the organization. Chapter 13 focuses on motivating people, with implications for enhancing performance. Chapter 14 examines work teams, including the management of relationships between groups. Finally, Chapter 15 addresses a vital management activity: communication. Here, you will learn how to maximize your effectiveness in communicating with other people throughout the organization.

Chapter Twelve
Leadership

Every soldier has a right to competent command.

—*Julius Caesar*

Chapter Outline

Vision
Leading and Managing
Leading and Following
Power and Leadership
    Sources of Power
Traditional Approaches to Understanding
    Leadership
    Leader Traits
    Leader Behaviors
    Situational Approaches to Leadership
Contemporary Perspectives on Leadership
    Charismatic Leadership
    Transformational Leadership
    Post-Heroic Leadership
Developing Your Leadership Skills

Learning Objectives

After studying Chapter 12, you will know:

1. What it means to be a leader.

2. How a good vision helps you be a better leader.

3. How to understand and use power.

4. The personal traits and skills of effective leaders.

5. The behaviors that will make you a better leader.

6. What it means to be a charismatic and transformational leader.

7. How to further your own leadership development.

Setting the Stage

A Few Good Leaders

- Carley Fiorina of Hewlett-Packard and Debby Hopkins of Lucent are two of the most powerful women in U.S. business. They share a philosophy of nurturing the company, not as just an income sheet and a balance sheet, but as "an organic, living, breathing thing" (p. 132). States Fiorina, "A company is people—people with brains and hearts and guts. If you're a leader, you've got to capture the whole person. People want to see you . . . challenge the mind and capture the heart" (p. 139).

- Bill Ford Jr., chairman of Ford Motor, says that the way to enhance Ford's brand, sell more cars and services, and boost Ford's share price is to take care of Ford's employees, its community, and its environment. He means it. "I'm in this for my children and my grandchildren. I want them to inherit a legacy they're proud of. I don't want anybody . . . to have to apologize for working for Ford Motor Co. In fact, I want the opposite. I want them to look and say, 'What a difference we made!' " (p. 124).

- David S. Potrruck transformed Charles Schwab, the traditional financial services company, into a prototype of how a huge company can move quickly and compete successfully with the small, new players in the Internet age. He began by transforming himself into an executive who listens "to hear rather than to answer." He says, "The more I am known by those I want to follow me, and the more I can know them, the greater will be our ability to do great things together."

Debby Hopkins, CFO of Lucent, is one of the most powerful women in U.S. businesss.
[Gail Halaban/SABA]

- Francis Collins, director of the National Institute of Health's National Human Genome Research Institute, and J. Craig Venter, CEO of Celera Genomics, are direct competitors. They don't like each other. But, they share a vision. In 2000 they jointly announced that their organizations had deciphered the biochemical "letters" of human DNA. Knowing the genetic codes will transform medicine and lead to a revolution in the diagnosis and treatment of diseases. The joint announcement by these two visionaries marks the beginning of the genomic era.

Sources: P. Sellers, "The 50 Most Powerful Women in Business," Fortune, October 16, 2000, pp. 130–60; B. Morris, "This Ford Is Different: Idealist On Board," Fortune, April 3, 2000, pp. 122–36; F. Andrews, "Hard Lessons Learned at Schwab," The New York Times, April 30, 2000, Section 3, p. 7; F. Golden and M. D. Lemonick, "The Race Is Over," Time, July 3, 2000.

People get excited about the topic of leadership. They want to know: What makes a great leader? Executives at all levels in all industries are interested in this question. They believe the answer will bring improved organizational performance and personal career success. They hope to acquire the skills that will transform an "average" manager into a true leader like the ones described in Setting the Stage.

Fortunately, leadership can be taught—and learned. According to one source, "Leadership seems to be the marshaling of skills possessed by a majority but used by a minority. But it's something that can be learned by anyone, taught to everyone, denied to no one."[1]

What is leadership? To start with, a leader is one who influences others to attain goals. The greater the number of followers, the greater the influence. And the more successful the attainment of worthy goals, the more evident the leadership. But we must explore beyond this bare definition to capture the excitement and intrigue that devoted followers and students of leadership feel when they see a great leader in action, and to understand what organizational leaders really do and what it really takes to gain entry into *Fortune's* Hall of Fame for U.S. Business Leadership.

Outstanding leaders combine good strategic substance and effective interpersonal processes to formulate and implement strategies that produce results and sustainable competitive advantage.[2] They may launch enterprises, build organization cultures, win wars, or otherwise change the course of events.[3] They are strategists who seize opportunities others overlook, but "they are also passionately concerned with detail—all the small, fundamental realities that can make or mar the grandest of plans."[4]

Vision

vision A mental image of a possible and desirable future state of the organization.

"The leader's job is to create a vision," states Robert L. Swiggett, former chair of Kollmorgen Corporation.[5] Until a few years ago, vision was not a word one heard managers utter. But today, having a vision for the future and communicating that vision to others are known to be essential components of great leadership. "If there is no vision, there is no business," maintains entrepreneur Mark Leslie.[6] Joe Nevin, an MIS director, described leaders as "painters of the vision and architects of the journey."[7] Practicing businesspeople are not alone in this belief; academic research shows that a clear vision, and communication of the vision, lead to higher venture growth in entrepreneurial firms.[8]

A **vision** is a mental image of a possible and desirable future state of the organization. It expresses the leader's ambitions for the organization.[9] The best visions are both ideal and unique.[10] If a vision conveys an *ideal,* it communicates a standard of excellence and a clear choice of positive values. If the vision is also *unique,* it communicates and inspires pride in being different from other organizations. The choice of language is important; the words should imply a combination of realism and optimism, an action orientation, and resolution and confidence that the vision will be attained.[11]

Great leaders imagine an ideal future for their organizations that goes beyond the ordinary and beyond what others may have thought possible. They strive to realize significant achievements that others have not. In short, as the following examples show, leaders must be forward looking and clarify the directions in which they want their organizations, and even entire industries, to move.

Visions in action

Here are some examples of leaders and their visions:

- Craig McCaw is a cable television and telecommunications entrepreneur and one of the boldest leaders of the information age. One of his visions is for Teledesic, a futuristic network of 288 satellites providing high-speed video, data, and voice communications all over the planet. With the recent bankruptcy of Iridium in the same industry, some are

AOL Chairman and CEO Steve Case's vision of "ruling the Internet" involves an interactive future where software takes a backseat. *[AP/WIDE WORLD PHOTOS]*

skeptical of McCaw's Teledesic vision. But he loves big problems and big opportunities, and no one else thinks as big as he does.

- Vern Raburn's vision would do for air travel what the PC did for computing. With a revolutionary jet engine, new manufacturing techniques, and an all-digital avionics system, he intends to build a six-seater jet that goes just as far, almost as fast, and burns much less fuel at a fraction of the cost of competing jets. The plan is to open up private air travel to far more people than can now afford it. He'll go after business travelers and wealthy individuals, and also create air-limo services that will compete with major airlines' first- and business-class fares. The editor of *Flying* magazine calls the idea "mind-boggling. It would be unprecedented in the history of aviation" (p. 136). Critics think it will be impossible. But as the designer of the revolutionary jet engine says, "They think we can't do it because *they* can't. It's the 'if it doesn't exist, it can't exist' theorem" (p. 136).

- Steve Case and Bill Gates have visions that are simultaneously the same and different. Each wants to rule the Internet, and each wants a company with the largest market capitalization in the world. But they differ as to what "ruling the Internet" will look like. For Gates and Microsoft, the vision is domination via software. For Case and AOL Time Warner, the vision is an interactive future in which software takes a backseat to content, brands, marketing, customer relationships, and the creation of Internet communities—a "superstore of interactivity" (p. 68). The two seem headed for a showdown, rather than toward a future that encompasses both visions complementarily.

- Phil Turner was facilities manager at Raychem Corporation, fixing toilets and air conditioners. But rather than believing that the workers in the facilities were performing menial jobs and making only trivial contributions to the organization, Turner viewed their work as a mission—to make people feel good, "to lift people's spirits through beauty, cleanliness, and functionality, enthusiasm, good cheer, and excellence."

Sources: J. Kouzes and B. Posner, *The Leadership Challenge* (San Francisco: Jossey-Bass, 1995); E. Schonfeld, "The Little (Jet) Engine That Could," *Fortune,* July 24, 2000, pp. 132–42; J. Nocera, "The Men Who Would Be King," *Fortune,* February 7, 2000, pp. 66–69; B. Morris and B. J. Feder, "Can Craig McCaw Keep His Satellites from Crashing?," *The New York Times,* June 4, 2000, Section 3, pp. 1, 6, 7. ●

As you can see, visions can be small or large and can exist throughout all organizational levels as well as at the very top. The important points are that (1) a vision is necessary for effective leadership; (2) a person or team can develop a vision for any job, work unit, or organization; and (3) many people, including managers who do not develop into strong leaders, do not develop a clear vision—instead, they focus on performing or surviving on a day-by-day basis.

Put another way, leaders must know what they want.[12] And other people must understand what that is. The leader must be able to articulate the vision, clearly and often. Other people throughout the organization should understand the vision and be able to state it clearly themselves. That's a start. But the vision still means nothing until the leader and followers take action to turn the vision into reality.[13]

Two metaphors reinforce the important concept of vision.[14] The first is the jigsaw puzzle. It is much easier to put a puzzle together if you have the picture on the box cover in front of you. Without the picture, or vision, the lack of direction is likely to result in frustration and failure. The second metaphor is the slide projector. Imagine a projector that is out of focus. If you had to watch blurred images for a long period of time, you would get confused, impatient, and disoriented. You would stop following the presentation and lose respect for the presenter. It is the leader's job to focus the projector. That is what communicating a vision is all about: making it clear where you are heading.

Not just any vision will do, either for the leader or for the company. Whereas vision is very important for success, visions can be inappropriate, and even fail, for a variety of reasons.[15] First, an inappropriate vision may reflect merely the leader's personal needs. Such a vision can be unethical, or may fail because of lack of acceptance by the market or by those who must implement it.

Second (and related to the first), an inappropriate vision may ignore stakeholder needs. You learned about assessing stakeholders in earlier chapters. Third, the leader must stay abreast of environmental changes. Although effective leaders maintain confidence and persevere despite obstacles, the time may come when the facts dictate that the vision must change. You will learn more about change and how to manage it later in the text.

Leading and managing

Effective managers are not necessarily true leaders. Many administrators, supervisors, and even top executives execute their responsibilities without being great leaders. But these positions afford opportunity for leadership. The ability to lead effectively, then, will set the excellent managers apart from the average ones.

Managers must deal with the ongoing, day-to-day complexities of organizations. True leadership includes effectively orchestrating important change.[16] While managing requires planning and budgeting routines, leading includes setting the direction (creating a vision) for the firm. Management requires structuring the organization, staffing it with capable people, and monitoring activities; leadership goes beyond these functions by inspiring people to attain the vision. Great leaders keep people focused on moving the organization toward its ideal future, motivating them to overcome whatever obstacles lie in the way.

Many observers believe that U.S. business lost its competitive advantage because of a lack of strong leadership.[17] While many managers focus on superficial activities and worry about short-term profits and stock prices, too few have emerged as leaders who foster innovation and attainment of long-term goals. And whereas many managers are overly concerned with "fitting in" and not rocking the boat, those who emerge as leaders are more concerned with making important decisions that may break with tradition but are humane, moral, and right. The leader puts a premium on substance rather than on style.

It is important to be clear here about several things. First, management and leadership are both vitally important. To highlight the need for more leadership is not to minimize the importance of management or managers. It is to say that leadership involves unique processes that are distinguishable from basic management processes.[18] Moreover, just because they involve different processes does not mean that they require different, separate people. The same individual can exemplify effective managerial processes, leadership processes, both, or neither.

Some people still will dislike the idea of distinguishing between management and leadership, maintaining it is artificial or derogatory toward the managers and management processes that make orgnizations run. Perhaps a better or more useful distinction is between supervisory and strategic leadership.[19] **Supervisory leadership** is behavior that provides guidance, support, and corrective feedback for the day-to-day activities of work unit members. **Strategic leadership** gives purpose and meaning to organizations. *Strategic leadership* involves anticipating and envisioning a viable future for the organization, and working with others to initiate changes that create such a future.[20]

supervisory leadership Behavior that provides guidance, support, and corrective feedback for the day-to-day activities of work unit members.

strategic leadership Behavior that gives purpose and meaning to organizations, envisioning and creating a positive future.

Leading and following

Organizations succeed or fail not only because of how well they are led but because of how well followers follow. Just as managers are not necessarily good leaders, people are not always good followers. The most effective followers are capable of independent thinking and at the same time are actively committed to organizational goals.[21] Robert Townsend, who led a legendary turnaround at Avis, says that the most important characteristic of a follower may be the willingness to tell the truth.[22] Great leaders do the same.[23]

As a manager, you will be asked to play *both* roles. As you lead the people who report to you, you will report to your boss. You will be a member of some teams and committees, and you may chair others. While the leadership roles get the glamour and therefore are the roles that many people covet, followers must perform their responsibilities conscientiously as well.

Effective followers are distinguished from ineffective ones by their enthusiasm and commitment to the organization and to a person or purpose—an idea, a product—other than themselves or their own interests. They master skills that are useful to their organizations, and they hold performance standards that are higher than required. Effective followers may not get the glory, but they know their contributions to the organization are valuable. And as they make those contributions, they study leaders in preparation for their own leadership roles.[24]

Power and leadership

power The ability to influence others.

Central to effective leadership is **power**—the ability to influence other people. In organizations, this often means the ability to get things done or accomplish one's goals despite resistance from others.

Sources of power

One of the earliest and still most useful approaches to understanding power suggests that leaders have five important potential sources of power in organizations.[25] Figure 12.1 shows these power sources.

Legitimate power   The leader with *legitimate power* has the right, or the authority, to tell others what to do; employees are obligated to comply with legitimate orders. For example, a supervisor tells an employee to remove a safety hazard, and the employee removes the hazard because he has to obey the authority of his boss. In contrast, when a staff person lacks the authority to give an order to a line manager, the staff person has no legitimate power over the manager. As you might guess, managers have more legitimate power over their direct reports than they do over their peers, bosses, and others inside or outside their organizations.[26]

Reward power   The leader who has *reward power* influences others because she controls valued rewards; people comply with the leader's wishes in order to receive those rewards. For example, a manager works hard to achieve her performance goals to get a positive performance review and a big pay raise from her boss. On the other hand, if company policy dictates that everyone receive the same salary increase, a leader's reward power decreases because he or she is unable to give higher raises.

Coercive power   The leader with *coercive power* has control over punishments; people comply to avoid those punishments. For instance, a manager implements an absenteeism policy that administers disciplinary actions to offending employees. A manager has less coercive power if, say, a union contract prohibits him or her from punishing employees harshly. In general, lower-level managers have less legitimate, coercive, and reward power than do middle- and higher-level managers.[27]

figure 12.1
Sources of power

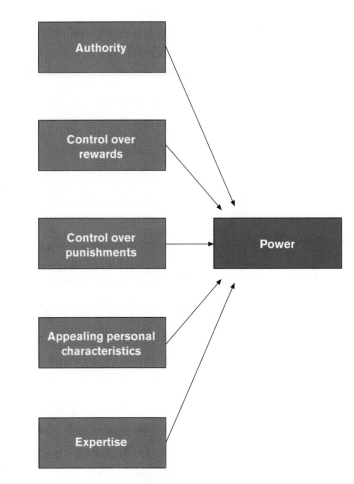

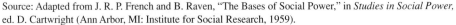

Source: Adapted from J. R. P. French and B. Raven, "The Bases of Social Power," in *Studies in Social Power,* ed. D. Cartwright (Ann Arbor, MI: Institute for Social Research, 1959).

Referent power The leader with *referent power* has personal characteristics that appeal to others; people comply because of admiration, a desire for approval, personal liking, or a desire to be like the leader. For example, young, ambitious managers emulate the work habits and personal style of a successful, charismatic executive. An executive who is incompetent, disliked, and commands little respect has little referent power.

Expert power The leader who has *expert power* has certain expertise or knowledge; people comply because they believe in, can learn from, or can otherwise gain from that expertise. For example, a sales manager gives her salespeople some tips on closing a deal. The salespeople then alter their sales techniques because they respect the manager's expertise. On the other hand, this manager may lack expert power in other areas, such as finance; thus, her salespeople may ignore her advice concerning financial matters.

People who are in a position that gives them the right to tell others what to do, who can reward and punish, who are well liked and admired, and who have expertise on which other people can draw will be powerful members of the organization. All of these sources of power are potentially important. Although it is easy to assume that the most powerful bosses are those who have high legitimate power and control major rewards and punishments, it is important not to underestimate the more "personal" sources like expert and referent power. These personal sources of power are the ones most closely related to people's motivation to perform to their managers' expectations.[28]

Traditional approaches to understanding leadership

Three traditional approaches to studying leadership are the trait approach, the behavioral approach, and the situational approach.

Leader traits

trait approach A leadership perspective that focuses on individual leaders and attempts to determine the personal characteristics that great leaders share.

The **trait approach** is the oldest leadership perspective and was dominant for several decades. This approach seems logical for studying leadership: It focuses on individual leaders and attempts to determine the personal characteristics (traits) that great leaders share. What set Winston Churchill, Alexander the Great, Gandhi, Napoleon, and Martin Luther King apart from the crowd? The trait approach assumes the existence of a leadership personality and assumes that leaders are born, not made.

From 1904 to 1948, over 100 leadership trait studies were conducted.[29] At the end of that period, management scholars concluded that no particular set of traits is necessary for a person to become a successful leader. Enthusiasm for the trait approach diminished, but some research on traits continued. By the mid-1970s, a more balanced view emerged: Although no traits ensure leadership success, certain characteristics are potentially useful. The current perspective is that some personality characteristics—many of which a person need not be born with but can strive to acquire—do distinguish effective leaders from other people.[30]

1. **Drive.** *Drive* refers to a set of characteristics that reflect a high level of effort. Drive includes high need for achievement, constant striving for improvement, ambition, energy, tenacity (persistence in the face of obstacles), and initiative. In several countries, the achievement needs of top executives have been shown to be related to the growth rates of their organizations.[31] But the need to achieve can be a drawback if leaders focus on personal achievement and get so personally involved with the work that they do not delegate enough authority and responsibility. And whereas need for achievement has been shown to predict organizational effectiveness in entrepreneurial firms, it does not predict success for division heads in larger and more bureaucratic firms.[32]

2. **Leadership motivation.** Great leaders not only have drive; they *want to lead*. They have a high need for power, preferring to be in leadership rather than follower positions. A high power need induces people to attempt to influence others, and sustains interest and satisfaction in the process of leadership. When the power need is exercised in moral and socially constructive ways, rather than to the detriment of others, leaders will inspire more trust, respect, and commitment to their vision.

3. **Integrity.** *Integrity* is the correspondence between actions and words. Honesty and credibility, in addition to being desirable characteristics in their own right, are especially important for leaders because these traits inspire trust in others.

4. **Self-confidence.** *Self-confidence* is important for a number of reasons. The leadership role is challenging, and setbacks are inevitable. Self-confidence allows a leader to overcome obstacles, make decisions despite uncertainty, and instill confidence in others.

5. **Knowledge of the business.** Effective leaders have a high level of *knowledge* about their industries, companies, and technical matters. Leaders must have the intelligence to interpret vast quantities of information. Advanced degrees are useful in a career, but ultimately less important than acquired expertise in matters relevant to the organization.[33]

Finally, there is one personal skill that may be the most important: the ability to perceive the needs and goals of others and to adjust one's personal leadership approach accordingly.[34] Effective leaders do not rely on one leadership style; rather, they are capable of using different styles as the situation warrants.[35] This quality is the cornerstone of the situational approaches to leadership, which we will discuss shortly.

Leading an Avon makeover

Andrea Jung is CEO of Avon Products, and is tackling what may be the toughest turnaround challenge in consumer products. Avon is at a crucial turning point in its history. Founded in 1886, it pioneered door-to-door selling and hit its peak when the mothers of most of today's women tried their first lipstick. The direct sales model, tremendously successful when most women didn't work, is now antiquated. It is up to Jung to make sure this old company with an old model survives in the modern era.

Jung had very little operating experience when she took over in 1999. Suddenly she was running a company with 3 million independent sales reps and operations in 137 countries. Her vow is to make Avon as big in the women's beauty business as Disney is in entertainment. She wants Avon to be the "ultimate relationship marketer of products and services for women."

Jung needs to rebuild the company from the ground up. Much more than selling cosmetics door-to-door, Avon will be the source for anything and everything a woman wants to buy. Possible products include vitamins and nutritional supplements, in-store spa facials and massages, and financial services and legal advice targeted toward women. And each customer will have three choices for how to buy: through an Avon rep, in a store, or online.

Avon has never engaged in traditional retailing, so as not to compete against its independent sales reps. But the company is now moving aggressively into retail channels. Avon experimented with kiosks in shopping malls to attract younger customers unfamiliar with Avon products, and is now franchising kiosks to its reps. Avon also announced it will create a separate line of products to sell at a store-within-a-store at a major mass retailer, possibly Kmart or Wal-Mart.

But the highest hopes lie with the Web. The biggest challenge: figuring out how the Avon reps will fit in. The reps produce 98 percent of the company's revenues, and they have been the backbone of the company, and of its brand image, forever. Jung says, "if we don't include them in everything we do, then we're just another retail brand, just another Internet site, and I don't see the world needing more of those" (p. 140). Jung surveyed the reps about the Website and created incentives for them to get involved. She is involving both the computer-savvy and the computer-illiterate in the process. Among other things, the site asks customers if they want a personal eRepresentative in their zip code. "What we do is about relationships, affiliations, being with other people. That is never going to go out" (p. 140).

Jung needs the support of those millions of independent sales reps and employees to get today's women to buy an old brand. Addressing 13,000 reps at a sales convention, she stated, "Avon is first and foremost about you. I stand here before you and promise you that that will never change" (p. 138). To women in a Chinese factory, she said "We will change the future of women around the world!" (p. 138).

The performance pressure is huge. Jung is one of the most-watched CEOs in the United States. So far, the sales reps are responding enthusiastically, and few observers are betting against her.

Source: N. Byrnes, "Avon: The New Calling," *Business Week*, September 18, 2000, pp. 137–48. ●

Leader behaviors

behavioral approach A leadership perspective that attempts to identify what good leaders do—that is, what behaviors they exhibit.

The **behavioral approach** to leadership attemps to identify what good leaders do. Should leaders focus on getting the job done or on keeping their followers happy? Should they make decisions autocratically or democratically? In the behavioral approach, personal characteristics are considered less important than the actual behaviors leaders exhibit.

Three general categories of leadership behavior have received particular attention: behaviors related to task performance, group maintenance, and employee participation in decision making.

Task performance
Leadership requires getting the job done. **Task performance behaviors** are the leader's efforts to ensure that the work unit or organization reaches its goals. This dimension is variously referred to as *concern for production, directive leadership, initiating structure,* or *closeness of supervision.* It includes a focus on work speed, quality and accuracy, quantity of output, and following the rules.[36]

Group maintenance
In exhibiting **group maintenance behaviors,** leaders take action to ensure the satisfaction of group members, develop and maintain harmonious work relationships, and preserve the social stability of the group. This dimension is sometimes referred to as *concern for people, supportive leadership,* or *consideration.* It includes a focus on people's feelings and comfort, appreciation of them, and stress reduction.[37]

What *specific* behaviors do performance- and maintenance-oriented leadership imply? To help answer this question, assume you are asked to rate your boss on these two dimensions. If a leadership study were conducted in your organization, you would be asked to fill out a questionnaire similar to the one in Table 12.1. The behaviors indicated in the first set of questions represent performance-oriented leadership; those indicated in the second set represent maintenance-oriented leadership.

One theory of leadership, **Leader-Member Exchange (LMX) theory,**[38] highlights the importance of leader behaviors not just toward the group as a whole but toward individuals on a personal basis. The focus is primarily on the leader behaviors historically

task performance behaviors Actions taken to ensure that the work group or organization reaches its goals.

group maintenance behaviors Actions taken to ensure the satisfaction of group members, develop and maintain harmonious work relationships, and preserve the social stability of the group.

Leader-Member Exchange (LMX) theory Highlights the importance of leader behaviors not just toward the group as a whole but toward individuals on a personal basis.

table 12.1
Questions assessing task performance and group maintenance leadership

Task performance leadership

1. Is your superior strict about observing regulations?
2. To what extent does your superior give you instructions and orders?
3. Is your superior strict about the amount of work you do?
4. Does your superior urge you to complete your work by a specified time?
5. Does your superior try to make you work to your maximum capacity?
6. When you do an inadequate job, does your superior focus on the inadequate way the job is done?
7. Does your superior ask you for reports about the progress of your work?
8. How precisely does your superior work out plans for goal achievement each month?

Group maintenance leadership

1. Can you talk freely with your superior about your work?
2. Does your superior generally support you?
3. Is your superior concerned about your personal problems?
4. Do you think your superior trusts you?
5. Does your superior give you recognition when you do your job well?
6. When a problem arises in your workplace, does your superior ask your opinion about how to solve it?
7. Is your superior concerned about your future benefits, such as promotions and pay raises?
8. Does your superior treat you fairly?

Source: Reprinted from J. Misumi and M. Peterson, "The Performance-Maintenance (PM) Theory of Leadership: Review of a Japanese Research Program," *Administrative Science Quarterly* 30, no. 2 (June 1985), by permission of *Administrative Science Quarterly,* © 1985 by Cornell University.

considered group maintenance.[39] According to LMX theory, and supported by research evidence, maintenance behaviors such as trust, open communication, mutual respect, mutual obligation, and mutual loyalty form the cornerstone of relationships that are satisfying and perhaps more productive.[40]

Remember, though, the potential for cross-cultural differences. Maintenance behaviors are important everywhere, but the specific behaviors can differ from one culture to another. For example, in the United States, maintenance behaviors include dealing with people face-to-face; in Japan, written memos are preferred over giving directions face-to-face, thus avoiding confrontation and permitting face-saving in the event of disagreement.[41]

participation in decision making Leader behaviors that managers perform in involving their employees in making decisions.

autocratic leadership A form of leadership in which the leader makes decisions on his or her own and then announces those decisions to the group.

democratic leadership A form of leadership in which the leader solicits input from subordinates.

laissez-faire A leadership philosophy characterized by an absence of managerial decision making.

Participation in decision making
How should a leader make decisions? More specifically, to what extent should leaders involve their people in making decisions?[42] The **participation-in-decision-making** dimension of leadership behavior can range from autocratic to democratic. **Autocratic leadership** makes decisions and then announces them to the group. **Democratic leadership** solicits input from others. Democratic leadership seeks information, opinions, and preferences, sometimes to the point of meeting with the group, leading discussions, and using consensus or majority vote to make the final choice.

The effects of leader behavior
How the leader behaves influences people's attitudes and performance. Studies of these effects focus on autocratic versus democratic decision styles or on performance- versus maintenance-oriented behaviors.

Decision styles
The classic study comparing autocratic and democratic styles found that a democratic approach resulted in the most positive attitudes, whereas an autocratic approach resulted in somewhat higher performance.[43] A **laissez-faire** style, in which the leader essentially made no decisions, led to more negative attitudes and lower performance. These results seem logical and probably represent the prevalent beliefs among managers about the general effects of these decision-making approaches.

However, democratic styles, appealing though they may seem, are not always the most appropriate. When companies are in dire straits and need to be turned around quickly, democratic decision making may be too slow, or people may demand decisiveness from the leader.[44] Whether a decision should be made autocratically or democratically depends on characteristics of the leader, the followers, and the situation.[45] Thus, a situational approach to leader decision styles, discussed later in the chapter, is appropriate.

Performance and maintenance behaviors
The performance and maintenance dimensions of leadership are independent of each other. In other words, a leader can behave in ways that emphasize one, both, or neither of these dimensions. Some research indicates that the ideal combination is to engage in both types of leader behaviors.

In the well-known Ohio State studies, a team of Ohio State University researchers investigated the effects of leader behaviors in a truck manufacturing plant of International Harvester.[46] Generally, supervisors who were high on *maintenance behaviors* (which the researchers termed *consideration*) had fewer grievances and less turnover in their work units than supervisors who were low on this dimension. The opposite held for *task performance behaviors* (which the team called *initiating structure*). Supervisors high on this dimension had more grievances and higher turnover rates.

When maintenance and performance leadership behaviors were considered together, the results were more complex. But one conclusion was clear: When a leader must be high on performance-oriented behaviors, he or she should *also* be maintenance oriented. Otherwise the leader will have employees with high rates of turnover and grievances.

At about the same time the Ohio State studies were being conducted, an equally famous research program at the University of Michigan was studying the impact of the same leader behaviors on groups' job performance.[47] Among other things, the researchers concluded that the most effective managers engaged in what they called *task-oriented behavior*: planning, scheduling, coordinating, providing resources, and setting performance goals. Effective managers also exhibited more *relationship-oriented behavior*:

demonstrating trust and confidence, acting friendly and considerate, showing appreciation, keeping people informed, and so on. As you can see, these dimensions of leader behavior are essentially the task performance and group maintenance dimensions.

After the Ohio State and Michigan findings were published, it became popular to talk about the ideal leader as one who is always both performance and maintenance oriented. The best-known leadership training model to follow this style is Blake and Mouton's Leadership Grid.®[48] In grid training, managers are rated on their performance-oriented behavior (called *concern for production*) and maintenance-oriented behavior (*concern for people*). Then their scores are plotted on the grid shown in Figure 12.2. The highest score is a 9 on both dimensions.

As the figure shows, joint scores can fall at any point on the grid. Managers who did not score a 9,9—for example, those who were high on concern for people but low on concern for production—would then receive training on how to become a 9,9 leader.

For a long time, grid training was warmly received by U.S. business and industry. Later, however, it was criticized for embracing a simplistic, one-best-way style of leadership and ignoring the possibility that 9,9 is not best under all circumstances. For example, even 1,1 could be appropriate if employees know their jobs (and therefore don't need to receive directions). Also, they may enjoy their jobs and their co-workers enough that whether or not the boss shows personal concern for them is not very important. Nonetheless, if the manager is uncertain how to behave, it probably is best to exhibit behaviors that are related to both task performance and group maintenance.[49]

As the following examples show, a wide range of effective leadership styles exists. Organizations that understand the need for diverse leadership styles will have a competitive advantage in the modern business environment over those that believe there is only "one best way."

figure 12.2
The Leadership Grid®

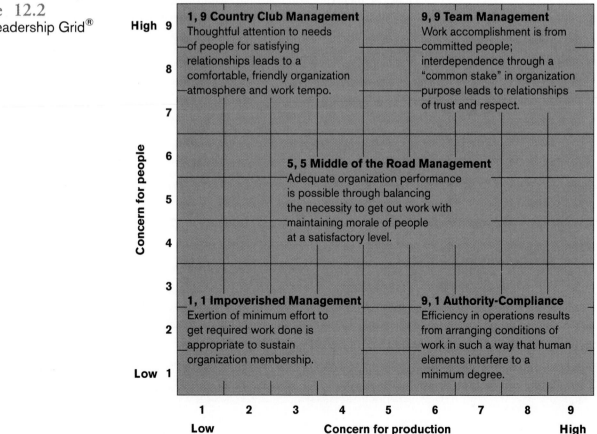

Source: The Leadership Grid® Figure from *Leadership Dilemmas—Grid Solutions,* p. 29, by Robert R. Blake and Anne Adams McCanse. Copyright © 1991, by Robert R. Blake and the Estate of Jane S. Mouton. Used with permission. All rights reserved.

Men and women leaders: (How) do they differ?

Admiral Louise Wilmot was the highest-ranking woman in the U.S. Navy when she retired.
[From the personal archives of Rear Admiral Louise Wilmot]

On the average, men and women are equally effective as leaders. However, the situation may make a difference: Male leaders tend to be more effective in military settings, and women are usually more effective in educational, social service, and government organizations. Why this is so is not completely clear.

Think about it for a moment: Do women and men behave differently in leadership roles? Is there a "male" leadership style, and, if so, does it differ from the "female" style?

According to an article in *Harvard Business Review,* the first female executives had to behave like men to get to the top. But today, women are moving into top management by drawing on unique skills and attitudes that men are less likely to possess. Men, says author Judy Rosener, are more likely to rely on their formal authority and on rewards and punishments (legitimate, reward, and coercive powers), whereas women tend to use their charisma, interpersonal skills, hard work, and personal contacts. In Rosener's study, women leaders claimed to encourage participation, share power and information, and enhance other people's self-worth. Additional academic research confirms that women managers tend to be more participative than males.

Admiral Louise Wilmot was the highest-ranking woman in the U.S. Navy when she retired. Her leadership style emphasized teamwork and interpersonal relationships. When asked if her style arose because she is a woman, she replied that as a leader you should "preserve your person and preserve whatever you are that is good and wholesome and makes you interesting and different from everyone else. There is no reason in the world to surrender your soul, your person, or your spirit" (p. 89).

Cisco's John Chambers is one Silicon valley male who sees tremendous strengths in women leaders. He believes that great female leadership talent is waiting to be tapped, and is about to explode onto the Silicon Valley scene. Support for this comes from Harvard's Rosabeth Moss Kanter's comment, "women get high ratings on exactly those skills needed to succeed in the global Information Age, where teamwork and partnering are so important" (p. 76).

Source: J. B. Rosener, "Ways Women Lead," *Harvard Business Review* 68 (May–June 1990), pp. 103–11; A. Eagly, S. Karom, and M. Makhijani, "Gender and the Effectiveness of Leaders: A Meta-Analysis," *Psychological Bulletin,* 1995, pp. 125–45; V. H. Vroom, "Leadership and the Decision-making Process," *Organizational Dynamics,* Spring 2000, pp. 82–93; P. Sellers, "The 50 Most Powerful Women in Business," *Fortune,* October 16, 2000, pp. 131–16, E. Fagenson-Eland and P. J. Kidder, "A Conversation with Rear Admiral Louise Wilmot: Taking the Lead and Leading the Way," *Organizational Dynamics,* Winter 2000, pp. 80–91; and R. Sharpe, "As Leaders, Women Rule," *Business Week,* November 20, 2000, pp 74–84. ●

situational approach
Leadership perspective proposing that universally important traits and behaviors do not exist, and that effective leadership behavior varies from situation to situation.

Situational approaches to leadership

According to proponents of the **situational approach** to leadership, universally important traits and behaviors don't exist. They believe effective leader behaviors vary from situation to situation. *The leader should first analyze the situation and then decide what to do.* In other words, look before you lead.

Democracy *and* autocracy

A head nurse in a hospital described her leadership style:

My leadership style is a mix of all styles. In this environment I normally let people participate...

But in a code blue situation where a patient is dying I automatically become very autocratic: "You do this; you do that; you, out of the room; you all better be quiet; you, get Dr. Mansfield." The staff tell me that's the only time they see me like that. In an emergency like that, you don't have time to vote, talk a lot, or yell at each other. It's time for someone to set up the order.

I remember one time, one person saying, "Wait a minute, I want to do this." He wanted to do the mouth-to-mouth resuscitation. I knew the person behind him did it better, so I said, "No, he does it." This fellow told me later that I hurt him so badly to yell that in front of all the staff and doctors. It was like he wasn't good enough. So I explained it to him: that's the way it is. A life was on the line. I couldn't give you warm fuzzies. I couldn't make you look good because you didn't have the skills to give the very best to that patient who wasn't breathing anymore.

A similar business example comes from a division manager in a food and beverage company. When appointed to her position, the division was performing poorly, morale was terrible, and her charge was to turn the division around. The manager started participatively, with one-on-one conversations to get to know people and hear their opinions. She then held a three-day off-site meeting so people could offer solutions for various problems. After consensus emerged about the problems, priorities, and action plans, she shifted into a more autocratic style. She assigned specific managers to be responsible and accountable for each action step. Then, during the first few weeks of implementation, she continually reminded people of the new vision, the urgency, and the serious consequences if people failed to meet their responsibilities. "I had to be brutal about this follow-up and make sure this stuff happened. It was going to take discipline and focus" (p. 89). Seven months after the manager entered the crisis situation and started the turnaround efforts, the division exceeded its profit target by $5 million.

Source: J. Wall, *Bosses* (Lexington, MA: Lexington Books, 1986), pp. 103–4; and D. Goleman, "Leadership that Gets Results," *Harvard Business Review,* March–April 2000, pp. 78–90. ●

These leaders have their own intuitive situational approach to leadership. They know the potential advantages of the participatory approach to decision making, but they also know that in some circumstances they must make decisions on their own.

The first situational model of leadership was proposed in 1958 by Tannenbaum and Schmidt. In their classic *Harvard Business Review* article, these authors described how managers should consider three factors before deciding how to lead: forces in the manager, forces in the subordinate, and forces in the situation.[50] Forces in the manager include the manager's personal values, inclinations, feelings of security, and confidence in subordinates. Forces in the subordinate include the employee's knowledge and experience, readiness to assume responsibility for decision making, interest in the task or problem, and understanding and acceptance of the organization's goals. Forces in the situation include the type of leadership style the organization values, the degree to which the group works as a unit effectively, the problem itself and the type of information needed to solve it, and the amount of time the leader has to make the decision.

Consider which of these forces makes an autocratic style most appropriate and which dictates a democratic, participative style. By engaging in this exercise, you are constructing a situational theory of leadership.

Although the Tannenbaum and Schmidt article was published almost a half-century ago, most of its arguments remain valid. Since that time, other situational models have emerged. We will focus here on two of them: the Vroom model for decision making, and path-goal theory. The others are summarized in the appendix to this chapter.

The Vroom model of leadership style

This situational model follows in the tradition of Tannenbaum and Schmidt. The **Vroom model** emphasizes the participative dimension of leadership: how leaders go about making decisions. The model uses the basic situational approach of assessing the situation before determining the best leadership style.[51]

Table 12.2 shows the situational factors used to analyze problems. Each is based on an important attribute of the problem the leader faces and should be assessed as either high or low.

Vroom model A situational model of leadership that focuses on how leaders go about making decisions.

table 12.2
Situational factors for problem analysis

Situational factors for problem analysis	
Decision significance:	The significance of the decision to the success of the project or organization.
Importance of commitment:	The importance of team members' commitment to the decision.
Leader's expertise:	Your knowledge or expertise in relation to this problem.
Likelihood of commitment:	The likelihood that the team would commit itself to a decision that you might make on your own.
Group support for objectives:	The degree to which the team supports the organization's objectives at stake in this problem.
Group expertise:	Team members' knowledge or expertise in relation to this problem.
Team competence:	The ability of team members to work together in solving problems.

Source: V. Vroom, "Leadership and the Decision-Making Process," *Organizational Dynamics,* Spring 2000, pp. 82–94.

The Vroom model, shown in Figure 12.3, operates like a funnel. You answer the questions one at a time, sometimes skipping some questions as you follow the appropriate path. Eventually, you reach one of 14 possible endpoints. For each endpoint, the model

figure 12.3
Vroom's model of leadership style

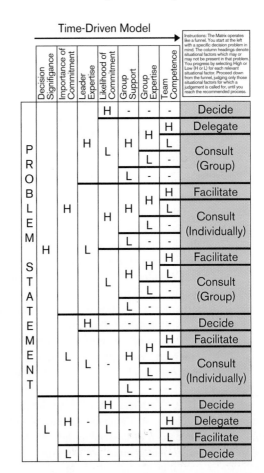

Source: V. Vroom, "Leadership and the Decision-Making Process," *Organizational Dynamics,* Spring 2000, pp. 82–94.

figure 12.4
Vroom's leader decision styles

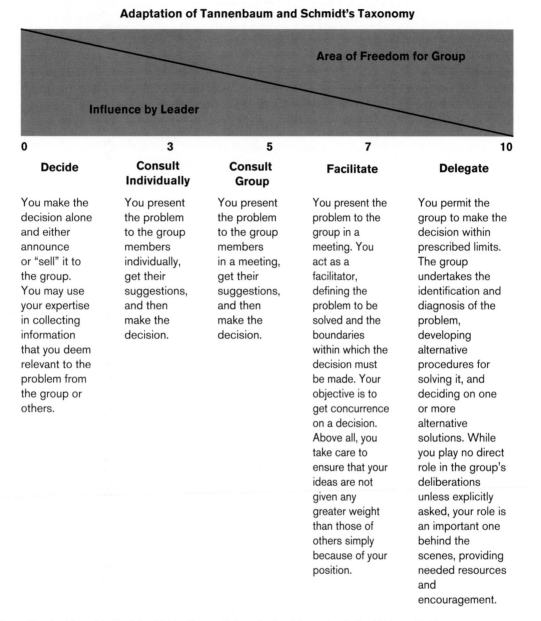

Adaptation of Tannenbaum and Schmidt's Taxonomy

Area of Freedom for Group

Influence by Leader

0	3	5	7	10
Decide	**Consult Individually**	**Consult Group**	**Facilitate**	**Delegate**
You make the decision alone and either announce or "sell" it to the group. You may use your expertise in collecting information that you deem relevant to the problem from the group or others.	You present the problem to the group members individually, get their suggestions, and then make the decision.	You present the problem to the group members in a meeting, get their suggestions, and then make the decision.	You present the problem to the group in a meeting. You act as a facilitator, defining the problem to be solved and the boundaries within which the decision must be made. Your objective is to get concurrence on a decision. Above all, you take care to ensure that your ideas are not given any greater weight than those of others simply because of your position.	You permit the group to make the decision within prescribed limits. The group undertakes the identification and diagnosis of the problem, developing alternative procedures for solving it, and deciding on one or more alternative solutions. While you play no direct role in the group's deliberations unless explicitly asked, your role is an important one behind the scenes, providing needed resources and encouragement.

Source: V. Vroom, "Leadership and the Decision-Making Process," *Organizational Dynamics,* Spring 2000, pp. 82–94.

states which of the five decision styles is most appropriate. Several different decision styles may work, but the style recommended is the one in the feasible set that takes the least amount of time.

Figure 12.4 defines the types of leader decision styles. The five styles indicate that there are several shades of participation, not just autocratic or democratic.

The following example presents a managerial decision for you to work through the model.

Applying the Vroom model of leadership style

Setting: Banking
Your Position: President & Chief Executive Officer
The bank examiners have just left, insisting that many of your commercial real estate

loans be written off, thereby depleting already low capital. Along with many other banks in your region, your bank is in serious danger of being closed by the regulators. As the financial problems surfaced, many of the top executives left to pursue other interests, but fortunately, you were able to replace them with three highly competent younger managers. While they had no prior acquaintance with one another, each is a product of a fine training program with one of the money center banks in which they rotated through positions in each of the banking functions.

Your extensive experience in the industry leads you to the inevitable conclusion that the only hope is a two-pronged approach involving reduction of all but the most critical expenses and the sale of assets to other banks. The task must be accomplished quickly since further deterioration of the quality of the loan portfolio could result in a negative capital position forcing regulators to close the bank.

The strategy is clear to you, but you have many details that will need to be worked out. You believe that you know what information will be needed in order to get the bank on a course for future prosperity. You are fortunate in having three young executives to help you out. While they have had little or no experience in working together you know that each is dedicated to the survival of the bank. Like you, they know what needs to be done and how to do it.

Source: V. Vroom, "Leadership and the Decision-Making Process," *Organizational Dynamics,* Spring 2000, pp. 82–94.

Answer to the boxed Vroom banker problem: Answers are H H H L H H L. The preferred decision style is to consult your group.

path-goal theory A theory that concerns how leaders influence subordinates' perceptions of their work goals and the paths they follow toward attainment of those goals.

Of course, not every managerial decision warrants this complicated analysis. But the model becomes less complex after one works through it a couple of times. Also, using the model for major decisions ensures that you consider the important situational factors and alerts you to the most appropriate style to use.

Path-goal theory

Perhaps the most generally useful situational model of leadership effectiveness is path-goal theory. Developed by Robert House, **path-goal theory** gets its name from its concern with how leaders influence followers' perceptions of their work goals and the paths they follow toward goal attainment.[52]

The key situational factors in path-goal theory are (1) personal characteristics of followers and (2) environmental pressures and demands with which followers must cope to attain their work goals. These factors determine which leadership behaviors are most appropriate.

The four pertinent leadership behaviors are (1) *directive leadership,* a form of task performance-oriented behavior; (2) *supportive leadership,* a form of group maintenance-oriented behavior; (3) *participative leadership,* or decision style; and (4) *achievement-oriented leadership,* or behaviors geared toward motivating people, such as setting challenging goals and rewarding good performance.

These situational factors and leader behaviors are merged in Figure 12.5. As you can see, appropriate leader behaviors—as determined by characteristics of followers and the work environment—lead to effective performance.

figure 12.5
The path-goal framework

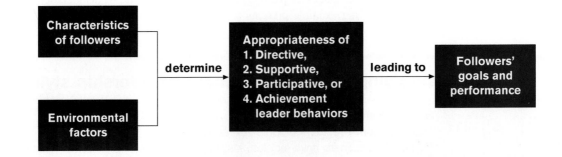

The theory also specifies *which* follower and environmental features are important. There are three key follower characteristics. *Authoritarianism* is the degree to which individuals respect, admire, and defer to authority. *Locus of control* is the extent to which individuals see the environment as responsive to their own behavior. People with an *internal* locus of control believe that what happens to them is their own doing; people with an *external* locus of control believe that it is just luck or fate. Finally, *ability* is people's beliefs about their own abilities to do their assigned jobs.

Path-goal theory states that these personal characteristics determine the appropriateness of various leadership styles. For example, the theory makes the following propositions:

- A directive leadership style is more appropriate for highly authoritarian people, because such people respect authority.
- A participative leadership style is more appropriate for people who have an internal locus of control, because these individuals prefer to have more influence over their own lives.
- A directive style is more appropriate when subordinates' ability is low. The directive style helps people understand what has to be done.

Appropriate leadership style is also determined by three important environmental factors: people's tasks, the formal authority system of the organization, and the primary work group.

- Directive leadership is inappropriate if tasks already are well structured.
- If the task and the authority or rule system are dissatisfying, directive leadership will create greater dissatisfaction.
- If the task or authority system is dissatisfying, supportive leadership is especially appropriate, because it offers one positive source of gratification in an otherwise negative situation.
- If the primary work group provides social support to its members, supportive leadership is less important.

Path-goal theory offers many more propositions. In general, the theory suggests that the functions of the leader are to (1) make the path to work goals easier to travel by providing coaching and direction; (2) reduce frustrating barriers to goal attainment; and (3) increase opportunities for personal satisfaction by increasing payoffs to people for achieving performance goals.

How best to do these things depends on your people and on the work situation. Again: Analyze, then adapt your style accordingly.

Substitutes for leadership   Sometimes leaders don't have to lead—or, situations constrain their ability to lead effectively. The situation may be one in which leadership is unnecessary or has little impact. **Substitutes for leadership** can provide the same influence on people that leaders otherwise would have.

substitutes for leadership Factors in the workplace that can exert the same influence on employees that leaders would provide.

Certain follower, task, and organizational factors are substitutes for task performance-oriented and group maintenance-oriented leader behaviors.[53] For example, group maintenance behaviors are less important and will have less impact if people already have a closely knit group, they have a professional orientation, the job is intrinsically satisfying, or there is great physical distance between leader and followers. Physicians who are strongly concerned with professional conduct, enjoy their work, and work independently do not need social support from hospital administrators.

Task performance leadership is less important and will have less positive effect if people have a lot of experience and ability, feedback is supplied to them directly from the task or by computer, or the rules and procedures are rigid. If these factors are operating, the leader does not have to tell people what to do or how well they are performing.

The concept of substitutes for leadership does more than indicate when a leader's attempts at influence will and will not work. It provides useful and practical prescriptions for how to manage more efficiently.[54] If the manager can develop the work situation to the point where a number of these substitutes for leadership are operating, less time will need to be spent in direct attempts to influence people. The leader will be free to spend more time on other important activities.

Contemporary perspectives on leadership

So far, you have learned the major classic approaches to understanding leadership. Now we will discuss a number of new developments that are revolutionizing our understanding of this important aspect of management. These developments include charismatic leadership, transformational leadership, and post-heroic leadership.

Charismatic leadership

Like many great leaders, Ronald Reagan had charisma. Lee Iacocca, Thomas Watson, Alfred Sloan, and Steve Jobs are good examples of charismatic leaders in industry. Herb Kelleher of Southwest Airlines is a highly charismatic leader whose departure from the company has people seriously worried about whether anyone can succeed in his place.[55]

Charisma is a rather evasive concept; it is easy to spot but hard to define. When executive recruiter Korn/Ferry International advised CEO wannabes to "develop charisma," *Business Week* responded sarcastically, "What's next? Grow a third eye? Master telekinesis?" (p. 86).[56]

What *is* charisma, and how does one acquire it? According to one definition, "Charisma packs an emotional wallop for followers above and beyond ordinary esteem, affection, admiration, and trust . . . The charismatic is an idolized hero, a messiah and a savior . . ."[57] As you can see from this quotation, many people, particularly North Americans, value charisma in their leaders. But some people don't like the term *charisma*;[58] it can be associated with the negative charisma of evil leaders with blind followers.[59]

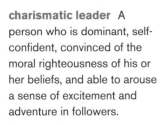

charismatic leader A person who is dominant, self-confident, convinced of the moral righteousness of his or her beliefs, and able to arouse a sense of excitement and adventure in followers.

Charismatic leaders are dominant and exceptionally self-confident and have a strong conviction in the moral righteousness of their beliefs.[60] They strive to create an aura of competence and success and communicate high expectations for and confidence in followers.

Charismatic Martin Luther King was a brilliant leader who had a compelling vision, a dream for a better world.
[Flip Schulke/Black Star]

The charismatic leader articulates ideological goals and makes sacrifies in pursuit of those goals.[61] Martin Luther King had a dream for a better world, and John F. Kennedy spoke of landing a human on the moon. In other words, such leaders have a compelling vision. The charismatic leader also arouses a sense of excitement and adventure. He or she is an eloquent speaker who exhibits superior verbal skills, which helps communicate the vision and motivate followers. Walt Disney was able to mesmerize people with his storytelling, had enormous creative talent, and instilled in his organization strong values of good taste, risk taking, and innovation.[62]

Leaders who possess these characteristics or do these things inspire in their followers trust, confidence, acceptance, obedience, emotional involvement, affection, admiration, and higher performance.[63] Evidence for the positive effects of charismatic leadership has been found in a wide variety of groups, organizations, and management levels, and in countries including India, Singapore, The Netherlands, China, Japan, and Canada.[64]

Transformational leadership

transformational leader A leader who transforms a vision into reality and motivates people to transcend their personal interests for the good of the group.

transactional leaders
Management through transactions in which leaders use their legitimate, reward, and coercive powers to give commands and exchange rewards for services rendered.

Charisma contributes to transformational leadership. **Transformational leaders**[65] get people to transcend their personal interests for the sake of the larger community.[66] They generate excitement and revitalize organizations. At Hewlett-Packard, the ability to generate excitement is an explicit criterion for selecting managers.

The transformational process moves beyond the more traditional *transactional* approach to leadership. The concept of **transactional leaders** views management as a series of transactions in which leaders use their legitimate, reward, and coercive powers to give commands and exchange rewards for services rendered. Unlike transformational leadership, transactional leadership is dispassionate; it does not excite, transform, empower, or inspire people to focus on the interests of the group or organization. However, transactional approaches may be more effective for individualists than for collectivists[67] (recall Chapter 6).

Generating excitement   Transformational leaders generate excitement in three primary ways.[68] First, they are *charismatic,* as described earlier. Second, they give their followers *individualized attention.* Transformational leaders delegate challenging work to deserving people, keep lines of communication open, and provide one-on-one mentoring to develop their people. They do not treat everyone alike, because not everyone *is* alike.

Third, transformational leaders are *intellectually stimulating.* They arouse in their followers an awareness of problems and potential solutions. They articulate the organization's opportunities, threats, strengths, and weaknesses. They stir the imagination and generate insights. Therefore, problems are recognized and high-quality solutions are identified and implemented with the full commitment of followers.

Skills and strategies   At least four skills or strategies contribute to transformational leadership.[69] First, transformational leaders *have a vision*—a goal, an agenda, or a results-orientation that grabs people's attention. Second, they *communicate their vision;* through words, manner, or symbolism, they relate a compelling image of the ultimate goal. Third, transformational leaders *build trust* by being consistent, dependable, and persistent. They position themselves clearly by choosing a direction and staying with it, thus projecting integrity. Finally, they have a *positive self-regard.* They do not feel self-important or complacent; rather, they recognize their personal strengths, compensate for their weaknesses, nurture and continually develop their talents, and know how to learn from failure. They strive for success rather than merely trying to avoid failure.

Transformational leadership has been identified in industry, the military, and politics.[70] Examples of transformational leaders include Henry Ford, General George Patton, Lee Iacocca, and Jan Carlzon.[71] As with studies of charisma, transformational leadership and its positive impact on follower satisfaction and performance[72] have been demonstrated in countries the world over, including Egypt, Germany, China, England, and Japan.[73]

Transforming leaders   Importantly, transformational leadership is not the exclusive domain of presidents and chief executives. Ford Motor Company, in collaboration with the University of Michigan School of Business, has put thousands of middle managers through a program designed to stimulate transformational leadership.[74] The training included analysis of the changing business environment, company strategy, and personal reflection and discussion about the need to change. Participants assessed their own leadership styles and developed a specific change initiative to implement after the training—a change that would make a needed and lasting difference.

Over the next six months, the managers implemented change on the job. Almost half of the initiatives resulted in transformational changes in the organization or work unit; 54 percent of the changes were smaller, more incremental, or more personal. Whether managers made small or transformational changes depended on their attitude going into the training, their level of self-esteem, and the amount of support they received from others on the job for their efforts. Thus, some managers did not respond as hoped. But almost half embraced the training, became more transformational in orientation, and tackled significant transformational changes for the company.[75]

Post-heroic leadership

A common view of leaders is that they are heroes. Phenomenally talented, they step forward in difficult times and save the day. But in these complex times, it is foolhardy to assume that a great top executive can solve all problems by himself or herself.[76] No one person can deal with all of today's rapid-fire changes, competitive threats, and escalating customer demands.

Therefore, it is a big mistake to cruise along assuming Arnold Schwarzenegger will intervene and make things right. The hope that a single leader can save the firm is usually a prescription for disappointment. Effective leadership must permeate the organization, not reside in one or two superstars at the top.

To do this, you can paint a clear picture of great performance, and engage individuals—their hearts, minds, and hands—in making the business better. This requires the leader to coach, develop, and challenge every individual to continually improve his or her abilities and make greater contributions.

Great leadership is impossible without the full involvement, cooperation, and initiatives of followers.[77] The leader's job becomes one of spreading leadership abilities throughout the firm.[78] Make people responsible for their own performance. Create an environment in which each person can figure out what needs to be done and then do it well. Point the way and clear the path so people can succeed. Give them the credit they deserve. Make heroes out of *them*.

Post-heroic leadership for the 21st century

What is now required of leaders is less the efficient management of resources, and more the effective unleashing of intellectual capital and human resources. In other words, you should *capitalize on all the brains and talent in your organization.*

Five key roles personify post-heroic leadership in the 21st century:

1. *Using vision to motivate and inspire.* A recent survey showed that executives consider this to be the most important skill for future global leaders. According to Percy Barnevik, perhaps the most admired business leader in Europe, "It is important that people in an organization have something to be proud of ... Our employees ... like to see a purpose that goes beyond numbers. It is important that a company can be perceived as changing the world in a positive way" (pp. 19–20).

2. *Empowering employees at all levels.* Ken Melrose, CEO of Toro, says "You best lead by serving the needs of your people. You don't do their jobs for them; you enable them to learn and progress on the job" (p. 22). Most people want to expand their own knowledge, feel involved in their organization, and contribute to its success.

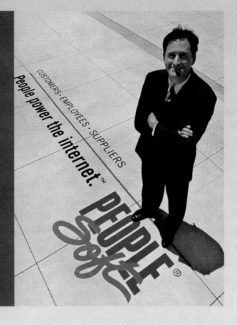

At PeopleSoft, everyone from CEO Steve Zarate to the newest recruit receives the same top-of-the-line laptop.
[AP/WIDE WORLD PHOTOS]

3. *Accumulating and sharing internal knowledge.* At PeopleSoft, everyone from the CEO (Steve Zarate) to the newest recruit gets the same top-of-the line laptop with lots of performance enhancements. The purpose to to break down hierarchical status differences and support the global communications network. The laptop isn't a device for personal productivity; it's the entry point for a worldwide information infrastructure. According to Zarate, "The objective is to have all 4,500 people know what matters" (p. 25).

4. *Gathering and integrating external information.* Fred Taylor of Gateway notes that the company talks to 100,000 people per day through its shopping, orders, and support requests. "The time it takes for an idea to enter this organization, get processed, and then go to customers for feedback is down to minutes. We've designed the company around speed and feedback" (p. 28). More generally, information about the business environment and specific stakeholders, including customers, competitors, and potential collaborators, must be constantly sought, assessed, and used.

5. *Challenging the status quo and enabling creativity.* The philosophy of encouraging risk taking in the pursuit of innovation prompts Wood Dickinson, CEO of the Dickinson movie theatre chain, to tell his managers to try new things and not worry about having "intelligent failures in the pursuit of service excellence" (p. 31). The new competitive landscape is swarming with opportunities that are best addressed via innovation and creativity.

Sources: G. G. Dess and J. C. Picken, "Changing Roles: Leadership in the 21st Century," *Organizational Dynamics,* Winter 2000, pp. 18–33; and R. D. Ireland and M. A. Hitt, "Achiving and Maintaining Strategic Competitiveness in the 21st Century: The Role of Strategic Leadership," *Academy of Management Executive,* February 1999, pp. 43–57. ●

A note on courage

To be a good leader, you need the courage to create a vision of greatness for your unit; identify and manage allies, adversaries, and fencesitters; and to execute your vision, often against opposition. This does not mean you should commit career suicide by alienating too many powerful people; it does mean taking reasonable risks, with the good of the firm at heart, in order to produce constructive change.

Specifically, some acts of courage required to fulfill your vision will include:[79] (1) seeing things as they are and facing them head-on, making no excuses and harboring no wishful illusions; (2) saying what needs to be said to those who need to hear it; and (3) putting up with, and persisting despite, resistance, criticism, abuse, and setbacks. Courage includes stating the realities, even when they are harsh, and publicly stating what you will do to help and what you want from others. This means laying the cards on the table honestly: Here is what I want from you . . . What do you want from me?[80]

Developing your leadership skills

As with other things, you must work at *developing* your leadership abilities. Great musicians and great athletes don't become great on natural gifts alone. They also pay their dues by practicing, learning, and sacrificing. Leaders in a variety of fields, when asked how they become the best leader possible, offered the following comments:[81]

- "I've observed methods and skills of my bosses that I respected."
- "By taking risks, trying, and learning from my mistakes."
- "Reading autobiographies of leaders I admire to try to understand how they think."
- "Lots of practice."
- "By making mistakes myself and trying a different approach."
- "By purposely engaging with others to get things done."
- "By being put in positions of responsibility that other people counted on."

How do you go about developing your leadership abilities? Start by thinking about your potential employer. Look for how it develops leadership talent. Best practices include paying close executive-level attention to the development of people, providing assignments that stretch the abilities of up-and-coming talent, creating individualized development plans, and providing multirater feedback.[82] Companies best at leadership development include Johnson & Johnson, Hewlett-Packard, Shell International, Arthur Andersen, General Electric, and the World Bank.[83]

More generally, get out of your "comfort zone." That is, don't seek out and remain in easy, nonchallenging situations; enter, create, and face situations that require you to adapt and change. This is the best way to learn, and it is the way great executives learn.[84]

More specifically, here are some developmental experiences you should seek:[85]

- *Assignments:* Building something from nothing; fixing or turning around a failing operation; taking on project or task force responsibilities; accepting international assignments.
- *Other people:* Having exposure to positive role models; increasing visibility to others; working with people of diverse backgrounds.
- *Hardships:* Overcoming ideas that fail and deals that collapse; confronting others' performance problems; breaking out of a career rut.
- *Other events:* Formal courses; challenging job experiences; supervision of others; experiences outside work.

These experiences do not guarantee that you will develop into an effective leader. But without them, your development will surely be constrained. Seek these experiences; expect mistakes and don't beat yourself up over them; and take time to learn from your experiences.

Key terms

Summary of learning objectives

Now that you have studied Chapter 12, you should know:

What it means to be a leader.

A leader is one who influences others to attain goals. Leaders orchestrate change, set direction, and motivate people to overcome obstacles and move the organization toward its ideal future.

How a good vision helps you be a better leader.

Outstanding leaders have vision. A vision is a mental image that goes beyond the ordinary and perhaps beyond what others thought possible. The vision provides the direction in which the leader wants the organization to move.

How to understand and use power.

Having power and using it appropriately are essential attributes of an effective leader. Managers have five potential sources of power: legitimate, reward, coercive, referent, and expert. These power sources are potentially available to managers at all organizational levels and should be used appropriately.

The personal traits and skills of effective leaders.

The old idea that leaders have certain traits or skills fell into disfavor but lately has been resurrected. Important leader characteristics include drive, leadership motivation, integrity, self-confidence, and knowledge of the business. Perhaps the most important skill is the ability to accurately perceive the situation and then change behavior accordingly.

The behaviors that will make you a better leader.

Important leader behaviors include task performance, group maintenance, and participation in decision making. Exhibiting more rather than fewer of these behaviors will enhance your effectiveness in the long run. The Vroom model helps a leader decide how much participation to use in making decisions. Path-goal theory assesses characteristics of the followers, the leader, and the situation; it then indicates the appropriateness of directive, supportive, participative, or achievement-oriented leadership behaviors.

What it means to be a charismatic and transformational leader.

To have charisma is to be dominant and self-confident, to have a strong conviction of the righteousness of your beliefs, to create an aura of competence and success, and to communicate high expectations for and confidence in your followers. Charisma is one component of transformational leadership. Transformational leaders translate a vision into reality by getting people to transcend their individual interests for the good of the larger community. They do this through charisma, individualized attention to followers, intellectual stimulation, formation and communication of their vision, building of trust, and positive self-regard.

How to further your own leadership development.

You can develop your own leadership skills not only by understanding what effective leadership is all about, but also by seeking challenging developmental experiences. Such important life experiences come about from taking challenging assignments, through exposure in working with other people, by overcoming hardships and failures, by taking formal courses, and by other actions.

Discussion questions

1. What elements from the chapter do you see in the leaders described in "Setting the Stage"?

2. Is there a difference between effective management and effective leadership? Explain your views and learn from others' views.

3. Identify someone you think is an effective leader. What traits and skills does this individual possess that make him or her effective?

4. Do you think most managers can be transformational leaders? Why or why not?

5. In your own words, define courage. What is the role of courage in leadership? Give examples of acts of leadership you consider courageous.

6. Do you think men and women differ in their leadership styles? If so, how? Do men and/or women prefer different styles in their bosses? What evidence do you have for your answers?

7. Who are your heroes? Try to identify some traditional heroes and also some that are "post-heroic." What makes them heroes, and what can you learn from them in general? What can you learn from them about leadership in particular?

8. Assess yourself as a leader based on what you have read in this chapter. What are your strengths and weaknesses?

9. Identify the developmental experiences you have had that may have strengthened your ability to lead. What did those experiences teach you? Also identify some developmental experiences you need to acquire, and how you will seek them. Be specific.

10. Consider a couple of decisions you are facing that could involve other people. Use the Vroom model to decide what approach to use to make the decisions.

11. Consider an organization of which you are a leader or a member. What could great transformational leadership accomplish in the organization?

12. Consider a job you hold or have held in the past. Consider how your boss managed you. How would you describe him or her as a leader? What substitutes for leadership would you have enjoyed being put into place?

Concluding Case
Following a legend

From the Pages of
BusinessWeek

Jeffrey Immelt is following a legend. He is succeeding GE's CEO Jack Welch, who created more shareholder value—almost $500 billion—than anyone in history. *Business Week* describes Welch as the epitome of the "CEO as maximum leader for all seasons—a human dynamo who through sheer force of personality and brilliance of vision can transform any company, no matter how big or how complicated, into an engine of perpetual outperformance" (p. 88). During his 20-year reign at GE, Welch's face graced countless book and magazine covers; he was one of the most famous businesspeople on the planet; and he was the most admired executive in the United States. He is widely considered the best CEO in America, and some consider him the best manager of the century.

Even Welch made mistakes early in his tenure. Obviously, he survived those mistakes. But today's environment, faced by Immelt, is more unforgiving. Times are tough, characterized by more turbulence in executive suites than in the past. Honeymoons are short. Impatience runs high when the investment community isn't quickly made happy. Two-thirds of all companies worldwide have replaced their CEO at least once since 1995. More than 1,000 U.S. CEOs left office in 2000 alone. And *Business Week* speculates about an even bigger epidemic of CEO firings yet to come.

Immelt's college classmates call him a natural leader; Welch says simply, "People follow him." He has been successful at inspiring innovation. A major customer is impressed with Immelt's decisiveness. The customer had a longstanding request that he couldn't convince others at GE to act on. "The first time I met Jeff . . . he made the decision in a minute. He told me, 'That makes total sense. We'll do it'" (p. 97).

Immelt faces major challenges. Although Immelt's title is CEO, it is not clear how much authority he has. Welch will stay on for one year beyond the Immelt announcement, and the two will work together closely. Despite his retirement announcement, Jack Welch is still highly vigorous and involved.

Immelt says he is very comfortable with the way GE is run. But he has experience in only 3 of 10 GE divisions, most of it in GE's highly entrepreneurial Plastics Division. And he has never worked overseas. Nonetheless, he sees great opportunities in global expansion and weaving the Internet into everything GE does.

GE is merging with Honeywell, the biggest merger in its history. The Honeywell merger greatly enlarges GE's Power Systems and Aircraft Engines units. But those units are losing key leaders. Moreover, Honeywell was underperforming, and decisions must be made about what to sell and what to build. In addition, the economy in late 2000 slowed down seriously.

GE's Appliances Division is struggling, and NBC (owned by GE) is facing daunting competition. Wall Street likes "pure plays," but GE is a highly complex conglomerate in many different industries. Some suspect that only someone of Welch's skills and stature could hold it together. With Wall Street's preference for companies to focus on fewer industries than GE does, and high expectations for profitability, Immelt could face enormous pressure to break up GE. And his position may be shaky if he doesn't deliver results.

Questions

1. Imagine that you are in Jeffrey Immelt's position. Assume that you are more experienced than you are now, and that you legitimately earned your way into the position. What would you feel emotionally?

2. Immelt has huge responsibilities and faces major challenges. How would you advise him to proceed? What should he do as leader?

3. What has Immelt been doing lately, and how is GE faring?

4. What skills and knowledge do you have now that would be useful in an important business leadership position? What skills and knowledge do you need to acquire? What is your plan to develop as a leader?

Sources: Bianco and L. Lavell, "The CEO Trap," *Business Week,* December 11, 2000, pp. 86–92; and P. Moore with N. Byrnes, "The Man Who Would Be Welch," *Business Week,* December 11, 2000, pp. 94–97. ●

As if following a legend wasn't enough, GE's CEO Jefferey Immelt (right) also faces today's impatient investment community.
[AFP/CORBIS]

Experiential Exercises
12.1 Power and influence

Objective

To explore the nature of power and influence, and your attitudes toward different kinds of power and influence.

Instructions

Read the introductions, "A. Power" and "B. Influence," to the Power and Influence Worksheet, and complete those sections of the worksheet. Then read and complete "C. Power and influence."

Power and influence worksheet

A. Power

A number of people have made statements about power and winning (e.g., P. T. Barnum, Mao Tse-tung, Leo Durocher, Lord Action, Vince Lombardi). Some of these statements are listed in the table that follows. Indicate how you feel about each of the statements by circling number 1 if you strongly disagree, number 5 if you strongly agree, and so on.

	Strongly disagree	Disagree	Neutral	Agree	Strongly agree
Winning is everything.	1	2	3	4	5
Nice guys finish last.	1	2	3	4	5
There can only be one winner.	1	2	3	4	5
There's a sucker born every minute.	1	2	3	4	5
You can't completely trust anyone.	1	2	3	4	5
All power rests at the end of the gun.	1	2	3	4	5
Power seekers are greedy and can't be trusted.	1	2	3	4	5
Power corrupts; absolute power corrupts absolutely.	1	2	3	4	5
You get as much power as you pay for.	1	2	3	4	5

B. Influence

During the past week or so you have come in contact with many people. Some have influenced you positively, some negatively. Try to recall recent experiences with employers, peers, teachers, parents, clergy, and the like who may have influenced you in some way. Then try to think about how and why they influenced you as they did.

1. On the following table, list the names of all those who influenced you during the past week or so according to the kind of power that person used. The same person's name may appear under more than one type of social power if that person used multiple power bases. Also, indicate whether the influence was positive (+) or negative (−).

Social power base	Names and whether (+) or (−)
Legitimate authority	_____
Reward	_____
Coercive	_____
Referent	_____
Expert	_____

2. After examining your list, check (✓) the following questions.

	Yes	No
a. Was there one person who had + marks appearing under several social power bases?	_____	_____
b. Was there one person who had − marks appearing under several social power bases?	_____	_____
c. Did you find that most of the people with + marks tended to fall under the same power bases?	_____	_____
d. Did you find that most of the people with − marks tended to fall under the same power bases?	_____	_____

3. From your answers to the last two questions, list which social power bases you found to be positive (+) and which you found to be negative (−).

+	−
_____	_____
_____	_____
_____	_____
_____	_____
_____	_____

Do you think you personally prefer to use those power bases you listed under + when you try to influence people? Do you actually use them?

C. Power and influence

From the table in Part B, find the one person whom you think had the strongest positive influence on you (Person 1), and the one who had the strongest negative influence (Person 2). These are most likely the persons whose names appear most frequently.

In the following table, place a 1 on the line for each statement that best indicates how you think Person 1 would respond to that statement. Put a 2 on the line for each statement that reflects how you think Person 2 would respond to that item.

	Strongly disagree	Disagree	Neutral	Agree	Strongly agree
Winning is everything.	_____	_____	_____	_____	_____
Nice guys finish last.	_____	_____	_____	_____	_____
There can only be one winner.	_____	_____	_____	_____	_____
There's a sucker born every minute.	_____	_____	_____	_____	_____
You can't completely trust anyone.	_____	_____	_____	_____	_____
All power rests at the end of the gun.	_____	_____	_____	_____	_____
Power seekers are greedy and can't be trusted.	_____	_____	_____	_____	_____
Power corrupts; absolute power corrupts absolutely.	_____	_____	_____	_____	_____
You get as much power as you pay for.	_____	_____	_____	_____	_____

Now compare your responses in Part A to those in Part C. Do you more closely resemble Person 1 or Person 2? Do you prefer to use the kinds of power that person uses? Which kinds of power do you use most frequently? Which do you use least frequently? When do you feel you have the greatest power? When do you have the least power? How do these answers compare to what you found in Part B3?

Source: Excerpted from Lawrence R. Jauch, Arthur G. Bedian, Sally A. Coltin, and William F. Glueck, *The Managerial Experience: Cases, Exercises, and Readings,* 4th ed. Copyright © 1986 by The Dryden Press. Reprinted by permission of the publisher.

12.2 Evaluating your leadership style

Objectives

1. To examine your personal style of leadership.

2. To study the nature of the leadership process.

3. To identify ways to improve or modify your leadership style.

Instructions

1. Working alone, complete and score the Leadership Style Survey.

2. In small groups, exchange scores, compute average scores, and develop responses to the discussion questions.

3. After the class reconvenes, group spokespersons present group findings.

Discussion Questions

1. In what ways did your experience or lack of experience influence your responses to the survey?

2. In what ways did student scores and student responses to survey test items agree? In what ways did they disagree?

3. What do you think accounts for differences in student leadership attitudes?

4. How can students make constructive use of the survey results?

Leadership style survey

This survey describes various aspects of leadership behavior. To measure your leadership style, respond to each statement according to the way you would act (or think you would act) if you were a work group leader.

	Always	Frequently	Occasionally	Seldom	Never
1. I would allow team members the freedom to do their jobs in their own way.	5	4	3	2	1
2. I would make important decisions on my own initiative without consulting the workers.	5	4	3	2	1
3. I would allow the team members to make their own decisions.	5	4	3	2	1
4. I would not try to socialize with the workers.	5	4	3	2	1
5. I would allow team members to do their jobs as they see fit.	5	4	3	2	1
6. I would consider myself to be the group's spokesperson.	5	4	3	2	1
7. I would be warm, friendly, and approachable.	5	4	3	2	1
8. I would be sure that the workers understand and follow all the rules and regulations.	5	4	3	2	1
9. I would demonstrate a real concern for the workers' welfare.	5	4	3	2	1
10. I would be the one to decide what is to be done and how it is to be done.	5	4	3	2	1

	Always	Frequently	Occasionally	Seldom	Never
11. I would delegate authority to the workers.	5	4	3	2	1
12. I would urge the workers to meet production quotas.	5	4	3	2	1
13. I would trust the workers to use good judgment in decision making.	5	4	3	2	1
14. I would assign specific tasks to specific people.	5	4	3	2	1
15. I would let the workers establish their own work pace.	5	4	3	2	1
16. I would not feel that I have to explain my decisions to workers.	5	4	3	2	1
17. I would try to make each worker feel that his or her contribution is important.	5	4	3	2	1
18. I would establish the work schedules.	5	4	3	2	1
19. I would encourage workers to get involved in setting work goals.	5	4	3	2	1
20. I would be action oriented and results oriented.	5	4	3	2	1
21. I would get the workers involved in making decisions.	5	4	3	2	1
22. I would outline needed changes and monitor action closely.	5	4	3	2	1
23. I would help the group achieve consensus on important changes.	5	4	3	2	1
24. I would supervise closely to ensure that standards are met.	5	4	3	2	1
25. I would consistently reinforce good work.	5	4	3	2	1
26. I would nip problems in the bud.	5	4	3	2	1
27. I would consult the group before making decisions.	5	4	3	2	1

The 411 on . . .

Classic Contingency Models of Leadership

The chapter described some situational or contingency models of leadership; here are two more, presented here in the interest of conserving chapter space.

Fiedler's contingency model

Fiedler's contingency model of leadership effectiveness states that effectiveness depends on two factors: the personal style of the leader and the degree to which the situation gives the leader power, control, and influence over the situation.[1] Figure 12.A.1 illustrates the contingency model. The upper half of the figure shows the situational analysis, and the lower half indicates the appropriate style. In the upper portion, three questions are used to analyze the situation:

1. Are leader–member relations good or poor? (To what extent is the leader accepted and supported by group members?)

2. Is the task structured or unstructured? (To what extent do group members know what their goals are and how to accomplish them?)

3. Is the leader's position power strong or weak (high or low)? (To what extent does the leader have the authority to reward and punish?)

These three sequential questions create a decision tree in which a situation is classified into one of eight categories. The lower the category number, the more favorable the situation is for the leader; the higher the number, the less favorable the situation. Originally, Fiedler called this variable "situational favorableness" but now calls it "situational control." Situation 1 is the best: Relations are good, task structure is high, and power is high. In the least favorable situation (8), in which the leader has very little situational control, relations are poor, tasks lack structure, and the leader's power is weak.

Different situations dictate different leadership styles. Fiedler measured leadership styles with an instrument assessing the leader's *least preferred coworker* (LPC); that is, the attitude toward the follower the leader liked the least. This was considered an indication more generally of leaders' attitudes toward people. If a leader can single out the person she likes the least, but her attitude is not all that negative, she received a high score on the LPC scale. Leaders with more negative attitudes toward others would receive low LPC scores.

Based on the LPC score, Fiedler considered two leadership styles. **Task-motivated leadership** places primary emphasis on

figure 12.A.1

Fiedler's analysis of situations in which the task- or relationship-motivated leader is more effective

Leader–member relations	Good				Poor			
Task structure	Structured		Unstructured		Structured		Unstructured	
Leader position power	High	Low	High	Low	High	Low	High	Low
	1	2	3	4	5	6	7	8

Favorable for leader →→→→→→→→→→→→→→→→→ Unfavorable for leader

Type of leader most effective in the solution	Task-motivated	Task-motivated	Task-motivated	Relation-ship-motivated	Relation-ship-motivated	Relation-ship-motivated	Relation-ship-motivated	Task-motivated

Source: D. Organ and T. Bateman, *Organizational Behavior,* 4th ed. (Burr Ridge, IL: Richard D. Irwin, 1990).

completing the task and is more likely exhibited by leaders with low LPC scores. **Relationship-motivated leadership** emphasizes maintaining good interpersonal relationships and is more likely from high-LPC leaders. These leadership styles correspond to task performance and group maintenance leader behaviors, respectively.

The lower part of Figure 12.A.1 indicates which style is situationally appropriate. For situations 1, 2, 3, and 8, a task-motivated leadership style is more effective. For situations 4 through 7, relationship-motivated leadership is more appropriate.

Fiedler's theory was not always supported by research. It is better supported if three broad rather than eight specific levels of situational control are assumed: low, medium, and high. It was quite controversial in academic circles; among other arguable things, it assumed that leaders cannot change their styles but must be assigned to situations that suit their styles. However, the model has withstood the test of time and still receives attention. Most important, it initiated and continues to emphasize the importance of finding a fit between the situation and the leader's style.

Hersey and Blanchard's situational theory

Hersey and Blanchard developed an important situational model that added another factor the leader should take into account before deciding whether task performance or maintenance behaviors are more important. Originally called the *life cycle theory of leadership,* their **situational theory** highlights the maturity of the followers as the key situational factor.[2] **Job maturity** is the level of the

follower's skills and technical knowledge relative to the task being performed; **psychological maturity** is the follower's self-confidence and self-respect. High-maturity followers have both the ability and the confidence to do a good job.

The theory proposes a simple, linear relationship between a follower's maturity and the degree of task performance behaviors a leader should use. The more mature the followers, the less the leader needs to organize and explain tasks. The required amount of maintenance behaviors is a bit more complex. As in Fiedler's model, the relationship is curvilinear: Maintenance behaviors are not important with followers of low or high levels of maturity but are important for followers of moderate maturity. For low-maturity followers, the emphasis should be on performance-related leadership; for moderate-maturity followers, performance leadership is somewhat less important and maintenance behaviors become more important; and for high-maturity followers, neither dimension of leadership behavior is important.

Little academic research has been done on this situational theory, but the model is extremely popular in management training seminars. Regardless of its scientific validity, Hersey and Blanchard's model provides a reminder that it is important to treat different people differently. Moreover, it suggests the importance of treating the same individual differently from time to time as he or she changes jobs or acquires more maturity in her or his particular job.[3]

Appendix key terms

Fiedler's contingency model of leadership effectiveness A situational approach to leadership postulating that effectiveness depends on the personal style of the leader and the degree to which the situation gives the leader power, control, and influence over the situation, p. 408

Hersey and Blanchard's situational theory A life cycle theory of leadership developed by Hersey and Blanchard postulating that a manager should consider an employee's psychological and job maturity before deciding whether task performance or maintenance behaviors are more important, p. 409

job maturity The level of the employee's skills and technical knowledge relative to the task being performed, p. 409

psychological maturity An employee's self-confidence and self-respect, p. 409

Relationship-motivated leadership Leadership that places primary emphasis on maintaining good interpersonal relationships, p. 409

task-motivated leadership Leadership that places primary emphasis on completing a task, p. 408

Chapter Thirteen

Motivating for Performance

The worst mistake a boss can make is not to say well done.

—John Ashcroft

The reward of a thing well done is to have done it.

—Ralph Waldo Emerson

Chapter Outline

Learning Objectives

After studying Chapter 13, you will know:

1. The kinds of behaviors managers need to motivate in people.

2. How to set challenging, motivating goals.

3. How to reward good performance.

4. The key beliefs that affect people's motivation.

5. The ways in which people's individual needs affect their behavior.

6. How to create a motivating, empowering job.

7. How people assess fairness and how to achieve fairness.

8. The causes and consequences of a satisfied workforce.

Setting the Stage

Different Approaches to Motivation

Harvard Business School publishes 35,000 cases worldwide. The case purchased most often is about Lincoln Electric Company of Cleveland. Lincoln Electric produces industrial electric motors and is the world's largest manufacturer of arc welding products.

The attraction of the case is Lincoln's success at motivating workers by tying pay to performance. All of its people—most of whom are factory workers, and many without college degrees—participate in the company's incentive plan. All but two share in the annual bonus—the president and the chair. The two top executives are paid based on a percentage of sales; if sales go down, they take the first pay cut.

Lincoln also has a piecework rate, with which workers earn money based on how much they produce. All jobs in the company have pay ranges (hourly or salary) so that individuals who perform at their highest capability can move up to the top of the range for their particular job.

Every six months, the CEO personally reviews all merit ratings. Everyone is rated in four performance categories: output, quality, dependability (ability to work without supervision), and cooperation and ideas. Over the 50-plus years in which the system has been in place, the average year-end bonus has been 95.5 percent of base. In other words, employees commonly double their annual income by virtue of the annual bonus.

Lincoln Electric Company's merit pay plan allows most workers to double their base salary via their annual bonus.
[Courtesy of The Lincoln Electric Company, Cleveland, Ohio]

Lincoln has been number one in its business worldwide for the entire life of the incentive system. Most people's performance is outstanding—and they don't require much supervision. The foreman-to-worker ratio is 1:100. Typically it's 1:25, even 1:10 in some plants. The cost savings help pay the bonus.

Lincoln Electric has outlasted giants like Westinghouse to dominate a fiercely competitive industry. Managers attribute their company's success to a philosophy: a strong belief in the power of unfettered capitalism.

AES Corporation, the global electricity giant with 40,000 employees, espouses a different philosophy about motivating people. Chairman Roger Sant and CEO Dennis Bakke built their company around the principles of fairness, integrity, social responsibility, and fun. The employees are truly "empowered." That is, frontline employees make and execute important decisions without interference from above.

Sant speaks about one of the key principles: "The word *fun* can be misleading . . . AES is fun . . . because the people who work here are fully engaged. They have total responsibility for decisions. They are accountable for results. What they do every day matters to the company, and it matters to the

Chapter Fourteen
Managing Teams

No one can whistle a symphony. It takes an orchestra to play it.

—Halford E. Luccock

Chapter Outline

Learning Objectives

After studying Chapter 14, you will know:

1. How teams contribute to your organization's effectiveness.

2. What makes the new team environment different from the old.

3. How groups become teams.

4. Why groups sometimes fail.

5. How to build an effective team.

6. How to manage your team's relationships with other teams.

7. How to manage conflict.

Setting the Stage

Two High-Impact Teams

"The Internet is going to have as much of an impact on the automobile industry as Henry Ford's mass-merchandising and production methods did in the 1920s" (p. 120), states Lee Sage, global leader of Ernst & Young's automotive-industry consulting practice. At Ford and Toyota, two work teams are trying to make that happen.

At Ford, Thor Ibsen leads the unit that is trying to change the entire company by using the Internet to give consumers total choice in finding or creating exactly the vehicle they want. One of Ibsen's teams is the eConsumer Group, which wants to make Ford the first automaker modeled after Dell's build-to-order business model. Lead times for autos are too long to offer build-to-order service for every customer, but the team does want it to be an option if a specific car or truck isn't already somewhere in the channel from factory to dealer.

In the beginning, senior executives often didn't reply to Thor's e-mail messages. But thanks to the efforts and talents of Ibsen's team, Jim Schroer, Ford's VP for global marketing, now says the Internet team has generated a momentum that is impossible to ignore. "We have an enormous opportunity as the industry shifts to e-business . . . we intend to lead the industry in e-business" (p. 124).

Thor Ibsen's eConsumer Group wants to make Ford the first automaker to offer customers a build-to-order service option.
[Zubin Shroff]

At Toyota, Peter Dames leads the electronic-commerce strategy team that wants to "convince the rest of the company that those things have an impact on everything else—our budget, our strategy, our margins. Half the work we do here is evangelizing" (p. 120).

Toyota is history-rich, very profitable, and proud. Dames's goal is to show the rest of the company that playing by old rules, revering tradition, and sticking to familiar processes don't cut it in the Internet economy. His team members don't adhere to the unwritten shirt-and-tie dress code; they wear jeans and sneakers. They designed their own business cards with images of a spaceman and a toy robot—very different from Toyota's standard cards. Dames wants his team to be rebellious, and to be highly visible within Toyota.

One team member said, "We've been involved with every major Internet initiative at the company and technology has never been the problem." Another picked up the theme: "It's always been about getting people to work differently and redefining business processes. That's the toughest nut to crack" (p. 136). Dames concludes, "The rest of the company used to be Internet skeptics, and now, for the most part, they're believers" (p. 138).

Source: S. Kirsner, "Collision Course," *Fast Company, January-February 2000, pp. 118–44.*

Scorecard:

Round	Minutes	Choice Red team	Choice Blue team	Cumulative points Red team	Cumulative points Blue team
1	3				
2	3				
3*	3 (reps.) 3 (teams)				
4	3				
5	3				
6*	3 (reps.) 3 (teams)				
7**	3 (reps.) 3 (teams)				
8**	3 (reps.) 3 (teams)				

*Payoff points are doubled for this round. **Payoff points are squared for this round. (Retain the minus sign.)
Source: Dorothy Hai, "Prisoner's Dilemma," in *Organizational Behavior: Experiences and Cases* (St. Paul, MN: West, 1986), pp. 125–27.
Reprinted by permission. Copyright © 1986 by West Publishing Company. All rights reserved.

14.2 The traveler's check scam group exercise

Instructions

1. (3 min.) Group selects an observer. The observer remains silent during the group problem-solving process, recording the activities of the group on the Observer's Report Form.
2. (15 min.) Group members read the following problem and proceed to solve it.
3. (2 min.) When the group has a solution to the problem upon which all members agree, it will be written on a note and handed to the instructor.
4. (5 min.) The observer briefs the group on the problem-solving processes observed during the exercise.
5. (25 min.) The small group discusses the following topics:
   a. Did the group decide on a problem solution process before it attempted to solve the problem? If so, what was it?
   b. Was the solution of the problem hindered in any way by the lack of an appropriate agreed-upon group problem-solving process? Explain.
   c. Who were the leaders of the group during the exercise? What did they do? Critique their leadership activities.
   d. What communications patterns were used by the group during the exercise? Who participated the most? Who participated the least? Describe individual behaviors.
   e. Did the group solve the problem? How many members of the group discovered the correct answer on their own?
   f. Was using the group to solve this problem better than assigning the problem to one person? Explain the rationale for your answer.

The case of Mickey the Dip

Mickey the Dip, an expert pickpocket and forger, liked to work the Los Angeles International Airport on busy days. His technique was to pick the pockets of prosperous-looking victims just before they boarded planes to the East Coast. This gave Mickey five hours to use stolen credit cards before the owners could report their losses.

One morning Mickey snatched a fat wallet from a traveler and left the airport to examine his loot. To his surprise he found no credit cards but instead $500 in traveler's checks. After 20 minutes of practice, Mickey could sign a perfect imitation of the victim's signature. He then proceeded to a large department store where all suits were being sold for 75 percent of the regular price. Mickey purchased a suit for $225 and paid for it with $300 in stolen traveler's checks. After the clerk who served him went to lunch, he bought another suit for $150 and paid for it with the remaining $200 of stolen traveler's checks. Later, Mickey switched the labels on the two suits and, using the receipt from the $225 suit, returned the $150 suit at a centralized return desk for a refund. The refund clerk took the suit and gave Mickey eleven $20 bills, which he stuffed into his pocket and disappeared.

When the department store deposited the traveler's checks, they were returned as forgeries. Assuming the store normally sold suits at twice their wholesale price and used 10 percent of sales as an overhead cost figure, what was the cash value of the loss suffered by the store as a result of Mickey's caper? Do not consider taxes in your computations.

The traveler's check scam exercise observer's report

1. What happened during the first few minutes the group met after members finished reading the problem? (List behaviors of specific group members.)

2. Identify the group role played by each group member during the exercise. Give examples of the behavior of each.

3. Were there any conflicts within or among group members during the exercise? Explain the nature of the conflicts and the behavior of the individual(s) involved.

4. How were decisions made in the group? Give specific examples.

5. How could the group improve its problem-solving skills?

Source: Peter P. Dawson, *Fundamentals of Organizational Behavior* (Englewood Cliffs, NJ: Prentice–Hall, 1985), pp. 419–22. © 1985. Reprinted by permission of Prentice–Hall, Inc., Englewood Cliffs, N.J. ●

Chapter Fifteen
Communicating

Electronic engineers have yet to devise a better interoffice communications system than the water cooler.

—Leo Ellis

Chapter Outline

Interpersonal Communication
    One-Way versus Two-Way Communication
    Communication Pitfalls
    Mixed Signals and Misperception
    Oral and Written Channels
    Electronic Media
    Communications Networks
    Media Richness
    Efficiency and Effectiveness
Improving Communication Skills
    Improving Sender Skills
    Nonverbal Skills
    Improving Receiver Skills
    Effective Supervision
Organizational Communication
    Downward Communication
    Upward Communication
    Horizontal Communication
    Formal and Informal Communication
    Boundarylessness

Learning Objectives

After studying Chapter 15, you will know:

1. The important advantages of two-way communication.

2. Communications problems to avoid.

3. When and how to use the various communications channels.

4. Ways to become a better "sender" and "receiver" of information.

5. How to improve downward, upward, and horizontal communications.

6. How to work with the company grapevine.

7. The advantages and characteristics of the boundaryless organization.

Setting the Stage

The Power of Dialogue

A steel mill in the Midwest had endured 30 years of labor–management animosity. People called each other names, threw chairs, stormed out of meetings, and staged work slowdowns. Neither management nor labor trusted the other, and both sides doubted that reconciliation was possible. But tough competition from mini-mills forced them to try to cooperate. So they agreed to try a participative total quality improvement process, and formed joint problem solving committees.

In the initial meetings, consultants helped the groups to communicate more constructively. Instead of placing blame and resurrecting old conflicts, people tried to step away from the past and really think about the present and the future. They began talking honestly about concerns, and openly considered other viewpoints.

The process was not an easy one; it took time, effort, and courage. But eventually, for the first time, both managers and union personnel began to talk about the business as theirs. They came to recognize that they all were part of the same organization, and they began to think together rather than separately.

According to the union president, the old antagonism is a thing of the past. "That's gone. Now we're looking at the future." The CEO describes it this way: "The process became a method of exchanging thoughts and realizing that none of us have the answer, but together we might have a better answer."

Although it took time, eventually managers and union personnel began to think together rather than separately.
[Corbis Stock Market/William Taufic]

At KPMG Netherlands, chairman Ruud Koedikj knew his firm had to move into new growth areas, but wasn't sure where they were or how to identify them. So he met with all 300 partners, and described how he saw the firm's history, current business realities, and future challenges. He then asked how they could go about changing as a firm, and asked for their perspectives. Instead of announcing a new strategy, he engaged the partners in dialogue, thereby building trust and credibility. The partners responded by releasing 100 people from daily responsibilities so they could devote 60 percent of their time, over several months, to work on the strategic challenges faced by the firm.

Dialogue is a powerful tool with people outside the firm as well. While some companies ignore customers, others engage them in active dialogue in order to strengthen both products and customer relationships. At Cisco, customers have open access to Cisco's information, knowledge base, and user community via an online service, and they engage in dialogue, solving each other's problems. Some companies have extensive conversations with customers and potential customers about product features. Likewise, Ford's suppliers collaborate in developing new vehicles.

Thus, in progressive companies, customers and other outsiders step out of their traditional roles and become co-creators of value. The best conversations are a dialogue of equals. Done right, customers and others outside the firm become a source of competitive advantage. Effective dialogue is the source of that source.

Source: Used with permission of the publisher, from Organizational Dynamics, Autumn 1993, copyright © 1993. American Management Association, New York. All rights reserved. Also, N. M. Dixon, "The Hallways of Learning," Organizational Dynamics, Spring 1997, pp. 23–34; R. Heifetz and D. Laurie, "The Work of Leadership," Harvard Business Review, January–February 1996, pp. 124–34; and C. K. Prahalad and V. Ramaswamy, "Co-opting Customer Competence," Harvard Business Review, January–February 2000, pp. 79–87.

Two types of discourse work together to help a group become a team and an organization become a more effective organization. The two types—and their impact—are illustrated in "Setting the Stage." **Discussion** is like a ping-pong match, with people hitting the ball back and forth.[1] Each person is trying to win a debate, in the sense of having his or her view accepted by the group. Discussions can be polite, and useful, but they can also work at cross-purposes and become destructive.

Dialogue, on the other hand, has the goal of going beyond one person's understanding. The goal is not to "win," but for the team to come to a common, deep understanding. Dialogue explores complex issues from many viewpoints.[2] It requires a commitment to the truth, honesty about people's own beliefs, true listening, and open-mindedness toward others' beliefs. Free exploration of ideas helps individuals, and the group as a unit, to think and learn.[3]

Every group and organization should have both. The most common danger is plenty of discussion and argument, but not much in the way of real dialogue.

Discussion and dialogue are examples of how people communicate. Effective communication is a fundamental aspect of job performance and managerial effectiveness.[4] In this chapter, we will present important communication concepts and some practical guidelines for improving your effectiveness. We will discuss both interpersonal and organizational communication.

discussion A type of discourse in which each person attempts to win a debate by having his or her view accepted by the group.

dialogue A discourse in which members explore complex issues from many viewpoints in order to come to a common, deeper understanding.

Interpersonal communication

communication The transmission of information and meaning from one party to another through the use of shared symbols.

Communication is the transmission of information and meaning from one party to another through the use of shared symbols. Figure 15.1 shows a general model of the communication process.

The *sender* initiates the process by conveying information to the *receiver*—the person for whom the message is intended. The sender has a *meaning* he or she wishes to communicate and *encodes* the meaning into symbols (e.g., the words chosen for the message). Then the sender *transmits,* or sends, the message through some *channel,* such as a verbal or written medium.

The receiver *decodes* the message (e.g., reads it) and attempts to *interpret* the sender's meaning. The receiver may provide *feedback* to the sender by encoding a message in response to the sender's message.

The communication process often is hampered by *noise,* or interference in the system, that blocks perfect understanding. Noise could be anything that interferes with accurate conversation: ringing telephones, thoughts about other things, or simple fatigue or stress.

figure 15.1
A model of the communication process

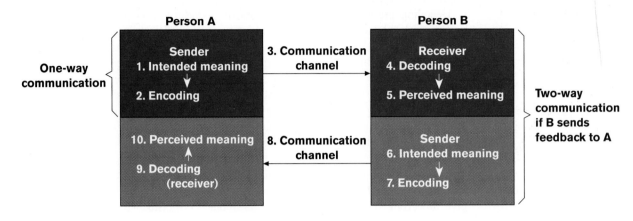

The model in Figure 15.1 is more than a theoretical treatment of the communication process: It points out the key ways in which communications can break down. Mistakes can be made at each stage of the model. A manager who is alert to potential problems can perform each step carefully to ensure more effective communication. The model also helps explain the differences between one-way and two-way communication, communications pitfalls, misperception, and the various communication channels.

One-way versus two-way communication

one-way communication A process in which information flows in only one direction—from the sender to the receiver, with no feedback loop.

In **one-way communication,** only the top half of the model in Figure 15.1 is operating. Information flows in only one direction—from the sender to the receiver, with no feedback loop. A manager sends a memo to a subordinate without asking for an immediate response. A boss gives an order over the phone. A father scolds his son and then storms out of the room.

When receivers do respond to senders, completing the Figure 15.1 model, **two-way communication** has occurred. One-way communication in situations like those just described can become two-way if the manager follows up her memo with a phone call and asks the receiver if he has any questions, the boss on the telephone listens to alternative suggestions for carrying out her order, and the father calms down and listens to his son's side of the story.

two-way communication A process in which information flows in two directions—the receiver provides feedback and the sender is receptive to the feedback.

True two-way communication means not only that the receiver provides feedback but also that the sender is receptive to the feedback. In these constructive exchanges, information is shared between both parties rather than delivered from one person to the other.

One-way communication is much more common than it should be because it is faster and easier for the sender. The busy executive finds it easier to dash off a memo than to discuss the issue with the subordinate. Also, he doesn't have to deal with questions or be challenged by someone who disagrees.

Two-way communication is more difficult and time-consuming than one-way communication. However, it is more accurate; fewer mistakes occur and fewer problems arise. Receivers have a chance to ask questions, share concerns, make suggestions or modifications, and consequently understand more precisely what is being communicated and what they should do with the information.[5]

Communication pitfalls

The sender's intended message does not always "get across" to the receiver. You are operating under an illusion if you think there is a perfect correlation between what you say and what people hear.[6]

Errors can occur in all stages of the communication process. In the encoding stage, words can be misused, decimal points typed in the wrong places, facts left out, or ambiguous phrases inserted. In the transmission stage, a memo gets lost on a cluttered desk, the words on an overhead transparency are too small to read from the back of the room, or words are spoken with ambiguous inflections.

Decoding problems arise when the receiver doesn't listen carefully or reads too quickly and overlooks a key point. And, of course, receivers can misinterpret the message, as a reader draws the wrong conclusion from an unclear memo, a listener takes a general statement by the boss too personally, or a sideways glance is taken the wrong way.

More generally, people's perceptual and filtering processes create misinterpretations. **Perception** is the process of receiving and interpreting information. As you know, such processes are not perfectly objective. They are subjective, as people's self-interested motives and attitudes toward the sender and toward the message create biased interpretations.

perception The process of receiving and interpreting information.

Filtering is the process of withholding, ignoring, or distorting information. Senders do this, for example, when they tell the boss what they think the boss wants to hear, or give unwarranted compliments rather than honest criticism. Receivers can also filter information; they may fail to recognize an important message, or attend to some aspects of the message but not others.

filtering The process of withholding, ignoring, or distorting information.

Filtering and subjective perception pervade one interesting aspect of the communications dynamic: how men and women differ in their communicating styles. In the workplace, choices made at different stages of the model—choices in which senders and receivers filter and perceive different things—"affect judgments of competence and confidence, as well as who gets heard, who gets credit, and what gets done."[7] According to Deborah Tannen, a popular writer and respected communications scholar at Georgetown University, men speak in ways to establish power, gain personal credit, and minimize the appearance of uncertainty. They have trouble admitting fault or weakness, ask fewer questions, and ritually disagree with others. In contrast, women are more likely to speak in ways to establish rapport, to downplay their accomplishments (assuming they will get the credit they deserve), to help others save face, and to be more indirect in telling others what to do. Women, says Tannen, are more likely to say "we" in situations where men say "I."[8]

A manager at a magazine who tended to phrase the assignments she gave her reporters as questions—"How would you like to do the X project with Y?" and "I was thinking of putting you on the X project, is that okay?"—was criticized by her male boss, who told her she did not portray the proper demeanor with her staff.[9] Another, the owner of a retail operation, told one of her store managers to do something by saying, "The bookkeeper needs help with the billing. How would you feel about helping her out?" He said fine, but didn't do it. Whereas the boss thought he meant he would do it, he said he meant he would think about how he would feel about helping. He decided he had better things to do.[10]

Because of such filtering and perceptual differences, you cannot assume the other person means what you think he means, or understands the meanings you intend. Managers need to excel at reading interactions, and adjusting their communication styles and perceptions to the people with whom they interact.[11] The very human tendencies to filter and perceive subjectively underlie many of the ineffective communications, and the need to engage in more effective communication practices, that you will read about through the rest of this chapter.

Mixed signals and misperception

A common thread underlying the discussion so far is that people's perceptions can undermine attempts to communicate. People do not pay attention to everything going on around them. They inadvertently send mixed signals that can undermine their intended messages. Different people attend to different things, and people interpret the same thing in different ways. All of this creates problems in communication.

If the communication is between people from different cultures, these problems are magnified.[12] Communication "breakdowns" often occur when business transactions take place between people from different countries. Chapter 6 introduced you to the importance of these cultural issues. Table 15.1 offers suggestions for communicating effectively with someone who speaks a different language.

The following examples further highlight the operation of mixed signals and misperceptions. A bank CEO knew that to be competitive he had to downsize his organization, and the employees who remained would have to commit to customer service,

table 15.1

What do I do if they do not speak my language?

Verbal behavior

- *Clear, slow speech.* Enunciate each word. Do not use colloquial expressions.
- *Repetition.* Repeat each important idea using different words to explain the same concept.
- *Simple sentences.* Avoid compound, long sentences.
- *Active verbs.* Avoid passive verbs.

Nonverbal behavior

- *Visual restatements.* Use as many visual restatements as possible, such as pictures, graphs, tables, and slides.
- *Gestures.* Use more facial and appropriate hand gestures to emphasize the meaning of words.
- *Demonstrations.* Act out as many themes as possible.
- *Pauses.* Pause more frequently.
- *Summaries.* Hand out written summaries of your verbal presentation.

Accurate interpretation

- *Silence.* When there is a silence, wait. Do not jump in to fill the silence. The other person is probably just thinking more slowly in the nonnative language or translating.
- *Intelligence.* Do not equate poor grammar and mispronunciation with lack of intelligence; it is usually a sign of nonnative language use.
- *Differences.* If unsure, assume difference, not similarity.

Comprehension

- *Understanding.* Do not just assume that they understand; assume that they do not understand.
- *Checking comprehension.* Have colleagues repeat their understanding of the material back to you. Do not simply ask if they understand or not. Let them explain what they understand to you.

Design

- *Breaks.* Take more frequent breaks. Second language comprehension is exhausting.
- *Small modules.* Divide the material to be presented into smaller modules.
- *Longer time frame.* Allocate more time for each module than you usually need for presenting the same material to native speakers of your language.

Motivation

- *Encouragement.* Verbally and nonverbally encourage and reinforce speaking by nonnative language participants.
- *Drawing out.* Explicitly draw out marginal and passive participants.
- *Reinforcement.* Do not embarrass novice speakers.

Source: N. Adler, *International Dimensions of Organizational Behavior,* 3rd ed. (Cincinnati: Southwestern, 1997).

become more empowered, and really *earn* customer loyalty.[13] Knowing that his employees would have doubts and concerns about the coming reorganization, he decided to make a promise to them that he would do his best to guarantee employment, growth, and training.

What signals did the CEO communicate to his people by his promises? One positive signal was that he cared about his people. But he also signaled that *he* would take care of *them,* thus undermining his goal of giving them more responsibility and empowering them. The employees wanted management to take responsibility for the market challenge that *they* needed to face—to handle things for them when *they* needed to learn the new ways of doing business. Inadvertently, the CEO spoke to their backward-looking need for security when he had meant to make them see that the bank's future depended on *their* efforts.

A CEO of another firm talked repeatedly about the importance of empowerment throughout the organization.[14] But during one meeting, when a young manager brought up a problem that the home office was not handling for him as he had requested, the CEO thanked the manager, told him to whom to talk, and assured him that he would pave the way. Many executives in attendance even praised the CEO for empowering the manager.

But the CEO could have given a better, much more empowering response. The CEO could have taken the opportunity to ask the manager how the organization could be redesigned so that he and other people like him felt they had the freedom to take the initiative and get results on their own. Promising to help one person on one issue, by invoking CEO power, does not communicate to people the goal of their true and permanent empowerment to make positive things happen on their own.[15]

Consider how many problems could be avoided—and how much more effective communication could be—if people took the time to (1) ensure that the receivers attend to the message they are sending; (2) consider the other party's frame of reference and attempt to convey the message from that perceptual viewpoint; (3) take concrete steps to minimize perceptual errors and improper signals, in both sending and receiving; and (4) send *consistent* messages. You should make an effort to predict people's interpretations of your messages and think in terms of how they could *misinterpret* your messages. It helps to say not only what you mean but also what you *don't* mean. Every time you say, "I am not saying *X,* I am saying *Y,*" you eliminate a possible misinterpretation.[16]

Oral and written channels

Communication can be sent through a variety of channels (steps 3 and 8 in the Figure 15.1 model) including oral, written, and electronic. Each channel has advantages and disadvantages.

Oral communication includes face-to-face discussion, telephone conversations, and formal presentations and speeches. Advantages are that questions can be asked and answered; feedback is immediate and direct; the receiver(s) can sense the sender's sincerity (or lack thereof); and oral communication is more persuasive and sometimes less expensive than written. However, oral communication also has disadvantages: It can lead to spontaneous, ill-considered statements (and regret), and there is no permanent record of it (unless an effort is made to record it).

Written communication includes memos, letters, reports, computer files, and other written documents. Advantages to using written messages are that the message can be revised several times, it is a permanent record that can be saved, the message stays the same even if relayed through many people, and the receiver has more time to analyze the message. Disadvantages are that the sender has no control over where, when, or if the message is read; the sender does not receive immediate feedback; the receiver may not understand parts of the message; and the message must be longer to contain enough information to answer anticipated questions.[17]

You should weigh these considerations when deciding whether to communicate orally or in writing. Also, sometimes use both channels, such as following up a meeting with a confirming memo or writing a letter to prepare someone for your phone call.

Electronic media

A special category of communication channels is electronic media. Managers use computers not only to gather and distribute quantitative data but to "talk" with others electronically. In electronic decision rooms, software supports simultaneous access to shared files, and allows people to share views and do work collectively.[18] Other means of electronic communication include *teleconferencing* in which groups of people in different locations interact over telephone lines (*audioconferencing*) and perhaps also see one another on television monitors as they participate in group discussions (*videoconferencing*).

Advantages   *Advantages* of electronic communication technology are numerous and dramatic. Within firms, the advantages include the sharing of more information, and speed and efficiency in delivering routine messages to large numbers of people across vast geographic areas. It can reduce time spent traveling, talking, and photocopying. It's also cheap: A message that costs $16 for overnight delivery, or $3 through snail mail, costs pennies via e-mail.[19] Alcoa reduced its cost base by over $1 billion by installing a system that enables it to manage in real time—that is, making decisions immediately, on the basis of accurate information communicated "live," as it happens.[20]

Some companies, including Boeing, use brainstorming software that allows anonymous contributions, presuming this will add more honesty to internal discussions. Some research indicates more data sharing and critical argumentation, and higher-quality decisions, with a group decision support system than that found in face-to-face meetings.[21] But anonymity also offers great potential for lies, gossip, insults, threats, harassment, and the release of confidential information.[22]

Disadvantages   *Disadvantages* of electronic communication include the difficulty of solving complex problems, which require more extended, face-to-face interaction, and the inability to pick up subtle, nonverbal, or inflectional clues about what the communicator is thinking or conveying. E-mail is most appropriate, then, for routine messages that do not require the exchange of large quantities of complex information. It is less suitable for confidential information, resolving conflicts, or negotiating.[23]

One inevitable consequence of electronic mail is "flaming": hurling insults, sending "nastygrams," venting frustration, snitching on co-workers to the boss, and otherwise breaching bureaucratic protocol.[24] E-mail liberates people to type and send things they would not say to a person's face. The lack of nonverbal cues can result in "kidding" remarks being taken seriously, causing resentment and regret. It is not unheard of for confidential messages, including details about people's personal lives and insulting, embarrassing remarks, to become public knowledge through electronic leaks.

Other downsides to electronic mail are important to know.[25] Different people and sometimes different working units latch onto different channels as their medium of choice. For example, an engineering division might use e-mail most; but a design group might rely primarily on voice mail or printed faxes, and neglect e-mail.[26] Another disadvantage is that e-mail messages sometimes are monitored or seen inadvertently by those for whom they are not intended. Deleting messages does not destroy them; they are saved elsewhere. Recipients can forward them to others, unbeknownst to the original sender. And they can be used in court cases to indict individuals or companies. E-mail messages are private property—but the private property of the system's owner, not of the sender.[27]

From the Pages of   ## Dialogue with Computers

IBM was first to market with an affordable speech program that transforms spoken sentences into text. Now powerful speech-recognition technology is bursting into the marketplace as machines learn how to recognize and understand "natural language" spoken by humans. The new generation of speech technology will have a profound impact on how we work and live.

Speech may be the ultimate bridge between people and machines; Bill Gates calls speech "not just the future of Windows, but the future of computing itself."

Speech-recognition software programs will do for you (rather, with you), such things as get airline reservations, trade stocks, and retrieve voice-mail, e-mail, and faxes from a unified mailbox. Voice-controlled Web-browsing programs will mean that you won't have to click for hours on end. You will be able to surf the Net without typing on a keyboard, by giving oral commands on the phone. And Tellme Networks wants to offer you a single toll-free number that would be the last one you ever need to dial, on which you can simply say "Connect me with the nearest muffler shop" or "Call my mother." You won't get a dial tone, but a personal virtual assistant that will call your friend or anyone you want at your command.

Business Week stated, "We can't guess what kinds of dialogs will evolve among humans and machines in the next century. But it's certain we'll all soon be spending a lot more time chatting with computers." For example, a Toyota team is attempting to use the Internet to put two-way communications into the automobile. My Car Universe is a prototype 3-D Website created in partnership with Intel, HP, Compaq, and design agency Spike Australia. The computer and driver both convey and receive information, asking questions and taking desired action. The computer informs when the brake pads are low, and asks if the driver wants to book an appointment with the local Toyota dealership. The car tells the user that concert tickets for a certain favorite band are going on sale, and offers to plan a route to buy tickets. It states when gas is needed, and tells the driver where she can get some en route. It can send security messages to a pager or Palm Pilot, notifying the owner if someone is struggling to get into the car. Real-time traffic data and an MP3 jukebox aren't far off.

Source: N. Gross, P. Judge, O. Port, and S. Wildstrom, "Let's Talk!" *Business Week,* February 23, 1998, pp. 45–53; E. Nee, "Who wants to talk to the Web?" *Fortune,* November 13, 2000, pp. 317–24; and S. Kirsner, "Collision Course," *Fast Company,* January–February 2000, pp. 118–44. ●

The virtual office

Many entrepreneurs conduct business via open "offices" on the Internet, working off their computers from wherever they happen to be. Similarly, major companies like IBM, AT&T, GE, and Chiat/Day are slashing office space and giving people laptops or powerful notebook computers, telecommunications software, voice mail, and other communications technologies so they can work virtually anywhere, anytime.[28] Based on the philosophy that management's focus should be on what people do, not where they are, the **virtual office** is a mobile office in which people can work anywhere—their home, car, airport, customers' offices—as long as they have the tools to communicate with customers and colleagues.[29] One observer calls the virtual office "the most radical redefinition of the workplace since the Industrial Revolution."[30]

virtual office A mobile office in which people can work anywhere, as long as they have the tools to communicate with customers and colleagues.

In the short run, at least, the benefits appear substantial. Compaq Computer has reduced sales costs and administrative expenses from 22 percent of revenue to 12 percent. Perkin-Elmer, which makes scientific equipment, was able to close 35 branch offices. AT&T says mobile offices allow salespeople to spend 15 to 20 percent more time with customers.[31] And most people like the flexibility it gives them.

But what will be the longer-term impact on productivity and morale? We may be in danger of losing too many "human moments," those authentic encounters that happen only when two people are physically together.[32] Some people hate being forced to work at home. Some valuable people have quit. Some send faxes, e-mail, and voice mail in the middle of the night—and others receive them. Some work around the clock and still feel they are not doing enough. The long hours of being constantly close to the technical

Many entrepreneurs conduct business via open "offices," working off their computers from wherever they happen to be.
[David Young-Wolff/ PhotoEdit]

tools of work can cause burnout. And some companies are learning that direct supervision at the office is necessary to maintain the quality of work, especially when employees are inexperienced and need guidance. One company president says, "As soon as I separate my supervisors from the people they're supposed to be developing, I make it difficult for effective coaching to occur.[33]

At the moment, it appears that most people are pleased to have changed to mobile offices, and that they believe they are being more productive. But questions have arisen, and some companies are being careful with the new idea. AT&T no longer makes mobile offices mandatory. And many companies experiment with the idea and give people options as they try to win people's approval of the new tools.

Most people believe that by working in a mobile office they are being more productive.
[©Tim O'Hara/CORBIS]

Horizontal communication has several important functions.[96] First, it allows sharing of information, coordination, and problem solving among units. Second, it helps solve conflicts. Third, by allowing interaction among peers, it provides social and emotional support to people. All of these factors contribute to morale and effectiveness.

Managing horizontal communication   The need for horizontal communication is similar to the need for integration, discussed in Chapter 8. Particularly in complex environments, in which decisions in one unit affect another, information must be shared horizontally. As examples of good horizontal communications, Motorola holds an annual conference for sharing best learnings across functional and business groups throughout the company. NASA co-locates scientists from different disciplines. Hewlett-Packard uses common data-bases for different product groups to share information and ideas.[97]

GE offers a great example of how to use productive horizontal communications as a competitive weapon.[98] GE consists of different divisions, including plastics, medical systems, financial services, and NBC. CEO Jack Welch uses the term "integrated diversity" to describe how GE coordinates its different businesses.

GE's businesses could operate completely independently. But each is supposed to help the others. They transfer technical resources, people, information, ideas, and money among themselves. GE accomplishes this high level of communication and cooperation through easy access between divisions and to the CEO; a culture of openness, honesty, trust, and mutual obligation; and quarterly meetings in which all the top executives get together informally to share information and ideas. The same kinds of things are done at lower levels as well.

Formal and informal communication

Organizational communications differ in formality. *Formal communications* are official, organization-sanctioned episodes of information transmission. They can move upward, downward, or horizontally and often are prearranged and necessary for performing some task.

Informal communication is more unofficial. People gossip;[99] employees complain about their boss; people talk about their favorite sports teams; they whisper secrets about their co-workers; work teams tell newcomers about how they operate.

grapevine Informal communication network.

The **grapevine** is the social network of informal communications that helps people interpret the organization, translates management's formal messages into "employee language," and conveys information that the formal system leaves unsaid. On the other hand, the grapevine can be destructive when irrelevant or erroneous gossip and rumors proliferate and harm operations.[100]

Managing informal communication   Most of the suggestions for improving personal skills and organizational communication—writing, speaking, listening, facilitating and reinforcing upward communication, and so on—typically are applied to improving formal communication. But they can help improve informal communication as well. Additional considerations also apply to managing informal communication effectively.

Rumors start over any number of topics, including who's leaving, who's getting a promotion, salaries, job security, and costly mistakes. Rumors can destroy people's faith and trust in the company—and in each other. But the grapevine cannot be eliminated. Therefore, managers need to *work with* the grapevine.

The grapevine can be managed in several ways.[101] First, if the manager hears a story that could get out of hand, he or she should *talk to the key people* involved to get the facts and their perspectives.

Second, suggestions for *preventing* rumors from starting include: explain things that

Experiential Exer

15.1 Nonverbal communication

Objective

To become more conscious of nonverbal messages.

Instructions

Following is a list of nonverbal communication "methods." Pick a day on which you will attempt to keep track of these methods.

Think back at the end of the day to three people who communicated in some way. Record how people in terms of their nonverbal commu... tify those that had the greatest and least e...

Nonverbal communication worksheet

Medium	What was the message?	How did you respond?	Whi... your mos...
How they shook hands			
Their posture			
Their facial expressions			
Their appearance			
Their voice tones			
Their smiles			
The expressions in their eyes			
Their confidence			
The way they moved			
The way they stood			
How close they stood to you			

are important but have not been explained; dispel uncertainties by providing facts; and work to establish open communications and trust over time.[102]

Third, *neutralize* rumors once they have started: disregard the rumor if it is ridiculous (has no credence with others); openly confirm any parts that are true; make public comments (no comment is seen as a confirmation of the rumor); deny the rumor, if the denial is based in truth (don't make false denials); make sure communications about the issue are consistent; select a spokesperson of appropriate rank and knowledge; and hold town meetings if needed.[103]

Boundarylessness

boundaryless organization
Organization in which there are no barriers to information flow.

Many executives and management scholars today consider free access to information in all directions to be an organizational imperative. Jack Welch of GE is the leading advocate and practitioner of what he has termed "boundarylessness." A **boundaryless organization** is one in which there are no barriers to information flow. Instead of boundaries separating people, jobs, processes, and places, ideas, information, decisions, and actions move to where they are most needed.[104] This does not imply a random free-for-all of unlimited communication and information overload. It implies information available *as needed* moving quickly and easily enough so that the organization functions far better as a whole than as separate parts.[105]

Steve Kerr is GE's chief learning officer. When he teaches managers, he says, "I bet every one of you goes home at night with stuff in your head that would help the company. . . and you don't tell your boss" because "it's awkward or risky. Imagine if you could just unleash the power of the collective knowledge right in this room; imagine the good it would do."[106] Kerr uses the metaphor of the organization as a house having three kinds of boundaries: the floors and ceilings, the walls that separate the rooms, and the outside walls. These barriers[107] correspond in organizations to the boundaries between different organizational levels, different units and departments, and the organization and its external stakeholders—for example, suppliers and customers. GE adds a fourth wall: global boundaries separating domestic from global operations.

GE's famous Workout program is a series of meetings for members of a business across multiple hierarchical levels, characterized by extremely frank, tough discussions that break down vertical boundaries. Workout has involved over 222,000 GE people; in any given week over 20,000 are participating in a Workout program.[108] Workout is also

GE's successful Workout program shows the benefits of open dialogue across boundaries.
[Courtesy of GE]

Concluding

Would you really do it?

Imagine that you own and manage a small or mid-sized company. You pick the industry; you pick the location. Imagine, the firm is all yours.

You read in *Inc.* or *Fast Company* or *Harvard Business Review* about the latest management innovation: open-book management. You read about the original success story: Jack Stack bought Springfield ReManufacturing from International Harvester in 1983. It was collapsing after being rocked by a highly leveraged buyout. It had a first-year operating loss of about $60,000, over 100 employees who needed to be paid, and a debt-to-equity ratio of 89:1. Jack Stack opened the books, trained his people, and persuaded them to view the business as a game they could learn to play and win. The company returned to profitability, and is now written up in magazines and books as a brilliant model of how to do it.

You learn also of a number of companies that realized great results through opening the books, and understand the reasons why from taking a management course. And then you learn that Springfield ReManufacturing now holds seminars to teach other companies how to practice open-book management. You go to one, and you participate in exercises, simulations, and games to learn more about it. You are impressed, and are inclined to give it a try.

But there are downsides, as you learn when you get home and read another article. Your company has been around for a while, and the operating norms are pretty well established. How will people respond to this idea of opening the books? Will they understand? What will they think of the numbers? Will they want higher pay? Do they want a more active role in the company affairs? Do they even want to know the numbers?

Importantly, you will need to train them. You will need to commit to a lengthy, time-consuming learning period. Some of your managers and accountants, who had been privy to the confidential information, might not like the idea. They might fear they will lose power and status, or they might not trust the workers with the information. Possibly some confidential information will leak to competitors.

There are a few other issues as well. Changes in accounting and

financial systems and statements will be
measures will need to be linked with fina
system of rewards linked to performance n
system must be understood by everyone ar
fair.

An intriguing issue here is pay. Pay is j
kept secret at AES, where financial and m:
details of pot
sions, are w
though some |
mation will be
However, eve
crecy may be
Dennis Bakke
pensation issu
we're not ever
the case" (p. 1

You are no
tial downsides
or the implem
everyone will
your friends, v
panies.

Question

1. You have t
make this dec:
Yes or no: Wo
open-book sy:

2. If the answ
you do and sa
ple came to y

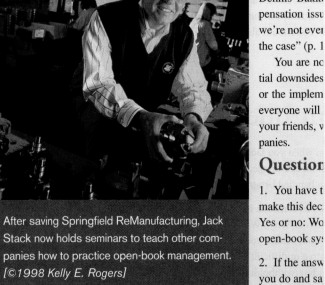

After saving Springfield ReManufacturing, Jack Stack now holds seminars to teach other companies how to practice open-book management. [©1998 Kelly E. Rogers]

3. If you are undecided, would you conver the idea? If so, how would you handle the 1

4. If your answer is yes, how would you p

5. What do you think about the issue of pa your opinion—both as an employee and as you were president, what would you do ab

Sources: J. Case, "Opening the Books," *Harvard* March–April 1997, pp. 118–27; and R. T. V. Da Management: Its Promise and Pitfalls," *Organiz* Winter 1997, pp. 7–20; S. Wetlaufer, "Organizir An Interview with AES's Roger Sant and Denni *Business Review,* January–February 1999, pp. 1

Case Incidents

Suggestion system policy

OFFICE OF THE PRESIDENT
Memorandum
Date: Friday, November 18
From: Bob Adams, president
To: John Sullens, vice president for human resources

Employee suggestion systems have been around for a long time. The positive financial impact of suggestion systems is significant in some organizations, according to my reading. For example, the National Association of Suggestions Systems estimates that 80 percent of the 500 largest U.S. corporations have such programs and that employee suggestions save the nation's companies more than $500 million a year.

The negative aspect of the suggestion system is that employees may become disgruntled about how the company runs the system. You may recall that two United Airlines employees charged in court that United stole their suggestion for a reduced-fare plan for employees of all airlines, that United successfully implemented the plan, and that United cheated them out of hundreds of thousands of dollars that they had coming under the company's suggestion system. They cited a provision of United Airlines' suggestion system rules that stated, "An employee is entitled to 10 percent of a typical year's profits resulting from an idea submitted through the suggestion system and successfully implemented."

During the trial, expert witnesses testified that in a typical year of operations under the reduced-fare plan, United earned $3 million attributable to the plan, of which 10 percent, or $300,000, rightfully belongs to the two employees who submitted the suggestion. The jury found that the company acted in bad faith by failing to pay off under the suggestion system and assessed $1.8 million in damages against the airline, which a judge later reduced to $368,000.

We can't afford to risk such financial peril! It's crucial, therefore, that you promptly review our suggestion system rules and policies and that you give me recommendations on the following issues. Include advantages and disadvantages associated with your policy recommendations.

1. *Calculation of award amount.* Should we offer a flat amount of money for each accepted suggestion, or should the award be based on a percentage of the savings (earnings) during some period? What percentage? What period?

2. *Maximum award.* Should we have a maximum limit on the payoff for any single suggestion (perhaps $10,000), or should it be open ended?

3. *Time of award payment.* Should we pay the award in full when the suggestion is accepted or as the savings (earnings) are realized annually?

4. *Joint award allocation.* When two or more employees combine on a suggestion, how should we allocate the award among them?

5. *Originality.* Should we pay off for suggestions that help us, even if they aren't original with the employee(s) making the suggestion?

6. *Impetus award.* Are you in favor of an "impetus award" in the range of $100 to $500 to recognize a suggestion that hastens an action initiated by the company before receipt of the suggestion?

7. *Written rules.* Do you think we need to spell out in writing every aspect of our suggestion system, or will an informal approach be more conducive to employee participation?

8. *Proof of knowledge.* Should we require all employees to sign a form stating that they have read and understand the suggestion system's rules (if we decide to write them up)?

9. *Another limitation.* Should an employee be limited to suggestions relating only to his or her area of the organization?

10. *An exclusion.* Should our marketing function and financial policy (including product and service pricing) be excluded from the suggestion system?

11. *Evaluation.* Do you have any suggestions on a procedure for evaluating suggestions?

12. *Abandonment.* Maybe dropping the suggestion system would be easier. What do you think?

We are reviewing all aspects of our suggestion system policy. Our attorney recommends abandonment. Let me hear from you as soon as possible. Treat this as a priority item.

Source: J. M. Champion and J. H. James, *Critical Incidents in Management: Decision and Policy Issues,* 6th ed. (Burr Ridge, IL: Richard D. Irwin, 1989).

Quality circle consequence

John Stevens, plant manager of the Fairlead Plant of Lockstead Corporation, which manufactures structural components for aircraft wings and bodies, became interested in using quality circles to improve performance in his plant. *Quality circles* was the name used to describe joint labor-supervision participation teams operating at the shop-floor level at Lockstead. Other companies called quality circles by names such as "productivity groups," "people involvement programs," and "departmental teams." Whatever the name, the purpose of quality circles was to improve the quality of manufacturing performance.

The subject of quality circles was a hot topic in the press. Stevens had seen books on Japanese management and productivity successes, which featured the use of quality circles. All these books featured the slogan "None of us is as smart as all of us."

Other books related quality circles to productivity gains. Articles on quality circles appeared often in trade journals and in business magazines, including *Business Week*.

Stevens also had a pamphlet from a management consulting firm announcing a "new and improved" training course for quality circle leaders, scheduled consecutively in Birmingham, Alabama; Williamsburg, Virginia; and Orlando, Florida. Another consultant offered "a program that will teach your managers and supervisors how to increase productivity and efficiency without making costly investments . . . by focusing on techniques germane to the quality circle process." Stevens was impressed enough to attend an advanced management seminar at a large midwestern university. A large part of the program concentrated on quality circles.

Professor Albert Mennon particularly impressed Stevens with his lectures on group discussion, team problem solving, and group decision making. Mennon convinced Stevens that employees meeting in quality circle teams with adequate leaders could effectively consider problems and formulate quality decisions that would be acceptable to employees. The staff conducting this state-of-the-art seminar covered five areas: (1) how to train quality circle members in the six-step problem sequence; (2) a description of what leaders and facilitators should do during the quality circle sessions; (3) planning and writing a policy guide; (4) developing an implementation plan; and (5) measuring quality circle progress and success.

Both the company and its employees were expected to benefit from a successfully implemented quality circle program. The list of payoffs included increased job satisfaction, productivity improvement, efficiency gains, and improved performance and labor relations. Moreover, it was expected that a reduction would occur in areas such a grievance loads, absenteeism, and costs.

Returning to his plant after the seminar, Stevens decided to practice some of the principles he had learned. He called together the 25 employees of Department B and told them that production standards established several years ago were too low in view of the recent installation of automated equipment. He gave the workers the opportunity to discuss the mitigating circumstances and to decide among themselves, as a group, what their standards should be. On leaving the room, he believed that the workers would establish much higher standards than he would have dared propose.

After an hour of discussion, the group summoned Stevens and notified him that, contrary to his opinion, they had decided the standards already were too high and, since they had been given the authority to establish their own standards, they were making a reduction of 10 percent. Stevens knew these standards were far too low to provide a fair profit on the owner's investment. Yet he believed his refusal to accept the group decision would be disastrous. Stevens thought of telephoning Professor Mennon for consultation on the quality circle dilemma, but he chose to act on his own.

Several options filled Steven's mind: (1) He could accept the blame for the quality circle experiment having gone awry and tell them to begin anew; (2) he could establish incentive pay adjustment linkages between the quality circle's decisions and productivity improvement; (3) he might even operate at a loss for a short while to prove that the original quality circle decision had been unacceptable; or (4) he might abandon the participative team program. Stevens needed a decision, an operational policy for the quality circle program, and an implementation plan.

Source: J. H. Champion and J. H. James, *Critical Incidents in Management: Decision and Policy Issues,* 6th ed. (Burr Ridge, IL: Richard D. Irwin. 1989). ●

Part Five

Controlling: Learning and Changing

Foundations of Management

Managing
The External Environment
Managerial Decision Making

↓

**Planning:
Delivering Strategic Value**

Planning and Strategic Management
Ethics and Corporate Responsibility
International Management
New Ventures

Strategy Implementation

**Organizing: Building
a Dynamic Organization**

Organization Structure
The Responsive Organization
Human Resources Management
Managing the Diverse Workforce

**Leading:
Mobilizing People**

Leadership
Motivating for Performance
Managing Teams
Communicating

**Controlling:
Learning and Changing**

Managerial Control
Managing Technology and Innovation
Creating and Managing Change

In Parts 1 through 4, you learned about the foundations of management, planning and strategy, and how to implement plans by organizing, staffing, and leading. Part 5 concludes with three chapters about controlling and changing what the organization and its people are doing. Chapter 16 describes managerial control, including issues related to culture as well as techniques for ensuring that intended activities are carried out and goals are accomplished.

The last two chapters focus on change and renewal. Chapter 17 discusses technology and innovation, including a strategic approach to new technologies and the creation of a culture for innovation. Chapter 18 examines an ongoing challenge for the modern executive: Becoming world class through the management of change. In that chapter, we describe the nature of this challenge and how managers can deal with it. Some of the topics you learned about in earlier chapters play central roles in the change process; Chapter 18 should remind you how your understanding of them will continually benefit your managerial career.

Chapter Sixteen
Managerial Control

More than at any time in the past, companies will not be able to hold themselves together with the traditional methods of control: hierarchy, systems, budgets, and the like . . . The bonding glue will increasingly become ideological.

—Collins & Porras[1]

Use your good judgment in all situations. There will be no additional rules.

—Nordstrom's employee manual

Chapter Outline

Learning Objectives

After studying Chapter 16, you will know:

1. Why companies develop control systems for employees.

2. How to design a basic bureaucratic control system.

3. The purposes for using budgets as a control device.

4. How to intrepret financial ratios and other financial controls.

5. The procedures for implementing effective control systems.

6. The different ways that market control mechanisms are used by organizations

7. How clan control can be approached in an empowered organization.

Setting the Stage

Can Chrysler Stop the Skid?

In Chapter 6, we opened with a story of the merger between Daimler and Chrysler. Let's pick up that story again to introduce this chapter on control.

Recall, when Jurgen E. Schrempp made his bold deal to merge Daimler-Benz with Chrysler Corp. in 1998, all of Detroit buzzed with fears that overbearing Germans would march in and big-foot the American carmaker. Now, investors might wish they had. After suffering one disaster after another, Schrempp and his team perhaps gave U.S. managers too much free rein, even as problems careened out of control. Now that they are in the driver's seat, will the Germans do better? The problems are enormous, and the German management may be seriously out of touch.

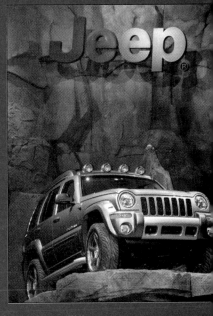

The ugly truth is that Chrysler is in financial trouble. Chrysler minivans and SUVs face stiff competition, mostly from Japanese models such as Honda's Odyssey. Chrysler sales are falling despite huge incentives it is offering customers, as costs soar. Even more discouraging is the U.S. slowdown. And Chrysler is usually the first in Detroit to feel a downdraft. "Chrysler has always been the canary in the mine shaft," says researcher Sean McAlinden at the Center for Automotive Research in Ann Arbor, Michigan. The slowdown has already hit. U.S. automakers assemble 8.6 million minivans and light trucks a year. That capacity will grow nearly 20 percent over the next three years. But demand is starting to soften.

Chrysler hopes its new Jeep Liberty will be more competitive with Japanese SUVs.
[Bryan Mitchell/Liaison]

For now, Daimler has given vague signs of how it will restructure and reposition Chrysler. But Chrysler CEO Dieter Zetsche is expected to cut production and eliminate unsuccessful models. The big unknown is how deep the cuts will go. Chrysler has already pared its product-development funds from $48 billion to $36 billion. More staff cuts are expected.

Chrysler's 4,400 dealers aren't likely to be spared, either. Zetsche is expected to streamline the network—the same tactic he used to help turn Mercedes around in the mid-1990s. Although painful at the time, it paid off, as he weaned Mercedes clients off incentives. And Zetsche could get surprisingly little opposition. Dealers themselves say they realize the unwieldy network is part of the problem. "There are just too many domestic dealerships. We're competing with each other," says Herb Chambers, owner of Chambers Motorcars in Boston.

This sort of downsizing usually cheers up stockholders. But share prices have slid, and the company's market capitalization is now just $39 billion, about 20 percent less than Daimler-Benz sported before it bought Chrysler. Investors aren't likely to become believers again until solid signs of a recovery come in.

Schrempp doesn't bear the biggest share of blame for Chrysler's downward spiral, of course. But by waiting so long to install his own team, Schrempp lost a crucial opportunity to get a grip on Chrysler's woes. Now it falls squarely on him and his German lieutenants to fix the mess in a tougher, grimmer economic environment.

Source: Christine Tierney and Jeff Green, "Can Schrempp Stop the Careening at Chrysler?," Business Week, December 4, 2000, p. 40.

control The process of measuring progress toward planned performance and applying corrective measures to ensure that performance is in line with managers' objectives.

Ｈow does a respected company like Daimler Chrysler get so out of control? Left on their own, people may knowingly or unknowingly act in ways that they perceive to be beneficial to them individually but that may work to the detriment of the organization as a whole. This is what happened at Chrysler. Without some means of regulating what people do, the organization can literally fall apart. In this regard, control is one of the fundamental forces that keeps the organization together.[1]

Control is typically defined as any process that directs the activities of individuals toward the achievement of organizational goals. Some managers don't want to admit it (see Table 16.1), but control problems—the lack of controls or the wrong kinds of controls—frequently cause irreparable damage to organizations. Ineffective control systems result in problems ranging from employee theft to peeling tire tread problems to escalating fuel prices in California. Employees simply wasting time costs U.S. employers billions of dollars each year![2]

Control has been called one of the Siamese twins of management. The other twin is planning. Some means of control are necessary because once managers form plans and strategies, they must ensure the plans are carried out. This means making sure that other people are doing what needs to be done and not doing inappropriate things. If plans are

table 16.1
The leadership symptoms of an out-of-control company

David Ferrari, president of Argus Management Corporation, maintains that many businesses are in big trouble without the CEO even knowing it. The symptoms:

- **Misplaced confidence**—believing that everything they do is right and they cannot make mistakes.

- **Blame deflection**—if they admit they are in trouble, they blame everything but themselves.

- **Avoidance**—doing "busy work" that is easy to handle rather than tackling the big, companywide issues.

- **An eye to the past**—justifying current practices by saying, "We've always done it that way."

- **Blind optimism**—refusing to believe bad numbers and believing that things will take care of themselves.

- **Setting a poor example**—spending lavishly on perks for themselves rather than living up to the same stringent standards expected of others.

- **Isolation**—other people—subordinates, directors, outsiders—don't send warning signals or stand up to the CEO to convince him or her that things are perilously out of control.

Source: Reprinted with permission from *Inc.* magazine, July 1990. Copyright © 1990 by Goldhirsh Group, Inc., 38 Commercial Wharf, Boston, MA 02110.

not carried out properly, management must take steps to correct the problem. This is the primary control function of management. Ensuring creativity, enhancing quality, reducing costs—managers must figure out ways to control what occurs in their organizations.

Not surprisingly, effective planning facilitates control, and control facilitates planning. Planning lays out a framework for the future, and in this sense, provides a blueprint for control. Control systems, in turn, regulate the allocation and utilization of resources, and in so doing, facilitate the process of planning. In today's complex organizational environment, both functions have become more difficult to implement at the same time they have become more important in every department of the organization. Managers today must control their people, inventories, quality, and costs, to mention just a few of their responsibilities.

According to William Ouchi of the University of California at Los Angeles, managers can apply three broad strategies for achieving organizational control: bureaucratic control, market control, and clan control.[3] **Bureaucratic control** is the use of rules, regulations, and formal authority to guide performance. It includes such things as budgets, statistical reports, performance appraisals, and the like to regulate behavior and results. **Market control** involves the use of pricing mechanisms to regulate activities in organizations as though they were economic transactions. Business units may be treated as profit centers and trade resources (services or products) with one another via such mechanisms. Managers who run these units may be evaluated on the basis of profit and loss. **Clan control,** unlike the first two types, does not assume that the interests of the organization and individuals naturally diverge. Instead, clan control is based on the idea that employees may share the values, expectations and goals of the organization and act in accordance with them. When members of an organization have common values and goals—and trust one another—formal controls may be less necessary. Clan control is based on many of the interpersonal processes described in Chapter 12 on leadership and Chapter 14 on groups and teams (e.g., group norms and cohesiveness).

Table 16.2 summarizes the main features of bureaucratic, market, and culture controls. We use this framework as a foundation for our discussions throughout the chapter.

bureaucratic control The use of rules, regulations, and authority to guide performance.

market control Control based on the use of financial and economic information.

clan control Control based on the norms, values, shared goals, and trust among group members.

Bureaucratic control systems

Bureaucratic (or formal) control systems are designed to measure progress toward planned performance and, if necessary, to apply corrective measures to ensure that performance is in line with managers' objectives. Control systems detect and correct significant variations, or discrepancies, in the results obtained from planned activities.

table 16.2
Characteristics of controls

System control	Features and requirements
Bureaucratic control	Uses formal rules, standards, hierarchy, legitimate authority. Works best where tasks are certain and workers are independent.
Market control	Uses prices, competition, profit centers, exchange relationships. Works best where tangible output can be identified and market can be established between parties.
Clan control	Involves culture, shared values, beliefs, expectations, and trust. Works best where there is "no one best way" to do a job and where employees are empowered to make decisions.

Sources: W. G. Ouchi, "A Conceptual Framework for the Design of Organizational Control Mechanisms," *Management Science* 25 (1979), pp. 833–48; W. G. Ouchi, "Markets, Bureaucracies, and Clans," *Administrative Science Quarterly* 25 (1980), pp. 129–41; and Richard D. Robey and C. A. Sales, *Designing Organizations* (Burr Ridge, IL: Richard D. Irwin, 1994).

The control cycle

Figure 16.1 shows a typical control system with four major steps: (1) setting performance standards, (2) measuring performance, (3) comparing performance against the standards and determining deviations, and (4) taking corrective action.

standard Expected performance for a given goal; a target that establishes a desired performance level, motivates performance, and serves as a benchmark against which actual performance is assessed.

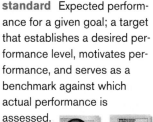

Step 1: Setting performance standards Every organization has goals, including profitability, innovation, satisfaction of constituencies, and so on. A **standard** is the level of expected performance for a given goal. Standards are performance targets that establish desired performance levels, motivate performance, and serve as benchmarks against which to assess actual performance. Standards can be set for any activity—financial activities, operating activities, legal compliance, charitable contributions, and so on.[4]

We have discussed setting performance standards in other parts of the text. For example, employee goal setting for motivation is built around the concept of specific, measurable performance standards. Such standards should be challenging and typically should aim for improvement over past performance. Typically, performance standards are derived from job requirements. Examples might include increasing market share by 10 percent, reducing costs 20 percent, or answering customer complaints within 24 hours. But performance standards don't just apply to people in isolation—they frequently reflect the integration of human and system performance. BAE Systems Controls, for example, makes control systems for aircraft engines (these controls are essentially computers mounted on the engines to monitor performance, control speed, and optimize fuel efficiency). These controls have to withstand extreme temperatures and vibration. And because they're used on a wide variety of military and commercial aircraft, they must be highly reliable. "Every four seconds, one of our engine controls takes off," notes Dave Herr, director of operations. "At this instant there are a quarter of a million people flying somewhere, trusting our engine control." In producing these controls, workers in BAE's plant set very stringent performance standards for quality and reliability. The failure rate (termed a "shutdown rate") of the engine controls is just 0.7 incidents per million hours. That means you'd have to fly 24 hours a day, every day for a century, to experience one in-flight engine shutdown. That's a pretty incredible standard.[5]

figure 16.1
The control process

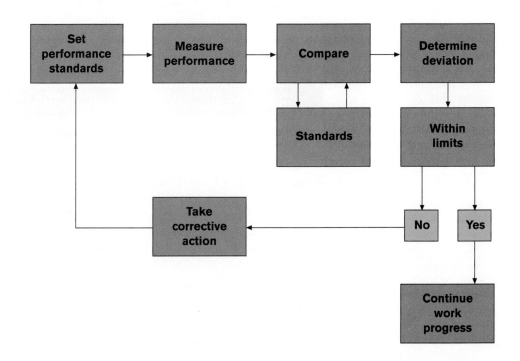

Performance standards can be set with respect to (1) quantity, (2) quality, (3) time used, and (4) cost. For example, production activities include volume of output (quantity), defects (quality), on-time availability of finished goods (time use), and dollar expenditures for raw materials and direct labor (cost). Many important aspects of performance, such as customer service, can be measured by the same standards—for example, adequate supply and availability of products, quality of service, speed of delivery, and so forth.

One word of caution: The downside of establishing performance targets and standards is that they may not be supported by other elements of the control system. Each piece of the system is important and dependent on the others. Otherwise the system can get terribly out of balance. Let's look at some of the other pieces.

Step 2: Measuring performance

The second step in the control process is to measure performance levels. For example, managers can count units produced, days absent, papers filed, samples distributed, and dollars earned. Performance data commonly are obtained from three sources: written reports, oral reports, and personal observations.

Written reports include computer printouts. Thanks to computers' increasing capabilities and decreasing costs, both large and small companies can gather huge amounts of performance data.

One common example of *oral reports* occurs when a salesperson contacts his or her immediate manager at the close of each business day to report the accomplishments, problems, or customers' reactions during the day. The manager can ask questions to gain additional information or clear up any misunderstandings. When necessary, tentative corrective actions can be worked out during the discussion.

Personal observation involves going to the area of activities and watching what is occurring. The manager can observe work methods, employees' nonverbal signals, and the general operation. Personal observation gives an intimate picture of what is going on. But it also has some disadvantages. It does not provide accurate quantitative data; the information usually is general and subjective. Also, employees can misconstrue personal observation as mistrust or a lack of confidence. Nevertheless, many managers believe there is no good substitute for firsthand observation. As you learned in earlier chapters, personal contact can increase leadership visibility and upward communication. It also provides valuable information about performance to supplement written and oral reports.

Step 3: Comparing performance with the standard

The third step in the control process is comparing performance with the standard. In this process, the manager evaluates the performance. For some activities, relatively small deviations from the standard are acceptable, while in others a slight deviation may be serious. Managers who perform the controlling work therefore must carefully analyze and evaluate the results.

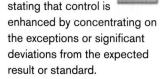

principle of exception A managerial principle stating that control is enhanced by concentrating on the exceptions or significant deviations from the expected result or standard.

The managerial **principle of exception** states that control is enhanced by concentrating on the exceptions, or significant deviations, from the expected result or standard. In comparing performance with the standard, managers need to direct their attention to the exception. For example, controlling the quality of components produced on an assembly line might show that only five pieces per 1,000 fall out of line. These five components are the exceptions and should be investigated further.[6]

With the principle of exception, only exceptional cases require corrective action. The manager should not be concerned with performance that equals or closely approximates the expected results. This principle is important in controlling. Managers can save much time and effort if they apply the principle of exception.

Step 4: Taking corrective action

The last step in the control process is to take action to correct significant deviations. This step ensures that operations are adjusted where necessary to achieve the initially planned results. Where significant variances are discovered, the manager should take immediate and vigorous action. Effective control cannot tolerate needless delays, excuses, or exceptions.

An alternative approach is for the corrective action to be taken not by higher-ups but by the operator at the point of the problem. In computer-controlled production technology, two basic types of control are feasible: specialist control and operator control. With *specialist control,* operators of computer-numerical-control (CNC) machines must notify engineering specialists of malfunctions. With this traditional division of labor, the specialist takes corrective action. With *operator control,* multiskilled operators can rectify their own problems as they occur. At companies such as Harley-Davidson, not only is this strategy more efficient (because deviations are controlled closer to their source), but operators benefit by virtue of a more enriched job.[7]

The appropriate corrective action depends on the nature of the problem. The corrective action may involve a change in a procedure or method, a disciplinary action, a new way to check the accuracy of manufactured parts, or a major organizational modification. Or it may simply be an inexpensive investment in employee training. At Corning, the source of major quality and production problems was traced to minute drafting errors by the engineering group. One of the solutions was quite simple: An engineer was sent to a proofreading class.[8]

Approaches to bureaucratic control

The three approaches to bureaucratic control are feedforward, concurrent, and feedback. **Feedforward control** takes place before operations begin and includes policies, procedures, and rules designed to ensure that planned activities are carried out properly. Examples include inspection of raw materials and proper selection and training of employees. **Concurrent control** takes place while plans are being carried out. It includes directing, monitoring, and fine-tuning activities as they occur. **Feedback control** focuses on the use of information about results to correct deviations from the acceptable standard after they arise.

Feedforward control

feedforward control The control process used before operations begin, including policies, procedures, and rules designed to ensure that planned activities are carried out properly.

concurrent control The control process used while plans are being carried out, including directing, monitoring, and fine-tuning activities as they are performed.

feedback control Control that focuses on the use of information about previous results to correct deviations from the acceptable standard.

Feedforward control Feedforward control (sometimes called *preliminary control*) is future oriented; its aim is to prevent problems before they arise. Instead of waiting for results and comparing them with goals, a manager can exert control by limiting activities in advance. For example, companies have policies defining the scope within which decisions are made. A company may dictate that managers adhere to clear ethical and legal guidelines when making decisions. Formal rules and procedures also prescribe people's actions before they occur. Stating that a financial officer must approve expenditures over $1,000 or that only components that pass all safety tests can be used in a product specifies in advance which actions can and cannot be taken. To prevent loan defaults, banks may require extensive loan documentation, reviews, and approvals by bank officers before authorizing a loan.[9]

Concurrent control Concurrent control, which takes place while plans are carried out, is the heart of any control system. On the production floor, all efforts are directed toward producing the correct quantity and quality of the right products in the specified amount of time. In an airline terminal, the baggage must get to the right airplanes before flights depart. In factories, materials must be available when and where needed, and breakdowns in the production process must be repaired immediately. Concurrent control also is in operation when supervisors watch employees to ensure they work efficiently and avoid mistakes. Advances in information technology have created powerful concurrent controls. Computerized systems give managers immediate access to data from the most remote corners of their companies. For example, managers can continuously update budgets based on an ongoing flow of performance data. In production facilities, monitoring systems that track errors per hour, machine speeds, and other measures allow managers to continuously correct small production problems before they become disasters.

Feedback control Feedback control implies that performance data were gathered and analyzed and the results returned to someone (or something) in the process to make corrections. When supervisors monitor behavior, they are exercising concurrent control. When they point out and correct improper performance, they are using feedback as a means of control.

Timing is an important aspect of feedback control. Long time lags often occur between performance and feedback, such as when actual spending is compared against the quarterly budget or when some aspect of performance is compared to the projection made a year ago. If feedback on performance is not timely, managers cannot quickly identify and eliminate the problem and prevent more serious harm.[10]

Some feedback processes are under real-time (concurrent) control, such as a computer-controlled robot on an assembly line. Such units have sensing units, which continually determine whether they are in the correct position to perform their functions. If not, a built-in control device makes immediate corrections.

Six sigma and quality control at Motorola

In the mid-1980s, Motorola was being consistently beaten in the competitive marketplace by foreign firms that were able to produce higher-quality products at a lower cost. Bob Galvin, Motorola's then-CEO, started the company on a quality path now known as "six sigma." Sigma is the Greek letter used in statistics to designate the estimated standard deviation or variation in a process. The lower the "sigma level," the more variation or defects in the process. The higher the sigma level, the fewer the defects.

"Sigma level" is often used as a shorthand notation for indicating the number of defects per million opportunities (DPMO) involved with a process. For example, a "two sigma level" process has 308,537 DPMO (not a very controlled process). As shown in Table 16.3, if a process has a "three sigma level," it has 6,210 DPMO. So, what is six sigma? Six sigma means operating at less than 3.4 DPMO. That's essentially being defect-free 99.99966 percent of the time. The six sigma program at Motorola provided an intense management focus on preventing defects in products, processes, and services; reducing cycle times; and controlling costs in order to generate value to the customer.

The results were dramatic. Motorola became the market leader and won the Malcolm Baldridge National Quality Award in 1988. Six sigma has since been embraced by many other companies, most notably General Electric (GE), Honeywell, and Merck. This process has led to significant cost reductions, increased market share, and superior financial performance. For example, at GE, in less than three years, the company's operating margin soared to a record 16.7 percent. In dollar amounts, six sigma delivered more than $300 million to GE's 1997 productivity gains and profits (Pyzdek). At Honeywell's former AlliedSignal operations, application of six sigma methods saved $600 million in 1999 (Honeywell International Inc.).

Source: Excerpted from Tom Rancour and Mike McCracken, "Applying 6 Sigma Methods for Breakthrough Safety Performance," *Professional Safety*, October 2000, 45, no. 10, pp. 29–32. ●

table 16.3
Relationship between sigma level and defects per million opportunities

Sigma level	DPMO	Is four sigma good enough?
2σ	308,537	Consider these everyday examples of four sigma quality. . .
3σ	66,807	• 20,000 lost articles of mail per hour
4σ	6,210	• Unsafe drinking water 15 minutes per day
5σ	233	• 5,000 incorrect surgical operations per week
6σ	3.4	• 200,000 wrong prescriptions each year
		• No electricity for 7 hours each month

Source: Tom Rancour and Mike McCracken, "Applying 6 Sigma Methods for Breakthrough Safety Performance," *Professional Safety*, October 2000, 45, no. 10, 29–32.

Management audits

management audits An evaluation of the effectiveness and efficiency of various systems within an organization.

Over the years, **management audits** have developed as a means for evaluating the effectiveness and efficiency of various systems within an organization, from social responsibility to accounting control. Management audits may be external or internal. Managers conduct external audits of other companies and internal audits of their own company. Some of the same tools and approaches are used for both types of audits.[11]

external audit An evaluation conducted by one organization, such as a CPA firm, on another.

External audits   An **external audit** occurs when one organization evaluates another organization. Typically an external body such as a CPA firm conducts financial audits of an organization (accounting audits are discussed later). But any company can also conduct external audits of competitors or other companies for strategic decision-making purposes. This type of analysis (1) investigates other organizations for possible merger or acquisition; (2) determines the soundness of a company that will be used as a major supplier; or (3) discovers the strengths and weaknesses of a competitor to maintain or better exploit the competitive advantage of the investigating organization. Publicly available data usually are used for these evaluations.[12]

External audits were used in feedback control in the discovery and investigation of the savings and loan scandals. They also are useful for preliminary control because they can prevent problems from occurring. If a company gathers adequate, accurate information about acquisition candidates, it is more likely to acquire the most appropriate companies and avoid unsound acquisitions.

internal audit A periodic assessment of a company's own planning, organizing, leading, and controlling processes.

Internal audits   **Internal audits** assesses (1) what the company has done for itself and (2) what it has done for its customers or other recipients of its goods or services. The company can be evaluated on a number of factors, including financial stability, production efficiency, sales effectiveness, human resources development, earnings growth, public relations, civic responsibility, or other criteria of organizational effectiveness. The audit reviews the company's past, present, and future.[13]

To perform a management audit, a list of desired qualifications is drawn up and weights are attached to each qualification. Among the more common undesirable practices uncovered by a management audit are the performance of unnecessary work; duplication of work; poor inventory control; uneconomical use of equipment and machines; procedures that are more costly than necessary; and wasted resources. Square D, the electrical equipment manufacturer, discovered it could throw away four manuals with 760 rules and regulations in favor of 11 policy statements. At Heinz, a quality program aimed mostly at eliminating waste and rework is estimated to save $250 million over three years. Oryx, the world's largest independent oil and gas producer, now takes six weeks instead of seven months to produce the annual budget and has cut in half the average time and cost of finding new oil and gas reserves.[14]

Budgetary controls

Budgetary control is one of the most widely recognized and commonly used methods of managerial control. It ties together feedforward control, concurrent control, and feedback control, depending on the point at which it is applied. *Budgetary control* is the process of finding out what's being done and comparing the results with the corresponding budget data to verify accomplishments or to remedy differences. Budgetary control commonly is called **budgeting.**

budgeting The process of investigating what is being done and comparing the results with the corresponding budget data to verify accomplishments or remedy differences. Also called budgetary controlling.

Fundamental budgetary considerations   In private industry, budgetary control begins with an estimate of sales and expected income. Table 16.4 shows a budget with estimates for sales and expenses for the first three months of the year. There is space to enter the actual accomplishments to expedite comparison between expected and actual results. Note that the total expenses plus estimated gross profit equal the total sales expectancy.

Budgeting information is supplied to the entire enterprise or to any of its units; it is not confined to financial matters. Units other than dollars typically can be used. For example, industry uses budgeting of production in physical units and of labor by different skills.

A primary consideration of budgeting is the length of the budget period. All budgets are prepared for a definite time period. Many budgets are for one, three, or six months or for one year. The length of time selected depends on the primary purpose of the budgeting. The period chosen should include the enterprise's complete normal cycle of activity. For example, seasonal variations should be included both for production and for sales. The budget period commonly coincides with other control devices, such as managerial reports, balance sheets, and statements of profit and loss. In addition, the extent to which reasonable forecasts can be made should be considered in selecting the length of the budget period.

Budgetary control proceeds through several stages. *Establishing expectancies* starts with the broad plan for the company and the estimate of sales, and it ends with budget approval and publication. The *budgetary operations* stage, then, deals with finding out what is being accomplished and comparing the results with expectancies. The last stage, as in any control process, involves taking corrective action when necessary.

Although practices differ widely, a member of top management often serves as the chief coordinator for formulating and using the budget. Usually the treasurer, controller, or chief accountant has these duties. He or she needs to be less concerned with the details than with resolving conflicting interests, recommending adjustments when needed, and giving official sanction to the budgetary procedures.

Types of budgets

There are many types of budgets. Some of the more common types are as follows:

- *Sales budget.* Usually data for the sales budget are prepared by month, sales area, and product.
- *Production budget.* The production budget commonly is expressed in physical units. Required information for preparing this budget includes types and capacities of machines, economic quantities to produce, and availability of materials.

table 16.4
A sales-expense budget

	January		February		March	
	Expectancy	Actual	Expectancy	Actual	Expectancy	Actual
Sales	$1,200,000		$1,350,000		$1,400,000	
Expenses						
General overhead	310,000		310,000		310,000	
Selling	242,000		275,000		288,000	
Producing	327,000		430,500		456,800	
Research	118,400		118,400		115,000	
Office	90,000		91,200		91,500	
Advertising	32,500		27,000		25,800	
Estimated gross profit	80,100		97,900		112,900	

• *Cost production budget.* The information in the cost production budget sometimes is included in production budgets. Comparing production cost with sales price shows whether or not profit margins are adequate.

• *Cash budget.* The cash budget is essential to every business. It should be prepared after all other budget estimates are completed. The cash budget shows the anticipated receipts and expenditures, the amount of working capital available, the extent to which outside financing may be required, and the periods and amounts of cash available.

• *Master budget.* The master budget includes all major activities of the business. It brings together and coordinates all the activities of the other budgets and can be thought of as a "budget of budgets."

Accounting records must be inspected periodically to ensure they were properly prepared and are correct. **Accounting audits,** which verify accounting reports and statements, are essential to the control process. This audit is performed by members of an outside firm of public accountants. Knowing that accounting records are accurate, true, and in keeping with generally accepted accounting practices (GAAP) creates confidence that a reliable base exists for sound overall controlling purposes.[15]

accounting audits Procedures used to verify accounting reports and statements.

Activity-based costing It is now widely recognized that traditional methods of cost accounting may be inappropriate in today's business environment because they are based on outdated methods of rigid hierarchical organization. Instead of assuming that organizations are bureaucratic "machines" that can be separated into component functions such as human resources, purchasing, or maintenance, companies such as Chrysler, Hewlett-Packard, and GE have begun using **activity-based costing (ABC)** to allocate costs across business processes.

activity-based costing (ABC) A method of cost accounting designed to identify streams of activity, and then to allocate costs across particular business processes according to the amount of time employees devote to particular activities.

ABC starts with the assumption that organizations are collections of people performing many different but related activities to satisfy customer needs. The ABC system is designed to identify those streams of activity, and then to allocate costs across particular business processes. The basic procedure works as follows (see Figure 16.2): First, employees are asked to break down what they do each day in order to define their *basic activities.* For example, employees in Dana Corporation's material control department engage in a number of activities ranging from processing sales orders and sourcing parts to requesting engineering changes and solving problems. These activities form the basis for ABC. Second, managers look at total expenses computed by traditional accounting—

figure 16.2
How Dana discovers
what its true costs are

	Salaries	Fringes	Supplies	Fixed costs
Process sales order				$144,846
Source parts				$136,320
Expedite supplier orders				$ 72,143
Expedite internal processing				$ 49,945
Receive supplier quality				$ 47,599
Reissue purchase orders				$ 45,235
Expedite customer orders				$ 27,747
Schedule intracompany sales				$ 17,768
Request engineering change				$ 16,704
Resolve problems				$ 16,648
Schedule parts				$ 15,390

Old-style accounting identifies costs according to the category of expense. The new math tells you that your real costs are what you pay for the different tasks your employees perform. Find that out and you will manage better.

Salaries
$371,917

Fringes
$118,069

Supplies
$76,745

Fixed Costs
$23,614

Total $590,345

Total $590,345

Source: Courtesy Dana Corp.

such as fixed costs, supplies, salaries, fringe benefits, and so on—and spread total amounts over the activities according to the amount of time spent on each activity. At Dana, customer service employees spend nearly 25 percent of their time processing sales orders and only about 3 percent on scheduling parts. So 25 percent of the total cost ($144,846) goes to order processing and 3 percent ($15,390) goes to scheduling parts. As can be seen in Figure 16.2, both the traditional and ABC systems reach the same bottom line. However, because the ABC method allocates costs across business processes, it provides a more accurate picture of how costs should be charged to products and services.[16]

Perhaps more important than the accuracy of ABC, the system highlights where wasted activities are occurring or if activities cost too much relative to the benefits they provide to customers. By providing this type of information, ABC has quickly become a valuable method for streamlining business processes. The example below from Alcoa shows how.

Alcoa masters its ABCs

In the high-tech world of aerospace manufacturing, where a few products can account for most of a factory's output, a bad production decision can cause trouble for years down the road. So in early 1999, when managers at Alcoa Inc.'s metal-forging plant in Cleveland foresaw a downturn in the aviation sector, one of its key markets, managers needed to figure out which of their aircraft products were pulling in the most profits. The plant's complex processes, varied output, and long product cycles made it tough to determine which lines produced the highest fixed overhead costs. With three- to five-year commitments, "we had to make sure that we could make money on products," says Jeffrey A. Weeks, the plant's aerospace business analyst.

Alcoa's solution has been a cost-assessment system known as activity-based costing, or ABC. This analytical approach breaks down all activities in a manufacturing plant and determines the portion of overhead used to make each product. "It's like splitting the bill at a restaurant," says Anthony A. Atkinson, a professor of accountancy at Canada's University of Waterloo. "Where traditional accounting divides the bill evenly between all the diners, ABC determines who had the T-bone and who had the burger."

With the cost of every product in clear view, managers can perform once-impossible analytical feats. Suddenly, they can understand how scarce funds may have been misapportioned, or how a formerly marginal customer may in fact be a profit spinner. Alcoa employed ABC to capture indirect costs such as machine set-ups, quality control, and packing and shipping. After crunching this sort of information in ABC software developed by Hyperion Solutions Corp. in Sunnyvale, California, Alcoa is beginning to make smarter production decisions. Managers can now ask: "Do we want to be in a line of business, or a particular product line, or do we want to sell off certain assets?" says Weeks. And while Alcoa is still assessing the complex conclusions of its ABC self-study, it is already using the results to rejigger its prices.

Source: Condensed from Hugh Filman, "Manufacturing Masters Its ABCs," *Business Week Online*, August 7, 2000. ●

Financial controls

In addition to budgets, businesses commonly use other statements for financial control. Two financial statements that help control overall organizational performance are the balance sheet and the profit and loss statement.

balance sheet A report that shows the financial picture of a company at a given time and itemizes assets, liabilities, and stockholders' equity.

assets The values of the various items the corporation owns.

liabilities The amounts a corporation owes to various creditors.

stockholders' equity The amount accruing to the corporation's owners.

The balance sheet

The **balance sheet** shows the financial picture of a company at a given time. This statement itemizes three elements: (1) assets, (2) liabilities, and (3) stockholders' equity. **Assets** are the values of the various items the corporation owns. **Liabilities** are the amounts the corporation owes to various creditors. **Stockholders' equity** is the amount accruing to the corporation's owners. The relationships among these three elements is as follows:

$$\text{Assets} = \text{Liabilities} + \text{Stockholders' equity}$$

Table 16.5 shows an example of a balance sheet. During the year, the company grew because it enlarged its building and acquired more machinery and equipment by means of long-term debt in the form of a first mortgage. Additional stock was sold to help finance the expansion. At the same time, accounts receivable were increased and work in process reduced. Observe that Total assets ($3,053,367) = Total liabilities ($677,204 + $618,600) + Stockholders' equity ($700,000 + $981,943 + $75,620).

Summarizing balance sheet items over a long period of time uncovers important trends and gives a manager further insight into overall performance and areas in which adjustments need to be made.

profit and loss statement An itemized financial statement of the income and expenses of a company's operations.

The profit and loss statement

The **profit and loss statement** is an itemized financial statement of the income and expenses of the company's operations. Table 16.6 shows a comparative statement of profit and loss for two consecutive years. In this illustration, the operating revenue of the enterprise has increased. Expense also has increased, but at a lower rate, resulting in a higher net income. Some managers draw up tentative profit and loss statements and use them as goals. Then performance is measured against these goals or standards. From comparative statements of this type, a manager can identify trouble areas and correct them.

Controlling by profit and loss is most commonly used for the entire enterprise and, in the case of a diversified corporation, its divisions. However, if controlling is by departments, as in a decentralized organization in which department managers have control over both revenue and expense, a profit and loss statement is used for each department. Each department's output is measured, and a cost, including overhead, is charged to each department's operation. Expected net income is the standard for measuring a department's performance.

Financial ratios

An effective approach for checking on the overall performance of an enterprise is to use key financial ratios. Ratios help indicate possible strengths and weaknesses in the company's operations. Key ratios are calculated from selected items on the profit and loss statement and the balance sheet. We will briefly discuss three categories of financial ratios: liquidity, leverage, and profitability.

current ratio A liquidity ratio which indicates the extent to which short-term assets can decline and still be adequate to pay short-term liabilities.

debt-equity ratio A leverage ratio which indicates the company's ability to meet its long-term financial obligations.

return on investment (ROI) A ratio of profit to capital used, or a rate of return from capital.

• **Liquidity ratios.** *Liquidity ratios* indicate the company's ability to pay short-term debts. The most common liquidity ratio is *current assets to current liabilities,* called the **current ratio** or *net working capital ratio.* This ratio indicates the extent to which current assets can decline and still be adequate to pay current liabilities. Some analysts set a ratio of 2 to 1, or 2.00, as the desirable minimum.

• **Leverage ratios.** *Leverage ratios* show the relative amount of funds in the business supplied by creditors and shareholders. An important example is the **debt-equity ratio,** which indicates the company's ability to meet its long-term financial obligations. If this ratio is less than 1.5, the amount of debt is not considered excessive.

• **Profitability ratios.** *Profitability ratios* indicate management's ability to generate a financial return on sales or investment. For example, **return on investment (ROI)** is a ratio of profit to capital used, or a rate of return from capital.

Using financial ratios

Although ratios provide both performance standards and indicators of what has occurred, exclusive reliance on financial ratios can have negative consequences as well. Because ratios usually are expressed in compressed time horizons

table 16.5
A comparative balance sheet

Comparative balance sheet for the years ending December 31	This year	Last year
Assets		
Current assets:		
Cash	$161,870	$119,200
U.S. Treasury bills	250,400	30,760
Accounts receivable	825,595	458,762
Inventories:		
Work in process and finished products	429,250	770,800
Raw materials and supplies	251,340	231,010
Total current assets	1,918,455	1,610,532
Other assets:		
Land	157,570	155,250
Building	740,135	91,784
Machinery and equipment	172,688	63,673
Furniture and fixtures	132,494	57,110
Total other assets before depreciation	1,202,887	367,817
Less: Accumulated depreciation and amortization	67,975	63,786
Total other assets	1,134,912	304,031
Total assets	$3,053,367	$1,914,563
Liabilities and stockholders' equity		
Current liabilities:		
Accounts payable	$ 287,564	$441,685
Payrolls and withholdings from employees	44,055	49,580
Commissions and sundry accruals	83,260	41,362
Federal taxes on income	176,340	50,770
Current installment on long-term debt	85,985	38,624
Total current liabilities	667,204	622,021
Long-term liabilities:		
15-year, 9 percent loan, payable in each of the years 2002–2015	210,000	225,000
5 percent first mortgage	408,600	
Registered 9 percent notes payable		275,000
Total long-term liabilities	618,600	500,000
Stockholders' equity:		
Common stock: authorized 1,000,000 shares, outstanding last year 492,000 shares, outstanding this year 700,000 shares at $1 par value	700,000	492,000
Capital surplus	981,943	248,836
Earned surplus	75,620	51,706
Total liabilities and stockholders' equity	$3,053,367	$1,914,563

management myopia
Focusing on short-term earnings and profits at the expense of longer-term strategic obligations.

(monthly, quarterly, or yearly), they often cause **management myopia**—managers focus on short-term earnings and profits at the expense of their longer-term strategic obligations.[17] Control systems using long-term (e.g., three-to-six-year) performance targets can reduce management myopia and focus attention farther into the future.

A second negative outcome of ratios is that they relegate other important considerations to a secondary position. Research and development, management development,

table 16.6
A comparative statement
of profit and loss

Comparative statement of profit and loss for the years ending June 30			
	This year	Last year	Increase or decreases
Income:			
Net sales	$ 253,218	$ 257,636	$ 4,418*
Dividends from investments	480	430	50
Other	1,741	1,773	32
Total	255,439	259,839	4,400*
Deductions:			
Cost of goods sold	180,481	178,866	1,615
Selling and administrative expenses	39,218	34,019	5,199
Interest expense	2,483	2,604	121*
Other	1,941	1,139	802
Total	224,123	216,628	7,495
Income before taxes	31,316	43,211	11,895*
Provision for taxes	3,300	9,500	6,200*
Net income	$ 28,016	$ 33,711	$ 5,695*

*Decrease.

progressive human resources practices, and other considerations may receive insufficient attention. Therefore, the use of ratios should be supplemented with other control measures. Organizations can hold managers accountable for market share, number of patents granted, sales of new products, human resources development, and other performance indicators.

The downside of bureaucratic control

So far, you have learned about control from a mechanical viewpoint. But organizations are not strictly mechanical; they are composed of people. While control systems are used to constrain people's behavior and make their future behavior predictable, people are not machines that automatically fall into line as the designers of control systems intend. In fact, control systems can lead to dysfunctional behavior. A control system cannot be effective without consideration of how people will react to it. For effective control of employee behavior, managers should consider three types of potential responses to control: rigid bureaucratic behavior, tactical behavior, and resistance.[18]

Rigid bureaucratic behavior   Often people act in ways that will help them look good on the control system's measures. This tendency can be useful, because it causes people to focus on the behaviors management requires. But it can result in rigid, inflexible behavior geared toward doing *only* what the system requires.

Rigid bureaucratic behavior occurs when control systems prompt employees to stay out of trouble by following the rules. Unfortunately, such systems often lead to poor customer service and make the entire organization slow to act (recall the discussion of bureaucracy in Chapter 10).

We have perhaps all been victimized at some time by rigid bureaucratic behavior. Reflect for a moment on this now classic story of a "nightmare" at a hospital:

At midnight, a patient with eye pains enters an emergency room at a hospital. At the reception area, he is classified as a nonemergency case and referred to the hospital's eye clinic. Trouble is, the eye clinic doesn't open until the next morning. When he arrives at the clinic, the nurse asks for his referral slip, but the emergency room doctor had forgotten to give it to him. The patient has to return to the emergency room and wait for another physician to screen him. The physician refers him back to the eye clinic and to a social worker to arrange payment. Finally, a third doctor looks into his eye, sees a small piece of metal, and removes it—a 30-second procedure.[19]

Stories such as these have, of course, given bureaucracy a bad name. Some managers will not even use the term *bureaucratic control* because of its potentially negative connotation. That is unfortunate because the control system itself is not the problem. The problems occur when the systems are no longer viewed as tools for running the business, but as rules for dictating rigid behavior.

Tactical behavior

Control systems will be ineffective if employees engage in tactics aimed at "beating the system." The most common type of tactical behavior is to manipulate information or report false performance data. People may produce two kinds of invalid data: about what *has* been done and about what *can* be done. False reporting about the past is less common, because it is easier to identify someone who misreports what happened than someone who gives an erroneous prediction or estimate of what might happen. Still, managers sometimes change their accounting systems to "smooth out" the numbers. Also, people may intentionally feed false information into a management information system to cover up errors or poor performance.[20]

More commonly, people falsify their predictions or requests for the future. When asked to give budgetary estimates, employees usually ask for larger amounts than they need. On the other hand, they sometimes submit unrealistically *low* estimates when they believe a low estimate will help them get a budget or a project approved. Budget-setting sessions can become tugs-of-war between subordinates trying to get slack in the budget and superiors attempting to minimize slack. Similar tactics are exhibited when managers negotiate unrealistically low performance standards so that subordinates will have little trouble meeting them; when salespeople project low forecasts so they will look good by exceeding them; and when workers slow down the work pace when time-study analysts are setting work pace standards. In these and other cases, people are concerned only with their own performance figures rather than with the overall performance of their departments or companies.[21]

Resistance to control

Often people strongly resist control systems. This occurs for several reasons. First, comprehensive control systems increase the accuracy of performance data and make employees more accountable for their actions. Control systems uncover mistakes, threaten people's job security and status, and decrease people's autonomy.

Second, control systems can change expertise and power structures. For example, management information systems can make the costing, purchasing, and production decisions previously made by managers. Thus, individuals fear a loss of expertise, power, and decision-making authority.

Third, control systems can change the social structure of the organization. They can create competition and disrupt social groups and friendships. People may end up competing against those with whom they formerly had comfortable, cooperative relationships. Because people's social needs are so important, they will resist control systems that reduce social need satisfaction.

Fourth, control systems may be seen as an invasion of privacy. The following illustration shows that some control systems are controversial, particularly when their accuracy is suspect or when they are viewed as unnecessary.

Drug testing: A controversial control system

Employee drug use is a serious problem. Possible consequences of employee drug use include injuries, illness, absenteeism, breakage, theft, and reduced productivity. A recent report by the U.S. Department of Health and Human Services reveals that nearly 10 percent of persons under the age of 50 admitted to taking illicit drugs on a regular basis. It is estimated that in the United States the use of illegal drugs by employees costs industry $25 billion a year. The magnitude of the problem has challenged managers to find ways to discourage or prevent employee drug use. One common approach is to implement a drug-testing program.

Many people favor employee drug testing as a control measure, but some change their minds when they are asked to personally submit a urine speciman. [Charles Gupton/The Stock Market]

Virtually all of the *Fortune* 200 companies have drug-testing programs, though a study by the Substance Abuse & Mental Health Services Adminstration indicates that testing is more likely for blue-collar employees than for white-collar employees. Companies test for cause (e.g., an accident or excessive absenteeism), randomly, on all employees, or on all applicants. Home Depot, for example tests all job applicants and all those receiving promotions. The most common test is a urinalysis; the employee supplies a urine sample that is chemically tested for traces of drugs in his or her system.

Some people have strongly resisted drug testing, though nearly 20 percent reveal positive drug use. Nevertheless, many object to it on philosophical and constitutional grounds. They claim the tests intrude on their personal lives, particularly because the tests reveal drug use during personal time, the effects of which may have worn off. They also claim the tests violate the right to privacy and constitute unreasonable search and seizure. People also object because the urinalysis tests are not 100 percent accurate. "False positive" test results—which indicate illegal drugs when there are none in the person's system—can be triggered by some foods and legal over-the-counter drugs.

Employees have responded to this control system in ways beyond verbal protest. Many have challenged the programs by filing lawsuits. Others take the tests but try not to get caught with drugs in their systems. They change the timing or substance of their drug use, submit friends' urine samples as their own, or put substances in their own samples that will make the drugs less detectable. Also, clean urine samples can be purchased. When drug testing first became popular in the mid-1980s, people sold samples on the streets. Now they can even be purchased online.

Employers have responded by tightening the control system. A common technique is to have someone watch employees submit their samples to make sure no one cheats. Some companies use expensive and accurate chemical tests, and some even use undercover agents and drug-sniffing dogs. At least one company is now marketing an alternative approach: a video game that tests eye-hand coordination to assess fitness for work duty.

Sources: M. Boles, "Blue-Collar Workers Face More Drug Tests," *Workforce* 76, no. 8 (August 1997), p. 22; M. Ligos, "Are Your Reps High?" *Sales & Marketing Management* 149, no. 11 (October 1997), pp. 80–86; M. Crant and T. Bateman, "Employee Responses to Drug-Testing Programs," *Employee Responsibilities and Rights Journal,* 1989; Lee Fletcher, "Employee Drug Testing Has Pitfalls," *Business Insurance* 34, no. 43, pp. 1, 69, Richard Rosenberg, "The Workplace on the Verge of 21st Century," *Journal of Business Ethics,* October 1999, 27, no. 1, pp. 3–14; and Gillian Flynn, How to Prescribe Drug Testing, *Workforce,* January 1999, 78, no. 1, pp. 107–9. ●

Designing effective control systems

Effective control systems maximize the potential benefits and minimize dysfunctional behaviors. To achieve this, management needs to design control systems that (1) are based on valid performance standards, (2) communicate adequate information to employees, (3) are acceptable to employees, (4) use multiple approaches, and (5) recognize the relationship between empowerment and control.

Establish valid performance standards
An effective control system must be based on valid and accurate performance standards. The most effective standards, as discussed earlier, tend to be expressed in quantitative terms; they are objective rather than subjective. Also, the measures should not be capable of being easily sabotaged or faked. Moreover, the system must incorporate all important aspects of performance. As you learned earlier, unmeasured behaviors are neglected. But management must also defend against another problem: too many measures that create overcontrol and employee resistance. To make many controls tolerable, managers can devote attention to a few key areas while setting "satisfactory" performance standards in others. Or they can establish simple priorities. The purchasing agent may have to meet targets in the following sequence: quality, availability, cost, inventory level. Finally, managers can set tolerance ranges. For example, in financial budgeting optimistic, expected, and minimum levels sometimes are specified.

Many companies' budgets set cost targets only. This causes managers to control spending, but also to neglect earnings. At Emerson Electric, profit rather than cost is the key measure. If an unanticipated opportunity to increase market share arises, managers can spend what they need to go after it. The phrase "it's not in the budget" is less likely to stifle people at Emerson than at most other companies.

This principle applies to nonfinancial aspects of performance as well. At Motorola, the recruiting department used to be measured by how much money it spent for each new hire. Now it is measured by how well its recruits subsequently perform.[22]

Provide adequate information
Management must adequately communicate to employees the importance and nature of the control system. Then people must receive feedback about their performance. Feedback motivates people and provides information that enables them to correct their own deviations from performance standards. Allowing people to initiate their own corrective action encourages self-control and reduces the need for outside supervision.

Information should be as accessible as possible, particularly when people must make decisions quickly and frequently. For example, a national food company with its own truck fleet had a difficult problem. The company wanted drivers to go through customer sales records every night, insert new prices from headquarters every morning, and still make their rounds—an impossible set of demands. To solve this control problem, the company installed PCs in more than 1,000 delivery trucks. Now drivers use their PCs for constant communication with headquarters. Each night drivers send information about the stores, and each morning headquarters sends prices and recommended stock mixes.

In general, a manager designing a control system should evaluate the information system in terms of the following questions:

1. Does it provide people with data relevant to the decisions they need to make?
2. Does it provide the right amount of information to decision makers throughout the organization?
3. Does it provide enough information to each part of the organization about how other related parts of the organization are functioning?[23]

Ensure acceptability to employees
Employees are less likely to resist a control system and exhibit dysfunctional behaviors if they accept the system. They are more likely to accept systems that have useful performance standards but are not overcontrolling. One Food Lion (a supermarket chain) store manager said to a *Fortune* reporter

about standards he considered unreasonable, "I put in more and more and more time—a hundred hours a week—but no matter . . . I could never satisfy the supervisors . . . They wanted 100 percent conditions, seven days a week, 24 hours a day. And there's no . . . way you could do it."[24] Employees will find systems more acceptable if they believe the standards are possible to achieve.

The control system should emphasize positive behavior rather than focus on controlling negative behavior alone. As noted earlier, companies like Emerson look at profits rather than costs. Jean-Marie Descarpentries of Franco-British CMB Packaging clearly prefers to highlight the positive: He has the heads of 94 profit centers project their best possible performance if everything goes perfectly. He wants his managers to "dream the impossible dream." Then he avoids penalizing people who just miss their lofty goals by assessing them based on how they performed this year versus last year and against the performances of the best managers in the industry.[25]

One of the best ways to establish reasonable standards and thus gain employee acceptance of the control system is to set standards participatively. As we discussed in Chapter 4, participation in decision making secures people's understanding and acceptance and results in better decisions. Allowing employees to participate in control system decisions that directly affect their jobs will help overcome resistance and foster acceptance of the system.

Use multiple approaches

Multiple controls are necessary. For example, casinos exercise control over card dealers by (1) requiring them to have a card dealer's license before being hired; (2) using various forms of direct scrutiny, including up to three levels of direct supervision, closed-circuit cameras, and observation through one-way mirrors; and (3) requiring detailed paperwork to audit transfers of cash and cash equivalents.[26] As you learned earlier in this chapter, control systems generally should include both financial and nonfinancial performance targets and incorporate aspects of preliminary, concurrent, and feedback control.

The other controls: Markets and clans

Although the concept of control has always been a central feature of organizations, the principles and philosophies underlying its use are changing. In the past, control has been almost exclusively focused on bureaucratic (and market) mechanisms. Generations of managers have been taught that they could maximize productivity by regulating what employees did on the job—through standard operating procedures, rules, regulations, and close supervision. To increase output on an assembly line, for example, managers in the past tried to identify the "one best way" to approach the work and then to monitor employee activities to make certain that they followed standard operating procedures. In short, they controlled work by dividing and simplifying tasks, a process we referred to in Chapter 1 as *scientific management*.

Although formal bureaucratic control systems are perhaps the most pervasive in organizations (and the most talked about in management textbooks), they are not always the most effective. *Market controls* and *clan controls* may both represent more flexible, though no less potent, approaches to regulating performance.

Market control

In contrast to bureaucratic controls, market controls involve the use of economic forces—and the pricing mechanisms that accompany them—to regulate performance. The system works like this: In cases where output from an individual, department, or business unit has value to other people, a price can be negotiated for its exchange. As a market for these transactions becomes established, two effects occur:

- Price becomes an indicator of the value of the product or service.
- Price competition has the effect of controlling productivity and performance.

The basic principles that underlie market controls can actually operate at the corporate level, the business unit (or department) level, and the individual level. Figure 16.3 shows a few different ways that market controls are used in an organization.

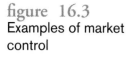

figure 16.3
Examples of market
control

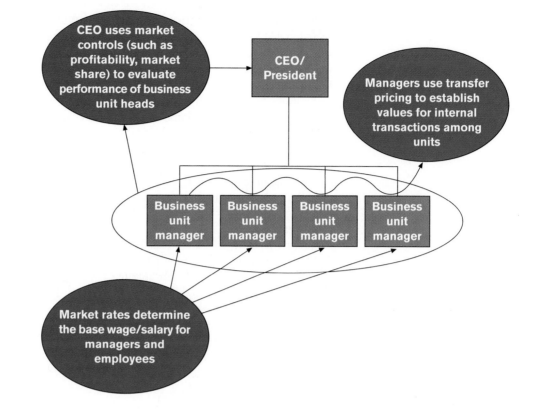

Market controls at the corporate level

In large, diversified companies, market controls are often used to regulate independent business units. Particularly in large conglomerate firms that act as holding companies, business units are typically treated as profit centers that compete with one another. Top executives may place very few bureaucratic controls on business unit managers, but use profit and loss data for evaluating performance. So while decision making and power are decentralized to the business units, market controls ensure that business unit performance is in line with corporate objectives.

Use of market control mechanisms in this way has been criticized by those who insist that economic measures do not adequately reflect the complete value of an organization. Employees often suffer as diversified companies are repeatedly bought and sold based on market controls.

Market controls at the business unit level

Market control can also be used within business units to regulate exchanges among departments and functions. Transfer pricing is one method that organizations use to try to reflect market forces for internal transactions. A **transfer price** is the price charged by one unit in the organization for a product or service that it supplies to another unit of the same organization. For example, in automobile manufacturing, a transfer price may be affixed to components and subassemblies before they are shipped to subsequent business units for final assembly. Ideally the transfer price reflects the price that the receiving business unit would have to pay for that product or service in the marketplace.

transfer price Price charged by one unit for a product or service provided to another unit within the organization.

As organizations have more options to outsource products and services to external partners, market controls such as transfer prices provide natural incentives to keep costs down, and quality up. Consider the situation where training and development activities can be done internally by the human resources department or outsourced to a consulting firm. If the human resources department cannot supply quality training at a reasonable price, then there may be no reason for that department to exist inside the firm. Organizations such as Continental Airlines, IBM, and Corning have placed strict market controls on their human resources functions in order to manage costs and performance.[27]

Market controls at the individual level   Market controls are also used at the individual level. For example, in situations where organizations are trying to hire employees, the supply and demand for particular skills influence the wages employees can expect to receive and the rate organizations are likely to pay. Employees or job candidates that have more valuable skills tend to be paid a higher wage. Of course, wages don't always reflect market rates—sometimes they are set (perhaps arbitrarily) based on internal resource considerations—but the market rate is often the best indicator of an employee's potential worth to a firm.

Market-based controls such as these are important in that they provide a natural incentive for employees to enhance their skills and offer them to potential firms. Even after individuals gain employment, market-based wages are important as controls in that persons with higher economic value may be promoted faster to higher positions in the organization.

Market controls are often used by boards of directors to manage CEOs of major corporations. Ironically, CEOs are usually seen as the ones controlling everyone else in the company, but the fact is that the CEO is accountable to the board of directors, and the board must devise ways to ensure that the CEO acts in their interest. Believe it or not, CEOs often do not want to accept the associated risk required to achieve higher profits for the owners, and consequently may act in ways that make them look good personally (such as making the company bigger or more diversified) but that don't translate into higher profits for the firm.

To attach some strings to the actions of CEOs, boards typically use at least two types of incentives on top of base salary: First, some type of bonus is tied to short-term profit targets such as return on equity. In large U.S. companies, fully 79 percent of the pay of CEOs is now at risk, meaning it's variable depending on the performance of the company. In addition to short-term incentives, boards also use some type of long-term incentives linked to the firm's share price, usually through stock options. More than half of a CEO's pay typically depends on delivering superior performance over time. According to Pearl Meyer, an executive pay consultant in New York, the typical CEO pay package is 21 percent salary, 27 percent short-term (annual) incentives, 16 percent long-term incentives, and 36 percent stock-based pay (mostly options, which usually cannot be exercised for three years).[28]

Clan control: The role of empowerment and culture

Increasingly, managers are discovering that control systems based solely on bureaucratic and market mechanisms are insufficient for directing today's workforce. There are several reasons for this.

• *Employees' jobs have changed.* The nature of work is evolving. Employees working with computers, for example, have more variability in their jobs, and much of their work is intellectual, and therefore invisible. Because of this, there is no one best way to perform a task, and programming or standardizing jobs becomes extremely difficult. Close supervision is also unrealistic since it is nearly impossible to supervise activities like reasoning and problem solving.

• *The nature of management has changed.* The role of managers is evolving, too. It used to be the case that managers knew more about the job than employees did. Today, it is typical for employees to know more about their jobs than anyone else. We refer to this as the shift from touch labor to knowledge work. When real expertise in organizations exists at the very lowest levels, hierarchical control becomes impractical.[29]

• *The employment relationship has changed.* The social contract at work is being renegotiated. It used to be that employees were most concerned about issues such as pay, job security, the hours of work, and the like. Today, however, more and more employees want to be more fully engaged in their work, taking part in decision making, deriving solutions to unique problems, and receiving assignments that are challenging and involving. They want to use their brains.

For these three reasons, the concept of *empowerment* has not only become more and more popular in organizations, but it has become a necessary aspect of a manager's repertoire of control. With no "one best way" to approach a job, and no way to scrutinize what employees do every day, managers must empower employees to make decisions and trust that they will act in the best interests of the firm. But this does not mean giving up control. Instead it means that managers need to make better use of clan control, as opposed to authoritarian control.[30] As we noted at the beginning of this chapter, *clan control* involves creating relationships built on mutual respect, and encouraging each individual to take responsibility for his or her actions. Employees work within a guiding framework of values, and they are expected to use good judgment. At Nordstrom, the fashion retailer, for example, instead of a thick manual laying out company policies, employees are simply given a five-by-eight-inch card that reads: "Use good judgment in all situations. There will be no additional rules." The emphasis in an empowered organization is on satisfying customers, not on pleasing the boss. Mistakes are tolerated, as the unavoidable by-product of dealing with change and uncertainty, and viewed as opportunities to learn. And team members learn together. Table 16.7 provides a set of guidelines for managing in an empowered world.

Understanding culture's role in control
Organization culture is the foundation of clan control. **Organization culture** is the set of important assumptions about the organization and its goals and practices that members of the company share. It is a system of shared values about what is important and beliefs about how the world works. In this way, a company's culture provides a framework that organizes and directs people's behavior on the job. That's the essence of control.[31]

organization culture The set of important assumptions about the organization and its goals and practices that members of the company share.

Cultures can be strong or weak; strong cultures can have great influence on how people think and behave. A strong culture is one in which everyone understands and believes in the firm's goals, priorities, and practices. A strong culture can be a real advantage to the organization if the behaviors it encourages and facilitates are appropriate ones. At several points in this textbook, we have alluded to strong cultures at companies such as Southwest Airlines, Starbuck's Coffee, or the Walt Disney Company that encourage extraordinary devotion to customer service. Employees in these companies don't need rule books to dictate how they act; their actions are rooted in their companies' cultures.

table 16.7
Management control in an empowered setting

1. *Put control where the operation is.* Layers of hierarchy, close supervision, and checks and balances are quickly disappearing and being replaced with self-guided teams. For centuries even the British Empire—as large as it was—never had more than six levels of management including the Queen.

2. *Use "real time" rather than after-the-fact controls.* Issues and problems must be solved at the source by the people doing the actual work. Managers become a resource to help out the team.

3. *Rebuild the assumptions underlying management control to build on trust rather than distrust.* Today's "high-flex" organizations are based on empowerment, not obedience. Information must facilitate decision making, not police it.

4. *Move to control based on peer norms.* Clan control is a powerful thing. Workers in Japan, for example, have been known to commit suicide rather than disappoint or lose face within their team. Although this is extreme, it underlines the power of peer influence. The Japanese have a far more homogeneous culture and set of values than we do. In North America, we must build peer norms systematically and put much less emphasis on managing by the numbers.

5. *Rebuild the incentive systems to reinforce responsiveness and teamwork.* The twin goals of adding value to the customer and team performance must become the dominant raison d'être of the measurement systems.

Source: Gerald H. B. Ross, "Revolution in Management Control," *Management Accounting,* November 1990, pp. 23–27. Reprinted by permission.

At Nordstrom, the fashion retailer, employees are simply given a five-by-eight-inch card with one rule on it. *[Courtesy of Nordstrom, Inc.]*

On the other hand, a strong culture that encourages the wrong behaviors can severely hinder the company's efforts to bring about appropriate changes. IBM, for example, is frequently discussed as an organization that had a very strong culture that served it well for several decades. But the uniformity and conformity established by IBM's culture was ill-suited for creating a more dynamic and flexible organization needed today. One of Lou Gerstner's first tasks after taking over as CEO was to transform the culture to focus on creativity, innovation, and radical thinking. One symbolic gesture in that regard was relaxing IBM's traditional dress code of white shirts and blue pin-striped suits. The dress code itself was not important. But it represented the stodgy old IBM that Gerstner wanted to change.

In contrast to strong cultures, weak cultures have the following characteristics: Different people hold different values, there is confusion about corporate goals, and it is not clear from one day to the next what principles should guide decisions. As you can guess, such a culture fosters confusion, conflict, and poor performance. Most managers would agree that they want to create a strong culture that encourages and supports goals and useful behaviors that will make the company more effective.[32]

Diagnosing culture   Let's say that you want to understand a company's culture. Perhaps you are thinking about working there and you want a good "fit," or perhaps you are working there right now and you want to expand your repertoire of clan control. How would you go about making the diagnosis? A variety of things will give you useful clues about culture:

• *Corporate mission statements and official goals* are a starting point, as they will tell you the firm's desired public image. But you still need to figure out whether the public statements truly reflect how the firm conducts business.

• *Business practices* can be observed. How a company responds to problems, makes strategic decisions, and treats employees and customers tells a lot about what top management really values.

• *Symbols, rites, and ceremonies* give further clues about culture. For instance, status symbols can give you a feel for how rigid the hierarchy is and for the nature of relationships between lower and higher levels. Who is hired and fired—and why—and the activities that are rewarded indicate the firm's real values.

• *The stories people tell* carry a lot of information about their company's culture. Every company has its myths, legends, and true stories about important past decisions and actions that convey the company's main values. Traditionally, Frito-Lay tells service stories, J&J tells quality stories, and 3M tells innovation stories. The stories often feature the company's heroes: persons once or still active possessed of the qualities and characteristics that the culture especially values, who act as models for others about how to behave.

In general, cultures can be categorized according to whether they emphasize flexibility versus control and whether their focus is internal or external to the organization. By juxtaposing these two dimensions, we can describe four types of organizational cultures (see Figure 16.4):

• **Group culture.** A group culture is internally oriented and flexible. It tends to be based on the values and norms associated with affiliation. An organizational member's compliance with organizational directives flows from trust, tradition, and long-term commitment. It tends to emphasize member development and values participation in decision making. The strategic orientation associated with this cultural type is one of implementation through consensus building. Leaders tend to act as mentors and facilitators.

• **Hierarchical culture.** The hierarchical culture is internally oriented by more focus on control and stability. It has the values and norms associated with a bureaucracy. It values stability and assumes individuals will comply with organizational mandates when roles are formally stated and enforced through rules and procedures.

figure 16.4
Competing values model of culture

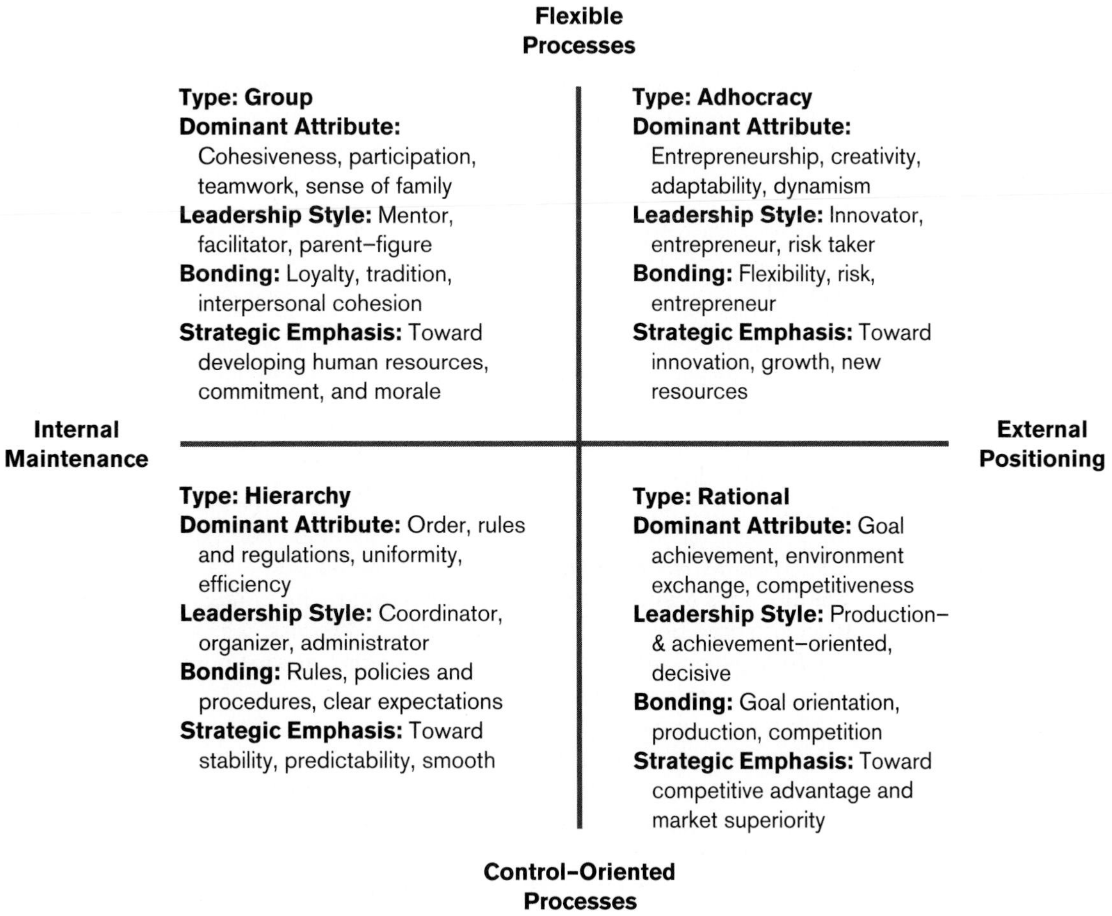

Flexible Processes

Type: Group
Dominant Attribute:
  Cohesiveness, participation, teamwork, sense of family
Leadership Style: Mentor, facilitator, parent–figure
Bonding: Loyalty, tradition, interpersonal cohesion
Strategic Emphasis: Toward developing human resources, commitment, and morale

Type: Adhocracy
Dominant Attribute:
  Entrepreneurship, creativity, adaptability, dynamism
Leadership Style: Innovator, entrepreneur, risk taker
Bonding: Flexibility, risk, entrepreneur
Strategic Emphasis: Toward innovation, growth, new resources

Internal Maintenance   **External Positioning**

Type: Hierarchy
Dominant Attribute: Order, rules and regulations, uniformity, efficiency
Leadership Style: Coordinator, organizer, administrator
Bonding: Rules, policies and procedures, clear expectations
Strategic Emphasis: Toward stability, predictability, smooth

Type: Rational
Dominant Attribute: Goal achievement, environment exchange, competitiveness
Leadership Style: Production– & achievement–oriented, decisive
Bonding: Goal orientation, production, competition
Strategic Emphasis: Toward competitive advantage and market superiority

Control-Oriented Processes

Source: Kim S. Cameron and Robert E. Quinn, *Diagnosing and Changing Organizational Culture* (Englewood Cliffs, NJ: Addison-Wesley 1988).

• **Rational culture.** The rational culture is externally oriented and focused on control. Its primary objectives are productivity, planning, and efficiency. Organizational members are motivated by the belief that performance that leads to the desired organizational objectives will be rewarded.

• **Adhocracy.** The adhocracy is externally oriented and flexible. This culture type emphasizes change in which growth, resource acquisition, and innovation are stressed. Organizational members are motivated by the importance or ideological appeal of the task. Leaders tend to be entrepreneurial and risk takers. Other members tend to have these characteristics as well.[33]

The Procter & Gamble story that follows shows how important—and difficult—culture is to manage. Changing an organization's culture is a monumental task.

Is P&G's culture makeover only skin deep?

When Durk I. Jager became chief executive of Procter & Gamble, he announced that the consumer-products giant would also adopt an open attitude that would help the company respond better to the changing demands of its markets. Jager, however, was attempting to remake a corporate culture of secrecy and strict discipline that had been calcifying for 162 years.

So, how is Jager's cultural revolution going? P&G insiders say there are big changes afoot. Employees who not long ago were obliged to wear dresses or suits with blue or white shirts are going casual. Rewriting memos 20 times is out, as are many of the review committees that killed initiative. Disgruntled employees are encouraged to complain anonymously on the company Intranet. They also can visit the "Ask Durk" site and request a direct answer from Jager. And, yes, he responds.

Jager is also orchestrating Organization 2005, a shakeup designed to break apart the "Proctoid" mentality, speed up ideas, and get products to market faster. "You want to create an environment where you can screw up. You have to be able to fail. You just can't have a risk-averse consensus," says Andrew Shore of PaineWebber, Inc., who is impressed with the changes so far.

There is evidence that Jager's ways are working. Procter finished its $1 billion acquisition of Iams pet food in a mere 60 days, instead of the typical year or more. It has managed to get two new products, an electrostatic mop called Swiffer and a dry-cleaning product called Dryel, which works in home dryers, to market in under two years, instead of four or five. A new Internet joint venture called reflect.com, which uses the Web to sell beauty products, also took just a few months.

Another sign: Procter executives announced they were giving away 40 patents to a Milwaukee engineering school. "Historically," admits Gordon F. Brunner, P&G's chief technology officer, "we've pretty much kept such patents to ourselves. But we're changing." Giving away patents also helps—Procter has 25,000—more than it knows what to do with. The company is also starting to license technology to competitors to get some cash rather than spend money in patent litigation. It has already licensed its process for putting more absorbable calcium in orange juice to Tropicana.

Meanwhile, rapid deployment of new products is helping profits. But there are still some skeptics. "This makes me laugh. This is a company that monitors every move they make, reporters' phone calls, employees' health records, everything," says Alecia Swasy, the author of *Soap Opera: The Inside Story of Procter & Gamble.* While reporting for *The Wall Street Journal,* Procter tried to shut down Swasy's sources at the company by unsuccessfully asking a court for her phone records. Chris Hoyt, a former Procter exec, says the changes are merely window dressing: "They are still the same old Procter on the important stuff."

Ultimately, however, Procter has no choice. Its old methods can't survive the pace of the Internet age. Its flagship Crest toothpaste has been overtaken by Colgate, and its high hopes for fat-substitute Olestra have flopped. Nor can Procter count on its vaunted clout in consumer goods. Its usually brilliant marketing is being hurt as television, its major ad outlet, is splintered by new media. Mass retailers such as Wal-Mart Stores, Inc. are grabbing more power, so it can no longer boss retailers around on matters such as slotting in grocery stores. There may be a new and improved Procter out there. But it's a reluctant makeover, and it's late in coming.

Source: Peter Glaauszka, "Is P&G's Makeover Only Skin Deep?," *Business Week,* November 15, 1999, 3655, p. 52. ●

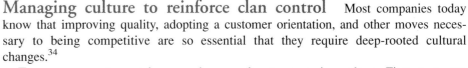

Managing culture to reinforce clan control   Most companies today know that improving quality, adopting a customer orientation, and other moves necessary to being competitive are so essential that they require deep-rooted cultural changes.[34]

Top management can take several approaches to managing culture. First, corporate leadership should espouse lofty ideals and visions for the company that will inspire the organization's members. (We first spoke of vision in Chapter 4 on strategy, and we discussed it more fully in Chapter 12 on leadership.) The vision—whether it concerns quality, integrity, innovation, or whatever—should be articulated over and over until it becomes a tangible presence throughout the organization.

Second, executives must give constant attention to the mundane details of daily affairs such as communicating regularly, being visible and active throughout the company, and setting examples. The CEO should not only talk about the vision; he or she should embody it day in and day out. This makes the CEO's pronouncements credible, creates a personal example others can emulate, and builds trust that the organization's progress toward the vision will continue over the long run.

Important here are the moments of truth when hard choices must be made. Imagine top management trumpeting a culture that emphasizes quality and then discovering that a part used in a batch of assembled products is defective. The decision whether to replace the part at great expense in the interest of quality or to ship the defective part just to save time and money will go a long way toward either reinforcing or destroying a quality-oriented culture.

All along, it is essential that the CEO and other executives celebrate and reward those who exemplify the new values. Another key to managing culture involves hiring, socializing newcomers, and promoting based on the new corporate values. In this way, the new culture will begin to permeate the organization. While this may seem a time-consuming approach to building a new culture, executives must recognize that it can take years to replace a long-time culture of traditional values with one that embodies the competitive values needed in the future.

The resiliency and time investment of clan control are a "double-edged sword." Clan control takes a long time to develop, and an even longer time to change. This gives an organization stability and direction during periods of upheaval in the environment or the organization (e.g., during changes in the top management). And yet if managers want to establish a new culture—a new form of clan control—they must help employees unlearn the old values and embrace the new. We will talk about this transition process more in the final chapter of this book (Chapter 18, "Creating and Managing Change").

Key terms

Summary of learning objectives

Now that you have studied Chapter 16, you should know:

Why companies develop control systems for employees.

Left to their own devices, employees may act in ways that do not benefit the organization. Control systems are designed to eliminate idiosyncratic behavior and keep employees directed toward achieving the goals of the firm. Control systems are a steering mechanism for guiding resources, for helping each individual act in behalf of the organization.

How to design a basic bureaucratic control system.

The design of a basic control system involves four steps: (1) setting performance standards; (2) measuring performance; (3) comparing performance with the standards; and (4) eliminating unfavorable deviations by taking corrective action. Performance standards should be valid, and should cover issues such as quantity, quality, time, and cost. Once performance is compared with the standards, the principle of exception suggests that the manager needs to direct attention to the exceptional cases that have significant deviations. Then the manager takes the action most likely to solve the problem.

The purposes for using budgets as a control device.

Budgets combine the benefits of feedforward, concurrent, and feedback controls. They are used as an initial guide for allocating resources, a reference point for using funds, and a feedback mechanism for comparing actual levels of sales and expenses to their expected levels. Recently, companies have modified their budgeting processes to allocate costs over basic processes (such as customer service) rather than to functions or departments. By changing the way they prepare budgets, many companies have discovered ways to eliminate waste and improve business processes.

How to interpret financial ratios and other financial controls.

The basic financial statements are the balance sheet and the profit and loss statement. The balance sheet compares the value of company assets to the obligations it owes to owners and creditors. The profit and loss statement shows company income relative to costs incurred. In addition to these statements, companies look at liquidity ratios (whether the company can pay its short-term debts), leverage ratios (the extent to which the company is funding operations by going into debt), and profitability ratios (profit relative to investment). These ratios provide a goal for managers as well as a standard against which to evaluate performance.

The procedures for implementing effective control systems.

To maximize the effectiveness of controls, managers should (1) design control systems based on valid performance standards, (2) ensure that employees are provided with adequate information about their performance, (3) encourage employees to participate in the control system's design, (4) see that multiple approaches are used (such as bureaucratic, market, and clan control), and (5) recognize the relationship between empowerment and control.

The different ways that market control mechanisms are used by organizations.

Market controls can be used at the level of the corporation, the business unit or department, or the individual. At the corporate level, business units are evaluated against one another based on profitability. At times less profitable, businesses are sold while more profitable businesses receive more resources. Within business units, transfer pricing may be used to approximate market mechanisms to control transactions among departments. At the individual level, market mechanisms control the wage rate of employees and can be used to evaluate the performance of individual managers.

How clan control can be approached in an empowered organization.

Increasingly, it is not practical to approach control from a centralized, mechanistic viewpoint. In today's organizations, it is difficult to program "one best way" to approach work, and it is often difficult to monitor performance. To be responsive to customers, companies must harness the expertise of employees and give them the freedom to act on their own initiative. To maintain control while empowering employees, companies should (1) use self-guided teams, (2) allow decision making at the source of the problems, (3) build trust and mutual respect, (4) base control on a guiding framework of norms, and (5) use incentive systems that encourage teamwork.

Discussion questions

1. Can you think of an instance in which an organization did not use some form of control? What happened?

2. How are leadership and control different? How are planning and control different? How are structure and control different?

3. Of the four steps in the control process, which is the most important?

4. What are the pros and cons of bureaucratic controls such as rules, procedures, supervision, and the like?

5. How effective is organizational culture as a control mechanism? What are its strengths? Its limitations? When would a manager rely on clan control the most?

6. Does empowerment imply the loss of control? Why or why not?

Concluding Case
Is Your Airline Out of Control?

Like many people, Paul Reutlinger has a Saturday morning ritual: He goes to a neighborhood cafe, where he's greeted as a regular, orders coffee, and reads the local paper. The routine doesn't vary—only the country. Moving from his native Switzerland to Belgium and now to France, Reutlinger is a traveling Mr. Fix-It for ailing airlines.

In an industry where national pride and politics still hold sway, Reutlinger is a professional outsider. A Swissair marketing executive who has lived all over Europe and in Latin America, he was recruited in 1996 to head Belgium's Sabena after Swissair's parent, SAirGroup, took a 49% stake in the former state-run Belgian carrier. Within two years, he engineered a turnaround that put Sabena in the black for the first time in 40 years. Now, Reutlinger has come to France as CEO of Air Liberte, Air Littoral, and AOM, three carriers in the midst of a difficult merger.

Reutlinger, 57, combines a hard-nosed management style with the skill of a diplomat. After arriving at Sabena, he immersed himself in local culture, making friends with politicians and journalists over leisurely lunches and hanging art by the Belgian surrealist René Magritte in his office. Despite this, Reutlinger also slashed costs and, by taking a more conciliatory tone, extracted concessions from labor unions. "I had an advantage because I didn't have a history in Sabena and was seen as more or less a neutral person," he acknowledges.

Reutlinger's task in France looks even more difficult. He enjoys strong backing from SAirGroup, which holds minority stakes in the three regional carriers and wants to merge them to strengthen its hand against Air France, but all three companies are losing money and have been plagued by worker strikes in opposition to the merger. Reutlinger also has the delicate task of cohabiting with Alexandre Couvelaire, the French former chairman of AOM and Air Liberte, who could chafe at relinquishing management control. But Reutlinger is confident he can pull the group out of the red by 2003 by negotiating new labor deals and taking advantage of operating efficiencies from the merger.

Questions

1. How does Paul Reutlinger do it? What is his secret for turning around an airline that's in a nosedive?

2. How does Reutlinger harness the talents and energies of employees to make certain they are working to make the organization successful?

3. Left on their own, people may act in ways that they perceive to be individually beneficial but that may work to the detriment of the organization. Without some means of regulation the organization can literally fall apart. In this regard, what are some of the more important managerial activities that define control?

Source: Carol Matlack, "Got a Busted Airline? He's the Man to Fix It," Business Week Online (Nov. 20, 2000).

Experiential Exercises

16.1 Safety Program

Objective

To understand some of the specific activities that fall under the management functions *planning, organizing, controlling and staffing,* and *directing.*

Instructions

After reading the following case, briefly describe the kinds of steps you would take as production manager in trying to solve your safety problem. Be sure to specifically relate your answer to the activities of *planning, organizing, controlling and staffing,* and *directing.*

Managing the Vamp Co. Safety Program

If there are specific things that a manager does, how are they done? What does it "look like" when one manages? The following describes a typical situation in which a manager performs managerial functions:

As production manager of the Vamp Stamping Company, you've become quite concerned over the metal stamping shop's safety record. Accidents that resulted in operators' missing time on the job have increased quite rapidly in the past year. These more serious accidents have jumped from 3 percent of all accidents reported to a current level of 10 percent.

Because you're concerned about your workers' safety as well as the company's ability to meet its customers' orders, you want to reduce this downtime accident rate to its previous level or lower within the next six months.

You call the accident trend to the attention of your production supervisors, pointing out the seriousness of the situation and their continuing responsibility to enforce the gloves and safety goggles rules. Effective immediately, every supervisor will review his or her accident reports for the past year, file a report summarizing these accidents with you, and state their intended actions to correct recurring causes of the accidents. They will make out weekly safety reports as well as meet with you every Friday to discuss what is being done and any problems they are running into.

You request the union steward's cooperation in helping the safety supervisor set up a short program on shop safety practices.

Because the machine operators are having the accidents, you encourage your supervisors to talk to their workers and find out what they think can be done to reduce the downtime accident rate to its previous level.

While the program is going on, you review the weekly reports, looking for patterns that will tell you how effective the program is and where the trouble spots are. If a supervisor's operators are not decreasing their accident rate, you discuss the matter in considerable detail with the supervisor and his or her key workers.

Source: Reprinted with the permission of Simon & Schuster, Inc., from the Macmillan college text by Theodore T. Herbert, *The New Management: Study Guide,* 4th ed., p. 41. Copyright © 1988 by Macmillan College Publishing Company, Inc.

16.2 Preliminary, Concurrent, and Feedback Control

Objectives

1. To demonstrate the need for control procedures.

2. To gain experience in determining when to use preliminary, concurrent, and feedback controls.

Instructions

1. Read the text materials on preliminary, concurrent, and feedback control.

2. Read the Control Problem Situation and be prepared to resolve those control problems in a group setting.

3. Your instructor will divide the class into small groups. Each group completes the Preliminary, Concurrent, and Feedback Control Worksheet by achieving consensus on the types of control that should be applied in each situation. The group also develops responses to the discussion questions.

4. After the class reconvenes, group spokespersons present group findings.

Discussion Questions

1. For which control(s) was it easier to determine application? For which was it harder?

2. Would this exercise be better assigned to groups or to individuals?

Control Problem Situation

Your management consulting team has just been hired by Technocron International, a rapidly growing producer of electronic surveillance devices that are sold to commercial and government end users. Some sales are made through direct selling and some through industrial resellers. Direct-sale profits are being hurt by what seem to be exorbitant expenses paid to a few of the salespeople, especially those who fly all over the world in patterns that suggest little planning and control. There is trouble among the resellers because standard contracts have not been established and each reseller has an entirely different contractual relationship. Repayment schedules also vary widely from customer to customer. Also, profits are reduced by the need to specialize most orders, making mass production almost impossible. However, no effort has been made to create interchangeable components. There are also tremendous inventory problems. Some raw materials and parts are bought in such small quantities that new orders are being placed almost daily. Other orders are so large that there is hardly room to store everything. Many of these purchased components are later found to be defective and unusable, causing production delays. Engineering changes are made that make large numbers of old compo-

nents still in storage obsolete. Some delays result from designs that are very difficult to assemble, and assemblers complain that their corrective suggestions are ignored by engineering. To save money, untrained workers are hired and assigned to experienced "worker-buddies" who are expected to train them on the job. However, many of the new people are too poorly educated to understand their assignments, and their worker-buddies wind up doing a great deal of their work. This, along with the low pay and lack of consideration from engineering, is causing a great deal of worker unrest and talk of forming a union. Last week alone there were nine new worker grievances filed, and the U.S. Equal Employment Opportunity Commission has just announced intentions to investigate two charges of discrimination on the part of the company. There is also a serious cash flow problem, as a number of long-term debts are coming due at the same time. The cash flow problem could be relieved somewhat if some of the accounts payable could be collected.

The CEO manages corporate matters through five functional divisions: operations, engineering, marketing, finance, and human resources management and general administration.

Preliminary, Concurrent, and Feedback Control Worksheet

Technocron International is in need of a variety of controls. Complete the following matrix by noting the preliminary, concurrent, and feedback controls that are needed in each of the five functional divisions.

Divisions	Preliminary controls	Concurrent controls	Feedback controls
HRM and general administration	_____	_____	_____
Operations	_____	_____	_____
Engineering	_____	_____	_____
Marketing	_____	_____	_____
Finance	_____	_____	_____

Chapter Seventeen

Managing Technology and Innovation

A wise man will make more opportunities than he finds.

—Francis Bacon

I've got vision, and the rest of the world wears bifocals.

—Paul Newman, in Butch Cassidy and the Sundance Kid

Chapter Outline

Learning Objectives

After studying Chapter 17, you will know:

1. The processes involved in the development of new technologies.

2. How technologies proceed through a life cycle.

3. How to manage technology for competitive advantage.

4. How to assess technology needs.

5. Where new technologies originate and the best strategies for acquiring them.

6. How people play a role in managing technology.

7. How to develop an innovative organization.

8. The key characteristics of successful development projects.

Setting the Stage

e-Merging Technology and Medicine

Sheryl S. Alderton recently checked herself into Brigham & Women's Hospital in Boston for a lumpectomy, a common surgical procedure for breast cancer. Like all patients, Alderton didn't want to stay in the hospital longer than necessary. Thanks to a novel program run by cancer surgeon Dr. Yvedt L. Matory, she didn't have to. Two days after the procedure—and two days earlier than normal—Matory sent Alderton home, equipped with a Sony Vaio computer complete with a video lens and speakerphone. Twice during her first week home, Alderton booted up the Vaio and checked in with trained breast-cancer nurses, who looked at the incision while talking to her. When an infection developed during a bad snowstorm, Alderton set up an online appointment with Matory, who prescribed an antibiotic. Without the Vaio, Alderton doubts Matory would have been able to examine her at all, because she lives in a small town 2½ hours from Boston, and all the major roads were blocked. "This took a lot of stress off the surgery," says Alderton. "I got more rest at home, and if anything, they were more responsive to my needs. "The hospital hopes to set up similar programs for patients with congestive heart failure, asthma, and colon cancer.

The Internet is being used to extend health care far beyond the hospital's walls.
[Corbis Stock Market/Ed Wheeler]

Most of the world's medical centers are still technologically challenged compared to banks, manufacturing plants, and dot.coms. But a few hospitals, such as Brigham & Women's and its sister hospital, Massachusetts General Hospital, boast staffs of doctors and clinicians who are using information technology to revolutionize medicine. Here, the paper records that were the hallmark of medicine are giving way to electronic medical records, which are instantly accessible and constantly updated. Doctors are entering their orders, from prescriptions to lab tests, into a computer system loaded with software that instantly catches errors. In the radiology department, old-fashioned films that can easily be lost are being replaced with digital images. Perhaps most striking, the Internet is being used to extend care far beyond the hospital's walls, from Martha's Vineyard to Indonesia.

The Brigham and the General, as they're known, are the cornerstones of Harvard Medical School and rank among the world's best hospitals. Yet even here, information technology has produced astonishing improvements. It has cut the frequency of serious medication errors by 55 percent and the number of overall medication errors by 81 percent. The Institute of Medicine has reported that such medical errors kill at least 44,000 Americans a year—more than the number who die from AIDS or breast cancer. And because medical mistakes are so expensive, the order-entry system alone saves the Brigham up to $10 million a year—a 10-to-1 payback on its annual cost.

While such use of technology is hardly unusual in the business world, these hospitals "are way ahead of the state of U.S. medical practice," says Erica Drazen, a medical informatics expert at First Consulting Group. Some 95 percent of the nation's physicians and more than 90 percent of hospitals still rely almost exclusively on inefficient paper systems. "It is an outrage," says Dr. Russell J. Ricci, general manager of IBM Global Healthcare. "If an airplane crashed every day because maintenance records were kept on paper, the government would insist operations be computerized." But because "it is too emotionally unsettling" to recognize hospitals are unsafe, he argues, "the issue of how to use information technology to [improve] health care has not been [widely] addressed." To be sure, the cost and difficulty of converting to computer-based systems also has slowed adoption.

The Brigham saw the potential more than a decade ago and began building its own internally designed system. In the early 1990s, it started using a computer system to keep patient records and issue doctors' orders for its 720-bed hospital, which annually cares for 40,000 inpatients and 700,000 outpatients. When the Brigham merged with the General in 1994 to create partners, this system was extended to the other hospitals and physicians affiliated with Partners. It now includes 30,000 workstations in 150 different locations.

The rate of adoption of e-health practices will likely accelerate. One reason: The business community is demanding it. Recently, a group of 60 business, including heavyweights such as Ford Motor Corp. and General Electric Corp., announced they will send their workers to hospitals using computerized systems like those found at Brigham and the General. The two Boston pioneers may still be exceptions. But before the decade is out, health care experts, doctors—and patients—are hoping they become the norm.

Source: Condensed from William Symonds, "How e-Hospitals Can Save Your Life," Business Week, December 11, 2000, 3711, pp. EB70–EB74.

Technological innovation is daunting in its complexity and pace of change. And as you have no doubt figured out, it is therefore vital for a firm's competitive advantage. Not long ago, new products took years to plan and develop, were standardized and mass produced, and were pushed onto the market through extensive selling and promotional campaigns. With sales lives for these products measured in decades, production processes used equipment dedicated to making only those standardized products and achieved savings through economies of scale. But today's customers often demand products that have yet to be designed. Product development is now a race to become the first to introduce innovative products—products whose lives often are measured in months as they are quickly replaced by other, even more technologically sophisticated products.

Managing today's technology requires that managers understand how technologies emerge, develop, and affect the ways organizations compete and the ways people work. In this chapter, we discuss how technology can affect an organization's competitiveness and how to integrate technology into the organization's competitive strategy. Then we assess the technological needs of the organization and the means by which these needs can be met.

Technology and innovation

technology The systematic application of scientific knowledge to a new product, process, or service.

In Chapter 9 ("The Responsive Organization") we defined **technology** as the methods, processes, systems, and skills used to transform resources into products. More broadly speaking, we can think about technology as the commercialization of science; the systematic application of scientific knowledge to a new product, process, or service. In this sense, technology is embedded in every product, service, and procedure used or produced.[1]

innovation A change in technology; a departure from previous ways of doing things.

If we find a better product, process, or procedure to accomplish our task, we have an innovation. **Innovation** is a change in technology—a departure from previous ways of doing things. Two fundamental types of innovation are product and process innovation. *Process innovations* are changes that affect the methods of producing outputs. In Chapter 9 we discussed flexible manufacturing practices such as just-in-time, massed customization, simultaneous engineering, and the like. Each of these innovations has changed the way products are manufactured and distributed. In contrast, *product innovations* are changes in the actual outputs (products and services) themselves.[2]

There are definable and predictable patterns in the way technologies emerge, develop, and are replaced. Critical forces converge to create new technologies, which then follow well-defined, life-cycle patterns. Understanding the forces driving technological development and the patterns they follow can help a manager anticipate, monitor, and manage technologies more effectively.

- First, there must be a *need,* or *demand,* for the technology. Without this need driving the process, there is no reason for technological innovation to occur.
- Second, meeting the need must be theoretically possible, and the *knowledge* to do so must be available from basic science.
- Third, we must be able to *convert* the scientific knowledge into practice, in both engineering and economic terms. If we can theoretically do something, but doing it is economically impractical, the technology cannot be expected to emerge.
- Fourth, the *funding, skilled labor, time, space,* and *other resources* needed to develop the technology must be available.
- Finally, *entrepreneurial initiative* is needed to identify and pull all the necessary elements together.

technology life cycle A predictable pattern followed by a technological innovation starting from its inception and development to market saturation and replacement.

The technology life cycle

Technological innovations typically follow a relatively predictable pattern called the **technology life cycle.** Figure 17.1 depicts the pattern. The cycle begins with the recognition of a need and a perception of a means by which the need can be satisfied through applied science or knowledge. The knowledge and ideas are brought together and

figure 17.1
The technology life cycle

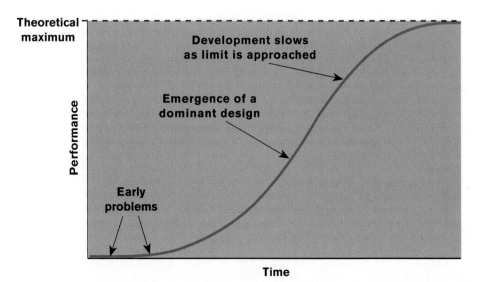

developed, culminating in a new technological innovation. Early progress can be slow in these formative years as competitors experiment a great deal with product design and operational characteristics to meet consumer needs. Here is where the rate of product innovation tends to be highest. For example, during the early years of the auto industry, companies tried a wide range of machines including electric- and steam-driven cars to determine which product would be most effective. Eventually the internal combustion engine emerged as the dominant design, and the number of product innovations leveled off.

Once early problems are resolved and a dominant design emerges, improvements come more from process innovations to refine the technology. It is at this point that companies can gain an advantage by pursuing process efficiencies and cost competitiveness. In the auto example, as companies settled on a product standard, they began leveraging the benefits of mass production and vertical integration to improve productivity. These process innovations were instrumental in lowering production costs and bringing the price of automobiles in line with consumer budgets.[3]

Eventually the new technology begins to reach the upper limits of both its performance capabilities and the spread of its usage. Development slows and becomes increasingly costly, and the market becomes saturated (i.e., there are few new customers). The technology can remain in this mature stage for some time—as in the case of autos—or be quickly replaced by another technology offering superior performance or economic advantage. As we shall see later in the chapter, U.S. auto companies are working right now on new aerospace technologies that will transform the automobile industry. The evolution of life cycles can take decades or even centuries, as in the case of iron and steelmaking technologies. A dramatic example of technology evolution can be found in spatial auditory devices for the blind.

As this example of KASPA shows, a technology life cycle can be made up of many individual *product* life cycles. Each of these products is an incremental improvement over its predecessors. In this way, technological development involves significant innovations, often representing entirely new technologies, followed by a large number of small, incremental innovations. Ongoing development of a technology increases the benefits gained through its use, makes the technology easier to use, and allows more applications. In the process, the use of the technology expands to new adopters.

From the Pages of BusinessWeek

A man with vision

Bats and dolphins find their way around with natural sonar systems that enable them to perceive the dimensions of their world with reflected sound. So why not humans? It's an idea that Leslie Kay, an expert in submarine sonar from New Zealand, has devoted nearly 40 years to researching. He's developing sonar systems to help the visually impaired navigate their darkened world.

Due to radical improvements in his technology, Kay's latest device may be on the verge of becoming accepted by the blind as an essential mobility tool alongside the venerable cane and seeing-eye dog. Dubbed KASPA, for Kay's Auditory Spatial Perception Aid, the device is worn like a headband. It emits frequency-modulated ultrasound signals similar to those of some animals. Embedded a few inches apart in the band are two receptors that produce stereophonic sounds in earphones, just as the distance between our eyes produces stereovisual images permitting depth perception. The sounds change in pitch to reflect the distance and dimension of objects around the KASPA wearer. In tests, blind children have used KASPA to ride bikes through obstacle courses, and one blind child even batted a softball. Kay has high hopes that KASPA will give the blind the previously unimaginable ability to accurately perceive and visualize their physical surroundings, as bats and dolphins do. "The stage has been reached when blind persons can walk about like sighted persons do in a busy shopping area, going in and out of shops. They'll be able to recognize their location relative to the many landmarks on the way," Kay says.

Leslie Kay's KASPA may become as essential a mobility tool to the blind as the cane and seeing-eye dog.
[Courtesy of Dr. Leslie Kay]

Kay, who is nearing 80, developed his first sonar device for the blind in the 1970s. Called the SonicGuide, it looked like a pair of eyeglasses. Similar to KASPA, a module over the nosepiece radiated pulses of high-frequency ultrasound. Two matching receivers captured the reflected signals and transmitted them as audible sound to a pair of earphones. By learning to interpret the changing echoes, wearers would develop an "acoustic picture" of their surroundings.

But the blind didn't share Kay's vision. Fewer than 1,000 of the units were sold before they were finally withdrawn from the market in 1998. "The technology was never marketed or promoted very well." says Daniel Kish, who teaches the blind techniques for getting around Los Angeles and is blind himself. "Many teachers in the field were intimidated by it, so it was not passed on to students."

The rejection didn't prompt Kay to stop his research, however, and KASPA is the fruit of that labor. Tests with the improved device has turned up some impressive results. In one test, 14 blind schoolchildren with very low to high intelligence were able to navigate with KASPA after 20 hours of training in 40 exercises over several weeks. "We believe we can bring movement for the blind to a level never thought possible," Kish says. "The impact on the blind's functional capacities could be staggering." If he's right, someday soon blind people will be playing soccer and baseball and racing through the woods on mountain bikes.

Source: Alan Hall, "Sonar Sight for the Blind?," *Business Week Online*, December 11, 2000. ●

The diffusion of technological innovations

The spread in the use of a new technology over time follows an S-shaped pattern (see Figure 17.2). This pattern, first observed in 1903, has been verified with many new technologies and ideas in a wide variety of industries and settings.[4] The adopters of a new technology fall into five groups.

The first group, representing approximately 2.5 percent of adopters, is the *innovators*. Typically innovators are adventurous, but some might consider them headstrong or even extreme.

The next 13.5 percent of adopters are *early adopters*. This group is critical to the success of a new technology, because its members include well-respected opinion leaders. Early adopters often are the people or organizations to whom others look for leadership, ideas, and up-to-date technological information. The next group, representing 34 percent of adopters, is the *early majority*. These adopters are more deliberate and take longer to decide to use something new. Often they are important members of a community or industry, but typically not the leaders.

Representing the next 34 percent are the late *majority*. Members of this group are more skeptical of technological change and approach innovation with great caution, often adopting only out of economic necessity or increasing social pressure.

figure 17.2

Technology dissemination
pattern and adopter
categories

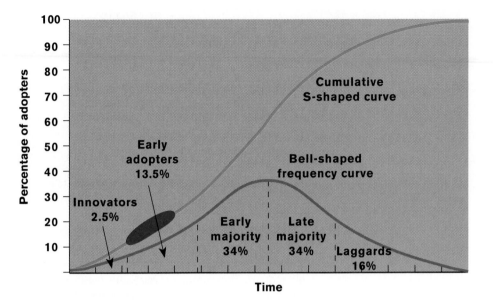

figure 17.2

Technology dissemination
pattern and adopter
categories

The final 16 percent are *laggards*. Often isolated and highly conservative in their views, laggards are extremely suspicious of innovation and change.

Much of the speed with which an innovation spreads depends on five attributes. An innovation will spread quickly if it:

1. Has a great advantage over its predecessor.
2. Is compatible with existing systems, procedures, infrastructures, and ways of thinking.
3. Has less rather than greater complexity.
4. Can be easily tried or tested without significant cost or commitment.
5. Can be easily observed and copied.

Designing products with these technological considerations in mind can make a critical difference in their success.

Technological innovation in a competitive environment

Discussions about technology life cycles and diffusion patterns may imply that technological change occurs naturally or automatically. Just the opposite; change is neither easy nor natural in organizations (we discuss change more fully in the next chapter). Decisions about technology and innovation are very strategic and need to be approached in a systematic way.

In Chapter 4, we discussed two generic strategies a company can use to position itself in the market: low cost and differentiation. With *low-cost* leadership, the company maintains an advantage because it has a lower cost than its competitors. With a *differentiation* strategy, the advantage comes from having a unique product or service for which customers are willing to pay a premium price.[5] Technological innovations can support either of these strategies: They can be used to gain cost advantage through pioneering lower-cost product designs and creating low-cost ways to perform needed operations or they can support differentiation by pioneering unique products or services that increase buyer value and thus command premium prices.

In some cases, a new technology can completely change the rules of competition within an industry.[6] Leading companies that respond ineffectively to technological opportunities can falter while new companies emerge as the dominant competitors. The stories of how Microsoft and Intel grew from the opportunities provided by IBM are now well known.

But industries are seldom transformed overnight. Typically, signals of a new technology's impact are visible well in advance, leaving time for companies and people to respond. For example, most any competitor in the telecommunications industry fully understands the potential value of cellular technology. Often the key issue is not *whether* to adopt a new technology but *when* to adopt it and how to integrate the change with the organization's operating practices and strategies.

Technology leadership

The adage "timing is everything" is applied to many things, ranging from financial investments to telling jokes. It also applies to the development and exploitation of new technologies. Industry leaders such as Xerox, 3M, Hewlett-Packard, and Merck built and now maintain their competitive positions through early development and application of new technologies. However, technology leadership imposes costs and risks, and it is not the best approach for every organization (see Table 17.1).[7]

Advantages of technology leadership

What makes innovators and technology leadership attractive is the potential for high profits and first-mover advantages. Being the first to market with new technologies can provide significant competitive advantage. If technology leadership increases an organization's efficiency relative to competitors, it achieves a cost advantage. It can use the advantage to either reap greater profits than competitors or attract more customers by charging lower prices. Similarly, if a company is first to market with a new technology, it may be able to charge a premium price because it faces no competition. Higher prices and greater profits can defray the costs of developing new technologies.

This one-time advantage of being the technology leader can be turned into a sustainable advantage. Sustainability of a lead depends on competitors' ability to duplicate the technology and the organization's ability to keep building on the lead quickly enough to outpace competitors. It can do this in several ways. The reputation for being an innovator can create an ongoing advantage and even spill over to the company's other products. For example, 3M's reputation for innovation and quality differentiates some of its standard products such as adhesive tape and allows the product to command a premium price. A competitor may be able to copy the product but not the reputation. Patents and other institutional barriers also can be used to block competitors and maintain leadership. Polaroid has successfully kept industry giant Kodak out of the instant-photography market for years through a series of patents and new products such as JoyCam and i-Zone. However, digital photography may be changing all of the rules.[8]

The first mover can also preempt competitors by occupying the best market niches. If it can establish high switching costs (recall Chapter 2) for repeat customers, these positions can be difficult for competitors to capture. Microsoft has dominated the software market for computers with its Windows operating system because of the large library of software that is packaged with it. Although other companies can offer more advanced

table 17.1
Advantages and disadvantages of technology leadership

Advantages	Disadvantages
First-mover advantage	Greater risks
Little or no competition	Cost of technology development
Greater efficiency	Costs of market development and customer education
Higher profit margins	
Sustainable advantage	Infrastructure costs
Reputation for innovation	Costs of learning and eliminating defects
Establishment of entry barriers	
Occupying of best market niches	Possible cannibalization of existing products
Opportunities to learn	

software, their products are not as attractive because they are not bundled as the Windows-based systems are (Ironically, this advantage was so intractable that it was viewed as monopolistic in court.)[9]

Technology leadership can provide a significant learning advantage. While competitors may be able to copy or adopt a new technology, ongoing learning by the technology leader can keep the company ahead by generating minor improvements that are difficult to imitate. Many Japanese manufacturers use several small, incremental improvements generated with their *kaizen* programs (recall Chapter 9) to continuously upgrade the quality of their products and processes. All of these minor improvements cannot be easily copied by competitors, and collectively they can provide a significant advantage.[10]

Disadvantages of technology leadership   However, being the first to develop or adopt a new technology does not always lead to immediate advantage and high profits. While such potential may exist, technology leadership imposes high costs and risks that followers are not required to bear. Being the leader thus can be more costly than being the follower. These costs include educating buyers unfamiliar with the new technology, building an infrastructure to support the technology, and developing complementary products to achieve the technology's full potential. Also, regulatory approval may be needed. For example, the cost of producing a new drug, including testing and the expense of obtaining FDA approval, is estimated at around $200 million. While followers do not get the benefits of being first to market, they can copy the drug for a fraction of this cost once the original patents expire.[11]

Being a pioneer carries other risks. If raw materials and equipment are new or have unique specifications, a ready supply at a reasonable cost may not be available. Or the technology may not be fully developed and may have problems yet to be resolved. In addition, the unproved market for the technology creates uncertainty in demand. Finally, the new technology may have an adverse impact on existing structures or business. It may cannibalize current products or make existing investments obsolete.

Technology followership

Not all organizations are equally prepared to be technology leaders, nor would leadership benefit each organization equally. Much of the difference in choosing to be a technology leader or follower depends on how a company positions itself to compete, the benefits gained through the use of a technology, and the characteristics of the organization.

Interestingly, technology followership also can be used to support both low-cost and differentiation strategies. If the follower learns from the leader's experience, it can avoid the costs and risks of technology leadership, thereby establishing a low-cost position. PC manufacturers have been successful with this type of followership strategy. IBM's personal computer market share within the United States has never matched that of its mainframes largely because of low-cost technology followers such as Dell and Gateway. Followership can also support differentiation. By learning from the leader, the follower can adapt the products or delivery systems to more closely fit buyers' needs.

Adoption timing is dependent on the organization's strategic needs and technology skills as well as the potential benefits of the new technology. As discussed earlier, technologies do not emerge in their final state; rather, they undergo *development over time* (see Figure 17.3). Development makes the technology easier to use and more adaptable to various strategies. At the same time, *complementary products and technologies* may be developed and introduced that make the main technology more useful. For example, software and printer technologies traditionally lag computer hardware technology, thereby limiting the usefulness of hardware technology breakthroughs.

These complementary products and technologies combine with the *gradual diffusion* of the technology to form a shifting competitive impact from the technology. The appropriate time for an organization to adopt technological innovations is when the costs and risks of switching to the technology are outweighed by the benefits. This point differs among organizations and depends largely on the company's characteristics and strategies.[12]

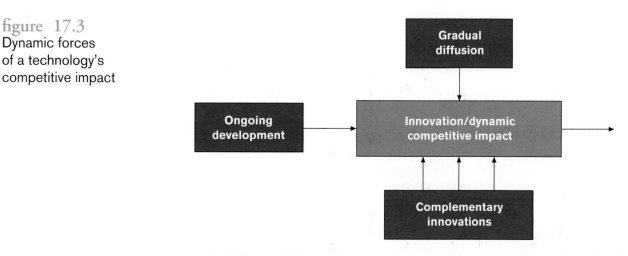

Source: D. M. Schroeder, "A Dynamic Perspective on the Impact of Process Innovation upon Competitive Strategies," *Strategic Management Journal* 11 (January 1990), pp. 25–42.

Assessing technology needs

A decade ago, the major U.S. steel companies suffered from significant cost disadvantages relative to non-U.S. producers. These high costs were due largely to poor productivity resulting from aging plants and obsolete equipment. U.S. companies lagged their European and Japanese counterparts in adopting new, productivity-enhancing process technologies such as the basic oxygen furnace and the continuous-casting process. Had the U.S. companies accurately assessed and adopted these technologies in a timely manner, the massive layoffs (about 60 percent) of the industry's workforce could have been avoided.

Assessing the technology needs of the organization involves measuring current technologies as well as external trends affecting the industry.

Measuring current technologies

technology audit Process of clarifying the key technologies upon which an organization depends.

Before organizations can devise strategies for developing and exploiting technological innovation, they must gain a clear understanding of their current technology base. A **technology audit** helps to clarify the key technologies upon which the organization depends. The most important dimension of a new technology is its competitive value. One technique for measuring competitive value categorizes technologies as emerging, pacing, key, and base.[13]

- *Emerging technologies* are still under development and thus are unproved. They may, however, significantly alter the rules of competition in the more distant future.
- *Pacing technologies* have yet to prove their full value but have the potential to alter the rules of competition by providing significant advantage.
- *Key technologies* have proven effective, but they also provide a strategic advantage because not everyone uses them. Knowledge and dissemination of these technologies are limited and they continue to provide some first-mover advantages.
- *Base technologies* are those that are commonplace in the industry; everyone must have them to be able to operate. Thus, they provide little competitive advantage.

Technologies can evolve rapidly through these categories. For example, electronic word processing was considered an emerging technology in the late 1970s. By the early 1980s, it could be considered pacing. While promising advantages, the technology's cost and capabilities restricted its usefulness to a limited number of applications. With continued improvements and more powerful computer chips, electronic word processing quickly became a key technology. Its costs dropped, its usage spread, and it demonstrated the capacity to enhance productivity. By the late 1980s, it was considered a base technology in most applications. Word processing technology is now so widely used that it is viewed as a routine activity in almost every office.

Assessing external technological trends

Just as with any planning, decisions about technology must balance internal capabilities (strengths and weaknesses) with external opportunities and threats. There are several techniques that organizations use to better understand how technology is changing within an industry.

Benchmarking
As mentioned in Chapter 4, *benchmarking* is the process of comparing the organization's practices and technologies with those of other companies. The ability to benchmark technologies against those of competitors can vary among industries. While competitors understandably are reluctant to share their secrets, information trading for benchmarking is not uncommon and can prove highly valuable. For example, Harley-Davidson's recovery of its reputation for manufacturing quality motorcycles began only after company executives toured Honda's plant and witnessed firsthand the weaknesses of Harley's manufacturing technologies and the vast potential for improvement. In fact, Japanese companies often are willing to show U.S. competitors their operations because they believe the U.S. companies won't use the information!

It is important to benchmark against potential competitors in other nations. There may be key or pacing technologies in use that can easily be imported and offer significant advantage. Also, overseas firms may be more willing to share their knowledge if they are not direct competitors and if they are anxious to exchange information for the benefit of both companies.

Scanning
Whereas benchmarking focuses on what is being done currently, *scanning* focuses on what can be done and what is being developed. In other words, benchmarking examines key and perhaps some pacing technologies, while scanning seeks out pacing and emerging technologies—those just being introduced and still in their development.

Scanning typically involves a number of tactics, many of them the same as those used in benchmarking. However, scanning places greater emphasis on identifying and monitoring the sources of new technologies for an industry. It may also dictate that executives read more cutting-edge research journals and attend research conferences and seminars. The extent to which scanning is done depends largely on how close to the cutting edge of technology the organization needs to operate.

Framing decisions about technological innovation

Once an organization has done a thorough job of analyzing its current technological position, it can begin to make decisions about how to proceed into the future to either develop or exploit emerging technological innovations. Decisions about technological innovations must balance many interrelated factors. The most effective approach to technology depends not only on the technology's potential to support the organization's strategic needs, but also on the organization's skills and capabilities to successfully exploit the technology. The organization's competitive strategy, the technical abilities of its employees to deal with the new technology, the fit of the technology with the company's operations, and the company's ability to deal with the risks and ambiguities of adopting a new technology all must be timed to coincide with the dynamic forces of a developing technology. This does not always mean waiting for the technology to develop. Often it requires changing the capabilities and strategies of the organization to match the needs of the technology. This could include hiring new people, training existing employees, changing internal policies and procedures, and changing strategies. These considerations are discussed next.

Anticipated market receptiveness

The first consideration that needs to be addressed when developing a strategy around technological innovation is market potential. In many cases, innovations are stimulated by external demand for new products and services. For example, current work to develop low earth-orbiting satellites (LEOs) for wireless communications is motivated by a clear understanding of its worldwide market potential. Telecommunications companies such as Motorola, TRW, and Loral are working diligently to develop innovative technologies in this arena.[14]

In assessing market receptiveness, executives need to make two determinations. In the short run, there should be an immediate application that demonstrates the value of the new technology. In the long run, there needs to be a set of applications that show the technology is the proven means to satisfy a market need. For example, despite the recent dominant use of audio compact discs (CDs), the shift to technologies such as MP3 may result in CDs becoming less attractive. LPs, cassettes, and 8-tracks (does anyone remember these?) are virtually nonexistent today.

From the Pages of
BusinessWeek

This is not your dad's PC

It's hard to imagine that a product selling more than 150 million units a year could be past its prime. But looking at the plunging shares of one-time highfliers like Gateway, Dell, and Apple, you would think the personal computer industry has one foot in the grave.

The simple fact is that after years as the bellwether of the technology sector, PC sales growth is slowing. The industry is poised to grow 16.6 percent in 2001, according to market researcher International Data Corp. That's a great number if you're selling cars. But if you sell PCs, which have seen average growth of more than 20 percent for nearly a decade, it's like a punch in the face. "The computers people have today are adequate, so that turns them into a discretionary purchase," says Forrester Research analyst Carl Howe.

Even as the PC takes it on the chin, though, the tech industry as a whole isn't necessarily heading for a TKO. Step outside the world of desktop PCs, and you'll find a number of niches, including laptops, that will continue to expand at 20 percent or better. That's good news for PC makers, because portables offer higher margins than desktops. What's more, consumer devices ranging from Palm-style handhelds to MP3 music players to digital cameras should get a lift as prices come down and features proliferate.

PC makers will share in the success of such devices and the peripherals that enhance them. A year ago, only five manufacturers sold digital music players, for example—none of them mainstream PC makers. Today, more than 50 companies sell them, including industry stalwarts such as Dell Computer Corp., which offers a $300 home digital jukebox, and Compaq Computer Corp., which will set you up with an MP3 player built into its iPaq handheld for $500. Even chipmaking giant Intel Corp. is planning a digital music player amid expectations that sales this year will grow 59 percent to $1 billion, according to Cahners In-Stat Group. They'll face tough competition, though, from upstarts such as SonicBlue Inc., which sells the market-leading Rio MP3 player for $200.

Handheld computers are also reaching a wider audience as the likes of Compaq and Hewlett-Packard duke it out with Palm, Casio, and upstart Handspring. Sales of the devices are expected to surge 31 percent to 8.7 million units, Cahners says. These devices will grow more powerful and spawn a host of peripherals. Already, thanks to lightweight wireless modems and memory cards, the $149 Handspring Visor can be turned into an MP3 player, cell phone, or global positioning device—a far cry from the simple task-scheduling machines available little more than a year ago.

Source: Excerpted from David Rocks, Peter Burrows, Cliff Edwards, and Andy Reinhardt, "Computers and Chips," *Business Week*, January 8, 2001, 3714, pp. 94–95. ●

Technological feasibility

In addition to market receptiveness, organizations must also consider the feasibility of technological innovations. Visions can stay unrealized for a long time. Technical obstacles may represent barriers to progress. Companies such as Intel and Cyrix face continual hurdles in developing newer and faster computer chips.

Since Intel brought the first microprocessor to market in 1971, chip makers have made dramatic advances in computing. The number of transistors on a chip, and its resulting performance, has doubled nearly every 18 to 24 months; upholding what has become known as Moore's Law (Gordon Moore is the cofounder of Intel).

But the frontier of microprocessor technology is being restricted by the combined forces of physics and economics. The wires that run between transistors right now are 400 times thinner than a human hair. Can they be made skinnier yet? Yes, but the task of continually doubling the speed of electrons passing wires of near-zero width will be tricky—and maybe impossible—at some point. Even if it's technically feasible, can companies afford the massive investments needed to do so?[15]

Other industries face similar technological hurdles. In the oil industry, for example, technological barriers prevent exploration and drilling in the deepest parts of the ocean. In medicine, scientists and doctors work continuously to identify the causes and cures for diseases such as cancer and AIDS. In aviation and aeronautics, researchers are working to develop technologies that allow pilots to "see" through clouds. Each of these potentially valuable innovations is slowed by the technical limits of currently available technologies.[16]

Economic viability

Closely related to technological feasibility is economic viability. Apart from whether a firm can "pull off" a technological innovation, executives must consider whether there is a good financial incentive for doing so. For example, the use of solar fusion to generate electricity has been technically feasible for years. However, its cost remains prohibitively higher than the cost of fossil fuels. Similarly, the use of fuel-cell technology for automobiles is almost technically feasible, but its costs are still way too high (we highlight this issue later).

The issue of economic viability takes us back to our earlier discussion of adoption timing. Earlier adopters may have first-mover advantages, but there are costs associated with this strategic approach. The development costs of a particular technological innovation may be quite high, such as in pharmaceuticals, chemicals, software, and the like. Patents and copyrights often help organizations recoup the costs of their investments in technological innovations. Without such protection, the investments in research and development might not be justifiable.

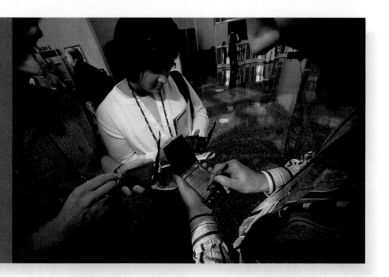

Handheld computers will continue to grow more powerful and spawn a host of peripherals.
[Mark Richards/PhotoEdit]

An exception to the "economic viability" rule might be the now-classic story of Merck and the drug Mectizan. Mectizan is the commercial name for a drug called *ivermectin* developed by Merck scientists to cure river blindness (onchocerciasis). The success rate of the drug has been astoundingly high, but governments in the third-world countries where it is needed cannot afford it. Seeing no economic viability, Merck executives decided to commercialize the drug anyway and donate it to those who need it. Merck has gotten help from 13 organizations including the World Health Organization (WHO), The United Nations Development Programme, and The Carter Center. Millions of people in Africa, the Middle East, and Latin America have gotten treatment.[17]

Anticipated competency development

It has been repeatedly stated in this text that organizations should (and do) build their strategies based on core competencies. This advice applies to technology and innovation strategies as well. Frequently, we can view technological innovations that are the tangible product of intangible—or tacit—knowledge and capabilities that make up a firm's core competence. The Merck and Intel examples illustrate instances in which core competencies in research and development lead to new technological innovations.

In contrast, the example of Brigham and General hospitals in "Setting the Stage" illustrates a situation in which hospitals must develop new competencies in order to embrace new technologies. Recall from Chapter 4 ("Planning and Strategic Management") that Hard Rock Cafe and Toys 'R' Us faced a similar situation in utilizing the Internet. To regain competitiveness, these companies had to bolster their competencies in information technology, and this has not been easy to do.

The upshot from this is that while certain technologies may have tremendous market applicability, firms must have (or develop) the internal competencies needed to execute their technology strategy. Without the skills needed to implement an innovation, even promising technological advances may prove disastrous.

Organizational suitability

The final issues that tend to be addressed when deciding on technological innovations have to do with the culture of the organization, the interests of managers, and the expectations of stakeholders. Companies such as 3M and Sony who are seen as proactive "technology-push" innovators tend to have cultures that are more outward-looking and opportunistic. Executives accord considerable priority to developing and exploiting technological expertise, and decision makers tend to have bold intuitive visions of the future. Typically there are technology champions who articulate competitively aggressive, first-mover technological strategies. In many cases, executives are more concerned about the opportunity costs of not taking action than they are about the potential to fail.

By contrast, *defender* firms such as Rolls Royce tend to adopt a more circumspect posture toward innovation. Their strategies are focused more on deepening their capability base through complementary technologies that extend rather than replace their current ones. Strategic decisions are likely to be based on careful analysis and experience in the industry setting. A hybrid *analyzer* firm like Matsushita (see the Concluding Case) tends to allow others to demonstrate solid demand in new arenas before it responds. As we noted earlier, these types of firms tend to adopt an early-follower strategy to grab a dominant position more from their strengths in marketing and manufacturing than through technological innovation.[18]

Every company has different capabilities to deal with new technology. As discussed previously, early adopters have characteristics different from late adopters. Early adopters of new technologies tend to be larger, more profitable, and more specialized. Therefore, they are in an economic position to absorb the risks associated with early adoption while profiting more from its advantages. In addition, the people involved in early adoption are more highly educated, have a greater ability to deal with abstraction, can more effectively cope with uncertainty, and have strong problem-solving capabilities. Thus, early adopters can more effectively manage the difficulties and uncertainty of a less fully developed technology.[19]

table 17.2
Framing decisions about
technological innovation

Considerations	Examples
Market Receptiveness—Assess external demand for the technology (short/long run).	Cell phones, MP3, personal digital assistants (PDAs), HDTV, etc.
Technological Feasibility—Evaluate technical barriers to progress.	Deep-sea oil exploration, physical size of PC microprocessors
Economic Viability—Examine any cost considerations and forecast profitability.	Solar fusion, fuel cell for automobiles, missile defense system
Competency Development—Determine if current competencies are sufficient.	Information technology in hospitals, digital technology in cameras
Organizational Suitability—Assess the fit with culture and managerial systems.	Steel companies focusing on creativity and innovation

As shown in Table 17.2, these five considerations (market receptiveness, technological feasibility, economic viability, competency development, and organizational suitability) all jointly influence decisions about technology innovations. Even one of these can derail an otherwise promising project.

From the Pages of BusinessWeek

Bell Labs: The original and still the best

Alexander Graham Bell uttered his now famous request, "Mr. Watson, come here I need you," on March 10, 1876. Forty-nine years later, the merger of AT&T and Western Electric's research-and-development operations gave birth to Bell Labs, a unique blend of economic savoir faire and basic discovery that continues to lead the communications and microelectronics revolutions. To carry the mission into the new century, the laboratories' present corporate parent, Lucent Technologies, recently appointed William F. Brinkman as vice-president for research. An affable, down-to-earth physicist who blends pure research with an impressive track record of transforming technology into marketable products, Brinkman now oversees the work of 1,200 researchers from his office at Bell Labs' headquarters in Murray Hill, New Jersey.

Brinkman takes the reins of a research operation that he helped revive after it faltered in the period following the 1982 breakup of AT&T. Over the past few years, Bell Labs has won a steady stream of accolades for its research and has spawned a host of new products. Its research won the 1998 Nobel prize for physics and the 1998 National Medal of Technology. In 1999, the labs racked up a record 1,020 patents. Here are some of Brinkman's views on the future of communications, technology, and industrial R&D.

Q: What are the key attributes required to manage a large and diverse R&D laboratory?
A: The ability to recognize excellent people, set directions, and provide support for the people trying to make things happen. One must be careful to distinguish innovation from discovery. You can only manage discovery by setting direction and hiring people to work in that direction with the hope of great discoveries. Innovation, the process of taking a discovery or idea to the market, is something that must be managed carefully, and we work hard to do this.

Q: What do you see as the main challenge of your new position at Bell Labs?
A: Bell Labs must deliver value to its parent, and that means quickly turning major research breakthroughs into significant new product lines. We've had considerable success at this in the past several years, with products like a central-office

switch-router, the first software-based network switch for both data and voice networks, and the first all-optical router. We must keep these kinds of innovations coming.

Q: Today, few industrial research organizations do any basic research. Will basic science continue to be emphasized at Bell Labs?

A: Yes, definitely. For example, we have a group working on neural computation because we believe that new ideas of broad importance will emerge from a better understanding of the brain that we will gain from this basic research. My guess is that 10 percent to 20 percent of our research budget goes to basic science, but we really don't keep track of the basic- vs. applied-spending breakdown. We try to integrate all of our research into a holistic program.

Q: What would you choose as the most important recent advance in communications technology?

A: I would say the optical amplifier. This is a device that boosts light signals in an optical fiber by amplifying the light signal itself without first converting it to electricity. Invented at Bell Labs in 1986, these amplifiers gave a tremendous boost to fiber-optic transmission systems. Instead of requiring a regenerator every 20 to 25 miles, optical amplifiers are placed 75 miles apart. Without optical amplifiers, there would be no Internet as we know it.

Q: What trends do you see driving the development of technology in the new century?

A: Photonics and silicon-integrated circuits are going to drive high-bit-rate communication all the way home to the individual, enabling him or her to access many new kinds of information. In addition, high-speed wireless-data access will free us from the desktop and office.

Q: How will Bell Labs position itself to make a contribution?

A: There is going to be a marriage of electronics and photonics, united by system engineers and software engineers. This marriage will create extremely complex networks that will serve a broad spectrum of consumer needs. Bell Labs will need to maintain its expertise in all four of these technologies— electronics, photonics, systems engineering, and software.

Q: We hear much less about the threat of Japanese and "foreign" competition these days. Has the United States won back its leadership position?

A: It depends what we are talking about. The United States certainly holds the leading position in communications technology. In basic research, the Japanese have been making major investments that have put them in a much stronger position than in the past. However, I believe the United States is still in the lead.

Q: Is the United States still behind in competitiveness and innovation?

A: With the large number of recent startups, it's hard to say there's a crisis in innovation. However, I do think government funding of physical-science research at universities has suffered as research in the biological sciences has been built up and defense funding has decreased.

Source: Excerpted from Alan Hall, "Why Bell Labs Sticks to the Basics," *Business Week,* March 20, 2000, pp. 18F–18H. ●

Sourcing and acquiring new technologies

Developing new technology may conjure up visions of scientists and product developers working in R&D laboratories like that of Bell Labs. However, new technology can also come from many other sources, including suppliers, manufacturers, users, other industries, universities, the government, and overseas companies. While every source of innovation should be explored, each industry usually has specific sources for most of its new technologies. For example, because of the limited size of most farming operations, innovations in farming most often come from manufacturers, suppliers, and government extension services. Seed manufacturers develop and market new, superior hybrids; chemical producers improve pesticides and herbicides; and equipment manufacturers design improved farm equipment. Land-grant universities develop new farming techniques, and extension agents spread their usage.

In many industries, however, the primary sources of new technology are the organizations that use the technology. For instance, over three-fourths of scientific innovations are developed by the users of the scientific instruments being improved and may subsequently be licensed or sold to manufacturers or suppliers.[20]

make-or-buy decision The question an organization asks itself about whether to acquire new technology from an outside source or develop it itself.

Essentially, the question of how to acquire new technology is a **make-or-buy decision.** In other words, should the organization develop the technology itself or acquire it from an outside source? However, the decision is not that simple. There are many alternatives, and each has advantages and disadvantages. Some of the more common options are discussed in the following paragraphs.

Internal development

Developing a new technology within the company has the potential advantage of keeping the technology proprietary (exclusive to the organization). This provides an important advantage over competitors.

Purchase

Most technology already is available in products or processes that can be openly purchased. For example, a bank that needs sophisticated information-processing equipment need not develop the technology itself. It can simply purchase the technology from manufacturers or suppliers. In most situations, this is the simplest, easiest, and most cost-effective way to acquire new technology.

Contracted development

If the technology is not available and a company lacks the resources or time to develop it internally, it may choose to contract the development from outside sources. Possible contractors include other companies, independent research laboratories, and university and government institutions.

Licensing

Certain technologies that are not easily purchased as part of a product can be licensed for a fee. Pioneers of the VHS format for videocassette recorders held the critical patents, but they freely licensed the technology and the right to use it to competing manufacturers of video equipment. This practice helped make VHS the dominant format (over Beta) by providing other manufacturers with easy access to the technology, thereby creating an industry standard.

Technology trading

Technology trading is another way to gain access to new technologies. Ironically, this tactic sometimes is used between rival companies. For example, U.S. steel producers that use the minimill concept freely trade a great deal of know-how among one another. In some cases, this activity extends to training (without charge) a competitor's employees on new process improvements. While not all industries are amenable to technology sharing, trading is becoming increasingly common because of the high cost of developing advanced technologies independently.[21]

Research partnerships and joint ventures

As discussed in the following fuel cell example, research partnerships are arrangements designed to jointly pursue specific new-technology development. Typically, each member enters the partnership with different skills or resources needed for successful new-technology development. An effective combination is an established company and a start-up. Joint ventures are similar in most respects to research partnerships, but they tend to have greater permanence and their outcomes result in entirely new companies.[22]

Acquisition of an owner of the technology

If a company lacks the needed technology but wishes to acquire proprietary ownership of it, one option is to purchase the company that owns the technology. This transaction can take a number of forms, ranging from an outright purchase of the entire company to a minority interest sufficient to gain access to the technology. Sun Microsystem's CEO, Scott McNealy, readily acknowledges that part of his firm's strategy is to acquire companies with emerging technologies. In the fast-paced world of Internet computing, there is no way one firm can do it all itself.[23]

Choosing among these alternatives can be simplified by asking the following basic questions:

1. Is it important (and possible) in terms of competitive advantage that the technology remain proprietary?
2. Are the time, skills, and resources for internal development available?
3. Is the technology readily available outside the company?

As Figure 17.4 illustrates, the answers to these questions guide the manager to the most appropriate technology acquisition option.

Technology and managerial roles

chief technology officer (CTO) Executive in charge of technology strategy and development.

In organizations, technology traditionally has been the responsibility of vice presidents for research and development (R&D). These executives are directly responsible for corporate and divisional R&D laboratories. Typically their jobs have a functional orientation. But increasingly companies are creating the position of **chief technology officer (CTO).** The CTO is a senior position at the corporate level with broad, integrative responsibilities. CTOs coordinate the technological efforts of the various business units,

figure 17.4
Technology acquisition options

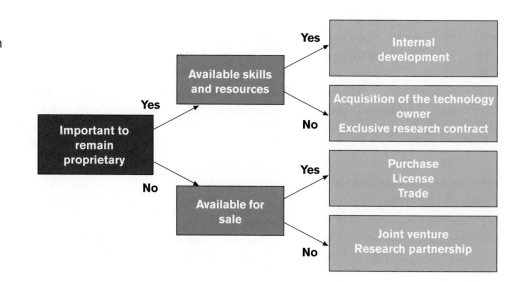

act as a voice for technology in the top management team, supervise new-technology development, and assess the technological implications of major strategic initiatives such as acquisitions, new ventures, and strategic alliances.[24]

CTOs also perform an important boundary role: They work directly with outside organizations. For example, they work with universities for funding research to stay abreast of technical developments and with regulatory agencies to ensure compliance with regulations, identify trends, and influence the regulatory process.

Other people play a variety of critical roles in developing new technology. Recall from Chapter 7 that it is the *entrepreneur* who, in an effort to exploit untried technologies, invents new products or finds new ways to produce old products. The entrepreneur opens up new possibilities that change the competitive structure of entire industries.[25] For example, Steven Jobs started Apple Computer in his garage and launched the multi-billion-dollar personal computer industry.

Key roles in acquiring and developing new technologies are the technical innovator, product champion, and executive champion.[26] The **technical innovator** develops the new technology or has the key skills needed to instill and operate the technology. This person possesses the requisite technical skills, but he or she may not have the managerial skills needed to push the idea forward and secure acceptance within the organization. This is where the product champion gets involved. Introducing new technology into an organization requires that someone promote the idea. The **product champion**—often at the risk of his or her position and prestige—promotes the idea throughout the organization, searching for support and acceptance. The champion can be a high-level manager, but often this is not the case. If the champion lacks the power and financial resources to make the required changes independently, she or he must convince people who have such authority to support the innovation. In other words, product champions must get sponsorship.

Sponsorship comes from the **executive champion,** who has the status, authority, and financial resources to support the project and protect the product champion. Without this support and protection, the product champion, and thus the new technology, could not succeed. Resources needed to develop the innovation would be unavailable, and without protection the champion would not be allowed to continue promoting the change.

technical innovator A person who develops a new technology or has the key skills to install and operate the technology.

product champion A person who promotes a new technology throughout the organization in an effort to obtain acceptance and support for it.

executive champion An executive who supports a new technology and protects the product champion of the innovation.

From the Pages of BusinessWeek

Hey, wanna ride in my new car?

The innovation is fuel cell technology. Through a chemical reaction between hydrogen and oxygen, fuel cells generate the juice to power an electric motor—and the only emission out the tailpipe is a trickle of water. The technology could result in the eventual demise of the internal combustion engine (and all of its pollution). Cost—not surprising—is the roadblock (a Ford Taurus would cost over $100,000 today). A good deal more work is needed to make the technology commercially feasible. That's what is leading to a good many research partnerships and alliances:

- BASF, BP, DaimlerChrysler, Methanex, Statoil, and fuel cell manufacturer Xcellsis (Kirchheim, Germany) plan to collaborate to develop and commercialize methanol fuel cells to power cars. The companies will immediately begin a two-year technology, infrastructure, and market study. They aim to sign a formal agreement on developing the methanol fuel cell market—beginning with tests on a trial fleet of fuel cell cars—if the study yields a positive conclusion.
- DaimlerChrysler, Ford Motor Co., fuel cell maker Ballard Power Systems, three oil companies, and the State of California announced a precedent-setting program to field a fleet of fuel cell vehicles in a program called the California Fuel Cell Partnership. The collaboration aims to put roughly 50 pollution-free, fuel-cell-powered passenger vehicles on the road between 2000 and 2003; that includes about 20 buses.
- BMW, Renault, and Delphi Automotive Systems have established a solid-oxide fuel cell development agreement. BMW intends to use the solid-oxide fuel cell as an auxiliary source for gasoline-powered passenger cars, while Renault will install them in light- and heavy-duty diesel trucks.

- General Motors Corp. and its Adam Opel AG division showed off their joint effort in advanced vehicle technology and outlined their "alternative fuel" plan for the both near- and long-term. GM and Opel say their brand-new prototype is the world's most advanced "operational" hydrogen-powered vehicle—and it may be hard to argue. The technology is stowed away in a single Opel Zafira MPV minivan. The Zafira is a full 5-seat minivan propelled by a 75-hp, three-phase electric motor that is powered by a fuel cell that consumes hydrogen. Unlike previous efforts with a fuel cell fed by hydrogen reformed onboard from methanol, the HydroGen1 is fueled by pure hydrogen (although currently there is next to no infrastructure to deliver hydrogen for public consumption).
- In an unusual partnership that combines oil industry refining expertise with General Motors Corp's fuel cell technology, GM and ExxonMobil Corp. announced they have developed a new highly efficient gasoline fuel processor for fuel cell vehicles. The on-board processor turns ordinary gasoline into a high-quality stream of hydrogen that powers a fuel cell, enabling vehicles to be "gassed up" at the corner station like a conventional car or truck. The development promises to be a big breakthrough because it could eliminate two of the biggest current problems for the technology: storing hydrogen on board and lack of a hydrogen-refueling infrastructure.

Sources: Keith Naughton, "Detroit's Impossible Dream," *Business Week,* March 2, 1998, pp. 66–67; Alex Scott, "Chemical-auto Industry Alliance Drives Fuel Cell Agreement," *Chemical Week,* September 20, 2000, 162, no. 35, p. 20; Drew Winter; "GM, ExxonMobil in Fuel Cell Advance," *Ward's Auto World,* September 2000, 36, no. 9, p. 79; "Renault Joins Fuel Cell Venture," *Ward's Auto World,* June 2000, 36, no. 6, p. 32; Bob Krantz, "New Sell for Fuel Cell," *Ward's Auto World,* August 2000, 36, no. 8, pp. 54–56; and Bill Visnic, "New Alliance Hastens Fuel Cell Development," *Ward's Auto World,* May 1999, 35, no. 5, p. 136. ●

Organizing for innovation

Organizing for innovation requires a balance between unleashing people's creative energies and capabilities and controlling the results to meet market needs in a timely manner.

Unleashing creativity

As discussed in Chapter 7 (New Ventures), 3M has a strong orientation toward *intrapreneurship,* and derives about one-third of its revenues from new products. 3M, along with other companies such as Merck, Hewlett-Packard, and Rubbermaid, have well-established histories of producing many successful new technologies and products. What sets these and other continuous innovators apart? The one thing these companies have in common is an organizational culture that encourages innovation.[27]

Consider the 3M legend from the early 1920s of inventor Francis G. Okie. Okie dreamed up the idea of using sandpaper instead of razor blades for shaving. The aim was to reduce the risk of nicks and avoid sharp instruments. The idea failed, but rather than being punished for the failure, Okie was encouraged to champion other ideas, which included 3M's first blockbuster success: waterproof sandpaper. A culture that permits failure is crucial for fostering the creative thinking and risk taking required for innovation.

As strange as it may seem, *celebrating* failure can be vital to the innovation process.[28] Failure is the essence of learning, growing, and succeeding. Innovative companies have many balls in the air at all times, with many people trying many new ideas. A majority of the ideas will fail—but it is only through this process that the few big "hits" will emerge that make a company an innovative star.

3M uses the simple set of rules listed in Table 17.3 to help foster innovation. These rules can be—and are—copied by other companies. But 3M has an advantage in that it has followed these rules since its inception and ingrained them in its culture. This culture is shared and passed on in part through stories. One such legend is about the 3M engineer who was fired because he refused to stop working on a project that his boss thought was wasting resources. Despite being fired, the engineer came to work as usual, finished the project, and demonstrated the value of his innovation. The engineer eventually was promoted to head a new division created to manufacture and market the innovation.

table 17.3
3M's rules for an
innovative culture

- **Set goals for innovation.** By corporate decree, 25 to 30 percent of annual sales must come from new products that are five years old or less.

- **Commit to research and development.** 3M invests in R&D at almost double the rate of the average U.S. company. One R&D goal is to cut in half the time it takes to introduce new products.

- **Inspire intrapreneurship.** Champions are encouraged to run with new ideas, and they get a chance to manage their products as if they were running their own businesses. 3Mers are allowed to spend 15 percent of their time pursuing personal research interests unrelated to current company projects.

- **Facilitate, don't obstruct.** Divisions are kept small and allowed to operate with a great deal of independence but have constant access to information and technical resources. Researchers with good ideas are awarded $50,000 Genesis grants to develop their brainstorms into new products.

- **Focus on the customer.** 3M's definition of quality is to demonstrate that the product can do what the customer—not some arbitrary standard—dictates.

- **Tolerate failure.** 3Mers know that if their ideas fail, they will still be encouraged to pursue other innovative ideas. Management knows that mistakes will be made, and that destructive criticism kills initiative.

Sources: Company reports; R. Mitchell, "Masters of Innovation: How 3M Keeps Its New Products Coming," *Business Week,* April 10, 1989, pp. 58–63; T. Katauskas, "Follow-Through: 3M's Formula for Success," *R&D,* November 1990; and Thomas J. Martin, "Ten Commandments for Managing Creative People," *Fortune,* January 16, 1995, pp. 135–36.

Bureaucracy busting

Bureaucracy is an enemy of innovation. While bureaucracy is useful to maintain orderliness and gain efficiencies, it also can work directly against innovativeness. Developing radically different technologies requires a more fluid and flexible (organic) structure that does not restrict thought and action. However, such a structure can be chaotic and disruptive to normal operations. Consequently, companies often establish special temporary project structures that are isolated from the rest of the organization and allowed to operate under different rules. These units go by many names, including "skunkworks" (recall Chapter 7), "greenhouses," and "reserves."

In Japan, *angura is* an "underground research" policy that allows scientists to spend up to 20 percent of their time pursuing projects about which only the immediate supervisor knows.[29] When Apple developed the Macintosh, Steve Jobs took a small group of young engineers and programmers and set up operations apart from the remainder of the plant. They started from scratch, trying to completely rethink the personal computer. A pirate's flag was flown over their operation to demonstrate that they were not part of the regular bureaucratic operating structure and defied conventional rules. The result was a very successful new product.

As shown in Figure 17.5, other managerial systems can facilitate innovation. At steel companies such as Chaparral and Nucor, employees work in *cross-functional teams* to solve problems and create innovative solutions. These *flat structures* help create an enviornment that encourages collaboration and creativity. Teams focus on present issues and problems as well as future concerns and opportunities. In addition, teams work with outside partners to bring knowledge into the organization so that it can be integrated with existing ideas and information to create innovations. All the while, teams are supported by values of egalitarianism, information sharing, openness to outside ideas, and positive risk. The aim is to destroy the traditional boundaries between functions and departments in order to create less bureaucratic "learning laboratories."[30]

figure 17.5
The learning laboratory

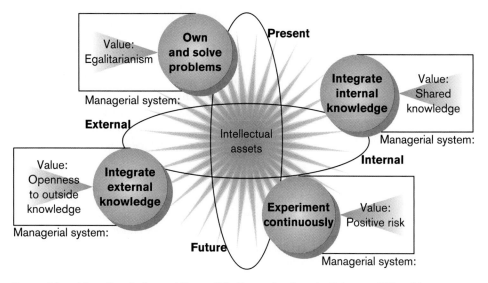

Source: Adapted from Dorothy Leonard-Barton, "The Factory As a Learning Laboratory," *Sloan Management Review*, Fall, 1992, pp. 23–38.

Implementing development projects

development project A focused organizational effort to create a new product or process via technological advances.

A powerful tool for managing technology and innovations is the **development project.**[31] A development project is a focused organizational effort to create a new product or process via technological advances. For example, several years ago Eastman Kodak launched a development project to create the FunSaver Camera. The concept was simple: to package film in an inexpensive plastic camera body so that after the pictures were taken, the consumer could simply drop the whole assembly with a photo finisher. While the FunSaver utilized existing design knowledge, it was developed on a unique computer-aided design and manufacturing (CAD/CAM) system. Two years earlier, Hewlett-Packard had initiated a development project of its own to design a new class of low-cost computer printers based on ink-jet technology. HP's Deskjet Printer was one of the company's first attempts to integrate manufacturing, marketing, and R&D. The development project allowed the company to achieve an unprecedented advantage in both cost and speed.

In general, development projects fall into one of four categories: (1) *research or advanced development projects* designed to invent new science for application in a specific project; (2) *breakthrough development projects* designed to create the first generation of a product or process; (3) *platform development projects* that establish the basic architecture for a whole set of follow-on projects; and (4) *derivative development projects* that are narrower in scope and are designed to provide incremental improvements to an existing product or process.[32]

Development projects such as these typically feature a special cross-functional team that works together on an overall concept or idea. Like most cross-functional teams, their success depends on how well individuals work together to pursue a common vision. And in the case of development projects, teams must frequently interact with suppliers and customers—making the complexity of their task that much greater. Because of their urgency and strategic importance, most development projects are conducted under intense time and budget pressures, thus presenting a real-time test of the company's ability to innovate.

Managers should recognize that development projects have multiple benefits. Not only are they useful for creating new products and processes, but they frequently cultivate skills and knowledge that can be used for future endeavors. In other words, the capabilities that companies derive from a development project frequently can be turned into a source of competitive advantage. For example, when Ford created a development project to design an air-conditioning compressor to outperform its Japanese rival, executives also discovered they had laid the foundation for new processes that Ford could use in future projects. Their new capability in integrated design and manufacturing helped Ford reduce the costs and lead times for other product developments. Thus, *organizational learning* had become an equally important criterion for evaluating the success of the project.

For development projects to achieve their fullest benefit, they should build on core competencies (recall Chapters 4 and 9); have a guiding vision about what must be accomplished and why (Chapter 12); have a committed team (Chapters 12 and 14); instill a philosophy of continuous improvement (Chapter 9); and generate integrated, coordinated efforts across all units (Chapters 8 and 9).

Technology, job design, and human resources

Adopting a new technology typically requires changes in the way jobs are designed. Often the way the task is redefined fits people to the demands of the technology to maximize the technology's operation. But this often fails to maximize total productivity, because it ignores the human part of the equation. The social relationships and human aspects of the task may suffer, lowering overall productivity.

sociotechnical systems An approach to job design that attempts to redesign tasks to optimize operation of a new technology while preserving employees' interpersonal relationships and other human aspects of the work.

The **sociotechnical systems** approach to work redesign specifically addresses this problem. This approach redesigns tasks in a manner that jointly optimizes the social and technical efficiency of work. Beginning with studies on the introduction of new coal-mining technologies in 1949, the sociotechnical systems approach to work design focused on small, self-regulating work groups.[33] Later it was found that such work arrangements could operate effectively only in an environment in which bureaucracy was limited. Today's trends in bureaucracy "bashing," lean and flat organizations, work teams, and an empowered workforce are logical extensions of the sociotechnical philosophy of work design. At the same time, the technologies of the information age—in which people at all organizational levels have access to vast amounts of information—make these leaner and less bureaucratic organizations possible.

Managers face several choices regarding how to apply a new technology. Technology can be used to limit the tasks and responsibilities of workers and "deskill" the workforce, thus turning workers into servants of the technology.

Alternatively, managers can select and train workers to master the technology, using it to achieve great accomplishments and improve the quality of their lives. Technology, when managed effectively, can empower workers as it improves the competitiveness of organizations.

Hewlett-Packard undertook a development project that resulted in the inkjet printer, a product that gave the company an unprecedented advantage in both cost and speed. *[Courtesy of Hewlett-Packard Company]*

table 17.4
Compensation practices in traditional and advanced manufacturing firms

Type of Compensation Practice	Traditional factory	Integrated manufacturing
Performance contingent	Focus on *individual incentives* reflects division of labor and separation of stages and functions.	Extensive use of *group incentives* to encourage teamwork, cooperation, and joint problem solving.
Job contingent	Use of *hourly wage* assumes that the differences in employee contribution are captured in job classifications and that performance is largely determined by the production system.	Use of *salary* assumes that employees' contributions transcend the job per se to substantially affect output. The distinctions between classes of employment are diminished.
Person contingent	*Seniority pay* rewards experience as a surrogate for knowledge and skill in a stable environment and rewards loyalty to reduce uncertainty within the system.	*Skill-based* pay rewards continuous learning and the value-added derived from increased flexibility in a dynamic environment.

Source: Scott A. Snell and James W. Dean, Jr., "Strategic Compensation for Integrated Manufacturing. The Moderating Effects of Jobs and Organizational Inertia," *Academy of Management Journal* 37, no. 5 (1994) pp. 1109–40.

However, as managers make decisions about how to design jobs and manage employees, they also need to consider other human resource systems that complement the introduction of new technology. Table 17.4, for example, shows how compensation systems can be changed to facilitate the implementation of advanced manufacturing technology. In the contemporary setting, use of group incentives, salary, and skill-based pay systems helps reinforce collective effort (recall the use of cross-functional teams), professionalism, empowerment, and flexibility required for knowledge work. If a company's pay system is not aligned with the new technologies, it may not reward behavior that is needed to make the changes work. Worse yet, existing reward systems may actually reinforce old behaviors that run counter to what is needed for the new technology.

Taken as a whole, these ideas provide a set of guidelines for managing the strategic and organizational issues associated with technology and innovation. In Chapter 18, we expand this discussion to focus on how organizations can reshape themselves to adapt to a dynamic marketplace. Managing change and organizational learning are central elements of what it takes to become a world-class organization.

Key terms

Chief technology officer (CTO), p. 553
Development project, p. 557
Executive champion, p. 554
Innovation, p. 534
Make-or-buy decision, p. 552
Product champion, p. 554

Sociotechnical systems, p. 558
Technical innovator, p. 554
Technology, p. 539
Technology audit, p. 545
Technology life cycle, p. 539

Summary of learning objectives

Now that you have studied Chapter 17, you should know:

The processes involved in the development of new technologies.

Forces that compel the emergence of a new technology include (1) a need for the technology, (2) the requisite scientific knowledge, (3) technical convertibility of this knowledge, (4) the capital resources to fund development, and (5) the entrepreneurial insight and initiative to pull the components together.

How technologies proceed through a life cycle.

New technologies follow a predictable life cycle. First, a workable idea about how to meet a market need is developed into some product innovation. Early progress can be slow as competitors experiment with product designs. Eventually a dominant design emerges as the market accepts the technology, and further refinements to the technology occur from process innovations. As the technology begins to approach both the theoretical limits to its performance potential and market saturation, growth slows and the technology matures. At this point the technology can remain stable or be replaced by a new technology.

How to manage technology for competitive advantage.

Adopters of new technologies are categorized according to the timing of their adoption: innovators, early adopters, the early majority, the late majority, and laggards. Technology leadership has many first-mover advantages, but also poses significant disadvantages. The same may be said for followership. After that, technology that helps improve efficiency will support a low-cost strategy, while technologies that help make products more distinctive or unique will support a differentiation strategy. Determining an appropriate technology strategy depends on the degree to which the technology supports the organization's competitive requirements and, if a technology leadership strategy is chosen, the company's ability, in terms of skills, resources, and commitment, to deal with the risks and uncertainties of leadership.

How to assess technology needs.

Assessing the technology needs of a company begins by benchmarking, or comparing, the technologies it employs with those of both competitors and noncompetitors. Benchmarking should be done on a global basis to understand practices used worldwide. Technology scanning helps identify emerging technologies and those still under development in an effort to project their eventual competitive impact.

Where new technologies originate and the best strategies for acquiring them.

New technologies can be acquired or developed. Options include internal development, purchase, contracted development, licensing, trading, research partnerships and joint ventures, and acquisition. The approach used depends on the existing availability of the technology, the skills, resources, and time available, and importance of keeping the technology proprietary.

How people play a role in managing technology.

People play many different roles in managing technology. For example, the chief technology officer (CTO) is the person with broad, integrative responsibility for technological innovation. In addition, the entrepreneur is the person who recognizes the competitive potential of the technology and finds new ways to exploit opportunities. The technical innovator has the key skills needed to develop or install and operate the technology. The product champion is the person who promotes the new idea(s) in order to gain support throughout the organization. The executive champion is the person with status and resources to support the project.

How to develop an innovative organization.

Organizing for innovation involves unleashing the creative energies of employees while directing their efforts toward meeting market needs in a timely manner. Culture, structure, development projects, and job design are critical for building an innovative organization.

The key characteristics of successful development projects.

For development projects to achieve their fullest benefit, they should (1) build on core competencies; (2) have a guiding vision about what must be accomplished and why; (3) have a committed team; (4) instill a philosophy of continuous improvement; and (5) generate integrated, coordinated efforts across all teams and units.

Discussion questions

1. At the beginning of this chapter there is a quote by Francis Bacon that reads, "A wise man will make more opportunities than he finds." What does this have to do with technology and innovation? What does it have to do with competitive advantage?

2. What examples of technological innovation can you identify? What forces led to the commercialization of the science behind these technologies? Did the capability exist before the market demand, or was the demand there before the technology was available?

3. Thomas Edison once said that most innovations are 10 percent inspiration and 90 percent perspiration. How does this match with what you know about technology life cycles?

4. Why would a company choose to follow rather than lead technological innovations? Is the potential advantage of technological leadership greater when innovations are occurring rapidly, or is it better in this case to follow?

5. If you were in the grocery business, who would you benchmark for technological innovations? Would the companies be inside or outside your industry? Why?

6. How would you see the executive champion, the chief technology officer, and the product champion working together? Could the roles all be played by the same individual? Why or why not?

Concluding Case
Matsushita: Organizing for Innovation

When Kunio Nakamura was tapped to become president and CEO at Matsushita Electric Industrial Co. last March, he had one big demand: to keep doing what he'd been doing. As a senior exec at the world's largest consumer electronics conglomerate, Nakamura had reshaped almost everything he'd gotten his hands on—including U.S. operations. So when he assumed his new duties on June 29, the tall, tanned 61-year-old was given free rein to restructure the sprawling company. "I didn't want to be a CEO unless I could implement my own policies," he says, "My job is to instigate change."

It's about time. Nakamura must transform a stodgy giant, with 290,000 employees in 46 countries, into a fleet-footed player in the information technology age. He must also keep its edge in components for next-generation electronics. In what promises to be the largest shake-up in the 82-year-old company's history, nothing will be sacred—not Matsushita's $68 billion in sales, and not its cherished tradition of career-long job security. "Preserving sales levels and the size of the workforce are no longer key factors for us," Nakamura told *Business Week*. "It'll be necessary for people to adjust their skills to the IT Age."

Nakamura has a lot of ground to cover. True, the Panasonic brand is still immensely popular, and the company commands top market share in Japan for Net-capable phones, car-navigation systems, and DVD products. But it has never produced a mega-hit like Sony's Walkman. And it has been battered by falling profits on conventional items such as TVs and VCRs. Operating profit for consumer products fell 60 percent in the year to March 31; group operating profit dropped 18 percent to $1.8 billion.

Management-wise, Nakamura inherits a creaky machine. Matsushita lags far behind Sony, NEC, and others in terms of restructuring. Its bureaucracy is mammoth, with too many business divisions—some 140 in Japan alone. No wonder investors have been less than exuberant about the stock: Over the past year, it has underperformed, both in the broad market and the electronics sector.

So Nakamura is moving fast. A day after taking over, he pledged in a videotaped speech to "empower" employees by rewarding proven talent, not age or seniority. Nakamura also handed out 500 Net-ready cell phones to senior execs. "This way they can be reached anytime," says Nakamura. He plans to invest $1 billion

Matsushita Electric CEO Kunio Nakamura must transform the stodgy giant into a fleet-footed player in the information technology age.
[©AFP/CORBIS]

over the next three years to boost Matsushita's IT capacities.

Nakamura's forte seems to be just such lightning-fast makeovers. After streamlining Matsushita's U.S. operations, he turned all 35 of Matsushita's money-losing Chinese subsidiaries into profitable units in less than two years. "He carried out drastic restructuring in the United States and China," points out Kazushige Hata, consumer electronics analyst at ING Barings Securities (Japan) Ltd. "He should be able do it here, too."

WARY ANALYSTS. Under Nakamura, Matsushita will make a serious push into e-commerce. In October, it will begin selling Panasonic products online via a new portal site, LifeVit.com. Plans are also in the works to convert 7,000 of its 20,000 retail shops around Japan into e-commerce hubs that will supply and service goods ordered online. If it flies, the site will be recreated in the United States and Europe.

With a reorganization plan due in October, analysts are looking over Nakamura's shoulder. They want him to fold the subsidiary JVC, a maker of audiovisual equipment, into the consumer electronics division. They advocate a similar move for Matsushita Electric Works Ltd., a maker of lighting equipment and building materials. Nakamura hasn't ruled out such moves. He also aims to boost sales 5 percent annually by leveraging his strengths in five key areas: cell phones, high-end chips, digital TV, displays, and DVD and other optical discs. These already generate 20 percent of group revenue.

While investors are cautiously upbeat now that Nakamura has been named CEO, the new mood will evaporate fast if setbacks materialize. Nakamura hasn't a moment to spare.

Questions

1. What do you think is Matsushita's technology strategy?

2. What are the main reasons that Nakamura (and other executives) believe there is a need for change?

3. What kinds of things should Nakamura consider in changing the company?

Source: Irene M. Kunii, "A Bold Mechanic for a Creaky Machine," *Business Week*, August 7, 2000, p. 58H.

Experiential Exercises

17.1 Planning for Innovation

Objectives

1. To brainstorm innovative ideas for a company that has become stagnant.
2. To explore the elements of a good innovation plan.

Instructions

1. Read the Mason, Inc., scenario.
2. Individually or in small groups, offer a plan for encouraging innovation at Mason, Inc. Discuss staffing, rewards, organizational structure, work design, and any other facets of organizational behavior that apply.
3. In small groups, or with the entire class, share the plans you developed.

Discussion Questions

1. What elements do these plans have in common?
2. How well do the plans follow the innovation process?
3. Do the plans incorporate provisions for fulfilling the various roles required for innovation?
4. What are the strengths and weaknesses of each plan?
5. What should be the components of an effective plan?

Source: J. Gordon, *A Diagnostic Approach to Organizational Behavior* (Englewood Cliffs, N. J.: Prentice-Hall, 1983), p. 654. Reprinted by permission of Prentice-Hall, Inc., Englewood Cliffs, N.J.

Mason, Inc., Scenario

Mason, Inc., is a *Fortune 500* company that designs, develops, and manufactures personal grooming products. From 1950 to 1980 it was a leader in introducing new, profitable products into the marketplace. Its Research and Development Division grew from 20 to 150 professionals during that time. Since 1980, however, the company has relied on its past successes and has failed to introduce any significant innovative product into the marketplace. Top management wants to reestablish Mason's reputation as the number-one innovator in the industry.

17.2 Innovation for the Future

Objective

To look ahead into the future.

Instructions

Choose a partner. Together, develop an innovative product or service that will be popular in the year 2025. As you develop your product or service, ask yourselves the following questions:

1. What trends lead you to believe that this product or service will be successful?
2. What current technologies, services, or products will be replaced by your idea?

Present your idea to the class for discussion.

The 411 on . . .

Operations Management in the New Economy

The business of a company—any company—is to take certain inputs and, by means of a process, transform them into outputs. Bringing these outputs (the product) to market cost effectively will ensure the company's continued existence and well-being. The methods, systems, and mental framework by which a company transforms its inputs into outputs characterize its *operations*. A company maintains the health of its transformation process through *management* of these operations. *Operations management* is the analysis and implementation of this process.

Many varied factors impinge on a company's operations and its managers. As company size increases, so do the number of variables. Effective management of the operation and its variables contributes in no small measure to the company's success, whether the company is small or large, diversified or devoted to core businesses, a network organization or a highly structured, centralized body. It holds true whether the company sells a tangible product (goods) or an intangible one (services), for in both cases, the customer is buying the object of a desire, or the satisfaction of a need.

Effects of Change

We often read that operations management is in transition today. In actuality, it has always been in transition, because the world is always changing. Changes may take the form of new products (imagine the first traders bringing spices to Europe in the early Middle Ages), new distribution channels (Federal Express completely revamped our expectations about package delivery), alterations in the labor pool (women assumed many factory jobs during World War II, when men were at war), or new technologies (gunpowder altered all the rules of war in 14th-century Europe).

Characteristic of the current age is the quickening *rate* at which change occurs, placing pressure on individuals to adapt quickly, and rewarding those able to easily shift mental gears, personal habits, and priorities. Indeed, survival of the fittest applies not only to physical attributes, but also to mental agility. Operations managers must be among the most "fit" to function effectively in today's world.

The Context of Operations Management

What does it mean to be an effective manager of an operation? It means responding to the needs of diverse parties *within* the company, ensuring smooth movement through all stages of the transformation process. We can even take the viewpoint that, within the process, the "customer" is the department receiving the result of the preceding stage. For example, in a printing company, the operator of the press is the customer of the pre-press area. An effective manager works with this awareness, ensuring that each area supplies what the next one expects.

Operations management also means satisfying parties in the *larger* arena. For example, investors may want to know how well a new product line is faring in the market, or whether a new manufacturing process is delivering as promised. The community may want assurances that wastes from the production process will not cause quality of life to suffer. The government may demand an accounting of any number of activities covered by regulations. Thus, the manager of an operation does not exist in isolation, but is part of an ongoing interaction among any number of parties.

In ages past, the world was home to many different societies or cultures, which were mostly different one from another, but each more homogeneous than is the case today. Buyers in a given community needed the same products. Everyone knew what these products were, and common agreement on quality prevailed. Also prevalent was a common understanding of the entitlements of various social levels (what goods at what quality were the prerogative of the wealthy, for example). Because items were individually made, customization was the norm, for there was no other way to do business.

As the industrial age dawned in the 19th century, this situation changed. Suddenly the "customer" was no longer a few identifiable individuals, but a growing mass of less well-defined persons, any of whom, with money, could have what was formerly the prerogative of the few. With industrialization came mass production, and one product for all buyers became the norm, because there was no other cost-effective way to do business.

The modern-day corporation took shape against this background, and marketing was born. Now in the digital age, we are witnessing a phenomenon that once would have sounded like an oxymoron: mass customization. What are the implications for today's managers?

When the product is static, or has few variations, operations management quite justifiably focuses on the product (and its cost). This perspective has produced the orientation of traditional operations management. With the ability to manufacture many variations of the same product, with access to increasing amounts of information, the focus today has shifted to the customer's *experience* of the product: how he or she perceives to have been served by the vendor. The customer assesses whether the product contains the desired characteristics and quality, at the best price. Management of an operation with this awareness will likely spell the success or failure of the company in today's environment.

But is today's customer truly different? Yes and no, for despite the fact that things change, things also stay the same. Human beings still engage in the same activities: They create community; they raise the next generation; they trade; they provide for themselves; and in the process, they learn, fight, and play. And today's managers still shuttle inputs through the transformation process into successful outputs. Most of the traditional notions about human activity still apply.

To explain any activity, however, one may use a variety of lenses (Galileo's lens was different from Ptolemy's, so he derived a different explanation of the universe). A manager may view the process from the standpoint of product specifications, cost limitations, customer satisfaction, or any number of viewpoints. The lens chosen will reflect a particular view of the world and its priorities, as well as the company's priorities.

Sometimes there are no right or wrong choices, only consequences. The lens that adequately explained a given phenomenon at one time may not serve today. What is reflected through the lens will form the guidelines for decisions, however, so the choice has far-reaching repercussions.

New Perspectives

From time to time, particular orientations or viewpoints burst onto the stage, altering perceptions and leaving changed priorities in their wake. Such is the case with W. Edward Deming's *total quality management,* now an article of faith for many of today's managers. The Japanese readily embraced Deming's principles, taking an enviable and now imitated approach to customer satisfaction (see Chapter 9 of the text for Deming's fourteen points). Western nations paid scant attention until they saw the results of offering quality in a customer-oriented operation.

For most of us, quality is what we see in the end result (does the product meet manufacturing specifications?). In his lengthy essay *Zen and the Art of Motorcycle Maintenance,* Robert Pirsig associated achievement of quality with a state of mind: "Skilled mechanics and machinists of a certain sort . . . have patience, care and attentiveness to what they're doing, a kind of inner peace of mind that isn't contrived but results from a kind of harmony with the work . . ."[1] More characteristic of the Eastern mindset, this statement means that quality (good or bad) is not an attribute of the end product, but rather is inherent in the way an individual interacts with the subject of his or her attention.

To achieve good quality requires knowing what is good, and then having the mindset suitable for achieving it. This attentiveness is related to the Japanese *kaizen,* a willingness and desire to constantly improve. Since the 1980s, Japanese business practices have been the object of study and implementation by Westerners, from specific procedures (such as *kanban,* the basis of just-in-time inventory management), to general philosophies (the *kaizen* that is part of Japanese general operations strategy). A manager anywhere today would be ill-served by neglect of these concepts.

Likewise, companies that involve employees in the process are on the way to understanding that the people interface with the product is crucial to their success. We will see how important this view is in a few pages.

Corporate Organization

There are many ways to structure a company, and some of today's companies have taken their present form as the result of trends in the economy: mergers or acquisitions, diversification, alliances. With all, there are still certain functions identifiable in most corporate organizations. The operation of that function is what commands the attention of its managers. Let us consider how some of these common functions support the operations management system.

Strategic Planning
On the highest level, guiding the corporation from the broadest perspective, is strategic, or long-range, planning. The firm's upper-level managers provide the corporation's direction, defining and refining its mission in the process. Management of this function entails answering questions such as: What business are we in? What business should or will we be in? Who are our customers? How can or should we serve them? Do we want to focus on core businesses or diversify? Answers to these questions will help develop corporate goals, which, filtered through the company's management levels, give direction to its operation.

As stated earlier, the world is always changing. Good strategic planning seeks to *anticipate* change and then plan for it. Good planners also foster a feeling of confidence about what is likely to produce success. During the 1990s, when the rallying cry of much of corporate management was to stick to core businesses, G.E. chief Jack Welch built a successful conglomerate of widely diverse businesses, finding people of the mindset to operate well within that structure, and achieving effective coordination of all functions through its many divisions.

Marketing
Of all the company's functions, marketing is closest to the customer. Its job is to identify customer needs (latent or manifest) and translate them back to the firm for its reaction. Its role in supporting the operations management system is therefore critical. Operations managers must then restate what marketing has communicated in terms that will bring about the needed response from the production mechanism. To support its efforts, marketing works with advertising to state the company's offerings in terms that are attractive to the buyer. Sales is a part of the marketing function also, sales people being those who take action to sell within an identified market. This is the front line, the place where information about customer needs and desires penetrate and gain the attention of the company.

A story told in sales circles is about the ABC Company (a shoe manufacturer), whose marketing head visited a remote area of the world to assess the market. He returned to report to his boss, "There's no market; they don't wear shoes." The marketing head of competitor XYZ Company made the same trip for the same purpose, reporting to *his* boss: "It's a terrific market! They've got no shoes!" Marketing's response to a circumstance can take the firm into new areas.

Research and Engineering Suppose the marketing function has identified a new need or potential market. Enter the design and engineering people, whose function is the development and refinement of the product and the processes that manufacture it. They design, develop, and test the product through all stages until it is ready for market launch. They interact with customers who participate in testing of a new product prior to launching. They also interact with operations—the product attributes and the processes required to make them will become the responsibility of the operations management system. Even as a product is still on the drawing board, its design may change based on customer response, manufacturing procedures (i.e., what is feasible in the current setup), or prices of material or labor.

As researchers and developers, this part of the company is most in touch with what will be available in the future, and one of their functions is identification and implementation of solutions not currently in use. The end result of the designers' work will affect purchasing (of parts, equipment, materials), inventory management (quantities of items to keep on hand), shop floor operation (equipment may need rearrangement), capacity requirements (maximum rate of production), and human resources (human skills needed and cost of acquisition).

Human Resources This brings us to the next function: human resources. A company *is* its people. They form the culture, produce the product, and deliver it. The human resources function must seek, attract, and keep individuals having the skills, human qualities, and experience required by the operations management system. Effective management of human resources thus directly impacts the entire production process. Any company wishing to build a plant in a geographically desirable area would be foolish not to take into account the human component: educational level, work ethic, habits, and expectations of the labor pool.

Some believe that there are no bad employees, only employees placed in wrong positions. Effective use of employees will provide operations managers with a valuable source of innovation and productivity gains, for the employees are actually in contact with the product (and with the customer, in the case of a service business). They are the interface where quality is born. It cannot be stressed too heavily that one of the most valuable attributes of any employee is the ability to communicate: to articulate what's right about the work experience, what's wrong, and how to improve it. Dissatisfaction unexpressed is potential trouble; ideas not presented represent lost potential.

Purchasing Just as human inputs matter, so do materials. Selecting inputs that will support the company's orientation and vision is the crucial role played by the purchasing function. Optimally, it is a source of expertise for the operations management system, providing information about the variety of materials and systems available for use by the production process. The performance of any operating division is ultimately dependent on goods and services supplied to it by purchasing. Will the materials produce the result intended by the design of the product? Will they allow themselves to be molded as intended by the production process? Will they support the level of quality promised?

Cost-effective supply of the right materials potentially represents enormous savings for the company. A purchasing manager was once heard to say: "The sales division would have to close $500,000 in new business to produce the money I just saved by changing suppliers."

Logistics The logistics of moving inputs through transformation may or may not benefit from an overview of the entire process, for the flow may take different names depending on its location in the process. It may be called "inventory management" as inputs arrive, "scheduling" while in the transformation process, and "distribution" when outputs are en route to the customer. Smooth or poor coordination of the flow from supplier of materials to delivery to the customer has repercussions throughout the channel. If materials are not ready for a specific section of the production apparatus at the right time, equipment and machinery sit idle (a drain on profitability). Delays in delivery to customers mean delays in payment received, which has an impact on the company's cash flow.

From the Pages of BusinessWeek

Pricing and inventory woes put Apple in the red

When Apple CEO Steve Jobs announced that the company was going to lose $250 million in 2001's fourth quarter, many people wrote it off as yet another disappointment from a company that has produced so many of them. Apple lovers are a loyal bunch, and they'll probably stick with the company. But Jobs's dream of becoming the world's biggest computer-maker will likely remain just that—a dream.

What's contributing to Apple's woes? Plenty—but let's start with an insane pricing policy. The most recent product launch under Jobs was the Cube, a beautiful piece of engineering, but consumers weren't prepared to pay $1,800 for a computer that is technologically run of the mill. Apple's top-of-the-line G4 costs $7,598; a similar model offered by Gateway goes for $2,549. Take out the huge

Apple CEO Steve Jobs' dream of becoming the world's biggest computer-maker will likely remain a dream.
[©AFP/CORBIS]

$4,000 Apple flat-panel monitor and the $700 Gateway monitor, and there's still an $1,800 price differential.

Apple's next biggest problem is its hardware, which just can't compete with Intel's. Apple's chips are made by IBM, which has essentially stopped spending money on developing them, but Apple has refused to lower prices.

Even more frightening is Apple's inventory mismanagement. Apple is notorious for either being over- or understocked. Under competitor Dell's legendary inventory management, its shelves contain no more than a few days' worth of computers. Apple planned to reduce inventory to a five-week supply, but Jobs admitted that the company had close to an 11-week stock of computers.

Probably Apple's biggest problem is its failure to extend the popularity of its computers beyond graphic design and education. Growth depends on being able to broaden that narrow band of users. Bear Stearns analyst Andrew Neff noted that Apple's "installed base replenishes itself but does not grow."

New product lines may help. The handheld market is particulaly open to an Apple product. The iMac made users forget they were using a different operating system. It's possible that the company can come up with some snazzy new products that persuade non-Apple customers to jump on the bandwagon. Whole lines of new products take many months, if not years, to create, however.

Source: Sam Jaffe, "Why Apple Is Losing Its Appeal Again," *Business Week Online,* December 11, 2000. ●

Finance   This latter instance brings us to the finance area. This function serves as an interface between the firm's managers and the financial community: banks, investment firms, and stockholders. These entities have a stake in the company's success or failure, and at all times are poised to assist, advise, provide support, or withdraw it. Finance must adequately explain the company's performance so as to elicit the maximum amount of support from financial institutions. In so doing, it makes use of the accounting department. Not merely a mechanism for tracking costs, the accounting department provides information useful to managers in understanding the cost implications of their decisions. Such cost-monitoring information can help managers understand how their own costs compare with standard costs, for example. Accounting can also help derive the cost implications of introducing new equipment or technologies.

In another of its roles, the finance function must be knowledgeable about the firm's creditworthiness. Any decline in the company's ability to pay its bills will weaken its position vis-à-vis competitors. Finance must also monitor the creditworthiness of suppliers. If suppliers are not financially able to deliver what they promise, the operations management system will feel the impact immediately. The financial community watches the impact of all these decisions, basing its ratings (and therefore support) on the wisdom of the decision makers.

A Team Operation The fineness with which one breaks down the preceding functions can vary, but it should be clear at this point that the operations management system is only one of those operating within the corporate context. In the best of all possible worlds, operations management works hand-in-glove with the other functions, alert to any harmful fragmentation or lack of communication. Communication is, of course, a two-way street, and, just as operations people must be aware of the workings of the other functions, the latter must know what the operations management system perceives, needs, and expects.

Satisfying customer expectations is a corporate activity, the work of one body (from *corpus*, Latin for "body"), with the whole dependent on how well its parts work individually and how well they work together. Neglect of any one organ affects the body's ability to perform at optimum level.

Preparing for the Future in the New Economy

In addition to awareness of how the company is operating at present, every good manager will give thought to what *could* happen, what is likely to happen, and what is possible, both for the company as a whole, and for his or her own sphere of influence. Stated another way, an effective manager has a sense of vision. This means being aware of changes or potential changes in customer demands, and changes in the company's resources (technology, labor pool, financial support). A good manager must listen, being attentive to all facts, and then select the useful facts from among the many supplied. A manager must constantly ask, "What if . . . ?"

With good vision and a healthy curiosity, a manager will more adequately handle factors impinging on the operations management system. The objective is to develop a sense of vision adequate to anticipate conceivable consequences. Let us consider some of today's challenges in what is often referred to as the **"new economy."**

Globalization A company's sphere of activity has always been what could be reached easily by current means of communication and transportation. What is reachable has constantly expanded. The entire world is today's operating arena, both for buying inputs and for selling outputs. This circumstance presents the operations management system with a new range of possibilities.

The possibility of outsourcing has always been present. That is, do we make a particular component of the product, or do we send it out for manufacture pursuant to our specifications? Today, a manager may outsource locally, or to any facility in the world offering the capability of supplying the need. It takes a lot of information, as well as sound judgment, to know which part of the process would benefit from being handled out of house.

The success of producing elsewhere depends in part on the characteristics of the "elsewhere." In the 20th century, U.S. companies based in northern states would sometimes move certain manufacturing operations to the southern part of the country, taking advantage of lower labor costs. While this required some adjustment in expectations, the adjustment is slight compared to manufacturing in Pacific Rim countries or Latin America, for example. The reason is simple: Each culture handles things in a particular way. A wise manager will not assume that a different culture will respond to expectations in the same manner as an American labor force would, and this circumstance may work to one's advantage or to one's detriment. Those who can adequately anticipate potential problem areas are ahead of the game in the decision to manufacture offshore.

Then there is the globe as *marketplace*. To sell globally requires product design that accounts for differing tastes throughout the world's cultures. A small manufacturer of skincare products based on formulas from India began marketing her line in America some years ago. She reports that she had to make alterations to account for the fact that Americans would not use a product with an unusual smell, no matter how beneficial for the skin.[2] Nescafe markets its products all over the globe, but the instant coffee sold in Brazil does not taste like that sold in the United States—in each instance, the product must satisfy the taste of a different culture.[3]

The ease with which the operations management system can make these alterations has increased dramatically in the last few decades. Digital technology has made flexibility in manufacturing a much more attainable situation than was previously the case, offering enormous potential to vary the produce.

Environment Another challenge facing today's manager is the environment, meaning both the world and the milieu in which the company operates. In an earlier time, negative effects from a manufacturing process were unobtrusively absorbed by surroundings. As population density increased and consumption skyrocketed, particularly in the Western nations, this ceased to be true. What occurs in one place on the planet has an impact on the rest of it. The manager's challenge is to care enough about the future without imperiling today's operations, and the decisions are not simple.

It is unfortunate that the issue of environmental responsibility has traditionally been cast in ethical terms. While this stance is valid, and ultimately *the* reason for being good stewards of the planet, it does not help managers handle all the information required to make good decisions, nor does it quantify what is needed for decision making. In addition, consumers are often inconsistent, demanding recycled paper, for instance, then choosing to buy whiter paper that is not recycled.

Certainly the last few decades have witnessed significant progress in the handling of the most blatantly offensive effects of manufacturing processes (waste streaming, emissions control). But making the right decision is not a clear-cut path. Consider the simple example of the supermarket checkout stand. "Would you like paper or plastic for your groceries?" The environmentally responsible buyer must choose between less-than-desirable alternatives. Paper (even if recycled) uses trees; plastic uses hydrocarbons and is not as easy to recycle. Decisions faced by operations managers are infinitely more complex.

Furthermore, if managers do not see to their societal responsibility, others will demand compliance. A corporation is not its own island in community waters, for others are affected by its decisions: property owners, investors, the larger public, and tomorrow's adults. Surely we have learned by now that groups that do not effectively police their own ranks are sure targets for policing by others, be they governmental agencies or community organizations.

The alternatives for an operations manager are therefore to react or to take a leadership role, becoming knowledgeable about potential negative effects of the process managed by him or her, and proposing ways to handle them. In the long term, if we are to manage our economy's activities for tomorrow rather than today, responsibility for the environment is not a choice.

Knowledge and Information

One of the features of the new economy is that in the transformation process, the major input is intellectual property: knowledge, research, information, and design. These have supplanted (in value) the material inputs required to build physical units. When knowledge is the major raw material, launching of the first unit of a product represents millions of dollars; the cost of the second and thereafter is miniscule.

The products themselves are of a different nature, and it often takes greater sophistication to use a new-economy product—thus, for example, people's reluctance to switch from a PC to a Mac, or vice versa. As a result, customers are not as likely to be swayed by advertising, but rather by their increasing knowledge of the product and its technology. Successful companies will be those that increase a customer's knowledge base in general, and skill with their own products in particular.

As the information explosion continues to feed today's consumers and today's workforce, the knowledge acquired gives rise to expectations. As we will discuss a few pages hence, today's consumers are far from being locked into only a few sources for their information. Rather, they swim in an ocean of facts, figures, perspectives, and opportunities.

Nor are today's employees like those of yesteryear. It is rather the case that, depending on his or her own personal needs or aspirations, an employee is drawn to (and will stay with) a specific job in a given company for two reasons: (1) the possibility of experiencing personal satisfaction or growth, and (2) satisfaction in the human interaction prevalent at that company. The balance of these factors varies with the individual, but everyone draws from these

two wells. Today's managers must therefore provide more than the means for an employee to put bread on the table. The company must offer ongoing professional development, opportunity for increased responsibility in the firm, and a satisfying place to work. Today's employees do not expect to be *supervised,* but rather *coached* along the path of success. Needless to say, the manager must also be knowledgeable and continue to grow, increasing in value as a mentor.

Technology   The challenge of technology will occupy us for the rest of these pages. Technology has always existed and has always been neutral. That is, just as a knife serves to feed the family or to kill an adversary, so can new technologies be used to help or harm. As with any challenge, managers can view technological innovation as something to react to, something to anticipate, something to plan for, or something from which to derive potential improvements and growth.

Technologies exist in various stages of development; that is, some are ready and available for use by the operations management system, some will be cost effective in five or ten years, and some are in embryo. Any forward-looking manager will be aware of all three. Technology companies (those who market the latest of a given technology; e.g., cellular phones) must monitor technology on two fronts. They must be aware of similar products on the market, constantly assessing the limits of their own products. They must also be aware of technologies potentially useable by their own operations, just as any nontechnology company would.

In its development, a technology tends to move to the hands of the user. Take the clock as example. At one time in history, the only clock in the community was the one in the town square. Then, wealthier people could purchase large timepieces known as "grandfather clocks." By the middle of the 20th century, most adults owned a wristwatch, often a special gift received at graduation. Today, children and adults have access to many timepieces, from those on their wrists to the many in the home, office, or car. We could trace a similar progression for other technologies, such as engines, and, of course, computers (where the transition from mainframes to PCs occurred within a few decades of the last century).

The shift of a technology to the user is not always smooth. One of the potential stumbling blocks when a company embraces a technology is to discount the human factor involved in its use. We see this in small businesses constantly. The local copy shop brings in the latest copying and finishing equipment, offering everything from doublesided, spiral-bound reports graced with halftone photos, to personalized, artistic party invitations. The resulting product, however, is in part dependent on the skill and experience of the operator and the availability of sufficient personnel to work with customers.

Larger industrial equipment offers a similar scenario. At an earlier time in history, the operator of, for example, a multi-story printing press would have 30 years to become familiar with the operation of that equipment before a new generation came on stream. In today's offices, the word-processing staff barely becomes proficient at using the current popular software when a new product is embraced by management. These "improvements" provide fertile ground for inefficiencies, for in the final analysis, technology can advance only at the rate at which human beings can effectively use it.

With this knowledge, any effective operations manager will have some type of formal technology management in place—some means of looking ahead, preparing for the effects of new technologies. When envisioning the potential of new technology (or technology in embryo), the best human characteristics to bring to the table are:

1. Awareness (information plus perspective); and

2. Imagination (the ability to create new scenarios from existing ones).

Awareness is the easiest to acquire. In fact, it can be bought from the many consultants standing ready to assist corporations in preparing for the future. One must cultivate powers of imagination within oneself.

The Internet

That brings us to the current challenge for one's imaginative powers: the Internet. Opportunities and pitfalls abound in the Web. What follows are some noteworthy experiences gained from successful and unsuccessful uses of the Internet. By the time this material sees print, much will have changed.

The invention of writing made it possible to maintain information, growing it over the centuries, no longer dependent on what the human memory could hold. Printing made the information available to increasingly large numbers of people, at a cost that decreased over the centuries. In the computer age, we have the ability to move information around, making it tangible; that is, captured on paper, temporarily whenever and wherever needed.

Having made more and more tasks computer-dependent, managers are now grappling with the Internet. As with anything new and exciting, emotion interferes with decision making. Beset on all sides by promises, claims of potential benefits, and warnings about the consequences of failing to implement certain ideas, today's managers are facing decisions that have the force to make or break them.

Three ways are emerging as options for exploiting Internet operation: in-house development of a Web-based arm—an adjunct to traditional **"bricks and mortar"** operation; formation of a

partnership with a dot.com company; or formation of a **"pure-play"** dot.com operation. Shall we make products available on the Web, alongside our traditional physical presence; that is, become a **"clicks and bricks"** operation? Should we just close our physical doors and become a cyber company exclusively? Should we buy a dot.com operation as the best means of acquiring a Web presence?

Hesitancy in addressing Web potential is *not* an option for today's managers. In addition, the company as a whole must participate in formulating answers to these questions, for all points in the transformation process will be affected. A manager must ask, "At what points along the chain from inputs to outputs does the Web play a role?" And once we know that, what should the next move be?

Let us take a look at the country's three largest retailers (Sears, Kmart, and J. C. Penney) and the diverse ways they have reacted. When Amazon.com began selling online in 1997, none of these three had a Web presence. Since that time, all three have given **e-commerce** a role in their brand marketing and to enhance in-store sales.

Sears.com was launched in 1998 as an outlet for Craftsman tools and large appliances. Although the retailer added other products, the offerings were not uniform, leaving holes in its service. At present, Sears maintains a growing Website staff, treating the venture as a mere adjunct to its traditional business (as would a store-based retailer moving into catalog sales), not even breaking out financial information for its Website. The operation has not been without its set of challenges. For example, Sears discovered that selling online to individuals was not well served by its distribution network, which was designed to ship large quantities rather than single items.

J. C. Penney treats its Web operation as a division of its catalog unit, but, unlike Sears, breaks out the site's financial performance. The retailer is gradually increasing the number of products available online (like Sears), and experimenting with pricing models, such as auctions and automatic markdowns. Penney's approach to human resources needed to handle online sales is to train its catalog division's customer service staff for Web-based sales. As in catalog sales, satisfactory fulfillment will be the factor governing success.

Meanwhile, the giant Kmart has contracted its Internet business to a partially owned subsidiary, Web "pureplay" BlueLight. Homemaker guru Martha Stewart, part owner of BlueLight, is simultaneously moving Kmart upscale and high tech.

From the Pages of BusinessWeek: Three ways to add clicks to bricks

When online retailer Amazon burst onto the scene in 1997, retailers Sears Roebuck, Kmart, and J. C. Penney had no presence on the Internet. Three years later, they are the "big three" brick-and-mortar chains with the most retailing impact on the Net. The three rivals' Web strategies offer contrasting case studies in how established brick-and-mortar retailers are growing more serious about **e-tailing.**

Kmart contracted its Internet business to a partially owned subsidiary, Blue-Light.com. "That's our Internet strategy," explains Kmart spokeswoman Mary

Lorencz. BlueLight serves as Kmart's e-commerce arm and has its work cut out for it, considering that other Net companies are already offering a far more extensive range of discounted goods. Penney and Sears, by contrast, have in-house Websites.

Sears is reluctant to provide specific figures on how the site is doing. "We consider Sears.com basically an extension of our other businesses. It's not a separate entity," says Sears e-commerce spokeswoman Ann Woolman. Sears.com serves as an outlet for Craftsman tools, washers, dryers, small appliances, electronics, housewares, and other product lines from its stores. There are still gaping holes in the service. "Regardless of what Sears says about its site, buying products online and in the stores are two entirely separate businesses, and the company should treat them as such," Internet.com analyst Tom Taulli says.

Penney, on the other hand, treats its Web operation as a wholly-owned division of the catalog unit, while also separating out the site's financial performance. Penney views www.jcpenney.com as a revenue source that operates independently, the company says, rather than as a marketing expense, which is how Sears lists its site on the balance sheet. J. C. Penney is saving money by training its catalog division to handle customer service for Website sales. It has much of the cost for the Website spread across several divisions of the company. "We're working to put the entire selection of the J. C. Penney catalog online," Penney's Paul Pappajohn says. His team is also experimenting with several pricing models and is pushing automatic markdowns on the Website.

All three retailers are learning from the mistakes of pure-play online retailers that have lost millions of dollars or gone into bankruptcy by trying to develop the kind of brand name on the Web that Sears, Penney, and Kmart already enjoy at the mall. One example is the defunct furniture seller www.Living.com, which was unable to attract the Web customer base it had hoped for. Amazon's business model is still a work in progress and its chances for profitability remain slim in the near term.

All three still have shortcomings, and all offer only a limited range of in-store products as they move toward making fulfillment their highest priority. Just how the three traditional department-store chains fare selling kitchenware, DVDs, and bathrobes over the Web could determine the most effective model in clicks-and-bricks retailing. It appears that Penney has the advantage. And if it hits profitability before the others, we'll all know whose clicks-and-bricks strategy is working best.

Source: David Shook, "Comparing the Big Three of Clicks-and-Bricks," *Business Week Online,* October 5, 2000. ●

Alongside Web sales, retailers are in various stages of deploying new technologies to offer the benefits of online shopping at the retail site. For example, a kiosk on the shopping floor can make information available electronically, providing shoppers the information they need to make a buying decision. The Motorquest Automotive Group (parent of the car dealership chain) has refurbished existing locations to create a comfortable environment where customers can access all the information they want. At customer computers, buyers use MotorQuest's home page to wind their way through information from the various auto manufacturers, as well as options for pricing, loans, leasing, and reviews about the various makes and models.

These retailers, along with others such as Nordstrom, Eddie Bauer, and Radio Shack, are building on brand-name presence and a familiarity already created at the mall, in the dealership, and through catalog sales—an advantage not enjoyed by companies operating exclusively on the Web.

Enter now companies that have come at the opportunity from the other side: those who have existed as Web-based operations from the start, being not only retailers, but also industrial suppliers. Endowed with varying degrees of experience and varying business models, the success of these operations has varied. Most familiar to the general consumer are Amazon.com, eBay, and Priceline. Some have made the decision to supplement their Web-based presence

An alliance with Amazon.com and redesigned stores featuring new departments are two steps Toys 'R' Us has taken to woo back customers.
[AP/Wide World Photos]

with physical operations. For example, Amazon.com is now building a three-million square foot warehouse for its products, thus moving from a "clicks only" operation to "clicks and bricks."

Business models for the e-world are still in formation, as entrepreneurs live and learn. Analogous to computer manufacturers when the PC was new, the dot.com industry will continue to experience a shakeout, with wild successes, colossal failures, recoveries, and metamorphoses into more viable operations. Marketing strategies are developed and revised daily and business strategies revisited as managers learn about the Web and its effect on theiroperation. Success requires good judgment and steadfastness in the face of temptation from get-rich-quick schemes. Customers still want speed, convenience, and information—reliable information sometimes being more valuable than touching the merchandise. Customers may be initially attracted by the glitz of Web offerings, but ultimately will cast their votes for those who provide satisfaction in their experience with the product.

In what may turn out to be a successful recovery from a setback, Toys 'R' Us has formed an alliance with Amazon.com, attempting to mix the strengths of both physical presence and Web operation. Christmas of 1999 saw the toy giant turn away customers because of inability to fill orders generated from its Website. In the new alliance—expected to be the best of both worlds—Amazon.com develops the Website and handles order fulfillment, while Toysrus.com manages the inventory. Each has expertise the other needs in order to successfully sell online.

These arrangements are not without consequences for the consumer. A father was heard to lament the decision to give his children Amazon.com gift certificates for Christmas: "I thought they would buy books, but Amazon is now in league with Toys 'R' Us, and the kids are going crazy buying toys!"

Other issues crop up in these types of restructurings. One may ask, for example, whether more than one bookseller or toyseller is needed online, because "e-tailers" do not add value to the consumer. If you can get any item you want from the Amazon/Toys site, will the market support more than one? It remains to be seen how well the very successful Borders will fare in its Borders.com operation. Meanwhile, whether a company is a retailer or not, all of its areas of operation are affected by the Web, offering unimagined challenges for its operations management system.

Company-wide Resonance

Sales and marketing data collection is turned on its head by the Internet, as companies go to the **"cookie"** jar to see what is served up by the small text files that record information about a user's habits during a Website visit. Many retailers are of the opinion that this type of **data-mining** will make or break the operation in the future. That is, the ability to collect and use information from on-line customers will be crucial to successful marketing decisions.

The marketing function has an extremely versatile new tool,

but, as is true of any tool, its value is realized through skillful use. The advertising field sprouts **cyberagencies** daily, to help companies work with the new medium. A company's Web page can make it easy or hard for the customer to get the information leading to a purchase. As some have learned the hard way, it is not enough to simply take images that are successful in print and place them on the Web, for each medium has its own characteristics. Like stage actors learning new techniques for the movies, then newer techniques for television, companies cannot assume that their presentation will transfer flawlessly to the new medium. Thus is born a new industry: Web-page design, with success to those who can demonstrate that their conceptualizations do the job intended.

Design of the company's Website has a company-wide impact. For example, if a customer on the Web can verify that an item is available, chances of closing the sale are increased. If a customer can find out the expected delivery date of the product and the means, chances of sale are increased even more. In this scenario, front- and back-end operations touch, and delivering the goods is still key to success.

Mountains of Data The purchasing function benefits from the Web through sheer availability of information, as well as ease of response to questions. With resources such as the Thomas Register online, and the ability to e-mail, a purchasing manager need not wait for a visit from a sales representative. In fact, under the impact of the Web, businesses are seeing a realignment of the traditional relationships among producers, wholesalers, distributors, and retailers. In the business-to-business world, buyers previously faced a number of obstacles to getting the best deal: Suppliers were distant, research time was scarce, intermediaries controlled most of the information. Enter FreeMarkets OnLine Inc., a Web-based marketplace for industrial goods. Purchasing need only put out a contract on the Web, and a flood of bids from suppliers may be the response. In a sense, Web-based companies are becoming the new intermediaries, the conduit between producers and buyers.

FreeMarkets OnLine Inc. for industrial goods, GoFish for seafood, National Transportation Exchange for trucking, Chemdex for biochemical supplies, IMX Exchange for mortgage brokers to find loans, and this is only the start.

The Internet is also becoming the intermediary between employers and employees, and human resources departments can avail themselves of numerous Web-based tools to find candidates. Not only are there gigantic job exchanges such as Monster.com, but specialized networks exist to keep a job search within the small arena of interested parties. Job seekers and potential employers can access one another's information based on geographic preference, salary range, or skill sets. As of this writing, job offerings appear both in print and on the Web, so as to ensure maximum coverage during what is clearly a time of transition in recruitment and hiring.

Logistics, scheduling, and distribution tasks are increasingly plugged into Web-based networks, benefiting from the ease of gathering weather data, traffic patterns, and late-breaking news. Tracking information about shipments can be downloaded from Federal Express. Zip codes are available online from the U.S. Post Office. These factors affect the company's ability to deliver the product on time and the availability of materials from suppliers, effects ultimately felt by the operations management system.

Changing Information Patterns Information handling in general is in flux, as companies decide what information to make available to customers, investors, the general public, and the government, although the latter usually tells the company what it *must* make available, either in print or online. From information supplied on paper in the digital age, companies moved to information supplied on CD-ROM, whence a quick transition to supplying it on the Web.

In order to reduce printing costs, as well as act responsibly in the environment, companies required to supply compliance documentation are turning to read-only formats displayed on the Web. The solution is not without its obstacles, however, for not all interested parties necessarily have the same capacity for reading and printing out information. For example, an environmental group may not have a printer capable of handling the lengthy, image-rich report generated by the builder of a power plant.

Production of documentation is also affected—a given body of information can be generated (written, edited, captured electronically) by individuals residing in places distant one from the other. While offering cost advantages, this arrangement brings its own set of challenges, sometimes creating miscommunication that was relatively easy to work out when all production people resided under one roof.

Corporations must take these circumstances into account when deciding how to make use of the Web, for the decisions affect each of the company's functioning units. Certain kinds of information do not usually cause problems. For example, providing company address(es), phone numbers, hours of operation, and the like are

Companies can easily track their shipments by downloading the information directly from Federal Express. [©AFP/CORBIS]

more economically provided on the Web than by a live employee answering the telephone. Many inquiries that in the print age were handled by mailing out an annual report, for example, may be handled more cost-effectively on the Web.

Supplying other types of information, however, might not be as free of repercussions as the preceding examples. Depending on whether the company is a business-to-business or a business-to-consumer operation, buyers will want product information, forms and terms of payment, special sales, return policies, status of an order, shipping rates and turnaround, possibility of changing a current order, tracking information, or status of an order.

Providing and maintaining only one piece of this information—for example, change in an order—affects at least three departments: accounting, distribution, and marketing. Each department supplying the information must be aware of the consequences of making the information available and have a mechanism for handling changes. Coordination becomes an issue as well. For example, charges to a credit-card account must not occur before the merchandise is shipped. Whether selling to another business or to consumers, online operation requires new networks. Companies forge ahead in the learning curve in this burgeoning technology, confident in the knowledge that the potential advantages are well worth the temporary discomfort.

Intellectual Property

We have already mentioned that a characteristic of the new economy is the nature of the product: knowledge, design, and engineering, rather than hard manufacturing. Let us look at an environmental engineering firm and how the Web affects its operation. The business of such a firm might include devising solutions to improve power-plant operation. The activities of firms involved in planning of any such industrial facility are subject to compliance with governmental regulations. Handling of engineering projects, for example, a new power plant, requires submission of an enormous amount of data, to demonstrate that the firm has complied with and planned for all impacts on the community. A requirement might be, for example, that notification be given to every property owner within a certain radius of the plant. **Downloading** that information from title companies, then monitoring the notification process, is only one of a multitude of tasks potentially manageable on the Web.

The firm must provide the information to the various parties in certain forms, which gives rise to new information needs. For example, one way to verify that it has indeed shipped the requisite print or CD-ROM copies is by downloading tracking information from Federal Express. It can also make its compliance documentation available in a read-only format on the Web, allowing printing of sections by those who wish to do so.

In preparing to build a plant, all federal, state, and local regulations must be accounted for. The firm must provide information on how its power plant will affect traffic patterns, cultural resources, schools, water supply, flora and fauna, and air quality. It must also state its plans for handling hazardous materials generated during construction and operation of the plant.

Managing the enormous body of information to respond in the ways illustrated would have been a near impossibility before computer management of data.

Pitfalls

The scenarios described offer exciting possibilities. But what has been the experience of those who have moved forward, who have taken the leap over any number of canyons, and what can we learn from it? We have already mentioned Toys 'R' Us and its inability to respond to orders on the Web. In addition to losing business, it, along with other retailers such as Macys.com, CDNow, and Dbkids.com, was subject last year to Federal Trade Commission investigation and fines regarding rules for order fulfillment. The FTC regulation states that if retailers cannot meet promised deadlines, they must notify customers, giving them the option of canceling the order. Could the management of these companies have foreseen the inability to fill orders, and if so, how?

Confidentiality of information is an issue. The media reported last December that Toys 'R' Us must respond to the New Jersey Division of Consumer Affairs regarding its privacy policies. Class-action lawsuits claim that the retailer allowed market researchers to access consumer data from its Website. The retailer has responded that it hired a marketing firm to analyze customer data in order to improve customers' shopping experiences on the site. Although breach of confidentiality predates the Web, the enormity of any breach is compounded by the staggering amounts of data available for tapping.

Customer familiarity is another issue. Despite what seems to be a flurry of online buying, media reports suggest that many customers are not buying online at all, or only infrequently, or only certain products. As with catalog shopping, the online industry will mature as consumers become more familiar with offerings, and as Web retailers improve in presentation and fulfillment.

Some customers are concerned about credit-card data transmitted online, and are therefore hesitant to shop. The misuse of credit-card data is present, however, every time a clerk in a store records the data during a purchase. Although more perception than a real problem, perception motivates people's actions, preventing some from making the leap into **cybershopping.**

Circumstances such as these are forcing the formation of new business models, as companies grapple with all the variables, spurred on by the potential benefits.

New Needs and Desires

Customers themselves are changing, as it becomes possible to satisfy latent needs or desires. We have already alluded to mass customization. Here are some specific examples of varying product features.

Setting up an assembly line or installing production equipment is part of the cost of manufacturing. Speaking of color choice in automobiles, Henry Ford once said: "They can have any color they want, as long as it's black." Alteration of a manufacturing process to vary a product feature was very costly. With flexible manufacturing available in the digital age, manufacturers have the option of producing multiple flavors of bottled water, bluejeans tailored for different bodies, and a veritable artist's palette for automobile colors. Levi Strauss and Brooks now offer machine-customized garments, accommodating a vast array of body measurements. Barbie's friends can have hair and skin color, clothing, and even personalities picked by their young owners. Digital technology fuels the manufacturing capability; the Web spurs demand.

The result is that customer desire for customization and personalization has been moved to a new level. Shoppers previously settled for a product that was mostly, or approximately, what they wanted. They are now beginning to see that sometimes they can have a product endowed with *precisely* the features they want. The experience of product acquisition is therefore changing.

The Value of Human Attributes

What are the implications of all this change for traditional operations management? Changes are remembered as negative or positive, depending on how well one has survived them. There is no reason to believe that technological change is any more threatening than other kinds of change. Traditional human qualities still serve: vision, awareness, alertness, imagination, courage, steadfastness, persistence, flexibility, attentiveness, and goodwill.

Today's managers must be aware, noticing shifts in trends, habits and customs, possibilities, and ground rules. They must have or develop the vision to foresee the range of possibilities, and then the imagination to create solutions. They must have courage to strike out in new directions, and be alert to adjustments required by the new direction. An effective manager will be flexible enough to make an adjustment, and steadfast in the face of misunderstandings and mistakes. A manager will need to be persistent in following the chosen path, with attentiveness to all facets of the surroundings. Chances of success in any challenge are enhanced by goodwill.

Lastly, he or she will need luck. Some say "it comes to you," some say "you make your own." Most think that both are true.

Key terms

bricks and mortar, p. 570
clicks and bricks, p. 570
cookie, p. 572
cyberagency, p. 572
cybershopping, p. 574
data-mining, p. 572

download, p. 574
e-commerce, p. 570
e-tailing, p. 570
new economy, p. 568
pureplay, p. 570

Discussion Questions

1. Does every business have the same output? Explain your answer.

2. What is "mass customization"? How can products be mass produced yet still be differentiated to appeal to individual market sectors? How has mass customization affected management's focus on the product?

3. Why was Deming's "total quality management" embraced by the Japanese long before Deming's philosophy became key to U.S. operations management? How does it relate to operations management?

4. How does the corporate structure relate to operations management? Is there a relationship between finance and operations management?

5. What are the effects of globalization on operations management?

6. How has the new economy changed operations management? What is the major input in the operations process as a result?

7. What must business consider in deciding to take advantage of new technology? How does new technology affect operations management decisions?

8. Why were many dot.com companies so short-lived at the end of the century? Why would Amazon and Toys 'R' Us form an alliance? Which firm is likely to benefit more? Explain.

9. How can the Internet improve a firm's operations management?

10. What are the implications for operations management of customers being able to satisfy purchasing needs immediately using the Internet? Will e-business functions fundamentally change the way firms do business in the long run? Explain.

Chapter Eighteen
Creating and Managing Change

The world hates change, yet that is the only thing that has brought progress.

—*Charles Kettering*

My interest is in the future because I am going to spend the rest of my life there.

—*Charles Kettering*

Learning Objectives

After studying Chapter 18, you will know:

1. What it takes to be world class.

2. How to manage change effectively.

3. Ideas for how to create a successful future.

Setting the Stage

Change Agents Talk about Change

- "Want a tough job? Try leading an organization through major change . . . Almost without exception, executives claim it's the hardest work they've ever done."—T. A. Stewart, *Fortune.*

- "People always ask, 'Is the change over? Can we stop now?' You've got to tell them, 'No, it's just begun.'"—Jack Welch, General Electric.

- "We're on a journey that never ends. And the day we think we've got it made, that's the day we'd better start worrying about going out of business."—Rich Teerlink, CEO, Harley-Davidson.

- "Only the paranoid survive."—Andrew Grove, Chairman, Intel.

- "The capacity to change is a key success factor. You have to constantly reinvent yourself."—Edgardo Pappacena, partner, Arthur Andersen.

- Being a change agent is lonely. Greg Titus, who was in charge of taking Scudder Kemper Investments online, says "Resentment from other departments is a fact of life. I was walking down the executive corridor, and as I went past one of the offices I heard someone say, 'There goes Greg Titus, e-commerce god.' And it wasn't meant as a compliment."—Greg Titus.

Companies need to improve constantly in order to achieve world-class excellence.
[©Tony Arruza/CORBIS]

- "The brutal fact is that about 70 percent of all change initiatives fail."—Michael Beer and Nitin Nohria.

- At Corning's Sullivan Park research facility, "People say, 'we could revolutionize the world if we did this.' They don't say, 'We could make $100 million if we did this.'" —Adam Ellison.

- "In a world that keeps changing, perhaps the most valuable capability of all—for a company, for a team, for an individual—is the capacity for leading change. If you want to make a difference, you have to help your colleagues make change—in how they think, in how they behave, and in how they work together."—*Fast Company.*

- "You know how it is in the music business. Fickle! Here today, gone today!"—Chris Rock, comedian.

Sources: M. Gunther, "This Gang Controls Your Kids' Brains," Fortune, October 27, 1997, pp. 104–10; A. Grove, Only the Paranoid Survive, Currency/Doubleday, 1996; T. A. Stewart, "How to Lead a Revolution," Fortune, November 28, 1994, pp. 48–61; L. Kraar, Fortune, December 8, 1997, pp. 64–68; S. Sherman, "A Master Class in Radical Change," Fortune, December 13, 1993, pp. 82–90; G. Imperato, "Harley Shifts Gears," Fast Company, June–July 1997, pp. 194–213; J. McCune, Management's Brave New World," Management Review, October 1997, pp. 11–14; C. Fishman, "Creative Tension," Fast Company, November 2000, pp. 358–88; M. Beer and N. Nohria, "Cracking the Code of Change," Harvard Business Review, May-June 2000, pp. 133–41; and "Who's Fast," Fast Company, November 2001, p. 148.

These executives—and Chris Rock—are all talking about the same things: the difficulties and challenges of creating change, and the need to improve constantly in order to achieve world-class excellence and competitive advantage for the future.

Change happens—constantly and unpredictably. The economic environment shifts; competitors pop up everywhere; markets emerge and disappear. The challenge for organizations is not just producing innovative new products—it is to balance a culture that is both innovative and that builds a sustainable business.[1] And for individuals, the ability to cope with change is related to their job performance and the rewards they receive.[2]

Becoming world class

Managers today want, or *should* want, their organizations to become world class.[3] To some people, striving for world-class excellence seems a lofty, impossible, unnecessary goal. But it is a goal that is essential to survival and success in today's intensely competitive business world.

Being world class requires applying the best and latest knowledge and ideas, and having the ability to operate at the highest standards of any place anywhere.[4] Thus, becoming world class does not mean merely improving. It means becoming one of the very best in the world at what you do. Some have estimated that for most companies, becoming world class requires increasing quality by 100 to 1,000 times, decreasing costs by 30 percent to 50 percent, increasing productivity by two to four times, decreasing order-to-delivery time by a factor of 5 to 10, and decreasing new-product development times by 30 percent to 60 percent. And even if your firm realizes these dramatic improvements, it still will have to keep on getting better![5]

World-class companies create high-value products and earn superior profits over the long run. They demolish the obsolete methods, systems, and cultures of the past that have impeded their competitive progress, and apply more effective and competitive organizational strategies, structures, processes, and management of human resources. The result is an organization capable of competing successfully on a global basis.[6]

Sustainable, great futures

Two Stanford professors, James Collins and Jerry Porras, studied 18 corporations that had achieved and maintained greatness for half a century or more.[7] The companies include Sony, American Express, Ford, Motorola, Merck, Marriott, Johnson & Johnson, Disney, 3M, Hewlett-Packard, Citicorp, Wal-Mart, and others. Over the years, these companies have been widely admired, been considered the premier institutions in their industries, and made a real *impact* on the world. Although every company goes through periodic downturns—and these are no exceptions, over their long histories—these companies consistently prevailed across the decades. They turn in extraordinary performance *over the long run,* rather than fleeting greatness. This study is reported in the book called *Built to Last*—which is what these great organizations were and are.

The researchers sought to identify the essential characteristics of enduringly great companies. What characteristics did they discover? Among other things, these great companies have strong core values in which they believe deeply, and they express and live the values consistently. They are driven by goals—not just incremental improvements or business-as-usual goals, but stretch goals (recall Chapter 13). They change continuously, driving for progress via adaptability, experimentation, trial and error, opportunistic thinking, and fast action. And they focus not on beating the competition; they focus primarily on beating themselves. They continually ask, "How can we improve ourselves to do better tomorrow than we did today?"

But underneath the action and the changes, the core values and vision remain steadfast and uncompromised. Table 18.1 displays the core values of several of the companies that were "built to last." Note that the values are not all the same. In fact, there was

table 18.1
Core ideologies in
built-to-last companies

3M	Innovation; "Thou shalt not kill a new product idea"
	Absolute integrity
	Respect for individual initiative and personal growth
	Tolerance for honest mistakes
	Product quality and reliability
	"Our real business is solving problems"
American Express	Heroic customer service
	Worldwide reliability of services
	Encouragement of individual initiative
Boeing	Being on the leading edge of aeronautics; being pioneers
	Tackling huge challenges and risks
	Product safety and quality
	Integrity and ethical business
	To "eat, breathe, and sleep the world of aeronautics"
Sony	To experience the sheer joy that comes from the advancement, application, and innovation of technology that benefits the general public
	To elevate the Japanese culture and national status
	Being pioneers—not following others, but doing the impossible
	Respecting and encouraging each individual's ability and creativity
Wal-Mart	"We exist to provide value to our customers"—to make their lives better via lower prices and greater selection; all else is secondary
	Swim up-stream, buck conventional wisdom
	Be in partnership with employees
	Work with passion, commitment, and enthusiasm
	Run lean
	Pursue ever-higher goals
Walt Disney	No cynicism allowed
	Fanatical attention to consistency and detail
	Continuous progress via creativity, dreams, and imagination
	Fanatical control and preservation of Disney's "magic" image
	"To bring happiness to millions" and to celebrate, nurture, and promulgate "wholesome American values"

Source: From *Built to Last* by James C. Collins and Jerry I. Porras. Copyright © 1997 by James C. Collins and Jerry I. Porras. Reprinted by permission of HarperCollins Publishers, Inc.

no set of common values that consistently predicted success. Instead, the critical factor is that the great companies *have* core values, *know* what they are and what they mean, and *live* by them—year after year after year.

The tyranny of the "*or*"

tyranny of the "or" The belief that things must be either A or B, and cannot be both; that only one goal and not another can be attained.

Many companies, and individuals, are plagued by what the authors of *Built to Last* call the **"tyranny of the *or.*"** This refers to the belief that things must be either A or B, and cannot be both. The authors provide many common examples:[8] beliefs that you must choose either change or stability; be conservative or bold; have control and consistency or creative freedom; do well in the short-term or invest for the future; plan methodically or be opportunistic; create shareholder wealth or do good for the world; be pragmatic or idealistic. Such beliefs—that only one goal but not another can be attained—often are invalid and certainly are constraining—unnecessarily so.

The genius of the "*and*"

genius of the "and" The ability to pursue multiple goals at once.

In contrast to the "tyranny of the *or*," the **"genius of the *and*"** is the ability to pursue multiple goals at once. We have discussed earlier in the book the importance of delivering multiple competitive values to customers; performing all the management functions; reconciling hard-nosed business logic with ethics; leading and empowering; and others. Authors Collins and Porras add their own list,[9] which includes:

- Purpose beyond profit *and* pragmatic pursuit of profit.
- Relatively fixed core values *and* vigorous change and movement.
- Conservatism with the core values *and* bold business moves.
- Clear vision and direction *and* experimentation.
- Stretch goals *and* incremental progress.
- Control based on values *and* operational freedom.
- Long-term thinking and investment *and* demand for short-term results.
- Visionary, futuristic thinking *and* daily, nuts-and-bolts execution.

You have learned about all of these things throughout this course and should not lose sight of any of them—either in your mind or in your actions. To achieve them all requires the continuous and effective management of change.

Managing change

Every manager needs a clear understanding of how to manage change effectively. Organizational change is managed effectively when[10]

1. The organization is moved from its current state to some planned future state that will exist after the change.
2. The functioning of the organization in the future state meets expectations; that is, the change works as planned.
3. The transition is accomplished without excessive cost to the organization.
4. The transition is accomplished without excessive cost to individual organizational members.

People are the key to successful change.[11] For an organization to be great, or even just to survive, people have to care about its fate, and know how they can contribute. But typically, leadership lies with only a few people at the top. Too few take on the burden of change. The number of people who care deeply, and who make innovative contributions, is too small. People throughout the organization need to take a greater interest and a more active role in helping the business as a whole. They have to believe they can make a difference. And they have to identify with the entire organization, not just with their unit and close colleagues.

These important attitudes and feelings are not unusual in start-ups and very small organizations. Too often they are lost with growth and over time. In large, traditional corporations, they are all too rare. There needs to be a permanent rekindling of individual creativity and responsibility, a true change in the behavior of people throughout the organization. The essential task is to motivate people fully to keep changing in response to new business challenges.

Motivating people to change

People must be *motivated* to change. But often they resist changing. For example, if your boss were to tell you, "We have to become world class," what would be your reaction?

Many people settle for mediocrity rather than aspire to world-class status. They resist the idea of striving mightily for excellence; they say things such as the following:

- "Those world-class performance numbers are ridiculous! I don't believe them, they are impossible! Maybe in some industries, some companies . . . but ours is unique . . . "
- "Sure, maybe some companies achieve those numbers, but there's no hurry . . . We're doing all right. Sales were up 5 percent this year, costs were down 2 percent. And we've got to keep cutting corners . . . "
- "We can't afford to be world class like those big global companies, we don't have the money or staff . . . "
- "We don't believe this stuff about global markets and competitors. We don't need to expand internationally. One of our local competitors tried that a few years ago and lost its shirt."
- "It's not a level playing field . . . the others have unfair advantages . . ."

To deal with such reactions, and successfully implement positive change, it is important to understand why people often resist change. Figure 18.1 shows the common reasons for resistance. Some reasons are general and arise in most change efforts. Other reasons for resistance relate to the specific nature of a particular change.

General reasons for resistance

Several reasons for resistance arise regardless of the actual content of the change.[12]

- *Inertia.* Usually people don't want to disturb the status quo. The old ways of doing things are comfortable and easy, so people don't want to shake things up and try something new. For example, it is easier to keep living in the same apartment or house than to move to another.
- *Timing.* People often resist change because of poor timing. Maybe you would like to move to a different place to live, but do you want to move this week? Even if a place were available, you probably couldn't take the time. If managers or employees are unusually busy or under stress, or if relations between management and workers are strained, the timing is wrong for introducing new proposals. Where possible, managers should introduce change when people are receptive.
- *Surprise.* One key aspect of timing and receptivity is surprise. If the change is sudden, unexpected, or extreme, resistance may be the initial—almost reflexive—reaction. Suppose your university announced an increase in tuition, effective at the beginning of next term. Resistance would be high. At the very least, you would want to know about this change far enough in advance to give you time to prepare for it.
- *Peer pressure.* Sometimes work teams resist new ideas. Even if individual members do not strongly oppose a change suggested by management, the team may band together in opposition. If a group is highly cohesive and has antimanagement norms (recall Chapter 14), peer pressure will cause individuals to resist even reasonable changes.

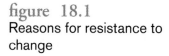

figure 18.1
Reasons for resistance to change

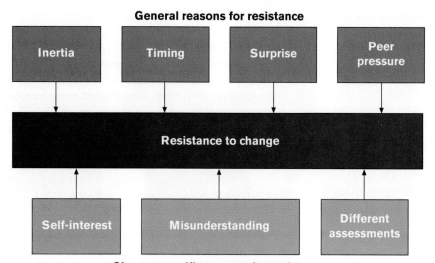

Change-specific reasons for resistance   Other causes of resistance arise from the specific nature of a proposed change. Change-specific reasons for resistance stem from what people perceive as the personal consequences of the change.[13]

• *Self-interest.* Most people care less about the organization's best interest than they do about their own best interests. They will resist a change if they think it will cause them to lose something of value.

What could people fear to lose? At worst, their jobs, if management is considering closing down a plant. A merger or reorganization, or technological change, could create the same fear. Despite assurances that no one will be laid off or fired, people might fear a cut in pay or loss of power and status under the new arrangement.

• *Misunderstanding.* Even when management proposes a change that will benefit everyone, people may resist because they don't fully understand its purpose. One company met resistance to the idea of introducing flexible working hours, a system in which workers have some say regarding the hours they work. This system can benefit employees, but a false rumor circulated among plant employees that people would have to work evenings, weekends, or whenever their supervisors wanted. The employees' union demanded that management drop the flexible-hours idea. The president was caught completely off guard by this unexpected resistance, and complied with the union's demand.

• *Different assessments.* Employees receive different—and usually less—information than management receives. Even within top management ranks, some executives know more than others do. Such discrepancies cause people to develop different assessments of proposed changes. Some may be aware that the benefits outweigh the costs, while others may see only the costs and not perceive the advantages. This is a common problem when management announces a change, say, in work procedures and doesn't explain to employees why the change is needed. Management expects advantages in terms of increased efficiency, but workers may see the change as another arbitrary, ill-informed management rule that causes headaches for those who must carry it out.

It is important to recognize that employees' assessments can be more accurate than management's; they may know a change won't work even if management doesn't. In this case, resistance to change is beneficial for the organization. Thus, even though management typically considers resistance a challenge to be overcome, it may actually represent an important signal that a proposed change requires further, more open-minded scrutiny.[14]

A general model for managing resistance   Figure 18.2 shows that motivating people to change often requires three basic stages: unfreezing, moving to institute the change, and refreezing.[15]

unfreezing Realizing that current practices are inappropriate and that new behavior must be enacted.

In the **unfreezing** stage, management realizes that its current practices are no longer appropriate and the company must break out of (unfreeze) its present mold by doing things differently. Unfreezing often results from an assessment of the company's adjustment to its present environment and its readiness for the future. The diagnosis should be thorough and unbiased. If management concludes that the fit between the company and its present or anticipated environment is poor, change is needed.

Particularly in turnaround situations, top management must take steps to unfreeze the old organization culture. People must come to recognize that some of the past ways of thinking, feeling, and doing things are obsolete.[16] Perhaps the most effective way to do this is to communicate to people the negative consequences of the old ways by comparing

figure 18.2
Implementing change

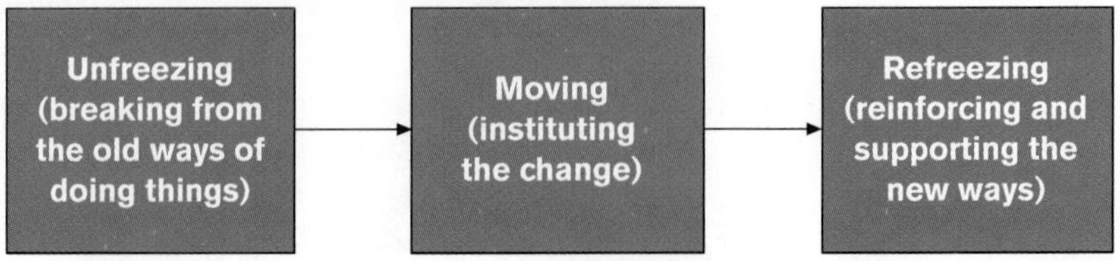

the organization's performance to its competitors'. As discussed in Chapter 15, management can share with employees data about costs, quality, and profits.[17] However, care must be taken not to arouse people's defensiveness by pinning the blame directly and entirely on them.[18]

An important contributor to unfreezing is the recognition of a performance gap, which can be a precipitator of major change. A **performance gap** is the difference between actual performance and the performance that should or could exist.[19] A gap typically implies poor performance; for example, sales, profits, stock price, or other financial indicators are down. This situation attracts management's attention, and management introduces changes to try to correct things.

performance gap The difference between actual performance and the desired performance.

Another, very important form of performance gap can exist. This type of gap can occur when performance is good but someone realizes that it could be better. Thus, the gap is between what is and what *could be*. This is where entrepreneurs seize opportunities and where companies that engage in strategic maneuvering gain a competitive edge. Whereas many change efforts begin with the negative, it often is more valuable to identify strengths and potential and then develop new modes of operating from that positive perspective.[20]

As an impetus for change, a performance gap can apply to the organization as a whole; it also can apply to departments, groups, and individuals. If a department or work group is not performing as well as others in the company, or if it sees an opportunity that it can exploit, that unit will be motivated to change. Similarly, an individual may receive negative performance feedback or see a personal opportunity on which to capitalize. Under these circumstances, unfreezing begins, and people can be more motivated to change than if no such gap exists.

moving Instituting the change.

Moving to institute the change begins with establishing a vision of where the company is heading. You learned about vision in the leadership and other sections of the course. The vision can be realized through strategic, structural, cultural, and individual change. Strategic ideas are discussed throughout the book. Changes in structure may involve moving to the divisional, matrix, or some other appropriate form (discussed in Chapters 8 and 9). Cultural changes (Chapter 9) are institutionalized through effective leadership (Chapters 12 through 15). Individuals will change as new people join the company (Chapters 10 and 11) and as people throughout the organization adopt the leader's new vision for the future.

refreezing Strengthening the new behaviors that support the change.

Finally, **refreezing** means strengthening the new behaviors that support the change. The changes must be diffused and stabilized throughout the company. Refreezing involves implementing control systems that support the change (Chapter 16), applying corrective action when necessary, and reinforcing behaviors and performance (Chapter 13) that support the agenda. Management should consistently support and reward all evidence of movement in the right direction.[21]

In today's organizations, refreezing is not always the best third step, if it creates new behaviors that are as rigid as the old ones. The ideal new culture is one of continuous change. Refreezing is appropriate when it permanently installs behaviors that maintain essential core values, such as a focus on important business results and those maintained by the companies that are "built to last." But refreezing should not create new rigidities that might become dysfunctional as the business environment continues to change.[22] The behaviors that should be refrozen are those that promote continued adaptability, flexibility, experimentation, assessment of results, and continuous improvement. In other words, lock in key values, capabilities, and strategic mission, but not necessarily specific management practices and procedures.

Specific approaches to enlist cooperation

As discussed earlier, management must enlist the cooperation of its people to implement a change. But how can managers get people to cooperate? How, specifically, can it manage employees' resistance to change?

Most managers underestimate the variety of ways they can influence people during a period of change.[23] Several effective approaches to managing resistance and enlisting cooperation are available, as described in Table 18.2:

table 18.2
Methods for dealing with resistance to change

Approach	Commonly used in situations	Advantages	Drawbacks
Education and communication	Where there is a lack of information or inaccurate information and analysis.	Once persuaded, people will often help with the implementation of the change.	Can be very time-consuming if lots of people are involved.
Participation and involvement	Where the initiators do not have all the information they need to design the change, and where others have considerable power to resist.	People who participate will be committed to implementing change, and any relevant information they have will be integrated into the change plan.	Can be very time-consuming if participators design an inappropriate change.
Facilitation and support	Where people are resisting because of adjustment problems.	No other approach works as well with adjustment problems.	Can be time-consuming and expensive, and still fail.
Negotiation and agreement	Where someone or some group will clearly lose out in a change, and where that group has considerable power to resist.	Sometimes it is a relatively easy way to avoid major resistance.	Can be too expensive in many cases if it alerts others to negotiate for compliance.
Manipulation and cooptation	Where other tactics will not work, or are too expensive.	It can be a relatively quick and inexpensive solution to resistance problems.	Can lead to future problems if people feel manipulated.
Explicit and implicit coercion	Where speed is essential, and the change initiators possess considerable power.	It is speedy and can overcome any kind of resistance.	Can be risky if it leaves people angry at the initiators.

Source: Reprinted by permission of the *Harvard Business Review.* An exhibit from "Choosing Strategies for Change" by John P. Kotter and Leonard A. Schlesinger (March–April 1979). Copyright © 1979 by the President and Fellows of Harvard College; all rights reserved.

1. **Education and communication.** Management should educate people about upcoming changes before they occur. It should communicate not only the *nature* of the change but its *logic.* This process can include one-on-one discussions, presentations to groups, or reports and memos. For Amy Radin of Citibank, "Getting buy-in across the organization takes a lot of education. If you have a core group of people who are focused only on e-commerce, then you've got to keep everyone else informed about what you're doing on the e-commerce front" (p. 363).[24]

2. **Participation and involvement.** It is important to listen to the people who are affected by the change. They should be involved in the change's design and implementation. When feasible, management should use their advice. Often it will be useful, and it may lead to consideration of important issues previously overlooked.

As you learned in Chapter 3, people who are involved in decisions understand them more fully and are more committed to them. People's understanding and commitment are important ingredients in the successful implementation of a change. Participation also provides an excellent opportunity for education and communication.

3. **Facilitation and support.** Management should make the change as easy as possible for employees and be supportive of their efforts. Facilitation involves providing the training and other resources people need to carry out the change and perform their jobs under the new circumstances. This step often includes decentralizing authority and empowering people, that is, giving them the power to make the decisions and changes needed to improve their performance.

Offering support involves listening patiently to problems, being understanding if performance drops temporarily or the change is not perfected immediately, and generally being on the employees' side and showing consideration during a difficult period.

4. **Negotiation and rewards.** When necessary, management can offer concrete incentives for cooperation with the change. Perhaps job enrichment is acceptable only with a higher wage rate, or a work rule change is resisted until management agrees to a concession on some other rule (say, regarding taking breaks). Even among higher-level managers, one executive might agree to another's idea for a policy change only in return for support on some other issue of more personal importance. Rewards such as bonuses, wages and salaries, recognition, job assignments, and perks can be examined and perhaps restructured to reinforce the direction of the change.[25]

When people trust one another, change is easier. But change is further facilitated by demonstrating its benefits to people.[26] Janiece Webb, who creates change at Motorola, says that nobody wins unless everybody wins, and that you must demonstrate to others how your work benefits them.[27] Amy Radin of Citibank says, "One lesson that I've learned is to create a financial incentive so that business units will support an Internet initiative. We are planning to create a shadow P&L for our e-commerce efforts to track how everything is going. But the benefits, all of the revenues created, will be allocated to the operating units . . . You're helping people meet their own goals."

5. **Manipulation and cooptation.** Sometimes managers use more subtle, covert tactics to implement change. One form of manipulation is cooptation, which involves giving a resisting individual a desirable role in the change process. The leader of a resisting group often is coopted. For example, management might invite a union leader to be a member of an executive committee or ask a key member of an outside organization to join the company's board of directors. As a person becomes involved in the change, he or she may become less resistant to the actions of the coopting group or organization.

6. **Coercion.** Some managers apply punishment or the threat of punishment to those who resist change. With this approach, managers use force to make people comply with their wishes. For example, a boss might insist that subordinates cooperate with the change and threaten them with job loss, denial of a promotion, or an unattractive work assignment. Sometimes you just have to lay down the law: The game is changing, and you need to play by the new rules or play somewhere else.[28]

Each approach to overcoming resistance has advantages and drawbacks, and, like many of the other situational or contingency management approaches described in the text, each is useful in different situations. Table 18.2 summarizes the advantages, drawbacks, and appropriate circumstances for these approaches to managing resistance to change. As the table implies, managers should not use just one or two general approaches, regardless of the circumstances. Effective change managers are familiar with the various approaches and know how to apply them according to the situation.

Throughout the process, change leaders need to build in stability. Recall from the companies that were "built to last," they all have essential core characteristics of which they don't lose sight. In the midst of change, turmoil, and uncertainty, people need anchors onto which they can latch.[29] This means keeping some things constant and visible, such as the organization's values and mission. It can help further to maintain the visibility of key people, continue key assignments and projects, and make announcements about which organizational components will not change. Such anchors will reduce anxiety and help overcome resistance.

Harmonizing multiple changes

There are no "silver bullets" or single-shot methods of changing organizations successfully. Single shots rarely hit a challenging target. Usually, many issues need simultaneous attention, and any single, small change will be absorbed by the prevailing culture and disappear. **Total organization change** involves introducing and sustaining multiple policies, practices, and procedures across multiple units and levels.[30] Such change affects the thinking and behavior of everyone in the organization, can enhance the organization's culture and success, and can be sustained over time.

A survey at a Harvard Business School conference found that the average attendee's company had five major change efforts going on at once.[31] The most common change programs were the things you have studied in this course: continuous improvement,

total organization change
Introducing and sustaining multiple policies, practices, and procedures across multiple units and levels.

TQM, time-based competition, and creation of a learning organization, a team-based organization, a network organization, core competencies, and strategic alliances. The problem is, these efforts usually are simultaneous but not coordinated. Things get muddled, people lose focus.[32] The result for the people involved is confusion, frustration, low morale, and low motivation.

Because companies introduce new changes constantly, many people complain about their companies' "flavor-of-the-month" approach to change. That is, employees often see many change efforts as just the company's jumping on board the latest bandwagon or fad. The more these change fads come and go, the more cynical people become, and the more difficult it is to get them committed to making the change a success.[33]

In this context, it helps tremendously to avoid fads. If a change initiative is nothing more than a passing fad, why should people invest their energy and time in it? Before initiating change, management should ask:[34] Will it really make a difference in results? Will it help provide employees with information, knowledge, power, and rewards to become more fully involved in making the business succeed and thrive? Does it really help people add value throughout their work? Does it help us focus better on customers and the things they value?

Management also needs to "connect the dots"—that is, integrate the various efforts into a coherent picture that people can see, understand, and get behind.[35] You connect the dots by understanding each change program and what its goals are, by identifying similarities among the programs and identifying their differences, and by dropping programs that don't meet priority goals with a clear results orientation. Most important, you do it by communicating to everyone concerned the common themes among the various programs: their common rationales, objectives, and methods. You show them how the various parts fit the strategic big picture, and how the changes will make things better for the company and its people. You must communicate these things thoroughly, honestly, and frequently.[36]

Leading change

Successful change requires managers to actively lead it. The essential activities of leading change are summarized in Figure 18.3.

A useful start for change leaders is to *establish a sense of urgency*.[37] This requires examining current realities and pressures in the marketplace and the competitive arena, identifying both crises and opportunities, and being frank and honest about them. This is an important component, in part because so many large companies have grown complacent.

Figure 18.4 shows some of the common reasons for complacency. To stop complacency and create urgency, the manager can talk candidly about weaknesses compared to competitors, making a point of backing up statements with data. Other tactics include setting stretch goals, putting employees in direct contact with unhappy customers and shareholders, distributing worrisome information to all employees instead of merely engaging in management "happy talk," eliminating excessive perks, and highlighting to everyone the future opportunities that exist but that the organization so far has not pursued.

Ultimately, urgency is driven by compelling business reasons for change. Survival, competition, and winning in the marketplace are compelling; they provide a sense of direction and energy around change. Change becomes not a hobby, a luxury, or something nice to do, but a business necessity.[38]

To *create a guiding coalition* means putting together a group with enough power to lead the change. Change efforts fail when a sufficiently powerful coalition is not formed.[39] Major organization change requires leadership from top management, working as a team. But over time, the support must gradually expand outward and downward throughout the organization. Middle managers and supervisors are essential. Groups at

figure 18.3
Leading change

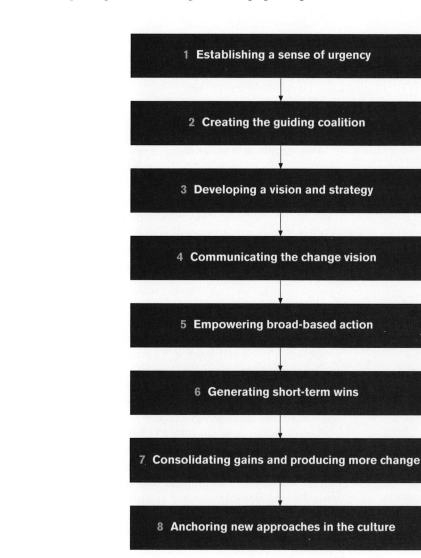

Source: J. Kotter, *Leading Change* (Boston: Harvard Business School Press, 1996).

all levels are the glue that can hold change efforts together, the medium for communicating about the changes, and the means for enacting new behaviors.[40]

Developing a vision and strategy, as discussed in earlier chapters, will direct the change effort. This process involves determining the idealized, expected state of affairs after the change is implemented. Because confusion is common during a major organizational change, the clearest possible image of the future state must be developed and conveyed to everyone.[41] This image, or vision, will be a target or guideline that can clarify expectations, dispel rumors, and mobilize people's energies. The portrait of the future also should communicate how the transition will occur, why the change is being implemented, and how people will be affected by the change. The power of a compelling vision is one of the most important aspects of change, and should not be underestimated or underutilized.

Communicating the change vision requires using every possible channel and opportunity to talk up and reinforce the vision and required new behaviors. It is said that aspiring change leaders undercommunicate the vision by a factor of 10, or even 100 or 1,000, seriously undermining the chances of success.[42] Chris Crosby, senior VP and director of Internet at Dain Rauscher Corp., advises you to "Draw pictures that take people where they want to go. Make the idea as tangible as possible. I had to take management out

figure 18.4
Sources of complacency

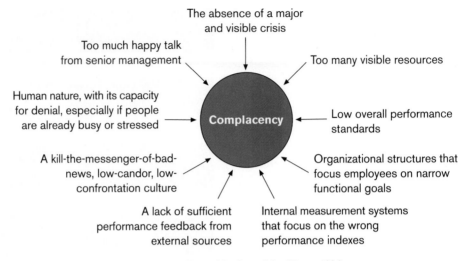

Source: J. Kotter, *Leading Change* (Boston: Harvard Business School Press, 1996).

18 months and say, 'Here's what the Web site will look like in a year and a half.' Once people could see it and touch it, they could understand it" (p. 358).[43]

Empowering broad-based action means getting rid of obstacles to success, including systems and structures that constrain rather than facilitate. Encourage risk taking and experimentation, and empower people by providing information, knowledge, authority, and rewards, as described in Chapter 13.

Generate short-term wins. Don't wait for the ultimate grand realization of the vision. You need results. As small victories accumulate, you make the transition from isolated initiative to an integral part of the business.[44] Plan for and create small victories that indicate to everyone that progress is being made. Recognize and reward the people who made the wins possible, doing it as visibly as you can so people notice and the positive message permeates the organization.

Make sure you *consolidate gains and produce more change.* With the well-earned credibility of previous successes, keep changing things in ways that support the vision. Hire, promote, and develop people who will further the vision. Reinvigorate the organization and your change efforts with new projects and change agents.

Finally, *anchor new approaches in the culture.*[45] Highlight positive results, communicate the connections between the new behaviors and the improved results, and keep developing new change agents and leaders. Continually increase the number of people joining you in taking responsibility for change.[46]

Shaping the future

reactive change A response that occurs when events in the environment have already affected the firm's performance; problem-driven change.

proactive change A response that is initiated before a performance gap has occurred.

Most change is reactive. A better way to change is to be proactive. **Reactive change** means responding to pressure, after the problem has arisen. It also implies being a follower. **Proactive change** means anticipating and preparing for an uncertain future. It implies being a leader and *creating* the future you want.

On the road to the future, there are drivers, passengers, and road kill. Put another way: On the road to the future, who will be the windshield, and who will be the bug?[47]

Needless to say, it's best to be a driver.[48] How do you become a driver? By being proactive more than merely reactive. By exercising foresight, learning continuously, pursuing growth, seizing advantage, and creating futures.

Exercising foresight

If you think only about the present, or wallow in the uncertainties of the future, your future is just a roll of the dice. It is far better to exercise foresight, set an agenda for the future, and pursue it with everything you've got.

So, contemplate and envision the future.

Envisioning the future

At Taco Bell, the anywhere, anytime vision is for great-tasting food, delivered fast, customized, and yet low-priced. Taco Bell had 9,000 points of access (POAs) in 1993, including not only restaurants but also carts, kiosks, vans, and express units in high school and college cafeterias, airports, malls, gas stations, convenience stores, and the Moscow subway station. Its goal was to have 200,000 POAs by the time you read this.

Oticon, the Danish hearing aid manufacturer, leveraged an approach it calls the "Human Link"—combining the expertise of scientists, physicians, hearing care professionals, and users—to create hearing aids that are molded and tuned to the precise needs of each customer's needs and preferences. Now it is introducing a new generation of digital hearing aids. Its Digifocus hearing aids "learn." They can process over 100 sound differentiating parameters, tuned and adapted to each individual, and adjust automatically to different sound environments. The vision is a product and service that can sense, respond, and adapt continually to customer experiences.

Lynne Franks is on a mission to help women entrepreneurs start businesses that are community-minded, values-driven, and family-friendly, through a global network of entrepreneurs who change the role of business all over the world.

William Edwin Swing is founder of the United Religions Initiative (URI), an international interfaith organization. He had no idea how to create a global organization, but he did know that existing international interfaith groups included different religions but excluded each other. Each was trying to corner the interfaith market. He took an entrepreneurial approach, looking elsewhere to find knowledge on collaboration and organization design, including a business-school professor and a former banker. The URI now is a network through which organizations leverage one another's resources while pursuing both mutual and individual goals. "We're trying to change world history" (p. 236).

Disney and Virgin are brands that transcend particular businesses. Disney's business is not theme parks, but "three-dimensional entertainment," and it is succeeding not only with parks but also cruise ships, Broadway shows, and many other ventures. A Virgin executive said "There is no assumption about what business Virgin should be in or shouldn't be in . . . The culture is one of why not rather than why" (p. 102). Virgin will enter industries where it thinks it can challenge existing rules, provide customers with better value, be more entertaining, and harass complacent industry incumbents.

Sources: J. Pine, B. Victor, and A. Boynton, "Making Mass Customization Work," *Harvard Business Review*, September–October 1993, pp. 108–22; J. Slocum, Jr., M. McGill, and D. Lei, "The New Learning Strategy: Anytime, Anything, Anywhere," *Organizational Dynamics*, Autumn 1994, pp. 33–47; B. Victor and A. Boynton, *Invented Here*. (Boston: Harvard Business School Press, 1998); C. Dahle, "How to Make your Mark," *Fast Company*, December 2000, pp. 204–20; C. Salter, "William Edwin Swing," *Fast Company*, November 2000, pp. 230–38; 234; and G. Hamel, "Reinvent your Company," *Fortune*, June 12, 2000, pp. 98–118. ●

If you and your bosses think you know what you need to do to succeed in the future, you probably need a dose of humility—it is impossible to know the future with certainty. But this does not need to be a reactive, defeatist view. It can be highly proactive, in a subtle but vitally important way. Managers may acknowledge that they don't know exactly what customers will want in the future, and what products they will have to deliver. But they *can* know that they have, or can acquire, the *capabilities* to deliver.[49] Thus, the focus is on identifying and building core competencies, as discussed in earlier chapters, and on improving continuously in the activities that will enable your firm to succeed in the future.

Taco Bell's "anywhere, anytime" vision led to a goal of creating 200,000 points of access by the time you read this.
[Courtesy of Taco Bell Corporation]

Learning continuously

Continuous learning is a vital route to renewable competitive advantage.[50] To learn continuously, your firm (and you!) need (1) a clear, strategic goal to learn new capabilities and (2) a commitment to constant experimentation.

Companies and individuals striving for world-class excellence must improve constantly. Continuous improvement, the concept made legendary by Toyota Motor Company, is a relentless drive to be better in every way: to find faster, more-efficient, low-cost methods to develop new, high-quality products. When Toyota became so successful at making low-cost, defect-free cars, it set the quality standard.[51]

In an environment of continuous improvement, everyone engages in exploration, discovery, and action, continually learns what is effective and what is not, and adjusts and improves accordingly. Figure 18.5 elaborates. With this philosophy, and the appropriate approaches, your company *can* have it all: low cost, high quality, flexibility, responsiveness, innovation, and speed. This process also generates learning on a more individual level, generating personal growth and development.

As described in other chapters, experimentation means trying new things in the spirit of continuous improvement, investing in research and long-term development projects, encouraging risks, and tolerating failures. Companies like J&J, 3M, and Bally Engineering practice self-obsolescence. That is, they try to make their own products obsolete. Why? Because the products will become obsolete sooner or later, and it's better to replace them with their own new products than to have competitors beat them to it. Home Depot will even close a thriving store and open two smaller ones in an effort to keep improving customers' shopping experiences.[52]

Similarly, Sony and Mitsubishi use "systematic abandonment" of their products.[53] When they introduce a new product, they establish a "sunset date" at which they will drop the product. Thus, they create a deadline for introducing a future product that will replace the brand new product, and begin those development efforts immediately. Their goal is to create three new products for every one they phase out: an incrementally improved product, a new product spin-off, and an entirely new innovation.

figure 18.5
Learning cycle: explore, discover, act

Explore

The first step is to explore current reality.
The aim is to be as honest and open as possible
about what is happening at present.

- Identify the problem/opportunity area
- Check with the customers, suppliers or
  other key stakeholders
- Reveal hidden issues
- Gather data
- Look for root causes
- Rethink the issue

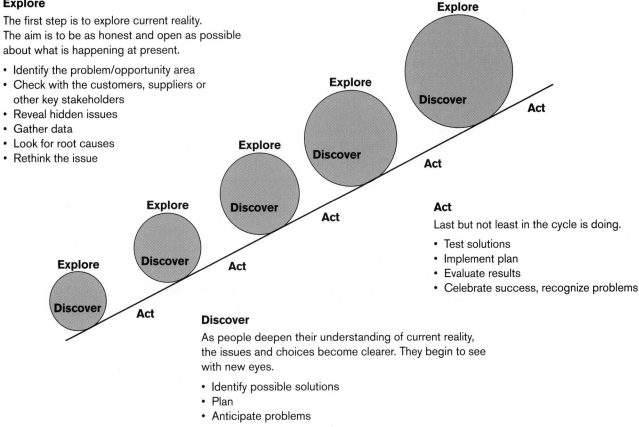

Act

Last but not least in the cycle is doing.

- Test solutions
- Implement plan
- Evaluate results
- Celebrate success, recognize problems

Discover

As people deepen their understanding of current reality,
the issues and choices become clearer. They begin to see
with new eyes.

- Identify possible solutions
- Plan
- Anticipate problems

Source: From *Leaning into the Future: Changing the Way People Change Organizations* by George Binney and Colin Williams; published by Nicholas Brealey Publishing Ltd., 1997. Tel: (0171) 430-0224, Fax: (0171) 404-8311. Reprinted by permission.

Pursuing growth

Cutting costs can be vitally important, but can only get you so far. Downsizing, reengineering, and other approaches to cost cutting sooner or later will reach their limits. You must also be able to go for growth by increasing revenues. This requires focusing on things such as technology, investment, product development, and creation of new markets. For example, in early 2001, Nestle was a favored refuge for investors fleeing tech companies, the top pick in the food-processing sector. The new CEO began his tenure by reducing operational costs, because "these were things which you can feel and you can touch" (p. 358).[54] But he is focusing also on innovation, coordination among its different businesses, maximizing sales, and building highly-targeted communities of consumers.

In other words, you can raise profits by shrinking expenses (the denominator in financial ratios), and also by increasing revenues (the numerator).[55] For traditional companies cutting costs was relatively easy; increasing revenues is more difficult. In the 1990s, the numerator did not receive nearly the emphasis it deserves. Stated an influential management expert, "We've produced a generation of denominator managers in the U.S."[56] On the other hand, hordes of Internet companies generated high revenues but went out of business because their costs were far too high.

Cisco Systems survived the shakeout while other companies died in the recent economic slowdown. Despite the economy, CEO John Chambers promised to generate incredible growth again.[57] He intends to do so by stepping up Cisco's efforts in two booming markets—wireless and optical—through acquisitions, new product innovation, creative use of the Net, and outsourcing.

A *Fortune* article concluded, "Without doubt, it's easier to get a dollar of profit growth by cutting costs than by raising revenues. But investors, the final arbiters of value, well know that those two dollars are very unlike in terms of the future they presage."[58] In other words, cost cutting is a start and cost control is essential, but additionally essential to long-term great success are revenue growth and a proactive eye to the future.

Seizing advantage

In a recent 10-year period, 17 companies in the *Fortune 1000* grew total shareholder return by 35 percent or more per year.[59] How did they do it? They invented totally new industries, or completely reinvented existing industries. Harley-Davidson turned around by selling not just motorcycles, but nostalgia. Amgen broke the rules of the biotech industry by focusing not on what customers wanted, but on great science. Starbuck's took a commodity and began selling it in trendy stores. CarMax and other companies reinvented the auto industry.[60]

To create new markets or transform industries—these are perhaps the ultimate forms of proactive change.[61] Competing for the future thus involves creating and dominating emerging opportunities. Consider:

Instead of . . .	Why not . . . ?
• fitting the firm to the environment	• change the environment to fit the firm
• preserving old advantages	• create new advantages
• locking in old markets	• create new markets
• investing in fixed assets	• invest in evolving/emerging opportunities

You need to create advantages. The challenge is not to maintain your position in the current competitive arena, but to create new competitive arenas, transform your industry, and imagine a future that others don't see. Creating advantage is better than playing catch-up through downsizing and reengineering. At best, such restructuring buys time; it cannot get you out ahead of the pack and buy world-class excellence.[62]

How many companies pictured at this electronics convention do you think practice "systematic abandonment?" How many products represented will be spun-off or dropped by the time you read this? *[Courtesy of Softbank COMDEX]*

So, which should you and your firm do?

- Take the path of greatest familiarity, or the path of greatest opportunity, wherever that may lead?
- Be only a good benchmarker, or a pathbreaker?
- Focus just on product time to market, or on time to global preeminence?
- Be a product leader, or also a core competence leader?
- Place priority on short-term financial returns, or on making a real, long-term impact?
- Look to the past, or live for the future?
- Do only what seems doable, or what is difficult and worthwhile?
- Change what is, or create what isn't?
- Solve problems, or create entirely new opportunities?

Creating the future

adapters Companies that take the current industry structure, and its future evolution, as givens.

shapers Companies that try to change the structure of their industries, creating a future competitive landscape of their own design.

Companies can try different strategic postures to prepare to compete in an uncertain future. **Adapters** take the current industry structure, and its future evolution, as givens. They choose where and how to compete. This posture is taken by most companies in fairly predictable environments, by conducting standard strategic analysis and choosing how to compete.

In contrast, **shapers** try to change the structure of their industries, creating a future competitive landscape of their own design.[63] For example, Federal Express entered the mail-and-package delivery industry with a strategy of delivering overnight. FedEx almost went bankrupt in its first two years, but ultimately reshaped the industry. Its bet paid off hugely, forcing others like United Parcel Service to adapt.

To get ahead of the pack, create the future.

Creating futures

- General Magic, a consortium including Motorola, Philips, AT&T, and others, envisions a world in which people use hand-held devices to visit a "virtual downtown" of travel agents, banks, libraries, and so on. "Information agents" in cyberspace make reservations, review financial data, or retrieve magazine articles. Has this world yet become a reality? Maybe not, but it never will, without the vision to create it. But vision and foresight, of course, must also be followed by creation.
- Dreamworks SKG was created by Steven Spielberg, Jeffrey Katzenberg, and David Geffen. Spielberg directed *ET* and *Jurassic Park,* among other great films. Katzenberg was responsible for the great recent animated films from the Disney Co. Geffen is the music executive and producer associated with Nirvana, Guns N' Roses, the Eagles, Tom Cruise movies, and Cats. Now they have joined forces to create what *Time* magazine calls the "prototype plugged-in multimedia company of the new millennium."
- Mondex International is a consortium of financial services providers and technology companies attempting to establish universal electronic-cash standards. It is spending big money on product development, infrastructure, and pilot experiments to gain quick customer acceptance.
- Helena Luczywo and Wanda Rapaczynski have turned a small underground newspaper in Poland into a local media empire, Agora SA. Theirs is one of the most remarkable success stories in post-communist Europe. Says Luczywo, "I've been fighting for freedom of expression for many years. I believe that our newspaper should stand for important things and should not avoid difficult topics. It should tell the truth, even when the truth goes against the popular grain, the government, or advertisers." Says Rapaczynski, "We aren't liked by everybody . . . We take seriously our role in this country as an institution of democracy." They both believe that the way to guarantee their independence as an agent of democracy is to become highly profitable, so as not to be vulnerable to outside economic pressure. States Luczywo, "If you want to be independent, then you must be financially independent."
- Ken Kutaragi of Sony knew that his company was behind in three hot, new digital markets: videogames, personal computers, and cell phones. Sony's historical strengths were in the analog technologies found in TVs, VCRs, and tape players. He went on a mission

Jeffrey Katzenberg, Steven Spielberg, and David Geffen joined forces to create Dreamworks SKG. The company has been billed as the "prototype plugged-in multimedia company of the new millennium," according to *Time* magazine.
[AP/Wide World Photos]

to convince senior management of the importance of computer entertainment, and that Sony had to convert to digital. He threatened to quit if Sony didn't fund his R&D efforts in a videogame project, and promised he could create a platform for Sony's future growth. Two years later, the PlayStation was born. By 1999, Sony had sold 55 million worldwide and 430 million copies of videogame software. Kutaragi then led the engineering team for the PlayStation II, a $1 billion development project.

Sources: G. Hamel and C. K. Prahalad, *Competing for the Future* (Boston: Harvard Business School Press, 1994); R. Corliss, "Hey, Let's Put On a Show!" *Time,* March 27, 1995, pp. 54–60; H. Courtney, J. Kirkland, and P. Viguerie, "Strategy under Uncertainty," *Harvard Business Review,* November-December 1997, pp. 66–79; G. Hamel, ``Driving Grassroots Growth,'' *Fortune,* September 4, 2000, pp. 173–87; and P. Kruger, ``Helena Luczywo & Wanda Rapaczynski,'' *Fast Company,* November 2000, pp. 152–66. ●

Creating the future is not for the faint-hearted; it requires high-stakes bets.[64] Eastman Kodak is spending $500 million per year to develop digital photography products. The company *hopes* it will change fundamentally the way people create, view, and store pictures. But Hewlett-Packard is pursuing its own, competing vision for reshaping the industry, centered around photo processing done in the home rather than in shops. Which will win? Or will they both? Or neither?

The Microsoft Network (MSN) aimed to become the standard for conducting transactions between networked computers. Microsoft bet big—not only with developmental costs, but in terms of attention, exposure, and credibility—that it could create the proprietary network and shape the evolution of electronic commerce. But it became clear that open networks would prevail, and Microsoft refocused its MSN concept around the Internet. Thus, Microsoft's shaping posture failed, but it responded quickly by becoming an adapter. It adapted successfully because it closely monitored the evolution of the market (for example, growth in the numbers of MSN and Internet subscribers), was willing to cut its losses, and learned useful lessons from the experience. For example, its engineers had acquired useful new learning about general programming and product development.

Figure 18.6 illustrates the vast opportunity to create new markets. Articulated needs are those that customers acknowledge and try to satisfy. Unarticulated needs are those that customers have not yet experienced. Served customers are those to whom your company is now selling, and unserved customers are untapped markets.

Business-as-usual concentrates on the lower-left quadrant. The leaders who recreate the game are constantly trying to create new opportunities in the other three quadrants.[65]

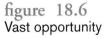

figure 18.6
Vast opportunity

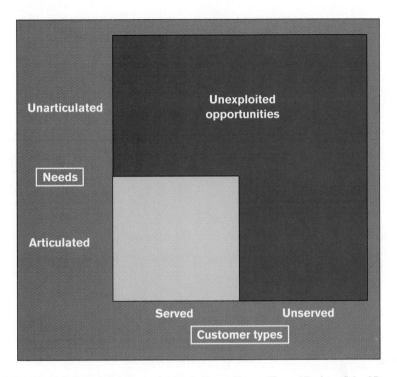

Source: G. Hamel and C. K. Prahalad, *Competing for the Future* (Boston: Harvard Business School Press, 1994).

For example, you can pursue the upper-left quadrant by imagining how you can satisfy a larger proportion of your customers' total needs.[66] Nike realized its customers didn't want only shoes and running apparel, but also specialized sunglasses, watches, and wearable MP3 music players. GE's Power Systems business learned that major electric utilities would pay not only for turbines and transformers, but also for a wide range of consulting and maintenance services, which have much higher margins.

More generally, Royal Dutch/Shell has institutionalized its "GameChanger" process to generate new businesses or new approaches to existing businesses, and GE Capital convenes annual "dreaming sessions." The company makes full use of its youngest managers to find business opportunities that their stodgier elders might miss.[67]

Shaping your own future

If you are an organizational leader, and your organization operates in traditional ways, your key goal should be to create a revolution, genetically reengineering your company before it becomes a dinosaur of the modern era.[68] What should be the goals of the revolution? You've been learning about them throughout this course.

But maybe you are not going to lead a revolution. Maybe you just want a successful career and a good life. You still must be able to deal with an economic environment that is increasingly competitive and fast-moving.[69] Creating the future you want for yourself requires setting high personal standards. Don't settle for mediocrity; don't assume that "good" is necessarily good enough—for yourself or for your employer. Try to avoid companies and industries that are less competitive than the world norm.[70]

Table 18.3 helps you think about how you can continually add value to your employer and also to yourself, as you upgrade your skills, your ability to contribute, your security with your current employer, and your ability to find alternative employment if necessary.

More advice from the leading authors on career management:[71] Consciously and actively manage your own career. Develop marketable skills, and keep developing more. Make career choices based on personal growth, development, and learning opportunities.

table 18.3
Adding value, personally

Go beyond your job description:

- volunteer for projects.
- identify problems.
- initiate solutions.

Seek out others and share ideas and advice.

Offer your opinions and respect those of others.

Take an inventory of your skills every few months.

Learn something new every week.

Discover new ways to make a contribution.

Engage in active thought and deliberate action.

Take risks based on what you know and believe.

Recognize, research, and pursue opportunity.

Differentiate yourself.

Source: Compiled from C. Hakim, *We Are All Self-Employed* (San Francisco: Berrett-Koehler, 1994).

Look for positions that stretch you, and for bosses who develop their protégés. Seek out environments that provide training and opportunity to experiment and innovate. And know yourself: Assess your strengths and weaknesses, your true interests, and ethical standards. If you are not already thinking in these terms and taking commensurate action, you should start now.

Additionally: Become indispensable to your organization. Be happy and enthusiastic in your job, and committed to doing great work, but don't be blindly loyal to one company. Be prepared to leave if necessary. View your job as an opportunity to prove what you can do and increase what you can do, not as a comfortable niche for the long term.[72] Go out on your own if it meets your skills and temperament.

This points out the need to maintain your options. More and more, contemporary careers can involve leaving behind the large organization and going entrepreneurial, becoming self-employed in the "post-corporate world."[73] In such a career, independent individuals are free to make their own choices. They can flexibly and quickly respond to demands and opportunities. Developing start-up ventures, consulting, accepting temporary employment, doing project work for one organization and then another, working in professional partnerships, being a constant deal-maker—these can be the elements of a successful career. Ideally, this self-employed model can help provide a balanced approach to working and to living life at home and with family, because people have more control over their work activities and schedules.

This can sound like the ideal world. It also has downsides. The independence can be frightening, the future unpredictable. It can isolate "road warriors" who are always on the go, working from their cars and airports, and interfere with social and family life.[74] Effective self-management is needed to keep things in perspective and in control.

Into the future   Commit to lifelong learning. Lifelong learning includes being willing to seek new challenges and to reflect honestly on successes and failures.[75] Lifelong learning requires occasionally taking risks; moving outside of your "comfort zone;" honestly assessing the reasons behind your successes and failures; aggressively asking for and listening to other people's information and opinions; and being open to new ideas.

Honored as one of the best management books of the year in Europe, *Leaning into the Future* gets its title from a combination of the words "leading" and "learning."[76] The two perspectives, on the surface, appear very different. But they also are powerful when

figure 18.7
Leaning into the future

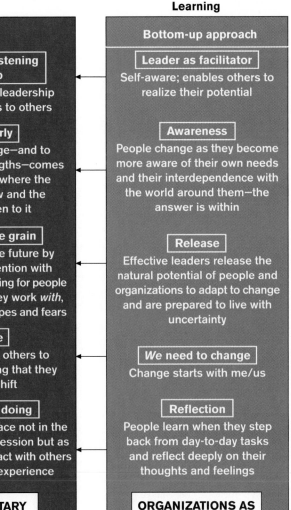

Source: From *Leaning into the Future: Changing the Way People Change Organizations* by George Binney and Colin Williams; published by Nicholas Brealey Publishing Ltd., 1997. Tel: (0171) 430-0224, Fax: (0171) 404-8311. Reprinted by permission.

pursued in complementary ways. Figure 18.7 captures the synergies of combining both leading and learning. Success in the future will come from shaping the future *and* adapting to the world; being clear about what you want to change *and* being responsive to others' perspectives; passionately pursuing your vision *and* understanding current realities; leading *and* learning.

This is another example of an important concept from the beginning of the chapter. For yourself, as well as for your organization, recognize and live the genius of the *and*.

Key terms

Adapters, p. 593
Genius of the "and," p. 580
Moving, p. 583
Performance gap, p. 583
Proactive change, p. 588
Reactive change, p. 588

Refreezing, p. 583
Shapers, p. 593
Total organization change, p. 585
Tyranny of the "or," p. 579
Unfreezing, p. 582

Summary of learning objectives

Now that you have studied Chapter 18, you should know:

What it takes to be world class.

You should strive for world-class excellence, which means using the very best and latest knowledge and ideas to operate at the highest standards of any place anywhere. Sustainable greatness comes from, among other things, having strong core values, living those values constantly, striving for continuous improvement, experimenting, and always trying to do better tomorrow than today. It is essential to not fall prey to the tyranny of the *or*; that is, the belief that one important goal can be attained only at the expense of another. The genius of the *and* is that multiple important goals can be achieved simultaneously and synergistically.

How to manage change effectively.

Effective change management occurs when the organization moves from its current state to a desired future state without excessive cost to the organization or its people. People resist change for a variety of reasons, including inertia, poor timing, surprise, peer pressure, self-interest, misunderstanding, and different information about (and assessments of) the change.

Motivating people to change requires a general process of unfreezing, moving, and refreezing, with the caveat that appropriate and not inappropriate behaviors be "refrozen." More specific techniques to motivate people to change include education and communication, participation and involvement, facilitation and support, negotiation and rewards, manipulation and cooptation, and coercion. Each approach has strengths, weaknesses, and appropriate uses, and multiple approaches can be used. More generally, it is important to harmonize the multiple changes that are occurring throughout the organization.

Effective change requires active leadership, including creating a sense of urgency, forming a guiding coalition, developing a vision and strategy, communicating the change vision, empowering broad-based action, generating short-term wins, consolidating gains and producing more change, and anchoring the new approaches in the culture.

Ideas for how to create a successful future.

Preparing for an uncertain future requires a proactive approach. Being proactive includes exercising foresight, learning continuously, pursuing growth, seizing advantages, and creating the future. You can proactively shape your own future by actively managing your career and your personal development, and becoming an active leader and a lifelong learner.

Discussion questions

1. Review the quotes on page 581, describing "resistance to becoming world class." Why do some people resist the goal of becoming world class? What lies behind the quotes? How can this resistance be overcome?

2. Generate specific examples of world-class business that you have seen as a consumer. Also, generate examples of poor business practice. Why and how do some companies inspire world-class practices, while others fail?

3. How can you make the concept of continuous improvement useful to you in your personal life and your career?

4. Generate and discuss examples of problems and opportunities that have inspired change, both in businesses and in you, personally.

5. Choose some specific types of changes you would like to see happen in groups or organizations with which you are familiar.

Imagine that you were to try to bring about these changes. What sources of resistance should you anticipate? How would you manage the resistance?

6. How would you "exercise foresight" with regard to your personal life and career?

7. Develop a specific plan for becoming a "continuous learner."

8. Consider a business with which you are familiar and discuss some ideas for how it should pursue a growth strategy. What are some pros and cons to your ideas? How might the best ideas be implemented?

9. In your own words, what does the idea of "creating the future" mean to you? How can you put this concept to good use? Again, generate some specific ideas that you can really use.

Concluding Case

Making Your Mark

Making your mark means making a distinctive contribution, by making the best use of your talents.

Neil Gershenfel is building "brains" for chairs, musical instruments, and other objects that up to now were considered inanimate. For example, he developed a computer for car seats that senses who is sitting in them, so they don't deploy potentially deadly airbags for small children.

Louis Monier invented Alta Vista, and therefore is one of the architects of the Web as we know it today. He was not one of the big financial winners, but he made his mark in a way that was far more important to him than just cashing in. With "my baby, my creation . . . I was able to see my experiment all the way to the end. I suppose I could have just taken one of the offers and joined another search engine or portal, and I would have been a lot richer today. It probably would have been less painful—and less interesting—than sticking with Alta Vista. But I don't think I would have learned as much" (p. 216). "I'd rather do something interesting, solve an interesting problem, than do something boring and get rich" (p. 220).

Dean Jernigan, owner of the Triple A Memphis Redbirds, wanted to build a different kind of sports team, not dominated by greedy players and greedier owners. He believed a baseball team should be part of the soul of a community. The goal should not be maximum return to owners; the goal should be maximizing returns to the community. Conventional wisdom said build a new stadium in the heart of Memphis's eastern-suburban sprawl. Jernigan took a risk and built it in the heart of downtown Memphis, creating a central-Memphis revival. And he registered his company as a nonprofit organization, with all income above expenses going to two local charities.

Dan Morrell is founder and CEO of Future Forests Ltd. He applies market incentives and marketing know-how to an immense challenge: climate change and global warming. "The future belongs to issue-focused groups who can make themselves attractive to CFOs as companies prepare for environmental taxes and regulations. At first, we found ourselves in companies' marketing budgets. Now we're migrating into their operations budgets—because clients recognize that environmental planning is a core function"(p. 338).

Ken Kutaragi, the developer of Sony's PlayStation whom you read about earlier, could have started his own videogame company, but he knew he wanted to leverage Sony's money, manufacturing capabilities, and marketing muscle. "If I had started this business as a venture outside a big company, it would have worked, but the moving speed would not have been fast enough. Sony had great human resources, capital, and manufacturing capability, but it did not have a vision. My team had the vision" (p. 180).

Brian Sugar was proud of the fact that he was moving to California to a new job as chief Web officer, and partnering with Yahoo! He was less proud of the fact that the company he was working for is Kmart's Internet subsidiary, BlueLight.com. "I grew up with the connotation of Kmart not being cool." (p. 214). But he is creating major, important change, and loving it. It was the ultimate clicks-and-mortar challenge. In this arena, Kmart has topped Wal-Mart. An analyst says, "It's been a while since Kmart's had any leading role in innovation" (p. 214). BlueLight.com is reinvigorating Kmart's brand and improving morale.

Heather Killen is an e-vangelist and the ultimate global citizen, building a truly global Internet company. Under her leadership, Yahoo! has become not just a U.S. company with international operations, but a truly global company. She tells her colleagues, "Don't think about 'international' as being *part* of our business. It *is* our business!" Yahoo! attracts users outside the United States by generating content locally. Says Killen, "We don't squirt English-language news through a translation engine and then put it up on our China or Argentina sites. That would never work" (p. 194). Yahoo! Chief Jerry Yang says of Killen, "She's our ambassador. Being a female executive in a global business can be very intimidating. But Heather is fearless, and she's found the right mix of showing respect yet not being a pushover" (p. 194).

Donald Winkler is dyslexic, and chairman and CEO of Ford Motor Credit Co. He struggles to process the world the way others do, but also he often sees the world in ways that others don't. A friend says that Winkler is motivated not by money but by success. "He always views himself as the underdog. He likes to surface from out of nowhere and win" (p. 266). Winkler's principles for effective leadership include: Set real priorities and real commitments; set and demand standards of excellence; and be willing to see failure as a stepping stone to success.

Vice President of International Operations Heather Killen has turned Yahoo! into a truly global company.
[James D. Wilson/Liaison Agency]

Questions

1. Consider the champions of change described here and in other parts of the chapter (for example, Lynne Franks, William Edwin Swing, Helena Luczywo, and Wanda Rapaczynski). Whom do you admire the most, and whom would you choose as a role model? Why? What do your choices teach you about yourself?

2. Choose any one individual from this group and generate an action plan for implementing the change he or she envisions.

3. What will be the mark *you* make? What is your plan for learning and leading the way to achieving your personal vision?

Sources: N. Stein, "Inventing Tomorrow Today," *Fortune,* March 6, 2000, pp. F-35–F-39; S. Koudsi, "Attention Kmart Bashers, "*Fortune,* November 13, 2000, pp. 213–22; C. Dahle, "How To Make Your Mark," *Fast Company,* December 2000, pp. 204–20; G. Calkins, "Dean Jernigan, "*Fast Company,* November 2000, pp. 170–84. A. Markels, "Heather Killen," *Fast Company,* November 2000, pp. 190–200; K. H. Hammonds, "Donald Winkler," *Fast Company,* November 2000, pp. 260–68; I. Wylie, "Dan Morrell," *Fast Company,* November 2000, pp. 336–42; and G. Hamel, "Driving Grassroots Growth," *Fortune,* September 4, 2000, pp. 173–87.

Experiential Exercises
18.1 A force-field analysis

Objective

To introduce you to force-field analysis of organizations and challenges facing them.

Instructions

Read the following force-field analysis, and come up with an organizational problem of your own to analyze.

Force-field analysis

A force-field analysis is one way to assess change in an organization. This concept reflects the forces, driving and restraining, at work at a particular time. It helps to assess organizational strengths and to select forces to add or remove in order to create change. The theory of change suggested by Kurt Lewin, who developed the force-field analysis, is that while driving forces may be more easily affected, shifting them could increase opposition (tension and/or conflict) within the organization and add restraining forces.

Therefore, it may be more effective to remove restraining forces to create change.

The use of the force-field analysis will demonstrate the range of forces pressing on an organization at a particular time. This analysis can increase people's optimism that it is possible to strategize and plan for change.

Example—Trying to increase student participation in student government.

Driving forces	Restraining forces
More money allocated for student government activities ⟶	⟵ High emphasis on grades—a need to study more.
Better publicity and public relations programs for student government. ⟶	⟵ Other activities—cultural, social, sports—divert interest.
Student government representatives go to classes and explain positive effects of student decisions. ⟶	⟵ Not much public relations work in the past.
Special career programs offered for student government participants. ⟶	⟵ Students do not see student government as effective or helping them get a job.

Present balance point

Force-field analysis worksheet

1. (10–15 min.) Choose an organizational change in process, complete the Problem Analysis section, and fill in the model.

2. (20 min.) In groups of three or four, discuss the driving and restraining forces in each person's problem.

3. (10 min.) Class discussion

Problem analysis

1. Describe the problem in a few words.

_____

_____

_____

_____

_____

_____

2. A list of forces *driving* toward change would include:

a. _____

b. _____

c. _____

a. Why is it useful to break a problem situation up into driving and restraining forces?

b. Would the model be used any differently whether applied to an individual or organizational problem?

d. _____

e. _____

f. _____

3. A list of forces *restraining* change would include:

a. _____

b. _____

c. _____

d. _____

e. _____

f. _____

4. Put the driving and restraining forces of the problem on this force-field analysis, according to their degree of impact on change.

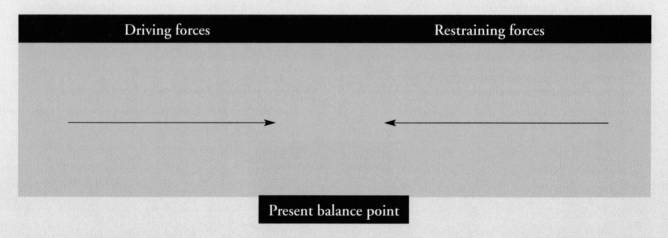

Driving forces	Restraining forces

Present balance point

18.2 Sears versus Kmart

Objective

To analyze operations at two well-known retail firms, with a view to making recommendations for changes that will improve profitability, sales, and customer service.

Instructions

Your group, Fastalk Consultants, is known as the shrewdest, most insightful, and most overpaid management consulting firm in the country. You have been hired by the president of Sears to make recommendations for improving the motivation and performance of personnel in their operations. Let us assume that the key job activity in store operations is dealing with customers.

Recently, the president of Sears has come to suspect that his company's competitor, Kmart, is making heavy inroads into Sears'

market. He has also hired a market research firm to investigate and compare the relative merits of products and prices in the two establishments, and has asked the market research firm to assess the advertising campaigns of the two organizations. Hence, you will not need to be concerned with marketing issues, except as they may have an impact on employee behavior. The president wants you to look into the organization of the two stores to determine the strengths and weaknesses of each.

The president has established an unusual contract with you. He wants you to make your recommendations based upon your observations *as a customer*. He does not want you to do a complete diagnosis with interviews, surveys, or behind-the-scenes observations. He wants your report in two parts.

Sears versus Kmart worksheet

1. Given his organization's goals of profitability, sales volume, and fast and courteous service, he wants an analysis that will compare and contrast Sears and Kmart in terms of the following concepts:

Organizational Goals

Conflict?_____

Clarity?_____

Environment

Stable/Changing?_____

Simple/Complex?_____

Certain/Uncertain?_____

Size

Large?_____

Medium?_____

Small?_____

Personnel

Knowledgeable?_____

Well Trained?_____

Jobs

Variety?_____

Wholeness?_____

Interaction?_____

Freedom?_____

Time of Work?_____

Location of Work?_____

Horizontal Division of Labor

Formalized Policies?_____

Departmentalization?_____

Standardization of Rules?_____

Vertical Division of Labor

Number of Levels?_____

Span of Control?_____

Centralization?_____

Communication?

Direction?_____

Openness?_____

Leadership Style

Task Oriented?_____

People Oriented?_____

Employee Motivation

Type?_____

Intrinsic/Extrinsic?_____

Rewards?_____

Support?_____

Coordination?_____

Decision Making?_____

1. How do Sears and Kmart differ in these aspects? Which company has the best approach?

_____

_____

2. Given the corporate goals listed under part 1, what specific changes might Sears' management make in the following areas to achieve these goals (profitability, sales volume, fast and courteous service)?

- Job design and work flow

_____

_____

- Organization structure (at the individual store level)

_____

_____

- Employee incentives

_____

_____

- Leadership

_____

_____

- Employee selection

_____

_____

3. Having completed your contract with the president of Sears, prepare a report for presentation to class. This should include specific recommendations you have considered in part 2.

Source: Excerpted from Lawrence R. Jauch, Arthur G. Bedeian, Sally A. Coltrin, and William F. Glueck, *The Managerial Experience: Cases, Exercises, and Readings*, 4th ed. Copyright © 1986 by The Dryden Press. Reprinted by permission of the publisher. ●

Integrating Case
The Transformation at General Electric

Jack Welch Jr. was appointed chairman and chief executive officer of General Electric in April 1981. Recently, Welch announced that he would retire. His tenure in the job was characterized by constant strategic and organizational change at GE. Among the initiatives with which Welch is associated are

1. *Changing the shape of the business portfolio.* Welch established two sets of criteria for redefining the business portfolio of GE. The first was to declare, "We will only run businesses that are number one or number two in their global markets— or, in the case of services, that have a substantial position— and are of a scale and potential appropriate to a $50 billion enterprise." Second, Welch defined three broad areas of business for GE: core, high-technology, and service businesses. As a result of these criteria, during the 1980s GE sold or closed businesses accounting for $10 billion in assets and acquired businesses amounting to $18 billion in assets. Divestment included Utah International, housewares and small appliances, consumer electronics, and semiconductors. Additions included RCA; Employers Reinsurance Corp.; Kidder Peabody Group; Navistar Financial; several new plastics ventures; Thomson's medical electronics business; and joint ventures with Fanuc (factory automation), Robert Bosch (electric motors), GEC (major appliances and electrical equipment), and Ericsson (mobile communications).

2. *Changing strategic planning.* Welch largely dismantled the highly elaborate strategic planning system that had been built up at GE over the previous decade. Documentation was drastically reduced, and the planning review process was made more informal—the central element was a meeting between Welch, his two vice chairmen, and top management of each SBU (Strategic Business Unit), which focused on identifying and discussing a few key themes. By 1984 the 200-strong corporate planning staff had been halved. The broad objective was "to get general managers talking to general managers about strategy rather than planners talking to planners."

3. *Delayering.* The changes in planning were one aspect of a more general change in the role of headquarters staff from being "checker, inquisitor, and authority figure to facilitator, helper, and supporter." This change involved a substantial reduction in reporting and paper generation and an increase in individual decision-making authority. These changes permitted a substantial widening of spans of control and the removal of several layers of hierarchy. In most of GE, levels of management were reduced from nine to four.

4. *Destaffing.* Divesting pressures, removing management layers, reducing corporate staffs, and increasing productivity resulted in enormous improvements. Between 1980 and 1990, GE's sales more than doubled while its numbers of employees fell from 402,000 to 298,000.

5. *Values.* A persistent theme in Welch's leadership was a commitment to values. Welch continually emphasized the importance of the company's "software" (values, motivation, and commitment) over its "hardware" (businesses and management structure). Welch's philosophy was articulated in 10 key principles and values:

Being number one or two in each business.
Becoming and staying lean and agile.
"Ownership"—individuals taking responsibility for decisions and actions.
"Stewardship"—individuals ensuring that GE's resources were leveraged to the full.
"Entrepreneurship."
"Excellence"—the highest personal standards.
"Reality."
"Candor."
"Open communications"—both internally and externally.
Financial support—earning a return needed to support success.

This emphasis on values was supported by a type of leadership that put a huge emphasis on communicating and disseminating these values throughout the company. Welch devoted a large portion of his time to addressing meetings of employees and management seminars at GE's Crotonville Management Development Institute.

New Culture, New Systems

During his first 5 years in office, Welch's priorities were strategy and structure. GE's business portfolio was radically transformed, and within its main businesses GE's strategies gave a much greater emphasis to local presence and global success and to the development and application of new technology. In terms of organizational structure, Welch's crusade against excess costs, complacency, and administrative inefficiencies resulted in a drastic pruning of the corporate hierarchy and a much flatter organization.

At the root of the "new culture" Welch sought to build at GE was a redefinition of the relational contract between GE and its employees:

"Like many other large companies in the United States, Europe and Japan, GE has had an implicit psychological contract based upon perceived lifetime employment . . . This produced a paternal, feudal, fuzzy kind of loyalty. You put in your time, worked hard, and the company took care of you for life. That kind of loyalty tends to focus people inward . . . The psychological contract has to change. People at all levels have to feel the risk-reward tension.

My concept of loyalty is not "giving time" to some corporate entity and, in turn, being shielded and protected from the outside world. Loyalty is an affinity among people who want to grapple with the outside world and win . . . The new psychological contract, if there is such a thing, is that jobs at GE are the best in the world for people who are willing to compete. We have the best training and development resources and an environment committed to providing opportunities for personal and professional growth."[1]

Creating a new attitude requires a shift from an internal focus to an external focus:

"What determines your destiny is not the hand you're dealt, it's how you play your hand. The best way to play your hand is to face reality—see the world as it is and act accordingly. . . For me, the idea is: to shun the incremental and go for the leap. Most bureaucracies—

and ours is no exception—unfortunately still think in incremental terms rather than in terms of fundamental change. They think incrementally because they think internally. Changing the culture—opening it up to quantum change—means constantly asking, not how fast am I going, how well am I doing versus how well I did a year or two before, but rather, how fast and how well am I doing versus the world outside."[2]

Critical to building a new culture and changing the "old ways" of GE was not just the bureaucracy itself, but the habits and attitudes that had been engendered by bureaucracy:

"The walls within a big, century-old company don't come down like Jericho's when management makes some organizational changes or gives a speech. There are too many persistent habits propping them up. Parochialism, turf battles, status, "functionalities" and, most important, the biggest sin of a bureaucracy, the focus on itself and its inner workings, are always in the background."[3]

The Work-Out Program—a Generic View

GE's Work-Out Program was a response to the desire to speed the process of organizational change in GE. Welch conceived the idea of Work-Out in September 1988. Welch conducted a session at every class of GE managers attending Management Development Institute at Crotonville, New York. He was impressed by the energy, enthusiasm, and flow of ideas that his open discussion sessions with managers were capable of generating. At the same time, he was frustrated by the resilience of many of GE's bureaucratic practices and the difficulty of transferring the ideas that individual managers possessed into action. After a particularly lively session at Crotonville, Welch and GE's education director, James Braughman, got together to discuss how the interaction in these seminars could be replicated throughout the company in a process that would involve all employees and would generate far-reaching changes within GE. In the course of a helicopter ride from Crotonville to GE's Fairfield headquarters, Welch and Braughman sketched the concept and the framework for the Work-Out process.

A model for GE's Work-Out was a traditional New England town hall meeting where citizens gather to vent their problems, frustrations, and ideas, and people eventually agree on certain civic actions. Welch outlined the goals of Work-Out as follows:

"Work-Out has a practical and an intellectual goal. The practical objective is to get rid of thousands of bad habits accumulated since the creation of General Electric. . . The second thing we want to achieve, the intellectual part, begins by putting the leaders of each business in front of 100 or so of their people, eight to ten times a year, to let them hear what their people think. Work-Out will expose the leaders to the vibrations of their business opinions, feelings, emotions, resentments, not abstract theories of organization and management."[4]

A generic summary of the Work-Out Program reveals three interrelated purposes: to fuel a process of continuous improvement and change; to foster cultural transformation characterized by trust, empowerment, elimination of unnecessary work, and a boundaryless organization; and to improve business performance.

The Structure of the Work-Out Process

The central idea of the Work-Out process was to create a forum where a cross-section of employees in each business could speak their minds about how their business was managed without fear of retribution. Because those doing the work were often the best people to recommend improvements in how their work should be managed, such interaction was seen as a first step in taking actions to remove unnecessary work and improve business processes. In January 1989, Welch announced Work-Out at an annual meeting of GE's 500 top executives. A broad framework was set out, but considerable flexibility was given to each of GE's 14 core businesses in how they went about the program. The key elements of Work-Out were

- *Off-site meetings.* Work-Out was held as a forum and to get away from the company environment. Two-to-three-day Work-Out events were held off-site.
- *Focus on issues and key processes.* There was a strong bias toward action-oriented sessions. The initial Work-Out events tended to focus on removing unnecessary work. This is what Braughman referred to as the "low-hanging fruit." As the programs developed, Work-Out focused more on more complex business processes. For example, in GE Lighting, groupwide sessions were held to accelerate new product development, improve fill rates, and increase integration between component production and assembly. In plastics

the priorities were quality improvement, lower cycle times, and increased cross-functional coordination.

- *Cross-sectional participation.* Work-Out sessions normally involved between 50 and 100 employees drawn from all levels and all functions of a business. Critical to the process was the presence of the top management of the particular business.
- *Small groups and town meetings.* Work-Out events normally involved a series of small group meetings that began with a brainstorming session followed by a plenary session (or "town meeting") in which the suggestions developed by the small groups were put to senior managers and then openly debated. At the end of each discussion, the leader was required to make an immediate decision: to adopt, reject, or defer for further study.
- *Follow-up.* A critical element of Work-Out was a follow-up process to ensure that what had been decided was implemented.

The Results of Work-Out

The results from Work-Out were remarkable. During its first 4 years, more than 3,000 Work-Out sessions had been conducted in GE, resulting in thousands of small changes eliminating "junk work" as well as much more complex and further-reaching changes in organizational structure and management processes. The terms *rattlers* and *pythons* were introduced to describe the two types of problem. Rattlers were simple problems that could be "shot" on sight. Pythons were more complex issues that needed unraveling.

As well as tangible structural changes and performance gains, some of the most important effects were changes in organizational culture. In GE Capital, one of the most centralized and bureaucratized of GE's businesses, one employee described the changes as follows: "we've been suppressed around here for a long time. Now that management is finally listening to us, it feels like the Berlin Wall is coming down.[5]

In 5 years, more than 300,000 employees, customers, and suppliers went through Work-Out sessions. A large variety of impressive and significant performance and efficiency improvements are reported in GE's internal documents, following introduction of the Work-Out processes. For example, the Gas Engine Turbines business unit at Albany, New York, reported an 80 percent decrease in production time to build gas engine turbines; Aircraft Engines at Lynn, Massachusetts, reduced jet engine production time from 30 to 4 weeks. GE's Financial Services Operation reported a reduction in operating costs from $5.10 to $4.55 per invoice, invoices paid per employee were up 34 percent, costs per employee paid fell 19 percent, and employees paid per payroll worker rose 32 percent. The Aerospace plant at Syracuse, New York, reported that as a result of the Work-Out Program, beyond achieving 100 percent compliance with pollution regulations, the production of hazardous waste materials was reduced from 759 tons in 1990 to 275 tons in 1992.

Managing Work-Out

Work-Out was intended as a bottom-up process in which (1) employees throughout each business would be free to challenge their leaders and (2) management's role was primarily to perpetuate the program and to ensure that decisions, once made, were implemented. But Work-Out could not be just a populist movement within the corporation. It needed to be directed toward creating the kind of corporation that GE needed to be to survive and prosper in the 1990s. To this extent Jack Welch saw his role as communicating and disseminating the principles, values, and themes that would permit GE's continued success.

In 1989 Welch crystallized his ideas about GE's management around three themes: speed, simplicity, and self-confidence:

"We found in the 1980s that becoming faster is tied to becoming simpler. Our businesses, with tens of thousands of employees, will not respond to visions that have sub-paragraphs and foot-notes. If we're not simple we can't be fast . . . and if we're not fast, we can't win.

Simplicity, to an engineer, means clean, functional, winning designs, no bells and whistles. In marketing it might manifest itself as clear, unencumbered proposals. For manufacturing people it would produce a logical process that makes sense to every individual on the line. And on an individual, interpersonal level it would take the form of plain speaking, directness, honesty.

But as surely as speed flows from simplicity, simplicity is grounded in self-confidence. Self-confidence does not grow in someone who is just another appendage on the bureaucracy; whose authority rests on little more than a title. People who are freed from the confines of their box on the organization chart, whose status rests on real world achievement—those are the people who develop the self-confidence to be simple, to share every bit of information available to them, to listen to those above, below and around them and then move boldly.

But a company cannot distribute self-confidence. What it can do—what we must do—is to give our people an opportunity to win, to contribute, and hence earn self-confidence themselves. They don't get that opportunity, they can't taste winning if they spend their days wandering in the muck of a self-absorbed bureaucracy.

Speed . . . simplicity . . . self-confidence. We have it in increasing measure. We know where it comes from . . . and we have plans to increase it in the 1990s.[6]

Best Practices

One of the Work-Out Program's many impressive outcomes is that it's a catalyst for new improvement programs. One such program, Best Practices, is aimed at increasing productivity. The GE business-development staff focused on 24 credible companies from an initial pool of 200 that had achieved faster productivity growth than GE and sustained it for at least 10 years. From this list, one dozen companies agreed to take part in GE's proposal to send its employees to their companies to learn their secrets to success. In exchange, GE offered to share the results of the study as well success stories with the participating companies. This learning for the Best Practices program involved companies such as Ford, Hewlett-Packard, Xerox, and Chaparral Steel plus three Japanese firms.

GE was less concerned with the actual work done at the companies than with management practices and attitudes of the employees. The difference between Best Practices and traditional benchmarking is that the former does not require keeping score. The focus on learning alternative successful management practices and managing processes was identified as the most critical component for long-term productivity improvements. The basic assumption that through multiple exposure to alternative management practices, managers and employees will be stimulated to continuously improve their own practices, continues to guide the program. Best Practices has evolved into a formal course taught to at least one dozen employees and managers per month in each business unit.

Questions

1. Based on the information presented, describe the overall planned change approach and phases led by Jack Welch.

2. Identify and briefly describe the major characteristics of the Work-Out Program.

3. Discuss how the organizational culture changed. What caused the change? What effects did the culture change have on human behavior and organizational performance and effectiveness?

Source: This case was written by R. Grant and A. B. (Rami) Shani for classroom use. The case draws heavily on the following sources: N. M. Tichy and S. Sherman, *Control Your Destiny or Someone Else Will* (New York: Doubleday, 1992); R. Slater, *The New GE: How Jack Welch Revived an American Institution* (Burr Ridge, IL: Irwin, 1993); R. N. Ashkenas and T. D. Jick, "From Dialogue to Action in GE Work-Out," in W. A. Pasmore and R. Woodman (eds.), *Research in Organization Change and Development,* vol. 6. (Greenwich. CT: JAI Press, 1993), pp. 267–87; "Jack Welch's Lessons for Success," *Fortune,* February 25, 1993, pp. 86–90.

Case Incidents

Robot repercussion

Victor Principal, vice president of industrial relations for General Manufacturing, Inc., sat in his office reviewing the list of benefits the company expected to realize from increasing its use of industrial robots. In a few minutes, he would walk down to the labor-management conference room for a meeting with Ralph McIntosh, president of the labor union local representing most of the company's industrial employees. The purpose of this meeting would be to informally exchange views and positions preliminary to the opening for formal contract negotiations later in the month, which would focus on the use of computer-integrated robotics systems and the resulting impact on employment, workers, and jobs.

Both Principal and McIntosh had access to similar information flows relevant to industrial robots, including the following. Unlike single-task machines, installed in earlier stages of automation, robots can be programmed to do one job and then reprogrammed to do another one. The pioneering generation of robots is mainly programmed to load machines, weld, forge, spray paint, handle materials, and inspect auto bodies. The latest generation of robots includes vision-controlled robots, which enable the machines to approximate the human ability to recognize and size up objects by using laser-beam patterns recorded by television cameras and transmitted to "smart" computers. The computer software interprets and manipulates the images relayed by the camera in a "smart" or artificially intelligent way.

Experts concluded that the impact of robot installation on employment would be profound, although the extent of the worker replacement was not clear. The inescapable conclusion was that robot usage had the capacity to increase manufacturing performance and to decrease manufacturing employment.

Principal walked down to the conference room. Finding McIntosh already there, Principal stated the company's position regarding installation of industrial robots: "The company needs the cooperation of the union and our workers. We don't wish to be perceived as callously exchanging human workers for robots." Then Principal listed the major advantages associated with robots: (1) improved quality of product as a result of the accuracy of robots; (2) reduced operating costs, as the per-hour operational cost of robots was about one-third of the per-hour cost of wages and benefits paid to an average employee; (3) reliability improvements, as robots work tirelessly and don't require behavioral support; and (4) greater manufacturing flexibility, because robots are readily reprogrammable for different jobs. Principal concluded that these advantages would make the company more competitive, which would allow it to grow and increase its workforce.

McIntosh's response was direct and strong: "We aren't Luddites racing around ruining machines. We know it's necessary to increase productivity and that robotic technology is here. But we can't give the company a blank check. We need safeguards and protection." McIntosh continued, "We intend to bargain for the following contract provisions:

1. Establishment of labor–management committees to negotiate *in advance* about the labor impact of robotics technology and, of equal importance, to have a voice in deciding how and whether it should be used.
2. Rights to advance notice about installation of new technology.
3. Retraining rights for workers displaced, to include retraining for new positions in the plant, the community, or other company plants.
4. Spreading the work among workers by use of a four-day workweek or other acceptable plan as an alternative to reducing the workforce.

McIntosh's final sentence summed up the union's position: "We in the union believe the company is giving our jobs to robots to reduce the labor force."

Their meeting ended amiably, but Principal and McIntosh each knew that much hard bargaining lay ahead. As Principal returned to his office, the two opposing positions were obvious. On his yellow tablet, Principal listed the requirements as he saw them: (1) A clearly stated overall policy was needed to guide negotiation decisions and actions; (2) it was critical to decide on a company position regarding each of the union's announced demands and concerns; and (3) a plan must be developed.

As Principal considered these challenges, he idly contemplated a robot possessing artificial intelligence and vision capability that could help him in his work. Immediately a danger alarm sounded in his mind. A robot so constructed might be more than helpful and might take over this and other important aspects of his job. Slightly chagrined, Principal returned to his task. He needed help—but not from any "smart" robot.

Source: J. Champion and J. James, *Critical Incidents in Management: Decision and Policy Issues,* 6th ed. (Burr Ridge, Ill.: Richard D. Irwin, 1989). ●

Implementing strategic change

James Fulmer, chief executive officer of Allied Industries, reviewed three notes he had exchanged with Frank Curtis, director of fiscal affairs, now president of a company owned by Allied. The two executives were going to meet in a few minutes to discuss problems that had recently surfaced. During the past decade, Allied had aggressively pursued a growth objective based on a conglomerate strategy of acquiring companies in distress. CEO Fulmer's policy was to appoint a new chief operating officer for each acquisition with instructions to facilitate a turnaround. Fulmer reviewed two of the notes he had written to Curtis.

Date: January 15, 2000.

Memorandum

To: Frank Curtis, Director of Fiscal Affairs, Allied Industries

From: James Fulmer, Chairman, Allied Industries

Subject: Your Appointment as President, Lee Medical Supplies

You are aware that Allied Industries recently acquired Lee Medical Supplies. Mr. John Lee, founder and president of the company, has agreed to retire, and I am appointing you to replace him. Our acquisitions group will brief you on the company, but I want to warn you that Lee Medical Supplies has a history of mismanagement. As a distributor of medical items, the company's sales last year totaled approximately $300 million, with net earnings of only $12 million. Your job is to make company sales and profits compatible with Allied standards. You are reminded that it is my policy to call for an independent evaluation of company progress and your performance as president after 18 months.

Date: September 10, 2001.

Memorandum

To: Frank Curtis, President, Lee Medical Supplies

From: James Fulmer, Chairman, Allied Industries

Subject: Serious Problems at Lee Medical Supplies

In accord with corporate policy, consultants recently conducted an evaluation of Lee Medical Supplies. In a relatively short period of time, you have increased sales and profits to meet Allied's standards, but I am alarmed at other aspects of your performance. I am told that during the past 18 months, three of your nine vice presidents have resigned and that you have terminated four others. An opinion survey conducted by the consultants indicates that a low state of morale exists and that your managerial appointees are regarded by their subordinates as hard-nosed perfectionists obsessed with quotas and profits. Employees report that ruthless competition now exists between divisions, regions, and districts. They also note that the collegial, family-oriented atmosphere fostered by Mr. Lee has been replaced by a dog-eat-dog situation characterized by negative management attitudes toward employee feelings and needs. After you have studied the enclosed report from the consultants, we will meet to discuss their findings. I am particularly concerned with their final conclusion that "a form of corporate cancer seems to be spreading throughout Lee Medical Supplies."

As Fulmer prepared to read the third note, written by Frank Curtis, he reflected on his interview with the consultants. While Fulmer considered Curtis a financial expert and a turnaround specialist, his subordinates characterized Curtis as an autocrat and better suited to be a Marine boot camp commander.

Date: September 28, 2001.

Memorandum

To: James Fulmer

From: Frank Curtis

Subject: The So-Called Serious Problems at Lee Medical Supplies

I have received your memorandum dated September 10, and reviewed the consultants' report. When you appointed me to my present position I was instructed to take over an unprofitable company and make it profitable. I have done so in 18 months, although I inherited a family-owned business that by your own admission had been mismanaged for years. I found a group of managers and salespeople with an average company tenure of 22 years. Mr. Lee had centralized all personnel decisions so that only he could terminate an employee. He tolerated mediocre performance. All employees were paid on a straight salary basis, with seniority the sole criterion for advancement. Some emphasis was given to increasing sales each year, but none was given to reducing costs and increasing profits. Employees did indeed find the company a fun place to work, and the feeling of being a part of a family did permeate the company. Such attitudes were, however, accompanied by mediocrity, incompetence, and poor performance.

I found it necessary to implement immediate strategic changes in five areas: the organization's structure, employee rewards and incentives, management information systems, allocation of resources, and managerial leadership style. As a result, sales areas were reorganized into divisions, regions, and districts. Managers who I felt were incompetent and/or lacking in commitment to my objectives and methods were replaced. Unproductive and mediocre employees were encouraged to find jobs elsewhere. Authority for staffing and compensation decisions was decentralized to units at the division, region, and district levels. Managers of those units were informed that along with their authority went responsibility for reducing costs and for increasing sales and profits. Each unit was established as a profit center. A new department was established and charged with reviewing performance of those units. Improved accounting and control systems were implemented. A management-by-objectives program was developed to establish standards and monitor performance. Performance appraisals are now required for all employees. To encourage more aggressive action, bonuses and incentives are offered to managers of units showing increased profits. A commission plan based on measurable sales and profit performances has replaced straight salaries. Resources are allocated to units based on their performance.

My own leadership style has probably represented the most traumatic change for employees. Internal competition is a formally mandated policy throughout the company. It has been responsible for much of the progress achieved to date. Progress, however, is never made without costs, and I recognize that employees are not having as much fun as in the past. I was employed to achieve results and not to ensure that employees remain secure and happy in their work. Don't let a few crybabies unable to adjust to changes lead you to believe that problems take precedence over profits. Does it mean that I am not people oriented if I believe it is unlikely that a spirit of aggressiveness and competitiveness can coexist with an atmosphere of cooperativeness and family orientation? Do you feel that we are obligated to employees because of past practices? Frankly, I thought I had your support to do whatever was necessary to get this company turned around. In our meeting, tell me if you think my approaches have been wrong and, if so, tell me what I should have done differently.

Just as Fulmer finished reviewing the third memorandum, his secretary informed him that Curtis had arrived for their scheduled meeting. He realized he was undecided about how to communicate to Curtis his ideas and beliefs regarding how changes in an organization can best be implemented. One thing he did know: He didn't appreciate how Curtis had expressed his views in his memorandum, but he recognized that he probably should set aside emotions and respond to the questions Curtis posed.

Source: J. Champion and J. James, *Critical Incidents in Management: Decision and Policy Issues,* 6th ed. (Burr Ridge, Ill.: Richard D. Irwin, 1989).   ●

Glossary

A

accommodation A style of dealing with conflict involving cooperation on behalf of the other party but not being assertive about one's own interests.

accountability The expectation that employees perform a job, take corrective action when necessary, and report upward on the status and quality of their performance.

accounting audits Procedures used to verify accounting reports and statements.

activity-based costing (ABC) A method of cost accounting designed to identify streams of activity, and then to allocate costs across particular business processes according to the amount of time employees devote to particular activities.

adapters Companies that take the current industry structure, and its future evolution, as givens.

affective conflict Emotional disagreement directed toward other people.

arbitration The use of a neutral third party to resolve a labor dispute.

assessment center A managerial performance test in which candidates participate in a variety of exercises and situations.

assets The values of the various items the corporation owns.

authority The legitimate right to make decisions and to tell other people what to do.

autocratic leadership A form of leadership in which the leader makes decisions on his or her own and then announces those decisions to the group.

autonomous work groups Groups that control decisions about and execution of a complete range of tasks.

avoidance A reaction to conflict that involves either ignoring the problem by doing nothing at all, or by deemphasizing the disagreement.

B

balance sheet A report that shows the financial picture of a company at a given time and itemizes assets, liabilities, and stockholders' equity.

barriers to entry Conditions that prevent new companies from entering an industry.

behavioral approach A leadership perspective that attempts to identify what good leaders do—that is, what behaviors they exhibit.

benchmarking The process of comparing the organization's practices and technologies with those of other companies.

bootlegging Informal efforts by managers and employees to create new products and new processes.

boundaryless organization Organization in which there are no barriers to information flow.

bounded rationality A less-than-perfect form of rationality in which decision makers cannot conduct a complete, rational analysis because decisions are complex and complete information is unavailable.

brainstorming A process in which group members generate as many ideas about a problem as they can; criticism is withheld until all ideas have been proposed.

broker Persons who assemble and coordinate participants in a network.

budgeting The process of investigating what is being done and comparing the results with the corresponding budget data to verify accomplishments or remedy differences. Also called budgetary controlling.

buffering Creating supplies of excess resources in case of unpredictable needs.

bureaucratic control The use of rules, regulations, and authority to guide performance.

business ethics The moral principles and standards that guide behavior in the world of business.

business incubators Protected environments for new, small businesses.

business judgment rule allows management wide latitude in policy if the policy can be justified.

business plan A formal planning step in starting a new business that focuses on the entire venture and describes all the elements involved in starting it.

business strategy The major actions by which a business competes in a particular industry or market.

C

cafeteria benefit program Employee benefit program in which employees choose from a menu of options to create a benefit package tailored to their needs.

centralized organization An organization in which high-level executives make most decisions and pass them down to lower levels for implementation.

certainty The state that exists when decision makers have accurate and comprehensive information.

charismatic leader A person who is dominant, self-confident, convinced of the moral righteousness of his or her beliefs, and able to arouse a sense of excitement and adventure in subordinates.

chief technology officer (CTO) Executive in charge of technology strategy and development.

clan control Control based on the norms, values, shared goals, and trust among group members.

coaching Dialogue with a goal of helping another be more effective and achieve his or her full potential on the job.

coalition building Finding other organizations or groups of voters that share political interests on a particular legislative issue.

coalitional model Model of organizational decision making in which groups with differing preferences use power and negotiations to influence decisions.

cognitive conflict Issue-based differences in perspectives or judgments.

cohesiveness The degree to which a group is attractive to its members, members are motivated to remain in the group, and members influence one another.

collaboration A style of dealing with conflict involving emphasizing both cooperation and assertiveness in order to maximize both parties' satisfaction.

communication The transmission of information and meaning from one party to another through the use of shared symbols.

comparable worth Principle of equal pay for different jobs of equal worth.

competitive environment The immediate environment surrounding a firm;

includes suppliers, customers, competitors, and the like.

competitive intelligence   Information that helps managers determine how to compete better.

compliance-based ethics programs   Company mechanisms typically designed by corporate counsel to prevent, detect, and punish legal violations.

compromise   A style of dealing with conflict involving moderate attention to both parties' concerns.

computer-integrated manufacturing   The use of computer-aided design and computer-aided manufacturing to sequence and optimize a number of production processes.

concentration   A strategy employed for an organization that operates a single business and competes in a single industry.

concentric diversification   A strategy used to add new businesses that produce related products or are involved in related markets and activities.

conceptual and decision skills   Skills pertaining to a manager's ability to recognize complex and dynamic issues, examine the numerous and conflicting factors such issues involve, and resolve the problems for the benefit of the organization and its members.

concurrent control   The control process used while plans are being carried out, including directing, monitoring, and fine-tuning activities as they are performed.

conflict   Opposing pressures from different sources. Two levels of conflict are psychological conflict and conflict that arises among individuals or groups.

conglomerate diversification   A strategy used to add new businesses that produce unrelated products or are involved in unrelated markets and activities.

contingency plans   Alternative courses of action that can be implemented based on how the future unfolds.

continuous process   A process that is highly automated and has a continuous production flow.

control   The process of measuring progress toward planned performance and applying corrective measures to ensure that performance is in line with managers' objectives.

controlling   The management function of monitoring progress and making needed changes.

cooperative strategies   Strategies used by two or more organizations working together to manage the external environment.

coordination   The procedures that link the various parts of the organization for the purpose of achieving the organization's overall mission.

coordination by mutual adjustment   Units interact with one another to make accommodations so as to achieve flexible coordination.

coordination by plan   Interdependent units are required to meet deadlines and objectives that contribute to a common goal.

core competencies   The unique skills or knowledge an organization possesses that give it an edge over competitors.

corporate constituency programs   Organizational efforts to identify, educate, and motivate individuals to take political action that could benefit the organization.

corporate legitimacy   A motive for organizational involvement in the public policy process. The assumption is that organizations are legitimate to the extent that their goals, purposes, and methods are consistent with those of society.

corporate social responsibility   Obligation toward society assumed by business.

corporate social responsiveness   The process companies follow and the actions they take in the domain of corporate social responsibility.

corporate strategy   The set of businesses, markets, or industries in which an organization competes and the distribution of resources among those entities.

cost competitiveness   Keeping costs low in order to achieve profits and prices that are attractive to consumers.

culture shock   The disorientation and stress associated with being in a foreign environment.

current ratio   A liquidity ratio which indicates the extent to which short-term assets can decline and still be adequate to pay short-term liabilities.

customer service   The speed and dependability with which an organization can deliver what customers want.

custom-made solutions   The combination of ideas into new, creative solutions.

D

debt-equity ratio   A leverage ratio which indicates the company's ability to meet its long-term financial obligations.

decentralized organization   An organization in which lower-level managers make important decisions.

defenders   Companies that stay within a stable product domain as a strategic maneuver.

delegation   The assignment of new or additional responsibilities to a subordinate.

democratic leadership   A form of leadership in which the leader solicits input from subordinates.

demographics   Measures of various characteristics of the people who comprise groups of other social units.

deontology   focuses on rights of individuals.

departmentalization   Subdividing an organization into smaller subunits.

design for environment (DFE)   A tool for creating products that are easy to recover, reuse, or recycle.

development   Teaching managers and professional employees broad skills needed for their present and future jobs.

development project   A focused organizational effort to create a new product or process via technological advances.

devil's advocate   A person who has the job of criticizing ideas to ensure that different viewpoints are fully explored.

dialectic   A structured debate comparing two conflicting courses of action.

dialogue   A discourse in which members explore complex issues from many viewpoints in order to come to a common, deeper understanding.

differentiation   An aspect of the organization's internal environment created by job specialization and the division of labor.

differentiation strategy   A strategy an organization uses to build competitive advantage by being unique in its industry or market segment along one or more dimensions.

discount the future   A bias weighting short-term costs and benefits more heavily than longer-term costs and benefits.

discussion   A type of discourse in which each person attempts to win a debate by having his or her view accepted by the group.

diversity training   Programs that focus on identifying and reducing hidden biases against people with differences and developing the skills needed to effectively manage a diversified workforce.

division of labor   The assignment of different tasks to different people or groups.

divisional organization   Departmentalization that groups units around products, customers, or geographic regions.

domain defense   Activities intended to counter challenges to the organization's legitimacy.

downsizing   The planned elimination of positions or jobs.

downward communication   Information that flows from higher to lower levels in the organization's hierarchy.

dynamic network   Temporary arrangements among partners that can be assembled and reassembled to adapt to the environment.

E

ecocentric management   has as its goal the creation of sustainable economic development and improvement of quality of life worldwide for all organizational stakeholders.

economic responsibilities   are to produce goods and services that society wants at a price that perpetuates the business and satisfies its obligations to investors.

economies of scope   Economies in which materials and processes employed in one product can be used to make other, related products.

egoism   An ethical system defining acceptable behavior as that which maximizes consequences for the individual.

Emergent strategy   The strategy that evolves from all the activities engaged in by people throughout the organization.

empowerment   The process of sharing power with employees, thereby enhancing their confidence in their ability to perform their jobs and their belief that they are influential contributors to the organization.

entrepreneurial orientation   The tendency of an organization to engage in activities designed to identify and capitalize successfully on opportunities to launch new ventures by entering new or established markets with new or existing goods or services.

entrepreneurial venture   A new business having growth and high profitability as primary objectives.

entrepreneurship   The pursuit of lucrative opportunities by enterprising individuals.

environmental scanning   Searching for and sorting through information about the environment.

environmental uncertainty   Lack of information needed to understand or predict the future.

equity theory   A theory stating that people assess how fairly they have been treated according to key factors: outcomes and inputs.

ERG theory   A human needs theory developed by Alderfer postulating that people have three basic sets of needs which can operate simultaneously.

ethical climate   of an organization refers to the processes by which decisions are evaluated and made on the basis of right and wrong.

ethical issue   Situation, problem, or opportunity in which an individual must choose among several actions that must be evaluated as right or wrong.

ethical responsibilities   Meeting other social expectations, not written as law.

ethics   The system of rules governing the ordering of values.

executive champion   An executive who supports a new technology and protects the product champion of the innovation.

expatriates   Parent-company nationals who are sent to work at a foreign subsidiary.

expectancy   Employees' perception of the likelihood that their efforts will enable them to attain their performance goals.

expectancy theory   A theory proposing that people will behave based on their perceived likelihood that their effort will lead to a certain outcome and on how highly they value that outcome.

external audit   An evaluation conducted by one organization, such as a CPA firm, on another.

external environment   All relevant forces outside a firm's boundaries, such as competitors, customers, the government, and the economy.

extinction   Withdrawing or failing to provide a reinforcing consequence.

extrinsic reinforcers   Reinforces given to a person by the boss, the company, or some other person.

F

failure rate   The number of expatriate managers of an overseas operation that come home early.

feedback control   Control that focuses on the use of information about previous results to correct deviations from the acceptable standard.

feedforward control   The control process used before operations begin, including policies, procedures, and rules designed to ensure that planned activities are carried out properly.

filtering   The process of withholding, ignoring, or distorting information.

final consumer   Those who purchase products in their finished form.

flexible benefit programs   Benefit programs in which employees are given credits to spend on benefits that fit their unique needs.

flexible factories   Manufacturing plants that have short production runs, are organized around products, and use decentralized scheduling.

flexible processes   Methods for adapting the technical core to changes in the environment.

forcing   A style of dealing with conflict involving competitiveness, strong focus on one's own goals, and little or no concern for the other person's goals.

forecasting   Method for predicting how variables will change the future.

framing effects   A psychological bias influenced by the way in which a problem or decision alternative is phrased or presented.

frontline managers Lower-level managers who supervise the operational activities of the organization.

functional organization Departmentalization around specialized activities, such as production, marketing, human resources, etc.

functional strategies Strategies implemented by each functional area of the organization to support the organization's business strategy.

G

garbage can model Model of organizational decision making depicting a chaotic process and seemingly random decisions.

genius of the "and" The ability to pursue multiple goals at once.

glass ceiling An invisible barrier that makes it difficult for certain groups, such as minorities and women, to move beyond a certain level in the organizational hierarchy

global organization model An organization model consisting of a company's overseas subsidiaries and characterized by centralized decisionmaking and tight control by the parent company over most aspects of worldwide operations. Typically adopted by organizations that base their global competitive strategy on low cost.

global start-up A new venture that is international from the very beginning.

goal A target or end that management desires to reach.

goal displacement A condition that occurs when a decision-making group loses sight of its original goal and a new, possibly less important, goal emerges.

goal-setting theory A motivation theory that states people have conscious goals that energize them and direct their thoughts and behaviors toward one end.

grapevine Informal communication network.

group maintenance behaviors Actions taken to ensure the satisfaction of group members, develop and maintain harmonious work relationships, and preserve the social stability of the group.

groupthink A phenomenon that occurs in decision making when group members avoid disagreement as they strive for consensus.

growth need strength The degree to which individuals want personal and psychological development.

H

hierarchy The authority levels of the organizational pyramid.

high-involvement organization A type of organization in which top management ensures that there is consensus about the direction in which the business is heading.

horizontal communication Information shared among people on the same hierarchical level.

host-country nationals Natives of the country where an overseas subsidiary is located.

human capital The knowledge, skills, and abilities of employees that have economic value.

human resources management (HRM) Formal systems for the management of people within the organization. Divided into three major areas: staffing, rewarding, and designing work.

hygiene factors Characteristics of the workplace, such as company policies, working conditions, pay, and supervision, that can make people dissatisfied.

I

illusion of control People's belief that they can influence events, even when they have no control over what will happen.

incremental model Model of organizational decision making in which major solutions arise through a series of smaller decisions.

independent entrepreneur An individual who establishes a new organization without the benefit of corporate sponsorship.

independent strategies Strategies that an organization acting on its own uses to change some aspect of its current environment.

informing A team strategy that entails concentrating first on the internal team process to achieve a state of performance readiness, then informing outsiders of its intentions.

innovation A change in technology; a departure from previous ways of doing things. Also, introduction of new products.

instrumentality The perceived likelihood that performance will be followed by a particular outcome.

integration The degree to which differentiated work units work together and coordinate their efforts.

integrity-based ethics programs Company mechanisms designed to instill in people a personal responsibility for ethical behavior.

intermediate consumer Customers who purchase raw materials or wholesale products before selling them to final customers.

internal audit A periodic assessment of a company's own planning, organizing, leading, and controlling processes.

international organization model An organization model that is composed of a company's overseas subsidiaries and characterized by greater control by the parent company over the research function and local product and marketing strategies than is the case in the multinational model.

interpersonal and communication skills People skills; the ability to lead, motivate, and communicate effectively with others.

intrapreneurs New venture creators working in big corporations.

intrinsic reward Reward a worker derives directly from performing the job itself.

ISO 9000 A series of quality standards developed by a committee working under the International Organization for Standardization to improve total quality in all businesses for the benefit of both producers and consumers.

J

job analysis A tool for determining what is done on a given job and what should be done on that job.

job enlargement Giving people additional tasks at the same time to alleviate boredom.

job enrichment Changing a task to make it inherently more rewarding, motivating, and satisfying.

job rotation Changing from one routine task to another to alleviate boredom.

just-in-time (JIT) A system that calls for subassemblies and components to be manufactured in very small lots and delivered to the next stage of the production process just as they are needed.

K

Kohlberg's model of cognitive moral development classifies people into one of three categories based on their level of moral judgment.

L

labor relations The system of relations between workers and management.

laissez-faire A leadership philosophy characterized by an absence of managerial decision making.

large batch Technologies that produce goods and services in high volume.

law of effect A theory formulated by Edward Thorndike in 1911 stating that behavior that is followed by positive consequences will likely be repeated.

Leader-Member Exchange (LMX) theory Highlights the importance of leader behaviors not just toward the group as a whole but toward individuals on a personal basis.

leading The management function that involves the manager's efforts to stimulate high performance by employees.

lean manufacturing An operation that strives to achieve the highest possible productivity and total quality, cost effectively, by eliminating unnecessary steps in the production process and continually strives for improvement.

learning organization An organization skilled at creating, acquiring, and transferring knowledge, and at modifying its behavior to reflect new knowledge and insights.

legal responsibilities To obey local, state, federal, and relevant international laws.

liabilities The amounts a corporation owes to various creditors.

line departments Units that deal directly with the organization's primary goods and services.

logistics The movement of the right goods in the right amount to the right place at the right time.

low-cost strategy A strategy an organization uses to build competitive advantage by being efficient and offering a standard, no-frills product.

M

macroenvironment The most general environment; includes governments, economic conditions, and other fundamental factors that generally affect all organizations.

make-or-buy decision The question an organization asks itself about whether to acquire new technology from an outside source or develop it itself.

management audits An evaluation of the effectiveness and efficiency of various systems within an organization.

management by objectives (MBO) A process in which objectives set by a subordinate and supervisor must be reached within a given time period.

management myopia Focusing on short-term earnings and profits at the expense of longer-term strategic obligations.

Management teams Teams that coordinate and provide direction to the subunits under their jurisdiction and integrate work among subunits.

management The process of working with people and resources to accomplish organizational goals.

managing diversity Managing a culturally diverse workforce by recognizing the characteristics common to specific groups of employees while dealing with such employees as individuals and supporting, nurturing, and utilizing their differences to the organization's advantage.

market control Control based on the use of financial and economic information.

mass customization The production of varied, individually customized products at the low cost of standardized, mass-produced products.

matrix organization An organization composed of dual reporting relationships in which some managers report to two superiors—a functional manager and a product manager.

maximize A decision realizing the best possible outcome.

mechanistic organization A form of organization that seeks to maximize internal efficiency.

media richness The degree to which a communication channel conveys information.

mentors Higher level managers who help ensure that high-potential people are introduced to top management and socialized into the norms and values of the organization.

middle-level managers Managers located in the middle layers of the organizational hierarchy, reporting to top-level executives.

mission An organization's basic purpose and scope of operations.

monolithic organization An organization that has a low degree of structural integration—employing few women, minorities, or other groups that differ from the majority—and thus has a highly homogeneous employee population.

moral philosophy Principles, rules, and values people use in deciding what is right or wrong.

motivation Forces that energize, direct, and sustain a person's efforts.

motivators Factors that make a job more motivating, such as additional job responsibilities, opportunities for personal growth and recognition, and feelings of achievement.

moving Instituting the change.

multicultural organization An organization that values cultural diversity and seeks to utilize and encourage it.

multinational organization model An organization model that consists of the subsidiaries in each country in which a company does business, with ultimate control exercised by the parent company.

N

need hierarchy A conception of human needs organizing needs into five major types, and postulating that people satisfy them one at a time from bottom to top.

needs assessment   An analysis identifying the jobs, people, and departments for which training is necessary.

negative reinforcement   Removing or withholding an undersirable consequence.

network organization   A collection of independent, mostly single-function firms.

nonprogrammed decisions   New, novel, complex decisions having no proven answers.

norms   Shared beliefs about how people should think and behave.

North American Free Trade Agreement (NAFTA)   An economic pact that combined the economies of the United States, Canada, and Mexico into the world's largest trading block.

O

one-way communication   A process in which information flows in only one direction—from the sender to the receiver, with no feedback loop.

open-book management   Practice of sharing with employees at all levels of the organization vital information previously meant for management's eyes only.

operational planning   The process of identifying the specific procedures and processes required at lower levels of the organization.

opportunity analysis   A description of the product or service, an assessment of the opportunity, an assessment of the entrepreneur, specification of activities and resources needed to translate your idea into a viable business, and your source(s) of capital.

optimizing   Achieving the best possible balance among several goals.

organic structure   An organizational form that emphasizes flexibility.

organization chart   The reporting structure and division of labor in an organization.

organization culture   The set of important assumptions about the organization and its goals and practices that members of the company share.

organizational behavior modification (OB Mod)   The application of reinforcement theory in organizational settings.

organizing   The management function of assembling and coordinating human, financial, physical, informational and other resources needed to achieve goals.

orientation training   Training designed to introduce new employees to the company and familiarize them with policies, procedures, culture, and the like.

outcome   A consequence a person receives for his or her performance.

outplacement   The process of helping people who have been dismissed from the company to regain employment elsewhere.

P

parading   A team strategy that entails simultaneously emphasizing internal team building and achieving external visibility.

parallel teams   Teams that operate separately from the regular work structure, and exist temporarily.

participation in decision making   Leader behaviors that managers perform in involving their employees in making decisions.

path-goal theory   A theory that concerns how leaders influence subordinates' perceptions of their work goals and the paths they follow toward attainment of those goals.

perception   The process of receiving and interpreting information.

performance appraisal (PA)   Assessment of an employee's job performance.

performance gap   The difference between actual performance and the desired performance.

planning   The management function of systematically making decisions about the goals and activities that an individual, a group, a work unit, or the overall organization will pursue in the future.

plans   The actions or means that managers intend to use to achieve organizational goals.

plural organization   An organization that has a relatively diverse employee population and makes an effort to involve employees from different gender, racial, or cultural backgrounds.

political action committees (PACs)   Political action groups that represent an organization and make donations to candidates for political office.

positive reinforcement   Applying valued consequences that increase the likelihood that a person will repeat the behavior that led to it.

power   The ability to influence others.

principle of exception   A managerial principle stating that control is enhanced by concentrating on the exceptions or significant deviations from the expected result or standard.

proactive change   A response that is initiated before a performance gap has occurred.

probing   A team strategy that requires team members to interact frequently with outsiders, diagnose their needs, and experiment with solutions.

procedural justice   Using fair process in decision making and making sure others know that the process was as fair as possible.

product champion   A person who promotes a new technology throughout the organization in an effort to obtain acceptance and support for it.

profit and loss statement   An itemized financial statement of the income and expenses of a company's operations.

programmed decisions   Decisions encountered and made before, having objectively correct answers, and solvable by using simple rules, policies, or numerical computations.

project and development teams   Teams that work on long-term projects but disband once the work is completed.

prospectors   Companies that continuously change the boundaries for their task environments by seeking new products and markets, diversifying and merging, or acquiring new enterprises.

psychological contract   A set of perceptions of what employees owe their employers, and what their employers owe them.

public affairs department   A department that monitors key events and trends in the organization's political and social environments, analyzes their effects on the organization, recommends organizational responses, and implements political strategies.

punishment   Administering an aversive consequence.

Q

quality   The excellence of a product, including such things as attractiveness, lack of defects, reliability, and long-term dependability.

quality circles   Voluntary groups of people drawn from various production teams who make suggestions about quality.

quality of work life (QWL) programs   Programs designed to create a workplace that enhances employee well-being.

R

reactive change   A response that occurs when events in the environment have already affected the firm's performance; problem-driven change.

ready-made solutions   Ideas that have been seen or tried before.

recruitment   The development of a pool of applicants for jobs in the organization.

reflection   Process by which a person states what he or she believes the other person is saying.

refreezing   Strengthening the new behaviors that support the change.

reinforcers   Positive consequences that motivate behavior.

relativism   bases ethical behavior on the opinions and behaviors of relevant other people.

reliability   The consistency of test scores over time and across alternative measurements.

resources   Inputs to a system that can enhance performance.

responsibility   The assignment of a task that an employee is supposed to carry out.

return on investment (ROI)   A ratio of profit to capital used, or a rate of return from capital.

right to work   Legislation that allows employees to work without having to join a union.

rightsizing   A successful effort to achieve an appropriate size at which the company performs most effectively.

risk   The state that exists when the probability of success is less than 100 percent.

roles   Different sets of expectations for how different individuals should behave.

S

satisfice   To choose an option that is acceptable, although not necessarily the best or perfect.

scenario   A narrative that describes a particular set of future conditions.

selection   Choosing from among qualified applicants to hire into an organization.

self-designing teams   Teams with control over the design of the team, as well as the responsibilities of autonomous work groups.

self-managed teams   Autonomous work groups in which workers are trained to do all or most of the jobs in a unit, have no immediate supervisor, and make decisions previously made by first-line supervisors.

semiautonomous work groups   Groups that make decisions about managing and carrying out major production activities, but still get outside support for quality control and maintenance.

sexual harassment   Conduct of a sexual nature that has negative consequences for employment.

shapers   Companies that try to change the structure of their industries, creating a future competitive landscape of their own design.

side street effect   As you head down a road, unexpected opportunities begin to appear.

simultaneous engineering   A design approach in which all relevant functions cooperate jointly and continually in a maximum effort aimed at producing high-quality products that meet customers' needs.

situational analysis   A process planners use, within time and resource constraints, to gather, interpret, and summarize all information relevant to the planning issue under consideration.

situational approach   Leadership perspective proposing that universally important traits and behaviors do not exist, and that effective leadership behavior varies from situation to situation.

skunkworks   A project team designated to produce a new, innovative product.

small batches   Technologies that produce goods and services in low volume.

small business   A business having fewer than 100 employees, independently owned and operated, not dominant in its field, and not characterized by many innovative practices.

smoothing   Leveling normal fluctuations at the boundaries of the environment.

social facilitation effect   working harder when in a group than when working alone.

social loafing   working less hard and being less productive when in a group.

sociotechnical systems   An approach to job design that attempts to redesign tasks to optimize operation of a new technology while preserving employees' interpersonal relationships and other human aspects of the work.

span of control   The number of subordinates who report directly to an executive or supervisor.

specialization   A process in which different individuals and units perform different tasks.

speed   Fast and timely execution, response, and delivery of results.

spin-off   A new company started by managers who create independent businesses that split from the parent corporation.

staff departments   Units that support line departments.

stakeholders   Groups and individuals who affect and are affected by the achievement of the organization's mission, goals, and strategies.

standard   Expected performance for a given goal; a target that establishes a desired performance level, motivates performance, and serves as a benchmark against which actual performance is assessed.

standardization   Establishing common rules and procedures that apply uniformly to everyone.

stockholders' equity   The amount accruing to the corporation's owners.

stonewalling   The use of public relations, legal action, and administrative processes to prevent or delay the introduction of legislation and regulation that may have an adverse impact on the organization.

strategic alliance   A formal relationship created among independent organizations with the purpose of joint pursuit of mutual goals.

strategic control system   A system designed to support managers in evaluating the organization's progress regarding its strategy and, when discrepancies exist, taking corrective action.

strategic goals   Major targets or end results relating to the organization's long-term survival, value, and growth.

strategic leadership   Behavior that gives purpose and meaning to organization, emissioning and creating a positive future.

strategic management   A process that involves managers from all parts of the organization in the formulation and implementation of strategic goals and strategies.

strategic maneuvering   The organization's conscious efforts to change the boundaries of its task environment.

strategic planning   A set of procedures for making decisions about the organization's long-term goals and strategies.

strategic retreat   Efforts to adapt products and processes to changes in the political and social environments while minimizing the negative effects of those changes.

strategic vision   The long-term direction and strategic intent of a company.

strategy   A pattern of actions and resource allocations designed to achieve the organization's goals.

structured interview   Selection technique that involves asking each applicant the same questions and comparing their responses to a standardized set of answers.

substitutes for leadership   Factors in the workplace that can exert the same influence on employees that leaders would provide.

subunits   Subdivisions of an organization.

superordinate goals   Higher-level goals taking priority over specific individual or group goals.

supervisory leadership   Behavior that provides guidance, support, and corrective feedback for the day-to-day activities of work unit members.

survivor's syndrome   Loss of productivity and morale in employees who remain after a downsizing.

switching costs   Fixed costs buyers face when they change suppliers.

SWOT analysis   A comparison of strengths, weaknesses, opportunities, and threats that helps executives formulate strategy.

T

tactical planning   A set of procedures for translating broad strategic goals and plans into specific goals and plans that are relevant to a distinct portion of the organization, such as a functional area like marketing.

task performance behaviors   Actions taken to ensure that the work group or organization reaches its goals.

task specialist   An individual who has more advanced job-related skills and abilities than other group members possess.

team   A small number of people with complementary skills who are committed to a common purpose, set of performance goals, and approach for which they hold themselves mutually accountable.

team maintenance specialist   individual into develops and maintains team harmony.

team training   Training that provides employees with the skills and perspectives they need to work in collaboration with others.

technical innovator   A person who develops a new technology or has the key skills to install and operate the technology.

technical skill   The ability to perform a specialized task involving a particular method or process.

technology   The systematic application of scientific knowledge to a new product, process, or service.

technology audit   Process of clarifying the key technologies upon which an organization depends.

technology life cycle   A predictable pattern followed by a technological innovation starting from its inception and development to market saturation and replacement.

teleology   Considers an act to be morally right or acceptable if it produces a desired result.

termination interview   A discussion between a manager and an employee about the employee's dismissal.

third-country nationals   Natives of a country other than the home country or the host country of an overseas subsidiary.

360 degree appraisal   Process of using multiple sources of appraisal to gain a

comprehensive perspective of one's performance.

time-based competition (TBC)   Strategies aimed at reducing the total time it takes to deliver a product or service.

top-level managers   Senior executives responsible for the overall management and effectiveness of the organization.

total organization change   Introducing and sustaining multiple policies, practices, and procedures across multiple units and levels.

total quality management   An integrative approach to management that supports the attainment of customer satisfaction through a wide variety of tools and techniques that result in high-quality goods and services.

traditional work groups   Groups that have no managerial responsibilities.

training   Teaching lower-level employees how to perform their present jobs.

trait approach   A leadership perspective that focuses on individual leaders and attempts to determine the personal characteristics that great leaders share.

transactional leaders   Management through business transactions in which leaders use their legitimate, reward, and coercive powers to give commands and exchange rewards for services rendered.

transfer price   Price charged by one unit for a product or service provided to another unit within the organization.

transformational leader   A leader who transforms a vision into reality and motivates people to transcend their personal interests for the good of the group.

transnational organization model   An organization model characterized by centralization of certain functions in locations that best achieve cost economies; basing of other functions in the company's national subsidiaries to facilitate greater local responsiveness; and fostering of communication among subsidiaries to permit transfer of technological expertise and skills.

transnational teams   Work groups composed of multinational members whose activities span multiple countries.

two-factor theory   Herzberg's theory describing two factors affecting people's work motivation and satisfaction.

two-way communication   A process in which information flows in two directions—the receiver provides feedback and the sender is receptive to the feedback.

tyranny of the "or"   The belief that things must be either A or B, and cannot be both; that only one goal and not another can be attained.

U

uncertainty   The state that exists when decision makers have insufficient information.

unfreezing   Realizing that current practices are inappropriate and that new behavior must be enacted.

union shop   An organization with a union and union security clause specifying that workers must join the union after a set period of time.

unity-of-command principle   A structure in which each worker reports to one boss, who in turn reports to one boss.

universalism   The ethical system upholding certain values regardless of immediate result.

upward communication   Information that flows from lower to higher levels in the organization's hierarchy.

utilitarianism   An ethical system which states that the greatest good for the greatest number should be the overriding concern of decision makers.

V

valence   The value an outcome holds for the person contemplating it.

validity   The degree to which a selection test predicts or correlates with job performance.

value chain   Sequence of activities that flow from raw materials to the delivery of a product or service.

vertical integration   The acquisition or development of new businesses that produce parts or components of the organization's product.

vigilance   A process in which a decision maker carefully executes all stages of decision making.

virtual office   A mobile office in which people can work anywhere, as long as they have the tools to communicate with customers and colleagues.

virtue ethics   A perspective that what is moral comes from what a mature person with "good" moral character would deem right.

vision   A mental image of a possible and desirable future state of the organization.

voluntary responsibilities   Additional behaviors and activities that society finds desirable and that the values of the business support.

Vroom model   A situational model of leadership that focuses on how leaders go about making decisions.

W

work teams   Teams that make or do things like manufacture, assemble, sell, or provide.

Notes

Chapter One

1. P. Coy, "The Creative Economy," *Business Week,* August 21–28, 2000, pp. 76–82.

2. J.W. Cortada, *21st Century Business* (London: Financial Times/Prentice Hall, 2001).

3. J.A. Byrne, "Management by Web," *Business Week,* August 21–28, 2000, pp. 84–96.

4. A. Reinhardt, "From Gearhead to Grand High Pooh-Bah," *Business Week,* August 21–28, 2000, pp. 129–30.

5. A. Muoio, "Should I Go.Com?," *Fast Company,* July 2000, p. 164.

6. J.A. Byrne, "Visionary vs. Visionary," *Business Week,* August 28, 2000, pp. 210–14.

7. J. Useem, "Dot-coms: What have we learned?," *Fortune,* October 30, 2000, pp. 82–104.

8. Ibid.

9. *The Executive,* November 1990, pp. 70–84.

10. W.J. Holstein, "The Stateless Corporation," *Business Week,* May 14, 1990, pp. 98–105.

11. Coy, "Creative Economy."

12. Ibid.

13. Ibid.

14. N. Gross, "Mining a Company's Mother Lode of Talent," *Business Week,* August 28, 2000, pp. 135–37.

15. S. Cranor, *The Management Century* (San Francisco: Jossey-Bass, 2000).

16. Byrne, "Management by Web."

17. Ibid.

18. C. Loomis, (Ed.) "Mr. Buffet on the Stock Market," *Fortune,* November 22, 2000, pp. 212–20.

19. Ibid.

20. R. Henkoff, "Smartest and Dumbest Managerial Moves of 1994," *Fortune,* January 16, 1995, pp. 48–97.

21. E.E. Lawler III, *The Ultimate Advantage* (San Francisco: Jossey-Bass, 1992).

22. Useem, "Dot-coms."

23. Byrne, "Visionary vs. Visionary."

24. T. Ehrenfeld, "The New and Improved American Small Business," *Inc.,* January 1995, pp. 34–45.

25. T. Ehrenfeld, "The Demise of Mom and Pop?," *Inc.,* January 1995, pp. 46–48.

26. Ibid.

27. D.A. Garvin, "Manufacturing Strategic Planning," *California Management Review,* Summer 1993, pp. 85–106.

28. Byrne, "Management by Web."

29. Muio, "Should I Go.Com?"

30. M. Loeb, "How's Business?," *Fortune,* January 16, 1995, pp. 135–36.

31. N. Hutheesing, "10 to Watch," *Forbes,* November 3, 1997, pp. 150–54.

32. D. Kirkpatrick, "Now Everyone in PCs Wants to Be Like Mike," *Fortune,* September 8, 1997, pp. 47–48.

33. Ibid.

34. Cortada, *21st Century Business.*

35. J. Collins, "Don't Rewrite the Rules of the Road." *Business Week,* August 28, 2000, pp. 206–8.

36. Ibid.

37. R. Webber, "General Management Past and Future," *Financial Times Mastering Management,* 1997.

38. C. Bartlett and S. Goshal, "The Myth of the Generic Manager: New Personal Competencies for New Management Roles," *California Management Review,* 40, no. 1, (1997) pp. 92–116.

39. Ibid.

40. Ibid.

41. L.R. Sayles "Doing Things Right: A New Imperative for Middle Managers," *Organizational Dynamics,* Spring 1993, pp. 5–14.

42. R. Katz, "Skills of an Effective Administrator," *Harvard Business Review* 52 (September–October), pp. 90–102.

43. H. Mintzberg, "The Manager's Job: Folklore and Fact," *Harvard Business Review* 53 (July–August 1975), pp. 49–61.

44. A. Deutschman, "The Trouble with MBAs," *Fortune,* July 29, 1991, pp. 67–79.

45. S. Lehrman, "Putting Management Potential to the Test," *Bryan–College Station Eagle,* December 8, 1985, p. 3F.

46. M.W. McCall, Jr. *High flyers: Developing the next generation of leaders* (Boston: Harvard Business School Press, 1997).

47. P. Cappelli, "Career Jobs are Dead," *California Management Review,* Fall, 1999, pp. 146–67.

48. S.M. Jacoby, "Are Career Jobs Headed for Extinction?," *California Management Review,* Fall, 1999, pp. 123–45.

49. W. Kiechel III, "A Manager's Career in the New Economy," *Fortune,* April 4, 1994, pp. 68–72.

50. Ibid.

51. M. Conlin, "Write Your Own Title," *Business Week,* August 21–28, 2000, p. 148.

52. Kiechel, "A Manager's Career in the New Economy."

53. B. O'Brian, and G. Stern, "Nonstop Networking Propels an Accountant into U.S. Big Leagues," *The Wall Street Journal,* March 20, 1997, pp. 1, 2.

54. T. Peters, *Liberation Management* (New York: Alfred A. Knopf, 1992).

55. D. Brady, "Wanted: Eclectic Visionary with a Sense of Humor," *Business Week,* August 21–28, 2000, pp. 143–44.

56. T. Peters, "The New Wired World of Work," *Business Week,* August 21–28, 2000, p. 172–74.

57. Ibid.

58. J. Kotter, *The New Rules: How to Succeed in Today's Post-Corporate World* (New York: The Free Press, 1995).

59. Ibid.

Chapter One Appendix

1. C. George, *The History of Management Thought* (Englewood Cliffs, NJ: Prentice Hall, 1972).

2. Ibid.

3. A.D. Chandler, *Scale and Scope: The Dynamic of Industrial Capitalism* (Cambridge, MA: Belknap Press of Harvard University Press, 1990).

4. Ibid.

5. J. Baughman, *The History of American Management* (Englewood Cliffs, NJ: Prentice Hall, 1969), chap. 1.

6. George, *The History of Management Thought,* chaps. 5–7; F. Taylor, *The Principles of Scientific Management* (New York: Harper & Row, 1911).

7. J. Case, "A Company of Businesspeople," *Inc.,* April 1993, pp. 70–93.

8. H. Kroos and C. Gilbert, *The Principles of Scientific Management* (New York: Harper & Row, 1911).

9. H. Fayol, *General and Industrial Management,* trans. C. Storrs (Marshfield, MA: Pitman Publishing, 1949).

10. George, *The History of Management Thought,* chap. 9; J. Massie, "Management Theory," in *Handbook of Organizations,* ed. J. March (Chicago: Rand McNally, 1965), pp. 387–422.

11. C. Barnard, *The Functions of the Executive* (Cambridge, MA: Harvard University Press, 1938).

12. George, *The History of Management Thought;* Massie, "Management Theory."

13. E. Mayo, *The Human Problems of Industrial Civilization* (New York: Macmillan, 1933); F. Roethlisberger and W. Dickson, *Management and the Worker* (Cambridge, MA: Harvard University Press, 1939).

14. A. Maslow, "A Theory of Human Motivation," *Psychological Review* 50 (July 1943), pp. 370–96.

15. A. Carey, "The Hawthorne Studies: A Radical Criticism," *American Sociological Review* 32, no. 3 (1967), pp. 403–16.

16. M. Weber, *The Theory of Social and Economic Organizations,* trans. T. Parsons and A. Henderson (New York: Free Press, 1947).

17. George, *The History of Management Thought,* chap. 11.

18. D. McGregor, *The Human Side of Enterprise* (New York: McGraw-Hill, 1960).

19. C. Argyris, *Personality and Organization* (New York: Harper & Row, 1957).

20. R. Likert, *The Human Organization* (New York: McGraw-Hill, 1967).

21. L. von Bertalanffy, "The History and Status of General Systems Theory," *Academy of Management Journal* 15 (1972), pp. 407–26; D. Katz and R. Kahn, *The Social Psychology of Organizations,* 2nd ed. (New York: John Wiley & Sons, 1978).

22. J. Thompson, *Organizations in Action* (New York: McGraw-Hill, 1967); J. Galbraith, *Organization Design* (Reading, MA: Addison-Wesley, 1977); D. Miller and P. Friesen, *Organizations: A Quantum View* (Englewood Cliffs, NJ: Prentice Hall, 1984).

23. S. Crainer, *The Management Century* (San Francisco: Jossey-Bass, 2000).

24. Ibid.

Chapter Two

1. T. G. Donlan, "Editorial Commentary: Abusive Process," *Barron's,* June 12, 2000, 80, no. 24, p. 59.

2. D. Kadlec, "The Nasdaq: What a Drag!," *Time,* October 23, 2000, 156, no. 17, pp. 72–73.

3. Judith J. Friedman and Nancy DiTomaso, "Myths about Diversity: What Managers Need to Know About Changes in the U.S. Labor Force," *California Management Review* 38, no. 4 (Summer 1996), pp. 54–77.

4. Carol Vinzant, "Big Tobacco in the Crosshairs," *Fortune,* September 18, 2000, 142, no 6, p. 298; Ross D. Petty, "Tobacco Marketing Restrictions in the Multistate Attorneys General Settlement: Is This Good Public Policy?," *Journal of Public Policy & Marketing,* (Fall 1999), 18 no 2, pp. 249—57.

5. Johnathan R. Laing, "Just Spiffy," *Barron's* 77, no. 12 (March 24, 1997), pp. 37–42; Matthew J. Kiernan, "Get Innovative or Get Dead," *Business Quarterly* 61, no. 1 (Autumn 1996), pp. 51–58.

6. David J. Collis and Cynthis A. Montgomery, *Corporate Strategy: Resources and Scope of the Firm* (Burr Ridge, Il: McGraw-Hill/Irwin, 1997).

7. Roger Hallowell, "Southwest Airlines: A Case Study Linking Employee Needs, Satisfaction, and Organizational Capabilities to Competitive Advantage," *Human Resource Management* 35, no. 4 (Winter 1996), pp. 513–34; Wendy Zeller, "Greyhound Is Limping Badly," *Business Week,* August 22, 1994, p. 32.

8. Brian K. Schimmoller, "Magicians Wanted," *Power Engineering,* August, 2000, 104 no. 8, p. 3.

9. "Woods Is Fined By Actors' Union," *New York Times,* November 11, 2000, p. 7; Arthur Sherman, George Bohlander, and Scott Snell, *Managing Human Resources,* 11th ed. (Cincinnati, OH: Southwestern Publishing, 1998).

10. Brent Schlender, "The Adventures of Scott McNealy: Javaman," *Fortune,* 136, no. 7 (October 13, 1997), pp. 70–78.

11. P. Kotler, *Marketing Management: Analysis, Planning, Implementation and Control,* 9th ed. (Englewood Cliffs, NJ: Prentice Hall, 1990).

12. Aaron A. Buchko, "Conceptualization and Measurement of Environmental Uncertainty: An Assessment of the Miles and Snow Perceived Environmental Uncertainty Scale," *Academy of Management Journal* 37, no. 2 (April 1994), pp. 410–25.

13. Abdalla F. Hagen, "Corporate Executives and Environmental Scanning Activities: An Empirical Investigation." *SAM Advanced Management Journal* 60, no. 2 (Spring 1995), pp. 41–47; Richard L. Daft. "Chief Executive Scanning, Environmental Characteristics, and Company Performance: An Empirical Study," *Strategic Management Journal* 9, no. 2 (March/April 1988), pp. 123–39; Masoud Yasai-Ardekani, "Designs for Environmental Scanning Systems: Tests of a Contingency Theory," *Management Science* 42, no. 2 (February 1996), pp. 187–204.

14. Sumantra Ghoshal, "Building Effective Intelligence Systems for Competitive Advantage," *Sloan Management Review* 28, no. 1 (Fall 1986), pp. 49–58; Kenneth D. Cory, "Can Competitive Intelligence Lead to a Sustainable Competitive Advantage?," *Competitive Intelligence Review* 7, no. 3 (Fall 1996), pp. 45–55.

15. Paul J. H. Schoemaker, "Multiple Scenario Development: Its Conceptual and Behavioral Foundation," *Strategic Management Journal* 14, no. 3 (March 1993), pp. 193–213.

16. Robin R. Peterson, "An Analysis of Contemporary Forecasting in Small Business," *Journal of Business Forecasting Methods & Systems* 15, no. 2 (Summer 1996), pp. 10–12; Spyros Makridakis, "Business Forecasting for Management: Strategic Business Forecasting," *International Journal of Forecasting* 12, no. 3 (September 1996), pp. 435–37.

17. Irving DeToro, "The 10 Pitfalls of Benchmarking," *Quality Progress* 28, no. 1 (January 1995), pp. 61–63.

18. Martin B. Meznar, "Buffer or Bridge? Environmental and Organizational Determinants of Public Affairs Activities in American firms," *Academy of Management Journal* 38, no. 4 (August 1995), pp. 975–96.

19. David Lei, "Advanced Manufacturing Technology: Organizational Design and Strategic Flexibility," *Organization Studies* 17, no. 3 (1996), pp. 501–23; James W. Dean Jr. and Scott A. Snell, "The Strategic Use of Integrated Manufacturing: An Empirical Examination," *Strategic Management Journal* 17, no. 6 (June 1996), pp. 459–80.

20. C. Zeithaml and V. Zeithaml, "Environmental Management: Revising the Marketing Perspective," *Journal of Marketing* 48 (Spring 1984), pp. 46–53.

21. Willem P. Burgers, "Cooperative Strategy in High Technology Industries," *International Journal of Management* 13, no. 2 (June 1996), pp. 127–34; Jeffrey E. McGee, "Cooperative Strategy and New Venture Performance: The Role of Business Strategy and Management Experi-

ence," *Strategic Management Journal* 16, no. 7 (October 1995), pp. 565–80.

22. Richard A. D'Aveni, *Hypercompetition—Managing the Dynamics of Strategic Maneuvering* (New York, The Free Press 1994); Michael A. Cusumano, "Strategic Maneuvering and Mass-Market Dynamics: The Triumph of VHS over Beta," *Business History Review* 66, no. 1 (Spring 1992), pp. 51–94.

23. R. Miles and C. Snow, *Organizational Strategy, Structure, and Process* (New York: McGraw-Hill, 1978).

Chapter Three

1. T. Peters, *Liberation Management* (New York: Alfred A. Knopf, 1992).

2. M. Magasin and F. L. Gehlen, "Unwise Decisions and Unanticipated Consequences," *Sloan Management Review, 41,* (1999), pp. 47–60.

3. M. McCall and R. Kaplan, *Whatever It Takes: Decision Makers at Work* (Englewood Cliffs, NJ: Prentice Hall, 1985).

4. B. Bass, *Organizational Decision Making* (Homewood, IL: Richard D. Irwin, 1983).

5. J. March, "Bounded Rationality, Ambiguity, and the Engineering of Choice," *Bell Journal of Economics* 9 (1978), pp. 587–608.

6. D. Messick and M. Bazerman, "Ethical Leadership and the Psychology of Decision Making," *Sloan Management Review,* Winter 1996, pp. 9–22.

7. N. Carr, "On the Edge: An Interview with Akamai's George Conrades," *Harvard Business Review,* May–June 2000, pp. 118–25.

8. G. A. Garvin. "Building a Learning Organization," *Harvard Business Review,* July–August 1993, pp. 78–91.

9. McCall and Kaplan, *Whatever It Takes.*

10. K. MacCrimmon and R. Taylor, "Decision Making and Problem Solving," in *Handbook of Industrial and Organizational Psychology,* ed. M. D. Dunnette (Chicago: Rand McNally, 1976).

11. Q. Spitzer and R. Evans, *Heads, You Win! How the Best Companies Think* (New York: Simon & Schuster, 1997).

12. C. Gettys and S. Fisher, "Hypothesis Plausibility and Hypotheses Generation," *Organizational Behavior and Human Performance* 24 (1979), pp. 93–110.

13. E. R. Alexander, "The Design of Alternatives in Organizational Contexts: A Pilot study," *Administrative Science Quarterly* 24 (1979), pp. 382–404.

14. P. Nayak and J. Ketteringham, *Breakthroughs* (New York: Rawson Associates, 1986).

15. A. R. Rao, M. E. Bergen, and S. Davis, "How to Fight a Price War," *Harvard Business Review,* March-April 2000, pp. 107–16.

16. Ibid.

17. J. O'Toole, *Vanguard Management: Redesigning the Corporate Future* (Garden City, NY: Doubleday, 1985).

18. McCall and Kaplan, *Whatever It Takes.*

19. Spitzer and Evans, *Heads, You Win!*

20. K. Labich, "Four Possible Futures," *Fortune,* January 25, 1993, pp. 40–48.

21. McCall and Kaplan, *Whatever It Takes.*

22. M. B. Stein, "Teaching Steelcase to Dance," *New York Times Magazine,* April 1, 1990, pp. 22ff.

23. D. Siebold, "Making Meetings More Successful," *Journal of Business Communication* 16 (Summer 1979), pp. 3–20.

24. I. Janis and L. Mann, *Decision Making* (New York: Free Press, 1977); Bass, *Organizational Decision Making.*

25. J. W. Dean Jr. and M. Sharfman, "Does Decision Process Matter? a Study of Strategic Decision-Making Effectiveness," *Academy of Management Journal* 39 (1996), pp. 368–96.

26. R. Nisbett and L. Ross, *Human Inference: Strategies and Shortcomings* (Englewood Cliffs, NJ: Prentice Hall, 1980).

27. R. Lowenstein, *When Genius Failed.* (New York: Random House, 2000).

28. Messick and Bazerman, "Ethical Leadership."

29. T. Bateman and C. Zeithaml, "The Psychological Context of Strategic Decisions: A Model and Convergent Experimental Findings," *Strategic Management Journal* 10 (1989), pp. 59–74.

30. Messick and Bazerman, "Ethical, Leadership."

31. N. Adler, *International Dimensions of Organizational Behavior* (Boston: Kent, 1990).

32. K. M. Esenhardt, "Speed and Strategic Choice: How Managers Accelerate Decision Making," *California Management Review* 32 (Spring 1990), pp. 39–54.

33. Q. Spitzer and R. Evans, " New Problems in Problem Solving," *Across the Board,* April 1997, pp. 36–40.

34. G. W. Hill, "Group versus Individual Performance: Are n + 1 Heads Better than 1?" *Psychological Bulletin* 91 (1982), pp. 517–39.

35. N. R. F. Maier, "Assets and Liabilities in Group Problem Solving: The Need for an Integrative Function," *Psychological Review* 74 (1967), pp. 239–49.

36. Ibid.

37. R. Cosier and C. Schwenk, "Agreement and Thinking Alike: Ingredients for Poor Decisions," *The Executive,* February 1990, pp. 69–74.

38. A. Amason, "Distinguishing the Effects of Functional and Dysfunctional Conflict on Strategic Decision Making: Resolving a Paradox for Top Management Teams," *Academy of Management Journal* 39 (1996), pp. 123–48. R. Dooley and G. Fyxell, "Attaining Decision Quality and Commitment from Dissent: The Moderating Effects of Loyalty and Competence in Strategic Decision-making Teams," *Academy of Management Journal,* August 1999, pp. 389–402.

39. K. Eisenhardt, J. Kahwajy, and L. J. Bourgeois III, "Conflict and Strategic Choice: How Top Management Teams Disagree," *California Management Review,* Winter 1997, pp. 42–62.

40. Cosier and Schwenk, "Agreement and Thinking Alike."

41. Ibid.

42. C. Knowlton, "How Disney Keeps the Magic Going," *Fortune,* December 4, 1989, pp. 115–32.

43. P. LaBerre, "The Creative Revolution," *Industry Week,* May 16, 1994, pp. 12–19.

44. J. V. Anderson, " Weirder than Fiction: The Reality and Myths of Creativity," *Academy of Management Executive,* November 1992, pp. 40–47; J. Krohe Jr., "Managing Creativity," *Across the Board,* September 1996, pp. 17–21.

45. A. Farnham, "How to Nurture Creative Sparks," *Fortune,* January 10, 1994, pp. 94–100; T. M. Amabile, "A Model of Creativity and Innovation in Organizations," in *Research and Organizational Behavior,* ed. B. Straw and L. Cummings, vol. 10 (1988), pp. 123–68.

46. R. Sutton and A. Hargadon "Brainstorming Groups in Context: Effectiveness in a Product Design Firm," *Administrative Design Quarterly* 41 (1996), pp. 685–718.

47. Dean and Sharfman, "Does Decision Process Matter?"

48. K. Eisenhardt, J. Kahwajy, and L. J. Bourgeois III, "How Management Teams Can Have a Good Fight," *Harvard Management Review,* July–August 1997, pp. 77–85.

49. J. E. Jackson and W. T. Schantz, "Crisis Management Lessons: When Push Shoved Nike," *Business Horizons,* January–February 1993, pp. 27–35.

50. C. M. Pearson and I. I. Mitroff, "From Crisis Prone to Crisis Prepared: A Framework for Crisis Management," *The Academy of Management Executive,* February 1993, pp. 48–59.

51. J. Hickman, and W. Crandall, " Before Disaster Hits: A Multifaceted Approach to Crisis Management," *Business Horizons,* March–April 1997, pp. 75–79.

52. I. Mitroff, L. K. Harrington, and E. Gai, "Thinking about the Unthinkable," *Across the Board,* September 1996, pp. 44–48.

53. C. M. Pearson and D. A. Rondinelli, "Crisis Management in Central European Firms," *Business Horizons,* 41, May–June 1998, pp. 50–60.

54. G. Meyers with J. Holusha, *When It Hits the Fan: Managing the Nine Crises of Business* (Boston: Houghton Mifflin, 1986).

55. McCall and Kaplan, *Whatever It Takes.*

Chapter Four

1. J. Bracker and J. Pearson, "Planning and Financial Performance of Small Mature Firms," *Strategic Management Journal* 7 (1986), pp. 503–22; Philip Waalewijn and Peter Segaar, "Strategic Management: The Key to Profitability in Small Companies," *Long Range Planning,* 26, no. 2 (April 1993), pp. 24–30.

2. Aramark annual report, 1997.

3. "Y2K Planning Pays Off," *Government Executive,* February 2000, 32, no. 2, p. 9.

4. V. Viswanath and D. Harding, "The Starbuck Effect," *Harvard Business Review,* March/April, 2000; M. Hornblower, "Wake Up and Smell the Protest," *Time,* April 17, 2000; M. Gimein, "Right On: Starbucks Makes a Net Play," *Fortune,* March 6, 2000; L. Lee, "Now, Starbucks Uses Its Bean," *Business Week,* February 14, 2000; R. Papiernik, "Starbucks Starts Fiscal 2000 with 30% Profit Growth in 1st Q," *Nation's Restaurant News,* February 7, 2000; K. Holland, "Starbucks Thinks It Will Travel Well," *Business Week,* November 16, 1998; N. Weiss, "How Starbucks Impassions Workers to Drive Growth," *Workforce,* August, 1998; J Reese, "Starbucks: Inside the Coffee Cult," *Fortune,* December 9, 1997; K. Strauss, "Howard Schultz: Starbucks' CEO Serves a Blend of Community, Employee Commitment," *Nation's Restaurant News,* January 2000; "Interview with Howard Schultz: Sharing Success," *Executive Excellence,* November

1999; N. D. Schwartz, "Still Perking After All These Years," *Fortune,* May 24, 1999.

5. "Business: Fading Fads," *The Economist,* April 22, 2000, 355, no. 8167, pp. 60–61.

6. Steven W. Floyd and Peter J Lane, "Strategizing throughout the Organization: Management Role Conflict in Strategic Renewal," *Academy of Management Review,* January 2000, 25, no. 1, pp 154–177. Don MacRae, "Seeing Beyond Monday Morning," *Business Week,* November 22, 2000, online.

7. Shell Oil company documents, 1997. Raymond Saner, Lichia Yiu, and Mikael Sondergaard, "Business Diplomacy Management: A Core Competency for Global Companies," *The Academy of Management Executive,* February 2000, 14, no. 1, pp. 80–92; Don Daake and William P Anthony, "Understanding Stakeholder Power and Influence Gaps in a Health Care Organization: An Empirical Study," *Health Care Management Review,* Summer 2000, 25, no. 3, pp. 94–107.

8. Arthur A. Thompson and A. J. Strickland III, *Strategic Management: Concepts and Cases,* 8th ed. (Burr Ridge, IL: Richard D. Irwin, 1995), p. 23.

9. Roger Hallowell, "Southwest Airlines: A Case Study Linking Employee Needs Satisfaction and Organizational Capabilities to Competitive Advantage," *Human Resource Management,* 35, no. 4 (Winter 1996), pp. 513–34.

10. Collis and Montgomery, *Corporate Strategy.*

11. Ibid.

12. Thomas D. Sugalski, "Resource Link: Reestablishing the Employment Relationship in an Era of Downsizing," *Human Resource Management,* 34, no. 3 (Fall 1995) pp. 389–403.

13. Robert C. Camp, "A Bible for Benchmarking, by Xerox," *Financial Executive* 9, no. 4. (July/August 1993) pp. 23–27. See, also, Dawn Anfuso, "At L. L. Bean, Quality

Starts with People," *Personnel Journal* 73, no. 1, (January 1994), p. 60; Ken Stork, "Benchmarking: Analyze as You Go about Planning," *Purchasing,* October 19, 2000, 129, no. 7, p. 33.

14. Robert E. Hoskisson, "Corporate Divestiture Intensity in Restructuring Firms: Effects of Governance, Strategy, and Performance," *Academy of Management Journal,* 37, no. 5, (October 1994) pp. 1207–51; S. Gannes, "Merck Has Made Biotech Work," *Fortune,* January 19, 1987, pp. 58–64; Mark Maremont, "Why Kodak's Dazzling Spin-Off Didn't Bedazzle," *Business Week,* June 28, 1993, p. 34; Emily S. Plishner, "Eastman Chemical Spins Out of the Kodak Family Portrait," *Chemical Week,* 152, no. 24 (June 23, 1993), p. 7.

15. Stratford Sherman, "Why Disney Had to Buy ABC," *Fortune,* 132, no. 5, (September 4, 1995), p. 80.

16. M. Porter, *Competitive Advantage* (New York: Free Press, 1985). pp. 11–14.

17. John Huey, "Outlaw Flyboy CEOs," *Fortune,* November 13, 2000, 142, no. 11, pp. 237–250.

18. Anne Faircloth, "One-on-One Shopping," *Fortune,* July 7, 1997, pp. 235–236; Melanie Wells, "Are Dynasties Dying?," *Forbes,* March 6, 2000, p. 126.

19. R. A. Eisenstat, "Implementing Strategy: Developing a Partnership for Change," *Planning Review,* September–October 1993, pp. 33–36.

Chapter Five

1. A. Bernstein, "Too Much Corporate Power?" *Business Week,* September 11, 2000, pp. 145–58.

2. M. E. Guy, *Ethical Decision Making in Everyday Work Situations* (New York: Quorum Books, 1990).

3. O. C. Ferrell and J. Fraedrich, *Business Ethics: Ethical Decision Making and Cases,* 3rd ed. (Boston: Houghton Mifflin, 1997).

4. Ibid.

5. Guy, *Ethical Decision Making.*

6. Ferrell and Fraedrich, *Business Ethics.*

7. L. Kohlberg and D. Candee, "The Relationship of Moral Judgment to Moral Action" in *Morality, Moral Behavior, and Moral Development,* ed. W. M. Kurtines and J. L. Gerwitz (New York: John Wiley & Sons, 1984).

8. L. K. Trevino, "Ethical Decision Making in Organizations: A Person-Situation Interactionist Model," *Academy of Management Review,* pp. 601–17.

9. Ferrell and Fraedrich, *Business Ethics.*

10. J. Krohe Jr., "Ethics Are Nice, but Business Is Business," *Across the Board,* April 1997, pp. 16–22.

11. Ibid.

12. J. Badarocco Jr. and A. Webb, "Business Ethics: A View from the Trenches," *California Management Review,* Winter 1995, pp. 8–28.

13. G. Laczniak, M. Berkowitz, R. Brookes, and J. Hale, "The Business of Ethics: Improving or Deteriorating?" *Business Horizons,* January–February 1995, pp. 39–47.

14. S. Brenner and E. Molander, "Is the Ethics of Business Changing?" in *Ethics in Practice: Managing the Moral Corporation,* ed. K. Andrews (Cambridge, MA: Harvard Business School Press, 1989).

15. R. T. De George, *Business Ethics,* 3rd ed. (New York: Macmillan, 1990).

16. T. P. Paré, "Jack Welch's Nightmare on Wall Street," *Fortune,* September 5, 1994, pp. 40–48.

17. J. B. Ciulla, "Why Is Business Talking about Ethics? Reflections on Foreign Conversations," *California Management Review,* Fall 1991, pp. 67–80.

18. R. E. Allinson, "A Call for Ethically Centered Management," *Academy of Management Executive,* February 1995, pp. 73–76.

19. Krohe, "Ethics Are Nice."

20. D. Messick and M. Bazerman, "Ethical Leadership and the Psychol-

ogy of Decision Making," *Sloan Management Review,* Winter 1996, pp. 9–22.

21. Krohe, "Ethics Are Nice."

22. C. Handy, *Beyond Uncertainty: The Changing Worlds of Organizations* (Boston: Harvard Business School Press, 1996).

23. R. A. Cooke, "Danger Signs of Unethical Behavior: How to Determine if Your Firm Is at Ethical Risk," *Journal of Business Ethics,* April 1991, pp. 249–53.

24. Ciulla, "Why Is Business Talking about Ethics?"

25. A. Farnham, "State Your Values, Hold the Hot Air," *Fortune,* April 19, 1993, pp. 117–24.

26. G. R. Weaver, L. K. Trevino, and P. L. Cochran, "Corporate Ethics Programs as Control Systems: Influences of Executive Commitment and Environmental Factors," *Academy of Management Journal,* 42, (1999), pp. 41–57.

27. L. S. Paine, "Managing for Organizational Integrity," *Harvard Business Review,* March–April 1994, pp. 106–17.

28. F. Hall and E. Hall, "The ADA: Going beyond the Law," *The Academy of Management Executive,* February 1994, pp. 7–13; A. Farnham, "Brushing Up Your Vision Thing," *Fortune,* May 1, 1995, p. 129.

29. G. R. Weaver, L. K. Trevino, and P. L. Cochran, "Integrated and Decoupled Corporate Social Performance: Management Commitments, External Pressures, and Corporate Ethics Practices" *Academy of Management Journal,* 42, (1999), pp. 539–52.

30. Paine, "Managing for Organizational Integrity."

31. Krohe, "Ethics Are Nice."

32. Guy, *Ethical Decision Making;* D. Kirrane, "Managing Values: A Systematic Approach to Business Ethics," *Training and Development Journal,* November 1990, pp. 53–60.

33. R. P. Nielson, "What Can Managers Do about Unethical Management?" *Journal of Business Ethics,* May 1987, pp. 309–20.

34. L. Preston and J. Post, eds., *Private Management and Public Policy* (Englewood Cliffs, NJ: Prentice Hall, 1975).

35. Ferrell and Fraedrich, *Business Ethics.*

36. Ibid.

37. D. Quinn and T. Jones, "An Agent Morality View of Business Policy," *Academy of Management Review* 20 (1995), pp. 22–42.

38. M. Witzel, "Not for Wealth Alone: The Rise of Business Ethics," *Financial Times Mastering Management Review,* November 1999, pp. 14–19.

39. Ibid.

40. Ibid.

41. K. E. Goodpaster, "Business Ethics and Stakeholder Analysis," *Business Ethics Quarterly* 1 (1991), pp. 53–73.

42. D. C. Korten, *When Corporations Ruled the World* (San Francisco: Berrett–Koehler, 1995).

43. Handy, *Beyond Certainty.*

44. Quinn and Jones, "An Agent Morality View of Business Policy."

45. Handy, *Beyond Certainty.*

46. H. J. Reitz, J. A. Wall Jr., and M. S. Love, "Ethics in Negotiation: Oil and Water or Good Lubrication?" *Business Horizons,* May–June 1998, pp. 5–14.

47. D. Turban and D. Greening, "Corporate Social Performance and Organizational Attractiveness to Prospective Employees," *Academy of Management Journal* 40 (1997), pp. 658–72.

48. Handy, *Beyond Certainty.*

49. S. Waddock and N. Smith, "Corporate Responsibility Audits: Doing Well by Doing Good," *Sloan Management Review,* Winter 2000, pp. 75–83.

50. J. Collins and J. Porras, *Built to Last: Successful Habits of Visionary Companies* (London: Century Business, 1996).

51. Ibid.

52. R. Ackerman and R. Bauer, *Corporate Social Responsiveness* (Reston, VA: Reston, 1976).

53. M. B. E. Clarkson, "A Stakeholder Framework for Analyzing and Evaluating Corporate Social Performance," *Academy of Management Review* 20 (1995), pp. 92–117.

54. J. S. Harrison and R. E. Freeman, "Stakeholders, Social Responsibility, and Performance: Empirical Evidence and Theoretical Perspectives," *Academy of Management Journal,* 42 (1999), pp. 479–85.

55. Ibid.

56. Kanter, *World Class* (New York: Touchstone, 1995), p. 192.

57. Ibid., pp. 192–94.

58. Ibid.

59. J. Gale and R. A. Buchholz, "The Political Pursuit of Competitive Advantage: What Business Can Gain from Government," in *Business Strategy and Public Policy: Perspectives from Industry and Academia,* ed. A. A. Marcus, A. M. Kaufman, and D. R. Beam (Westport, CT: Greenwood Press, 1987), pp. 31–41.

60. T. Parsons and C. Perrow, *Complex Organizations,* 2nd ed. (Glenview, IL: Scott, Foresman, 1979).

61. B. Baysinger, "Domain Maintenance as an Objective of Business Political Activity," *Academy of Management Review* 9 (1984), pp. 248–58.

62. P. Andrews, "The Sticky Wicket of Evaluating Public Affairs: Thoughts about a Framework," *Public Affairs Review* 6 (1986), pp. 94–105.

63. S. Lusterman, *The Organization and Staffing of Corporate Public Affairs* (New York: Conference Board, 1987).

64. C. Zeithaml, G. Keim, and B. Baysinger, "Toward an Integrated Strategic Management Process: An Empirical Review of Corporate Political Strategy," *in Strategic Management Frontiers,* ed. John H. Grant (Greenwich, CT: JAI Press, 1988), pp. 377–93.

65. A. J. Hillman and M. A. Hitt, "Corporate Political Strategy Formulation: A Model of Approach, Participation, and Strategy Decisions," *Academy of Management Review* 24 (1999), pp. 825–42.

66. Bernstein, "Too Much Corporate Power?"

67. G. Keim and C. Zeithaml, "Corporate Political Strategy and Legislative Decision Making," *Academy of Management Review,* 1986, pp. 828–43.

68. S. L. Hart and M. B. Milstein, "Global Sustainability and the Creative Destruction of Industries," *Sloan Management Review,* Fall 1999, pp. 23–33.

69. J. Post, "Managing as if the Earth Mattered," *Business Horizons,* July–August 1991, pp. 32–38.

70. C. J. Corbett and L. N. Van Wassenhove, "The Green Fee: Internationalizing and Operationalizing Environmental Issues," *California Management Review,* Fall 1993, pp. 116–33.

71. N. Walley and B. Whitehead, "It's Not Easy Being Green," *Harvard Business Review,* May–June 1994, pp. 46–51.

72. "The Challenge of Going Green," letters, *Harvard Business Review,* July–August 1994, pp. 37–50.

73. F. Rice, "Who Scores Best on the Environment," *Fortune,* July 26, 1993, pp. 114–22.

74. P. Shrivastava, "Ecocentric Management for a Risk Society," *Academy of Management Review* 20 (1995), pp. 118–37.

75. Ibid.

76. Ibid.

77. Ibid.

78. Ibid.

79. M. Russo and P. Fouts, "A Resource-Based Perspective on Corporate Environmental Performance and Profitability," *Academy of Management Journal* 40 (1997), pp. 534–59, and R. D. Klassen and D. Clay Whybark, "The Impact of Environmental Technologies on Manufacturing Performance," *Academy of Management Journal,* 42 (1999), pp. 599–615.

80. H. Bradbury and J. A. Clair, "Promoting Sustainable Organizations with Sweden's Natural Step," *Academy of Management Executive,* November, 1999, pp. 63–74.

81. A. Fisher, "The World's Most Admired Companies," *Fortune,* October 27, 1997, pp. 40–58.

82. G. Pinchot and E. Pinchot, *The Intelligent Organization,* 1996, San Francisco: Berrett Koehler.

83. S. L. Hart, "Beyond Greening: Strategies for a Sustainable World," *Harvard Business Review,* January–February 1997, pp. 66–76.

Chapter Five Appendix B

1. P. Hawken, A. Lovins, and L. Hunter Lovins, *Natural Capitalism* (Boston: Little Brown, 1999).

2. F. Rice, "Who Scores Best on the Environment," *Fortune,* July 26, 1993, p. 114–22.

3. J. K. Hammitt. "Climate Change Won't Wait for Kyoto," *The Washington Post,* November 29, 2000, p. A39

4. A. Brown, "Business Leaders Respond to Rio with Self-Regulation," *International Herald Tribune,* June 23, 1997, p. 17.

5. Ibid.

6. K. W. Chilton, "Reengineering U.S. Environmental Protection," *Business Horizons,* March–April 2000, pp. 7–16

7. K. Dechant and B. Altman, "Environmental Leadership: From Compliance to Competitive Advantage," *The Academy of Management Executive,* August 1994, pp. 7–20.

8. R. Stavins, letter in "The Challenge of Going Green," *Harvard Business Review,* July–August 1994, pp. 37–50.

9. N. Walley and B. Whitehead, "It's Not Easy Being Green," *Harvard Business Review,* May–June 1994, pp. 46–51; C. J. Corbett and L. N. Van Wassenhove, "The Green Fee: Internationalizing and Operationalizing Environmental Issues, *California Management Review,* Fall 1993, pp. 116–33.

10. Walley and Whitehead, "It's Not Easy Being Green."

11. Stavins, "The Challenge of Going Green."

12. Ibid.

13. F. B. Cross, "The Weaning of the Green: Environmentalism Comes of Age in the 1990s," *Business Horizons,* September–October 1990, pp. 40–46.

14. "The Challenge of Going Green."

15. J. Singh, "Making Business Sense of Environmental Compliance," *Sloan Management Review,* Spring, 2000, pp. 91–100

16. H. Ellison, "Saving Nature while Earning Money," *International Herald Tribune,* June 23, 1997, p. 18.

17. E. Smith and V. Cahan, "The Greening of Corporate America," *Business Week,* April 23, 1990, pp. 96–103.

18. M. E. Porter, "America's Green Strategy," *Science,* April 1991, p. 168.

19. A. Kleiner, "What Does It Mean to Be Green?" *Harvard Business Review,* July–August 1991, pp. 38–47.

20. D. C. Kinlaw, *Competitive and Green: Sustainable Performance in the Environmental Age* (Amsterdam: Pfeiffer & Co., 1993).

21. Rice, "Who Scores Best on the Environment."

22. J. O'Toole, "Do Good, Do Well: The Business Enterprise Trust Awards," *California Management Review,* Spring 1991, pp. 9–24.

23. Rice, "Who Scores Best on the Environment?"

24. O'Toole, "Do Good, Do Well."

25. G. Hardin, "The Tragedy of the Commons," *Science* 162 (1968), pp. 1243–48.

26. D. Kirkpatrick, "Environmentalism: The New Crusade," *Fortune,* February 12, 1990, pp. 44–55.

27. Ibid.

28. R. Carson, *The Silent Spring* (Boston: Houghton Mifflin, 1962); R. Paehlke, *Environmentalism and the Future of Progressive Politics* (New Haven: Yale University Press, 1989), pp. 13–41, 76–143; R. Nash, ed., *The American Environment* (Reading, MA: Addison-Wesley, 1968); R. Revelle and H. Landsberg, eds., *America's Changing Environment* (Boston: Beacon Press, 1970); L. Caldwell, *Environment: A Challenge to Modern Society* (Garden City, NY: Anchor Books, 1971); J. M. Petulla,

Environmental Protection in the United States (San Francisco: San Francisco Study Center, 1987).

29. B. Commoner, *Science and Survival* (New York: Viking Press, 1963); B. Commoner, *The Closing Circle: Nature, Man and Technology* (New York: Bantam Books, 1971).

30. R. Paehlke, *Environmentalism and the Future of Progressive Politics* (New Haven: Yale University Press, 1989)

31. P. Shrivastava, "Ecocentric Management for a Risk Society," *Academy of Management Review* 20 (1995), pp. 118–37.

32. B. Commoner, *The Closing Circle: Nature, Man and Technology* (New York: Bantam Books, 1971).

33. Paehlke, *Environmentalism.*

34. Ibid.

35. Ibid.

36. P. Hawken, J. Ogilvy, and P. Schwartz, *Seven Tomorrows: Toward a Voluntary History* (New York: Bantam Books, 1982); Paehlke, *Environmentalism.*

37. Porter, "America's Green Strategy."

38. R.Y.K. Chan, "An Emerging Green Market in China: Myth or Reality?" *Business Horizons*, March–April, 2000, pp. 55–60.

39. S. Waddock and N. Smith, "Corporate Responsibility Audits: Doing Well by Doing Good," *Sloan Management Review*, Winter, 2000, pp. 75–83.

40. C. Morrison, *Managing Environmental Affairs: Corporate Practices in the U.S., Canada, and Europe* (New York: Conference Board, 1991).

41. Ibid.

42. Kleiner, "What Does It Mean to Be Green?"

43. K. Fischer and J. Schot, *Environmental Strategies for Industry* (Washington, DC: Island Press, 1993).

44. J. Howard, J. Nash, and J. Ehrenfeld, "Standard or Smokescreen? Implementation of a Voluntary Environmental Code," *California Management Review*, Winter, 2000, pp. 63–82.

45. Rice, "Who Scores Best on the Environment?"

46. Ibid.

47. Ibid.

48. S. L. Hart and M. B. Milstein, "Global Sustainability and the Creative Destruction of Industries," *Sloan Management Review*, Fall 1999, pp. 23–32.

49. H. Ellison, "Saving Nature while Earning Money."

50. Dechant and Altman, "Environment Leadership."

51. Smith and Cahan, "The Greening of Corporate America."

52. J. Elkington and T. Burke, *The Green Capitalists* (London: Victor Gullanez, 1989); M. Zetlin, "The Greening of Corporate America," *Management Review*, June 1990, pp. 10–17.

53. Smith and Cahan, "The Greening of Corporate America."

54. Hart and Milstein, "Global Sustainability."

55. J. Stevens, "Assessing the Health Risks of Incinerating Garbage," *EURA Reporter*, October 1989, pp. 6–10.

56. A. Lovins, L. Hunter Lovins, and P. Hawken, "A Road Map for Natural Capitalism," *Harvard Business Review*, May–June, 1999, pp. 145–58.

57. A. Kolk, "Green Reporting," *Harvard Business Review*, January–February, 2000, pp. 15–16.

58. L. Blumberg and R. Gottlieb, "The Resurrection of Incineration" and "The Economic Factors," in *War on Waste,* ed. L. Blumberg and R. Gottlieb (Washington, DC: Island Press, 1989).

59. L. Blumberg and R. Gottlieb, "Recycling's Unrealized Promise," in Blumberg and Gottlieb, *War on Waste*, pp. 191–226.

60. Lovins, Lovins, and Hawken, "A Road Map for Natural Capitalism."

61. J. Elkington, "Towards the Sustainable Corporation: Win-Win-Win Business Strategies for Sustainable Development," *California Management Review*, Winter 1994, pp. 90–100.

62. Lovins, Lovins, and Hawken, "A Road Map for Natural Capitalism."

63. Dechant and Altman, "Environmental Leadership."

64. Brown, "Business Leaders Respond to Rio with Self-Regulation."

65. H. Ellison. ,"Joint Implementation Promotes Cooperation on World Climate," *International Herald Tribune*, June 23, 1997, p. 21.

66. Corbett and Van Wassenhove, "The Green Fee."

67. Ibid.

68. R. D. Klassen and D. Clay Whybark, "The Impact of Environmental Technologies on Manufacturing Performance,"*Academy of Management Journal*, 42, 1999, pp. 599–615.

69. Hart and Milstein, "Global Sustainability."

70. Ibid.

71. Ibid.

72. Ibid.

73. Elkington, "Towards the Sustainable Corporation."

74. F. S. Rowland, "Chlorofluorocarbons and the Depletion of Stratospheric Ozone," American Scientist, January–February 1989, pp. 36–45.

75. Elkington, "Towards the Sustainable Corporation."

76. Corbet and Van Wassenhove, "The Green Fee."

77. H. Ellison,"Joint Implementation Promotes Cooperation on World Climate."

78. Elkington, "Towards the Sustainable Corporation."

79. H. Ellison, "The Balance Sheet," *International Herald Tribune,* June 23, 1997, p. 21.

80. Ibid.

81. P. B. Gray and D, Devlin, "Heroes of Small Business," *Fortune Small Business,* November, 2000, pp. 50–64.

82. S. Tully, "Water, Water Everywhere," *Fortune,* May 15, 2000, pp. 343–54.

Chapter Six

1. "European Foreign Policy: Unity by Machinery?" *The Economist,* March 2, 1996, pp. 46–47; "European Union: Wishful Thinking," *The*

Economist, September 24, 1994, pp. 84–85; "Europe: Shaping the Union," *The Economist,* December 2, 2000, 357, no. 8199, pp. 49–51; "Leaders: Europe's Choice," *The Economist,* December 2, 2000, 357, no. 8199, pp. 20–21.

2. "EU: MNCs Face New Challenges as Frontiers Merge," *Crossborder Monitor* 2, no. 10, March 16, 1994, p. 1; Jane Sasseen, "EU Dateline," *International Management* 49, no. 2 (March 1994), p. 5; Andrew Martin and George Ross, *The Brave New World of European Labor: European Trade Unions at the Millennium* (New York: Berghahn, 1999); Robert A. Feldman and C. Maxwell Watson, "Central Europe: From Transition to EU Membership," *Finance & Development,* September 2000, 37, no. 3, pp. 24–27.

3. Robert W. Bednarzik, "The Role of Enterpreneurship in U.S. and European Job Growth," *Monthly Labor Review,* July 2000, 123, no. 7, pp. 3–16; Wolf Sauter, *Competition Law and Industrial Policy in the Eu,* (Oxford, UK: Oxford University Press, 1998).

4. T. Peters, "Prometheus Barely Unbound," *The Executive,* November 1990, pp. 70–84.

5. Michael Shari, "Free Trade in Asia: Bogged Down Again," *Business Week,* December 4, 2000, 3710, p. 62; "Asia: Smaller Steps," *The Economist,* November 18, 2000, 357, no. 8197, p. 50.

6. James T. Peach, Richard V. Adkisson, "NAFTA and Economic Activity Along the U.S.-Mexico Border," *Journal of Economic Issues,* June 2000, 34, no. 2, pp. 481–89.

7. Gail M. Gerhart, "Can Africa Claim the 21st Century?" *Foreign Affairs,* November/December 2000, 79, no. 6, p. 191; Michael D. White, "Land of Promise," *World Trade,* September 1999, 12, no. 9, pp. 58–60.

8. Evangelos O. Simos, "International Economic Outlook: The World Economy in 2009," *The Journal of Business Forecasting Methods & Systems,* Fall 2000, 19, no. 3, pp. 31–35.

9. Roger Ahrens, "Going Global," *International Business* 9, no. 7 July/August 1996, pp. 26–30; Bill Javetski, "Old World, New Investment," *Business Week,* October 7, 1996, pp. 50–51.

10. Russell B. Scholl, "The International Investment Position of the United States at Yearend 1999," *Survey of Current Business,* July 2000, 80, no. 7, p. 46.

11. "Current International Trade Position of the U.S.: Imports Outpace Exports: Balance with Japan Improves," *Business America* 117, no. 6, June 1996, pp. 35–37.

12. James Barron, "Flower Power," *CIO,* September 15, 2000, 13, no. 25, pp. 108–12.

13. Anne-Wil Harzing, "An Empirical Analysis and Extension of the Bartlett and Ghoshal Typology of Multinational Companies," *Journal of International Business Studies* (2000), 31, 1, pp. 101–20; Don E. Schultz and Philip J. Kitchen, "Global Reach," *Adweek,* October 30, 2000, 41, no. 44, p. 51.

14. Steven E. Prokesch, "Making Global Connections at Caterpillar," *Harvard Business Review* 74, no. 2, March/April 1996, pp. 88–89; Laurie Freeman, "Caterpillar on a Roll," *B to B,* September 11, 2000, 85, no. 14, pp. 3, 44; Ian Buchanan, "The US Experience," *Asian Business,* May 1998, 34, no. 5, pp. 14–16.

15. Chang H. Moon, "The Choice of Entry Modes and Theories of Foreign Direct Investment," *Journal of Global Marketing* 11, no. 2 (1997), pp. 43–64; Isabelle Maignan and Bryan A. Lukas, "Entry Mode Decisions: The Role of Managers' Mental Models," *Journal of Global Marketing* 10, no. 4 (1997), pp. 7–22.

16. Maureen Nevin Duffy, "3M Lauds China Government Help," *Chemical Marketer Reporter* 251, no. 1, January 6, 1997, p. 19.

17. Charlene Marmer Solomon, "Staff Selection Impacts Global Success," *Personnel Journal,* January 1994, pp. 88–101.

18. Nancy J. Adler and Susan Bartholomew, "Managing Globally Competent People," *Academy of Management Executive* 6, no. 3 (1992), pp. 52–65; Cecil G. Howard, "Profile of the 21st-Century Expatriate Manager," *HRMagazine,* June 1992, pp. 93–100.

19. Scott A. Snell, Charles C. Snow, Sue Canney Davison, and Donald C. Hambrick, "Designing and Supporting Transnational Teams: The Human Resource Agenda," *Human Resource Management,* 1998: Charles C. Snow, Scott A. Snell, Sue Canney Davison, and Donald C. Hambrick, "Use Transnational Teams to Globalize Your Company," *Organizational Dynamics,* Spring 1996, pp. 50–67.

20. Donald C. Hambrick, James W. Fredrickson, Lester B. Korn, and Richard M. Ferry, "Reinventing the CEO," *21st Century Report* (New York: Korn/Ferry and Columbia Graduate School of Business, 1989).

21. Charlene Marmer Solomon, "Danger Below! Spot Failing Global Assignments," *Personnel Journal,* November 1996, pp. 78–85.

22. Reyer A. Swaak, "Expatriate Failures: Too Many, Too Much Cost, Too Little Planning," *Compensation & Benefits Review,* November/December 1995, pp. 50–52.

23. Howard, "Profile of the 21st-Century Expatriate Manager."

24. Nancy J. Adler, "Global Leadership: Women Leaders," *Management International Review* 37, no. 1 (Special issue, 1997), pp. 171–96; Nancy J. Adler and Fadna N. Israeli, "Competitive Frontiers. Women Managers in a Global Economy," *Organization Studies* 16, no. 4 (1995), pp. 724–25. See also Nancy J. Adler, "Pacific Basin Managers: A Gaijin, Not a Woman," *Human Resource Management* 26, no. 2 (1987), pp. 169–91; Hilary Harris, "Women in International Management: Opportunity or Threat?" *Women in Management Review* 8, no. 5 (1993), pp. 9–11.

25. Gretchen M. Sprietzer, Morgan W. McCall, and Joan D. Mahoney, "Early Identification of International

Executive Potential," *Journal of Applied Psychology* 82, no. 1 (1997), pp. 6–29; Ronald Mortensen, "Beyond the Fence Line," *HRMagazine,* November 1997, pp. 100–109; "Expatriate Games," *Journal of Business Strategy,* July/August 1997, pp. 4–5; "Building a Global Workforce Starts with Recruitment," *Personnel Journal* (Special Supplement), March 1996, pp. 9–11.

26. Gunnar Beeth, "Multicultural Managers Wanted," *Management Review,* May 1997, p. 21.

27. David Stamps, "Welcome to America," *Training,* November 1996, pp. 23–30.

28. Linda K. Trevino and Katherine A. Nelson, *Managing Business Ethics: Straight Talk about How to Do It Right* (New York: John Wiley & Sons, 1995).

29. Patricia Digh, "Shades of Gray in the Global Marketplace," *HRMagazine,* April 1997, pp. 91–98.

30. Charlene Marmer Solomon, "Put Your Global Ethics to the Test," *Personnel Journal,* January 1996, pp. 66–74.

31. Digh, "Shades of Gray"; Ashay B. Desai and Terri Rittenburg, "Global Ethics: An Integrative Framework for MNEs," *Journal of Business Ethics* 16 (1997), pp. 791–800; Paul Buller, John Kohls, and Kenneth Anderson, "A Model for Addressing Cross-Cultural Ethical Conflicts," *Business & Society* 36, no. 2 (June 1997), pp. 169–93.

Chapter Seven

1. S. Shane and S. Venkataraman, "The Promise of Entrepreneurship as a Field of Research, *Academy of Management Review, 25,* (2000), pp. 217–26.

2. J. A. Timmons, *New Venture Creation* (Burr Ridge, IL: Richard D. Irwin, 1994).

3. G. T. Lumpkin and G. G. Dess, "Clarifying the Entrepreneurial Orientation Construct and Linking It To Performance," *Academy of Management Review,* 1996, Volume 21, pp. 135–72.

4. R. W. Smilor, "Entrepreneurship: Reflections on a Subversive Activity," *Journal of Business Venturing 12* (1997), pp. 341–46.

5. W. Megginson, M. J. Byrd, S. R. Scott Jr., and L. Megginson, *Small Business Management: An Entrepreneur's Guide to Success,* 2nd ed. (Boston: Irwin McGraw-Hill, 1997).

6. Timmons, *New Venture Creation.*

7. T. Peters, "Thrashed by the Real World," *Forbes,* April 7, 1997, p. 100.

8. G. Pinchot, "How Intrapreneurs Innovate," *Management Today*, December 1985, pp. 54–61.

9. A. Marsh, "Promiscuous Breeding" *Forbes,* April 7, 1997, pp. 74–77.

10. B. O'Reilly, "The New Face of Small Business," *Fortune,* May 2, 1994, pp. 82–88.

11. Smilor, "Entrepreneurship," p. 341.

12. H. Aldrich, *Ethnic Entrepreneurs: Immigrant Business in Industrial Societies* (Newbury Park, CA: Sage, 1990).

13. W. A. Sahlman, "The New Economy Is Stronger than You Think," *Harvard Business Review,* November-December 1999, pp. 99–106.

14. P. Evans and T. S. Wurster, "Getting Real About Virtual Commerce," *Harvard Business Review,* November-December 1999, pp. 85–94.

15. J. Useem, "Dot-coms: What Have We Learned?" *Fortune,* October 30, 2000, pp. 82–104.

16. "How It Really Works: Introduction," *Business Week,* August 25, 1997, pp. 48–49.

17. P. Elstron, "It Must Be Something in the Water," *Business Week*, August 25, 1997, pp. 84–87.

18. T. Fuller, "Malaysia's Wired 'Supercorridor'," *International Herald Tribune,* November 15–16, 1997, pp. 1, 6.

19. A. Ebeling, "The Three Icons of the Old West," *Forbes,* November 17, 1997, pp. 152–54.

20. J. Collins and J. Porras, *Built to Last* (London: Century, 1996).

21. Ibid.

22. K. H. Vesper, *New Venture Mechanics* (Englewood Cliffs, NJ: Prentice Hall, 1993).

23. B. Schlender et al., "Cool Companies, Part 1," *Fortune,* July 7, 1997, pp. 50–60.

24. Ibid.

25. Shane & Venkataraman, "Promise of Entrepreneurship."

26. Vesper, *New Venture Mechanics.*

27. E. Schonfeld, "The Space Business Heats Up," *Fortune,* November 24, 1997, pp. 52–60.

28. Ibid.

29. Ibid.

30. E. Schonfeld, "Going Long," *Fortune,* March 20; 2000, pp. 172–92.

31. Vesper, *New Venture Mechanics.*

32. Timmons, *New Venture Creation.*

33. "Do Universities Stifle Entrepreneurship?" *Across the Board,* July/August 1997, pp. 32–38.

34. M. Sonfield and R. Lussier, "The Entrepreneurial Strategy Matrix: A Model for New and Ongoing Ventures," *Business Horizons,* May–June, 1997, pp. 73–77.

35. Hisrich and Peters, *Entrepreneurship.*

36. Ibid.

37. W. A. Sahlman, "How to Write a Great Business Plan," *Harvard Business Review,* July–August 1997, pp. 98–108.

38. Ibid.

39. Ibid.

40. Schlender et al., "Cool Companies."

41. Sahlman, "How to Write a Great Business Plan."

42. Ibid.

43. J. A. Fraser, "Do I Need to Plan Differently for a Dot-com Business?" *Inc.,* July 2000, pp. 142–43.

44. Ibid.

45. R. A. Baron and G. D. Markman, "Beyond Social Capital: How Social Skills Can Enhance Entrepreneurs' Success," *Academy of Management Executive,* February 2000, pp. 106–16.

46. R. Balu, "Starting your Startup," *Fast Company,* January–February, 2000 pp. 81–112.

47. Ibid.

48. S. McCartney, "Michael Dell—and His Company—Grow Up," *The Wall Street Journal*, January 31, 1995, pp. B1, B4.

49. A. F. Brattina, "The Diary of a Small-Company Owner," *Inc.*, May 1993, pp. 79–89, and June 1993, pp. 117–22.

50. L. Kroll, "My Partner, My Father," *Forbes*, June 2, 1997, pp. 66–70.

51. W. P. Barrett, "The Perils of Success," *Forbes*, November 3, 1997, pp. 129–37.

52. Ibid.

53. Ibid., p. 132.

54. O'Reilly, "The New Face of Small Business."

55. C. Burck, "The Real World of the Entrepreneur," *Fortune*, April 5, 1993, pp. 62–81.

56. Serwer, "Lessons from America's Fastest-Growing Companies," pp. 42–60.

57. R. Blunden, "A Framework for the Empirical Study of Venture Discontinuance," in *The Spirit of Entrepreneurship*, ed. R. G. Wycham et al. (Vancouver, BC: International Council of Small Business, 1987), p. 159.

58. P. F. Drucker, "How to Save the Family Business," *The Wall Street Journal*, August 19, 1994, p. A10.

59. Barrett, "The Perils of Success," p. 137.

60. L. Kroll, "The Graduates," *Forbes*, November 3, 1997, pp. 138–42.

61. Balu, "Starting your Startup."

62. B. Oviatt and P. P. McDougall, "Global Start-ups: Entrepreneurs on a Worldwide Stage," *Academy of Management Executive* 9 (1995), pp. 30–43.

63. Ibid.

64. Ibid.

65. M. Hordes, J. A. Clancy, and J. Baddaley, "A Primer for Global Start-ups," *Academy of Management Executive* 9, (1995), pp. 7–11.

66. Ibid.

67. R. M. Kanter et al., "Driving Corporate Entrepreneurship," *Management Review*, April 1987, pp. 14–16.

68. I. Chithelen, "Work in Progress," *Forbes*, November 12, 1990, pp. 226–27.

69. N. Venkatraman, "Five Steps to a Dot-com Strategy: How to Find your Footing on the Web," *Sloan Management Review*, Spring, 2000 pp. 15–28.

70. R. M. Kanter, *The Change Masters* (New York: Simon & Schuster, 1983).

71. D. Clark, "How a Woman's Passion and Persistence Made 'Bob'," *The Wall Street Journal*, January 10, 1995, pp. B1, B8.

72. Collins and Porras, *Built to Last*.

73. D. Roth, "Now, for All you Net Potatoes, Here's NBCi," *Fortune*, March 20, 2000 pp. 156–60.

74. J. B. Quinn, "Outsourcing Innovation: The New Engine of Growth," *Sloan Management Review*, Summer, 2000 pp. 13–28.

75. E. Nee, "Hewlett-Packard's New E-vangelist," *Fortune*, January 10, 2000, pp. 166–67.

76. Kanter et al., "Driving Corporate Entrepreneurship."

77. J. Argenti, *Corporate Collapse*: The Causes and Symptoms (New York: John Wiley & Sons, 1979).

78. Kanter et al., "Driving Corporate Entrepreneurship."

79. G. T. Lumpkin and G. G. Dess, "Clarifying the Entrepreneurial Orientation Construct and Linking It to Performance," *Academy of Management Review* 21 (1996), pp. 135–72.

80. T. Bateman and J. M. Crant, "The Proactive Dimension of Organizational Behavior," *Journal of Organizational Behavior*, 1993, pp. 103–18.

81. A. E. Serwer, "Michael Dell Turns the PC World Inside Out," *Fortune*, September 8, 1997, pp. 38–44.

82. Lumpkin and Dess, "Clarifying the Entrepreneurial Orientation Construct."

83. Collins and Porras, *Built to Last*.

84. G. Pinchot and E. Pinchot, *The Intelligent Organization* (San Francisco: Berrett-Koehler, 1996).

Chapter Eight

1. Ronald N. Ashkenas and Suzanne C. Francis, "Integration Managers: Special Leaders for Special Times," *Harvard Business Review,* November/December 2000, 78, no. 6, pp. 108–16.

2. Andrew West, "The Flute Factory: An Empirical Measurement of the Effect of the Division of Labor on Productivity and Production Cost," *American Economist,* Spring 1999, 43, no. 1, pp. 82–87.

3. P. Lawrence and J. Lorsch, *Organization and Environment* (Homewood, IL: Richard D. Irwin, 1969).

4. Ibid.; Thompson, *The New Manager's Handbook*. Also see S. Sharifi and K. S. Pawar, "Product Design as a Means of Integrating Differentiation," *Technovation* 16, no. 5 (May 1996), pp. 255–64; W. B. Stevenson and J. M. Bartunek, "Power, Interaction, Position, and the Generation of Cultural Agreement in Organizations," *Human Relations* 49, no. 1 (January 1996), pp. 75–104.

5. Abbas J. Ali, Robert C. Camp, and Manton Gibbs, "The Ten Commandments Perspective on Power and Authority in Organizations," *Journal of Business Ethics,* August 2000, 26, no. 4, pp. 351–61; Robert F. Pearse, "Understanding Organizational Power and Influence Systems," *Compensation & Benefits Management,* Autumn 2000, 16, no. 4, pp. 28–38.

6. Susan F. Shultz, *Board Book: Making Your Corporate Board a Strategic Force in Your Company's Success* (New York: AMACOM, 2000); Ralph D. Ward, *Improving Corporate Boards: The Boardroom Insider Guidebook* (New York: John Wiley & Sons, 2000).

7. John A. Byrne, "The Best & the Worst Boards," *Business Week,* January 24, 2000, 3665, pp. 142–52.

8. A. J. Michels, "Chief Executives as Idi Ahmin?" *Fortune,* July 1, 1991, p. 13; C. M. Daily and D. R. Dalton, "CEO and Board Chair Roles Held Jointly or Separately: Much Ado About Nothing?", *Academy of Management Executive* 11, no. 3 (August 1997), pp. 11–20.

9. Tony Simons, Lisa Hope Pelled, and Ken A. Smith, "Making Use of Difference: Diversity, Debate, and Decision Comprehensiveness in Top Management Teams," *Academy of Management Journal,* December 1999, 42, no. 6, pp. 662–73; C. Carl Pegels, Yong I Song, and Baik Yang, "Management Heterogeneity, Competitive Interaction Groups, and Firm Performance," *Strategic Management Journal,* September 2000, 21, no. 3, pp. 911–21.

10. Shawnee Vickery, Cornelia Droge, and Richard Germain, "The Relationship Between Product Customization and Organizational Structure," *Journal of Operations Management,* June 1999, 17, no. 4, pp. 377–91.

11. D. Van Fleet and A. Bedeian, "A History of the Span of Management," *Academy of Management Review* 2 (1977), pp. 356–72.

12. Philippe Jehiel, "Information Aggregation and Communication in Organizations," *Management Science,* May 1999, 45, no. 5, pp. 659–69; Ahnn Altaffer, "First-line Managers: Measuring Their Span of Control," *Nursing Management,* July 1998, 29, no. 7, pp. 36–40.

13. "Span of Control vs. Span of Support," *The Journal for Quality and Participation,* Fall 2000, 23, no. 4, p. 15; James Gallo and Paul R. Thompson, "Goals, Measures, and Beyond: In Search of Accountability in Federal HRM," *Public Personnel Management,* Summer 2000, 29, no. 2, pp. 237–48; Clinton O. Longenecker and Timothy C. Stansfield, "Why Plant Managers Fail: Causes and Consequences," *Industrial Management,* January/February 2000, 42, no. 1, pp. 24–32.

14. E. Beaubien, "Legendary Leadership," *Executive Excellence* 14, no. 9 (September 1997), p. 20; "How Well Do You Delegate," *Supervision* 58, no. 8 (August 1997), p. 26; J. Mahoney, "Delegating Effectively," *Nursing Management* 28, no. 6 (June 1997), p. 62; J. Lagges, "The Role of Delegation in Improving Productivity," *Personnel Journal,* November 1979, pp. 776–79.

15. G. Matthews, "Run Your Business or Build an Organization?" *Harvard Management Review,* March–April 1984, pp. 34–44.

16. Russ Forrester, "Empowerment: Rejuvenating a Potent Idea," *The Academy of Management Executive,* August 2000, 14, no. 3, pp. 67–80; Monica L. Perry, Craig L. Pearce, and Henry P. Sims, Jr., "Empowered Selling Teams: How Shared Leadership Can Contribute to Selling Team Outcomes," *The Journal of Personal Selling & Sales Management,* Summer 1999, 19, no. 3, pp. 35–51.

17. Suzy Wetlaufer, "Organizing for Empowerment: An Interview with AES's Roger Sant and Dennis Bakke," *Harvard Business Review,* January/February 1999, 77, no. 1, pp. 110–23.

18. E. E. Lawler III, "New Roles for the Staff Function: Strategic Support and Services," in *Organizing for the Future,* J. Galbraith, E. E. Lawler III, & Associates (San Francisco: Jossey-Bass, 1993).

19. Michael Porter, *Competitive Advantage: Creating and Sustaining Superior Performance* (New York: Free Press, 1985).

20. Rob Cross and Lloyd Baird, "Technology Is Not Enough: Improving Performance by Building Organizational Memory," *Sloan Management Review,* Spring 2000, 41, no. 3, pp. 69–78; R. Duncan, "What is the Right Organization Structure?", *Organizational Dynamics* 7 (Winter 1979), pp. 59–80.

21. George S. Day, "Creating a Market-Driven Organization," *Sloan Management Review,* Fall 1999, 41, no. 1, pp. 11–22.

22. R. Boehm and C. Phipps, "Flatness Forays," *McKinsey Quarterly* 3 (1996), pp. 128–43.

23. Bruce T. Lamont, V. Sambamurthy, Kimberly M. Ellis, and Paul G. Simmonds, "The Influence of Organizational Structure on the Information Received by Corporate Strategists of Multinational Enterprises," *Management International Review,* Third Quarter 2000, 40, no. 3, pp. 231–52.

24. Wilma Bernasco, Petra C. de Weerd-Nederhof, Harry Tillema, and Harry Boer, "Balanced Matrix Structure and New Product Development Process at Texas Instruments Materials and Controls Division," *R&D Management,* April 1999, 29, no. 2, pp. 121–31; J. K. McCollum, "The Matrix Structure: Bane or Benefit to High Tech Organizations?" *Project Management Journal* 24, no. 2 (June 1993), pp. 23–26; R. C. Ford, "Cross-Functional Structures: A Review and Integration of Matrix," *Journal of Management* 18, no. 2 (June 1992), pp. 267–94; H. Kolodny, "Managing in a Matrix," *Business Horizons,* March–April 1981, pp. 17–24.

25. David Cackowski, Mohammad K. Najdawi, and Q. B. Chung, "Object Analysis in Organizational Design: A Solution for Matrix Organizations," *Project Management Journal,* September 2000, 31, no. 3, pp. 44–51; J. Barker, "Conflict Approaches of Effective and Ineffective Project Managers: A Field Study in a Matrix Organization," *Journal of Management Studies* 25, no. 2 (March 1988), pp. 167–78; G. J. Chambers, "The Individual in a Matrix Organization," *Project Management Journal* 20, no. 4 (December 1989), pp. 37–42, 50; S. Davis and P. Lawrence, "Problems of Matrix Organizations," *Harvard Business Review,* May–June 1978, pp. 131–42.

26. Anthony Ferner, "Being Local Worldwide: ABB and the Challenge of Global Management Relations," *Industrielles,* Summer 2000, 55, no. 3, pp. 527–29; C. Bartlett and S. Ghoshal, "Matrix Management: Not a Structure, a Frame of Mind," *Harvard Business Review* 68 (July–August 1990), pp. 138–45.

27. Jasmine Tata, Sameer Prasad, and Ron Thorn, "The Influence of Organizational Structure on the Effectiveness of TQM Programs," *Journal of Managerial Issues,* Winter 1999, 11, no. 4, pp. 440–53; Davis and Lawrence, "Problems of Matrix Organizations."

28. J. G. March & H. A. Simon, *Organizations* (New York: John Wiley &

Sons, 1958); J. D. Thompson, *Organizations in Action* (New York: McGraw-Hill, 1967).

29. Paul S. Adler, "Building Better Bureaucracies," *The Academy of Management Executive,* November 1999, 13, no. 4, pp. 36–49.

30. M. Tushman and D. Nadler, "Implications of Political Models of Organization," in *Resource Book in Macro Organizational Behavior,* ed. R. H. Miles (Santa Monica, CA: Goodyear, 1980).

Chapter Nine

1. Rick Dove, "Agility = Knowledge Management + Response Ability," *Automotive Manufacturing & Production,* March 1999, 111, no.3, pp. 16–17; Patrick M Wright, Lee Dyer, and Michael G Takla, "What's Next? Key Findings from the 1999 State-of-the-Art & Practice Study," *Human Resource Planning* (1999), 22, no. 4, pp. 12–20.

2. T. Burns and G. Stalker, *The Management of Innovation* (London: Tavistock, 1961).

3. Krackhardt and Hanson, "Information Networks: The Company Behind the Chart," *Harvard Business Review,* July–August 1993, pp. 104–11.

4. B. Buell and R. Hof, "Hewlett-Packard Rethinks Itself," *Business Week,* April 1, 1991, pp. 76–79.

5. "Why Big Might Remain Beautiful," *The Economist,* March 24, 1990, p. 79; W. Zellner, "Go-Go Goliaths," *Business Week,* February 13, 1995, pp. 64–70.

6. "Chasing the Future," Microsoft Corporation essay (http://www.microsoft.com/ISSUES/essays/07-10research.asp).

7. Linda L Hellofs and Robert Jacobson, "Market Share and Customers' Perceptions of Quality: When Can Firms Grow their Way to Higher versus Lower Quality?," *Journal of Marketing,* January 1999, 63, no. 1, pp. 16–25.

8. M. Selz, "Small Manufacturers Display the Nimbleness the Times Require," *The Wall Street Journal,*

December 29, 1993, pp. A1, A2; (http://www.ultrapac.com/).

9. W. Cascio, "Downsizing: What Do We Know? What Have We Learned?" *Academy of Management Executive,* February 1993, pp. 95–104; Sarah J. Freeman, "The Gestalt of Organizational Downsizing: Downsizing Strategies As Package of Change," *Human Relations,* December 1999, 52, no. 12, pp. 1505–154.

10. R. E. Stross, "Microsoft's Big Advantage—Hiring Only the Supersmart," *Fortune,* November 25, 1996, pp. 159–62; R. Lieber, "Wired for Hiring. Microsoft's Slick Recruiting Machine," *Fortune,* February 5, 1996, pp. 123–24; Ibid.; M. Hitt, B. Keats, H. Harback, and R. Nixon, "Rightsizing: Building and Maintaining Strategic Leadership and Long-Term Competitiveness," *Organizational Dynamics,* Fall 1994, pp. 18–31.

11. Cascio, "Downsizing," and Jack Ciancio, "Survivor's Syndrome," *Nursing Management,* May 2000, 31, no. 5, pp. 43–45.

12. J. Galbraith, "Organization Design: An Information Processing View," *Interfaces* 4 (Fall 1974), pp. 28–36. See also S. A. Mohrman, "Integrating Roles and Structure in the Lateral Organization," in *Organizing for the Future,* J. Galbraith, E. E. Lawler III, & Associates (San Francisco: Jossey-Bass, 1993); Barbara B. Flynn and F. James Flynn, "Information-processing Alternatives for Coping with Manufacturing Environment Complexity," *Decision Sciences,* Fall 1999, 30, no. 4, pp. 1021–52.

13. Walden Paddlers, personal communication.

14. Galbraith, "Organization Design," Mohrman, "Integrating Roles and Structure."

15. K. Ohmae, *The Mind of the Strategist: Business Planning for Competitive Advantage* (New York: Penguin Books, 1982), Chap. 8; Harry Stern, "Succeeding in a 'customer-centric' Economy," *Foodservice Equipment & Supplies,* September 2000, 53, no. 10, pp. 27–28.

16. K. Ishikawa, *What Is Total Quality Control? The Japanese Way,* trans. David J. Lu (Englewood Cliffs, NJ: Prentice Hall, 1985); Bob Lewis, "Instead of Focusing Solely on Internal Customers, Look at Customers as Well," *InfoWorld,* October 25, 1999, 21, 43, p. 104.

17. Bill Creech, *The 5 Pillars of TQM: How to Make Total Quality Management Work for You* (New York: Plume Publishing, 1995,) James R. Evans and William M. Lindsay, *Management and Control of Quality* (Cincinnati: Southwestern College Publishing, 1998).

18. Mark Czarnecki, *Managing by Measuring: How to Improve Your Organization's Performance through Effective Benchmarking* (New York: AMACOM, 1999); Douglas Dow, Danny Samson, and Steve Ford, "Exploding the Myth: Do All Quality Management Practices Contribute to Superior Quality Performance?" *Production and Operations Management,* Spring 1999, 8, 1, pp. 1–27. See also, Janet Barnard, "Using Total Quality Principles in Business Courses: The Effect on Student Evaluations," *Business Communication Quarterly,* June 1999, 62, no. 2, pp. 61–73.

19. For more information about ISO 9000 (as well as newer programs such as ISO 14000 for environmental management), see the International Organization for Standardization's web page: http://www.iso.ch/welcome. html.

20. J. Champy, *Reengineering Management* (New York: HarperBusiness, 1995). See also M. Hammer and J. Champy, *Reengineering the Corporation* (New York: HarperCollins, 1992).

21. Joan Woodward, *Industrial Organization: Theory and Practice* (London: Oxford University Press, 1965).

22. James H. Gilmore and B. Joseph Pine, Ed., *Markets of One: Creating Customer-Unique Value through Mass Customization* (Cambridge: Harvard Business Review Press, 2000); B. Joseph Pine, *Mass Customization: The New Frontier in Business Competition* (Cambridge:

Harvard Business School Press, 1992).

23. Funda Sahin, "Manufacturing Competitiveness: Different Systems to Achieve the Same Results," *Production and Inventory Management Journal,* First Quarter 2000, 41, no. 1, pp. 56–65.

24. Subhash Wadhwa, and K. Srinivasa Rao, "Flexibility: An Emerging Meta-competence for Managing High Technology," *International Journal of Technology Management* 19, (2000) no. 7-8, pp. 820–45.

25. Jeff Green, "How Architects Are Giving Jeep New Traction," *Business Week,* October 2, 2000, p. 152H; Jeff Green, "Honda's Independent Streak," *Business Week,* October 2, 2000, pp. 152B–152H; Brett A. Peters and Leon F. McGinnis, "Strategic Configuration of Flexible Assembly Systems: A Single Period Approximation," *IIE Transaction,* April 1999, 31, no. 4, pp. 379–90.

26. A. Taylor III, "How Toyota Defies Gravity," *Fortune,* December 8, 1997, pp. 100–108; Gary S. Vasilash, "How Toyota Does It—Every Day," Automotive Manufacturing & Production, August 2000, 112, no. 8, pp. 48–49; Stephen R. Morrey, "Learning to Think Lean: A Roadmap and Toolbox for the Lean Journey," *Automotive Manufacturing & Production,* August 2000, 112, no. 8, p. 147; Funda Sahin, "Manufacturing Competitiveness: Different Systems to Achieve the Same Results," *Production and Inventory Management Journal,* First Quarter 2000, 41, no. 1, pp. 56–65.

27. Sahin, "Manufacturing Competitiveness"; Gary S. Vasilash, "Flexible Thinking: How Need, Innovation, Teamwork & a Whole Bunch of Machining Centers Have Transformed TRW Tillsonburg into a Model of Lean Manufacturing," *Automotive Manufacturing & Production,* October 1999, 111, no. 10, pp. 64–65.

28. Chen H. Chung, "Balancing the Two Dimensions of Time for Time-based Competition," *Journal of Managerial Issues,* Fall 1999, 11, no. 3, pp.

299–314; Denis R. Towill and Peter McCullen, "The Impact of Agile Manufacturing on Supply Chain Dynamics," *International Journal of Logistics Management* (1999), 10, no. 1, pp. 83–96; see also George Stalk and Thomas M. Hout, *Competing Against Time: How Time-Based Competition Is Reshaping Global Markets* (New York: Free Press, 1990).

29. R. Henkoff, "Delivering the Goods," *Fortune,* November 28, 1994, pp. 64–78; Tony Seideman, "A&P Uses Transportation Software to Wring New Efficiency Out of Supply Chain," *Stores,* September 2000, 82, no. 9, pp. 172–74.

30. "2001 in Review: Logistics," *Traffic World,* January 1, 2001, 265, no.1, p. 15; Morris A. Cohen, Carl Cull, Hau L Lee and Don Willen, "Saturn's Supply-chain Innovation: High Value in After-sales Service," *Sloan Management Review,* Summer 2000, 41, no. 4, pp. 93–101.

31. Tom Stundza, "Buyers Ask Service Centers: 'What Happened to JIT?'. . . and a Few Other Things," *Purchasing,* May 6, 1999, 126, 7, pp. 60–70; Damien Power and Amrik S. Sohal, "Human Resource Management Strategies and Practices in Just-in-time Environments: Australian Case Study Evidence," *Technovation,* July 2000, 20, 7, pp. 373–87.

32. M. Tucker and D. Davis, "Key Ingredients for Successful Implementation of Just-in-Time: A System for All Business Sizes," *Business Horizons,* May–June 1993, pp. 59–65; Helen L. Richardson, "Tame Supply Chain Bottlenecks," *Transportation & Distribution,* March 2000, 41, no. 3, pp. 23–28.

33. John E. Ettlie, "Product Development—Beyond Simultaneous Engineering," *Automotive Manufacturing & Production,* July 2000, 112, 7, p. 18; Utpal Roy, John M. Usher, and Hamid R. Parsaei, eds. *Simultaneous Engineering: Methodologies and Applications* (Newark, NJ: Gordon and Breach, 1999); Marilyn M. Helms and Lawrence P. Ettkin, "Time-based Competitiveness: A Strategic Per-

spective," *Competitiveness Review* (2000) 10, no. 2, pp. 1–14.

34. G. Hamel and C. K. Prahalad, "Competing for the Future," *Harvard Business Review,* July–August 1994, pp. 122–28.

35. G. Hamel and C. K. Prahalad, *Competing for the Future* (Boston: Harvard Business School Press, 1994).

36. R. E. Miles and C. C. Snow, *Fit, Failure, and the Hall of Fame* (New York: Free Press, 1994); Gillian Symon, "Information and Communication Technologies and Network Organization: A Critical Analysis," *Journal of Occupational and Organizational Psychology,* December 2000, 73, no. 4, pp. 389–95.

37. M. Lynne Markus, Brook Manville, and Carole E. Agres "What Makes a Virtual Organization Work?" *Sloan Management Review,* Fall 2000, 42, no. 1, pp. 13–26; William M. Fitzpatrick and Donald R. Burke, "Form, Functions, and Financial Performance Realities for the Virtual Organization," *S.A.M. Advanced Management Journal,* Summer 2000, 65, no. 3, pp. 13–20.

38. Miles and Snow, *Fit, Failure, and the Hall of Fame.*

39. Sherri Singer, "Diesel Engines Burn Leaner and Cleaner," *Machine Design,* October 7, 1999, 71, no. 19, pp. 64–69; P. P. Balestrini, "Globalization in the Automotive Industry: The Preferred External Growth Path," *Journal of International Marketing and Marketing Research,* October 2000, 25, no. 3, pp. 137–65.

40. Pamela Harper and D. Vincent Varallo, "Global Strategic Alliances," *Executive Excellence,* October 2000, 17, no.10, pp. 17–18.

41. R. M. Kanter, "Collaborative Advantage: The Art of Alliances," *Harvard Business Review,* July–August 1994, pp. 96–108; John B. Cullen, Jean L. Johnson, and Tomoaki Sakano, "Success Through Commitment and Trust: The Soft Side of Strategic Alliance Management," *Journal of World Business,* Fall 2000, 35, no. 3, pp. 223–40; Prashant Kale, Harbir Singh, and Howard Perlmutter,

"Learning and Protection of Proprietary Assets in Strategic Alliances: Building Relational Capital," *Strategic Management Journal,* March 2000, 21, no. 3, pp. 217–37.

42. P. Senge, *The Fifth Discipline* (New York: Doubleday Currency, 1990).

43. D. A. Garvin, "Building a Learning Organization," *Harvard Business Review,* July–August 1993, pp. 78–91; David A. Garvin, *Learning in Action: A Guide to Putting the Learning Organization to Work* (Boston: Harvard Business School Press, 2000); Victoria J. Marsick and Karen E. Watkins, *Facilitating Learning Organizations: Making Learning Count* (Aldershot, Hampshire, Gower Pub. Co, 1999).

44. Ibid.

45. Robert J. Vandenberg, Hettie A. Richardson, and Lorrina J. Eastman, "The Impact of High Involvement Work Processes on Organizational Effectiveness: A Second-order Latent Variable Approach," *Group & Organization Management,* September 1999, 24, no. 3, pp. 300–39; Gretchen M. Spreitzer and Aneil K. Mishra, "Giving Up Control without Losing Control. Trust and Its Substitutes' Effects on Managers' Involving Employees in Decision Making," *Group & Organization Management,* June 1999, 24, no. 2, pp. 155–87; Susan Albers Mohrman, Gerald E. Ledford, and Edward E. Lawler, III, *Strategies for High Performance Organizations—The CEO Report: Employee Involvement, TQM, and Reengineering Programs in Fortune 1000 Corporations,* (San Francisco: Jossey-Bass, 1998).

46. R. Ashkenas, D. Ulrich, T. Jick, and S. Kerr, *The Boundaryless Organization: Breaking the Chains of Organizational Structure* (San Francisco: Jossey-Bass, 1995); R. W. Keidel, "Rethinking Organizational Design," *Academy of Management Executive,* November 1994, pp. 12–27; Ron Ashkenas, Todd Jick, Dave Ulrich, and Catherine Paul-Chowdhury, *The Boundaryless Organization Field Guide: Practical Tools for Building the New Organization* (San Francisco: Jossey-Bass, 1999).

Chapter Ten

1. "The Importance of HR," *HRFocus,* March 1996, p. 14; John McMorrow, "Future Trends in Human Resources," *HR Focus,* September 1999, 76, no. 9, pp. 7–9; Albert A. Vicere, "New Economy, New HR," *Employment Relations Today,* Autumn 2000, 27, no. 3, pp. 1–11.

2. Thomas O. Davenport, "Workers As Assets: A Good Start But . . . ," *Employment Relations Today,* Spring 2000, 27, no. 1, pp. 1–18; Bruce Gilley, "Filling the Gap," *Far Eastern Economic Review,* September 14, 2000, 163, no. 37, pp. 44–46; "Filling the Skills Gap," *Business Europe,* May 17, 2000, 40, no. 10, p. 6.

3. Darin E. Hartley, *Job Analysis at the Speed of Reality* (Amherst, MA: HRD Press, 1999); Frederick P. Morgeson and Michael A. Campion, "Accuracy in Job Analysis: Toward an Inference-based Model," *Journal of Organizational Behavior,* November 2000, 21, no. 7, pp. 819–27; Jeffery S. Shippmann, Ronald A. Ash, Linda Carr, and Beryl Hesketh, "The Practice of Competency Modeling," *Personnel Psychology,* Autumn 2000, 53, no. 3, pp. 703–40.

4. Jeffery S. Schippmann, *Strategic Job Modeling: Working at the Core of Integrated Human Resources.* (Mahwah, NJ: Lawrence Erlbaum Associates, 1999).

5. David E. Terpstra, "The Search for Effective Methods," *HRFocus,* May 1996, pp. 16–17; Herbert G. Heneman III and Robyn A. Berkley, "Applicant Attraction Practices and Outcomes Among Small Businesses," *Journal of Small Business Management,* January 1999, 37, no. 1, pp. 53–74; Jean-Marie Hiltrop, "The Quest for the Best: Human Resource Practices to Attract and Retain Talent," *European Management Journal,* August 1999, 17, no. 4, pp. 422–30.

6. Kerri Koss Morehart, "How to Create an Employee Referral Program that Really Works," *HR Focus,* January 2001, 78, no. 1, pp. 3–5; Keith Swenson, "Maximizing Employee Referrals" *HR Focus,* January 1999,

76, no. 1, pp. 9–10; "Are Your Recruiting Methods Discriminatory?" *Workforce* May 2000, 79, no. 5, pp. 105–6.

7. "Pop Quiz: How Do You Recruit the Best College Grads?" *Personnel Journal,* August 1995, pp. 12–18; Shannon Peters Talbott, "Boost Your Campus Image to Attract Top Grads," *Personnel Journal,* March 1996, pp. 6–8; Cora Daniels, "Wall Street Says Please," *Fortune,* March 6, 2000, 141, no. 5, p. 420; Jean Buchanan, "Finding and Keeping Talent in a Shrinking Labor Pool," *Office Systems,* November 1999, 16, no. 11, pp. 42–46.

8. Malcolm Wheatley, "The Talent Spotters," *Management Today,* June 1996, pp. 62–64; Michael McDaniel, Deborah L. Whetzel, Frank L. Schmidt, and Steven D. Maurer, "The Validity of Employment Interviews: A Comprehensive Review and Meta-Analysis," *Journal of Applied Psychology* 79, no. 4 (August 1994), pp. 599–616; Michael A. Campion, James E. Campion, and Peter J. Hudson Jr., "Structured Interviewing: A Note on Incremental Validity and Alternative Question Types," *Journal of Applied Psychology* 79, no. 6 (December 1994), pp. 998–1002; R. A. Fear, *The Evaluation Interview* (New York: McGraw-Hill, 1984); Pamela Mendels, "Asking the Right Questions," *Business Week Online,* October 13, 2000; Matthew T. Miklave and A. Jonathan Trafimow "Ask Them If They Were Fired, But Not When They Graduated," *Workforce,* August 2000, 79, no. 8, pp. 90–93; Olivia Crosby, "Employment Interviewing: Seizing the Opportunity and the Job," *Occupational Outlook Quarterly,* Summer 2000, 44, no. 2, pp. 14–21.

9. Christopher E. Stenberg, "The Role of Pre-employment Background Investigations in Hiring," *Human Resource Professional* 9, no. 1 (January/February 1996), pp. 19–21; "The Final Rung: References," *Across the Board,* March 1996, p. 40; Paul Taylor, "Providing Structure to Interviews and Reference Checks," *Workforce,* May 1999, Supplement,

pp. 7–10; "Avoiding 'Truth or Dare' in Reference Checks," *HRFocus,* May 2000, 77, no. 5, pp. 5–6; "Fear of Lawsuits Complicates Reference Checks," *InfoWorld* February 1, 1999, 21, no. 5, p. 73; D. L. Hawley, "Background Checks on the Rise," *Legal Assistant Today,* May/Jun 2000, 17, no. 5, pp. 28, 40; David E. Terpstra, R. Bryan Kethley, Richard T. Foley, and Wanthanee Limpaphayom, "The Nature of Litigation Surrounding Five Screening Devices," *Public Personnel Management,* Spring 2000, 29, no. 1, pp. 43–54.

10. See also M. R. Barrick and M. K. Mount, "The Big Five Personality Dimensions and Job Performance: A Meta-Analysis," *Personnel Psychology* 44 (1991), pp. 1–26; Daniel P. O'Meara, "Personality Tests Raise Questions of Legality and Effectiveness," *HRMagazine,* January 1994, pp. 97–100; Lynn A. McFarland and Ann Marie Ryan, "Variance in Faking Across Noncognitive Measures," *Journal of Applied Psychology,* October 2000, 85, no. 5, pp. 812–21.

11. "Denny's Takes Drug-free Policy Nationwide," *Employee Benefit Plan Review,* October 2000, 55, no. 4, pp. 34–36; "Fewer Employers Are Currently Conducting Psych & Drug Tests," *HRFocus,* October 2000, 77, no. 10, p. 8; Debra R. Comer, "Employees' Attitudes Toward Fitness-for-duty Testing," *Journal of Managerial Issues,* Spring 2000, 12, no. 1, pp. 61–75; "ACLU Report Debunks Workplace Drug Testing," *HRFocus,* November 1999, 76, no. 4, p. 4.

12. Patrick M. Wright, Michele K. Kacmar, Gary C. McMahan, and Kevin Deleeuw, "P = f(M × A): Cognitive Ability as a Moderator of the Relationship between Personality and Job Performance," *Journal of Management* 21, no. 6 (1995), pp. 1129–2063; Paul R. Sackett and Daniel J. Ostgaard, "Job-Specific Applicant Pools and National Norms for Cognitive Ability Tests: Implications for Range Restriction Corrections in Validation Research," *Journal of Applied Psychology* 79, no. 5 (October

1994), pp. 680–84; F. L. Schmidt and J. E. Hunter, "Tacit Knowledge, Practical Intelligence, General Mental Ability, and Job Knowledge," *Current Directions in Psychological Science* 2, no. 1 (1993), pp. 3–13; Mary Roznowski, David N. Dickter, Linda L. Sawin, Valerie J. Shute, and Sehee Hong, "The Validity of Measures of Cognitive Processes and Generability for Learning and Performance on Highly Complex Computerized Tutors: Is the G Factor of Intelligence Even More General?" *Journal of Applied Psychology,* December 2000, 85, no. 6, 940–55; Jose M. Cortina, Nancy B. Goldstein, Stephanie C. Payne, H. Krisl Davison, and Stephen W. Gilliland, "The Incremental Validity of Interview Scores Over and Above Cognitive Ability and Conscientiousness Scores," *Personnel Psychology,* Summer 2000, 53, no. 2, 325–51.

13. Winfred Arthur Jr., David J. Woehr, and Robyn Maldegen, "Convergent and Discriminant Validity of Assessment Center Dimensions: A Conceptual and Empirical Reexamination of the Assessment Center Construct-related Validity Paradox," *Journal of Management* (2000), 26, no. 4, pp. 813–35; Raymond Randall, Eammon Ferguson, and Fiona Patterson, "Self-assessment Accuracy and Assessment Center Decisions," *Journal of Occupational and Organizational Psychology,* December 2000, 73, no. 4, p. 443.

14. Lynn A. McFarland and Ann Marie Ryan, "Variance in Faking Across Noncognitive Measures," *Journal of Applied Psychology,* October 2000, 85, no. 5, 812–21; David E. Terpstra; R. Bryan Kethley, Richard T. Folev, and Wanthanee Limpaphayom. "The Nature of Litigation Surrounding Five Screening Devices," *Public Personnel Management,* Spring 2000, 29, no. 1, pp. 43–54.

15. D. S. Ones, C. Viswesvaran, and F. L. Schmidt, "Comprehensive Meta-Analysis of Integrity Test Validities: Findings and Implications for Personnel Selection and Theories of Job Performance," *Journal of Applied Psychology* 78 (August 1993), pp. 679–703.

16. Rocki-Lee DeWitt, "The Structural Consequences of Downsizing," *Organization Science* 4, no. 1 (February 1993), pp. 30–40; Priti Pradhan Shah, "Network Destruction: The Structural Implications of Downsizing," *Academy of Management Journal,* February 2000, 43, no. 1, pp. 101–12; Jennifer Laabs, "Has Downsizing Missed Its Mark?" *Workforce,* April 1999, 78, no. 4, pp. 30–38.

17. See *Adair v. United States,* 2078 U.S. 161 (1908); Deborah A. Ballam, "Employment-at-will; The Impending Death of a Doctrine," *American Business Law Journal,* Summer 2000, 37, no. 4, pp. 653–87.

18. Anne Fisher, "Dumping Troublemakers, and Exiting Gracefully," *Fortune,* February 15, 1999, 139, no. 3, p. 174; Paul Falcone "Employee Separations: Layoffs vs. Terminations for Cause," *HRMagazine,* October 2000, 45, no. 10, pp. 189–96; Paul Falcone, "A Blueprint for Progressive Discipline and Terminations," *HRFocus,* August 2000, 77, no. 8, pp. 3–5.

19. See also John E. Lyncheski, "Mishandling Terminations Causes Legal Nightmares," *HRMagazine* 40, no. 5 (May 1995), pp. 25–30. Katherine A. Karl and Barry W. Hancock, "Expert Advice on Employment Termination Practices: How Expert Is It?" *Public Personnel Management,* Spring 1999, 28, no. 1, pp. 51–62.

20. *Employer EEO Responsibilities* (Washington, DC: Equal Employment Opportunity Commission, U.S. Government Printing Office, 1996); Nancy J. Edman and Michael D. Levin-Epstein, *Primer of Equal Employment Opportunity,* 6th ed. (Washington, DC: Bureau of National Affairs, 1994).

21. Robert Gatewood and Hubert Field, *Human Resource Selection,* 3rd ed. (Chicago, IL: Dryden Press, 1994), pp. 36–49; R. A. Baysinger, "Disparate Treatment and Disparate Impact Theories of Discrimination: The Continuing Evolution of Title VII of the 1964 Civil Rights Act," in *Readings in Personnel and Human Resource Management,* ed. R. S. Schuler, S. A. Youngblood, and V. L.

Huber (St. Paul, MN: West Publishing, 1987).

22. "Uniform Guidelines on Employee Selection Procedures," *Federal Register* 43, no. 166 (August 25, 1978), pp. 38290–309.

23. "Industry Report 2000: The Money," *Training,* October 2000, 37, no. 10, pp. 51–55; Skip Corsini, "The Great Training Robbery," *Training,* October 2000, 37, no. 10, p. 160.

24. A. P. Carnevale, *America and the New Economy: How New Competitive Standards Are Radically Changing American Workplaces* (San Francisco: Jossey-Bass, 1991); Marc Hequet, "Doing More with Less," *Training* 31 (October 1995), pp. 77–82; Robert M. Fulmer, Philip A. Gibbs, and Marshall Goldsmith, "Developing Leaders: How Winning Companies Keep On Winning," *Sloan Management Review,* Fall 2000, 42, no. 1, pp. 49–59; "Most Training Dollars Spent on Trainers, and Not Materials," *HR Focus,* December 2000, 77, no. 12, p. 8.

25. Sandra N. Phillips, "Team Training Puts Fizz in Coke Plant's Future," *Personnel Journal* 75, no. 1 (January 1996), pp. 39–42. See also George Bohlander and Kathy McCarthy, "How to Get the Most from Team Training," *National Productivity Review,* Autumn 1996, pp. 25–35.

26. For more information, see Kenneth Wexley and Gary Latham, *Increasing Productivity through Performance Appraisal* (Reading, MA; Addison-Wesley, 1994).

27. Mark Edwards and Ann J. Ewen, "How to Manage Performance and Pay with 360-Degree Feedback," *Compensation and Benefits* Review 28, no. 3 (May/June 1996), pp. 41–46. Also see Mary N. Vinson, "The Pros and Cons of 360-Degree Feedback: Making It Work," *Training and Development* 50, no. 4 (April 1996), pp. 11–12; John F. Milliman, Robert F. Zawacki, Carol Norman, Lynda Powell, and Jay Kirksey, "Companies Evaluate Employees from All Perspectives," *Personnel Journal* 73, no. 11 (November 1994), pp. 99–103; R. S. Schuler, *Personnel and Human Resource Management* (St. Paul, MN: West Publishing 1984).

28. G. W. Bohlander, S. A. Snell, and A. W. Sherman, Jr., *Managing Human Resources,* 12th edition, (Cincinnati, OH: Southwestern Publishing, 2001).

29. Garry M. Ritzky, "Incentive Pay Programs That Help the Bottom Line," *HRMagazine* 40, no. 4 (April 1995), pp. 68–74; Steven Gross and Jeffrey Bacher, "The New Variable Pay Programs: How Some Succeed, Why Some Don't," *Compensation and Benefits Review* 25, no. 1 (January–February 1993), p. 51; G. T. Milkovich and J. M. Newman, *Compensation* (New York: McGraw-Hill Irwin, 1999).

30. Theresa Welbourne and Luis Gomez-Mejia, "Gainsharing: A Critical Review and a Future Research Agenda," *Journal of Management* 21, no. 3 (1995), pp. 559–609; Luis P. Gomez-Mejia, Theresa M. Welbourne, and Robert M. Wiseman, "The Role of Risk Sharing and Risk Taking Under Gainsharing," *Academy of Management Review,* July 2000, 25, no. 3, pp. 492–507; Denis Collins, *Gainsharing and Power: Lessons from Six Scanlon Plans* (Ithaca, NY: ILR Press, 1998); P. K. Zingheim and J. R. Schuster, *Pay people right!* (San Francisco: Jossey Bass, 2000).

31. J. Savage, "Incentive Programs at Nucor Corporation Boost Productivity," *Personnel Administrator,* August 1981, pp. 33–36; Anil K. Gupta and Vijay Govindarajan, "Knowledge Management's Social Dimension: Lessons from Nucor Steel," *Sloan Management Review,* Fall 2000, 42, no. 1, pp. 71–80; Elaine C. Hollensbe and James P. Guthrie, "Group Pay-for-performance Plans: The Role of Spontaneous Goal Setting," *Academy of Management Review,* October 2000, 25, no. 4, pp. 864–72.

32. Kenneth W. Chilton, "Lincoln Electric's Incentive System: A Reservoir of Trust," *Compensation and Benefits Review* 25, no. 6 (November 1994); pp. 29–34. See also D. W. Meyers, *Human Management: Principles and Practice* (Chicago: Commerce Clearing House, 1986); James P. Guthrie, "Alternative Pay Practices and Employee Turnover: An Organization Economics Perspective," *Group & Organization Management,* December 2000, 25, no. 4, pp. 419–39.

33. Ellen C. Kearns and Monica Gallagher, eds., *The Fair Labor Standards Act* (Washington, DC: BNA, 1999).

34. Charles Fay and Howard W. Risher, "Contractors, Comparable Worth and the New OFCCP; Deja Vu and More," *Compensation and Benefits Review,* September/October 2000, 32, no. 5, pp. 23–33; Gillian Flynn, "Protect Yourself from an Equal-pay Audit," *Workforce,* June 1999, 78, no. 6, pp. 144–46.

35. Bohlander, Snell, and Sherman, *Managing Human Resources.*

36. Susan E. Gardner and Christopher Daniel, "Implementing Comparable Worth/Pay Equity: Experiences of Cutting-edge States," *Public Personnel Management,* Winter 1998, 27, no. 4, pp. 475–89.

37. T. Gup, "The Curse of Coal," *Time,* November 4, 1991, pp. 54–64.

38. Linda Kahn, *Primer of Labor Relations,* 25th ed. (Washington, DC: Bureau of National Affairs Books, 1994); A. Sloane and F. Witney, *Labor Relations* (Englewood Cliffs, NJ: Prentice Hall, 1985).

39. S. Premack and J. E. Hunter, "Individual Unionization Decisions," *Psychological Bulletin* 103 (1988), pp. 223–34; Leo Troy, *Beyond Unions and Collective Bargaining* (Armonk, NY: M. E. Sharpe, 1999); John A. McClendon, "Members and Nonmembers: Determinants of Dues-paying Membership in a Bargaining Unit," *Relations Industrielles,* Spring 2000, 55, no. 2, pp. 332–47.

40. Robert Sinclair and Lois Tetrick, "Social Exchange and Union Commitment: A Comparison of Union Instrumentality and Union Support Perceptions," *Journal of Organizational Behavior* 16, no. 6 (November 1995), pp. 669–79. See also Premack and Hunter, "Individual Unionization Decisions."

41. David Lewin and Richard B. Peterson, *The Modern Grievance Procedure in the United States,* (Westport CT: Quorum Books, 1998); Steven E. Abraham and Paula B. Voos, "Right-to-work Laws: New Evidence from the Stock Market," *Southern Economic Journal,* October 2000, 67, no. 2, pp. 345–62.

42. George Bohlander and Donna Blancero, "A Study of Reversal Determinants in Discipline and Discharge Arbitration Awards: The Impact of Just Cause Standards," *Labor Studies Journal* 21, no. 3 (Fall 1996), pp. 3–18.

Chapter Eleven

1. *Employment Projections,* (Washington DC: Bureau of Labor Statistics, U.S. Department of Labor, 2000) (http://stats.bls.gov/emplt981.htm); "Futurework: Trends and Challenges for Work in the 21st Century," *Occupational Outlook Quarterly,* Summer 2000, 44, no. 2, pp. 31–36.

2. Ibid.

3. *Employment Projections,* Bureau of Labor Statistics; Jennifer Laabs, "Celebrating National Business Women's Week," *Workforce,* October 2000, 79, no. 10, p. 32.

4. *Employment and Earnings,* (Washington, DC: Bureau of Labor Statistics, U.S. Department of Labor, July 1996), p. 152. See also Nacy Perry, "More Women Are Executive VPs," *Fortune,* July 12, 1993, p. 16; Jennifer Laabs, "Saturn Gets Female President, But Female Leaders Are Still a Corporate Oddity," *Workforce,* February 1999, 78, no. 2, p. 22.

5. Tom Dunkel, "The Front Runners," *Working Woman,* April 1996, pp. 30–35, 72, 75; Rosemary Cafasso, "The Diversity Gap," *Computerworld,* June 1996, pp. 35–37; Laabs, "Saturn Gets Female President," p. 22; Rochelle Sharpe, "As Leaders, Women Rule," *Business Week,* November 20, 2000, pp. 74–84.

6. George Bohlander, Scott Snell, Arthur Sherman, *Managing Human Resources,* 12th ed. (Cincinnati, OH: Southwestern Publishing, 2001); William Petrocelli and Barbar Kate Repa, *Sexual Harassment on the Job: What It Is and How to Stop It* (Berkeley, CA: Nolo Press, 1998).

7. Margaret L. Usdansky, "Minority Majorities in One in Six Cities," *USA Today,* June 9, 1993, p. 10A; "Charting the Projections: 1994–2005;" Margaret Blackburn White and Joseph Potts, "Just the Facts: Women of Color in U.S. Corporations," *Diversity Factor,* Spring 1999, 7, no. 3, pp. 8–15; Alberto Davila and Marie T Mora, "English Fluency of Recent Hispanic Immigrants to the United States in 1980 and 1990," *Economic Development and Cultural Change,* January 2000, 48, no. 2, pp. 369–89; Milford Prewitt, "Immigration Eyed As Fix for Labor-shortage Woes," *Nation's Restaurant News,* October 2, 2000, 34, no. 40, pp. 1,68.

8. Asra Q. Nomani, "Labor Letter," *The Wall Street Journal,* November 7, 1996, p. A1. See also, G. Evans Witt, "In the Eye of the Beholder," *American Demographics,* October 1999, 21, no. 10, p. 24.

9. "An ADA Checklist for Implementation and Review," *HRFocus,* July 1994, p. 19. Stephen Overall, "Firms Hire Fewer Disabled People in Unskilled Jobs," *People Management,* November 16, 1995, p. 10. James Jordan, *ADA Americans with Disabilities Act Compliance Manual for California* (Bristol, UK: Jordan Publishing, 1999).

10. "New ADA Enforcement Guides from the EEOC," *HR Focus,* December 2000, 77, no. 12, p. 2.

11. Gail Dutton, "The ADA at 10," *Workforce,* December 2000, 79, no. 12, pp. 40–46.

12. *Employment Projections,* Bureau of Labor Statistics.

13. Ibid.

14. "Low Literacy," *Training and Development,* January 1994, p. 12; Ruth E. Davidhizar and Kenneth Brownson "Literacy, Cultural Diversity, and Client Education," *The Health Care Manager,* September 1999, 18, no. 1, pp. 39–47.

15. Michael A. Verespej, "The Education Difference," *Industry Week* 245, no. 9 (May 6, 1996), pp. 11–14; Teresa L. Smith, "The Basics of Basic-Skills Training," *Training and Development* 49, no. 4 (April 1995), pp. 44–46; Teresa L. Smith, "Job Related Materials Reinforce Basic Skills," *HRMagazine,* July 1995, pp. 84–90.

16. Kenneth Labich, "No More Crude at Texaco," *Fortune,* September 6, 1999, 140, no. 5, pp. 205–12; *Good for Business: Making Full Use of the Nation's Human Capital* (Washington, D.C.: The Federal Glass Ceiling Commission, 1995).

17. N. Adler, *International Dimensions of Organizational Behavior,* 3rd ed. (Boston: PWS–Kent, 1997); T. Cox and S. Blake, "Managing Cultural Diversity: Implications for Organizational Competitiveness," *Academy of Management Executives* 5 (August 1991), pp. 45–56.

18. "Successful Companies Realize that Diversity Is a Long-Term Process, Not a Program," *Personnel Journal,* April 1993, p. 54; Joan Crockett, "Diversity: Winning Competitive Advantage through a Diverse Workforce," *HR Focus,* May 1999, 76, no. 5, pp. 9–10.

19. Adler, *International Dimensions of Organizational Behavior;* Cox and Blake, "Managing Cultural Diversity."

20. Adler, *International Dimensions of Organizational Behavior.*

21. Audrey J. Murrell, Faye J. Crosby, and Robin J. Ely. *Mentoring Dilemmas: Developmental Relationships Within Multicultural Organizations* (Mahwah, NJ: Lawrence Erlbaum Associates, 1999). See a review of this book by Mark L. Lengnick-Hall, "Mentoring Dilemmas: Developmental Relationships Within Multicultural Organizations," *Personnel Psychology,* Spring 2000, 53, no. 1, pp. 224–27.

22. A. Livingston, "What Your Department Can Do," *Working Woman,* January 1991, pp. 59–60; Mary Dean Lee, Shelley M. MacDermid, and Michelle L. Buck, "Organizational

Paradigms of Reduced-load Work: Accommodation, Elaboration, and Transformation," *Academy of Management Journal,* December 2000, 43, no. 6, pp. 1211–34.

23. Leslie E. Overmyer Day, "The Pitfalls of Diversity Training," *Training and Development* 49, no. 12 (December 1995), pp. 24–29; Sara Rynes and Benson Rosen, "A Field Survey of Factors Affecting the Adoption and Perceived Success of Diversity Training," *Personnel Psychology* 48, no. 2 (Summer 1995), pp. 247–70; Lynda Ford, "Diversity: From Cartoons to Confrontations," *Training & Development,* August 2000, 54, no. 8, pp. 70–71; "Diversity: A 'New' Tool for Retention," *HR Focus,* June 2000, 77, no. 6, pp. 1, 14; Lin Grensing-Pophal, "Is Your HR Department Diverse Enough?" *HRMagazine,* September 2000, 45, no. 9, pp. 46–52; John M. Ivancevich and Jacqueline A. Gilbert, "Diversity Management Time for a New Approach," *Public Personnel Management,* Spring 2000, 29, no. 1, pp. 75–92.

24. Michael Burkart, "The Role of Training in Advancing a Diversity Initiative," *Diversity Factor,* Fall 1999, 8, no. 1, pp. 2–5.

25. Nancy L. Mueller, "Wisconsin Power and Light's Model Diversity Program," *Training and Development,* March 1996, pp. 57–60; Robert J Grossman, "Is Diversity Workinng?" *HRMagazine,* March 2000, 45, no. 3, pp. 46–50.

26. Phyllis Shurn-Hannah, "Solving the Minority Retention Mystery," *The Human Resource Professional,* May/Jun 2000, 13, no. 3, pp. 22–27; Gillian Flynn, "Firm's diversity efforts even the playing field," *Personnel Journal* (January 1996) 56.

27. Margaret Blackburn White, "Organization 2005: New Strategies at P&G," *Diversity Factor,* Fall 1999, 8, no. 1, pp. 16–20.

28. William G. Bowen, Derek Bok, and Glenda Burkhart, "A Report Card on Diversity: Lessons for Business from Higher Education," *Harvard Business Review,* January/February 1999,

7, no. 1, pp. 38–45; Bryan Gingrich, "Individual and Organizational Accountabilities Reducing Stereotypes and Prejudice within the Workplace," *Diversity Factor,* Winter 2000, 8, no. 2, pp. 14–19; Joan Crockett, "Diversity: Winning Competitive Advantage through a Diverse Workforce," *HR Focus,* May 1999, 76, no. 5, pp. 9–10.

Part Three Integrating Case

1. Gloria M. Curry, "Package Delivery Service: The Options Are Plentiful," *Office,* August 1989, pp. 60–62.

2. Charles Arthur, "The War in the Air," *Business* [U.K.], November 1989, pp. 60–66.

3. Erik Guyot, "Air Courier Fight for Pacific Business," *Asian Finance* [Hong Kong], July 15, 1990, pp. 22–23.

4. James T. McKenna, "Airline Boosts International Cargo Services to Protect Market Shares," *Aviation Week & Space Technology,* November 20, 1989, pp. 124–25.

5. Dean Foust, "Mr. Smith Goes Global," *Business Week,* February 13, 1989, pp. 66–72.

6. Frederick W. Smith, "Empowering Employee," *Small Business Reports,* January 1991, pp. 15–20.

7. Perry A. Trunick, "Leadership and People Distinguish Federal Express," *Transportation & Distribution,* December 1989, pp. 18–22.

8. "Federal Express Spreads its Wings," *Journal of Business Strategy,* July–August 1988, pp. 15–20.

9. Foust, "Mr. Smith Goes Global."

10. "Federal Express Spreads Its Wings." pp. 3–10.

11. Erik Calonius, "Federal Express Battle Overseas," *Fortune,* 1990, December 3, 1990, pp. 137–40.

12. Foust, "Mr. Smith Goes Global."

13. James Ott, "Board Decision Muddle Rules on Union Role after Merger," *Aviation Week & Space Technology,* August 28, 1989, p. 68.

14. Foust, "Mr. Smith Goes Global."

Chapter Twelve

1. W. Bennis and B. Nanus, *Leaders* (New York: Harper & Row, 1985), p. 27.

2. J. Petrick, R. Schere, J. Brodzinski, J. Quinn, and M. Fall Ainina, "Global Leadership Skills and Reputational Capital: Intangible Resources for Sustainable Competitive Advantage," *Academy of Management Executive,* February 1999, pp. 58–69.

3. Bennis and Nanus, *Leaders.*

4. Ibid., p. 144.

5. J. Kouzes and B. Posner, *The Leadership Challenge,* 1st ed. (San Francisco: Jossey-Bass, 1987).

6. Ibid.

7. Ibid.

8. J. Baum, E. A. Locke, and S. Kirkpatrick, "A Longitudinal Study of the Relation of Vision and Vision Communication to Venture Growth in Entrepreneurial Firms," *Journal of Applied Psychology,* 83 (1998), pp. 43–54.

9. E. C. Shapiro, *Fad Surfing in the Boardroom* (Reading, MA: Addison-Wesley, 1995).

10. J. Kouzes and B. Posner, *The Leadership Challenge,* 2nd ed. (San Francisco: Jossey-Bass, 1995).

11. Ibid.

12. W. Bennis and Townsend, *Reinventing Leadership* (New York: William Morrow, 1995).

13. Ibid.

14. Kouzes and Posner, *The Leadership Challenge* (1987).

15. J. A. Conger, "The Dark Side of Leadership," *Organizational Dynamics* 19 (Autumn 1990), pp. 44–55.

16. J. P. Kotter, "What Leaders Really Do," *Harvard Business Review* 68 (May–June 1990), pp. 103–11.

17. A. Zaleznik, "The Leadership Gap," *The Executive* 4 (February 1990), pp. 7–22.

18. G. Yukl, *Leadership in Organizations,* 3rd ed. (Englewood Cliffs, NJ: Prentice Hall, 1994).

19. R. House and R. Aditya, "The Social Scientific Study of Leadership. Quo Vadis?" *Journal of Management* 23, (1997), pp. 409–73.

20. R. D. Ireland and M. A. Hitt, "Achieving and Maintaining Strategic Competitiveness in the 21st Century. The Role of Strategic Leadership," *Academy of Management Executive,* February 1999, pp. 43–57.

21. R. E. Kelly, "In Praise of Followers," *Harvard Business Review* 66 (November–December 1988), pp. 142–48.

22. Bennis and Townsend, *Reinventing Leadership.*

23. R. Heifetz and D. Laurie, "The Work of Leadership," *Harvard Business Review,* January–February 1997, pp. 124–34.

24. Kelly, "In Praise of Followers."

25. J. R. P. French and B. Raven, "The Bases of Social Power," in *Studies in Social Power,* ed. D. Cartwright (Ann Arbor, MI: Institute for Social Research, 1959).

26. G. Yukl and C. Falbe, "Importance of Different Power Sources in Downward and Lateral Relations," *Journal of Applied Psychology* 76 (1991), pp. 416–23.

27. Ibid.

28. Ibid.

29. R. M. Stogdill, "Personal Factors Associated with Leadership: A Survey of the Literature," *Journal of Psychology* 25 (1948), pp. 35–71.

30. S. Kirkpatrick and E. Locke, "Leadership: Do Traits Matter?" *The Executive* 5 (May 1991), pp. 48–60.

31. G. A. Yukl, *Leadership in Organizations,* 2nd ed. (Englewood Cliffs, NJ: Prentice Hall, 1989).

32. Heifetz and Laurie, "The Work of Leadership."

33. J. P. Kotter, *The General Managers* (New York: Free Press, 1982).

34. S. Zaccaro, R. Foti, and D. Kenny, "Self-Monitoring and Trait-Based Variance in Leadership: An Investigation of Leader Flexibility across Multiple Group Situations," *Journal of Applied Psychology* 76 (1991), pp. 308–15.

35. D. Goleman, "Leadership that Gets Results," *Harvard Business Review,* March–April 2000, pp. 78–90.

36. J. Misumi and M. Peterson, "The Performance-Maintenance (PM) Theory of Leadership: Review of a Japanese Research Program," *Administrative Science Quarterly* 30 (June 1985), pp. 198–223.

37. Ibid.

38. G. Graen and M. Uhl-Bien, "Relationship-Based Approach to Leadership: Development of Leader-Member Exchange (LMX) Theory of Leadership over 25 Years: Applying a Multi-level Multidomain Perspective," *Leadership Quarterly* 6, no. 2 (1995), pp. 219–47.

39. House and Aditya, "The Social Scientific Study of Leadership."

40. C. R. Gerstner and D. V. Day, "Meta-analytic Review of Leader-Member Exchange-Theory: Correlates and Construct Issues," *Journal of Applied Psychology,* 82 (1997), pp. 827–44.

41. House and Aditya, "Social Scientific Study."

42. J. Wagner III, "Participation's Effect on Performance and Satisfaction: A Reconsideration of Research," *Academy of Management Review,* April 1994, pp. 312–30.

43. R. White and R. Lippitt, Autocracy and Democracy: *An Experimental Inquiry* (New York: Harper & Brothers, 1960).

44. J. Muczyk and R. Steel, "Leadership Style and the Turnaround Executive," *Business Horizons,* March–April 1999, pp. 39–46.

45. A. Tannenbaum and W. Schmidt, "How to Choose a Leadership Pattern," *Harvard Business Review* 36 (March–April 1958), pp. 95–101.

46. E. Fleishman and E. Harris, "Patterns of Leadership Behavior Related to Employee Grievances and Turnover," *Personnel Psychology* 15 (1962), pp. 43–56.

47. R. Likert, *The Human Organization: Its Management and Value* (New York: McGraw-Hill, 1967).

48. R. Blake and J. Mouton, *The Managerial Grid* (Houston: Gulf, 1964).

49. Misumi and Peterson, "The Performance-Maintenance (PM) Theory."

50. Tannenbaum and Schmidt, "How to Choose a Leadership Pattern."

51. V. H. Vroom, "Leadership and the Decision-Making Process," *Organizational Dynamics,* Spring 2000, pp. 82–93.

52. R. J. House, "A Path Goal Theory of Leader Effectiveness," *Administrative Science Quarterly* 16 (1971), pp. 321–39.

53. J. Howell, D. Bowen, P. Dorfman, S. Kerr, and P. Podsakoff, "Substitutes for Leadership: Effective Alternatives to Ineffective Leadership," *Organizational Dynamics* 19 (Summer 1990), pp. 21–38.

54. R. G. Lord and W. Gradwohl Smith, "Leadership and the Changing Nature of Performance," in D. R. Ilgen and E. D. Pulakos, eds., *The Changing Nature of Performance* (San Francisco: Jossey-Bass, 1999).

55. K. Brooker, "Can Anyone Replace Herb?" *Fortune,* April 17, 2000, pp. 186–92.

56. A. Bianco and L. Lavell, "The CEO Trap," *Business Week,* December 11, 2000, pp. 86–92.

57. B. M. Bass, *Leadership and Performance Beyond Expectations* (New York: Free Press, 1985). (a)

58. Y. A. Nur, "Charisma and Managerial Leadership: The Gift that Never Was," *Business Horizons,* July–August 1998, pp. 19–26.

59. R. J. House, "A 1976 Theory of Charismatic Leadership," in *Leadership: The Cutting Edge,* ed. J. G. Hunt and L. L. Larson (Carbondale, IL: Southern Illinois University Press, 1977).

60. M. Potts and P. Behr, *The Leading Edge* (New York: McGraw-Hill, 1987).

61. S. Yorges, H. Weiss, and O. Strickland, "The Effect of Leader Outcomes on Influence, Attributions, and Perceptions of Charisma," *Journal of Applied Psychology,* 84 (1999), pp. 428–36.

62. Potts and Behr, "Leading Edge."

63. D. A. Waldman and F. J. Yammarino,

"CEO Charismatic Leadership: Levels-of-Management and Levels-of-Analysis Effects," *Academy of Management Review,* 24 (1999), pp. 266–85.

64. House and Aditya, "The Social Scientific Study of Leadership."

65. J. M. Howell and K. E. Hall-Merenda, The Ties that Bind: The Impact of Leader-Member Exchange, Transformational and Transactional Leadership, and Distance on Predicting Follower Performance," *Journal of Applied Psychology,* 84 (1999), pp. 680–94.

66. B. M. Bass, "Leadership: Good, Better, Best," *Organizational Dynamics,* Winter 1985, pp. 26–40.(b)

67. D. I. Jung and B. J. Avolio, "Effects of Leadership Style and Followers' Cultural Orientation on Performance in Group and Individual Task Conditions," *Academy of Management Journal,* 42 (1999), pp. 208–18.

68. Bass, *Leadership.*

69. Bennis and Nanus, *Leaders.*

70. B. Bass, B. Avolio, and L. Goodheim, "Biography and the Assessment of Transformational Leadership at the World-Class Level," *Journal of Management* 13 (1987), pp. 7–20.

71. K. Albrecht and R. Zemke, *Service America* (Homewood, IL: Dow Jones–Irwin, 1985).

72. T. A. Judge and J. E. Bono, "Five-Factor Model of Personality and Transformational Leadership," *Journal of Applied Psychology,* 85 (2000), pp. 751–65.

73. B. Bass, "Does the Transactional-Transformational Paradigm Transcend Organizational and National Boundaries?" *American Psychologist* 22 (1997), pp. 130–42.

74. G. Spreitzer and R. Quinn, "Empowering Middle Managers to Be Transformational Leaders," *Journal of Applied Behavioral Science* 32 (1996), pp. 237–61.

75. Ibid.

76. J. Huey, "The New Post-Heroic Leadership," *Fortune,* February 21, 1994, pp. 42–50.

77. W. Bennis, "The End of Leadership: Exemplary Leadership Is Impossible Without Full Inclusion, Initiatives, and Cooperation of Followers," *Organizational Dynamics,* Summer 1999, pp. 71–79.

78. Ibid.

79. P. Block, *The Empowered Manager* (San Francisco: Jossey-Bass, 1991).

80. Ibid.

81. Kouzes and Posner, *The Leadership Challenge* (1995).

82. J. Beeson, "Succession Planning: Building the Management Corps," *Business Horizons,* September–October, 61–66.

83. R. Fulmer, P. Gibbs, and M. Goldsmith, "Developing Leaders: How Winning Companies Keep On Winning," *Sloan Management Review,* Fall 2000, pp. 49–59.

84. M. McCall, *High Flyers* (Boston: Harvard Business School Press, 1998).

85. Ibid.

Chapter Twelve Appendix

1. F. E. Fiedler, *A Theory of Leadership Effectiveness* (New York: McGraw-Hill, 1967).

2. P. Hersey and K. Blanchard, *The Management of Organizational Behavior* (Englewood Cliffs, NJ: Prentice Hall, 1984).

3. Yukl, *Leadership in Organizations.*

Chapter Thirteen

1. R. Kreitner and F. Luthans, "A Social Learning Approach to Behavioral Management: Radical Behaviorists 'Mellowing Out,'" *Organizational Dynamics,* Autumn 1984, pp. 47–65.

2. D. Katz and R. L. Kahn, *The Social Psychology of Organizations* (New York: John Wiley & Sons, 1966).

3. E. Locke, "Toward a Theory of Task Motivation and Incentives," *Organizational Behavior and Human Performance 3* (1968), pp. 157–89.

4. W. F. Cascio, "Managing a Virtual Workplace," *Academy of Management Executive,* August 2000, pp. 81–90.

5. R. H. Schaffer, "Demand Better Results—and Get Them," *Harvard Business Review* 69 (March–April 1991), pp. 142–49.

6. T. Mitchell and W. Silver, "Individual and Group Goals When Workers Are Interdependent: Effects on Task Strategies and Performance," *Journal of Applied Psychology* 75 (1990), pp. 185–93.

7. P. C. Early, T. Connolly, and G. Ekegren, "Goals, Strategy Development, and Task Performance: Some Limits on the Efficacy of Goal Setting," *Journal of Applied Psychology* 74 (1989), pp. 24–33; C. E. Shalley, "Effects of Productivity Goals, Creativity Goals, and Personal Discretion on Individual Creativity," *Journal of Applied Psychology* 76 (1991), pp. 179–85.

8. J. Main, "Is the Baldridge Overblown?" *Fortune,* July 1, 1991, pp. 62–65.

9. E. Thorndike, *Animal Intelligence* (New York: Macmillan, 1911).

10. F. Luthans and A. D. Stajkovic, "Reinforce for Performance: The Need to Go Beyond Pay and Even Rewards," *Academy of Management Executive,* May 1999, pp. 49–57.

11. R. Levering and M. Moskowitz, "The 100 Best Companies to Work For," *Fortune,* January 8, 2001, pp. 148–68.

12. Cascio, "Managing a Virtual Workplace."

13. S. Kerr, "Organizational Rewards: Practical, Cost-neutral Alternatives that You May Know, But Don't Practice," *Organizational Dynamics,* Summer 1999, pp. 61–70.

14. S. C. Faludi, "At Nordstrom Stores, Service Comes First—but at a Big Price," *The Wall Street Journal,* February 20, 1990, pp. A1, A16.

15. K. Butterfield, L. K. Trevino, and G. Ball, "Punishment from the Manager's Perspective: A Grounded Investigation and Inductive Model," *Academy of Management Review* 39 (1996), pp. 1479–512.

16. S. Kerr, "On the Folly of Rewarding A, While Hoping for B," *Academy of Management Journal* 18 (1975), pp. 769–83.

17. J. Weber, "Farewell, Fast Track," *Business Week,* December 10, 1990, pp. 192–200.

18. D. Leonard, "They're Coming to Take You Away," *Fortune,* May 29, 2000, pp. 89–106.

19. A. Bennett, "When Money Is Tight, Bosses Scramble for Other Ways to Motivate the Troops," *The Wall Street Journal,* October 31, 1990, pp. B1, B5.

20. V. H. Vroom, *Work and Motivation* (New York: John Wiley & Sons, 1964).

21. R. E. Wood, P. W. B. Atkins, and J. E. H. Bright, "Bonuses, Goals, and Instrumentality Effects," *Journal of Applied Psychology,* 84 (1999), pp. 703–20.

22. Kerr, "Organizational Rewards."

23. A. H. Maslow, "A Theory of Human Motivation," *Psychological Review,* July 1943, pp. 370–96.

24. M. Wahba and L. Birdwell, "Maslow Reconsidered: A Review of Research on the Need Hierarchy Theory," *Organizational Behavior and Human Performance* 15 (1976), pp. 212–40.

25. F. Rose, "A New Age for Business?" *Fortune,* October 8, 1990, pp. 156–64.

26. G. Dessler, "How to Earn Your Employees' Commitment," *Academy of Management Executive,* May 1999, pp. 58–67.

27. Weber, "Farewell, Fast Track."

28. C. Alderfer, *Existence, Relatedness, and Growth: Human Needs in Organizational Settings* (Glencoe, IL: Free Press, 1972).

29. C. Pinder, *Work Motivation* (Glenview, IL: Scott, Foresman, 1984).

30. D. McClelland, *The Achieving Society* (New York: Van Nostrand Reinhold, 1961).

31. D. McClelland and R. Boyatzis, "Leadership Motive Pattern and Long-Term Success in Management," *Journal of Applied Psychology* 67 (1982), pp. 737–43.

32. N. Adler, *International Dimensions of Organizational Behavior,* 2nd ed. (Boston: Kent, 1991); G. Hofstede, *Cultures and Organizations* (London: McGraw-Hill, 1991).

33. E. E. Lawler III and D. Finegold, "Individualizing the Organization: Past, Present, and Future," *Organizational Dynamics,* Summer 2000, pp. 1–15.

34. Ibid.

35. T. M. Amabile, "A Model of Creativity and Innovation in Organizations," in *Research in Organizational Behavior,* ed. B. M. Staw and L. L. Cummings (Greenwich, CT: JAI Press, 1988), pp. 10, 123–67.

36. C. M. Ford, "A Theory of Individual Creative Action in Multiple Social Domains," *Academy of Management Review* 21 (1996), pp. 1112–42.

37. G. Oldham and A. Cummings, "Employee Creativity: Personal and Contextual Factors at Work," *Academy of Management Journal* 39 (1996), pp. 607–34.

38. T. Amabile, R. Conti, H. Coon, J. Lazenby, and M. Herron, "Assessing the Work Environment for Creativity," *Academy of Management Journal* 39 (1996), pp. 1154–84.

39. M. Campion and G. Sanborn, "Job Design," in *Handbook of Industrial Engineering,* ed. G. Salvendy (New York: John Wiley & Sons, 1991).

40. Lawler and Finegold, "Individualizing the Organization."

41. B. G. Posner, "Role Changes," *Inc.,* February 1990, pp. 95–98.

42. M. Campion and D. McClelland, "Interdisciplinary Examination of the Costs and Benefits of Enlarged Jobs: A Job Design Quasi-Experiment," *Journal of Applied Psychology* 76 (1991), pp. 186–98.

43. F. Herzberg, *Work and the Nature of Men* (Cleveland: World, 1966).

44. J. R. Hackman, G. Oldham, R. Janson, and K. Purdy, "A New Strategy for Job Enrichment," *California Management Review* 16 (Fall 1975), pp. 57–71.

45. T. Ehrenfeld, "Cashing In," *Inc.,* July 1993, pp. 69–70.

46. D. Fenn, "Bottoms Up," *Inc.,* July 1993, pp. 58–60.

47. R. Rechheld, "Loyalty-Based Management," *Harvard Business Review,* March–April, 1993, pp. 64–73.

48. D. Whitford, "A Human Place to Work," *Fortune,* January 8, 2001, pp. 108–18; 458–59.

49. G. Hamel, "Reinvent your Company," *Fortune,* June 12, 2000, pp. 98–118.

50. Levering and Moskowitz, "The 100 Best Companies."

51. A. Bianchi, "True Believers," *Inc.,* July 1993, pp. 72–73.

52. J. Finegan, "People Power," *Inc.,* July 1993, pp. 62–63.

53. Ibid.

54. T. Peters and N. Austin, *A Passion for Excellence* (New York: Random House, 1985).

55. Ehrenfeld, "Cashing In."

56. Finegan, "People Power."

57. Campion and Sanborn, "Job Design."

58. C. Argyris, "Empowerment: The Emperor's New Clothes," *Harvard Business Review,* May–June 1998, pp. 98–105.

59. R. Forrester, Empowerment: Rejuvenating a Potent Idea," *Academy of Management Executive,* August 2000, pp. 67–80.

60. R. C. Liden, S. J. Wayne, and R. T. Sparrowe, "An Examination of the Mediating Role of Psychological Empowerment on the Relations Between the Job, Interpersonal Relationships, and Work Outcomes," *Journal of Applied Psychology,* 85, (2000), pp. 407–16.

61. Peters and Austin, A *Passion for Excellence.*

62. K. Thomas and B. Velthouse, "Cognitive Elements of Empowerment: An 'Interpretive' Model of Intrinsic Task Motivation," *Academy of Management Review* 15 (1990), pp. 666–81.

63. Price Waterhouse Change Integration Team, *Better Change* (Burr Ridge, IL: Richard D. Irwin, 1995).

64. E. E. Lawler III. *The Ultimate Advantage: Creating the High Involvement Organization* (San Francisco: Jossey-Bass, 1992).

65. G. M. Spreitzer, "Social Structural Characteristics of Psychological Empowerment," *Academy of Man-*

agement Journal 39 (1996), pp. 483–504.

66. J. Kouzes and B. Posner, *The Leadership Challenge* (San Francisco: Jossey-Bass, 1995).

67. Price Waterhouse Change Integration Team, *Better Change.*

68. J. Jasinowski and R. Hamrin, *Making It in America* (New York: Simon & Schuster, 1995).

69. J. Adams, "Inequality in Social Exchange," in *Advances in Experimental Social Psychology,* ed. L. Berkowitz (New York: Academic Press, 1965).

70. M. Bloom, "The Performance Effects of Pay Dispersion on Individuals and Organizations," *Academy of Management Journal,* 42, (1999), pp. 25–40.

71. D. Skarlicki, R. Folger, and P. Tesluk, "Personality As a Moderator in the Relationships between Fairness and Retaliation," *Academy of Management Journal,* 42, (1999), pp. 100–108.

72. W. C. Kim and R. Mauborgne, "Fair Process: Managing in the Knowledge Economy," *Harvard Business Review,* July–August 1997, pp. 65–75.

73. Ibid.

74. D. Henne and E. Locke, "Job Dissatisfaction: What Are the Consequences?" *International Journal of Psychology* 20 (1985), pp. 221–40.

75. D. Bowen, S. Gilliland, and R. Folger, "HRM and Service Fairness: How Being Fair with Employees Spills Over to Customers," *Organizational Dynamics,* Winter 1999, pp. 7–23.

76. Levering and Moskowitz, "The 100 Best Companies."

77. Whitford, "A Human Place."

78. R. E. Walton, "Improving the Quality of Work Life," *Harvard Business Review,* May–June 1974, pp. 12, 16, 155.

79. E. E. Lawler III, "Strategies for Improving the Quality of Work Life," *American Psychologist* 37 (1982), pp. 486–93; J. L. Suttle, "Improving Life at Work: Problems and

Prospects," in *Improving Life at Work,* ed. J. R. Hackman and J. L. Suttle (Santa Monica, CA: Goodyear, 1977).

80. S. L. Robinson, "Trust and Breach of the Psychological Contract," *Administrative Science Quarterly* 41 (1996), pp. 574–99.

81. E. W. Morrison and S. L. Robinson, "When Employees Feel Betrayed: A Model of How Psychological Contract Violation Develops," *Academy of Management Review* 22 (1997), pp. 226–56.

82. D. Rousseau, "Changing the Deal while Keeping the People," *Academy of Management Executive* 10 (1996), pp. 50–58.

83. E. Ridolfi, "Executive Commentary," *Academy of Management Executive* 10 (1996), pp. 59–60.

84. E. E. Lawler III. *From the Ground Up* (San Francisco: Jossey-Bass 1996).

85. Ibid.

86. S. Ghoshal, C. Bartlett, and P. Moran, "Value Creation: The New Management Manifesto," *Financial Times Mastering Management Review,* November 1999, pp. 34–37.

88. Kim and Mauborgne, "Fair Process."

89. Rousseau, "Changing the Deal while Keeping the People;" Kim & Mauborgne, "Fair Process."

Chapter Fourteen

1. E. C. Wenger and W. M. Snyder, "Communities of Practice: The Organizational Frontier," *Harvard Business Review,* January–February 2000, pp. 139–45.

2. S. Cohen and D. Bailey "What Makes Teams Work: Group Effectiveness Research from the Shop Floor to the Executive Suite," *Journal of Management* 23 (1997), pp. 239–90.

3. B. Dumaine, "Who Needs a Boss?" *Fortune,* May 7, 1990, pp. 52–60.

4. Ibid.

5. K. Wexley and S. Silverman, *Working Scared* (San Francisco: Jossey-Bass, 1993).

6. B. Dumaine, "The Trouble with Teams," *Fortune,* September 5, 1994, pp. 86–92.

7. E. E. Lawler III, *From the Ground Up* (San Francisco: Jossey-Bass, 1996).

8. Wexley and Silverman, *Working Scared.*

9. Lawler, *From the Ground Up.*

10. Dumaine, "The Trouble with Teams."

11. Lawler, *From the Ground Up.*

12. R. M. Kanter, "Championing Change: An Interview with Bell Atlantic's CEO Raymond Smith," *Harvard Business Review,* January–February 1991, pp. 118–30.

13. R. Heifetz and D. Laurie, "The Work of Leadership," *Harvard Business Review,* January–February 1996, pp. 124–34.

14. Lawler, *From the Ground Up.*

15. Dumaine, "Who Needs a Boss?"

16. D. Nadler, J. R. Hackman, and E. E. Lawler III, *Managing Organizational Behavior* (Boston: Little, Brown, 1979).

17. P. B. Paulus and H. Yang, "Idea Generation in Groups: A Basis for Creativity in Organizations," *Organizational Behavior and Human Decision Processes,* 82, May 2000, pp. 76–87.

18. M. Cianni and D. Wnuck, "Individual Growth and Team Enhancement: Moving toward a New Model of Career Development," *Academy of Management Executive* 11 (1997), pp. 105–15.

19. Cohen and Bailey, "What Makes Teams Work."

20. J. Katzenback and D. Smith, "The Discipline of Teams," *Harvard Business Review,* March–April 1993, pp. 111–20.

21. J. Zenger and Associates, *Leading Teams* (Burr Ridge, IL: Business One Irwin, 1994).

22. S. Cohen, "New Approaches to Teams and Teamwork," in J. Galbraith, E. E. Lawler III, and Associates, *Organizing for the Future* (San Francisco: Jossey-Bass, 1993).

23. Cohen and Bailey, "What Makes Teams Work."

24. Ibid.

25. R. Banker, J. Field, R. Schroeder, and K. Sinha, "Impact of Work Teams on Manufacturing Performance: A Longitudinal Field Study," *Academy of Management Journal* 39 (1996), pp. 867–90.

26. D. Yeatts, M. Hipskind, and D. Barnes, "Lessons Learned from Self-Managed Work Teams," *Business Horizons,* July–August 1994, pp. 11–18.

27. B. Kirkman and D. Shapiro, "The Impact of Cultural Values on Employee Resistance to Teams: Toward a Model of Globalized Self-managing Work Team Effectiveness," *Academy of Management Review* 22 (1997), pp. 730–57.

28. B. Macy and H. Isumi, "Organizational Change, Design, and Work Innovation: A Meta-analysis of 131 North American Field Studies—1961–1991," *Research in Organizational Change and Development* 7 (1993), pp. 235–313.

29. Ibid.

30. B. W. Tuckman, "Developmental Sequence in Small Groups," *Psychological Bulletin* 63 (1965), pp. 384–99.

31. C. Snow, S. Snell, S. Davison, and D. Hambrick, "Use Transnational Teams to Globalize Your Company," *Organizational Dynamics,* Spring 1996, pp. 50–67.

32. C. J. G. Gersick, "Time and Transition in Work Teams: Toward a New Model of Group Development," *Academy of Management Journal,* 31 (1988), pp. 9–41.

33. J. R. Hackman, *Groups That Work (and Those That Don't)* (San Francisco: Jossey-Bass, 1990).

34. Zenger and Associates, *Leading Teams.*

35. R. Cross, "Looking Before You Leap: Assessing the Jump to Teams in Knowledge-based Work," *Business Horizons,* September–October 2000, pp. 29–36.

36. Dumaine, "The Trouble with Teams."

37. J. Case, "What the Experts Forgot to Mention," *Inc.,* September 1993, pp. 66–78.

38. A. Nahavandi and E. Aranda, "Restructuring Teams for the Reengineered Organization," *Academy of Management Executive,* November 1994, pp. 58–68.

39. J. Katzenback and D. Smith, *The Wisdom of Teams* (Boston: Harvard Business School Press, 1993).

40. Nadler, Hackman, and Lawler, *Managing Organizational Behavior.*

41. P. Petty, "Behind the Brands at P&G: An Interview with John Smale," *Harvard Business Review,* November–December 1985, pp. 78–80.

42. T. Peters and N. Austin, *A Passion for Excellence* (New York: Random House, 1985).

43. T. Kidder, *The Soul of a New Machine* (Boston: Little, Brown, 1981).

44. Nadler, Hackman, and Lawler, *Managing Organizational Behavior.*

45. Katzenback and Smith, "The Discipline of Teams."

46. Ibid.

47. C. Meyer, "How the Right Measures Help Teams Excel," *Harvard Business Review,* May–June 1994, pp. 95–103.

48. J. R. Katzenbach and J. A. Santamaria, "Firing Up the Front Line," *Harvard Business Review,* May–June 1999, pp. 107–17.

49. B. L. Kirkman and B. Rosen, "Powering Up Teams," *Organizational Dynamics,* Winter 2000, pp. 48–66.

50. Lawler, *From the Ground Up.*

51. M. Erez, "Is Group Productivity Loss the Rule or the Exception? Effects of Culture and Group–Based Motivation," *Academy of Management Journal* 39 (1996), pp. 1513–37.

52. Katzenbach and Smith, "The Discipline of Teams."

53. P. Pascarelloa, "Compensating Teams," *Across the Board,* February 1997, pp. 16–22.

54. T. R. Zenger and C. R. Marshall, "Determinants of Incentive Intensity in Group-based Rewards," *Academy*

of Management Journal, 43 (2000), pp. 149–63.

55. R. Wageman, "Interdependence and Group Effectiveness," *Administrative Science Quarterly* 40 (1995), pp. 145–80.

56. Cianni and Wnuck, "Individual Growth and Team Enhancement."

57. Lawler, *From the Ground Up.*

58. Wellins, Byham, and Dixon, *Inside Teams.*

59. Ibid.

60. J. M. Levine, E. T. Higgins, and H. Choi, "Development of Strategic Norms in Groups," *Organizational Behavior and Human Decision Processes,* 82 (2000), pp. 88–101.

61. J. O'Toole, *Vanguard Management: Redesigning the Corporate Future* (New York: Doubleday, 1985).

62. R. F. Bales, *Interaction Process Analysis: A Method for the Study of Small Groups* (Reading, MA: Addison-Wesley, 1950).

63. Katzenback and Smith, *The Wisdom of Teams.*

64. R. Wellins, R. Byham, and G. Dixon, *Inside Teams* (San Francisco: Jossey-Bass, 1994).

65. C. Stoner and R. Hartman, "Team Building: Answering the Tough Questions," *Business Horizons,* September–October 1993, pp. 70–78.

66. S. E. Seashore, *Group Cohesiveness in the Industrial Work Group* (Ann Arbor, MI: University of Michigan Press, 1954).

67. Banker et al., "Impact of Work Teams on Manufacturing Performance."

68. B. Mullen and C. Cooper, "The Relation Between Group Cohesiveness and Performance: An Integration," *Psychological Bulletin* 115 (1994), pp. 210–27.

69. D. P. Forbes and F. J. Milliken, "Cognition and Corporate Governance: Understanding Boards of Directors as Strategic Decision-making Groups," *Academy of Management Review,* 24 (1999), pp. 489–505.

70. T. Simons, L. H. Pelled, and K. A. Smith, "Making Use of Difference:

Diversity, Debate, and Decision Comprehensiveness in Top Management Teams," *Academy of Management Journal,* 42 (1999), pp. 662–73.

71. Seashore, *Group Cohesiveness in the Industrial Work Group.*

72. B. Lott and A. Lott, "Group Cohesiveness as Interpersonal Attraction: A Review of Relationships with Antecedent and Consequent Variables," *Psychological Bulletin,* October 1965, pp. 259–309.

73. B. L. Kirkman and B. Rosen, "Beyond Self-management: Antecedents and Consequences of Team Empowerment," *Academy of Management Journal,* 42 (1999) pp. 58–74.

74. Hackman, *Groups That Work.*

75. W. Bennis, *Organizing Genius* (Reading, MA: Addison-Wesley, 1997).

76. Cianni and Wnuck, "Individual Growth and Team Enhancement."

77. K. Jehn, "A Multimethod Examination of the Benefits and Detriments of Intragroup Conflict," *Administrative Science Quarterly* 40 (1995), pp. 245–82.

78. Wellins, Byham, and Dixon, *Inside Teams.*

79. D. G. Ancona, "Outward Bound: Strategies for Team Survival in an Organization," *Academy of Management Journal* 33 (1990), pp. 334–65.

80. Ibid.

81. L. Sayles, *Leadership: What Effective Managers Really Do, and How They Do It* (New York: McGraw-Hill, 1979).

82. Ibid.

83. S. Wetlaufer, "Common Sense and Conflict: An Interview with Disney's Michael Eisner," *Harvard Business Review,* January–February 2000, pp. 114–24.

84. Stoner and Hartman, "Team Building."

85. D. Tjosvold, *Working Together to Get Things Done* (Lexington, MA: Lexington Books, 1986).

86. M. Blum and J. A. Wall Jr., "HRM: Managing Conflicts in the Firm,"

Business Horizons, May–June 1997, pp. 84–87.

87. Ibid.

88. J. A. Wall Jr. and R. R. Callister, "Conflict and Its Management," *Journal of Management* 21 (1995), pp. 515–58.

89. K. W. Thomas, "Conflict and Conflict Management," in *Handbook of Industrial and Organizational Psychology,* ed. M. D. Dunnette (Chicago: Rand McNally, 1976).

90. K. W. Thomas, "Toward Multi-Dimensional Values in Teaching: The Example of Conflict Behaviors," *Academy of Management Review* (1977), pp. 484–89.

91. C. O. Longenecker and M. Neubert, "Barriers and Gateways to Management Cooperation and Teamwork," *Business Horizons,* September–October 2000, pp. 37–44.

Chapter Fifteen

1. D. Yankelovich, *The Magic of Dialogue: Transforming Conflict into Cooperation* (New York: Simon & Schuster, 1999).

2. P. Senge, *The Fifth Discipline* (New York: Doubleday, 1990).

3. Ibid.

4. L. Penley, E. Alexander, I. E. Jernigan, and C. Henwood, "Communication Abilities of Managers: The Relationship to Performance," *Journal of Management* 17 (1991), pp. 57–76.

5. W. V. Haney, "A Comparative Study of Unilateral and Bilateral Communication," *Academy of Management Journal* 7 (1964), pp. 128–36.

6. M. McCormack, "The Illusion of Communication," *Financial Times Mastering Management Review,* July 1999, pp. 8–9.

7. D. Tannen, "The Power of Talk: Who Gets Heard and Why," *Harvard Business Review,* September–October 1995, pp. 138–48.

8. Ibid.

9. Ibid.

10. Ibid.

11. Ibid.

12. L. K. Larkey, "Toward a Theory of Communicative Interactions in Culturally Diverse Workgroups," *Academy of Management Review,* April 1996, pp. 463–91.

13. C. Argyris, "Good Communication That Blocks Learning," *Harvard Business Review,* July–August 1994, pp. 77–85.

14. Ibid.

15. Ibid.

16. C. Deutsch, "The Multimedia Benefits Kit," *The New York Times,* October 14, 1990, sec. 3, p. 25.

17. T. W. Comstock, *Communicating in Business and Industry* (Albany, NY: Delmar, 1985).

18. J. Taylor and W. Wacker, *The 500 Year Delta: What Happens after What Comes Next* (New York: HarperCollins, 1997).

19. P. L. McLeod, "A Literary Examination of Electronic Meeting System Use in Everyday Organizational Life, *Human Relations,* 35 (1999), pp. 188–206.

20. T. A. Stewart, "How Cisco and Alcoa Make Real Time Work," *Fortune,* May 29, 2000, pp. 284–86.

21. S. S. K. Lam and J. Schaubroeck, "Improving Group Decisions by Better Pooling Information: A Comparative Advantage of Group Decision Support Systems," *Journal of Applied Psychology,* 85 (2000), pp. 565–73.

22. M. Schrage, "If You Can't Say Anything Nice, Say It Anonymously," *Fortune,* December 6, 1999, p. 352.

23. R. Rice and D. Case, "Electronic Message Systems in the University: A Description of Use and Utility," *Journal of Communication* 33 (1983), pp. 131–52; C. Steinfield, "Dimensions of Electronic Mail Use in an Organizational Setting," *Proceedings of the Academy of Management,* San Diego, 1985.

24. J. Solomon, "As Electronic Mail Loosens Inhibitions, Impetuous Senders Feel Anything Goes," *The Wall Street Journal,* October 12, 1990, pp. B1, B8.

25. B. Glassberg, W. Kettinger, and J. Logan, "Electronic

Communication: An Ounce of Policy Is Worth a Pound of Cure," *Business Horizons,* July–August 1996, pp. 74–80.

26. Ibid.

27. Ibid.

28. N. B. Kurland and D. E. Bailey, "Telework: The Advantages and Challenges of Working Here, There, Anywhere, Anytime," *Organizational Dynamics,* Autumn 1999, pp. 53–68.

29. K. Edelman "Open Office? Try Virtual Office," *Across the Board,* March 1997, p. 34.

30. S. Shellenbarger, "Overwork, Low Morale Vex Office Staff," *The Wall Street Journal,* August 17, 1994, pp. B1, B4.

31. Ibid.

32. E. M. Hallowell, "The Human Moment at Work," *Harvard Business Review,* January–February 1999, pp. 58–66.

33. "Home Alone: The Job," *Collections & Credit Risk,* May 1997, p. 23.

34. J. Stuller, "Overload," *Across the Board,* April 1996, pp. 16–22.

35. Taylor and Wacker, *The 500 Year Delta.*

36. Ibid.

37. R. Tetzeli, "Surviving Information Overload," *Fortune,* July 11, 1994, pp. 32–35.

38. Ibid.

39. T. W. Malone, "Is Empowerment Just a Fad? Control, Decision Making and IT," *Sloan Management Review,* Winter 1997, pp. 23–35.

40. J. W. Medcof, "Challenges in Managing Technology in Transnational Multipartner Networks," *Business Horizons,* January–February 1996, pp. 47–54.

41. R. Lengel and R. Daft, "The Selection of Communication Media as an Executive Skill," *Academy of Management Executive* 2 (1988), pp. 225–32.

42. J. R. Carlson and R. W. Zmud, "Channel Expansion Theory and the Experiential Nature of Media Richness Perceptions," *Academy of Management Journal,* 42, (1999), pp. 153–70.

43. L. Trevino, R. Daft, and R. Lengel, "Understanding Managers' Media Choices: A Symbolic Interactionist Perspective," in *Organizations and Communication Technology,* ed. J. Fulk and C. Steinfield (London: Sage, 1990).

44. J. Fulk and B. Boyd, "Emerging Theories of Communication in Organizations," *Journal of Management* 17 (1991), pp. 407–46.

45. P. G. Clampitt, *Communicating for Managerial Effectiveness* (London: Sage, 1991).

46. W. F. Cascio, "Managing a Virtual Workplace," *Academy of Management Executive,* August 2000, pp. 81–90.

47. Ibid.

48. Ibid.

49. M. McCall, M. Lombardo, and A. Morrison, *The Lessons of Experience: How Successful Executives Develop on the Job* (Lexington, MA: Lexington, 1988).

50. C. M. Kelly, "Effective Communications—Beyond the Glitter and Flash," *Sloan Management Review,* Spring 1985, pp. 69–74.

51. J. A. Conger, "The Necessary Art of Persuasion," *Harvard Business Review,* May–June 1998, pp. 84–95.

52. D. Sull, "The Rhetoric of Transformation," *Financial Times Mastering Management Review,* December/January 1999/2000, pp. 34–37.

53. N. Nohria and B. Harrington, *Six Principles of Successful Persuasion* (Boston: Harvard Business School Publishing Division, 1993).

54. R. Ashkenas, D. Ulrich, T. Jick, and S. Kerr, *The Boundaryless Organization* (San Francisco: Jossey-Bass, 1995).

55. H. K. Mintz, "Business Writing Styles for the 70's," *Business Horizons,* August 1972. Cited in *Readings in Interpersonal and Organizational Communication,* ed. R. C. Huseman, C. M. Logue, and D. L. Freshley (Boston: Allyn & Bacon, 1977).

56. C. D. Decker, "Writing to Teach Thinking," *Across the Board,* March 1996, pp. 19–20.

57. M. Forbes, "Exorcising Demons from Important Business Letters," *Marketing Times,* March–April 1981, pp. 36–38.

58. C. Krauthammer, "Make It Snappy: In Praise of Short Papers, Short Speeches, and, Yes, the Sound Bite," *Time* July 21, 1997, p. 84.

59. W. Strunk Jr. and E. B. White, *The Elements of Style,* 3rd ed. (New York: Macmillan, 1979); H. R. Fowler, *The Little Brown Handbook* (Boston: Little, Brown, 1986).

60. G. Ferraro, "The Need for Linguistic Proficiency in Global Business," *Business Horizons,* May–June 1996, pp. 39–46.

61. Ibid.

62. C. Chu, *The Asian Mind Game* (New York: Rawson Associates, 1991).

63. Ferraro, "The Need for Linguistic Proficiency in Global Business."

64. Comstock, *Communicating in Business and Industry.*

65. M. Korda, *Power: How to Get It, How to Use It* (New York: Random House, 1975).

66. A. Mehrabian, "Communication without Words," *Psychology Today,* September 1968, p. 52. Cited in M. B. McCaskey, "The Hidden Message Managers Send," *Harvard Business Review,* November–December 1979, pp. 135–48.

67. Ferraro, "The Need for Linguistic Proficiency in Global Business."

68. *Business Horizons,* May–June 1993. Copyright 1993 by the Foundation for the School of Business at Indiana University. Used with permission.

69. "Too Many in the New Workforce Are Lacking Basic Skills," *Research Alert,* November 15, 1996, p. 5.

70. A. Athos and J. Gabarro, *Interpersonal Behavior* (Englewood Cliffs, NJ: Prentice Hall, 1978).

71. "Have You Heard about Sperry?" *Management Review* 69 (April 1980), p. 40.

72. J. Kouzes and B. Posner, *The Leadership Challenge* (San Francisco: Jossey-Bass, 1995).

73. G. Graham, J. Unruh, and P. Jen-

nings, "The Impact of Nonverbal Communication in Organizations: A Survey of Perceptions," *Journal of Business Communications* 28 (1991), pp. 45–62.

74. Ibid.

75. D. Upton and S. Macadam, "Why (and How) to Take a Plant Tour," *Harvard Business Review,* May–June 1997, pp. 97–106.

76. S. Wetlaufer, "Common Sense and Conflict: An Interview with Disney's Michael Eisner," *Harvard Business Review,* January–February 2000, pp. 114–24.

77. N. Adler, *International Dimensions of Organizational Behavior,* 2nd ed. (Boston: Kent, 1991).

78. Chu, *The Asian Mind Game.*

79. W. C. Redding, *Communication within the Organization: An Interpretive Review of Theory and Research* (New York: Industrial Communication Council, 1972). Cited in F. M. Jablin, "Superior-Subordinate Communication: The State of the Art," *Psychological Bulletin* 86 (1979), pp. 1201–22.

80. Penley et al, "Communication Abilities of Managers."

81. J. W. Koehler, K. W. E. Anatol, and R. L. Applebaum, *Organizational Communication: Behavioral Perspectives* (Orlando, FL: Holt, Rinehart & Winston, 1981).

82. J. Waldroop and T. Butler, "The Executive as Coach," *Harvard Business Review,* November–December 1996, pp. 111–17.

83. D. T. Hall, K. L. Otazo, and G. P. Hollenbeck, "Behind Closed Doors: What Really Happens in Executive Coaching," *Organizational Dynamics,* Winter 1999, pp. 39–53.

84. T. Judge and J. Cowell, "The Brave New World of Coaching," *Business Horizons,* July–August 1997, pp. 71–77.

85. Ibid.

86. J. Gutknecht and J. B. Keys, "Mergers, Acquisitions, and Takeovers: Maintaining Morale of Survivors and Protecting Employees," *Academy of Management Executive,* August 1993, pp. 26–36.

87. D. Schweiger and A. DeNisi, "Communication with Employees Following a Merger: A Longitudinal Field Experiment," *Academy of Management Journal* 34 (1991), pp. 110–35.

88. J. Case, "The Open-Book Managers," *Inc.,* September 1990, pp. 104–13.

89. J. Case, "Opening the Books," *Harvard Business Review,* March–April 1997, pp. 118–27.

90. T. R. V. Davis, "Open-Book Management: Its Promise and Pitfalls," *Organization Dynamics,* Winter 1997, pp. 7–20.

91. Ibid.

92. W. V. Ruch, *Corporate Communications* (Westport, CT: Quorum, 1984).

93. Ashkenas et al., *The Boundaryless Organization.*

94. Ruch, *Corporate Communications.*

95. Ashkenas et al., *The Boundaryless Organization.*

96. Koehler, Anatol, and Applebaum, *Organizational Communication.*

97. Ashkenas et al., *The Boundaryless Organization.*

98. D. K. Denton, "Open Communication," *Business Horizons,* September–October 1993, pp. 64–69.

99. N. B. Kurland and L. H. Pelled, "Passing the Word: Toward a Model of Gossip and Power in the Workplace," *Academy of Management Review,* 25, (2000), pp. 428–38.

100. R. L. Rosnow, "Rumor as Communication: A Contextual Approach," *Journal of Communication* 38 (1988), pp. 12–28.

101. K. Davis, "The Care and Cultivation of the Corporate Grapevine," *Dun's Review,* July 1973, pp. 44–47.

102. N. Difonzo, P. Bordia, and R. Rosnow, "Reining in Rumors," *Organizational Dynamics,* Summer 1994, pp. 47–62.

103. Ibid.

104. Ashkenas et al., *The Boundaryless Organization.*

105. Ibid.

106. R. M. Hodgetts, "A Conversation with Steve Kerr," *Organizational Dynamics,* Spring 1996, pp. 68–79.

107. Ibid.

108. R. M. Fulmer, "The Evolving Paradigm of Leadership Development," *Organizational Dynamics,* Spring 1997, pp. 59–72.

109. Ibid.

110. Ashkenas et al., *The Boundaryless Organization.*

Chapter Sixteen

1. James C. Collins, and Jerry I. Porras, *Built to Last: Successful Habits of Visionary Companies* (New York: HarperBusiness, 1994).

2. Keith Naughton, "Spinning Out of Control," *Newsweek,* September 11, 2000, 136, no. 11, p. 58; Christopher Palmeri, "California's Utilities Doth Protest Too Much," *Business Week,* January 15, 2001, 3715, pp. 42–43.

3. W. G. Ouchi, "Markets, Bureaucracies, and Clans," *Administrative Science Quarterly* 25 (1980), pp. 129–41.

4. Robert Simons, Antonio Davila, and Robert S. Kaplan, *Performance Measurement & Control Systems for Implementing Strategy* (Englewood Cliffs, NJ: Prentice Hall, 2000).

5. Elaine D. Pulakos, Sharon Arad, Michelle A. Donovan, and Kevin E. Plamondon, "Adaptability in the Workplace: Development of a Taxonomy of Adaptive Performance," *Journal of Applied Psychology,* August 2000, 85, no. 4, pp. 12–24; John H. Sheridan, "Lean Sigma Synergy," *Industry Week,* October 16, 2000, 249, no. 17, pp. 81–82.

6. J. T. Burr, "Keys to a Successful Internal Audit," *Quality Progress* 30, no. 4 (April 1997), pp. 75–77; John E. Ettlie, "Surfacing Quality at GE," *Automotive Manufacturing & Production,* August 2000, 112, no. 8, pp. 44–46; Roy A. Maxion and Robert T. Olszewski, "Eliminating Exception Handling Errors with Dependability Cases: A Comparative, Empirical Study," *IEEE Transactions on Software Engineering,* September 2000, 26, no. 9, pp. 888–906.

7. Robert Della, "Harley Rides High on SPC Changes," *Quality,* January 2000, 39, no. 1, 40–43.

8. R. Henkoff, "Make Your Office More Productive," *Fortune,* February 25, 1990, pp. 40–49.

   R. Buchele, "How to Evaluate a Firm," *California Management Review,* Fall 1962, pp. 5–17.

9. George Ellis, "Feedforward for Faster Control Response," *Control Engineering,* October 2000, 47, no. 11, p. 104.

10. Vanessa Urch Druskat, "Effects and Timing of Developmental Peer Appraisals in Self-managing Work Groups," *Journal of Applied Psychology,* February 1999, 84, no. 1, p. 58.

11. Sandra Waddock and Neil Smith, "Corporate Responsibility Audits: Doing Well by Doing Good," *Sloan Management Review,* Winter 2000, 41, no. 2, pp. 75–83; Lynn L. Bergeson, "OSHA Gives Incentives for Voluntary Self-audits," *Pollution Engineering,* October 2000, 32, no. 10, pp. 33–34.

12. Janet, L. Colbert, "The Impact of the New External Auditing Standards," *The Internal Auditor,* December 2000, 5, no. 6, pp. 46–50.

13. G. A. Ewert, "How to Sell Internal Auditing," *Internal Auditor* 54, no. 5 (October 1997), pp. 54–57; J. T. Burr, "Keys to a Successful Internal Audit," *Quality Progress* 30, no. 4 (April 1997), pp. 75–77; Satina V. Williams and Benson Wier, "Value-added Auditing: Where Are the Efficiencies Realized?," *Internal Auditing,* July/August 2000, 15, no. 4, pp. 37–42; David B. Crawford, "Levels of Control," *The Internal Auditor,* October 2000, 57, no. 5, pp. 42–45.

14. R. Henkoff, "Cost Cutting: How to Do It Right," *Fortune,* April 9, 1990, pp. 40–49.

15. Carol J. Loomis, "I Pay More in Income Taxes than Cisco—So Do You," *Fortune,* December 18, 2000, 142, no. 14, pp. 44–46; Thomas G. Donlan, "Bridging the GAAP," *Barron's,* November 6, 2000, vol. 80, Iss. 45, p. 74.

16. P. C. Brewer and L. A. Vulinec, "Harris Corporation's Experiences with Using Activity-Based Costing," *Information Strategy: The Executive's Journal* 13, no. 2 (Winter 1997), pp. 6–16; Terence P. Pare, "A New Tool for Managing Costs," *Fortune,* June 14, 1993, pp. 124–29;

17. K. Merchant, *Control in Business Organizations* (Boston: Pitman, 1985); C. W. Chow, Y. Kato, and K. A. Merchant, "The Use of Organizational Controls and Their Effects on Data Manipulation and Management Myopia," *Accounting, Organizations, and Society* 21, nos. 2/3 (February/April 1996), pp. 175–92.

18. E. E. Lawler III and J. Rhode, *Information and Control in Organizations* (Pacific Palisades, CA: Goodyear, 1976); Anthony Ferner, "The Underpinnings of 'Bureaucratic' Control Systems: HRM in European Multinationals," *The Journal of Management Studies,* June 2000, 37, no. 4, pp. 521–39; Marilyn S. Fenwick, "Cultural and Bureaucratic Control in MNEs: The Role of Expatriate Performance Management," *Management International Review* (1999), vol. 39, pp. 107–25.

19. J. Veiga and J. Yanouzas, *The Dynamics of Organization Theory,* 2nd ed. (St. Paul, MN: West, 1984).

20. L. Schiff, "Downsizing Workplace Stress," *Business & Health* 15, no. 1 (November 1997), pp. 45–46; S. Albrecht, "Are Your Employees the Enemy?" *HRFocus* 74, no. 4 (April 1997), p. 21.

21. Michael Scott, "Seven Pitfalls for Managers When Handling Poor Performers and How to Overcome Them," *Manage,* February 2000, 51, no. 3, pp. 12–14.

22. Henkoff, "Make Your Office More Productive."; See also, Peggy Anderson and Marcia Pulich, "Recruiting Good Employees in Tough Times," *The Health Care Manager,* March 2000, 18, no. 3, pp. 32–40.

23. Lawler and Rhode, *Information and Control in Organizations; J. A.* Gowan, Jr. and R. G. Mathieu,

"Critical Factors in Information System Development for a Flexible Manufacturing System," *Computers in Industry* 28, no. 3 (June 1996), pp. 173–83.

24. T. A. Stewart, "Do You Push Your People Too Hard?" *Fortune,* October 22, 1990, pp. 121–28.

25. S. Tully, "The CEO Who Sees Beyond Budgets," *Fortune,* October 22, 1990, pp. 121–28.

26. Robert W. Rudloff, "Casino Fraud," *The Internal Auditor,* June 1999, 56, no. 3, pp. 44–49; Mike McNamee, "Faster, Cheaper Trading—Can the Regulators Keep up," *Business Week,* August 9, 1999, 3641, pp. 84; Bill Zalud, "Conquering Digital Marks CCTV Innovations," *Security,* April 2000, 37, no. 4, pp. 43–44.

27. Gillian Flynn, "Out of the Red, Into the Blue," *Workforce,* March 2000, 79, no. 3, pp. 50–52; Alison Stein Wellner, "Entrepreneurial HR," *HR Magazine,* March 2000, 45, no. 3, pp. 52–58.

28. T. A. Stewart, "CEO Pay: Mom Would be Proud," *Fortune* 135, no. 6 (March 31, 1997), pp. 119–20; Brian Dumaine, "A Knockout Year for CEO Pay," *Fortune,* July 25, 1994, pp. 94–103; "Worthy of His Hire?" *The Economist,* February 1, 1992, pp. 19–22.

29. S. A. Snell and J. W. Dean Jr., "Strategic Compensation for Integrated Manufacturing: The Moderating Effects of Jobs and Organizational Inertia," *Academy of Managent Journal* 37, no. 5 (1994), pp. 1109–40; M. A. Youndt, S. A. Snell, J. W. Dean Jr., and D. P. P. Lepak, "Human Resource Management, Manufacturing Strategy, and Firm Performance," *Academy of Management Journal* 39, no. 4, Special Issue (1996), pp. 836–66; Peter Drucker, "Knowledge Work," *Executive Excellence,* April 2000, 17, no. 4, pp. 11–12.

30. Ken Moores and Joseph Mula, "The Salience of Market, Bureaucratic, and Clan Controls in the Management of Family Firm Transitions: Some Tentative Australian Evidence," *Family Business Review,* June 2000,

13, no. 2, pp. 91–106; Anthony Walker and Robert Newcombe, "The Positive Use of Power on a Major Construction Project," *Construction Management and Economics,* January/February 2000, 18, no. 1, pp. 37–44.

31. Peter H. Fuchs, Kenneth E. Mifflin, Danny Miller, and John O. Whitney, "Strategic Integration: Competing in the Age of Capabilities," *California Management Review,* Spring 2000, 42, no. 3, pp. 118–47; Mary Ann Lando, "Making Compliance Part of Your Organization's Culture," *Healthcare Executive,* September/October 1999, 15, no. 5, pp. 18–22; Kenneth A. Frank and Kyle Fahrbach, "Organization Culture As a Complex System. Balance and Information in Models of Influence and Selection," *Organization Science,* May/June 1999, 10, no. 3, pp. 253–77.

32. Ralph H. Kilmann, Mary J. Saxton, and Roy Serpa, *Gaining Control of the Corporate Culture* (San Francisco: Jossey-Bass, 1985); Kim S. Cameron and Robert E. Quinn, *Diagnosing and Changing Organizational Culture: Based on the Competing Values Framework* (Englewood Cliffs, NJ: Addison-Wesley, 1998).

33. Cameron and Quinn, "Diagnosing and Changing Organizational Culture."

34. R. Leifer and P. K. Mills, "An Information Processing Approach for Deciding upon Control Strategies and Reducing Control Loss in Emerging Organizations," *Journal of Management* 22, no. 1 (1996), pp. 113–37; Scott A. Dellana and Richard D. Hauser, "Toward Defining the Quality Culture," *Engineering Management Journal,* June 1999, 11, no. 2, pp. 11–15; Don Cohen and Lawrence Prusak, *In Good Company: How Social Capital Makes Organizations Work* (Cambridge, MA: Harvard Business School Press, 2001).

Chapter Seventeen

1. Robert A. Burgelman, Modesto A. Maidique, and Steven C. Wheelwright, *Strategic Manage-*
ment of Technology and Innovation, (New York: McGraw-Hill Higher Education, 2000).

2. Donna C. L. Prestwood and Paul A. Schumann Jr., "Revitalize Your Organization," *Executive Excellence* 15, no. 2 (February 1998), p. 16; Carliss Y. Baldwin and Kim B. Clark, "Managing in an Age of Modularity," *Harvard Business Review* 75, no. 5 (September–October 1997), pp. 84–93; Shanthi Gopalakrishnan, Paul Bierly, and Eric H. Kessler, "A Reexamination of Product and Process Innovations Using a Knowledge-based View," *Journal of High Technology Management Research,* Spring 1999, 10, no. 1, pp. 147–66; John Pullin, "Bombardier Commands Top Marks," *Professional Engineering,* July 5, 2000, 13, no. 3, pp. 40–46.

3. Gary P. Pisano. *The Development Factory: Unlocking the Potential of Process Innovation* (Boston: Harvard Business School Press, 1996); Richard Leifer, Christopher M. McDermott, Gina Colarelli O'Connor, Lois S. Peters, Mark Rice, and Robert W. Veryzer, *Radical Innovation: How Mature Companies Can Outsmart Upstarts* (Cambridge MA: Harvard Business School Press, 2000).

4. Hugh M. O'Neill, Richard W. Pounder, and Ann K. Buchholtz, "Patterns in the diffusion of Strategies across Organizations: Insights from the Innovation Diffusion Literature," *Academy of Management Review* 23, no. 1 (January 1998), pp. 98–114; Everett M. Rogers, *Diffusion of Innovations* (New York: Free Press, 1995); Bernard Guilhon, ed., *Technology and Markets for Knowledge—Knowledge Creation, Diffusion and Exchange within a Growing Economy* (Economics of Science, Technology and Innovation (Volume 22) (Dordrecht, Netherlands: Kluwer Academic Publishing, 2000).

5. M. E. Porter, *Competitive Strategy* (New York: Free Press, 1980); "Ciba Specialty Chemicals Highlights Sustainable Growth through Innovation," *Chemical Market Reporter,* April 17, 2000, 257, no. 16, p. 5.

6. J. A. Schumpeter, *The Theory of Economic Development* (Boston: Harvard University Press, 1934); Kathleen DesMarteau, "Information Technology Trends Drive Dramatic Industry Change," *Bobbin,* August 2000, 41, no. 12, pp. 48–58.

7. Shaker A. Zahra, Sarah Nash, and Deborah J. Bickford. "Transforming Technological Pioneering in Competitive Advantage." *Academy of Management Executive* 9, no. 1 (1995), pp. 17–31; Michael Sadowski and Aaron Roth, "Technology Leadership Can Pay Off," *Research Technology Management,* November/December 1999, 42, no. 6, pp. 32–33.

8. Todd Wasserman, "Kodak, Polaroid to Duel in Malls over Gen Y Girls," *Brandweek,* January 31, 2000, 41, no. 5, p. 10; Joel Dreyfuss, "Pixel This: How To Choose a Digital Camera," *Fortune,* April 3, 2000, 141, no. 7, pp. 263–64.

9. Jared Sandberg, "Microsoft's Six Fatal Errors," *Newsweek,* June 19, 2000, 135, no. 25, pp. 22–28; "Leaders: Breaking Up Microsoft," *The Economist,* June 10, 2000, 355, no. 8174, p. 20.

10. Masaaki Imai and Gemba Kaizen, *A Commonsense, Low-Cost Approach to Management* (New York: McGraw-Hill, 1997); Masaaki Imai and Gemba Kaizen, *The Key to Japan's Competitive Success* (New York: McGraw-Hill, 1986).

11. Marc Bertucco, "FDA Under Fire," *Psychology Today,* January/February 2001, 34, no. 1, pp. 10–11; Jill Wechsler, "Carrying a Big Stick," *Pharmaceutic Executive,* September 2000, 20, no. 9, pp. 24–27; Robin Goldwyn Blumenthal, "Next Thing You Know, the FDA Will Be Profitable," *Barron's,* November 22, 1999, 79, no. 47, p. 12.

12. P. A. Geroski, "Models of Technology Diffusion," *Research Policy,* April 2000, 29, no. 4/5, pp. 603–25; Louis A. Thomas, "Adoption Order of New Technologies in Evolving Markets," *Journal of Economic Behavior & Organization,* April 1999, 38, no. 4, pp. 453–82.

13. Ronald E. Oligney and Michael I. Economides, "Technology As an Asset," *Hart's Petroleum Engineer International,* September 1998, 71, no. 9, p. 27.

14. Scott Blake Harris, "Fixing Financial Standards," *Satellite Communications,* March 1999, 23, no. 3, p. 22; Lauren E. Burns, "Still Avoiding Flameout, Globalstar Learns Iridium's Lessons," *Aviation Week & Space Technology,* July 3, 2000, 153, no. 1, p. s23.

15. "Computing's Outer Limits," *Popular Science,* March 1998, 252, no. 3, p. 64.

16. Peter G. Neumann, "Missile Defense," *Communications of the ACM,* September 2000, 43, no. 9, p. 128; Nancy Gohring, "New Spectrum Up for Grabs," *Telephony,* May 24, 1999, 236, no. 21, p. 14.

17. Jimmy Carter. "Corporate Giving Is Part of the Solutions Equation; Philanthropy: When Business Works with Individuals, Government and Nonprofits to Do Good, Success Is Boundless," *Los Angeles Times,* February 19, 1998, p. B9; Nancy Walsh D'Epiro, "Targeting River Blindness," *Patient Care* 31, no. 16 (October 15, 1997), p. 18; Joanne B Ciulla, "The Importance of Leadership in Shaping Business Values," *Long Range Planning,* April 1999, 32, no. 2, pp. 166–72.

18. Irene M. Kunii, "A Bold Mechanic for a Creaky Machine," *Business Week,* August 7, 2000, p. 58H; Sadanori Arimura, "How Matsushita Electric and Sony Manage Global R&D," *Research Technology Management,* March/April 1999, 42, no. 2, pp. 41–52; Richard Nathan, "Matsushita Hopes Silicon Valley Links Can Boost Its R&D," *Research Technology Management,* March/April 1999, 42, no. 2, pp. 4–5.

19. Rajiv Dewan, Bing Jing, and Abraham Seidmann, "Adoption of Internet-based Product Customization and Pricing Strategies," *Journal of Management Information Systems,* Fall 2000, 17, no. 2, pp. 9–28; P. A. Geroski, "Models of Technology Diffusion," *Research Policy,* April

2000, 29, no. 4/5, pp. 603–25; Everett M. Rogers, *Diffusion of Innovations* (New York: Free Press, 1995).

20. Eric Von Hippel, *The Sources of Innovation* (Oxford, UK: Oxford University Press, 1994); Dorothy Leonard, *Wellsprings of Knowledge: Building and Sustaining the Sources of Innovation* (Cambridge MA: Harvard Business School Press, 1998).

21. Ibid.

22. John Hagedoorn, Albert N. Link, and Nicholas S. Vonortas, "Research Partnerships," *Research Policy,* April 2000, 29, no. 4/5, pp. 567–86; Sang-Seung Yi, "Entry, Licensing and Research Joint Ventures," *International Journal of Industrial Organization,* January 1999, 17, no. 1, pp. 1–24.

23. Joseph F. Kovar, "Readers' Choice: Scott McNealy, Sun," *Computer Reseller News,* November 13, 2000, 920, pp. 129–30; Peter Burrows, Michael Moeller, and Steve Hamm, "Free Software from Anywhere?" *Business Week,* September 13, 1999, pp. 37–38; Gary K. Jones, Aldor Lanctot, Jr., and Hildy J. Teegan, "Determinants and Performance Impacts of External Technology Acquisition," *Journal of Business Venturing,* May 2000, 16, no. 3, pp. 255–83.

24. Michael Vizard, "It's the CTOs Who Help to Drive the Changing Role of IT in the World of Business," *InfoWorld,* November 29, 1999, 21, no. 48, p. 91; Gary H. Anthes, "The CIO/CTO Balancing Act," *Computerworld,* June 19, 2000, 34, no. 25, pp. 50–51.

25. Melanie Warner, "The New Way to Start Up in Silicon Valley," *Fortune* 137, no. 4 (March 2, 1998), pp. 168–74; Leon Richardson, "The Successful Entrepreneur," *Asian Business,* July 1994, p. 71; Charles Burck, "The Real World of the Entrepreneur," *Fortune,* April 5, 1993, pp. 42–55.

26. D. L. Day, "Raising Radicals: Different Processes for Championing Innovative Corporate Ventures," *Organization Science* 5, no. 2 (May

1994), pp. 148–72; Clifford Siporin, "Want Speedy FDA Approval? Hire a 'Product Champion,' " *Medical Marketing & Media,* October 1993, pp. 22–28; Clifford Siporin, "How You Can Capitalize on Phase 3B," *Medical Marketing & Media,* October 1994, pp. 72–72. Eric H. Kessler, "Tightening the Belt: Methods for Reducing Development Costs Associated with New Product Innovation," *Journal of Engineering and Technology Management,* March 2000, 17, no. 1, pp. 59–92.

27. Edgar Figueroa and Pedro Conceicao, "Rethinking the Innovation Process in Large Organizations: A Case Study of 3M," *Journal of Engineering and Technology Management,* March 2000, 17, no. 1, pp. 93–109; David Howell, "No Such Thing As a Daft Idea," *Professional Engineering,* February 23, 2000, 13, no. 4, pp. 28–29.

28. Lisa K. Gundry, Jill R. Kickul, and Charles W. Prather, "Building the Creative Organization," *Organizational Dynamics* 22, no. 2 (Spring 1994), pp. 22–36; Thomas Kuczmarski, "Inspiring and Implementing the Innovation Mind-Set," *Planning Review,* September–October 1994, pp. 37–48; Robert D. Ramsey, "How an Optimistic Outlook Can Give You an Edge," *Supervision* (Sep. 2000) 61 no. 9, pp. 6–8.

29. R. Neff, "Toray May Have Found the Formula for Luck," *Business Week,* June 15, 1990, p. 110.

30. Dorothy Leonard, *Wellsprings of Knowledge: Building and Sustaining the Sources of Innovation* (Cambridge MA: Harvard Business School Press, 1998); Dorothy Leonard-Barton "The Factory As a Learning Laboratory," *Sloan Management Review,* Fall 1992, pp. 23–38; Anil K. Gupta and Vijay Govindarajan, "Knowledge Management's Social Dimension: Lessons from Nucor Steel," *Sloan Management Review,* Fall 2000, 42, no. 1, pp. 71–80.

31. H. Kent Bowen, Kim B. Clark, Charles A. Holloway, and Steven C. Wheelwright, "Development Projects: The Engine of Renewal," *Harvard Business Review,*

September–October 1994, pp. 110–20; C. Eden, T. Williams, and F. Ackermann, "Dismantling the Learning Curve: The Role of Disruptions on the Planning of Development Projects," *International Journal of Project Management* 16, no. 3 (June 1998), pp. 131–38; Mohan V Tatikonda and Stephen R Rosenthal, "Technology Novelty, Project Complexity, and Product Development Project Execution Success: A Deeper Look at Task Uncertainty in Product Innovation," *IEEE Transactions on Engineering Management,* February 2000, 47, no. 1, pp. 74–87.

32. Robert H. Hayes, Kim B. Clark, and Steven C. Wheelwright, *Dynamic Manufacturing: Creating the Learning Organization* (New York: Free Press, 1988).

33. E. Trist, "The Evolution of Sociotechnical Systems as a Conceptual Framework and as an Action Research Program," in *Perspectives on Organizational Design and Behavior,* ed. A. Van de Ven and W. F. Joyce (New York: John Wiley & Sons, 1981), pp. 19–75; Alfonso Molina, "Insights into the Nature of Technology Diffusion and Implementation: The Perspective of Sociotechnical Alignment," *Technovation* 17, nos. 11/12 (November/December 1997), pp. 601–26.

34. S. Zuboff, *In the Age of the Smart Machine* (New York: Basic Books, 1988); Scott A. Snell and James W. Dean Jr., "Strategic Compensation for Integrated Manufacturing: The Moderating Effects of Jobs and Organizational Inertia," *Academy of Management Journal* 37, no. 5 (1994), pp. 1109–40; M. A. Youndt, S. A. Snell, J. W. Dean Jr., and D. P. Lepak, "Human Resource Management, Manufacturing Strategy, and Firm Performance," *Academy of Management Journal* 39, no. 4, Special Issue (1996), pp. 836–66.

Chapter Seventeen Appendix

1. Robert M. Pirsig, *Zen and the Art of Motorcycle Maintenance* (New York: William Morrow and Company, Inc., 1974).

2. Pratima Raichur, *Absolute Beauty* (New York: HarperPerennial, 1986).

3. Nescafe: Nestle (verified by Terri Haywood via 1/16/01 e-mail that Nescafe and Nesquik flavors are modified for the market in which they are sold).

Chapter Eighteen

1. M. Schrage, "Getting Beyond the Innovation Fetish," *Fortune,* November 13, 2000, pp. 225–32.

2. T. A. Judge, C. J. Thoresen, V. Pucik, and T. M. Welbourne, "Managerial Coping with Organizational Change: A Dispositional Perspective, "*Journal of Applied Psychology,* 84 (1999), pp. 107–22.

3. C. Giffi, A. Roth, and G. Seal, *Competing in World-Class Manufacturing: America's 21st Century Challenge* (Homewood, IL: Business One Irwin, 1990).

4. R. M. Kanter, *World Class: Thriving Locally in the Global Economy* (New York: Touchstone, 1995).

5. T. G. Gunn, *21st Century Manufacturing* (New York: HarperBusiness, 1992).

6. Giffi, Roth, and Seal, *Competing in World-Class Manufacturing.*

7. J. Collins and J. Porras, *Built to Last* (London: Century, 1996).

8. Ibid.

9. Ibid.

10. D. A. Nadler, "Managing Organizational Change: An Integrative Approach," *Journal of Applied Behavioral Science* 17 (1981), pp. 191–211.

11. R. Teerlink, "Harley's Leadership U-turn," *Harvard Business Review,* July–August 2000, pp. 43–48.

12. J. Stanislao and B. C. Stanislao, "Dealing with Resistance to Change," *Business Horizons,* July–August 1983, pp. 74–78.

13. J. P. Kotter and L. A. Schlesinger, "Choosing Strategies for Change," *Harvard Business Review,* March–April 1979, pp. 106–14

14. E. B. Dent and S. Galloway Goldberg, "Challenging Resistance to Change," *Journal of Applied Behavioral Science,* March 1999, pp. 25–41.

15. G. Johnson, *Strategic Change and the Management Process* (New York: Basil Blackwell, 1987); K. Lewin, "Frontiers in Group Dynamics," *Human Relations* 1 (1947), pp. 5–41.

16. E. H. Schein, "Organizational Culture: What It Is and How to Change It," in *Human Resource Management in International Firms,* ed. P. Evans, Y. Doz, and A. Laurent (New York: St. Martin's Press, 1990).

17. M. Beer, R. Eisenstat, and B. Spector, *The Critical Path to Corporate Renewal* (Cambridge, MA: Harvard Business School Press, 1990).

18. E. E. Lawler III. "Transformation from Control to Involvement," in *Corporate Transformation,* ed. R. Kilmann and T. Covin (San Francisco: Jossey-Bass, 1988).

19. D. Hellriegel and J. W. Slocum, Jr., *Management,* 4th ed. (Reading, MA: Addison-Wesley, 1986).

20. P. Harris, *New World, New Ways, New Management* (New York: American Management Association, 1983).

21. Schein, "Organizational Culture."

22. E. E. Lawler III, *From the Ground Up* (San Francisco: Jossey-Bass, 1995).

23. Kotter and Schlesinger, "Choosing Strategies for Change."

24. P. C. Judge, "It's Lonely on the Edge," *Fast Company,* September 2000, pp. 352–63.

25. Nadler, "Managing Organizational Change."

26. D. Rousseau and S. A. Tijoriwala, "What's a Good Reason to Change? Motivated Reasoning and Social Accounts in Promoting Organizational Change," *Journal of Applied Psychology,* 84 (1999), pp. 514–28.

27. P. C. Judge, "Janiece Webb," *Fast Company,* November 2000, pp. 218–26.

28. R. B. Reich, "Your Job Is Change," *Fast Company,* October 2000, pp. 140–60.

29. C. F. Leana and B. Barry, "Stability and Change As Simultaneous Experiences in Organizational Life," *Academy of Management Review,* 25 (2000), pp. 753–59.

30. B. Schneider, A. Brief, and R. Guzzo, "Creating a Climate and Culture for Sustainable Organizational Change," *Organizational Dynamics,* Spring 1996, pp. 7–19.

31. The Price Waterhouse Change Integration Team, *Better Change: Best Practices for Transforming Your Organization* (Burr Ridge, IL: Irwin, 1995).

32. M. Beer and N. Nohria, "Cracking the Code of Change," *Harvard Business Review,* May–June 2000, pp. 133–41.

33. N. Nohria and J. Berkley, "Whatever Happened to the Take-Charge Manager?" *Harvard Business Review,* January–February 1994, pp. 128–37.

34. Lawler, *From the Ground Up.*

35. The Price Waterhouse Change Integration Team, *Better Change.*

36. Ibid.

37. J. Kotter, *Leading Change* (Boston: Harvard Business School Press, 1996).

38. Lawler, *From the Ground Up.*

39. Kotter, *Leading Change.*

40. Schneider, Brief, and Guzzo, "Creating a Climate and Culture."

41. R. Beckhard and R. Harris, *Organizational Transitions* (Reading, MA: Addison-Wesley, 1977).

42. Kotter, *Leading Change.*

43. Judge, "It's Lonely on the Edge."

44. G. Hamel, "Waking Up IBM" *Harvard Business Review,* July–August 2000, pp. 137–46.

45. Kotter, *Leading Change.*

46. D. Smith, *Taking charge of Change* (Reading, MA: Addison-Wesley, 1996).

47. G. Hamel, "Killer Strategies That Make Shareholders Rich," *Fortune,* June 23, 1997, pp. 22–34.

48. G. Hamel and C. K. Prahalad, *Competing for the Future* (Boston: Harvard Business School Press, 1994).

49. B. J. Pine, B. Victor, and A. Boynton, "Making Mass Customization Work," *Harvard Business Review,* September–October 1993, pp. 108–19.

50. J. W. Slocum, Jr., M. McGill, and D. Lei, "The New Learning Strategy: Anytime, Anything, Anywhere," *Organizational Dynamics,* Autumn 1994, pp. 33–37.

51. Pine, Victor, and Boynton, "Making Mass Customization Work."

52. W. Zellner and D. Griesing, "Go-Go Galiaths," *Business Week,* February 13, 1995, pp. 64–70.

53. M. J. Kiernan, "The New Strategic Architecture: Learning to Complete in the Twenty-First Century," *The Academy of Management Executive,* February 1993, pp. 7–21.

54. R. Tomlinson, "Can Nestle Be the Very Best?" *Fortune,* November 13, 2000, pp. 353–60.

55. M. Magnet, "Let's Go for Growth," *Fortune,* March 7, 1994, pp. 60–72.

56. Ibid.

57. E. Nee, "Cisco: How it Aims to Keep Right On Growing," *Fortune,* February 5, 2001, pp. 90–96.

58. Magnet, "Let's Go for Growth,"

59. J. O'Shea and C. Madigan, *Dangerous Company: The Consulting Powerhouses and the Business They Save and Ruin* (New York: Times Books, 1997).

60. Ibid.

61. Hamel and Prahalad, *Competing for the Future.*

62. Ibid.

63. H. Courtney, J. Kirkland, and P. Viguerie, "Strategy under Uncertainty," *Harvard Business Review,* November–December 1997, pp. 66–79.

64. Ibid.

65. Hamel and Prahalad, *Competing for the Future.*

66. R. Charan and G. Colvin, "Managing for the Slowdown," *Fortune,* February 5, 2001, pp. 78–88.

67. G. Hamel, "Reinvent Your Company," *Fortune,* June 12, 2000, pp. 98–118.

68. J. Kotter, *The New Rules: How to Succeed in Today's Post-Corporate World* (New York: The Free Press, 1995).

69. Ibid.

70. Ibid.

71. Lawler, *From the Ground Up;* Kotter, *The New Rules.*

72. Lawler, *From the Ground Up.*

73. M. Peiperl and Y. Baruck, "Back to Square Zero: The Post-Corporate Career," *Organizational Dynamics,* Spring 1997, pp. 7–22.

74. Ibid.

75. Kotter, *The New Rules.*

76. G. Binney, and C. Williams, *Leaning into the Future* (London: Nicholas Brealey, 1997).

Name Index

A

Aaronsen, Jeffrey, 203
Abbott, John S., 288
Abraham, Steven E., n10.41
Abramson, Andy, 313
Abramson, Michael, 118
Achison, Thomas, 497
Ackerman, R., n5.52
Ackerman, Roger G., 288
Ackermann, F., n17.31
Adams, Bob, 500
Adams, J., n13.69
Aditya, R., n12.19, n12.39, n12.41, n12.64
Adkisson, Richard V., n6.6
Adler, N., 148, 358, 469; n3.31, n6.18, n6.24, n11.17, n11.19, n11.20, n13.32, n15.77
Adler, Paul S., n8.29
Agres, Carole E, n9.37
Ahrens, Roger, n6.9
Ainina, M. Fall, n12.2
Akasie, J., 220
Albrecht, K., n12.71
Albrecht, S., n16.20
Alderfer, C., n13.28
Alderton, Sheryl S., 537
Aldrich, H., n7.12
Alexander, E. R., n3.13, n15.4
Alexander, S., 320
Ali, Abbas J., n8.5
Alix, Jay, 23
Allen, Chris T., 213
Allinson, R. E., n5.18
Altaffer, Ahnn, n8.12
Altman, B., 180; n5B.7, n5B.50, n5B.63
Amabile, T. M., n3.45, n13.35, n13.38
Amason, A., n3.38
Anatol, K. W. E., n15.81, n15.96
Ancona, D. G., n14.79, n14.80
Anderson, J. V., n3.44
Anderson, Kenneth, n6.31
Anderson, Peggy, n16.22
Anderson, Ray, 164

Andrews, F., 379
Andrews, K., n5.14
Andrews, P., n5.62
Anfuso, Dawn, n4.13
Anthes, Gary H., n17.24
Anthony, William P., n4.7
Applebaum, R. L., n15.81, n15.96
Arad, Sharon, n16.5
Aranda, E., n14.38
Argenti, J., n7.77
Argyris, Chris, 38; n1A.19, n13.58, n15.13, n15.14, n15.15
Arimura, Sadanori, n17.18
Armstrong, Larry, 46
Arndt, Michael, 56, 67
Arnst, Catherine, 276
Arthur, Charles, n11IC.2
Arthur, Winfrid, Jr., n10.13
Ash, Mary Kay, 421
Ash, Ronald A., n10.3
Ashcroft, John, 410
Ashkenas, Ronald N., 608; n8.1, n9.46, n15.54, n15.93, n15.95, n15.97, n15.104, n15.105, n15.110, n18A.5
Athos, A., n15.70
Atkins, P. W. B., n13.21
Atkinson, Anthony A., 515
Austin, N., n13.54, n13.61, n14.42
Avolio, B. J., n12.67, n12.70
Axtell, Laurie, 312

B

Bacher, Jeffrey, n10.29
Bacon, Francis, 536
Badarocco, J., Jr., n5.12
Baddaley, J., n7.65, n7.66
Bailey, D., n14.2, n14.19, n14.23, n14.24, n15.28
Baird, Lloyd, n8.20
Bakke, Dennis, 264, 411, 412, 492; n8.17
Baldrige, Malcolm, 287, 288, 371, 511

Baldwin, Carliss Y., n17.2
Bales, R. F., n14.62
Balestrini, P. P., n9.39
Ball, G., n13.15
Ballam, Deborah A., n10.17
Ballard, L. Gregory, 12
Balu, R., 78; n7.46, n7.47, n7.61
Banker, R., 443; n14.25, n14.67
Banta, Vivian, 347
Bargas, Sylvia E., 192
Barker, E., 220
Barker, J., n8.25
Barnard, Chester, 35; n1A.11
Barnard, Janet, n9.18
Barnard, Kurt, 122
Barnes, Bear, 230
Barnes, D., 444; n14.26
Barnevik, Percy, 18, 398
Barnum, P. T., 404
Baron, James, 313
Baron, R. A., n7.45
Barrett, A., 75; n7.59
Barrett, W. P., n7.51, n7.52, n7.53
Barrick, M. R., n10.10
Barron, James, n6.12
Barry, B., n18.29
Bartholomew, Susan, n6.18
Bartlett, C., 19; n1.39, n1.40, n1.41, n8.26, n13.86
Bartlett, Christopher A., 196
Bartunek, J. M., n8.4
Baruck, Y., 22; n18.73, n18.74
Bass, B., n3.4, n3.24, n12.57, n12.66, n12.68, n12.70, n12.73
Bateman, T., 408, 418, 520; n3.29, n7.80
Bauer, R., n5.52
Baughman, J., n1A.5
Baum, J., n12.8
Baysinger, B., n5.61, n5.64
Baysinger, R. A., n10.21
Bazerman, M., n3.6, n3.30, n5.20
Beam, D. R., n5.59
Beaubien, E., n8.14

Beckhard, R., n18.41
Bedeian, Arthur G., 29, 604; n8.11
Bedian, Arthur G., 405, 494
Bednarzik, Robert W., n6.3
Beer, M., 130, 577, 577; n18.17, n18.32
Beeson, J., n12.82
Beeth, Gunnar, n6.26
Behr, P., n12.60, n12.62
Bell, Alexander Graham, 50, 550
Bennett, A., n13.19
Bennett, Cy, 374
Bennett, S., 6
Bennis, W., 444; n12.1, n12.3, n12.4, n12.12, n12.13, n12.22, n12.69, n12.77, n12.78, n14.75
Bentell, Nicholas J., 328
Bergen, M. E., n3.15, n3.16
Bergeson, Lynn L., n16.11
Berkley, J., n18.33
Berkley, Robyn A., n10.5
Berkowitz, L., n13.69
Berkowitz, M., n5.13
Bernasco, Wilma, n8.24
Bernstein, A., 142, 147, 154, 168; n5.1, n5.66
Bernstein, Sanford C., 122
Berra, Yogi, 482
Bertucco, Marc, n17.11
Bethune, Gordon, 127
Bezos, Jeff, 223
Bianchi, A., n13.51
Bianco, A., n12.56
Bickford, Deborah J., n17.7
Biederman, P. Ward, 444
Bierce, Ambrose, 218
Bierly, Paul, n17.2
Binney, G., 591, 597; n18.76
Birdwell, L., n13.24
Bissell, J., 460
Black, Cathie, 346
Blair, Tony, 153
Blake, Jim, 323
Blake, Robert R., 389; n12.48
Blake, S., n11.17, n11.19
Blancero, Donna, n10.42

Subject Index

References beginning with the letter "n" indicate a chapter number (and when necessary its appendix designation, e.g., "A" or "B") followed by a period and then an endnote number for that chapter. For example, "n1.11" refers to endnote 11 of Chapter 1; "n1A.11" refers to endnote 11 of Appendix A of Chapter 11 of the endnotes.